"Composed in the style of the great medieval *catenae*, this new anthology of patristic commentary on Holy Scripture, conveniently arranged by chapter and verse, will be a valuable resource for prayer, study and proclamation. By calling attention to the rich Christian heritage preceding the separations between East and West and between Protestant and Catholic, this series will perform a major service to the cause of ecumenism."

AVERY CARDINAL DULLES, S.J.
Laurence J. McGinley Professor of Religion and Society
Fordham University

"The initial cry of the Reformation was *ad fontes*—back to the sources! The Ancient Christian Commentary on Scripture is a marvelous tool for the recovery of biblical wisdom in today's church. Not just another scholarly project, the ACCS is a major resource for the renewal of preaching, theology and Christian devotion."

TIMOTHY GEORGE
Dean, Beeson Divinity School, Samford University

"Modern church members often do not realize that they are participants in the vast company of the communion of saints that reaches far back into the past and that will continue into the future, until the kingdom comes. This Commentary should help them begin to see themselves as participants in that redeemed community."

ELIZABETH ACHTEMEIER
Union Professor Emerita of Bible and Homiletics
Union Theological Seminary in Virginia

"Contemporary pastors do not stand alone. We are not the first generation of preachers to wrestle with the challenges of communicating the gospel. The Ancient Christian Commentary on Scripture puts us in conversation with our colleagues from the past, that great cloud of witnesses who preceded us in this vocation. This Commentary enables us to receive their deep spiritual insights, their encouragement and guidance for present-day interpretation and preaching of the Word. What a wonderful addition to any pastor's library!"

WILLIAM H. WILLIMON
Dean of the Chapel and Professor of Christian Ministry
Duke University

"Here is a nonpareil series which reclaims the Bible as the book of the church by making accessible to earnest readers of the twenty-first century the classrooms of Clement of Alexandria and Didymus the Blind, the study and lecture hall of Origen, the cathedrae of Chrysostom and Augustine, the scriptorium of Jerome in his Bethlehem monastery."

GEORGE LAWLESS
Augustinian Patristic Institute and Gregorian University, Rome

"Few publishing projects have encouraged me as much as the recently announced Ancient Christian Commentary on Scripture with Dr. Thomas Oden serving as general editor. . . . How is it that so many of us who are dedicated to serve the Lord received seminary educations which omitted familiarity with such incredible students of the Scriptures as St. John Chrysostom, St. Athanasius the Great and St. John of Damascus? I am greatly anticipating the publication of this Commentary."

FR. PETER E. GILLQUIST
Director, Department of Missions and Evangelism
Antiochian Orthodox Christian Archdiocese of North America

"The Scriptures have been read with love and attention for nearly two thousand years, and listening to the voice of believers from previous centuries opens us to unexpected insight and deepened faith. Those who studied Scripture in the centuries closest to its writing, the centuries during and following persecution and martyrdom, speak with particular authority. The Ancient Christian Commentary on Scripture will bring to life the truth that we are invisibly surrounded by a 'great cloud of witnesses.'"

FREDERICA MATHEWES-GREEN
Commentator, National Public Radio

"For those who think that church history began around 1941 when their pastor was born, this Commentary will be a great surprise. Christians throughout the centuries have read the biblical text, nursed their spirits with it and then applied it to their lives. These commentaries reflect that the witness of the Holy Spirit was present in his church throughout the centuries. As a result, we can profit by allowing the ancient Christians to speak to us today."

HADDON ROBINSON
Harold John Ockenga Distinguished Professor of Preaching
Gordon-Conwell Theological Seminary

"All who are interested in the interpretation of the Bible will welcome the forthcoming multivolume series Ancient Christian Commentary on Scripture. Here the insights of scores of early church fathers will be assembled and made readily available for significant passages throughout the Bible and the Apocrypha. It is hard to think of a more worthy ecumenical project to be undertaken by the publisher."

BRUCE M. METZGER
Professor of New Testament, Emeritus
Princeton Theological Seminary

ANCIENT CHRISTIAN
COMMENTARY ON SCRIPTURE

OLD TESTAMENT

XV

APOCRYPHA

EDITED BY

SEVER J. VOICU

GENERAL EDITOR
THOMAS C. ODEN

InterVarsity Press
Downers Grove, Illinois

InterVarsity Press
P.O. Box 1400, Downers Grove, IL 60515-1426
Internet: www.ivpress.com
E-mail: email@ivpress.com

InterVarsity Press® is the book-publishing division of InterVarsity Christian Fellowship/USA®, a movement of students and faculty active on campus at hundreds of universities, colleges and schools of nursing in the United States of America, and a member movement of the International Fellowship of Evangelical Students. For information about local and regional activities, write Public Relations Dept., InterVarsity Christian Fellowship/USA, 6400 Schroeder Rd., P.O. Box 7895, Madison, WI 53707-7895, or visit the IVCF website at <www.intervarsity.org>.

Scripture quotations, unless otherwise noted, are from the Revised Standard Version of the Bible, copyright 1946, 1952, 1971 by the Division of Christian Education of the National Council of the Churches of Christ in the U.S.A., and are used by permission.

Selected excerpts from Bede: On Tobit and on the Canticle of Habakkuk, edited and translated by Séan Connolly, ©1997. Used by permission of Four Courts Press, Dublin, Ireland.

Cover photograph: Scala/Art Resource, New York. View of the apse. S. Vitale, Ravenna, Italy.

Spine photograph: Byzantine Collection, Dumbarton Oaks, Washington D.C. Pendant cross (gold and enamel). Constantinople, late sixth century.

ISBN 978-0-8308-1485-5

Printed in the United States of America ∞

 InterVarsity Press is committed to protecting the environment and to the responsible use of natural resources. As a member of Green Press Initiative we use recycled paper whenever possible. To learn more about the Green Press Initiative, visit <www.greenpressinitiative.org>.

Library of Congress Cataloging-in-Publication Data

Apocrypha/edited by Sever J. Voicu; general editor, Thomas C.
Oden.
    p. cm.—(Ancient Christian commentary on Scripture; 15)
    Includes bibliographical references and indexes.
    ISBN 978-0-8308-1485-5 (cloth: alk. paper)
    1. Bible. O. T. Apocrypha—Commentaries. I. Voicu, S. J. II. Oden,
Thomas C.
    BS1700.A67 2010
    229.0709—dc22

2009042061

P	23	22	21	20	19	18	17	16	15	14	13	12	11	10	9	8	7	6	5	4	3	2	1
Y	30	29	28	27	26	25	24	23	22	21	20	19	18	17	16	15	14	13	12	11	10		

ANCIENT CHRISTIAN COMMENTARY PROJECT RESEARCH TEAM

GENERAL EDITOR
Thomas C. Oden

ASSOCIATE EDITOR
Christopher A. Hall

OPERATIONS MANAGER AND TRANSLATIONS PROJECT COORDINATOR
Joel Elowsky

RESEARCH AND ACQUISITIONS DIRECTOR
Michael Glerup

GRADUATE RESEARCH ASSISTANTS
Jennifer T. Kaalund
Michael Nausner
Shanell T. Smith

ADMINISTRATIVE ASSISTANT
Judy Cincotta

Contents

GENERAL INTRODUCTION

The Ancient Christian Commentary on Scripture has as its goal the revitalization of Christian teaching based on classical Christian exegesis, the intensified study of Scripture by lay persons who wish to think with the early church about the canonical text, and the stimulation of Christian historical, biblical, theological and pastoral scholars toward further inquiry into scriptural interpretation by ancient Christian writers.

The time frame of these documents spans seven centuries of exegesis, from Clement of Rome to John of Damascus, from the end of the New Testament era to A.D. 750, including the Venerable Bede.

Lay readers are asking how they might study sacred texts under the instruction of the great minds of the ancient church. This commentary has been intentionally prepared for a general lay audience of nonprofessionals who study the Bible regularly and who earnestly wish to have classic Christian observation on the text readily available to them. The series is targeted to anyone who wants to reflect and meditate with the early church about the plain sense, theological wisdom and moral meaning of particular Scripture texts.

A commentary dedicated to allowing ancient Christian exegetes to speak for themselves will refrain from the temptation to fixate endlessly upon contemporary criticism. Rather, it will stand ready to provide textual resources from a distinguished history of exegesis that has remained massively inaccessible and shockingly disregarded during the last century. We seek to make available to our present day audiences the multicultural, multilingual, transgenerational resources of the early ecumenical Christian tradition.

Preaching at the end of the first millennium focused primarily on the text of Scripture as understood by the earlier esteemed tradition of comment, largely converging on those writers that best reflected classic Christian consensual thinking. Preaching at the end of the second millennium has reversed that pattern. It has so forgotten most of these classic comments that they are vexing to find anywhere, and even when located they are often available only in archaic editions and inadequate translations. The preached word in our time has remained largely bereft of previously influential patristic inspiration. Recent scholarship has so focused attention upon post-Enlightenment historical and literary methods that it has left this longing largely unattended and unserviced.

This series provides the pastor, exegete, student and lay reader with convenient means to see what Athanasius or John Chrysostom or the desert fathers and mothers had to say about a particular text for preaching, for study and for meditation. There is an emerging awareness among Catholic, Protestant and Orthodox laity that vital biblical preaching and spiritual formation need deeper grounding beyond the scope of the historical critical orientations that have governed biblical studies in our day.

Hence this work is directed toward a much broader audience than the highly technical and specialized scholarly field of patristic studies. The audience is not limited to the university scholar concentrating on the study of the history of the transmission of the text or to those with highly focused philological interests in textual morphology or historical critical issues. Though these are crucial concerns for specialists, they are not the paramount interests of this series.

This work is a Christian Talmud. The Talmud is a Jewish collection of rabbinic arguments and comments on the Mishnah, which epitomized the laws of the Torah. The Talmud originated in approximately the same period that the patristic writers were commenting on texts of the Christian tradition. Christians from the late patristic age through the medieval period had documents analogous to the Jewish Talmud and Midrash (Jewish commentaries) available to them in the *glossa ordinaria* and catena traditions, two forms of compiling extracts of patristic exegesis. In Talmudic fashion the sacred text of Christian Scripture was thus clarified and interpreted by the classic commentators.

The Ancient Christian Commentary on Scripture has venerable antecedents in medieval exegesis of both eastern and western traditions, as well as in the Reformation tradition. It offers for the first time in this century the earliest Christian comments and reflections on the Old and New Testaments to a modern audience. Intrinsically an ecumenical project, this series is designed to serve Protestant, Catholic and Orthodox lay, pastoral and scholarly audiences.

In cases where Greek, Latin, Syriac and Coptic texts have remained untranslated into English, we provide new translations. Wherever current English translations are already well rendered, they will be utilized, but if necessary their language will be brought up to date. We seek to present fresh dynamic equivalency translations of long-neglected texts which historically have been regarded as authoritative models of biblical interpretation.

These foundational sources are finding their way into many public libraries and into the core book collections of many pastors and lay persons. It is our intent and the publisher's commitment to keep the whole series in print for many years to come.

Thomas C. Oden
General Editor

A GUIDE TO USING THIS COMMENTARY

Several features have been incorporated into the design of this commentary. The following comments are intended to assist readers in making full use of this volume.

Pericopes of Scripture

The scriptural text has been divided into pericopes, or passages, usually several verses in length. Each of these pericopes is given a heading, which appears at the beginning of the pericope. For example, the first pericope in the commentary on Tobit is "1:1-2 Tobit's Historical Setting." This heading is followed by the Scripture passage quoted in the Revised Standard Version (RSV) across the full width of the page. The Scripture passage is provided for the convenience of readers, but it is also in keeping with medieval patristic commentaries, in which the citations of the Fathers were arranged around the text of Scripture.

Book titles, ordering and versification follow the RSV. For example, although the Prayer of Azariah and the Song of the Three Young Men is inserted between Daniel 3:23 and 3:24 of the Masoretic Text (yielding the versification of 3:24-90 in the Greek), here the text is versified independently (vv. 1-68) as in the RSV.

Overviews

Following each pericope of text is an overview of the patristic comments on that pericope. The format of this overview varies within the volumes of this series, depending on the requirements of the specific book of Scripture. The function of the overview is to provide a brief summary of all the comments to follow. It tracks a reasonably cohesive thread of argument among patristic comments, even though they are derived from diverse sources and generations. Thus the summaries do not proceed chronologically or by verse sequence. Rather they seek to rehearse the overall course of the patristic comment on that pericope.

We do not assume that the commentators themselves anticipated or expressed a formally received cohesive argument but rather that the various arguments tend to flow in a plausible, recognizable pattern. Modern readers can thus glimpse aspects of continuity in the flow of diverse exegetical traditions representing various generations and geographical locations.

Topical Headings

An abundance of varied patristic comment is available for each pericope of these letters. For this reason we have broken the pericopes into two levels. First is the verse with its topical heading. The patristic comments are then focused on aspects of each verse, with topical headings summarizing the essence of the patristic comment by evoking a key phrase, metaphor or idea. This feature provides a bridge by which modern readers can enter into the heart of the patristic comment.

Identifying the Patristic Texts

Following the topical heading of each section of comment, the name of the patristic commentator is given. An English translation of the patristic comment is then provided. This is immediately followed by the title of the patristic work and the textual reference—either by book, section and subsection or by book and verse references. If the notation differs significantly between the English-language source footnoted and other sources, alternate references appear in parentheses. Some differences may also be due to variant biblical versification or chapter and verse numbering.

The Footnotes

Readers who wish to pursue a deeper investigation of the patristic works cited in this commentary will find the footnotes especially valuable. A footnote number directs the reader to the notes at the bottom of the right-hand column, where in addition to other notations (clarifications or biblical cross references) one will find information on English translations (where available) and standard original language editions of the work cited. An abbreviated citation (normally citing the book, volume and page number) of the work is provided. A key to the abbreviations is provided on page xv. Where there is any serious ambiguity or textual problem in the selection, we have tried to reflect the best available textual tradition.

Where original language texts have remained untranslated into English, we provide new translations. Wherever current English translations are already well rendered, they are utilized, but where necessary they are stylistically updated. A single asterisk (*) indicates that a previous English translation has been updated to modern English or amended for easier reading. The double asterisk (**) indicates either that a new translation has been provided or that some extant translation has been significantly amended. We have standardized spellings and made grammatical variables uniform so that our English references will not reflect the odd spelling variables of the older English translations. For ease of reading we have in some cases edited out superfluous conjunctions.

For the convenience of computer database users the digital database references are provided to either the Thesaurus Linguae Graecae (Greek texts) or to the Cetedoc (Latin texts) in the appendix found on pages 475-84 and in the bibliography found on pages 514-24.

When patristic commentary concerns material not found in the RSV, the source of the material is noted. For example, see the notes accompanying Bede's commentary on Tobit 2:17 (p. 8, nn. 43, 44, 46), which identify the Vulgate as Bede's source.

ABBREVIATIONS

ACTHN   Origen. *Homilies on Numbers*. Translated with notes and introduction by Thomas P. Scheck. Edited by Christopher A. Hall. Ancient Christian Texts. Downers Grove, Ill.: IVP Academic, 2009.

ACW   Ancient Christian Writers: The Works of the Fathers in Translation. Mahwah, N.J.: Paulist Press, 1946-.

ANF   A. Roberts and J. Donaldson, eds. Ante-Nicene Fathers. 10 vols. Buffalo, N.Y.: Christian Literature, 1885-1896. Reprint, Grand Rapids, Mich.: Eerdmans, 1951-1956; Reprint, Peabody, Mass.: Hendrickson, 1994.

BP   Biblioteca Patristica. Florence: Nardini, 1984-.

BTACH   Seán Connolly, trans. *Bede: On Tobit and On the Canticle of Habakkuk*. Dublin: Four Courts Press, 1997.

CCCM   Corpus Christianorum. Continuatio mediaevalis. Turnhout, Belgium: Brepols, 1969-.

CCL   Corpus Christianorum. Series Latina. Turnhout, Belgium: Brepols, 1953-.

CS   Cistercian Studies. Kalamazoo, Mich.: Cistercian Publications, 1973-.

CSCO   Corpus Scriptorum Christianorum Orientalium. Louvain, Belgium, 1903-.

CSEL   Corpus Scriptorum Ecclesiasticorum Latinorum. Vienna, Austria, 1866-.

CTP   Collana di Testi Patristici. Rome: Città Nuova, 1961-.

EncJud   *Encyclopaedia Judaica*. 16 vols. Jerusalem: Encyclopaedia Judaica, 1972.

ESOO   J. S. Assemani, ed. *Sancti Patris nostri Ephraem Syri Opera omnia*. 6 vols. Rome, 1732-1746.

FC   Fathers of the Church: A New Translation. Washington, D.C.: Catholic University of America Press, 1947-.

FMTM   Fonti medievali per il terzo millennio. Rome: Città Nuova, n.d.

GCS   Die griechischen christlichen Schriftsteller der ersten Jahrhunderte. Leipzig and Berlin: Akademie-Verlag, 1897-.

GMO   Gregorii Magni opera = Opere di Gregorio Magno. Rome: Città Nuova, 1992-.

KRS   Clara Kraus Reggiani. *Storia della letteratura giudaico-ellenistica*. Milan: Mimesis, 2008.

LCC   J. Baillie et al., eds. The Library of Christian Classics. 26 vols. Philadelphia: Westminster, 1953-1966.

LCPM   Letture cristiane del primo millennio. Milan: Paoline, 1900-.

LEC (CUAP)   Library of Early Christianity. Washington, D.C.: Catholic University of America Press, 2007-.

LXX	Septuagint
MT	Masoretic Text
NBA	Nuova Biblioteca Agostiniana = Opere di Sant' Agostino. Rome: Città Nuova, 1967-.
NPNF	P. Schaff et al., eds. A Select Library of the Nicene and Post-Nicene Fathers of the Christian Church. 2 series (14 vols. each). Buffalo, N.Y.: Christian Literature, 1886-1900; reprint, Grand Rapids, Mich.: Eerdmans, 1952-1956; reprint, Peabody, Mass.: Hendrickson, 1994.
PG	J.-P. Migne, ed. Patrologiae cursus completus. Series Graeca. 166 vols. Paris: Migne, 1857-1886.
PL	J.-P. Migne, ed. Patrologiae cursus completus. Series Latina. 221 vols. Paris: Migne, 1844-1864.
PO	Patrologia Orientalis. Paris and Turnhout, Belgium: Brepols, 1903.
PTA	Dieter Hagedorn, Rudolf Kassel, Ludwig Koenen and Reinhold Merkelbach, eds. Papyrologische Texte und Abhandlungen. Bonn: R. Habelt, 1968-.
Pusey	P. E. Pusey, ed. "Fragmenta in sancti Pauli epistulam ii ad Corinthios." In *Sancti patris nostri Cyrilli archiepiscopi Alexandrini in D. Joannis evangelium.* Vol. 3, pp. 320-60. Oxford: Clarendon Press, 1872; reprint, Brussels: Culture et Civilisation, 1965.
SAEMO	Sancti Ambrosii Episcopi Mediolanensis Opera. Milan: Biblioteca Ambrosiana; Rome: Città Nuova, 1979-.
SC	H. de Lubac, J. Daniélou et al., eds. Sources Chrétiennes. Paris: Editions du Cerf, 1941-.
Simonetti UTET	Manlio Simonetti, ed. *I Principi di Origene.* Classici delle religioni. La religione cattolica. Turin, Italy: Unione Tipografico—Editrice Torinese, 1968.
Trad. Cola	Jerome. *Commento a Daniele.* Translated, introduced and annotated in Italian by Silvano Cola. Commenti patristici all' Antico Testamento. Rome, Città Nuova, 1966.
Trad. Corsini	Origen. *Commento al Vangelo di Giovanni.* Translated, introduced and annotated in Italian by Eugenio Corsini. Classici della filosofia. Turin, Italy: Unione Tipografico—Editrice Torinese, 1968.
Vg	Vulgate
VS	Verba Seniorum n.s. Rome: Studium, 1961-.
WSA	J. E. Rotelle, ed. *Works of St. Augustine: A Translation for the Twenty-First Century.* Hyde Park, N.Y.: New City Press, 1995.

Introduction to the Apocrypha

This volume of the Ancient Christian Commentary on Scripture is inherently different from its predecessors in that it focuses on texts whose canonical status is disputed. These variously regarded writings constitute part of the Old Testament in Catholic and Byzantine Orthodox editions of Scripture but are absent from Jewish and Protestant editions, differences of opinion which are reflected semantically: the Protestant tradition labels the writings apocrypha while among Catholics they are designated deuterocanonical.[1] Behind our present situation lies a complex history which predates the Christian era, a history whose main outlines will be summarized here.

Alexandria

These works were composed and initially transmitted among the Greek-speaking Jewish diaspora, the so-called Hellenistic Jews, whose primary intellectual center from the third century B.C. until the end of the first century A.D. was Alexandria in Egypt.[2]

Alexander the Great, following his rise to the Macedonian throne (336 B.C.) and after returning from his first Asian expedition, founded the city of Alexandria in 331 B.C. along the western edge of the Nile delta. After his death in 323 B.C., Alexander's empire was broken up and Alexandria was apportioned to the Ptolemaic dynasty, which preserved power in Egypt for nearly three centuries, until Cleopatra's suicide in 30 B.C.

In the so-called *Alexander Romance*, Alexander states his intention to make Alexandria "the capital of the inhabited world."[3] Although this vision was never fulfilled, the city underwent

---

[1]Whereas Orthodox Bibles reference the Greek manuscripts of the Septuagint, Catholic Bibles follow the canon defined by the Council of Trent, which essentially follows the Vulgate (the Latin version edited by Jerome). Since the Septuagint and Vulgate do not share a common canon, the Orthodox and Catholic canons are not identical, though they are very similar. Earlier situations were even more complex—Rabbinic Judaism used the works on occasion and some Protestant editions occasionally included select apocrypha; in neither case, however, was the normative character of the writings ever admitted. The situation has been different also for the Bibles of the Eastern Orthodox Churches. As for *deuterocanonical*, the term designates writings whose inclusion in the canon took place at a later, though unspecified, moment. On the history of the acceptance of the deuterocanonical books in the West, see Thomas O'Loughlin, "Inventing the Apocrypha: The Role of Early Latin Canon Lists," *Irish Theological Quarterly* 74 (2009): 53-74.

[2]A Greek-speaking Judaism also existed in Palestine and in many other regions of the ancient world, including Rome, though a significant part of the diaspora immigrated to Babylon (i.e., into a Semitic milieu). Almost all of the works receiving comment in the present volume, however, have significant ties to Alexandria.

[3]*Alexander Romance* 1.34. The *Alexander Romance* is a legendary version of the life of the Macedonian conqueror, composed perhaps in the third century A.D. The work is also known as Pseudo-Callisthenes, because in the manuscripts it appears under the name of Callisthenes, nephew of Aristotle and chronicler of the glorious deeds of Alexander who, nonetheless, had him executed in 327 B.C. This attribution is false, however; we do not know the actual author's name despite the text's wide circulation in late antiquity and the Middle Ages in many languages and versions. The text was even translated into Hebrew: see Giuliano Tamani, "La tradizione ebraica del Romanzo di

considerable development, especially under the first two Ptolemies, Ptolemy I Soter (reigned 323-282 B.C.) and Ptolemy II Philadelphus (reigned 286/5-246 B.C.), thanks in part to its strategic position as a port controlling trade between Egypt, an important grain producer, and the rest of the Mediterranean world. Alexandria was also an important cultural center, perhaps most famous for its extensive library, the first institution of its kind in the ancient world.[4]

Alexandria, whose first inhabitants were Greek-speaking, soon attracted emigrants from other regions, especially Palestine, which had remained partially under Egyptian control.[5] It was in this cosmopolitan milieu that many of the works constituting the Apocrypha were composed, translated or transmitted.

The Letter of Aristeas to Philocrates

The Jewish emigration to Alexandria faced various conflicts, including predictable linguistic and cultural challenges. The people gave up their ancestral language, namely Hebrew and/or Aramaic[6] in favor of Greek. Interactions with the surrounding culture tested the limits of Jewish religion, as Jews found themselves immersed in a pagan culture at a time when all civilian life was permeated with religious notions.

These pressures necessitated that important, normative literary witnesses of the Jewish community be translated into Greek. The Alexandrian context in which these translations took place can be illustrated from the curious *Letter of Aristeas to Philocrates*, composed probably in the second century B.C. The letter reports the story of seventy-two elders (reduced to seventy, for reasons unknown, in succeeding tradition)[7] who were sent from Palestine to Alexandria in order to translate the Hebrew Law, that is, the Pentateuch, from Hebrew into Greek. The task was carried out in seventy-two days, during a kind of exile on the gilded island of Pharos at the port of Alexandria.

Many incongruities, like the claim that Palestine possessed enough erudite, bilingual scholars capable of translating from Hebrew to Greek, or that (with some chronological discrepancies) the translation was promoted by Demetrius Phalereus to Ptolemy II Philadelphus for inclusion in the library of Alexandria, indicate that the episode is legendary. This notwithstanding, the *Letter of Aristeas* responded to some concrete needs of Alexandria's Jewish community. It was written to legitimate, through a complex of religious and philological arguments, the translation of the Law from the sacred Hebrew language into pagan Greek. It is impossible, however,

---

Alessandro," in *La diffusione dell'eredità classica nell'età tardoantica e medievale: Forme e modi di trasmissione. Atti del Seminario Nazionale (Trieste, 19-20 settembre 1996)*, ed. A. Valvo, L'eredità classica nel mondo orientale 1 (Alessandria, Italy: Edizioni dell'Orso, 1997), pp. 221-32.

[4]At Alexandria the first attempts were made to organize the transmission of the *Iliad* and the *Odyssey*, through collation of the various copies of the Homeric poems. Similar techniques were later applied by Origen in the Hexapla, pointing out differences between the Hebrew Old Testament and the Septuagint.

[5]See A. Jakab, "Le judaïsme hellénisé d'Alexandrie: Depuis la fondation de la ville jusqu'à la révolte sous Trajan," *Henoch* 21 (1999): 147-63.

[6]Although almost the whole Old Testament was written in Hebrew, some of the later parts, particularly in Daniel, were written in Aramaic.

[7]Thus the Greek translation is called the "Septuagint" ("of the Seventy").

to determine whether this polemical work was written in order to legitimize Jewish practices in the eyes of the Greeks, or in response to objections from Palestinian Judaism, or, perhaps most likely, in order to placate controversies that had arisen within the Alexandrian diaspora.

The *Letter of Aristeas* purports to legitimate only the Greek translation of the Pentateuch. However, beginning in the second century B.C., the Greek corpus of the diaspora was developed and enriched considerably. On the one hand numerous Hebrew or Aramaic religious works, including all of the books the Hebrew Bible presently comprises,[8] were translated into Greek. On the other hand numerous original works were written in Greek by Jewish authors, mostly for the purpose of proselytizing, since Judaism was then an actively proselytizing religion.[9] This latter body of works became known as Judaic-Hellenistic literature.[10]

The Septuagint

By the name *Septuagint* ("of the seventy"; abbreviated LXX), the Christian tradition designates a collection of Jewish religious and sapiential writings written in Greek and preserved in particular biblical manuscripts of the fourth and fifth centuries[11] and the later Greek tradition.

What we now know as the Septuagint represents a collection of literature spanning from the late third century B.C. to the first century A.D. Much of it consists of Greek translations, including all of what would later become the Hebrew Bible, from the Pentateuch to the Prophets,[12] but also translations of works that, though Hebrew or Aramaic in origin, were later forgotten or marginalized by Judaism. By 100 B.C. the translation of Semitic works into Greek was probably complete, though the Septuagint also includes works that were originally written in Greek among the Jewish diaspora. This period of Septuagintal writing concluded in the first century A.D. with the production of 4 Maccabees.[13]

---

[8]It would be anachronistic to speak of a "Hebrew Bible" contemporaneous with the *Letter of Aristeas*—a Hebrew Bible in the modern sense can only be spoken of much later, following the production of the first codices at the end of the first millennium. Nonetheless, even at the end of the first century A.D. one observes in Judaism, and especially in Palestinian Judaism, a tendency to delimit a canon of sacred texts.

[9]In some cases Jewish authors would adopt Hellenistic literary conventions with the same broad proselytizing purposes. This happened, for example, with Ezekiel the Tragedian's *Exagoge*, a versified rendering of the Exodus according to Hellenistic poetic conventions; see Pierluigi Lanfranchi, *L'Exagoge d'Ézéchiel le Tragique: Introduction, texte, traduction et commentaire*, Studia in Veteris Testamenti Pseudepigrapha 21 (Leiden: Brill, 2006); Rachel Bryant Davies, "Reading Ezekiel's Exagoge: Tragedy, Sacrificial Ritual, and Midrashic Tradition," *Greek, Roman and Byzantine Studies* 48 (2008): 393-415. It is thought that the so-called *Sibylline Oracles*, which are based on pagan traditions, were composed (or at least deeply reworked) in the context of Alexandrian Judaism; see KRS 102-4.

[10]Most of the writings produced by Greek-speaking Jews are lost or known just as fragments. However, almost the entire corpus of treatises by Philo of Alexandria (born probably in the last quarter of the first century B.C., died ca. A.D. 50) is preserved in Greek and Armenian. Another important Jewish author who wrote in Greek, though he was of Palestinian origin, was the historian Flavius Josephus (died early second century A.D.). Both authors were extensively used by Christians for exegetical and historical purposes.

[11]Most notable are codices Vaticanus, Sinaiticus and Alexandrinus, all of Christian production. The deuterocanonical content of these three manuscripts is not identical, suggesting that there was not yet unanimity concerning which works to include.

[12]Or, following the traditional Jewish order, the Torah, Prophets and Hagiographa. In contemporary Christian practice the books of the Old Testament, though translated from the Hebrew, are arranged in an order closer to the LXX than to the Masoretic Text. The present series (ACCS) follows this ordering by placing the book of Daniel after Ezekiel and among the Prophets. The characterization of Daniel as a prophetic book is not a Christian innovation—it is attested in the manuscripts of Qumran; cf. Julio Trebolle, "Canonical Reception of the Deuterocanonical and Apocryphal Books in Christianity," in *Flores Florentino: Dead Sea Scrolls and Other Early Jewish Studies in Honour of Florentino García Martínez*, ed. Anthony Hilhorst, Émile Puech and Eibert J. C. Tigchelaar, Supplements to the Journal for the Study of Judaism 122 (Leiden: Brill 2007), pp. 587-603, esp. p. 588.

[13]Although the Septuagint is comprised entirely of Jewish works, its collection into a single volume took place in a Christian context. In

The text of the Septuagint presents a number of differences in structure and content with respect to the Masoretic Text (MT).[14] These differences can be explained in part by the fact that the translation was based on ancient manuscripts different from those preserved later by Palestinian Judaism.[15]

These translations must have been considerably popular among broader diasporic Hellenistic Judaism since the Septuagint became the Bible not only of authors such as Philo, which would be considered normal given his Egyptian context, but also the Bible of many Jews with strong Palestinian ties, including the authors of the New Testament.[16]

Acceptance of the Deuterocanonical Books in Antiquity

Establishing the canon of Scripture was a long and complex process in the Judeo-Christian tradition.[17] For Palestinian Judaism, the discussion is traditionally considered to have closed toward the end of the first century A.D. with the synod of Jamnia, which accepted only those books for which a Hebrew or Aramaic original was available.[18] Determination of the Christian canon, however, extended until at least the end of the fourth century.[19]

Textual discrepancies between the Hebrew and Greek versions played a role in the controversies between Jews and Christians, and in the establishment of the Christian canon. Justin Martyr, writing in the mid-second century amid an atmosphere of reciprocal accusations of falsehood, noted some of these discrepancies in his work. About a century later, Origen (d. 253), writing from Caesarea in Palestine, promoted a philological approach to the issue with his Hexapla, a synopsis of the Hebrew and Septuagintal texts together with other Greek versions or revisions. This venture showed that some books were not traceable to Hebrew originals while others existed in Hebrew forms different from that translated into Greek. Origen often used

---

fact, before the appearance of parchment codices around the middle of the third century A.D., it was physically impossible to join all of the writings of the Hebrew Bible into a manageable single volume. Before then the Old Testament, along with all other ancient documents, had to be transmitted on scrolls.

[14]*Masoretic Text* is the technical term designating the text of the Hebrew Bible preserved in the great medieval Hebrew manuscripts.

[15]Note, for example, variations in the numeration of the Psalms, the addition of a Psalm 151 (which was rediscovered at Qumran) or differences in ordering the chapters in Jeremiah.

[16]See, for example, a basic citation such as Matthew 1:23 ("Behold, a virgin shall conceive") which repeats the Greek text of Isaiah 7:14, which differs from the Hebrew.

[17]Recent years have witnessed numerous investigations into the process of biblical canon formation, the results of which are better known than the dynamics involved. See, e.g., L. M. McDonald and J. A. Sanders, eds., *The Canon Debate: On the Origin and Formation of the Bible* (Peabody, Mass.: Hendrickson, 2002); J.-M. Auwers and H. J. de Jonge, eds., *The Biblical Canons*, Bibliotheca Ephemeridum theologicarum Lovaniensium 163 (Leuven: Leuven University Press, 2003).

[18]Cf., however, the reevaluation of the significance of this synod by J. P. Lewis, "Jamnia Revisited," in *The Canon Debate: On the Origin and Formation of the Bible*, ed. L. M. McDonald and J. A. Sanders (Peabody, Mass.: Hendrickson, 2002), pp. 146-62. Regardless, the predominance of Palestinian Judaism following the destruction of the Temple initiated the slow decline of Greek-speaking Judaism. On the latter's sporadic survival in the Byzantine world, see Patrick Andrist, "The Greek Bible Used by the Jews in the Dialogues *Contra Iudaeos* (4th-10th centuries CE)," in *Jewish Reception of Greek Bible Versions: Studies in Their Use in Late Antiquity and the Middle Ages*, ed. Nicholas de Lange, Julia G. Krivoruchko and Cameron Boyd-Taylor, Texts and Studies in Medieval and Early Modern Judaism 23 (Tübingen: Mohr Siebeck, 2009), pp. 235-62.

[19]In the Roman Catholic Church the biblical canon was formally defined only in the sixteenth century with the decisions of the Council of Trent, although the Council effectively limited itself to ratifying the previous Latin usage, as represented by the best available manuscripts of the Vulgate.

deuterocanonical material in his works, though his comments reveal that he was aware that they did not exist in Hebrew.

Later Christian authors took an approach similar to Origen's: they mentioned the special situation of the deuterocanonical books, implying a certain reservation, but generally accepted their use. This approach is modeled in Athanasius of Alexandria's *Festal Letter* 39, written for Easter 367, which lists the sacred books[20] and mentions in an appendix some deuterocanonical books whose reading he recommends to *beginners*.[21] Athanasius did not, however, refrain from using the deuterocanonical works occasionally in his own works.

Not long after Athanasius, at the end of the fourth century, Jerome announced his doctrine of *"hebraica veritas,"* according to which only books translated from a Hebrew original were recognized as authentically inspired. Jerome, however, did not dare exclude the deuterocanonical books from the Vulgate, since by his time they had gained a high level of acceptance among Christians.

Another manifestation of a certain reserve toward the deuterocanonical books are the cases—relatively frequent and exemplified in the present volume—where explicit and literal citations as well as allusions are made from deuterocanonical material without attribution.

A notable consequence of this state of affairs is the dearth of patristic commentaries dedicated to the deuterocanonical books. For example, Bede (d. 735) was the first author to write a (rather disjointed) series of interpretations on Tobit; with the deuterocanonical commentaries of Rabanus Maurus (d. 856) we are fully into the Carolingian era. The book of Baruch and the additions to Daniel represent exceptions to this rule, as they were generally commented on together with their protocanonical counterparts in Jeremiah and Daniel respectively.[22]

In contrast to the relative leniency patristic commentators exhibited toward Baruch and the additions to Daniel stands the extreme reticence shown toward the books of Maccabees. While the Maccabean brothers became models of Christian martyrdom,[23] this portion of their story is the only one mentioned with any frequency, and it generally appears without explicit reference to its source (2 Maccabees 7).

What was true for 1-4 Maccabees was true for many other deuterocanonical works. For this reason, the present volume contains commentary on a limited number of works: Tobit, the Wisdom of Solomon, Sirach, Baruch, the Letter of Jeremiah and the additions to Daniel. It was not possible to gather a sufficient quantity of ancient commentary on the other books to justify their inclusion in this volume.[24]

---

[20]See Gabriella Aragione, "La *Lettre festale* 39 d'Athanase. Présentation et traduction de la version copte et de l'extrait grec," in *Le canon du Nouveau Testament. Regards nouveaux sur l'histoire de sa formation*, ed. Gabriella Aragione, Eric Junod and Enrico Norelli, Le monde de la Bible 54 (Geneva: Labor et fides, 2005), pp. 197-219.

[21]*Beginners* probably indicates catechumens, who were not yet worthy to read the "authentic" Scriptures.

[22]See, e.g., Olympiodorus's glosses on Baruch, which cannot be considered a true commentary, and the inclusion of Baruch in Theodoret's commentary on Jeremiah. A similar situation holds with Hippolytus's commentary on Daniel.

[23]See Luigi F. Pizzolato and Chiara Somenzi, *I sette fratelli maccabei nella chiesa antica d'occidente*, Studia patristica Mediolanensia 25 (Milan: Vita e Pensiero, 2005); Gerard Rouwhorst, "The Cult of the Seven Maccabean Brothers and Their Mother in Christian Tradition," in *Saints and Role Models in Judaism and Christianity*, ed. Marcel Poorthuis and Joshua Schwartz, Jewish and Christian Perspectives Series 7 (Leiden: Brill, 2004), pp. 183-204.

[24]In fact, for Wisdom and Sirach, many of the passages included in this volume are from Rabanus Maurus, an author who cannot be con-

The following is a brief survey of deuterocanonical/apocryphal books that have been accepted in some Christian Bibles.[25]

Books of Esdras

Events pertaining to Ezra (*Esdras* in Greek), protagonist of the great postexilic religious restoration, are recounted in the Hebrew work of Ezra-Nehemiah (known in the Vulgate and older Catholic tradition as 1 and 2 Esdras, but collectively in the LXX as 2 Esdras [Esdras B]). The Septuagint transmits another book concerning Ezra known as 1 Esdras (Esdras A LXX; 3 Esdras in the Vulgate; 2 Esdras in Slavonic), regarding which a Semitic archetype is commonly hypothesized. This book contains some typically Hebrew motifs and was used by Flavius Josephus, circumstances which are compatible with the hypothesis of a Jewish-Hellenistic rewriting based on canonical traditions regarding Ezra.[26]

Ezra is also presented as the recipient of apocalyptic[27] revelations, the best-known of which is 2 Esdras (absent in the LXX; 4 Esdras in the Vulgate; 3 Esdras in Slavonic; in modern scholarly literature 2 Esdras 1–2 = 5 Ezra, 2 Esdras 3–14 = 4 Ezra, 2 Esdras 15–16 = 6 Ezra), lost in Greek but transmitted in other languages, and whose composition is fixed at around A.D. 100.[28]

Additions to Esther

The Septuagintal version of the book of Esther contains seven additions to the MT. These additions, which are inserted at different places in the text in the Greek manuscripts, have been grouped together at the end of the book in the Vulgate.[29]

The purpose of the additions is twofold and reveals the intention to use the Greek form in the service of proselytizing: on the one hand, the additions emphasize religious notions by mentioning God and introducing two prayers; on the other hand, they approach the story, not without

---

sidered ancient in that he is from the Carolingian era, even if his exegetical approach follows traditional guidelines and probably includes former interpretations which are otherwise lost. The use of later commentaries would have allowed considerable expansion of this volume, but would have altered its nature. Moreover, one of the most acute problems encountered in editing this volume was the frequency with which citations were taken from deuterocanonical books without commentary, but only for the purpose of lending support to reasoning based on other biblical passages.

[25]More detailed descriptions can be found in works such as L. Rost, *Judaism Outside the Hebrew Canon: An Introduction to the Documents* (Nashville: Abingdon, 1976); Clara Kraus Reggiani, *Storia della letteratura giudaico-ellenistica* (Milan: Mimesis, 2008); David A. deSilva, *Introducing the Apocrypha: Message, Context, and Significance* (Grand Rapids: Baker, 2002); George W. E. Nickelsburg, *Jewish Literature Between the Bible and the Mishnah: A Historical and Literary Introduction* (Minneapolis: Augsburg Fortress, 2005). For a helpful summary, see J. M. Grintz and Y. Dan, "Apocrypha and Pseudepigrapha," *EncJud* 3:181-187. An overview of exegesis of the deuterocanonical books in the patristic era may be found in Charles Kannengiesser, *Handbook of Patristic Exegesis: The Bible in Ancient Christianity*, 2 vols., The Bible in Ancient Christianity 1 (Leiden: Brill, 2004).

[26]See KRS 55-57; J. Petroff, "Ezra, Greek Book of," *EncJud* 6:1109-10.

[27]The term *apocalyptic*, which derives from the Greek *apokalypsis* ("revelation"), is used to designate works which recount, at times in obscure language, a divine revelation containing a message of messianic hope, liberation (including at the political level) or future salvation.

[28]See KRS 79-80; M. E. Stone, "Ezra, Apocalypse of," *EncJud* 6:1108-1109.

[29]The transmission of Esther is quite complicated. For a recent overview of the various forms of the book in Hebrew, Greek and Latin, see P.-M. Bogaert, "Les formes anciennes du livre d'Esther. Réflexions multiples à l'occasion de la publication du texte de l'ancienne version latine," *Revue théologique de Louvain* 40 (2009):66-77.

contradictions, in the style of a Hellenistic romance. The date of these additions is uncertain, but there are indications that they should be placed around 114 B.C.[30]

Additions to Daniel

With respect to the Masoretic Text, the book of Daniel includes additions and appendixes in its Septuagintal form and in its derivative versions. There are three passages where this occurs: (1) The Prayer of Azariah and the Song of the Three Young Men has been inserted between Dan. 3:23 and 3:24 (MT);[31] (2) the story of Susanna, which introduces the personage of Daniel the prophet as a young man, finds itself in various places in the text: in Greek it sometimes precedes the canonical book, or it has been placed in an appendix constituting the thirteenth chapter (this is paralleled by the Latin forms);[32] (3) the two novellas comprising Bel and the Dragon, which ridicule the worship of idols, close the book of Daniel (chapter 14) in the Septuagint and the Vulgate.[33] There is no consensus regarding the date of composition of these additions, but it is generally suggested that they were composed in the mid-second century B.C. Although they share affinities with Midrashic literature and the Babylonian context to which they make reference, these additions must have been profoundly reworked, if not composed entirely, in Greek.[34]

The additions to Daniel were generally interpreted as stories of God's intervening to free his righteous people. This is exemplified in Hippolytus's commentary on Susanna and discussions of the text by others, including Origen, Jerome and Augustine. The story depicts the final triumph of good over evil through the action of a youthful Daniel. Susanna was interpreted allegorically as an image of the persecuted church, especially in light of the false accusations of the elders, who were presented as an image of the synagogue.

The Prayer of Azariah and the Song of the Three Young Men were widely used in ancient Christian liturgy, particularly in the Easter vigil. The two constituent pericopes were variously interpreted: sometimes they were viewed as an appeal to conversion and penance, while at other times they brought to mind the creative power of the Lord and his absolute authority over creation, the ultimate consequence of his dominion being the liberation of the faithful. The interpretation of the Antiochene authors follows this line, especially Severian of Gabala, but also Chrysostom and Theodoret.

The episodes of Bel and the Dragon were little used in the patristic period, in part because the struggle against idols lost much of its importance with the advent of Constantinian rule.[35] Nevertheless Athanasius, Pseudo-Chrysostom, Palladius, Cyril of Jerusalem and other authors mention the episodes. Pseudo-Ephrem sees them as an image of the martyrs' struggle; elsewhere

---

[30]See KRS 57-58; B. M. Metzger, "Esther, Additions to the Book of," *EncJud* 6:913-14.

[31]See B. M. Metzger, "Song of the Three Children and the Prayer of Azariah," *EncJud* 15:154.

[32]See KRS 58-60; B. M. Metzger, "Susanna and the Elders," *EncJud* 15:532.

[33]See J. M. Grintz, "Bel and the Dragon," *EncJud* 4:412.

[34]This is especially true of the additions to chapter 3, whose language is strikingly similar to the LXX version of Psalms.

[35]Keep in mind, however, that the deuterocanonical episode of Daniel in the lions' den (Bel 31-41 [Dan 14:31-41 LXX]) is a partial duplicate of the protocanonical account (Dan 6:17-25). See Kenneth Stevenson and Michael Glerup, eds., *Ezekiel, Daniel*, ACCS OT 13 (Downers Grove, Ill.: InterVarsity Press, 2008), for interpretation of the protocanonical account.

they are understood as an exhortation to fight against temptations of the flesh or the enticements of the world.

The Prayer of Manasseh

This brief text takes its inspiration from 2 Chronicles 33:11-13, which mentions that king Manasseh repented of his sins when he was deported to Babylon. The guiding ideas of this prayer are the efficacy of authentic conversion and trust in God's infinite mercy.

Its composition is placed in the mid-first century B.C., but no consensus exists as to whether it was composed in Greek or translated from a Semitic original. Although it is passed down in the manuscripts of the Septuagint, the Prayer of Manasseh is not part of the canon of the Roman Church.[36] In the Byzantine office it is traditionally recited before bedtime.

Baruch and the Letter of Jeremiah

Baruch, friend and later secretary or confidant of Jeremiah (cf. Jer 36:4-8; Bar 1:1-14), is presented as the author of these two brief works that were transmitted together with the canonical book of Jeremiah. In the Greek tradition the two writings are clearly distinguished, the first being placed before Lamentations and the second after it; in the Vulgate, however, they are found together under the name of Baruch.[37] The accepted date of composition is the second century B.C., but Baruch 1:1–3:8 was probably translated from Hebrew, while the rest is thought to be of Greek origin.[38]

Thanks to his association with Jeremiah, Baruch is cited rather frequently in the patristic era and was commented on by Theodoret together with the book of the prophet; Olympiodorus composed glosses on the text in Alexandria in the early fifth century. The patristic tradition attributed a role of fundamental importance to passages susceptible to christological interpretation. Baruch 3:36-37 (3:37-38 LXX) was one of those passages, singled out already from the time of Irenaeus.[39] This is also true for Baruch 3:12 where the tradition, exemplified by Athanasius, identifies an allusion to the equality between the Father and the Son. Chapter 4, which describes the new heavens and the new earth and promises the restoration of Jerusalem, was also emphasized in antiquity.

Tobit

Many Aramaic and Hebrew fragments of this book have been found at Qumran, confirming the existence of a Semitic precursor since lost to us, traces of which may be found in the rabbinic tradition.[40]

---

[36]Cf. KRS 60; B. M. Metzger, "Manasseh, Prayer of," *EncJud* 11 (1972), coll. 854-55.

[37]This latter arrangement is followed in the present volume.

[38]See KRS 60; M. E. Stone, "Baruch, Book of," *EncJud* 4:272-73.

[39]The citation we have included from Quodvultdeus is only one example among many others; they are, however, very repetitive, and usually do not go beyond stating the prophecy.

[40]It is possible, however, that references to Tobit in rabbinic contexts are due to Christian influence.

The date of definitive composition could be as early as the second century B.C., even though the work transmits traditions that are much older. The Greek translation exists in three different forms, one of which corresponds to the Qumran fragments. There are considerable differences between the Vulgate and the Septuagint, particularly in the first chapters.[41]

The few pages that Bede dedicates to Tobit do not constitute a systematic commentary, but rather a type of anthology of its most important passages. In his interpretation which, like that of the entire tradition, is largely allegorical, the role attributed to Israel in the transmission of the Old Testament to the nations is stressed, as is Israel's future conversion. Tobit's father Tobiel, whose experiences are comparable to those of Job, is repeatedly presented as a just man who is saved in the end. Tobit and Sarah are depicted as the perfect couple whose piety defeats their enemies and overcomes every obstacle. An important element in the exegesis of the book is the consideration of the nature and role of angels as executors of the Lord's commands.

Judith

The story of Judith and Holofernes is a short novel apparently without historical basis. There are no traces of it in either Hebrew or Aramaic, though it was originally written in one of the two. Its composition was probably in the early second century B.C.

The book exists in Greek in several forms. The Latin of the Vulgate derives from a lost Aramaic summary and is probably the source of the medieval Hebrew versions.[42]

Ecclesiasticus, or the Wisdom of Jesus the Son of Sirach

This book was composed in Hebrew between 190-180 B.C. It is sometimes referred to by its Latin title, Ecclesiasticus,[43] but its original title seems to have been "Wisdom of Simeon, son of Joshua son of Eleazar son of Sira." In content and literary genre it is to a significant extent an elaboration of Proverbs.

The text of Sirach has a particularly complicated history. The first versions, in Greek, Latin and Syriac, go back to a translation of the book, rewritten and provided with a prologue by the author's grandson or great-grandson. The three forms, among other things, present significant editorial differences. The Semitic original was mentioned frequently and positively in the rabbinic tradition, but medieval Judaism had lost track of it by the end of the tenth century.

Between 1896 and 1900, long Hebrew fragments of Sirach were discovered in the genizah[44] of the old Cairo synagogue; other fragments were later found at Qumran between 1952 and 1955 and at Masada in 1964. These fragments, which contain essentially the same form of the text, have allowed the recovery of about two thirds of the original.[45]

---

[41]See KRS 60; Y. M. Grintz, "Tobit, Book of," EncJud 15:1183-86.

[42]See KRS 60-61; Y. M. Grintz, "Judith, Book of," EncJud 10 (1972), coll. 451-59.

[43]The name Ecclesiasticus was coined before the mid-third century, probably in Roman Africa, precisely to emphasize the book's acceptance by the church. It later became the book's exclusive designation in the Latin tradition.

[44]The genizah was a place where worn-out liturgical books were abandoned, since Judaism prohibited their destruction.

[45]See KRS 61-65; M. Z. Segal, "Ben Sira, Wisdom of," EncJud 4:550-53.

Sirach is a long and heterogeneous book, cited relatively infrequently by a patristic tradition aware of the problem of its canonicity. The first chapters, containing exhortations to the practice of virtue, were the most appreciated. Passages that could be interpreted as christological prophecies were of particular interest, including 1:1 and the discourse on wisdom in chapter 24. Prior to Rabanus Maurus's late commentary, the final chapters containing a recapitulation of Israel's history were little read.

The Wisdom of Solomon

This work, which the manuscript tradition attributes to Solomon, was evidently composed in Greek, although one cannot rule out the possibility that it was distantly inspired, especially in its beginning, by a Semitic original that has been completely lost. In any case the surviving text, which perhaps goes back to the mid-first century B.C., was written by an author skilled in Hellenistic Greek who displays an influence of Greek philosophy.[46]

Wisdom was used frequently by the Fathers, especially the passages that could be interpreted as allegorical references to Christ or the Holy Spirit. This is especially true of Wisdom 7:22-23, often cited due to the outbreak of the Arian controversy. The first known systematic commentary was written in the Carolingian era by Rabanus Maurus. His work may have been preceded by others, at least in Latin. Cassiodorus,[47] in Institutiones 5.5, records that the presbyter Ballatore dedicated to Wisdom an exposition in eight books, unfortunately lost, and mentions that Ambrose and Augustine preached on Wisdom.

Books of Maccabees

The Septuagint hands down four books of the Maccabees, of diverse provenance, related only by the mention of the protagonists of the revolt against Antiochus Epiphanes and his successors (165-135 B.C.). Three of these books were translated into Latin, but only the first two were transmitted in Jerome's Vulgate and considered canonical by the Catholic Church.[48]

1 Maccabees was translated from a Hebrew original most likely written around 100 B.C., now totally lost, though it seems to have left traces in medieval Jewish writings.[49]

2 Maccabees, in contrast, was composed in Greek, probably toward the end of the second century B.C., and summarizes the historical work of an otherwise unknown author, Jason of Cyrene.[50]

3 Maccabees was also composed in Greek, probably in Egypt in the first century B.C. Flavius Josephus seems to have known some of the traditions that came together in this work.[51]

4 Maccabees was written probably in the first century A.D. in Greek, perhaps at Antioch,

---

[46]See KRS 65-67; Y. M. Grintz, "Solomon, Wisdom of," *EncJud* 15:119-21.

[47]See R. A. B. Mynors, *Cassiodori senatoris Institutiones* (Oxford: The Clarendon Press, 1961), p. 24.

[48]See KRS 69-74.

[49]See Y. M. Grintz, "Maccabees, First Book of," *EncJud* 11:656-58.

[50]See Y. M. Grintz, "Maccabees, Second Book of," *EncJud* 11:658-60.

[51]See Y. Amir, "Maccabees, Third Book of," *EncJud* 11:660-61.

where the tomb of the Maccabees has traditionally been located. Possession of this tomb has been the subject of a bitter and protracted dispute between Jews and Christians.[52] Literarily the work is a unique compromise in that it contains expressive forms typical of the Greek panegyric tradition in the context of what is almost certainly a synagogal homily. Its date makes 4 Maccabees the last book of the Septuagint.[53]

The books of Maccabees are almost never explicitly cited by the Fathers. From the time of Origen, 2 Maccabees 7:28 was sometimes used to confirm the creation of the world *ex nihilo*. 4 Maccabees had a certain echo in the Christian tradition, in particular in the encomia of the martyrs.[54]

The passage of 2 Maccabees 12:43-45, in which Judas Maccabeus makes provision for an "atonement for the dead, that they might be delivered from their sin," played an important role in the controversy regarding the existence of purgatory at the time of the Protestant reformation. In the patristic era, however, the passage does not seem to have been used, since the formal doctrine of purgatory reached its full development only in the Late Middle Ages.[55]

An Appendix to the Psalter

In the Jewish and Christian traditions, the Psalter totals 150 Psalms, notwithstanding differences in the numbering of the Psalms. Since antiquity, however, an appendix of pseudo-Davidic Psalms has been added at the end of many translations of the Psalter.

The Septuagint and Vetus Latina[56] include so-called Psalm 151 under the title, "A Psalm written by the same David, apart from the received collection, when he conquered Goliath."

The Syriac version adds four other Psalms besides Psalm 151. The Semitic origin of these Psalms was recognized in the twentieth century, and they have even been translated back into Hebrew.[57] The Hebrew text of these Psalms and other similar compositions were discovered at Qumran (11Q5 [11QPsª]). Their redaction can most likely be placed somewhere around 100 B.C. Apparently they were never cited or commented on within the Christian tradition.[58]

---

[52]See Raphaëlle Ziadé, *Les martyrs Maccabées: de l'histoire juive au culte chrétien. Les homélies de Grégoire de Nazianze et de Jean Chrysostome*, Supplements to Vigiliae Christianae 80 (Leiden: Brill, 2007); M. Schatkin, "The Maccabean Martyrs," in *Vigiliae Christianae* 28 (1974): 97-113.

[53]See Giuseppe Scarpat, trans. and ed., *Quarto libro dei Maccabei*, Biblica 9 (Brescia, Italy: Paideia, 2006); Y. Amir, "Maccabees, Fourth Book of," *EncJud* 11:660-61.

[54]See Ton Hilhorst, "Fourth Maccabees in Christian Martyrdom texts," in *Ultima Aetas. Time, Tense and Transience in the Ancient World. Studies in Honour of Jan den Boeft*, ed. Caroline Kroon and Daan Den Hengst (Amsterdam: VU University Press, 2000), pp. 107-21.

[55]The doctrine of Martin Luther, which in 1518 still accepted purgatory, though very conditionally (cf. LW 31: 126), evolved to the point of a total and definitive rejection in the *Smalcald Articles*, written in 1537. The Western doctrine of purgatory was also rejected by the Orthodox Churches.

[56]The Vetus Latina is a Latin version of the Bible that precedes the Vulgate; it dates from around A.D. 200.

[57]Cf. M. Noth, "Die fünf syrisch überlieferten apokryphen Psalmen," *Zeitschrift für die alttestamentliche Wissenschaft* 48 (1930): 1-23.

[58]For a more detailed presentation, including an ample bibliography of the literature concerning the Psalms found at Qumran, cf. André Dupont-Sommer, "Écrits qoumrâniens. VI. Psaumes pseudo-davidiques," *La Bible. Écrits intertestamentaires*. I. Publié sous la direction d'André Dupont-Sommer et Marc Philonenko (Bibliothèque de la Pléiade 337), [S.l.]: Gallimard, 1987, pp. 301-331. See also James C. Vanderkam and Peter Flint, *The Meaning of the Dead Sea Scrolls: Their Significance for Understanding the Bible, Judaism, Jesus and Christianity*, (San Francisco: HarperSanFrancisco, 2002), pp. 189-193; Peter W. Flint, "The Psalms Scrolls from the Judaean Desert: Relationships and Textual Affiliations," *New Qumran Texts and Studies: Proceedings of the First Meeting of the International Organization*

Other Works Transmitted by Hellenistic Judaism

Besides the books generally accepted in the ancient Christian tradition, there are other texts of Jewish or Judaic-Hellenistic origin, transmitted in Greek and other languages. The normative status of these texts was conceded only sporadically and their circulation was relatively limited. Since the list is somewhat long, only some of the more important works will be mentioned here.[59]

The *Psalms of Solomon* were translated from a lost Hebrew original, written probably in the first century B.C.

The *Testaments of the Twelve Patriarchs*, possible fragments of which were found at Qumran, were widespread in Greek and Armenian. They were sometimes transmitted together with the Old Testament in the Armenian language.

Among apocalyptic books, we can cite *1 Enoch (Ethiopic Apocalypse)*, preserved entirely only in Ethiopic from a Greek version based on an Aramaic original, fragments of which were recovered from Qumran. The work still enjoys great prestige in the Ethiopian Orthodox Church today.[60]

The Semitic origin of *2 Enoch (Slavonic Apocalypse)* has not been demonstrated. The work, a sort of midrash of the story of Enoch, seems to be based on a Judaic-Hellenistic original, perhaps of the first century A.D.

The *Apocalypse of Moses*, which reports the last words of Moses to Joshua, is known only from a Latin fragment, translated from the Greek, which in turn derives from a Semitic original of the first to second century A.D.

2 Baruch (Syriac Apocalypse) is preserved only in Syriac. It derives, through a Greek intermediary, from a Hebrew or Aramaic original written perhaps in the first century A.D.

The book of *Jubilees*, composed during the mid-second century B.C. possibly among the Essenes, is extant entirely only in Ethiopic. Fragments have been found at Qumran and others are extant in Greek and Latin. The work, also known in Greek as *Little Genesis*, contains an elaborate retelling of Genesis and Exodus, up to the departure from Egypt.

Professor Thomas Oden entrusted this volume of the Ancient Christian Commentary on Scripture to me in 1994. Michael Glerup patiently kept up contact, offering friendly encouragement to continue the work in the frequent difficult moments. Examination of the Latin patristic citations would have been impossible without the lists of the *Patrologia Latina* provided by Michael Nausner. The English translation was carried out in particular by Ted Papa. Finally, this volume would never have arrived in port without the constant help of Joel Elowsky.

My thanks to all of them, and may the Lord bless each one.

---

for Qumran Studies, ed. George J. Brooke and Florentino García Martínez; Studies on the Texts of the Desert of Judah 15, (Leiden: Brill, 1994), pp. 31-52.

[59]See KRS 68, 76-86.

[60]The *Book of Enoch* is the only work of this category to be cited in the New Testament, the letter of Jude explicitly affirming its prophetic character (see Jude 14-15).

TOBIT

1:1-2 TOBIT'S HISTORICAL SETTING

¹*The book of the acts^a of Tobit the son of Tobiel, son of Ananiel, son of Aduel, son of Gabael, of the descendants of Asiel and the tribe of Naphtali, ²who in the days of Shalmaneser,^b king of the Assyrians, was taken into captivity from Thisbe, which is to the south of Kedesh Naphtali in Galilee above Asher.*

a Gk words   b Gk Enemessarus

Overview: The Fathers, especially Bede, found much that was useful in reading Tobit, especially from an allegorical perspective. Israel's perennial enemy, for instance, the king of Assyria, was depicted as the devil, the perennial adversary of Christians (BEDE).

1:1-2 The Acts of Tobit

THE USEFULNESS OF READING TOBIT. BEDE: The book of the holy father Tobit is clearly of saving benefit to its readers even in its superficial meaning, inasmuch as it abounds in both the noblest examples and the noblest counsels for moral conduct, and anyone who knows how to interpret it historically (and allegorically as well)

can see that its inner meaning excels the mere letter as much as the fruit excels the leaves. For if it is understood in the spiritual sense, it is found to contain within it the greatest mysteries of Christ and the church. ON TOBIT, FOREWORD.[1]

AN IMAGE OF THE DEVIL. BEDE: This captivity at the hands of the king of the Assyrians denotes the captivity of the human race whereby, through the king of all the perverse, that is, the devil, it was banished from the abode of its heavenly homeland and deported to its sojourn in this exile. ON TOBIT 1.2.[2]

---

[1]BTACH 39; CCL 119B:3. [2]BTACH 39; CCL 119B:3.

1:3-22* DEPORTATION

³*I, Tobit, walked in the ways of truth and righteousness all the days of my life, and I performed many acts of charity to my brethren and countrymen who went with me into the land of the Assyr-*

ians, to Nineveh. ⁴Now when I was in my own country, in the land of Israel, while I was still a young man, the whole tribe of Naphtali my forefather deserted the house of Jerusalem. This was the place which had been chosen from among all the tribes of Israel, where all the tribes should sacrifice and where the temple of the dwelling of the Most High was consecrated and established for all generations for ever.

⁵All the tribes that joined in apostasy used to sacrifice to the calf ᶜ Baal, and so did the house of Naphtali my forefather. ⁶But I alone went often to Jerusalem for the feasts, as it is ordained for all Israel by an everlasting decree. Taking the first fruits and the tithes of my produce and the first shearings, I would give these to the priests, the sons of Aaron, at the altar. ⁷Of all my produce I would give a tenth to the sons of Levi who ministered at Jerusalem; a second tenth I would sell, and I would go and spend the proceeds each year at Jerusalem; ⁸the third tenth I would give to those to whom it was my duty, as Deborah my father's mother had commanded me, for I was left an orphan by my father. ⁹When I became a man I married Anna, a member of our family, and by her I became the father of Tobias.

¹⁰Now when I was carried away captive to Nineveh, all my brethren and my relatives ate the food of the Gentiles; ¹¹but I kept myself from eating it, ¹²because I remembered God with all my heart. ¹³Then the Most High gave me favor and good appearance in the sight of Shalmaneser,ᵇ and I was his buyer of provisions. ¹⁴So I used to go into Media, and once at Rages in Media I left ten talents of silver in trust with Gabael, the brother of Gabrias. ¹⁵But when Shalmaneserᵇ died, Sennacherib his son reigned in his place; and under him the highways were unsafe, so that I could no longer go into Media.

¹⁶In the days of Shalmaneserᵇ I performed many acts of charity to my brethren. ¹⁷I would give my bread to the hungry and my clothing to the naked; and if I saw any one of my people dead and thrown out behind the wall of Nineveh, I would bury him. ¹⁸And if Sennacherib the king put to death any who came fleeing from Judea, I buried them secretly. For in his anger he put many to death. When the bodies were sought by the king, they were not found. ¹⁹Then one of the men of Nineveh went and informed the king about me, that I was burying them; so I hid myself. When I learned that I was being searched for, to be put to death, I left home in fear. ²⁰Then all my property was confiscated and nothing was left to me except my wife Anna and my son Tobias.

²¹But not fiftyᵈ days passed before two of Sennacherib'sᵉ sons killed him, and they fled to the mountains of Ararat. Then Esarhaddon,ᶠ his son, reigned in his place; and he appointed Ahikar, the son of my brother Anael, over all the accounts of his kingdom and over the entire administration. ²²Ahikar interceded for me, and I returned to Nineveh. Now Ahikar was cupbearer, keeper of the signet, and in charge of administration of the accounts, for Esarhaddonᶠ had appointed him second to himself.ᵍ He was my nephew.

---

b Gk *Enemessarus* c Other authorities read *heifer* d Other authorities read *fifty-five* e Gk *his* f Gk *Sacherdonus* g Or *a second time* * Tob 1:3-25 Vg. The Latin and the Septuagint are very different, especially because the Vulgate uses the first person and the Septuagint the third person.

OVERVIEW: Israel has received the Word of God, making it known to the pagans and later entrusting it to them until its own conversion. Tobit's adulthood is an image of Israel, who receives the Law. Tobias is Tobit's firstborn as Christ is the firstborn of the Father. The king is a symbol of the devil, who tries in vain to destroy the church and the synagogue. The unexpected change in the fortunes of Tobit is a symbol of the fortunes of the church (BEDE).

1:8 *The Third Tenth*

ISRAEL SHARES THE WORD OF GOD. BEDE: Tobit shared all he could get every day with captives who were of his own kin, but also he gave tithes to strangers and proselytes.[1] And the people of Israel through their teachers ministered the alms of God's Word not only to the unlettered audience of their own nation but also to those of the Gentiles who wished to convert to the religious observance of their way of life. For whatever natural good thing they could get that was not confiscated by the enemy who held them captive, they showed it all to their own folk as an instance of virtue. But also they always gave a certain portion of their saving knowledge even to the Gentiles, which explains the significance of Tobit's assigning a tithe of his property to strangers. ON TOBIT 1.2.[2]

1:9 *Marriage and Fatherhood*

ISRAEL'S MATURITY. BEDE: And this people, after they had grown up and increased in Egypt,[3] espoused the synagogue, which had been established by Moses with legal ceremonies. ON TOBIT 1.9.[4]

AN IMAGE OF CHRIST, THE FIRSTBORN OF THE FATHER. BEDE: He learned that Christ was to be born of his own kin, as Moses had said, "Your God will raise up for you a prophet like me from among your brethren; to him you shall listen";[5] and the Lord said to David, "One of the fruit of your womb I will set upon my throne."[6] He gave him his own name believing and confessing what the Father says of him, "And I will make him the firstborn,"[7] as he says of the people themselves, "Israel is my firstborn son."[8]

"He taught him from his infancy to fear God and refrain from all sin,"[9] believing and confessing that he would commit no sin and that no deceit would be found on his lips[10] but that the spirit of the fear of the Lord would fill him.[11] ON TOBIT 1.9.[12]

1:14 *Ten Talents of Silver Left in Trust*

ISRAEL LOANED THE OLD TESTAMENT TO THE PAGANS. BEDE: To Gabael his fellow kinsman who was in need, Tobit gave ten silver talents in trust.[13] And the people of God entrusted to the Gentiles through the seventy translators[14] the knowledge of the divine law that is contained in the Decalogue in order thereby to free them from the indigence of unbelief; but they gave it in trust, that is, on condition that it be repaid after they themselves got wealthy or the one who had given it asked it back.[15] On the other hand, the Gentiles received the Word of God from the people of Israel through the medium of translation because now after the Lord's incarnation they also understand it spiritually and work at acquiring the riches of the virtues; but they pay back the creditor when they receive into the unity of the church the Jews who believe at the end of the world;[16] and, as well as entrusting to them the mysteries of Christ for their salvation, they also unlock for them the secrets of the Scriptures. ON TOBIT 1.9.[17]

1:19 *Fleeing Persecution*

THE DEVIL PERSECUTES THE CHURCH AND THE SYNAGOGUE. BEDE: Orders were given by the king that Tobit be killed and all his property confiscated[18] on account of the good deeds he had done, but he with his son and wife fled naked and went into hiding because many people loved him.[19] And the devil did his utmost to bring about the spiritual death of the people of God through idolatry and strip them of all the

---

[1]Tob 1:3, 8 (1:3, 7 Vg). [2]BTACH 39; CCL 119B:3. [3]See Ex 1:7. [4]BTACH 40; CCL 119B:3. [5]Deut 18:15; see Acts 3:22. [6]Ps 132:11 (131:11 LXX). [7]Ps 89:27 (88:28 LXX). [8]Ex 4:22. [9]Tob 1:10 Vg. [10]Is 53:9; see 1 Pet 2:22. [11]See Is 11:3. [12]BTACH 40*; CCL 119B:3-4. [13]See Tob 1:14 (cf. 1:16-17 Vg); see Col 2:14. [14]The text alludes to the translation of the Septuagint, which is reported in the Letter of Aristeas. [15]See Tob 9:5 (cf. 9:6 Vg). [16]See Rom 11:25-26. [17]BTACH 40; CCL 119B:4. [18]Tob 1:19-20 (1:22 Vg). [19]Tob 1:23 Vg.

riches of their virtues but could not because there were many holy teachers among them who made provision for their life and salvation. However, he fled with his son and wife because the enemy could not rob them either of belief in the Lord's incarnation or of the synagogue as an institution, however ferociously he persecuted them, as became evident in the tortures of the Maccabees.[20] On Tobit 1.22-23.[21]

1:21 Sennacherib Assassinated

THE FORTUNES OF THE CHURCH CHANGE.

BEDE: But when the king was assassinated by his sons, all Tobit's belongings were restored to him because often after the devil had been overcome and condemned by reason of his crimes which he spawned like a thoroughly wicked brood, prosperity returned to the people of God.[22] In these vicissitudes we can see the church too as an institution being tossed to and fro like the waves after the Lord's incarnation. On Tobit 1.22-23.[23]

---

[20]See 2 Macc 6–7. [21]BTACH 40-41; CCL 119B:4. [22]Tob 1:21-22 (1:24-25 Vg). [23]BTACH 41; CCL 119B:4.

2:1–3:6* THE BLIND

[1]When I arrived home and my wife Anna and my son Tobias were restored to me, at the feast of Pentecost, which is the sacred festival of the seven weeks, a good dinner was prepared for me and I sat down to eat. [2]Upon seeing the abundance of food I said to my son, "Go and bring whatever poor man of our brethren you may find who is mindful of the Lord, and I will wait for you." [3]But he came back and said, "Father, one of our people has been strangled and thrown into the market place." [4]So before I tasted anything I sprang up and removed the body[b] to a place of shelter until sunset. [5]And when I returned I washed myself and ate my food in sorrow. [6]Then I remembered the prophecy of Amos, how he said,
"Your feasts shall be turned into mourning,
and all your festivities into lamentation."
And I wept.
[7]When the sun had set I went and dug a grave and buried the body.[b] [8]And my neighbors laughed at me and said, "He is no longer afraid that he will be put to death for doing this; he once ran away, and here he is burying the dead again!" [9]On the same night I returned from burying him, and because I was defiled I slept by the wall of the courtyard, and my face was uncovered. [10]I did not know that there were sparrows on the wall and their fresh droppings fell into my open eyes and white films formed on my eyes. I went to physicians, but they did not help me. Ahikar, however, took care of me until he[i] went to Elymais.

¹¹Then my wife Anna earned money at women's work. ¹²She used to send the product to the owners. Once when they paid her wages, they also gave her a kid; ¹³and when she returned to me it began to bleat. So I said to her, "Where did you get the kid? It is not stolen, is it? Return it to the owners; for it is not right to eat what is stolen." ¹⁴And she said, "It was given to me as a gift in addition to my wages." But I did not believe her, and told her to return it to the owners; and I blushed for her. Then she replied to me, "Where are your charities and your righteous deeds? You seem to know everything!"

3 Then in my grief I wept, and I prayed in anguish, saying, ²"Righteous art thou, O Lord; all thy deeds and all thy ways are mercy and truth, and thou dost render true and righteous judgment for ever. ³Remember me and look favorably upon me; do not punish me for my sins and for my unwitting offences and those which my fathers committed before thee. ⁴For they disobeyed thy commandments, and thou gavest us over to plunder, captivity, and death; thou madest us a byword of reproach in all the nations among which we have been dispersed. ⁵And now thy many judgments are true in exacting penalty from me for my sins and those of my fathers, because we did not keep thy commandments. For we did not walk in truth before thee. ⁶And now deal with me according to thy pleasure; command my spirit to be taken up, that I may depart and become dust. For it is better for me to die than to live, because I have heard false reproaches, and great is the sorrow within me. Command that I now be released from my distress to go to the eternal abode; do not turn thy face away from me."

h Gk *him*   **i** Other authorities read *I*   ***** The Vulgate not only has the text in the third person but also instead of Tob 2:10b has a long passage (Tob 2:12-18).

OVERVIEW: The Jews celebrate Easter and Pentecost as prefigurations of the Christian feasts (AUGUSTINE, ORIGEN). Works of mercy are more important than the earthly goods but less important than following Jesus (MAXIMUS OF TURIN). Those who neglect watchfulness and fall into lewdness and arrogance are like the blind (BEDE). The trials of the just are for their improvement in Christ (PSEUDO-AUGUSTINE). Scripture records any number of women who acted foolishly, whom blind Tobit ridicules (JULIAN OF ECLANUM). In spite of his blindness, Tobit could see spiritual matters better than his relatives (BEDE). There are many ways of glorifying God through prayer (ORIGEN).

2:1 At Pentecost

THE JEWISH PENTECOST PREFIGURES THE CHRISTIAN CELEBRATION. AUGUSTINE: Often we are asked, "If we celebrate Pentecost because of the coming of the Holy Spirit, why do the Jews celebrate it?" The Jews do, in fact, also celebrate Pentecost. You heard that earlier this morning when you followed with attention the reading of the book of Tobit as it was read at the memorial shrine of the blessed Theogenes.[1] There it was said that on the day of Pentecost Tobit prepared a lunch and invited some of his friends who were worthy to participate in this feast since they feared the Lord. It says, "On the day of Pentecost, that is, the holiest day of the weeks." In fact, seven times seven equals forty-nine; to this number, one is added for the sake of unity in order to be able to bring us back to the head, the beginning. Unity in fact provides cohesion to every multitude; and the multitude if it is not cemented in unity is an

[1]Theogenes (or Theagenes) is a martyr of Hippo whose date is unknown.

agglomerate of disputing and quarrelsome people. If, however, there is concord, they form a single soul. Scripture asserts just this when speaking about those who had received the Holy Spirit. It says that "they had a single soul and heart toward God."[2] Thus it makes fifty days, which is the mystery of Pentecost.

But why, then, do the Jews celebrate Pentecost, if not because in their celebration there was something prefigured there? Pay close attention to me! You know that among the Jews a lamb is killed and the Passover is celebrated thus, like a figure of the passion of the Lord that would happen later. No Christian can ignore what I am saying. You also know that they were commanded to find a lamb among the goats and the sheep.[3] But can a lamb be found among goats and sheep? That command, in itself, was impossible, but it pointed toward the possibility that the Christ would come in truth in our Lord Jesus, who according to the flesh was born from the seed of David[4] and drew his origin from both the sinners and the righteous. In the genealogy of the Lord, according to the generations that the Evangelist recorded,[5] we find many sinners, because he also came from sinners; and the church today is assembled from both the just and sinners. NEWLY DISCOVERED SERMONS 31.2.[6]

2:4 Removing the Body

FOLLOWING JESUS MAKES US FORGET EVERYTHING ELSE. MAXIMUS OF TURIN: We understand how devoted he was who, as he himself maintained, left his dead father so as to lay hold of the Lord of life. For he says, "First permit me to go and bury my father."[7] The one whom he had left behind as dead he begs that he might return and bury. Sorrow did not hold him nor death detain him, because he was hastening to life. He had not yet closed the eyes of the dead man, not yet buried the stiff limbs, but as soon as he learned that the Lord had come he forgot the feeling of paternal piety, believing that there

was a greater piety in loving Christ more than one's parents. Perhaps he had read the prophetic passage that says, "Forget your people and your father's house."[8] So he forgot his father and remembered his Savior. Perhaps he had also heard the Lord's Gospel words: "The one who loves his father or mother more is not worthy of me."[9] Thus, as Tobit is justified because he abandons his meal for the sake of a burial, this man is approved because he abandons the burial of his father for the sake of Christ. For the one is not afraid to pass over his meal because of some earthly work intervenes, while the other fears lest some delay cause him to omit the eating of heavenly bread.[10] Thus, although in consideration of Christ we owe burial to everyone, this man forsook his father's burial out of love for Christ. SERMONS 41.2.[11]

2:6 Feasts Turned into Mourning

JEWISH FESTIVALS TRANSFERRED TO CHRISTIANS. ORIGEN: Once the people fell down in the desert and died.[12] Aaron their chief priest came and "stood in the midst of those who died and of those who lived,"[13] so that the devastation of death might not advance even further among the rest. And then came the true high priest, my Lord, and he came into the midst between those dying and the living. That is, he came between those Jews who accepted his presence and those who not only did not accept but also killed themselves more completely than him, saying, "The blood of that one be on us and on our children!"[14] So also "all the righteous blood that has been poured forth on the earth, from the blood of the righteous Abel to the blood of Zechariah whom they killed between the sanctuary and the altar, will be required from that generation"[15] that said, "His blood on us and on our children."[16] Therefore, these are a part of the dead people because

---

[2]Acts 4:32. [3]See Ex 12:5 LXX. [4]See Rom 1:3. [5]See Mt 1:1-17; Lk 3:23-38. [6]NBA 35/2:811-13. [7]Mt 8:21. [8]Ps 45:11 (44:11 LXX). [9]Mt 10:37. [10]See Jn 6:31-32. [11]ACW 50:102. [12]See Num 17:12. [13]Num 17:13. [14]Mt 27:25. [15]Mt 23:35-36. [16]Mt 27:25.

they do not properly perform either the feast of unleavened bread or the feast days. But "their feast days have been turned into sorrow and their songs into lamentations,"[17] they who, even if they wished, could not celebrate the feast days in that place that the Lord God chose.[18] And indeed we ourselves did not say to them, "You will have no part in this altar or in the inheritance of the Lord," but they themselves of their own accord refute the true altar and the heavenly high priest and have been brought to such a point of unhappiness that they both lost the image and did not accept the truth.[19] Therefore it is said to them, "Behold, your house is left to you deserted."[20] For the grace of the Holy Spirit has been transferred to the nations; the celebrations have been transferred to us because the high priest has passed over to us, not the imagined but the true high priest, chosen "according to the order of Melchizedek."[21] It is necessary that he offer for us true sacrifices, that is, spiritual,[22] where "the temple of God is built from living stones,"[23] which is "the church of the living God"[24] and where true Israel exists. Homilies on Joshua 26.3.[25]

2:10 Sparrows on the Wall

Watchfulness Guards Against Lewdness and Arrogance. Bede: Do not be surprised, reader, that sometimes, typologically speaking, people's good deeds have a bad meaning and their bad deeds a good meaning; that "God is light"[26] would never have been written in black ink but always in bright gold[27] if this were not permissible. But even if you should write the name of the devil in pure white chalk, it still means deep darkness. Tobit's being blinded, therefore, denotes, as the apostle says, "that blindness has come on a part of Israel."[28] He was wearied with burying and blinded,[29] because the one who tirelessly perseveres in good works is never deprived of the light of faith; the one who neglects to watch and stand firm in the faith and act powerfully and be strengthened[30] spiritually lies down and sleeps from fa-

tigue. The apostle's saying fits him well: "Rise, you who sleep, and arise from the dead, and Christ will enlighten you."[31] Because of their swift flight, swallows[32] are a figure of pride and volatility of heart, since their uncleanness immediately blinds those over whom it holds sway.[33] For the one who recklessly enslaves his soul to the volatility of licentiousness and pride sleeps, as it were, lying down beneath a swallow's nest. Now this blindness got the better of the people of Israel especially as the coming of the Lord in the flesh was imminent, when they were both being oppressed by the yoke of Roman slavery and transgressing the precepts of the divine law by very immoral living. On Tobit 2.10-11.[34]

2:12[35] Trials and Patience

The Just Are Tested. Pseudo-Augustine: The righteous are tested in order to bring about their improvement. This is why we must be strong in the face of temptations, knowing they do not occur in order to humiliate us but in order to make us grow if we face them with a serene mind for the sake of Christ. Questions from Both Testaments 99.[36]

2:14 Where Are Your Righteous Deeds?

Blind Tobit Ridicules Uncharitable Women. Anonymous Anomoean: "Why have you spoken like one of the many foolish women?"[37] He says, O woman, there have been many foolish women since the beginning of the world. There are countless women who, from

---

[17]See also Amos 8:10. [18]See Deut 12:5. Origen alludes to the destruction of the temple in Jerusalem. [19]See Heb 10:1. [20]Lk 13:35. [21]See Heb 5:6. [22]See Rom 12:1. [23]See 1 Pet 2:5. [24]See 1 Tim 3:15. [25]FC 105:219-20. [26]1 Jn 1:5. [27]Bede alludes to manuscripts in which the text written with black ink alternates with golden initials. [28]See Rom 11:25. [29]See Tob 2:10-11 Vg. [30]See 1 Cor 16:13. [31]Eph 5:14. [32]See Tob 2:11 Vg (Tob 2:10 LXX). Only the Vulgate mentions swallows; the Septuagint says "sparrows." [33]See 2 Pet 2:19. [34]BTACH 41-43*; CCL 119B:5. [35]Vg. [36]PL 35:2300. [37]Job 2:10. The anonymous author understands the phrase literally.

the earliest times, have shown themselves unreasonable: some less so, others more, some carnally, others also spiritually. Rebecca was foolish when she said to Isaac, "Give me children,"[38] because in fact Isaac did not have the power to do so, since the power and initiative were God's. But even more foolish was that obscene Egyptian whore who, assaulting the chaste and righteous Joseph with the utmost godlessness, said, "Lie with me!"[39] Tobit's wife was foolish, who unjustly said to Tobiah, "Where are your alms? Where are your good works? See, this shows how you have been brought low!"[40] But even more foolish, because she was more wicked, was that abominable, filthy and lustful Delilah, who, having seduced Samson in secret, who loved her purely, ruthlessly consigned him to derision and death.[41] COMMENTARY ON JOB 2.54.[42]

2:17[43] Tobit's Rebuke

TOBIT SAW SPIRITUAL MATTERS. BEDE: Tobit's relatives taunted him,[44] and even his wife upbraided him as if he had served God in vain.[45] But he rebuked and instructed them[46] and turned to God in prayer. There were some among that people who with foolish temerity treated with derision the misfortunes of his people because they were already far from the original happiness of their holy ancestors who once nobly served God in their midst. But the same people earnestly took care to correct these through all their more learned and chosen ones and turned to imploring God's mercy to obtain eternal life. Nor should it seem absurd that this Tobit, blind as he was and preaching God's word, is said to signify both reprobate and elect alike. For the patriarch Jacob too, while wrestling with the angel, was both lamed and blessed, signifying, that is, by his limping the unbelievers of his nation and by his blessing the believers.[47] ON TOBIT 2.10-11.[48]

3:1 Praying in Anguish

EXAMPLES OF PRAYER FOR GOD'S GLORIFICATION. ORIGEN: Regarding the second kind of prayer,[49] see Daniel: "And Azarias standing up prayed in this manner and opening his mouth in the midst of the fire he said . . . ".[50] And Tobias: "And I began to pray with tears, saying, You are just, O Lord, and all your works are just and all your ways mercy and truth. And your judgments are true and just forever." And since the passage in Daniel has been obelized[51] on the ground that it is not found in the Hebrew text, and those of the circumcision reject the book of Tobias as not being canonical,[52] I shall quote the words of Anna from the first book of Kings: "And she prayed the Lord, shedding many tears. And she made a vow, saying, O Lord of hosts, if you will look down on the affliction of your servant," and so on.[53] And in Habakkuk: "A prayer of Habakkuk the prophet with song. O Lord, I have heard your voice and was afraid. O Lord, I reflected on your works and was astonished. In the midst of two animals you will be known; in the approach of the years you will be recognized."[54] The example just given illustrates very well the definition of prayer inasmuch as he who offers it unites it with praise of God. And again, in the book of Jonah: "Jonah prayed to the Lord his God out of the belly of the fish. And he said, I cried out of my affliction to the Lord my God, and he heard me. Out of the belly of hell you heard the screams of my voice. And you have thrown me into the deep in the heart of the sea, and a flood has surrounded me."[55] ON PRAYER 14.4.[56]

---

[38]Gen 30:1, but this verse makes reference to Rachel and Jacob. [39]Gen 39:7. [40]Tob 2:14 (2:16 Vg). The grammar seems to confirm that the anonymous writer confuses Tobias with Tobit. [41]See Judg 16:4-31. [42]CSEL 96:331. [43]Vg. [44]See Tob 2:15-16 Vg. This phrase appears only in the Vulgate. [45]See Tob 2:22-23 Vg (2:14 LXX). [46]See Tob 2:17-18 Vg. This phrase appears only in the Vulgate. [47]See Gen 32:24-29. [48]BTACH 43*; CCL 119B:5. [49]Origen distinguishes four kinds of prayer: supplication, glorification, intercession and thanksgiving. [50]Pr Azar 2 (Dan 3:25 LXX). [51]This was a text-critical mark that Origen used in his Hexapla. [52]Even if the additions to Daniel and Tobit are not recognized by the Jews, Origen would use them. [53]1 Sam 1:10-11. [54]Hab 3:1. [55]Jon 2:2-4. [56]ACW 19:55.

3:7-17* SARAH

⁷*On the same day, at Ecbatana in Media, it also happened that Sarah, the daughter of Raguel, was reproached by her father's maids,* ⁸*because she had been given to seven husbands, and the evil demon Asmodeus had slain each of them before he had been with her as his wife. So the maids*ʲ *said to her, "Do you not know that you strangle your husbands? You already have had seven and have had no benefit from*ᵏ *any of them.* ⁹*Why do you beat us? If they are dead, go with them! May we never see a son or daughter of yours!"*

¹⁰*When she heard these things she was deeply grieved, even to the thought of hanging herself. But she said, "I am the only child of my father; if I do this, it will be a disgrace to him, and I shall bring his old age down in sorrow to the grave."*ˡ ¹¹*So she prayed by her window and said, "Blessed art thou, O Lord my God, and blessed is thy holy and honored name for ever. May all thy works praise thee for ever.* ¹²*And now, O Lord, I have turned my eyes and my face toward thee.* ¹³*Command that I be released from the earth and that I hear reproach no more.* ¹⁴*Thou knowest, O Lord, that I am innocent of any sin with man,* ¹⁵*and that I did not stain my name or the name of my father in the land of my captivity. I am my father's only child, and he has no child to be his heir, no near kinsman or kinsman's*ᵐ *son for whom I should keep myself as wife. Already seven husbands of mine are dead. Why should I live? But if it be not pleasing to thee to take my life, command that respect be shown to me and pity be taken upon me, and that I hear reproach no more."*

¹⁶*The prayer of both was heard in the presence of the glory of the great God.* ¹⁷*And Raphael*ⁿ *was sent to heal the two of them: to scale away the white films from Tobit's eyes; to give Sarah the daughter of Raguel in marriage to Tobias the son of Tobit, and to bind Asmodeus the evil demon, because Tobias was entitled to possess her. At that very moment Tobit returned and entered his house and Sarah the daughter of Raguel came down from her upper room.*

j Gk *they*   k Other authorities read *have not borne the name of*   l Gk *to Hades*   m Gk *his*   n Other authorities read *the great Raphael. And he*   * Tob 3:7-25 Vg.

OVERVIEW: The seven men to whom Sarah was promised were symbols of pagan science, which cannot raise itself beyond the visible world (BEDE). The whole creation and every part of the human being direct their prayer to the Lord (AUGUSTINE). The angels present to the Lord the prayers of people and of the saints (ORIGEN). Raphael is a likeness of the Lord, who heals and frees from darkness (BEDE).

3:8 Given to Seven Husbands

BOUND GENTILES FREED FROM DEMONIC IDOLATRIES. BEDE: Sarah, Raguel's daughter, in a city of the Medes, who had been given to seven husbands whom a demon killed as soon as they went in to her, figuratively denotes the mass of the Gentiles. Their teachers all knew about life in this world only, which runs a course of seven days,[1] but were unable to

[1]See Gen 2:3. Seven is a symbol of the visible world, which was created in seven days. Eight was in the early church a sign of fullness and perfection and a symbol of the eternal life.

say anything about eternal life. And so they were all carried off by the devil inasmuch as they were given over to idolatry until the true bridegroom, our Lord, came. He overcame the enemy and through faith united them (i.e., the Gentiles) to himself, as Tobias took Sarah to wife after tying up the devil on the instructions and with the aid of the archangel.[2] On Tobit 3.7-8.[3]

3:12 Turning Toward the Lord

Everything Directs Its Prayer to the Lord. Augustine: Accept the sacrifice of my confession[4] as the offering of my tongue,[5] which you have formed and stimulated to confess to your name.[6] Heal all my bones[7] and let them say, "Lord, who is like you?"[8] Not that he who confesses to you teaches you anything of what goes on within him, for the heart that is closed does not shut your eye, nor does the hardness of human beings stay your hand. Rather, you soften it, when you desire, either in compassion or in punishment. "There is no one who can hide from your heat."[9] Rather, my soul praises you,[10] so that it may love you; let it confess to you your mercies,[11] so that it may praise you. Your whole creation never stops or grows silent in your praises—every spirit praises you[12] through the mouth that is turned to you,[13] and all animals and bodily things through the mouth of those who look on them—so that our soul springs up to you from its weakness, supported by those things that you have made and passing over to you who have made these things so wonderfully.[14] There is refreshment and true strength. Confessions 5.1.1.[15]

3:16 The Prayer of Both Was Heard

The Intercession of Angels. Origen: It is not only the high priest who prays with those who truly pray, but also the angels, who "have joy in heaven on one sinner who repents, more than on ninety-nine just who need no repentance,[16] and the souls of the saints who have passed away. This is clear from the case of Raphael offering a reasonable sacrifice to God for Tobias and Sarah.[17] For the Scripture says that after they had prayed, "the prayers of them both were heard in the sight of the glory of the great Raphael, and he was sent to heal them both." And Raphael, in revealing to them his mission to them both, enjoined on him as an angel by God, says, "When you prayed, you and your daughter-in-law Sarah, I offered the memory of your prayer before the Holy One";[18] and a little further on: "I am Raphael, one of the seven angels who hear the prayers of the saints and enter before the glory of the Holy One."[19] And so, according to the word of Raphael, "prayer is good with fasting and alms and justice."[20] And in the case of Jeremiah, who appears in the Maccabees as "admirable for age and glory" so that "an extraordinary dignity and greatness" was about him, and who "stretched forth his right hand and gave to Judas a sword of gold"[21]—to him another holy man[22] who had died bore witness saying, "This is he who prays much for the people and for all the holy city, Jeremiah the prophet of God."[23] On Prayer 11.1.[24]

3:17 Raphael Sent to Heal Them

Healed and Freed from Darkness. Bede: The reason why the Lord's holy angel Raphael (which means "the healing of God") was sent was to rid Tobit of blindness and Sarah of the demon.[25] The Lord, who says of himself, "It is not those who are well that need the physi-

---

[2]See Tob 6:15-17 (6:16-19 LXX); 8:2-3. [3]BTACH 43*; CCL 119B:6. [4]See Ps 51:21 (50:21 LXX). [5]See Prov 18:21. [6]See Ps 54:8 (53:8 LXX). [7]See Ps 6:3. [8]Ps 35:10 (34:10 LXX). [9]Ps 19:7 (18:7 LXX). [10]See Ps 119:175 (118:175 LXX); 146:2 (145:2 LXX). [11]See Ps 107:8, 15, 21, 31 (106:8, 15, 21, 31 LXX). [12]See Ps 150:6. [13]See Tob 3:12 (3:14 Vg); Ps 51:15 (50:15 LXX). [14]See Ps 72:18 (71:18 LXX); Ps 136:4 (135:4 LXX). [15]FC 21:101-2. [16]Lk 15:7. [17]See Tob 12:12. [18]Tob 12:12. [19]Tob 12:15. [20]Tob 12:8. [21]2 Macc 15:13. [22]See 2 Macc 15:12, where the high priest Onias is praised. [23]2 Macc 15:14. [24]ACW 19:43. [25]See Tob 3:17 (cf. 3:25 Vg).

cian but those who are ill,"²⁶ was sent into the world to redeem both the Jewish people from the darkness of unbelief and the Gentiles from the bondage of idolatry. And of him the prophet said, "And his name shall be called the angel of great counsel."²⁷ ON TOBIT 3.25.²⁸

²⁶Mt 9:12. ²⁷Is 9:6 LXX. ²⁸BTACH 44*; CCL 119B:6.

4:1-21* TOBIAS

¹*On that day Tobit remembered the money which he had left in trust with Gabael at Rages in Media, and he said to himself:* ²*"I have asked for death. Why do I not call my son Tobias so that I may explain to him about the moneyᵒ before I die?"* ³*So he called him and said, "My son, when I die, bury me, and do not neglect your mother. Honor her all the days of your life; do what is pleasing to her, and do not grieve her.* ⁴*Remember, my son, that she faced many dangers for you while you were yet unborn. When she dies, bury her beside me in the same grave.*

⁵*"Remember the Lord our God all your days, my son, and refuse to sin or to transgress his commandments. Live uprightly all the days of your life, and do not walk in the ways of wrongdoing.* ⁶*For if you do what is true, your ways will prosper through your deeds.* ⁷*Give alms from your possessions to all who live uprightly, and do not let your eye begrudge the gift when you make it. Do not turn your face away from any poor man, and the face of God will not be turned away from you.* ⁸*If you have many possessions, make your gift from them in proportion; if few, do not be afraid to give according to the little you have.* ⁹*So you will be laying up a good treasure for yourself against the day of necessity.* ¹⁰*For charity delivers from death and keeps you from entering the darkness;* ¹¹*and for all who practice it charity is an excellent offering in the presence of the Most High.*

¹²*"Beware, my son, of all immorality. First of all take a wife from among the descendants of your fathers and do not marry a foreign woman, who is not of your father's tribe; for we are the sons of the prophets. Remember, my son, that Noah, Abraham, Isaac, and Jacob, our fathers of old, all took wives from among their brethren. They were blessed in their children, and their posterity will inherit the land.* ¹³*So now, my son, love your brethren, and in your heart do not disdain your brethren and the sons and daughters of your people by refusing to take a wife for yourself from among them. For in pride there is ruin and great confusion; and in shiftlessness there is loss and great want, because shiftlessness is the mother of famine.* ¹⁴*Do not hold over till the next day the wages of any man who works for you, but pay him at once; and if you serve God you will receive payment.*

"Watch yourself, my son, in everything you do, and be disciplined in all your conduct. ¹⁵*And what you hate, do not do to any one. Do not drink wine to excess or let drunkenness go with you on your way.* ¹⁶*Give of your bread to the hungry, and of your clothing to the naked. Give all your surplus to charity, and do not let your eye begrudge the gift when you made it.* ¹⁷*Place your bread on the grave of the righteous, but give none to sinners.* ¹⁸*Seek advice from every wise man, and do not despise any useful counsel.* ¹⁹*Bless the Lord God on every occasion; ask him that your ways*

may be made straight and that all your paths and plans may prosper. For none of the nations has understanding; but the Lord himself gives all good things, and according to his will he humbles whomever he wishes.

"So, my son, remember my commands, and do not let them be blotted out of your mind. [20]*And now let me explain to you about the ten talents of silver which I left in trust with Gabael the son of Gabrias at Rages in Media.* [21]*Do not be afraid, my son, because we have become poor. You have great wealth if you fear God and refrain from every sin and do what is pleasing in his sight."*

o Other authorities omit *about the money*   * Tob 4:1-23 Vg.

OVERVIEW: A light different from the sun illuminates the just. The wicked complain when they are mistreated, but they do not change their behavior. It is better to remember piously the just than bring gifts to their tombs (AUGUSTINE).

4:10 Showing Charity

A SPECIAL LIGHT ILLUMINATES THE JUST. AUGUSTINE: "Light has arisen for the just person."[1] What light is there for a just man or woman? A certain light that does not rise for the unjust, different from the light that dawns on good and bad alike.[2] Another light rises on a righteous person, that light of which the unrighteous will confess at the end that it never dawned for them: "No doubt of it, we strayed from the path of truth. On us the light of righteousness did not shine, nor did the sun rise for us."[3] Reveling in the common light, they lay in darkness of heart. What did it profit to them to see daylight with their eyes, if their minds could not see the light beyond? Tobit was blind, yet he taught his son the way of God. You know this is true, because Tobit advised his son, "Give alms, my son, for almsdeeds save you from departing into darkness," yet the speaker was in darkness himself. Do you see from this that it is a different light that rises for a just person and good cheer for those of straightforward heart[4]? EXPOSITIONS OF THE PSALMS 96.18.[5]

4:15 Disciplined Conduct

THE WICKED PREFER WICKEDNESS TO

GOODNESS. AUGUSTINE: "You loved malice above kindness."[6] Do you want proof that an evil person can see both, malice and kindness, yet chooses malice and turns away from kindness? Here it is. Why do such people complain when suffering unjustly? Why do they, in that situation, exaggerate the injustice as much as possible while commending kindness and denounce the offender who in treating them so badly has put malice above kindness? Let such people be their own criterion; let them judge their own behavior by their experience. If they will only obey Scripture's injunction, "You shall love your neighbor as yourself,"[7] and "Whatever good you want people to do for you, do the same yourselves for them,"[8] they will have within themselves evidence that they must not treat others as they would not wish to be treated themselves. EXPOSITIONS OF THE PSALMS 51.10.[9]

4:17 Honoring the Righteous

THE JUST SHOULD BE REMEMBERED PIOUSLY. AUGUSTINE: It is obvious that a banquet does not benefit the dead, and that it is a custom of the pagans, and that it does not flow from the channel of justice derived from our ancestors the patriarchs; we read about their funerals being celebrated; we do not read of funeral sacrifices being offered for them. This can also be observed in the customs of the Jews, for while they

---

[1]Ps 97:11 (96:11 LXX). [2]See Mt 5:45. [3]Wis 5:6. [4]See Ps 32:11 (31:11 LXX). [5]NBA 27/1:395-97. [6]Ps 52:5 (51:5 LXX). [7]Lev 19:18; Mt 19:19; 22:39; Mk 12:31. [8]Mt 7:12. [9]WSA 3/17:22.

have not inherited from their ancestors the fruit of virtue, still they have retained the ancient customs in a number of their celebrations and ceremonies. And as for the objection some people bring forth from the Scriptures: "Break your bread and pour out your wine on the tombs of the just but do not hand it over to the unjust,"[10] this is not the occasion, indeed, to expatiate on it; but still I will say that the faithful can understand what is being said. It is well known, after all, to the faithful how the faithful do these things out of a religious respect for their dear departed; and that such rites are not to be granted to the unjust, that is, to unbelievers, because "the just person lives by faith."[11] SERMON 361.6.6.[12]

---

[10]Tob 4:17 (4:18 Vg). [11]Rom 1:17. [12]WSA 3/10:228.

5:1-21* A FELLOW TRAVELER

[1]Then Tobias answered him, "Father, I will do everything that you have commanded me; [2]but how can I obtain the money when I do not know the man?" [3]Then Tobit gave him the receipt, and said to him, "Find a man to go with you and I will pay him wages as long as I live; and go and get the money." [4]So he went to look for a man; and he found Raphael, who was an angel, [5]but Tobias did not know it. Tobias said to him, "Can you go with me to Rages in Media? Are you acquainted with that region?" [6]The angel replied, "I will go with you; I am familiar with the way, and I have stayed with our brother Gabael." [7]Then Tobias said to him, "Wait for me, and I shall tell my father." [8]And he said to him, "Go, and do not delay." So he went in and said to his father, "I have found some one to go with me." He said, "Call him to me, so that I may learn to what tribe he belongs, and whether he is a reliable man to go with you."

[9]So Tobias invited him in; he entered and they greeted each other. [10]Then Tobit said to him, "My brother, to what tribe and family do you belong? Tell me." [11]But he answered, "Are you looking for a tribe and a family or for a man whom you will pay to go with your son?" And Tobit said to him, "I should like to know, my brother, your people and your name." [12]He replied, "I am Azarias the son of the great Ananias, one of your relatives." [13]Then Tobit said to him, "You are welcome, my brother. Do not be angry with me because I tried to learn your tribe and family. You are a relative of mine, of a good and noble lineage. For I used to know Ananias and Jathan, the sons of the great Shemaiah, when we went together to Jerusalem to worship and offered the first-born of our flocks and the tithes of our produce. They did not go astray in the error of our brethren. My brother, you come of good stock. [14]But tell me, what wages am I to pay you—a drachma a day, and expenses for yourself as for my son? [15]And besides, I will add to your wages if you both return safe and sound." So they agreed to these terms.

[16]Then he said to Tobias, "Get ready for the journey, and good success to you both." So his son made the preparations for the journey. And his father said to him, "Go with this man; God who

dwells in heaven will prosper your way, and may his angel attend you." So they both went out and departed, and the young man's dog was with them.

[17]But Anna,[q] his mother, began to weep, and said to Tobit, "Why have you sent our child away? Is he not the staff of our hands as he goes in and out before us? [18]Do not add money to money, but consider it rubbish as compared to our child. [19]For the life that is given to us by the Lord is enough for us." [20]And Tobit said to her, "Do not worry, my sister; he will return safe and sound, and your eyes will see him. [21]For a good angel will go with him; his journey will be successful, and he will come back safe and sound." So she stopped weeping.

p Gk *he*   q Other authorities omit *Anna*   *Tob 5:1-28 Vg.

OVERVIEW: Raphael's words and deeds foretell in many ways the coming of Christ: his apparition to Tobias is viewed by the Fathers as an image of Christ's incarnation; when he affirms that Tobit will be healed, he anticipates the salvation brought by Christ; the names of his ancestors contain the promise of Christ's help and grace; when he assures that Tobias will return safely, he predicts the return of the Jewish people at the end of time (BEDE). Essential and absolute goodness is shared only by the Father, the Son and the Holy Spirit (ORIGEN).

5:4-5 *Raphael, an Angel*

CHRIST APPEARED TO THE WORLD. BEDE: An angel appeared to Tobias and offered himself as a companion through whom he might perform wonders for the people to whom he had been sent.[1] And the Son of God assumed the nature of a human being so that, thus visibly spending his life with human beings, he might save the human race.[2] ON TOBIT 3.25.[3]

5:12 *Azarias, a Relative*

RAPHAEL'S "ANCESTORS." BEDE: Azarias means "the Lord is my helper," Ananias, "the favor of the Lord." And the Lord intimates to those who believe in him that he is the one whom the prophet longed for when he sang, "Lord, you are my helper and liberator; do not delay,"[4] and of him too the Evangelist says, "And we saw his glory, the glory as it were of the Only-

begotten of the Father, full of grace and truth."[5] ON TOBIT 5.18.[6]

5:13[7] *Be of Good Courage*

CHRIST BRINGS HEALING. BEDE: And our Lord through the miracles he wrought in the flesh showed the Jewish people from whom he had taken flesh that he was the Son of God and the angel,[8] that is, the messenger, of his Father's will.[9] He also announced to them the joy of eternal salvation saying, "Do penance, for the kingdom of heaven will draw near";[10] and to those who despaired of obtaining heavenly light he said, "I am the light of the world; the one who follows me will not walk in darkness but will have the light of life."[11] ON TOBIT 5.11-13.[12]

5:15 *Traveling in Safety*

THE PEOPLE OF ISRAEL WILL RETURN. BEDE: The angel promises Tobit to bring his son to Rages, a city of the Medes, and bring him back to him.[13] The Lord promises the believers among the Jewish people (although this same people is largely blinded) that he will reveal the mysteries of his incarnation to the Gentile people, and again at the end of our times he will make them known more widely to his own people from

---

[1]See Lk 1:49. [2]See Bar 3:37 (3:38 Vg). [3]BTACH 44*; CCL 119B:6. [4]Ps 70:5 (69:6 LXX). [5]Jn 1:14. [6]BTACH 45*; CCL 119B:7. [7]Vg. [8]See Rom 9:5. [9]Bede alludes to the etymology of the Septuagint word *angelos*, which originally meant "messenger." [10]Mt 4:17. [11]Jn 8:12. [12]BTACH 45; CCL 119B:7. [13]See Tob 5:10-16 (5:14-15 Vg).

whom he had taken flesh,[14] when faith in his divinity will both accompany him everywhere and accomplish everything. Of the "bringing" to the Medes he says, "And I have other sheep which are not of this fold; these too I must bring," and so forth.[15] Of the "bringing back" the apostle says, "Until the fullness of the Gentiles should come in, and so all Israel should be saved."[16] On Tobit 5.11-13.[17]

5:21 A Good Angel

ONLY THE TRINITY IS ABSOLUTELY GOOD. ORIGEN: There is no other second goodness existing in the Son, except that which is in the Father. And therefore the Savior also rightly says in the Gospel, "There is none good except one only, God the Father."[18] With such an expression it may be understood that the Son is not of a different goodness but of that only that exists in the Father. He is rightly termed the image of the Father[19] because he proceeds from no other source but from that primal goodness. Otherwise there might appear to be in the Son a different goodness from that which is in the Father.

Nor is there any dissimilarity or difference of goodness in the Son. Therefore, no one should imagine that there is a kind of blasphemy, as it were, in the words, "There is none good except one only, God the Father,"[20] as if someone thinks this denies that either the Son or the Holy Spirit is good. However, as we have already said, the primal goodness is to be understood as residing in God the Father, from whom both the Son is born and the Holy Spirit proceeds,[21] retaining within them, without any doubt, the nature of that goodness that is in the source from which they are derived.[22] And if there is anything else in Scripture that is called good (angels, human beings,[23] servants,[24] treasure,[25] or a good heart[26] or a good tree[27]), the word *good* is not used with its proper meaning, since these uses refer to outward goodness, not an essential goodness. On First Principles 1.2.13.[28]

---

[14]See Rom 9:5. [15]Jn 10:16. [16]Rom 11:25-26. [17]BTACH 45*; CCL 119B:7. [18]Mk 10:18. [19]See Col 1:15. [20]Mk 10:18. [21]See Jn 15:26. [22]See Jn 15:26. [23]See Mt 12:35. [24]See Mt 25:21. [25]See Lk 6:45. [26]See Lk 8:15. [27]See Mt 7:17. [28]Simonetti UTET 162-63; ANF 4:251.

6:1-17* THE FISH

[1]Now as they proceeded on their way they came at evening to the Tigris river and camped there. [2]Then the young man went down to wash himself. A fish leaped up from the river and would have swallowed the young man; [3]and the angel said to him, "Catch the fish." So the young man seized the fish and threw it up on the land. [4]Then the angel said to him, "Cut open the fish and take the heart and liver and gall and put them away safely." [5]So the young man did as the angel told him; and they roasted and ate the fish.

And they both continued on their way until they came near to Ecbatana. [6]Then the young man said to the angel, "Brother Azarias, of what use is the liver and heart and gall of the fish?" [7]He replied, "As for the heart and liver, if a demon or evil spirit gives trouble to any one, you make a smoke from these before the man or woman, and that person will never be troubled again. [8]And as *for the gall, anoint with it a man who has white films in his eyes, and he will be cured."*

⁹When they approached Ecbatana,ʳ ¹⁰the angel said to the young man, "Brother, today we shall stay with Raguel. He is your relative, and he has an only daughter named Sarah. I will suggest that she be given to you in marriage, ¹¹because you are entitled to her and to her inheritance, for you are her only eligible kinsman. ¹²The girl is also beautiful and sensible. Now listen to my plan. I will speak to her father, and as soon as we return from Rages we will celebrate the marriage. For I know that Raguel, according to the law of Moses, cannot give her to another man without incurring the penalty of death, because you rather than any other man are entitled to the inheritance."

¹³Then the young man said to the angel, "Brother Azarias, I have heard that the girl has been given to seven husbands and that each died in the bridal chamber. ¹⁴Now I am the only son my father has, and I am afraid that if I go in I will die as those before me did, for a demon is in love with her, and he harms no one except those who approach her. So now I fear that I may die and bring the lives of my father and mother to the grave in sorrow on my account. And they have no other son to bury them."

¹⁵But the angel said to him, "Do you not remember the words with which your father commanded you to take a wife from among your own people? Now listen to me, brother, for she will become your wife; and do not worry about the demon, for this very night she will be given to you in marriage. ¹⁶When you enter the bridal chamber, you shall take live ashes of incense and lay upon them some of the heart and liver of the fish so as to make a smoke. ¹⁷Then the demon will smell it and flee away, and will never again return. And when you approach her, rise up, both of you, and cry out to the merciful God, and he will save you and have mercy on you. Do not be afraid, for she was destined for you from eternity. You will save her, and she will go with you, and I suppose that you will have children by her." When Tobias heard these things, he fell in love with her and yearned deeply for her.

---

r Other authorities read *Rages*   * Tob 6:1-22 Vg.

OVERVIEW: The dog shows how we should defend faith (AMBROSE), especially how those who preach Christ's message should act. The Lord was untouched by the sin, which is represented by the river Tigris. The fish is the devil, who tries to seize humankind but is defeated by Christ. Its tossings are the persecutions against the faithful. Its heart is a symbol of the shrewdness of the snake, its gall evokes circumspection, and its liver recalls reflection. Tobias's cry foretells Christ's anguish as his death was approaching. Christ's heat transforms those who were subject to the devil, and the salt is Christ's teaching. Raguel's and Sarah's names are figures of the church (BEDE).

6:1¹ *The Dog Followed Them*

THE GRATEFUL DOG DEFENDS THE FAITH.

AMBROSE: What shall I say about dogs, who have a natural instinct to show gratitude and to serve as watchful guardians of their masters' safety? Therefore Scripture cries out to the ungrateful, the slothful and the craven, telling them that they are "dumb dogs, not able to bark."² To dogs, therefore, is given the ability to bark in defense of their masters and their homes. Thus you should learn to use your voice for the sake of Christ, when ravening wolves attack his sheepfold. Have the word ready on your lips, lest, like a silent watchdog, you may appear because of your unfaithfulness to abandon the post entrusted to you. Such a dog was the friend and companion of an angel. Not without reason did Raphael in the prophetic book³ cause this

---

¹Vg. ²Is 56:10. ³Ambrose underlines that the book of Tobit is inspired, a position that was still occasionally questioned in his milieu.

dog to accompany the son of Tobias when he went on a journey, in order to drive out Asmodeus and thereby confirm the marriage.[4] The demon is driven out as the result of a grateful recognition, and the union is stabilized. And so, under the symbolism of a dumb animal, the angel Raphael, as director of the young man Tobias whom he had agreed to protect, was able to arouse sentiments of gratitude in him.[5] HEXAMERON 9.4.17.[6]

THOSE WHO PREACH CHRIST'S MESSAGE. BEDE: When the Lord came to save the Gentiles, holy preachers followed in his footsteps because they carried out what he had commanded: "Go and teach all the nations."[7] Finally the Lord filled the home of Cornelius with the Holy Spirit, and so Peter baptized them with water.[8] The teachers are called dogs because they defend their founder's spiritual home, property and sheep from thieves and beasts, that is, from unclean spirits and heretical people. ON TOBIT 6.1.[9]

THE TIGRIS RIVER REPRESENTS SIN. BEDE: Tobias stopped over by the waters of the Tigris because the Lord, when he appeared in the world, spent his life among sinners and mortals; but the water of sin did not touch him, nor did the prince of darkness, when he came, find in him anything of his own.[10] ON TOBIT 6.1-2.[11]

6:2 A Fish Leaped from the River

THE FISH IS THE DEVIL. BEDE: Here again the mystery of the Lord's passion is quite obviously signified. For the huge fish, which, since it wanted to devour him, was killed by Tobias on the angel's instructions, represents the ancient devourer of the human race, that is, the devil.[12] When the latter desired the death of humanity in our Redeemer, he was caught by the power of the divinity. The river Tigris, which, because of its swift current, takes its name from the tiger, a very swift animal, intimates the downward course of our death and mortality.[13] In it lurked

a huge fish, inasmuch as the invisible seducer of the human race held the power of death.[14] ON TOBIT 6.1-2.[15]

TOBIAS'S CRY FORETELLS CHRIST'S ANGUISH. BEDE: And the Lord as the critical moment of death was on him "began to tremble with fear and be deeply dismayed,"[16] not that he was greatly afraid of the devil but, through the natural frailty of the flesh, dreaded death, which "entered the world through the devil's envy."[17] This is why "he also prayed that, if it were possible, the hour might pass from him, and said, 'Abba, Father, all things are possible to you; remove this cup from me, but not what I will but what you will.'"[18] ON TOBIT 6.3.[19]

6:3 Catch the Fish

THE LORD RESCUED THOSE SEIZED BY THE DEVIL. BEDE: The Lord seized hold of the devil and by dying caught and conquered the one who wanted to catch him in death.[20] Moreover he seized him by the gill[21] so that, with the right hand of his power, he might separate his most wicked head from his entrapped body, that is, that he might remove the wickedness of the ancient enemy from the heart of those whom he had wickedly allied to himself and had made, as it were, one body with him, and that, as a merciful redeemer, he might graft them into the body of his church.[22] For a fish has a gill at the joining of its head and body. Now, just as our Lord is the head of his church and the church is his body, so the devil is the head of all the wicked and all the wicked are his head and members. The reason why the Lord

---

[4]See Tob 3:8; 8:3. [5]See also Tob 11:5 (11:9 Vg). [6]FC 42:236-37. [7]Mt 28:19. [8]See Acts 10:44-48. [9]BTACH 46*; CCL 119B:8. [10]See Jn 14:30. [11]BTACH 47; CCL 119B:8. [12]Tob 6:3 (6:4 Vg). [13]The connection between "Tigris" and "tiger" has no etymological foundation, even if it is traditional. [14]See Heb 2:14. [15]BTACH 46-47; CCL 119B:8. [16]Mk 14:33. [17]Wis 2:24. [18]Mk 14:35-36; see Mt 19:26; Mk 10:27; Lk 18:27. [19]BTACH 47*; CCL 119B:8-9. [20]See Heb 2:14. [21]See Tob 6:4 Vg. [22]See Eph 1:22-23; 5:23.

seized the very savage fish by the gill, dragged it towards him and cast it up on dry land[23] was that, in smashing them to pieces, he openly and boldly exposed the devil's capabilities in public and rescued from the power of darkness[24] those whom he foreknew to be children of light. ON TOBIT 6.4.[25]

6:4[26] *The Fish Began Tossing*

PERSECUTION PROVOKED BY THE DEVIL. BEDE: Although the Lord on overcoming the wickedness of the malicious enemy brought him forth into the light and exposed him to everyone, the latter was still arrogant and contrived to instigate persecution against the Lord's elect who are his feet because by their means the Lord, who is king in heaven over all things, walks on the earth. ON TOBIT 6.4.[27]

6:5 *Tobias Follows the Angel's Instructions*

THE MEANING OF HEART, LIVER AND GALL. BEDE: The Lord gutted the fish when he exposed more extensively to his saints the devil's wickedness and tore from their flesh, as it were, the secrets of his snares. He put away his heart for himself because he wanted to point out in the holy books his cunning, of which it is written, "Now the serpent was more cunning than any of the beasts of the earth";[28] and of this heart Paul too says, "For we are well aware of his intentions."[29] He also put away the gall, since, in his concern for caution he wanted the extent of the malicious fury with which he raged against the human race to be written about and put on record. The liver too he put away because he deigned to make known to us through the teachers of the truth the mischievous maturity of his intrigues against us. For they say that it is by the heat and power of the liver the hidden properties of the food that is eaten are "cooked out" and reach the system. But when with careful consideration we seek to find in what order the things we propose to do are to be carried out, we, as it were, cook out by the heat of the liver the foods received in the stomach. ON TOBIT 6.5.[30]

CHRIST'S HEAT TRANSFORMS THE FAITHFUL. BEDE: The amount of the fish they took for themselves signifies those who are changed from members of the devil into members of Christ, that is, are converted from unbelief to the faith; but the amount they left represents those who, on hearing God's Word, prefer to remain behind among the dead and decaying members of their deceiver rather than return to the companionship of the Savior. He broiled its flesh in those whom he found carnal but rendered spiritual and strong again by the fire of his love.[31] Finally the Holy Spirit came down on the apostles in a vision of fire.[32] "The rest,"[33] he says, "they salted," which is particularly applicable to teachers to whom it is said, "You are the salt of the earth."[34] Now they, that is, Tobias and the angel, salted it, because the same "mediator between God and people" both humanly taught the apostles by word and divinely gave them the salt of wisdom in their hearts.[35] ON TOBIT 6.6.[36]

6:10 *Raguel and Sarah*

FIGURES OF THE CHURCH. BEDE: Raguel stands for the people of the Gentiles whom the Lord deigned to visit through his preachers in order to take himself a bride from their stock, that is, make of the Gentiles a church for himself. Also Sarah's name befits the church because of Sarah, the patriarch Abraham's wife, who bore Isaac the son of the promise, that is, the free people of the church.[37] Raguel's name too, which means "God is his sustenance" or "God is my friend,"[38]

---

[23]Tob 6:4 Vg. [24]See Col 1:13. [25]BTACH 47-48; CCL 119B:9. [26]Vg. [27]BTACH 48*; CCL 119B:9. [28]Gen 3:1. [29]2 Cor 2:11. [30]BTACH 49*; CCL 119B:9-10. [31]See Tob 6:5 (6:6 Vg). [32]See Acts 2:3. [33]Tob 6:5 (6:6 Vg). [34]Mt 5:13. [35]See 1 Tim 2:5. [36]BTACH 50*; CCL 119B:10. [37]See Gal 4:28; Rom 9:7-9. [38]This etymology is traditional.

denotes the people who, after overcoming the devil's deceit, unite themselves and their folk to the community of the Lord and can say, "The Lord is my shepherd, and I shall want for nothing,"[39] and earn the reward of hearing, "I shall no longer call you servants" but "friends."[40] On Tobit 6.6.[41]

---

[39] Ps 23:1 (22:1 LXX). [40] Jn 15:11. [41] BTACH 50*; CCL 119B:10.

7:1-18* RAGUEL

[1] When they reached Ecbatana and arrived at the house of Raguel, Sarah met them and greeted them. They returned her greeting, and she brought them into the house. [2] Then Raguel said to his wife Edna, "How much the young man resembles my cousin Tobit!" [3] And Raguel asked them, "Where are you from, brethren?" They answered him, "We belong to the sons of Naphtali, who are captives in Nineveh." [4] So he said to them, "Do you know our brother Tobit?" And they said, "Yes, we do." And he asked them, "Is he in good health?" [5] They replied, "He is alive and in good health." And Tobias said, "He is my father." [6] Then Raguel sprang up and kissed him and wept. [7] And he blessed him and exclaimed, "Son of that good and noble man!" When he heard that Tobit had lost his sight, he was stricken with grief and wept. [8] And his wife Edna and his daughter Sarah wept. They received them very warmly; and they killed a ram from the flock and set large servings of food before them.

Then Tobias said to Raphael, "Brother Azarias, speak of those things which you talked about on the journey, and let the matter be settled." [9] So he communicated the proposal to Raguel. And Raguel said to Tobias, "Eat, drink, and be merry; [10] for it is your right to take my child. But let me explain the true situation to you. [11] I have given my daughter to seven husbands, and when each came to her he died in the night. But for the present be merry." And Tobias said, "I will eat nothing here until you make a binding agreement with me." [12] So Raguel said, "Take her right now, in accordance with the law. You are her relative, and she is yours. The merciful God will guide you both for the best." [13] Then he called his daughter Sarah, and taking her by the hand he gave her to Tobias to be his wife, saying, "Here she is; take her according to the law of Moses, and take her with you to your father." And he blessed them. [14] Next he called his wife Edna, and took a scroll and wrote out the contract; and they set their seals to it. [15] Then they began to eat.

[16] And Raguel called his wife Edna and said to her, "Sister, make up the other room, and take her into it." [17] So she did as he said, and took her there; and the girl[s] began to weep. But the mother[s] comforted her daughter in her tears, and said to her, [18] "Be brave, my child; the Lord of heaven and earth grant you joy[t] in place of this sorrow of yours. Be brave, my daughter."

s Gk *she*   t Other authorities read *favor*   * Tob 7:1-20 Vg.

Overview: Raguel is a figure of the pagans who welcome the preaching of the gospel. The seven husbands who died are the pagan sages who do not know eternal life (Bede).

7:1 Brought into the House

Pagans Welcome the Preaching of the Gospel. Bede: The Lord went to the Gentile people through the teachers of his word, and they gladly received it in a great many places, as the Acts of the Apostles testify. On Tobit 7.1.[1]

7:11 Seven Husbands

The Pagan Sages. Bede: The Gentile people, on hearing the message of the faith and being admonished by the apostles to form the church of Christ from their progeny throughout the world, were able (but only after reliable investigation) to undertake the obligations and rules of the new religion. For they knew that in former times they had had many teachers who all (comprised, as it were, in the number seven) knew about the joys of this life alone but had nothing reliable to say about eternal joys; and consequently the destruction of eternal death would have snatched them away without hope of immortal life. On Tobit 7.11.[2]

---

[1]BTACH 51; CCL 119B:11.   [2]BTACH 51*; CCL 119B:11.

8:1-21* THE TOMB

[1]When they had finished eating, they escorted Tobias in to her. [2]As he went he remembered the words of Raphael, and he took the live ashes of incense and put the heart and liver of the fish upon them and made a smoke. [3]And when the demon smelled the odor he fled to the remotest parts of Egypt, and the angel bound him. [4]When the door was shut and the two were alone, Tobias got up from the bed and said, "Sister, get up, and let us pray that the Lord may have mercy upon us." [5]And Tobias began to pray,
"Blessed art thou, O God of our fathers,
and blessed be thy holy and glorious name for ever.
Let the heavens and all thy creatures bless thee.
[6]Thou madest Adam and gavest him Eve his wife
as a helper and support.
From them the race of mankind has sprung.
Thou didst say, 'It is not good that the man should be alone;
let us make a helper for him like himself.'
[7]And now, O Lord, I am not taking this sister of mine because of lust, but with sincerity. Grant that I may find mercy and may grow old together with her." [8]And she said with him, "Amen." [9]Then they

both went to sleep for the night.

But Raguel arose and went and dug a grave, ¹⁰*with the thought, "Perhaps he too will die."* ¹¹*Then Raguel went into his house* ¹²*and said to his wife Edna, "Send one of the maids to see whether he is alive; and if he is not, let us bury him without any one knowing about it."* ¹³*So the maid opened the door and went in, and found them both asleep.* ¹⁴*And she came out and told them that he was alive.* ¹⁵*Then Raguel blessed God and said,*

"Blessed art thou, O God, with every pure and holy blessing.
  Let thy saints and all thy creatures bless thee;
  let all thy angels and thy chosen people bless thee for ever.
¹⁶*Blessed art thou, because thou hast made me glad.*
  It has not happened to me as I expected;
  but thou hast treated us according to thy great mercy.
¹⁷*Blessed art thou, because thou hast had compassion on two only children.*
  Show them mercy, O Lord;
  and bring their lives to fulfilment in health and happiness and mercy."
¹⁸*Then he ordered his servants to fill in the grave.*

¹⁹*After this he gave a wedding feast for them which lasted fourteen days.* ²⁰*And before the days of the feast were over, Raguel declared by oath to Tobias*^u *that he should not leave until the fourteen days of the wedding feast were ended,* ²¹*that then he should take half of Raguel's*^v *property and return in safety to his father, and that the rest would be his "when my wife and I die."*

u Gk *him*   v Gk *his*   * Tob 8:1-24 Vg.

OVERVIEW: Burning the entrails of the fish indicates the renunciation of Satan at baptism. The desert and Egypt are symbols of the hearts of the unbelieving, which are deserted and in the darkness. The doctors of faith are like cows who take on themselves the yoke of the gospel and like rams who govern the people. The four rams echo and prefigure many biblical themes—the cardinal virtues and the four Gospels to the four quarters of the world (BEDE).

8:2 *Ashes of Incense*

RENOUNCING SATAN TO JOIN THE LORD. BEDE: And the Lord, as he is about to receive the church from the Gentiles as his bride, bids it at first betrothal (in the person of each individual believer) to renounce Satan and all his works and all his pomps, and then to confess its faith in the holy Trinity for the remission of sins, which is the significance of burning up with live coals the innermost entrails of the fish.[1] On TOBIT 8.2.[2]

8:3 *The Demon Fled*

FREEING THE UNBELIEVING. BEDE: Both "desert" and "Egypt" refer to the hearts of unbelievers, which are deserts, that is, forsaken by God of whose indwelling they are unworthy; and according to the meaning of the name "Egypt," these same hearts are plunged into shadow by the darkness of their own unbelief.[3] And not without reason is the one who is deserted by the grace of divine light filled by the prince of darkness. The reason why the angel got hold of the demon that wanted to kill Tobias and bound him in the desert of upper Egypt is that the devil, while restrained from snatching away the faithful who are members of their Redeemer, is allowed by this Lord and redeemer of ours to have dominion over unbelievers only. And even

---

[1]Bede summarizes the ritual of baptism.   [2]*BTACH* 52*; CCL 119B:11.   [3]Often Egypt is characterized as the country from which the darkness of idolatry originates.

in their case the Lord holds him bound because even the wicked, the very ones of whom he is master, he is not allowed to harm as much as he longs to in his insatiable rage. ON TOBIT 8.3.[4]

8:19 Calves and Rams Slaughtered

SYMBOLS OF THE FAITH, THE GOSPELS AND THE VIRTUES. BEDE: Our own teachers are indeed like cattle[5] because they bear the light yoke of the gospel,[6] for by preaching they beget and nurture those also who would advance further toward bearing the same yoke. They are the rams too because they are the fathers and leaders of the peoples who follow them, of whom it is said, "Bring to the Lord the offspring of rams."[7] They are moreover fat cattle because they are teachers filled to overflowing with the grace of heavenly love, of which grace the psalmist prays, "Let my soul be filled as with marrow and fat."[8] They are the two slaughtered cattle because all who for Christ either voluntarily mortify their body themselves, that they may become a living victim,[9] or hand it over to the enemy to be killed, these assuredly have learned to withstand the enemy "with the weapons of uprightness to the right and to the left,"[10] that is, in prosperity and adversity. They are the four slaughtered rams because holy teachers and martyrs preserve the four books of the holy gospel by faith and action, because they are supported by the four cardinal virtues of prudence, fortitude, temperance and justice, for they instruct the flock of Christ throughout the whole world, which is divided up into four quarters. Raguel had cattle and rams slaughtered because the Gentile people taught that those who had come to the faith from their own stock were like those whom, because of their outstanding virtue, the enemy desired to tempt and succeeded not in conquering after they were tempted but rather in making victorious as martyrs.[11] Or at all events he had those killed whom he taught to crucify their flesh for Christ with its vices and passions.[12] ON TOBIT 8.22.[13]

---

[4]BTACH 52*; CCL 119B:11-12. [5]The Vulgate affirms that Raguel had had "two cows" slaughtered; the Septuagint speaks of "two calves." [6]See Mt 11:30. [7]Ps 29:1 (28:1 LXX), variant. [8]Ps 63:6 (62:6 LXX). [9]See Rom 12:1. [10]See 2 Cor 6:7. [11]See Tob 8:19 (8:22 Vg). [12]See Gal 5:24. [13]BTACH 53-54*; CCL 119B:12-13.

9:1–10:12* THE WEDDING

[1]Then Tobias called Raphael and said to him, [2]"Brother Azarias, take a servant and two camels with you and go to Gabael at Rages in Media and get the money for me; and bring him to the wedding feast. [3]For Raguel has sworn that I should not leave; [4]but my father is counting the days, and if I delay long he will be greatly distressed." [5]So Raphael made the journey and stayed over night with Gabael. He gave him the receipt, and Gabael[w] brought out the money bags with their seals intact and gave them to him. [6]In the morning they both got up early and came to the wedding feast. And Gabael blessed Tobias and his wife.[x]

---

10 Now his father Tobit was counting each day, and when the days for the journey had expired and they did not arrive, [2]he said, "Is it possible that he has been detained?[y] Or is it possible that Gabael has died and there is no one to give him the money?" [3]And he was greatly distressed. [4]And his wife said to him, "The lad has perished; his long delay proves it." Then she began to mourn for him, and said, [5]"Am I not distressed, my child, that I let you go, you who are the light of my eyes?" [6]But Tobit said to her, "Be still and stop worrying; he is well." [7]And she answered him, "Be still and stop deceiving me; my child has perished." And she went out every day to the road by which they had left; she ate nothing in the daytime, and throughout the nights she never stopped mourning for her son Tobias, until the fourteen days of the wedding feast had expired which Raguel had sworn that he should spend there.

At that time Tobias said to Raguel, "Send me back, for my father and mother have given up hope of ever seeing me again." [8]But his father-in-law said to him, "Stay with me, and I will send messengers to your father, and they will inform him how things are with you." [9]Tobias replied, "No, send me back to my father." [10]So Raguel arose and gave him his wife Sarah and half of his property in slaves, cattle, and money. [11]And when he had blessed them he sent them away, saying, "The God of heaven will prosper you, my children, before I die." [12]He said also to his daughter, "Honor your father-in-law and your mother-in-law; they are now your parents. Let me hear a good report of you." And he kissed her. And Edna said to Tobias, "The Lord of heaven bring you back safely, dear brother, and grant me to see your children by my daughter Sarah, that I may rejoice before the Lord. See, I am entrusting my daughter to you; do nothing to grieve her."

w Gk he   x Cn: Gk And Tobias blessed his wife   y One Gk Ms Lat: Gk they are put to shame or they are disappointed   * Tob 9:1-6; 10:1-12; (9:1-12; 10:1-13 Vg).

OVERVIEW: Servants and camels are the preachers of the faith serving those who evangelize. Tobit's affliction concerns the Jews' long wait for salvation (BEDE).

9:2 Take a Servant and Two Camels

THOSE WHO PREACH THE FAITH. BEDE: The preachers chosen from the Gentiles through whom the Lord gathers in others too are Raguel's servants and camels: servants because they serve the needs of those they evangelize; camels because with the deference of brotherly love they also carry the burdens of their infirmity.[1] But the reason why there were four servants and two camels has been shown above where two cows and four rams were slaughtered.[2] ON TOBIT 9.6.[3]

10:3 Greatly Distressed

THE LONG WAIT. BEDE: And now as Christ through faith delays in the church assembled from the Gentiles, all who are converted to faith in him individually from among the Jews are deeply distressed in spirit that the Lord, detained as he is among the Gentiles, is slow in coming to save them.[4] ON TOBIT 10.1-3.[5]

---

[1]See Is 53:4. [2]See Tob 8:19 (8:22 Vg). [3]BTACH 55; CCL 119B:13-14. [4]Bede plays on the two senses of the Latin word *mora* ("delay" and "stay"). [5]BTACH 55; CCL 119B:14.

11:1-19* THE EYES

¹After this Tobias went on his way, praising God because he had made his journey a success. And he blessed Raguel and his wife Edna.

So he continued on his way until they came near to Nineveh. ²Then Raphael said to Tobias, "Are you not aware, brother, of how you left your father? ³Let us run ahead of your wife and prepare the house. ⁴And take the gall of the fish with you." So they went their way, and the dog went along behind them.

⁵Now Anna sat looking intently down the road for her son. ⁶And she caught sight of him coming, and said to his father, "Behold, your son is coming, and so is the man who went with him!"

⁷Raphael said, "I know, Tobias, that your father will open his eyes. ⁸You therefore must anoint his eyes with the gall; and when they smart he will rub them, and will cause the white films to fall away, and he will see you."

⁹Then Anna ran to meet them, and embraced her son, and said to him, "I have seen you, my child; now I am ready to die." And they both wept. ¹⁰Tobit started toward the door, and stumbled. But his son ran to him ¹¹and took hold of his father, and he sprinkled the gall upon his father's eyes, saying, "Be of good cheer, father." ¹²And when his eyes began to smart he rubbed them, ¹³and the white films scaled off from the corners of his eyes. ¹⁴Then he saw his son and embraced him, and he wept and said, "Blessed art thou, O God, and blessed is thy name for ever, and blessed are all thy holy angels. ¹⁵For thou hast afflicted me, but thou hast had mercy upon me; here I see my son Tobias!" And his son went in rejoicing, and he reported to his father the great things that had happened to him in Media.

¹⁶Then Tobit went out to meet his daughter-in-law at the gate of Nineveh, rejoicing and praising God. Those who saw him as he went were amazed because he could see. ¹⁷And Tobit gave thanks before them that God had been merciful to him. When Tobit came near to Sarah his daughter-in-law, he blessed her, saying, "Welcome, daughter! Blessed is God who has brought you to us, and blessed are your father and your mother." So there was rejoicing among all his brethren in Nineveh. ¹⁸Ahikar and his nephew Nadab[z] came, ¹⁹and Tobias' marriage was celebrated for seven days with great festivity.

z Other authorities read *Nasbas*   * Tob 11:1-21 Vg.

OVERVIEW: The dog indicates those who labor announcing the salvation and rejoice when it arrives. The white films indicate the current blindness of the Jews, and the egg is a symbol of hope. The two meanings of number seven: the gifts of grace and the arrival of Israel's conversion (BEDE). There are both differences and similarities between the healings of the man born blind and Tobit's (ORIGEN).

11:4 The Dog Went Behind Them

THE DOG ANNOUNCES THE ARRIVAL OF SALVATION. BEDE: One must not dismiss with scorn the figure of this dog, which is a traveler and the companion of an angel. So, as we have also pointed out above, he represents the church's teachers who by combating heretics often drive off troublesome wolves[1] from the supreme pastor's fold.[2] To them fittingly applies the fact that it is natural to dogs to repay a favor to those who are kind to them and patrol in restless vigil for their masters' safety. The reason why the dog ran ahead is that the teacher first preaches salvation; then the Lord, the enlightener, cleanses hearts. And the writer made the charming observation, "arriving as if bringing the news,"[3] because, of course, every sincerely believing teacher is a messenger of truth; charmingly "did he show his joy by wagging his tail,"[4] for the tail, which is the end of the body, suggests the end of a good work, that is, its perfection, or at any rate the reward that is granted without end. The dog then showed his joy by wagging his tail when he saw once more his master's homestead from which he was absent for a long time; teachers rejoice at the results of their work when they realize that by means of their ministry Judea is to be brought together again by the Lord; they rejoice at receiving an eternal award, and with this same reward common to all the elect they cheer the hearts of those they preach to when they promise them that Christ's grace will come without delay. On Tobit 11.9.[5]

11:13 The White Films Scaled Off

Hope for the Current Blindness of the Jews. Bede: And the Jewish people, on realizing the very bitter malice of the most wicked enemy, will recover the light they have lost. The white film that had obstructed his eyes denotes the folly of self-indulgence. For "they have a zeal for God, but it is not based on knowledge," and as Paul says again, "seeking to establish their own righteousness, they did not submit to the righteousness of God."[6] The black pupil of the eye sees, the white one grows dark; and people who in their own estimation are wise, saying, "Are we also blind?"[7] in such people there is no truth.[8] But those who are aware of their frailty and ignorance and know how to say, "My God, enlighten my darkness," are destined to enjoy the light of life in the Lord.[9] Moreover, the white film was well compared with the skin of an egg. By the egg hope is surely indicated, because it is obviously not alive, not an animate creature, but it is hoped by the bird that laid it that sometime it may live, walk, run and fly. And the apostle says, "But if we hope for what we do not see, we wait for it with patience."[10] Thus in the Gospel parable by the terms "bread," "fish" and an "egg" the three supreme virtues, namely, faith, hope and love, are symbolized.[11] On Tobit 11.14-15.[12]

11:14 Tobit Sees His Son

The Man Born Blind and Tobit. Origen: It is necessary to observe the means of expression the Evangelist used as to whether he says to us that the eyes of the blind person were opened or that he saw. He expresses that he opened his eyes with the words, "It was the sabbath when Jesus made the mud and opened his eyes."[13] But it also says that he saw with the words, "He went and returned seeing."[14] We will be able to find the difference between the expressions from Tobit. When white patches had formed over his eyes, it is not written that his eyes were later opened but that he saw. Of the rest, you will be able to observe one or the other aspect in the course of the entire episode related concerning the blind person, where one person asserts one thing and another that, with quite a bit of dissent from each other.[15] Commentary on the Gospel of John, fragment 66.[16]

11:19 For Seven Days

Grace and Israel's Conversion. Bede: The seven days suggest the light of the grace of the

[1]See Acts 20:29. [2]See 1 Pet 5:4. [3]Tob 11:9 Vg. [4]See Tob 11:9 Vg. [5]BTACH 57*; CCL 119B:15. [6]Rom 10:2-3. [7]Jn 9:40. [8]See Jn 8:44; 1 Jn 2:4. [9]Ps 18:28 (17:29 LXX). [10]Rom 8:25. [11]See Lk 11:11-12. [12]BTACH 58-59*; CCL 119B:16. [13]Jn 9:14. [14]Jn 9:7. [15]See Jn 9:16. [16]Trad. Corsini 870.

Spirit, which is received in sevenfold form.[17] The reason why his son's wife arrives seven days after Tobit is given the light of vision[18] is that after Judea is given the light through faith, after it receives the grace of the Holy Spirit, the church will come in to it so that there may be "one fold and one shepherd"[19] and one house of Christ supported on one cornerstone.[20] On Tobit 11.16-18.[21]

---

[17]See Is 11:2-3. [18]See Tob 11:18 Vg. [19]Jn 10:16. [20]See Eph 2:20; 1 Pet 2:5-6. [21]BTACH 59-60*; CCL 119B:17.

12:1-22 RAPHAEL

[1]*Tobit then called his son Tobias and said to him, "My son, see to the wages of the man who went with you; and he must also be given more." [2]He replied, "Father, it would do me no harm to give him half of what I have brought back. [3]For he has led me back to you safely, he cured my wife, he obtained the money for me, and he also healed you." [4]The old man said, "He deserves it." [5]So he called the angel and said to him, "Take half of all that you two have brought back."*

[6]*Then the angel[a] called the two of them privately and said to them: "Praise God and give thanks to him; exalt him and give thanks to him in the presence of all the living for what he has done for you. It is good to praise God and to exalt his name, worthily declaring the works of God. Do not be slow to give him thanks. [7]It is good to guard the secret of a king, but gloriously to reveal the works of God. Do good, and evil will not overtake you. [8]Prayer is good when accompanied by fasting, almsgiving, and righteousness. A little with righteousness is better than much with wrongdoing. It is better to give alms than to treasure up gold. [9]For almsgiving delivers from death, and it will purge away every sin. Those who perform deeds of charity and of righteousness will have fulness of life; [10]but those who commit sin are the enemies of their own lives.*

[11]*"I will not conceal anything from you. I have said, 'It is good to guard the secret of a king, but gloriously to reveal the works of God.' [12]And so, when you and your daughter-in-law Sarah prayed, I brought a reminder of your prayer before the Holy One; and when you buried the dead, I was likewise present with you. [13]When you did not hesitate to rise and leave your dinner in order to go and lay out the dead, your good deed was not hidden from me, but I was with you. [14]So now God sent me to heal you and your daughter-in-law Sarah. [15]I am Raphael, one of the seven holy angels who present the prayers of the saints and enter into the presence of the glory of the Holy One." [16]They were both alarmed; and they fell upon their faces, for they were afraid. [17]But he said to them, "Do not be afraid; you will be safe. But praise God for ever. [18]For I did not come as a favor on my part, but by the will of our God. Therefore praise him for ever. [19]All these days I merely appeared to you and did not eat or drink, but you were seeing a vision. [20]And now give thanks to God, for I am ascending to him who sent me. Write in a book everything that has happened." [21]Then they stood up; but they saw him no more. [22]So they confessed the great and wonderful works of God, and acknowledged that the angel of the Lord had appeared to them.*

a Gk *he*

OVERVIEW: We should not spread the mysteries of the faith carelessly but should rather keep them in our hearts to be given only to those who will appreciate them (HILARY OF POITIERS). If you do not fast, give at least food to the hungry. Wealth is an occasion to make mercy to the poor (GAUDENTIUS). The angels rejoice when we worship God, whereas the devil wants to be worshiped (AUGUSTINE). Tobias and Raphael are symbols of Christ's humanity and divinity (BEDE). The angels nourish themselves from the vision of God; their mission is to praise and serve him (JOHN OF DAMASCUS).

12:7 Guard the Secret of a King

KEEPING IN OUR HEARTS THE MYSTERIES OF FAITH. HILARY OF POITIERS: "I have hidden your words in my heart, so as not to sin against you."[1] Recall that something similar is often read, where it says, "It is good to hide the mystery of the king." Recall that Paul also hid some divine words from the Corinthians, who were still young in the faith, saying, "I have given you milk to drink, not solid food. In fact, you were not yet ready, and neither are you now."[2] We also read in the Gospel of the treasure found in a fertile, fruitful field and that was hidden in the field once it was purchased.[3] We know also that pearls should not be thrown before swine, and what is sacred should not be given to dogs.[4] We thus understand that some things are enclosed in the secret of our hearts. If they were to be divulged, it would imply the guilt of an unpardonable sin. HOMILIES ON THE PSALMS 118.BETH.6.[5]

12:8-9 Prayer, Fasting, Almsgiving, Righteousness

PRETEXTS NOT TO HELP THE POOR. GAUDENTIUS OF BRESCIA: It is written that fasting with almsgiving is a good thing. It was necessary to do both, to mitigate the Lord's indignation. Perhaps you cannot fast, and you cannot because you do not want to—at least give food to someone who is hungry. You who cannot stand to fast for three hours past the usual hour can certainly understand what someone would suffer who unwillingly goes hungry because of his poverty. Your cruelty forces him to fast, you who, fattened by sumptuous banquets, do not think to relieve the poor person's hunger with even a little food. You point to the possibility of famine, you pretend to be in need, you complain of unfavorable circumstances. You beg more shamefully than that poor person—indeed, you behave toward God like an ingrate with your false complaining. But what if there was a famine? Would you perhaps be the only one to feel it, and not that poor person? How is it that every day you lay out new silver, beautify your houses with marble, buy silk garments, trade necklaces adorned with gold and gems? It is shameful to mention and painful even to think of the number of peasants who, living on the lands of people who live in the luxury we have described, have died of hunger or been supported by the alms of the church. SERMONS 13.21-23.[6]

ALMS ARE A TREASURE IN HEAVEN. GAUDENTIUS OF BRESCIA: Perhaps some rich person might object, "Therefore it must have been with malice that God gave us wealth, if because of it the rich are tormented."[7] Such people, in fact, advance the wrong-headed idea that God wants to see human beings make mistakes and therefore provides not only the mode of sin but also the reason for it. Not out of malice but out of providence has God made you rich. He intended that through your works of mercy you would again find medicine to treat the wounds of your sins. "Certainly alms freely given preserve one from death and purify from every sin." The rich man was not tormented because he was rich but because Lazarus suffered hunger while he banqueted.[8] Although holy Abraham had been

---

[1]Ps 119:11 (118:11 LXX). [2]1 Cor 3:2. [3]See Mt 13:44. [4]See Mt 7:6. [5]CTP 186:31-32. [6]CTP 129:125-26. [7]See Lk 16:22-31. [8]See Lk 16:19-21.

a rich man, he was a servant of the poor and indigent. Also, holy Job possessed the kingdom of Arabia,[9] but, as it is written, no one was deprived, no poor person left his house empty-handed.[10] And then, when he came to find himself in pain, he was excoriated by his wife for his works of mercy that she implied he had kept working at in vain. "And now," she says, "here you are suffering."[11] Whew! See how astutely this poisonous snake offers her venom! Since she could not make him recede from the good works he was doing as a servant of God, she was given to make him repent of the good he had accomplished because he lost the fruit of his goodness. The rich, therefore, should beware of the terrible example of those who enrich themselves at the expense of mercy so that they do not undergo similar tortures. Rather, they should practice almsgiving with generosity, frequency and joy; "God in fact loves one who gives with joy."[12] They distribute their wealth to the poor, acquiring "treasures in heaven where neither rust nor moth destroy or thieves dig and steal."[13] Thus, leaving this world, they will be able to find rest in the truly rich bosom of Abraham.[14] To Benivolus 21-27.[15]

12:12 Bringing a Reminder of Prayer

Angels and Satan. Augustine: If some human being, but also if any angel, seemingly, should wish to tempt you, either through some kind of apparition or through a dream, and say, "Do this for me, celebrate this rite for me, because I am," for example, "the angel Gabriel," don't believe him.[16] As for you, stick safely to worshiping the one God who is Father and Son and Holy Spirit. If it is really an angel, he will rejoice at your worshiping like that; but if he gets angry because you haven't given him something extra, then you must now understand him to be the one about whom the apostle says that he "transfigures himself into an angel of light."[17] He wants to block your way; he is intruding himself with evil intent; he is not the mediator who rec-

onciles but rather the one who separates. I mean, that angel in the Apocalypse and others like him do not want themselves, but God, to be adored.[18] They are messengers, announcing whatever message they have been given to announce; they are "attendants,"[19] doing whatever they have been ordered to do, presenting our prayers to God, not demanding them for themselves in God's stead. The angel says to the man, "I offered your petition in the presence of the glory of God," and yet the man was not pleading with the angel but with God; the attendant offered his prayer. Newly Discovered Sermons 198.48.[20]

12:15 I Am Raphael

Christ's Humanity and Divinity. Bede: By the latter, quite appropriately, the divinity of our Savior is signified, just as his humanity is by Tobias. And the fact that we say that by two persons, that is, an angel and a man, the one person of the mediator between God and people is denoted in a figure,[21] will be no surprise to the one who reads in the commentaries of the venerable Fathers that in Isaac who was offered up by his father on an altar, and in the ram that was immolated, was denoted in figure as the one person of him who suffered for the world's salvation.[22] He in his humanity was slaughtered like a sheep, but in his divinity he remains with God the Father incapable of suffering, just as Isaac came back home alive with his father.[23] For if the ram aptly represents the humanity of Christ and the man his godhead, why should not a man much more aptly signify his humanity and an angel his divinity? On Tobit 3.7-8.[24]

12:19 Not Eating or Drinking

The Nature and Mission of the Angels.

---

[9]See Job 42:17 LXX. [10]See Job 22:9. [11]Job 2:9. [12]2 Cor 9:7. [13]Mt 6:20. [14]See Lk 16:22. [15]CTP 129:25-26. [16]See Gal 1:8. [17]2 Cor 11:14. [18]See Rev 19:10; 22:9. [19]See Heb 1:14. [20]WSA 3/11:217. [21]See 1 Tim 2:5. [22]See Gen 22:10-13. [23]See Is 53:7; Acts 8:23. [24]BTACH 43-44*; CCL 119B:6.

JOHN OF DAMASCUS: The angels see God to such extent as is possible for them, and this is their food. Although, because they are incorporeal, they are superior to us and free of all bodily passion, they are certainly not passionless, because only the Divinity is passionless. They take whatever form the Lord may command, and thus they appear to people and reveal the divine mysteries to them. They live in heaven and have as their one work to sing the praises of God and minister to his sacred will. ORTHODOX FAITH 2.3.[25]

---

[25]FC 37:207-8.

13:1-18* ZION

[1]Then Tobit wrote a prayer of rejoicing, and said:
"Blessed is God who lives for ever,
    and blessed is his kingdom.
[2]For he afflicts, and he shows mercy;
    he leads down to Hades, and brings up again,
    and there is no one who can escape his hand.
[3]Acknowledge him before the nations, O sons of Israel;
    for he has scattered us among them.
[4]Make his greatness known there,
    and exalt him in the presence of all the living;
because he is our Lord and God,
    he is our Father for ever.
[5]He will afflict us for our iniquities;
    and again he will show mercy,
and will gather us from all the nations
    among whom you[b] have been scattered.
[6]If you turn to him with all your heart and with all your soul,
    to do what is true before him,
then he will turn to you
    and will not hide his face from you.
But see what he will do with you;
    give thanks to him with your full voice.
Praise the Lord of righteousness,
    and exalt the King of the ages.
I give him thanks in the land of my captivity,
    and I show his power and majesty to a nation of sinners.

Turn back, you sinners, and do right before him;
    who knows if he will accept you and have mercy on you?
[7]I exalt my God;
    my soul exalts the King of heaven,
    and will rejoice in his majesty.
[8]Let all men speak,
    and give him thanks in Jerusalem.
[9]O Jerusalem, the holy city,
    he will afflict you for the deeds of your sons,
    but again he will show mercy to the sons of the righteous.
[10]Give thanks worthily to the Lord,
    and praise the King of the ages,
    that his tent may be raised for you again with joy.
May he cheer those within you who are captives,
    and love those within you who are distressed,
    to all generations for ever.
[11]Many nations will come from afar to the name of the Lord God,
    bearing gifts in their hands, gifts for the King of heaven.
Generations of generations will give you joyful praise.
[12]Cursed are all who hate you;
    blessed for ever will be all who love you.
[13]Rejoice and be glad for the sons of the righteous;
    for they will be gathered together,
    and will praise the Lord of the righteous.
[14]How blessed are those who love you!
    They will rejoice in your peace.
Blessed are those who grieved over all your afflictions;
    for they will rejoice for you upon seeing all your glory,
    and they will be made glad for ever.
[15]Let my soul praise God the great King.
[16]For Jerusalem will be built with sapphires and emeralds,
    her[c] walls with precious stones,
    and her towers and battlements with pure gold.
[17]The streets of Jerusalem will be paved[d] with beryl and ruby and stones of Ophir;
    [18]all her lanes will cry 'Hallelujah!' and will give praise,
    saying, 'Blessed is God, who has exalted you for ever.'"

b Other authorities read *we*   c Gk *your*   d Or *inlaid*   * Tob 13:1-23 Vg.

OVERVIEW: Blessed are those who love God and everybody in and because of God (AUGUSTINE). In heaven the praise of God is eternally chanted (GREGORY THE GREAT). Heavenly Jerusalem is the place where there is every good thing and every rejoicing in the presence of God (PSEUDO-AUGUSTINE). The hallelujah is chanted during Eastertide as a pledge of perpetual joy (BEDE).

13:14 Blessed Are Those Who Love God

LOVE FRIENDS AND FOES IN GOD. AUGUSTINE:

Everything is loved among friends, and it is so loved that the human conscience feels guilty before itself if it does not love one who returns the love and if it does not give love for love, seeking nothing in a bodily way beyond the signs of good will. From this comes that lamentation, if someone dies, the darkness of sorrow and the heart steeped in tears, by sweetness turned to bitterness, and the death of the living arising from the lost life of the dead. Happy is one who loves God and his friend in God and his enemy because of God.[1] He alone loses no dear one, since all people are dear in God who is never lost. And who is this but our God, the God who is the maker of heaven and earth[2] and who fills them up[3] because he makes them by filling them? No one loses God unless he leaves God. And, because he leaves God, where can he go or flee[4] except from your pleasure into your ire? For where does he not find your law in his punishment? And "your law is the truth"[5] and "you are the truth."[6] CONFESSIONS 4.9.14.[7]

13:18 Crying "Hallelujah!"

PRAISE OF THE HEAVENLY JERUSALEM.
PSEUDO-AUGUSTINE: Will I ever be able to see what is so desirable, what the angels long to gaze on,[8] so I can say, "Look, now I see what I have so longed for, what I wanted I now possess!"? When will I come and appear before the face of the Lord,[9] to contemplate him in the blessedness of his elect, to know the joy of his people and to glory in his inheritance?[10] When will I see that city of which it is said, "Your squares, Jerusalem, will be paved with pure gold, and in you will resound a hymn of exultation, and in all your streets they will say, 'Alleluia!'"?[11] O holy city, O splendid city! I salute you from afar, I invoke you, I seek you. I desire to see you and to rest in you, but the flesh that holds me back does not let me do so. O desirable city! Your walls are a single stone, your guardian will be God, your citizens will always be glad, since they enjoy forever the vision of God. There is no corrup-

tion in you, or defect, or old age or anger—but perennial peace, unchanging glory, eternal joy, continual celebration. Truly there is only joy and exultation, the flower and confidence of youth and of complete salvation. In you there is neither yesterday nor past, but all is today, since yesterday is your tomorrow and the past is everlasting and the same. Health is in you, life is in you, to you belongs infinite peace, and for you God is everything. "Of you they say marvelous things, O city of God."[12] "All make their dwelling in you with joy."[13] In you there is no fear or sadness. Every desire is turned into joy, since everything that can be desired is within reach, and everything one could want is there in abundance. All your inhabitants will receive a full measure[14] of happiness, so that all might visibly rejoice together, without end. All will rejoice together, because the brothers and sisters will live together[15] when all will gather in a single place. Finally, all will be one, as he who was worthy of his prayer being heard deigned to pray for his family, "As you, Father, are in me and I in you, may they also be one in us."[16] BOOK ON THE SPIRIT AND THE SOUL 60.[17]

THE BIBLE REVEALS THE HEAVENLY SONGS.
GREGORY THE GREAT: So as to gladden you in the promise of the joy to come, you know the songs of eternal praise that are written in this book, "Blessed are those who dwell in your house, O Lord; forever they will sing your praise!"[18] And how through a certain wise man[19] it is said of the heavenly Jerusalem, "All your squares will be paved with precious stones, and in all your streets they will sing alleluia."[20] This song of the eternal homeland was proclaimed to us by its citizens, who together cried out,

[1]See Tob 13:15 (13:18 Vg); Mt 5:44; Lk 6:27. [2]See Gen 1:1. [3]See Jer 23:24. [4]See Ps 139:7 (138:7 LXX). [5]Ps 119:142 (118:142 LXX). [6]See Jn 14:6. [7]FC 21:85. [8]See 1 Pet 1:12. [9]Ps 42:3 (41:3 LXX). [10]See Ps 106:5 (105:5 LXX). [11]Tob 13:17-18 (13:22 Vg). [12]Ps 87:3 (86:3 LXX). [13]Ps 87:7, variant (86:7 LXX). [14]See Lk 6:38. [15]See Ps 133:1 (132:1 LXX). [16]Jn 17:21. [17]PL 40:824-25. [18]Ps 84:5 (83:5 LXX). [19]Gregory omits Tobit's name as if it were still not wholly proper to use the book. [20]Tob 13:17-18 (13:22 Vg).

"Glory to God in the highest heavens, and peace on earth to people of good will."[21] HOMILIES ON EZEKIEL 1.9.34.[22]

AN ANTICIPATION OF ETERNAL JOY. BEDE:
Thus our custom is to chant "Alleluia" more frequently and happily during these fifty days in memory of this, our most peaceful and blissful action.[23] Alleluia is a Hebrew word, and in Latin it means "praise the Lord!" Accordingly, where we chant in the psalms, "Praise the Lord," in place of this expression among the Jews "Alleluia" is always chanted. In his book of Revelation, John the Evangelist mentions that he had heard the throngs of heavenly virtues singing it.[24] And when the venerable father Tobit had understood from an angelic vision what the glory of the citizens on high is, and the great brightness of the heavenly Jerusalem, he said the following with mystical voice, "All its streets are paved with precious and shining stones, and throughout all its districts 'Alleluia' will be sung." [25]

It is most proper and beautiful that a general custom has prevailed in holy church of all the faithful throughout the world singing this word of praise in the Hebrew language, out of reverence for the primitive practice. This has come about so that, through the harmony of such a devotion, the whole church may be admonished that now it ought to consist in one faith, confession and love of Christ, and in the future it ought to hurry to that land in which there is no discord of minds, no disharmony of speech. For just as once in Jerusalem the heart and soul of the multitude of the believers was one and all things were theirs in common, so in the "vision of supreme peace" the heart and soul of the entire multitude of those who see God will be one, loving and praising him by whose grace they see that they have been saved. [26] There everything will truly be theirs in common, for, as the apostle says, "God will be all in all."[27] HOMILIES ON THE GOSPELS 2.16.[28]

---

[21]Lk 2:14. [22]CTP 17:203. [23]Bede refers to the Western liturgy, which sings the Alleluia at Eastertide, after having omitted it during the Lent. [24]See Rev 19:1. [25]Tob 13:17-18 (13:22 Vg). [26]See Acts 4:32. [27]1 Cor 15:28. [28]CS 111:154-55; CTP 90:414-15.

14:1-15* NINEVEH

[1]Here Tobit ended his words of praise. [2]He was fifty-eight years old when he lost his sight, and after eight years he regained it. He gave alms, and he continued to fear the Lord God and to praise him. [3]When he had grown very old he called his son and grandsons, and said to him, "My son, take your sons; behold, I have grown old and am about to depart this life. [4]Go to Media, my son, for I fully believe what Jonah the prophet said about Nineveh, that it will be overthrown. But in Media there will be peace for a time. Our brethren will be scattered over the earth from the good land, and Jerusalem will be desolate. The house of God in it will be burned down and will be in ruins for a time. [5]But God will again have mercy on them, and bring them back into their land; and they will rebuild the house of God,ᵉ though it will not be like the former one until the times of the age are com-

pleted. After this they will return from the places of their captivity, and will rebuild Jerusalem in splendor. And the house of God will be rebuilt there with a glorious building for all generations for ever, just as the prophets said of it. ⁶Then all the Gentiles will turn to fear the Lord God in truth, and will bury their idols. ⁷All the Gentiles will praise the Lord, and his people will give thanks to God, and the Lord will exalt his people. And all who love the Lord God in truth and righteousness will rejoice, showing mercy to our brethren.

⁸"So now, my son, leave Nineveh, because what the prophet Jonah said will surely happen. ⁹But keep the law and the commandments, and be merciful and just, so that it may be well with you. ¹⁰Bury me properly, and your mother with me. And do not live in Nineveh any longer. See, my son, what Nadab*f* did to Ahikar who had reared him, how he brought him from light into darkness, and with what he repaid him. But Ahikar was saved, and the other received repayment as he himself went down into the darkness. Ahikar*g* gave alms and escaped the deathtrap which Nadab*h* had set for him; but Nadab*f* fell into the trap and perished. ¹¹So now, my children, consider what almsgiving accomplishes and how righteousness delivers." As he said this he died in his bed. He was a hundred and fifty-eight years old; and Tobias*h* gave him a magnificent funeral. ¹²And when Anna died he buried her with his father.

Then Tobias returned with his wife and his sons to Ecbatana, to Raguel his father-in-law. ¹³He grew old with honor, and he gave his father-in-law and mother-in-law magnificent funerals. He inherited their property and that of his father Tobit. ¹⁴He died in Ecbatana of Media at the age of a hundred and twenty-seven years. ¹⁵But before he died he heard of the destruction of Nineveh, which Nebuchadnezzar and Ahasuerus had captured. Before his death he rejoiced over Nineveh.

e Gk *house* f Other authorities read *Aman* g Other authorities read *Manasses* h Gk *he* * Tob 14:1-17 Vg.

OVERVIEW: The prophets predicted the conversion of pagans, which stems from the cross (ATHANASIUS). The counsels given by Tobias are a model concerning the education of children (CYPRIAN).

14:6 Gentiles Will Turn to the Lord God

THE CONVERSION OF PAGANS. ATHANASIUS: See then what human beings considered the foolishness of God because of the cross,[1] how this has become above anything else the most honored. For our resurrection is stored up in it. No longer Israel alone, but from this time forward all the nations, as the prophet has foretold, abandon their idols and acknowledge the true God, the Father of Christ.[2] The illusion of demons has come to nothing, and he alone who is truly God is worshiped in the name of our Lord Jesus Christ.[3] DISCOURSES AGAINST THE ARIANS 1.43.1.[4]

14:9 Be Merciful and Just

A MODEL FOR THE EDUCATION OF CHILDREN. CYPRIAN OF CARTHAGE: Be to your children such a father as was Tobias. Give useful and salutary precepts to your pledges such as he gave to his son; command your children as he too commanded saying, "And now, sons, I command you, serve God in truth, and do before God what pleases him; and command your children that they do justice and almsdeeds and that they be mindful of God and bless God's name on every occasion." WORKS AND ALMSGIVING 20.[5]

---

[1]See 1 Cor 1:18. [2]See also Is 11:10. [3]See 1 Cor 3:16. [4]CTP 173:99-100; NPNF 1 4:331**. [5]FC 36:246.

WISDOM OF SOLOMON

1:1-15* THE SEARCH FOR GOD AND THE AVOIDANCE OF SIN

¹Love righteousness, you rulers of the earth,
think of the Lord with uprightness,
and seek him with sincerity of heart;
²because he is found by those who do not put
him to the test,
and manifests himself to those who do not
distrust him.
³For perverse thoughts separate men from
God,
and when his power is tested, it convicts the
foolish;
⁴because wisdom will not enter a deceitful
soul,
nor dwell in a body enslaved to sin.
⁵For a holy and disciplined spirit will flee from
deceit,
and will rise and depart from foolish thoughts,
and will be ashamed at the approach of
unrighteousness.

⁶For wisdom is a kindly spirit and
will not free a blasphemer from the guilt of
his words;
because God is witness of his inmost feelings,
and a true observer of his heart, and a hearer
of his tongue.
⁷Because the Spirit of the Lord has filled the
world,
and that which holds all things together knows
what is said;

⁸therefore no one who utters unrighteous
things will escape notice,
and justice, when it punishes, will not pass
him by.
⁹For inquiry will be made into the counsels of
an ungodly man,
and a report of his words will come to the
Lord,
to convict him of his lawless deeds;
¹⁰because a jealous ear hears all things,
and the sound of murmurings does not go
unheard.
¹¹Beware then of useless murmuring,
and keep your tongue from slander;
because no secret word is without result,ᵃ
and a lying mouth destroys the soul.

¹²Do not invite death by the error of your life,
nor bring on destruction by the works of your
hands;
¹³because God did not make death,
and he does not delight in the death of the
living.
¹⁴For he created all things that they might
exist,
and the generative forcesᵇ of the world are
wholesome,
and there is no destructive poison in them;
and the dominionᶜ of Hades is not on earth.
¹⁵For righteousness is immortal.

a Or *will go unpunished* b Or *the creatures* c Or *palace* * In this pericope, the Latin versions used by the Latin fathers, that is, the Vetus Latina and the Vulgate, often have variant readings that stem from a too-literal translation of the Greek original.

OVERVIEW: The pericope begins with the conditions necessary to approach God: the imitation of God's justice (DHUODA), a pure heart (CHROMATIUS), faith (AUGUSTINE) that affirms the equality of the Father and the Son (FULGENTIUS) and the faithful reception of God's light with simplicity (GREGORY THE GREAT), so as to see him truly (ORIGEN). The Holy Spirit does not enter a malicious heart (PSEUDO-AUGUSTINE). If malice dwells in our hearts, we are far from God and a number of unfortunate consequences ensue: God is hindered from influencing our thinking (FULGENTIUS); he cannot justify us (AMBROSIASTER), nor can we receive his Spirit (GREGORY OF NYSSA, ANONYMOUS ITALIAN). Neither schismatics nor heretics receive the Holy Spirit (AUGUSTINE). We must not reject our Lord and Savior (CHROMATIUS). The incarnation of the Son makes possible the gift of the Spirit (CYRIL OF ALEXANDRIA). The Spirit departs from the wicked and approaches the chosen (GREGORY THE GREAT). The Trinity is indivisible, whereas sin separates humankind from God (FULGENTIUS).

Next, the text discusses the Spirit, who is God (FULGENTIUS) and operates in the world (AMBROSE). The Holy Spirit is all-powerful (PSEUDO AUGUSTINE) and all-knowing; nothing escapes him (AUGUSTINE, CYRIL OF ALEXANDRIA). The Spirit hears and knows all things (EUCHERIUS, AUGUSTINE, FULGENTIUS). The Spirit's knowledge makes the swearing of oaths useless (CHROMATIUS). The law is within us. God judges in the conscience, condemning the wicked will. We ourselves kill our soul with our sins (AUGUSTINE) and with the lie that causes death (PSEUDO-AMBROSE).

The pericope ends with an exhortation to search wisdom, since we know that what is good comes from God and what is bad comes from humans (ORIGEN). GOD, who can heal fallen human nature (FULGENTIUS), calls us to repentance to free us from death (AMBROSE). It is Christ who frees us from sin and death (FASTIDIOSUS). Injustice does not last forever (DIDYMUS).

1:1 *Love Righteousness and Seek the Lord*

JUSTICE MAKES US SIMILAR TO GOD.
DHUODA OF SEPTIMANIA: "Love righteousness," so as to show yourself just in your affairs. In fact, "the Lord is righteous, and he has loved righteousness," and he always loves it; "his face has looked on uprightness."[1] In those days, he who said, "Love righteousness, you rulers of the earth," both loved righteousness greatly and counseled that it be loved. And another said, "If you speak of righteousness, judge uprightly."[2] In fact, it is written, "With the judgment that you judge, you will be judged."[3] MANUAL 4.8.[4]

A PURE HEART. CHROMATIUS OF AQUILEIA: The one who approaches the Lord with an insincere heart is rejected, while the Lord receives the one who approaches with a sincere heart and a well-disposed mind,[5] according to the thought of Scripture, "Seek the Lord with sincerity of heart." Therefore the one who believed by faith was received by the Lord into the boat, that is, into the church, where the chorus of the apostles is found. The scribe was not worthy to be received by the Lord; rather, he was rejected, since he showed that he had no faith.[6] Blessed is the disciple who deserved to be received by the Lord, though the scribe was rejected! TRACTATE ON MATTHEW 41.5.[7]

THE BEGINNING OF FAITH. AUGUSTINE: Christ died for the ungodly and sinners[8] so that we might be called to believe, not by merit but by grace, and thus by believing we might also establish merit. This is why sinners are commanded to believe, because by believing one purges himself from sins. Sinners, in fact, have no idea what they will see by living rightly. This is why—

---

[1]Ps 11:7 (10:7 LXX). [2]Ps 58:2 (57:2 LXX). [3]Mt 7:2. [4]SC 225:244. Dhuoda of Septimania (fl. 840) wrote a manual, Liber Manualis, for her son on moral and religious conduct; see Marie Anne Mayeski, Dhouda: Ninth-Century Mother and Theologian (Scranton, Pa.: University of Scranton Press, 1995). [5]See Mt 8:21-22. [6]See Mt 8:19-20. [7]CTP 47:48. [8]See Rom 5:6.

since they cannot see unless they live rightly, and they cannot live rightly unless they believe—it is obvious that they must begin by believing. In this way the commandments, by which those who believe separate themselves from the things of this world, purify their hearts—for only with a pure heart can one see God. "Blessed are the pure in heart, for they will see God."[9] Also, in the words of the prophecy it is sung, "Seek him in sincerity of heart." On Eighty-three Varied Questions 68.3.[10]

True Love Accepts the Equality of Father and Son. Fulgentius of Ruspe: Those who do not believe in the equality of the Father and the Son completely reject the coming of the Son from God the Father. Coming to the one who loves them, the Father and the Son make a single dwelling with him.[11] Now, there cannot be a single dwelling for them both, if they are loved in different ways. And if they are not equal, they will inevitably be loved in an unequal way. It is therefore not possible to prepare a single dwelling for them in a simple heart if they are not equal. Yet Scripture admonishes us to do so, saying, "Think of the Lord with uprightness, and seek him with simplicity of heart." How can one seek God with simplicity of heart if he makes a distinction in his love for God the Father and God the Son? Or how can one have a simple love for God if he is convinced that there is a diversity in the Divinity? One loves with a simple heart that Divinity whose nature he believes to be simple. But if he adores the Divinity making distinctions, this is not simplicity but duplicity of heart. And this is not true faith but false. On the Incarnation 10.[12]

A Simple Heart Receives God's Light. Gregory the Great: "Think of the Lord with uprightness, and seek him with sincerity of heart." Sincerity of heart is like a day not dimmed by fraud, not obscured by lies, not darkened by envy, not clouded by deception; it is a day illuminated by the light of truth, made re-

splendent by the dawning of the divine presence. As it is written, "He speaks with the sincere."[13] For God, to speak is to reveal to human minds, by the illumination of his presence, the mysteries of his will. This is why it is said that God speaks with the sincere, because, by the light of his inspiration, he enlightens with his heavenly mysteries the minds of those who are not darkened by even a shadow of duplicity. On the Seven Penitential Psalms 5.4.[14]

1:2 Those Who Do Not Put God to the Test

Truly Seeing Christ. Origen: Even if one who is pure of heart and another stained with impurity are found in the same place, the fact that they are in the same place cannot harm the one or benefit the other. The one whose heart is pure will see God; the one whose heart is not in the same condition, however, will not be able to see what the other sees. In my view, the same can also be said of Christ when he was visible in the body. Not all those who laid eyes on him were able to see him.

They saw the body of Christ, but they did not see Christ as Christ. His disciples, however, saw him and contemplated the greatness of his divinity. I think this is the reason why, when Philip asks him, "Lord, show us the Father, and it is enough for us,"[15] the Savior responds, "Have I been with you all this time and you do not know me? Philip, he who sees me sees the Father as well."[16] In fact, neither Pilate nor Judas the betrayer gazed on the Father, for while they were gazing at Jesus, neither Pilate nor Judas gazed on Christ as Christ. Nor did the crowd that pressed around him.[17] Only those whom Jesus deemed worthy of beholding him actually saw him. We too, therefore, should work in such a way that God might appear to us in the present (as the sacred words of Scripture promised, "He lets those

---

[9]Mt 5:8. [10]NBA 6/2:189-91. [11]See Jn 14:23. [12]CCL 91:320. [13]Prov 3:32 Vg. [14]PL 79:605. [15]Jn 14:8. [16]Jn 14:9. [17]See Mk 5:24; Lk 8:42.

find him who do not test him, and he appears to those who believe in him"). And, in the life to come, he may not be hidden from us. Rather, may we see him "face to face."[18] HOMILIES ON THE GOSPEL OF LUKE 3.[19]

1:3 Perverse Thoughts Separate Individuals from God

THE HOLY SPIRIT DOES NOT ENTER A MALICIOUS HEART. PSEUDO-AUGUSTINE: Certainly, every year we celebrate the day of the coming of the Holy Spirit.[20] However, we must act in such a way as to invite him, with pure actions and feelings, so that he comes to us every day. We must be pure and clean in our senses and in our thoughts, and we must dedicate ourselves to watching over our speech and our hearts, so as to render ourselves always worthy of his visitations and his illumination and so that it may be evident that we are free from all impurity in our thoughts. He has said in fact that "perverse thoughts separate people from God." Let us make every effort to be free from all backbiting and malice, because "wisdom will not enter a deceitful soul or dwell in a body enslaved to sin." By their anger and pride, the hearts of the careless find themselves without the vigilance and protection of the Holy Spirit. Therefore, let us not sadden the Holy Spirit by these passions. Rather, let us invoke him, that with the grace of humility and the mildness of peace he would enter our hearts and that we would gladden him by our works and our initiatives. He himself has said, "With whom will I make my resting place? With the humble one, who has a contrite spirit and trembles at my word."[21] SERMON 182.6.[22]

SIN SEPARATES US FROM THE TRINITY. FULGENTIUS OF RUSPE: In the book of Wisdom it is clear that what separates people from God is not the distance of place but evil thoughts and wicked actions. It says, "Perverse thoughts separate people from God; the excellence of virtue banishes fools, because wisdom will not

enter a heart that does evil or dwell in a heart enslaved to sin. The Holy Spirit of instruction flees deceit and departs from foolish speech."[23] Who cannot see that this alludes to the Trinity of persons, each according to their properties? In fact, it is said that "perverse thoughts separate people from God," using a name by which the person of God the Father can be recognized. Then it adds that "wisdom will not enter a heart that does evil"; by this name Christ is indicated, whom Paul calls "the power of God and the wisdom of God."[24] Then it says, "The Holy Spirit flees from deceit, and departs from foolish speech." Moreover, in order that no one would think that an evil or godless person could distance himself, spatially, from this holy Trinity who is the one, true and good God, Scripture then says, "Wisdom is a spirit that is a friend of people; but he will not leave unpunished one who blasphemes, because God is witness of his inmost feelings and a true observer of his heart, and he hears the words of his mouth. In fact, the Spirit of the Lord fills the universe." BOOK TO VICTOR AGAINST THE SERMON OF FASTIDIOSUS THE ARIAN 4.[25]

1:4 Wisdom Shuns Deceitful, Sinful People

THE SPIRIT JUSTIFIES US. AMBROSIASTER: "The body is dead because of sin, but the spirit is alive because of righteousness."[26] The apostle declares that the bodies of those who have been abandoned by the Holy Spirit are dead because of sin, yet their experience of death does not touch him, that is, the Spirit. In fact, the Spirit of God does not know how to sin: he is given for justification and to justify by his help. Because he does not know how to sin, he is life, and he certainly cannot die, given that death is a result of sin.[27] It is for this reason that the sinner harms himself, but not the Spirit whom

---

[18]1 Cor 13:12. [19]GCS Origenes 9:21-22. [20]See Acts 2:4. [21]Is 66:2 Vg. [22]PL 39:2090. [23]Wis 1:3-5 Vg. [24]1 Cor 1:24. [25]CCL 91:287-88. [26]Rom 8:10, variant. [27]See Rom 5:12.

he has received. The Spirit certainly cannot be affected—he whose purpose it is to justify. Thus, the sign of a person's justification consists in this: that through the one who lives in him, the justified one shows himself to be a child of God.[28] In fact "not in a false person or in a body enslaved to sin" can the Holy Spirit live, as Solomon says. Certainly, if one returns to a carnal life, abandoned by the Holy Spirit, he will die in his unrighteousness. ON THE LETTER TO THE ROMANS 8.10.[29]

GOD DWELLS IN THE JUST RATHER THAN THE WICKED. FULGENTIUS OF RUSPE: The Father, the Son and the Holy Spirit come and go in their own, incomprehensible way. One cannot speak of a "change of locality" of the Father or of the Son or of the Holy Spirit. They come and go in such a way that, physically, they neither go to a place nor depart from it. Consequently, this coming of the Father, of the Son and of the Holy Spirit does not demonstrate the mobility of God but his piety. It is said in fact that the unique divinity of the Trinity, who fills all things and contains all things, comes to the one to whom he deigns to manifest himself, and he distances himself from the one to whom he hides the light of his love. But this does not mean a local absence, when he justly abandons one who is unworthy; nor does he make himself present in a place if he visits with his mercy one whom he has made worthy. Therefore, even though God says, "I fill heaven and earth,"[30] of some it is said, "God is not with them."[31] And though the Father fills all things, the book of Wisdom says, "Perverse thoughts separate human beings from God." And if it also says of the Son—that is, of the wisdom of God,[32] "she reaches from end to end with power and orders all things well,"[33] the same Wisdom says of itself, "The perverse will seek me, but they will not find me."[34] And again, "Wisdom does not enter a soul who does evil or dwell in a body enslaved to sin." And of the Holy Spirit, of whom it is said that he is immense in every way, it is

said, "The Holy Spirit flees from deceit and departs from foolish speech." THREE BOOKS TO TRASAMUNDUS 2.11.[35]

DWELLING IN THE SOUL OF THE JUST. GREGORY OF NYSSA: The soul whose life is in God will find its pleasure in none of those things that are deceptively presented as something good. If that soul allows its heart to be defiled by one passion, at the same time it breaks the covenant of its spiritual marriage. And, as it says in Scripture, "Wisdom cannot enter the soul that does evil." It may, in a word, be truly said that the good spouse cannot come to live with a soul that is irascible or full of malice or that harbors any other similar defect. ON VIRGINITY 16.1.[36]

THE SPIRIT REJECTS THE ARROGANT. ANONYMOUS ITALIAN: See, brothers, what pride did and what humility merited. Pride divided the tongues, when people wanted to raise a tower that would reach heaven.[37] Before there existed but a single language, Hebrew, which was called the human language. But, so that the prideful could not complete what they had begun, seventy-two languages were born. In our day, however, when the faithful in their humility received the Holy Spirit, they began to speak in every language.[38] For this reason, keep pride far from you, because all the prideful are children of the devil; and be humble, so that you will be worthy to receive the grace of the Holy Spirit and to be called children of God.[39] May your bodies and your hearts be pure of all defilement of sin, because the Holy Spirit "does not dwell in a body enslaved to sin."[40] SERMON 13, FOR WHITSUNDAY 2.[41]

1:5 A Disciplined Spirit Flees Deceit and Foolishness

---

[28]See Jn 1:12. [29]CTP 43:188-89. [30]Jer 23:24. [31]Ps 10:4 (9:25 LXX). [32]See Cor 1:24. [33]Wis 8:1. [34]Prov 1:28. [35]PL 65:257-58. [36]SC 119:452. [37]See Gen 11:1-9. [38]Acts 2:3-4. [39]See Jn 1:12. [40]Wis 1:4. [41]SC 161:224-26.

THE LORD ADDRESSES THE BELIEVING CHURCH. CHROMATIUS OF AQUILEIA: The city from which the inhabitants went out, pleading with the Lord to leave them,[42] represents the synagogue, which did not want to accept the Lord and Savior of the human race, even after it had seen his divine miracles. Therefore he returned to his own city—rejected by the synagogue, he has come to his church; it is this latter that in a true and proper sense merits the name of the city of Christ. Thus one understands why the Gadarenes pleaded with the Lord to leave their town. We must, however, be attentive, that none of us find ourselves in a similar situation; I am alluding to the danger that someone, because of an unbelieving heart, would impel the Lord and Savior of the world to leave his heart, because it is written that "the Holy Spirit, the teacher of discipline, flees from one who is false; he will not dwell in a body enslaved to sin." TRACTATE ON MATTHEW 43.7.[43]

SCHISMATICS AND HERETICS DO NOT RECEIVE THE SPIRIT. AUGUSTINE: Nor can it be said that those who mingle with Christ's sheep in a merely physical and hypocritical way are either in the church or belong to the communion of the Spirit. For the Holy Spirit, the master of discipline, hates those who are hypocritical. That is why all those baptized in schismatic or heretical congregations—they might better be called segregations—have not been regenerated by the Spirit. They are similar, so to speak, to Ishmael, who was born from Abraham according to the flesh, and not like Isaac who was born according to the Spirit in virtue of the promise.[44] SERMON 71.19.32.[45]

CHRIST BECAME INCARNATE TO GIVE US THE SPIRIT. CYRIL OF ALEXANDRIA: The first man, formed of mud and earth ,[46] had in his power the choice between good and evil[47] and had under his control whether he inclined to the one or the other. He was snared by a grave deception and, fallen into disobedience,[48] returned to the mother earth from which he was born;[49] subject to corruption and death, he transmitted this punishment to all his descendents. Evil increased and multiplied among us, and our hearts fell ever lower; sin reigned,[50] and thus, finally, human nature was deprived of the Holy Spirit that had lived in it. "The Holy Spirit of instruction flees from deceit," as it is written, "and he does not dwell in a body enslaved to sin." Because, therefore, the first Adam did not preserve the grace given to him by God, God the Father sent us the second Adam[51] from heaven. He sent us his own Son, made in our likeness, who did not know change or alteration and did not know sin,[52] so that, just as by the disobedience of the first we merited divine wrath, so by the obedience [53] of the second we would escape the curse, and its evil would cease.[54] COMMENTARY ON THE GOSPEL OF JOHN 2.1.[55]

THE SPIRIT DRAWS NEAR TO THE ELECT. GREGORY THE GREAT: The Spirit goes elsewhere when his grace distances itself from the proud and from those who are insincere. Thus it is written, "The Holy Spirit of instruction flees deceit." Therefore Christ himself says in the Gospel, "The Spirit[56] blows where he wills, and you hear his voice, but you do not know where he comes from or where he goes."[57] The Spirit comes and goes, because he abandons the reprobate, taking to himself the elect. And because God's judgment is omnipotent and inscrutable,[58] human beings do not know where they come from or where they go. Indeed, it is not possible to know whether someone will persevere to the end in the grace he has received. It is said therefore that the Spirit leaves one who has fallen and goes to one who will persevere, because, in this earthly life, he abandons some and takes others

---

[42]See Mt 8:34. [43]CTP 47:70-71. [44]See Gal 4:22-29. [45]NBA 30/1:445. [46]See 1 Cor 15:47. [47]See Gen 2:17. [48]See Rom 5:19. [49]See Gen 3:19. [50]See Rom 5:21. [51]See 1 Cor 15:47. [52]See Rom 5:19. [53]See Heb 5:8. [54]See Rom 5:18. [55]CTP 111:196. [56]Here the Vulgate uses *spiritus*, which means "wind" and "spirit." [57]Jn 3:8. [58]See Rom 11:33.

to himself, whom he does not abandon. Six Books on 1 Kings 5.460.[59]

Sin Separates Human Beings from God.
Fulgentius of Ruspe: Let no one hold that the three persons are separable, since he would not be able to find any one of the persons existing or acting before another or after another or without another. Just as by nature there can be no separability of action, in the same way there remains, by nature, an immutable unity of the will. We will now consider in what way both angels and human beings have been separated from God, in order to enable us to grasp without a shadow of doubt that the Trinity is inseparable. For holy Scripture says, in fact, that "perverse thoughts separate people from God," and that "wisdom does not enter into a malignant spirit, nor does it dwell in a body given over to sin" and that "the Holy Spirit of discipline flees from deceit and distances himself from thoughts lacking in reason." In effect, Isaiah also proves that iniquities dig a trench between God and humanity.[60] The holy Trinity, therefore, is the same faithful God in whom no wickedness can exist: "The Son of God came to take away sins; there is no sin or iniquity in him."[61] Letters 14.14.[62]

1:6 God Witnesses Inmost Feelings

The Spirit Discerns the Thoughts of the Heart. Augustine: Often, in fact, when the Scriptures speak about the mouth, they refer to the intimate recesses of the heart, where one approves and determines what will eventually be spoken with the mouth, when one speaks the truth. It follows, then, that anyone who approves a lie is in his heart a liar. A person might not lie in his heart, however, if in saying something that is not in his heart, he does so knowing that what he does is evil, but he does so to avoid a greater evil—at the same time disapproving of both evils. Those who hold this principle say that Scripture, as well, must be understood in this sense when it says, "He who pronounces the truth in his heart."[63] With the heart, in fact, one must always speak the truth—but not always with the lips; for example, if someone is forced, so as to avoid a greater evil, to say with his voice something contrary to what is in his mind. . . . A response in fact cannot be known when it remains hidden from others, who cannot listen to the voice of the heart unless the voice of the body makes it heard. But that voice of the heart does reach the ears of the Spirit of the Lord who, as Scripture says in the text cited, fills the whole earth. In that same portion of Scripture it also speaks about lips, the voice and language; but saying that these are known to the Lord means nothing other than what refers to the heart. Thus, when it is said that a sound "reaches our ears," it means that it is no longer hidden even from human beings. On Lying 16.31.[64]

1:7 The Spirit Has Filled the World

The Spirit Works in the World. Ambrose: As the Lord fills all things, so too we read of the Spirit, "For the Spirit of the Lord fills the whole world." You see also that it was said of all those who were gathered with the apostles, "They were filled with the Holy Spirit, and they spoke the word of God with boldness."[65] You see that the Holy Spirit gives both fullness and boldness. It is his work that the archangel announces, saying to Mary, "The Holy Spirit shall come on you."[66] On the Holy Spirit 1.7.87.[67]

The Spirit Fills the World. Augustine: The words "the Spirit hovered over the waters"[68] do not require us, as some claim, to understand that spirit by which this corporal mass of the universe is animated, allowing bodily creatures to generate and preserve themselves, each according to their species. In fact, such a being would also be a creature. Also, regarding the

---

[59]PL 79:460. [60]See Is 59:2. [61]1 Jn 3:4-5. [62]CTP 149:288-89. [63]Ps 15:2 (14:2 LXX). [64]NBA 7/2:365-67. [65]Acts 4:31. [66]Lk 1:35. [67]PL 16:725. [68]Gen 1:3.

text, "The Spirit of the Lord fills the universe," there are those who understand by this that spirit which, as an invisible creature, encompasses and vivifies the entire visible creation with a universal breath. But even here I do not see what would prevent one from understanding the Holy Spirit, when God says in a prophet, "I fill the heavens and the earth."[69] God in fact does not fill heaven and earth without his Holy Spirit. What is strange, then, if it was said of his Holy Spirit, "he filled the universe"? Indeed, he fills in one way when he sanctifies, as was said of Stephen, "He was filled with the Holy Spirit,"[70] and of many others. In another way he fills with sanctifying grace, as happens with some saints, and in yet another way he fills everything with his manifest and ordering presence. In conclusion, I do not know whether it can be proven with certainty from Scripture that, when speaking of the Spirit of God or of the Spirit of the Lord without any further qualification, it refers to something other than the Holy Spirit. ON VARIOUS QUESTIONS TO SIMPLICIANUS 2.1.5.[71]

THE SPIRIT IS GOD. FULGENTIUS OF RUSPE: The true faith asserts that the Holy Spirit also is creator, not created. Indeed, how can one deny that he is creator, about whom it has been proven that he established the array of the heavens? David says, "By the word of the Lord the heavens were made, and by the Spirit of his mouth their entire array."[72] And elsewhere, "Send forth your Spirit, and they shall be created."[73] The one who made humanity is in fact the creator of all. Blessed Job calls him "the divine Spirit who made me."[74] Therefore, just as the Holy Spirit created all things, in the same way he pervades all things, without limit. And one who pervades all things is true God by nature. It is written, "The Spirit of the Lord fills the world." And even blessed David attests that the Spirit is everywhere, saying precisely of God, "Where will I go, far from your Spirit, and where will I flee from your face?"[75] Then how can the Arians deny that the Holy Spirit is God, given that we

are the temple of the Holy Spirit, just as we are the temple of the Father and the Son? Indeed, the apostle says, "Do you not know that you are the temple of God and that the Spirit of God dwells in you? If anyone defiles the temple of God, God will destroy him. In fact, the temple of God is holy, and that is what you are."[76] In the same letter, the apostle asserts that we are the temple of God in such a way as to say that we are also the temple of the Holy Spirit. He says, "Do you not know that your members are the temple of the Holy Spirit who is in you, whom you have from God?"[77] And precisely to show that the Holy Spirit is God, he adds, "Glorify and keep God in your hearts."[78] LETTERS 8.17.8.[79]

THE SPIRIT IS ALL-POWERFUL. PSEUDO-AUGUSTINE: We will show that the Scriptures say that the Son is almighty like the Father, so that not only reason, but the divine witness as well, would persuade the shameless minds of heretics. The Father is called almighty, because the prophet says, "Thus says the almighty God."[80] The Son is called almighty when the apostle John says in Revelation, "From Jesus Christ our Lord, who is, who was and who is to come, the almighty."[81] The Holy Spirit is also called almighty: "The Spirit of the Lord fills the universe, and he who embraces all things, knows." Is it possible that the one who encompasses everything not be almighty? SERMON ON THE CREED 4.8.[82]

1:8 Saying Unrighteous Things

NOT ONE THOUGHT ESCAPES GOD. AUGUSTINE: Do not think, therefore, that God is in a particular place! He is with you, and he will be as you are. What does it mean, "He will be as you are"? He will be good if you are good, and he will seem bad to you if you are bad. If you are

---

[69]Jer 23:24. [70]Acts 7:55. [71]NBA 6/2:357-59. [72]Ps 33:6 (32:6 LXX). [73]Ps 104:30 (103:30 LXX). [74]Job 33:4. [75]Ps 139:7 (138:7 LXX). [76]1 Cor 3:16-17. [77]1 Cor 6:19. [78]1 Cor 6:20. [79]CTP 149:195-96. [80]Hag 1:2 Vg, etc. [81]Rev 1:5, 8. [82]PL 40:641.

good, he will help you, but he will avenge himself if you are wicked. You have the judge within you. When you want to do evil, you withdraw from the town square to your house, where no enemy can see you. From the rooms of your house that are open and can be seen by others, you go into your own room. And even if in your room you fear indiscreet eyes, you hide in your heart, and there, within, you weave your plot. God is within you more deeply than your very heart. Wherever you flee to, he is there.[83] EXPOSITIONS OF THE PSALMS 74.9.[84]

THE SPIRIT KNOWS ALL THINGS. FULGENTIUS OF RUSPE: Divinely inspired, he speaks thus of the Holy Sprit: "Because the Spirit of the Lord fills the world, he embraces all things and knows what is said." One understands, moreover, that here the Scripture refers to the voice of the heart, not of the body. That is, not to the voice of speech among living beings, but that of one's most hidden thoughts, that resounding voice that only God hears, since he alone sees the one who ponders secretly.[85] Thus he continues, "Therefore, no one who utters unrighteous things can remain hidden, nor will he be spared his chastening judgment." To show further in what this wicked speech consists, so that it would be understood more as the expression of the conscience than of the tongue, the holy Scripture then explains, "There will be an inquiry into the reflections of the godless." I have said this because it says of the Holy Spirit, "because he encompasses all things, he knows what is said." Given that he encompasses all things, the Holy Spirit is not inferior to the Father or the Son. And because he has knowledge of hidden thoughts, he is recognized as the true God. LETTERS 14.4.[86]

1:9 Inquiry into the Counsels of the Ungodly

GOD JUDGES WITHIN THE CONSCIENCE. AUGUSTINE: Is God perhaps circumscribed by a place—he to whom every conscience is present,

angelic and human, not only good but also evil? This distinction is truly important: whereas to good consciences he is present as Father, to bad consciences he is present as judge. In fact, it is written, "God judges the righteous and the ungodly."[87] It is also written, "The thoughts of the ungodly will be examined." The Lord does not make himself heard to the ears of the body more strongly than he does in the secret of one's thoughts, where he alone listens, where he alone is heard. SERMON 12.3.3.[88]

GOD CONDEMNS A WICKED WILL. AUGUSTINE: Perhaps the good that has come to us from the Lord's passion should be attributed to the godless people who killed Christ? Absolutely not. They wanted to kill; God permitted it. They would have been guilty even if they had had only the intention. As for God, he would not have permitted the crime if it had not been just. Let us suppose that they had not been able to carry out their crime but had only wanted to: they would have been equally unjust, equally murderers. Who can doubt this? It is true that "the Lord scrutinizes the righteous and the godless,"[89] and "he will inquire into the counsels of the ungodly." God sees, therefore, what someone wants, and not only what he is able to do. It follows that, if the Jews had wanted to kill Christ but were unable to carry out their intention (and therefore actually would not have killed him), they would have still been guilty, while you would have been without the advantages of the passion of Christ. The godless therefore wanted to carry out actions worthy of condemnation and were allowed to do so in your favor. Desiring to do so is imputed to the unrighteousness of the godless, while being permitted to do so is attributed to the power of God. The godless therefore desired unjustly, whereas God permitted justly. EXPOSITIONS OF THE PSALMS 61.22.[90]

---

[83]See Ps 139:7-8 (138:7-8 LXX). [84]NBA 26:923. [85]See Mt 6:4. [86]CTP 149:271. [87]Ps 11:5 (10:6 LXX). [88]NBA 29:217. [89]Ps 11:5 (10:6 LXX). [90]NBA 26:381-83.

THE LAW IS WITHIN US. AUGUSTINE: So that human beings would not complain that they lacked something, what they were unable to read in their own hearts was written on tablets of stone. It is not true that they did not have a law written in their hearts. It is only that they refused to read it. What they should have read in their consciences was thus put before their eyes. People were urged to look into their hearts by the voice of God, coming, as it were, from without. As Scripture says, "He will inquire into the counsels of the godless." Now, where there is an inquiry, there must also be law. But, because human beings, in their desire for exterior things, had become strangers even to themselves, they were also given a written law. Not because the law had not already been written on their hearts, but because you had fled from your heart, and he who is everywhere wanted to find you again and compel you to return to yourself. And what does the written law call out to those who have distanced themselves from the law impressed on their hearts? "Transgressors, return to your hearts."[91] EXPOSITIONS OF THE PSALMS 57.1.[92]

1:10 God Hears All Things

NO THOUGHT ESCAPES GOD. CYRIL OF ALEXANDRIA: There is truth in the saying of Wisdom: "The Spirit of the Lord fills the universe," and "An attentive ear hears all things."[93] To those, then, who foolishly, even godlessly, think that their words remain hidden to the divine mind, the psalmist says somewhere, "Understand, you senseless among the people. Fools, when will you become wise? Does he who made the ear not hear?"[94] How is it possible that he who gave hearing to his creatures would not hear everything? And from this you understand, yet again, that the Lord is God by nature. He was not unaware of what the Jews murmured secretly among the crowd. Rather, as befits God, he heard it, even though they did not speak openly of him, for fear of their leaders.[95] COMMENTARY ON THE GOSPEL OF JOHN 4.5.[96]

GOD HEARS EVERYTHING. EUCHERIUS: It is said that God has hearing, because he listens to everything and nothing remains hidden to him in silence. About this, it is written in the book of Wisdom, "Heaven's ear listens to everything; even the whisper of murmurings are not hidden from him." BOOK OF FORMULAS 1.[97]

1:11 A Lying Mouth Destroys the Soul

OATHS SERVE NO PURPOSE. CHROMATIUS OF AQUILEIA: The Lord demands that there be no difference between our oaths and our ordinary speech.[98] If this were not so, then it could be admitted that there is a sort of deception in our oath. Likewise, there must be no lie whatsoever in our words, because both a deceiving oath and a lie fall under the condemnation of divine judgment. Scripture attests to this: "A lying mouth destroys the soul." To speak the truth is already an oath, given that we read, "The truthful witness does not lie."[99] For this reason Scripture justly asserts that God often utters oaths. God is true, and he cannot lie. Everything he says can be considered an oath, given that everything God says is entirely true. It is true, of course, that sometimes Scripture says that God swears an oath. If he does so, however, it is because human beings are incredulous. He swears, then, because of the devious infidelity of the Jews, who believe that truth is found only in words given with an oath. It is for this reason alone that God at times wanted to swear an oath, so that those who did not believe God when he spoke would at least believe when he gave an oath. TRACTATE ON MATTHEW 24.2.3-4.[100]

WE DESTROY OUR SOULS. AUGUSTINE: "Do not fear those who kill the body, but do not have power to kill the soul."[101] Whoever wants to kill you can so do in the body but not in the

---

[91]Is 46:8 Vg. [92]NBA 26:193. [93]Wis 1:10, variant. [94]Ps 94:8-9 (93:8-9 LXX). [95]See Jn 6:12-13. [96]CTP 111:569. [97]PL 50:731. [98]See Mt 5:33-37. [99]Prov 14:5. [100]CTP 46:211. [101]Mt 10:27.

soul. Your soul will not die, unless you yourself want to kill it. Another's wickedness can kill your flesh, but the truth would preserve your soul in righteousness. If you abandon the truth, what other evil could your enemy do to you that would be greater than what you have done to yourself? Your enemy, if he wanted to harm you, could at most kill your flesh. You, however, by giving false testimony, kill the soul. Listen to Scripture: "A lying mouth destroys the soul." Expositions of the Psalms 79.13.[102]

Can the Soul Die? Augustine: "I have the power to give my life and the power to take it up again."[103] In another passage of the Gospel it says that it is not only the Father who raises the Son but the Son also raises himself. "I will destroy this temple," he says, "and in three days I will raise it up again." And the Evangelist notes, "he spoke of the temple of his body."[104] In fact, he had to raise what had died; now, the Word is not dead, and neither is his soul. Could the Lord's soul die, when not even your soul dies? How do I know, you ask, that my soul does not die? If you do not kill it, it will not die. In what sense, you ask, can I kill my soul? "A lying mouth destroys the soul," to not speak of other sins. How can I be sure, you insist, that it does not die? Listen to the Lord, who gives this assurance to his servant: "You must not fear those who kill the body and, after that, can do nothing more."[105] And more exactly, what did he say? "Fear, rather, him who has the power to cause both body and soul to perish in Gehenna."[106] This proves that the soul both dies and does not die. Tractates on the Gospel of John 47.7-8.[107]

Lies Lead to Death. Pseudo-Ambrose: It is not lawful to deceive anyone, either by clever reasoning or with simple words, because whoever lies in any way, sins. In fact, it is written, "A lying mouth destroys the soul." And it adds, "The burning pool of fire and sulphur is reserved for all liars. This is the second death."[108] The Contest Between Vices and Virtue 19.[109]

1:13 God Does Not Delight in the Death of the Living

God Calls Us to Penance. Ambrose: God wants all to be saved. Thus Solomon says, "God did not make death, and he does not delight in the death of the living." He made the soul so that it would exist. He created human beings to be incorruptible, making them in his image.[110] But they, straying from their natural duty, have become subject to death and are corrupted, because they were made from the earth.[111] But, through trials, God compels them to penance, so that the evil that had appeared—wickedness— would be burned up, consumed and eliminated through penance, and the place in the soul that was dominated by the unrighteousness that had arisen would be opened to receive virtue and grace. Certainly the soul has a precious nature that, since it is made in the likeness of God,[112] is capable of receiving every virtue. Expositions on the Psalms 1.48.[113]

What Is Death? Augustine: Therefore death does not come from God. In fact, "God did not make death, and he does not delight in the death of the living." In fact, the supreme essence makes all that is to exist, and consequently he is called essence. Death forces what dies into non-being, to the degree that it dies. If in fact something that dies were to die completely, it would certainly arrive at nonexistence. But it dies only to the extent that it does not participate in the essence. In short, the less it exists, the more it dies. The body is less than any kind of life, because to the extent that it remains in its species, it does so thanks to life, whether this regards an animated being or the entire nature of the world. For this reason the body is more subject to death and closer to nonexistence. Thus the life that neglects God, delighting in the fruits of the body,

---

[102]NBA 26:1109. [103]Jn 10:18. [104]Jn 2:19, 21. [105]Lk 12:4. [106]Mt 10:28. [107]NBA 24:941. [108]Rev 21:8. [109]PL 17:1070. [110]See Gen 1:26-27. [111]See 1 Cor 15:47. [112]See Gen 1:26-27. [113]PL 14:947.

tends toward nonexistence. And this is wickedness. OF TRUE RELIGION 11.22.[114]

CHRIST FREES US FROM SIN AND DEATH.
FASTIDIOSUS: The God of justice is also the author of life. Indeed, he is our justice and our life. And he did not make human beings either for sin or for death, because Scripture says, "God did not make death, and he does not delight in the death of the living." The fact that human beings who were created by God are subject to death is not the work of God, the Creator, but of the devil, the deceiver. In fact, after the man was deceived by the devil, because he did evil willingly, he experienced death against his will. He transgressed unjustly and was punished justly. God saw both these things—sin and death— in human beings, the one that they perversely committed, the other that they justly received. Because they were bound by these two powerful chains, God commanded the Lord Christ to take on flesh,[115] not that he would owe a debt to sin but so that, not owing a debt to sin,[116] he would undergo an unjust death for the debtors.[117] SERMON.[118]

1:14 God Created All Things to Exist

GOOD COMES FROM GOD.
ORIGEN: "God did not make death, and he does not delight in the death of the living. For he created all things that they might exist, and the generative forces of the world are wholesome, and there is no destructive poison in them. And the dominion of Hades is not on earth." Then, a little further on in the text, it says, "But by the envy of the devil death entered the world."[119] If therefore God made everything for us in the best possible way, it is we who have caused evil and sins. HOMILIES ON JEREMIAH 2.1.[120]

GOD CAN HEAL FALLEN HUMAN NATURE.
FULGENTIUS OF RUSPE: Every human being is so corrupted by the voluntary sin of the first man that only God, if he wills, can heal a person's

will by his good will. In fact, it is written, "He created all things that they might exist, and the creative forces of the world he made wholesome." Still, lest human beings would ever think the beginning of their healing derived from themselves, the divine word immediately adds, "And there is no purging medicine in them."[121] Therefore, though the devil had deprived the first man of faith,[122] he nevertheless did not deprive God of the power to give again what he had first given. Nor could the devil corrupt human nature to such a degree that it could not receive once again what it had lost, thanks to the generosity of God. In fact, the Almighty, who was capable of forming human nature, can also reform and preserve it, healing its fragility through grace. LETTERS 17.23.45.[123]

1:15 Righteousness Is Immortal

INJUSTICE LASTS ONLY FOR A SEASON.
DIDYMUS THE BLIND: I saw a godless person who said, "By the power of my own hand I have acted, and with my wisdom, for I am shrewd. I have removed the boundaries of the peoples, and I have pillaged their treasures."[124] I saw him exalted. I went forward in my thoughts to the next life and considered the arrangements of Providence. I saw him no longer, nor did I find his place, even though I looked for it.[125] Godlessness will come to an end and will be no more. It is not included in what is immortal, as is said of righteousness, "Righteousness is immortal." ON THE PSALM 36.35-36.[126]

THE JUST WILL NOT WAVER.
DIDYMUS THE BLIND: When I prospered, sowing in righteousness and reaping the fruits of righteousness,[127] I was in such a state that I could never waver.[128] If "whoever does the will of God remains

[114]PL 34:132. [115]See Jn 1:14. [116]See 2 Cor 5:21. [117]See 1 Cor 15:3. [118]CCL 91:280. [119]Wis 2:24. [120]CTP 123:50. [121]Wis 1:14 Vg. The Latin is *medicamentum exterminii*. [122]See Gen 3:1-7. [123]CTP 149:446. [124]Is 10:13. [125]Ps 37:36 (36:36 LXX). [126]PTA 6:110. [127]See Hos 10:12. [128]Ps 30:7 (29:7 LXX).

forever"[129] and his "righteousness is immortal," I indeed said this when I received the fruits of righteousness and prospered. I spoke thus to my soul, just as with the word according to which "no one can say 'Jesus is Lord' . . . "[130] I confessed this with my soul and with my life when I prospered and bore fruits of virtue, because I will never waver, according to the word: "Who-ever believes, and whoever lives and believes, will never die,"[131] and "The righteousness of the Lord remains forever."[132] ON THE PSALM 29.7.[133]

---

[129]1 Jn 2:17. [130]1 Cor 12:3. The verse is unfinished and continues with "without the Holy Spirit." [131]Jn 11:25-26. [132]Ps 112:9 (111:9 LXX); 2 Cor 9:9. [133]PTA 8:28.

1:16–2:9 THE DESTINY OF THE WICKED

[16]*But ungodly men by their words and deeds*
    summoned death;[d]
considering him a friend, they pined away,
and they made a covenant with him,
because they are fit to belong to his party.
2 *For they reasoned unsoundly, saying to*
    themselves,
"Short and sorrowful is our life,
and there is no remedy when a man comes to
    his end,
and no one has been known to return from
    Hades.
[2]*Because we were born by mere chance,*
and hereafter we shall be as though we had
    never been;
because the breath in our nostrils is smoke,
and reason is a spark kindled by the beating
    of our hearts.
[3]*When it is extinguished, the body will turn*
    to ashes,
and the spirit will dissolve like empty air.
[4]*Our name will be forgotten in time,*
and no one will remember our works;

our life will pass away like the traces of a
    cloud,
and be scattered like mist
that is chased by the rays of the sun
and overcome by its heat.
[5]*For our allotted time is the passing of a*
    shadow,
and there is no return from our death,
because it is sealed up and no one turns back.

[6]*"Come, therefore, let us enjoy the good*
    things that exist,
and make use of the creation to the full as in
    youth.
[7]*Let us take our fill of costly wine and*
    perfumes,
and let no flower of spring pass by us.
[8]*Let us crown ourselves with rosebuds before*
    they wither.
[9]*Let none of us fail to share in our revelry,*
everywhere let us leave signs of enjoyment,
because this is our portion, and this our
    lot."

d Gk *him*

OVERVIEW: This pericope has several themes: the corruption born from bad faith (AUGUSTINE), the inner discourse of humankind (FULGENTIUS), ignorance concerning the future life (AUGUSTINE) and our origin from formless matter. (PSEUDO-AUGUSTINE). We are asked to choose between pleasure and good (AMBROSE), so that we may avoid desperation (PSEUDO-AUGUSTINE). We must live in line with the truth of the gospel (AUGUSTINE).

2:1 Unsound Reasoning

CORRUPTION ARISES FROM BAD FAITH. AUGUSTINE: "They are corrupt, they do abominable things, no one does what is right."[1] Listen to these corrupt people. They in fact "have spoken among themselves, reasoning unsoundly." Corruption begins with bad faith. From there it passes to depraved habits, later leading to the most violent injustice. This is, in general, the ladder one climbs. What, then, did they say among themselves, thinking badly, "our life is short and sorrowful"? From this mistaken conviction proceeds what the apostle also spoke of: "Let us eat and drink, because tomorrow we die." But in the book of Wisdom this wantonness is described more thoroughly: "Let us crown ourselves with rosebuds before they wither. Let us leave signs of our enjoyment." And after this more thorough description of wantonness, what do we read? "Let us kill the poor, just person,"[2] which is as much as to say, "God does not exist."[3] EXPOSITIONS OF THE PSALMS 52.3.[4]

WE THINK AS WE SPEAK TO OURSELVES. FULGENTIUS OF RUSPE: Our thought, which originates and is formed in the memory, is rightly called an interior word. Indeed, what is thought, if not an interior discourse? Thus it is written, "What you speak in your hearts on your bed, reflect on and be silent."[5] In fact, in the Gospel, when the Lord said to the paralytic he had healed, "Your sins are forgiven you,"[6] Luke the Evangelist adds, "The scribes and the Phari-

sees began to ask themselves, 'Who is this who speaks blasphemies? Who can forgive sins, but God alone?' But Jesus, knowing their thoughts, responded, 'What are you thinking in your hearts?' "[7] Whereas Luke said, "the scribes and the Pharisees began to ask themselves," Matthew says, "Then some scribes began to think, 'This man blasphemes!' But Jesus, knowing their thoughts, said, 'Why do you think evil things in your hearts?' "[8] The book of Wisdom also says of some, "They spoke among themselves, reasoning unsoundly." It is therefore clear that to think is the same as to speak within oneself. Thus, thought is invisible. That is, thoughts are said without the sound of the voice of the body, but they reach another's hearing only through bodily speech. BOOK TO VICTOR AGAINST THE SERMON OF FASTIDIOSUS THE ARIAN 15.[9]

IGNORANT CONCERNING THE FUTURE LIFE. AUGUSTINE: When you say to yourself, "The happiness of this world is false," though you dare not express it, I nevertheless see in your heart that perhaps you wrinkle up your nose, mockingly, and say to yourself, "Maybe it will go well for me here! What comes after, I don't know." And it is not a small thing that you at least say that you do not know, so as to not perhaps also say, "Our life is short and sorrowful, and there is no remedy when a person dies. No one has been known to return from Hades."[10] At least you say, "I don't know." Recognizing one's ignorance is a step toward knowledge. I speak to you, therefore, as if you were to say to me, "I don't know what there could be after death. I simply don't know whether the righteous will be blessed and sinners unhappy, or if both will cease to exist." Even not knowing, you would nevertheless not have the audacity to say that after death sinners will be blessed and the righteous unhappy. You cannot say, even if you suppose that both will

---

[1]Ps 53:2 (52:2 LXX). [2]Wis 2:10 Vg. [3]Ps 53:2 (52:2 LXX). [4]NBA 26:41. [5]Ps 4:5. [6]Lk 5:20. [7]Lk 5:20-21. [8]Mt 9:3-4. [9]PL 65:521-22. [10]Wis 2:1 Vg.

no longer exist, that after death the godless will enjoy a better state and the righteous will suffer. Not even your ignorance can lead you to speak like that. Say, therefore, "I don't know if after death it will go well for the righteous and badly for the godless, or if both the one and the other will exist insensibly." SERMON 301.4.3.[11]

2:2[12] Fashioned from Nothing

CREATED FROM FORMLESS MATTER. PSEUDO-AUGUSTINE: In Wisdom it says, "He who created the world from formless matter,"[13] and the opposite, "We were made from nothing." The sense of Scripture affirms that God created the elements all at once, and they were all mixed together, with darkness mixed in with them. And God called this confusion of elements (that is, air, fire, water, land, darkness) formless matter, as it says in Genesis, "The earth was a formless waste."[14] He created the universe from this confusion, establishing the firmament, so that, once the waters were gathered in it, in a single place,[15] the dwelling of the human race would be created. After having distinguished and separated the elements, he made an inhabitable dwelling in the cavity that remained. QUESTIONS FROM THE OLD TESTAMENT 2.20.[16]

2:6 Enjoying the Good Things That Exist

CHOOSE BETWEEN PLEASURE AND THE GOOD. AMBROSE: All these things will be left behind. No one will take anything with him, except what he has received through the pleasure of the body. Therefore I have arrived at this conclusion, and there is none truer except the one that says that the good is what is gentle and cheerful. Therefore you must give credit to philosophy, or rather to the Wisdom of Solomon. CAIN AND ABEL 1.4.14.[17]

THE SOURCE OF GENUINE DESPAIR. PSEUDO-

AUGUSTINE: These are the words of people who despair of eternal life and, hoping in the ephemeral corruption of the flesh, it is as if they put their hopes in the sand in a stream. SERMON 392.4.[18]

2:8 Crowning Ourselves with Rosebuds

LIVE IN LINE WITH THE TRUTH OF THE GOSPEL. AUGUSTINE: May it therefore never happen that we say to you, Live as you like! Don't worry! God will never condemn anyone—it is enough that you keep the Christian faith. He redeemed you, he shed his blood for you—he will not damn you. If the desire to go and enjoy a show comes over you, do that too! After all, what is so bad about that? And these festivals that they celebrate in the whole city, with people rejoicing and feasting and (so they think) amusing themselves—while they are actually ruining themselves—at public tables . . . you go too, celebrate, do not worry! God's mercy is so boundless, he will let everything slide! "Crown yourselves with rosebuds before they wither!" And in the house of your God, feast there too, whenever you want! Stuff yourselves with food and drink along with your friends. Indeed, these creatures were given that you might enjoy them. Can God have given these things to the godless and the pagans, and not to you? If we were to make speeches like this to you, perhaps more people would join us. And if some perhaps noticed that we were saying things that were not entirely correct, we would alienate those few, but we would gain the favor of the great majority. If we were to act in this way, however, we would be proclaiming to you not the words of God and of Christ but our own words. We would be shepherds who pasture themselves, and not the sheep. SERMON 46.3.8.[19]

---

[11]NBA 33:463. [12]Vg. [13]Wis 11:17. [14]Gen 1:2. [15]See Gen 1:6. [16]PL 35:2392. [17]PL 14:324. [18]PL 39:1708. [19]NBA 29:803-5.

2:10-20 FURY AGAINST THE RIGHTEOUS

¹⁰Let us oppress the righteous poor man;
let us not spare the widow
nor regard the gray hairs of the aged.
¹¹But let our might be our law of right,
for what is weak proves itself to be useless.

¹²Let us lie in wait for the righteous man,
because he is inconvenient to us and opposes
    our actions;
he reproaches us for sins against the law,
and accuses us of sins against our training.
¹³He professes to have knowledge of God,
and calls himself a childᵉ of the Lord.
¹⁴He became to us a reproof of our thoughts;
¹⁵the very sight of him is a burden to us,
because his manner of life is unlike that of
    others,
and his ways are strange.

¹⁶We are considered by him as something
    base,
and he avoids our ways as unclean;
he calls the last end of the righteous happy,
and boasts that God is his father.
¹⁷Let us see if his words are true,
and let us test what will happen at the end of
    his life;
¹⁸for if the righteous man is God's son, he will
    help him,
and will deliver him from the hand of his
    adversaries.
¹⁹Let us test him with insult and torture,
that we may find out how gentle he is,
and make trial of his forbearance.
²⁰Let us condemn him to a shameful death,
for, according to what he says, he will be
    protected.

e Or servant

OVERVIEW: This pericope continues ironically in the mocking voice of cynicism. But Christ who was made poor for us is the model of the just person (AMBROSE). The patriarch Joseph as a slave was a figure or type of Jesus (QUODVULTDEUS). The wicked person runs away from the example of just individuals such as Joseph or Christ. Even we cannot always immediately recognize the just person (AUGUSTINE). See how Jesus was rejected by the Jews (CYRIL OF ALEXANDRIA), though his passion was predicted (HILARY OF POITIERS) and he was glorified in it (ORIGEN). We are called to imitate his example (AUGUSTINE).

2:12 Lying in Wait for the Righteous

CHRIST IS THE MODEL OF THE JUST. AMBROSE: The Lord reproaches the Jews, "I made myself poor for you, I suffered for you, and you have raised impious hands, saying, 'Let us rid ourselves of the righteous one, because he is useless to us.'"[1] EXPOSITIONS ON THE PSALMS 35.3.[2]

THE JEWS REJECTED CHRIST. CYRIL OF ALEXANDRIA: Though they had arrested the all-powerful Lord, they bound him nonetheless,[3] the very one who came to free us from the snares of the devil and to loose the bonds of sin. They led him to Annas, the father-in-law of Caiaphas,[4] about whom it can be argued that, in

[1]Wis 2:12 Vg. [2]PL 14:954. [3]See Jn 18:12. [4]See Jn 18:13.

a certain way, he was the designer and instigator of the crime against Christ. It is likely that it was from him that the traitor, who had been paid off with money, requested the cohort to arrest Christ.[5] Christ was therefore first brought to him. It seemed that he wanted to render true and actually present what had been said through the words of the prophet, "Let us bind the righteous one, because he is useless to us."[6] And in fact Christ truly was useless to the Jews, not because he really was useless but because, lovers of sin and pleasure that they were, it seemed that he brought them nothing good. Rather, he brought a righteousness that exceeded the Law, clearly explaining what was pleasing to God, who loves virtue. The Law offered no such way, only indicating through shadows and darkness,[7] indirectly and with difficulty, what might be of benefit to its hearers. Thus, as sunlight is in a certain way useless for one with a disease of the eyes, and he receives no benefit because his illness prevents it; and as healthy food seems more useless to sick people than to others, though by it they would recover the health they desire; so also the Lord seemed useless to the Jews, though he was the author of salvation. They, in fact, did not love salvation. COMMENTARY ON THE GOSPEL OF JOHN 11.12.[8]

2:13 A Child of the Lord

A PREDICTION OF CHRIST'S PASSION. HILARY OF POITIERS: We see that all the powerful manifestations of God's judgments ring out through the words of the prophets, which, it seems to me, are here called cascades. "Deep calls unto deep, in the roar of the cascades."[9] After the preaching of the prophets came the judgments of God, as though echoing back to the voice that had predicted their coming. The voice of one cascade was, "Let us plot against the righteous one, because he is an embarrassment to us and opposes himself to our actions, calling himself a child of the Lord." Another sound of the cascade is, "He was like a lamb led to the slaughter, as a sheep

mute before his shearers, and he did not open his mouth."[10] There is another voice, also: "They have pierced my hands and my feet, I can count all of my bones."[11] Then the voice, "They divide my garments among them, for my clothing they cast lots, and when I was thirsty they gave me vinegar to drink."[12] And what need is there now to recall all the voices of the cascades, since the prophetic books are full of the insults directed at the Lord and of his passion? HOMILIES ON THE PSALMS 41.12.[13]

2:15 The Sight of Him Is a Burden[14]

DIFFICULT TO RECOGNIZE IMMEDIATELY A JUST PERSON. AUGUSTINE: If you . . . want to love the beauty of the house of God and the place where his glory dwells,[15] seek vessels for noble use. And do not say, "I looked for them but did not find them."[16] If you have sought and have not found them, it means that you have not sought. The similar tends toward the similar, the dissimilar flees the dissimilar. If you are a vessel for common use, it is natural that the vessel for noble use[17] is annoying to you, even to look at. Have you not heard how some people said of such a one, "It is unbearable for us just to look at him"? If merely to look at him is unbearable for you, how could he appear to you plainly, so you might find him? Because these vessels are found in the realm of the interior man. Certainly, when someone gives the impression of being righteous, it does not mean that he is righteous. The righteous and the unrighteous both have the same face. Both are human beings, but both are not God's house, even if they both call themselves Christians. One is a vessel, and so is the other, but both are not for noble use. Rather, one is for noble use, and the other for common. SERMON 15.2.2.[18]

---

[5]See Jn 18:12. [6]Wis 2:12 Vg. [7]See Heb 10:1. [8]CTP 113:394-95. [9]Ps 42:8 (41:8 LXX). [10]Is 53:7. [11]Ps 22:17-18 (21:17-18 LXX). [12]Ps 22:19; 69:22 (21:19; 68:22 LXX). [13]PL 9:907-8. [14]Some versions number this verse as Wis 2:14b. [15]See Ps 26:8 (25:8 LXX). [16]See Mt 7:7-8; Lk 11:9-10. [17]See 2 Tim 2:20-21. [18]NBA 29:257.

THE WICKED REJECT THE EXAMPLE OF THE JUST. AUGUSTINE: "Since the wicked went away from me, I did not know him."[19] What, then, does "I did not know him" mean? Does it refer to the fact that when a scoundrel meets a righteous person on a narrow street, the words from the Wisdom of Solomon run through his mind, "It annoys us just to see him," and he crosses the street, so as to not see that undesired person? But how many rascals there are, and how difficult it is for us to see them! They see us, and not only do they not depart from us, but also they run after us, hoping (at least sometimes) to carry out their wicked plans with our collaboration! This happens all the time. In what sense, then, do they go away? The person who is not like you departs from you. What does "he departs from you" mean? He does not follow you. And what does "He does not follow you" mean? He does not imitate your conduct. Or, "Since the wicked was far from me," that is, since he was not like me, neither did he want to imitate my conduct (he did not want to live according to the model that my life offered for his imitation), and thus, "I did not know him." What, then, does "I did not know him" mean? That I did not approve of him, and not that I did not actually know him. EXPOSITIONS OF THE PSALMS 100.7.[20]

2:17 Testing His Words

THE PATRIARCH JOSEPH IS A FIGURE OF JESUS. QUODVULTDEUS: Joseph is sent by his father to visit his brothers and the sheep.[21] Our Joseph, as well, Christ the Lord, says, "I have been sent only to the lost sheep of the house of Israel."[22] It is said, "The brothers hated Joseph because of his dreams."[23] And our Joseph, too—Christ—cried out concerning his brothers the Jews, "They hated me without reason."[24] Seeing Joseph, the brothers said, "Here comes the dreamer. Come, let us kill him, and see what becomes of his dreams."[25] The godless, as Solomon says, said about our Joseph, "Come, let us kill the righteous one, because he is displeasing

to us." And they continue, "He claims to possess knowledge of God and declares himself a son of God. Let's see if his words are true, and let's find out what will happen in the end." He confirms what is in the Gospel, when he says about the son sent to the vineyard workers, "This is the heir. Come, let us kill him, and the inheritance will be ours."[26] After seizing Joseph, the brothers stripped him of his many-colored tunic and threw him in a ditch.[27] Our Joseph, by the mouth of the prophet, says the same of his passion: "They threw me in the outer ditch, in darkness and the shadow of death."[28] By the Gospel's authority we are told how he was stripped of his tunic, which was woven from top to bottom and which the soldiers refused to divide among themselves, thus confirming the unity of the church. Heretics are excluded from this casting of lots, because it was to be that only one would possess it, that is, unity.[29] "Taking," Scripture says, "a kid from the goats, Joseph's brothers dipped the tunic in its blood"[30] and took it to their father, falsely saying that a wild beast had torn him to pieces.[31] THE BOOK OF PROMISES AND PREDICTIONS OF GOD 1.26.36-37.[32]

2:20 Condemned to a Shameful Death

CHRIST WAS GLORIFIED IN HIS HUMILIATION. ORIGEN: My Lord Jesus Christ, when he assumed the flesh of the Virgin for our salvation, was surely glorified, because "he came to seek what was lost,"[33] though he was not "glorified gloriously."[34] In fact, it is said precisely of him, "We saw him, and he had neither beauty nor splendor, and his face was more to be despised than all the sons of mortals."[35] He was glorified also when he went to the cross and suffered death. Do you know why he was glorified? He

---

[19]Ps 101:4 (100:4 LXX). [20]NBA 27:495. [21]See Gen 37:13-14. [22]Mt 15:24. [23]Gen 37:11. [24]Jn 15:25. [25]Gen 37:19-20. [26]Mt 21:38. [27]See Gen 37:23-24. [28]Ps 88:7 (87:7 LXX). [29]See Jn 19:23-24. [30]See Gen 37:31. [31]See Gen 37:32-33. [32]CTP 82:92-93. [33]Mt 18:11. [34]Ex 15:1. [35]Is 53:2-3.

said, "Father, the hour has come; glorify your Son, so that your Son may glorify you."[36] For him, therefore, even the passion of the cross was glory. This glory was not glorious, however, but humble. Finally, it is said of him, "He humbled himself even to death, death on a cross,"[37] and of this also the prophet had foretold, "Let us condemn him to a shameful death." But Isaiah also says of him, "He bore his judgment in humiliation."[38] Thus in all these events the Lord was glorified, but humbly, so to speak. He was not "glorified gloriously."[39] HOMILIES ON EXODUS 6.1.[40]

LET US IMITATE CHRIST IN HIS PASSION. AUGUSTINE: "Since, when he sees the death of the wise, he will not see death."[41] He who has wearied himself endlessly and will live to the very end,[42] "will not see death, when he sees the death of the wise." What do these words mean? He will not understand what death is when he sees the wise die. In fact, he says to himself, hasn't the one who was so wise, who was intimate with Wisdom, who worshiped God with such piety—hasn't he died also? I will therefore do what I like while I live. Indeed, if those who have wisdom could do something about it, they would not die. He sees the one who dies, yet fails to see what death is. "When he sees the death of the wise, he will not see death." In the same way, the Jews saw Christ hanging on the cross and mocked him, saying, "If he is the Son of God, he would come down from the cross."[43] They did not see, in short, what death is. O, if they had seen what death is, they would have understood it! He died in time, so as to live again forever.

They lived in time, so as to die forever. But since they saw him die, they did not see death, that is, they did not understand what true death is. What, in fact, do they say in Wisdom? "Let us condemn him to a shameful death, because, according to his own words, he will be protected. If he is truly a son of God, God will help him, and free him from the hands of his adversaries." That is, he will not allow his Son to die, if he truly is his Son. But when they saw him on the cross being insulted, and he did not descend from the cross, they said, "He was truly a man." It had already been said that one who could rise from the grave certainly could have descended from the cross. He taught us, however, to bear insults, to be patient before the tongues of people, to drink the bitter chalice[44] now so as to later receive eternal life. You who are sick, drink the bitter chalice if you want to be healthy, because now your viscera are not healthy. Do not tremble with fear, because the doctor drank it first, that you might not tremble.[45] The Lord, that is, drank the bitterness of the passion first. The one who had no sin drank,[46] the one who had nothing to be healed of. Drink, therefore, until the bitterness of this world passes, until that world comes where there will be no scandal, no anger, no sickness, no bitterness, no fever, no deceit, no enmity, no old age, no death, no quarrels. EXPOSITIONS OF THE PSALMS 48.1.11.[47]

---

[36]Jn 17:1. [37]Phil 2:8. [38]Is 53:8. [39]Ex 15:1. [40]CTP 27:110-11. [41]Ps 49:10-11 (48:10 LXX). [42]See Ps 49:10 (48:10 LXX). [43]See Mt 27:42-43. [44]See Jer 23:15. [45]See Mt 26:39 par. [46]See Heb 4:15. [47]NBA 25:1211-13.

2:21-24* THE MISTAKE OF THE UNBELIEVING

²¹*Thus they reasoned, but they were led astray,
for their wickedness blinded them,*
²²*and they did not know the secret purposes of God,
nor hope for the wages of holiness,
nor discern the prize for blameless souls;*

²³*for God created man for incorruption,
and made him in the image of his own eternity,*ᶠ
²⁴*but through the devil's envy death entered the world,
and those who belong to his party experience it.*

f Other ancient authorities read *nature*   * Wis 2:21-25 Vg.

OVERVIEW: The Jews erred about Jesus' nature (AUGUSTINE), since they did not recognize the light of Christ (ORIGEN). They were motivated among other things by envy, which cuts deeply (PSEUDO-AMBROSE); it is an attitude that is very difficult to heal (CASSIAN) and is the devil's weapon (PSEUDO-AMBROSE). Through envy the devil leads humans to death (CYPRIAN). Death itself spread from the first human being to all humanity (PSEUDO-AMBROSE). All have imitated the devil (PSEUDO-AMBROSE) and surrendered to his allurements. We are the authors of our own blindness and weakness (AUGUSTINE). However, we can choose good or evil (ANONYMOUS ANOMOEAN), blessedness or damnation (FULGENTIUS).

2:21 Blinded by Wickedness

THE JEWS ERRED ABOUT JESUS' NATURE.
AUGUSTINE: Because Jesus was crucified and not freed, they believed he was not the Son of God. Thus, insulting him as he hung on the cross, they shook their heads, saying, "If you are the Son of God, come down from the cross. He saved others, but he cannot save himself."[1]

With these words, as one reads in the book of Wisdom, "they thought thus but were mistaken. Their wickedness blinded them." What would have been so amazing about coming down from the cross, for one who rose from the grave without difficulty? But why did he want to be patient to death? To flee from the presence of Saul into the cave.[2] "Cave," here, can be understood as a lower part of the earth. It was attested, in fact, and known to all, that Jesus' body was placed in a grave that had been hewn out of rock.[3] This grave, then, was the cave, and Christ took refuge there from Saul. The Jews, in fact, persecuted him until he was placed in the cave. How can we show that they persecuted him until he had been put in the cave? They wounded him with a lance, when he was already dead on the cross.[4] But when, after the funeral practices, the corpse was wrapped in linen and placed in the cave, by then they had nothing to do with his flesh. It was then that the Lord arose, unharmed and

---

[1]Mt 27:40.42. [2]See 1 Sam 24:1-4; Ps 57:1 (56:1 LXX). Augustine interprets this event, whose hero is David, as a figure of Jesus' passion and death; he also identifies the persecutor Saul with the Jews who killed Jesus. [3]See Mt 27:60; Mk 15:46. [4]See Jn 19:34.

incorrupt, from the cave where he had taken refuge to flee the presence of Saul. He hid himself from the godless, whom Saul prefigured, and showed himself to his members.[5] Once risen, his bodily members were touched by his members,[6] the apostles. They touched the risen one and believed. Thus, Saul's persecution came to nothing. EXPOSITIONS OF THE PSALMS 56.4.[7]

THE BLINDNESS THAT SPRINGS FROM WICKEDNESS. AUGUSTINE: The third way in which sin itself is also the punishment for sin can be seen in the one who says, "I do the evil that I do not want to do."[8] To this third type also belong all those evil actions one does through ignorance, believing them not evil or even good. In fact, blindness of heart, if it were not a sin, would be unjustly reproved, and yet it is reproved justly where it says, "Blind Pharisee!"[9] as well as in a great many other passages of the Word of God. Moreover, if blindness itself were not a punishment for sin, it would not be said, "Their wickedness has blinded them." And if this did not happen by a judgment of God, we would not read, "Their eyes are darkened so they would not see; he weakens their backs forever."[10] Indeed, who would blind his heart by his own choice, when no one would want to be blind in his body? UNFINISHED TRACTATE AGAINST JULIAN 1.47.[11]

2:22 The Purposes of God

THE JEWS RECOGNIZED THE PROPHETS. ORIGEN: Though such a great light had arisen, and though the Logos had been made manifest, declaring, "Here is a man whose name is Orient,"[12] they did not see the light, because "their wickedness blinded them, and they did not know the mysteries of God." Something paradoxical took place with that people and with the pagan nations. The Jews did see a lamp in each of the prophets, but they did not recognize the Sun of righteousness[13] that arose. Therefore, even though it seemed that they had a lamp, this

was taken from them. On the other hand, "the people"—the pagans—"who were in darkness saw a great light."[14] Not a small light, as with Israel (though each of the prophets was actually not a small light), but "the people who were in darkness saw a great light," our Lord and Savior Jesus Christ. His light shines, "extending from one end of the earth to the other with power and governing" the churches "with goodness,"[15] since his Spirit fills the whole earth. Thus the prophecy is fulfilled that says, "In the last days the mountain of God will be visible." And now, "all the nations stream toward it."[16] This mountain is Jesus Christ. COMMENTARY ON MATTHEW 16.3.[17]

2:23 Created for Incorruption

WE DESIRED OUR OWN WEAKNESS. AUGUSTINE: If, because of the sorrows the soul has conceived by its love of the world, we are not yet able to taste how sweet the Lord is, let us at least believe what the divine authority wanted said in the holy Scriptures regarding his Son, "born," as the apostle says, "of the seed of David according to the flesh."[18] In fact, as it is written in the Gospel, "Everything was made through him, and without him nothing was made."[19] He is the one who had compassion on our weakness, a weakness that we merited, not by his work but by our will. "Indeed, God created human beings for immortality" and gave them free will. A person would not be excellent if he were to observe God's commandments out of necessity and not through his own will. CHRISTIAN COMBAT 10.11.[20]

2:24 The Devil's Envy

THE FIRST CREATURE TO BE LOST. CYPRIAN OF CARTHAGE: The devil, seeing that human

---

[5]See 1 Cor 12:12-27 par. [6]See Lk 24:39. [7]NBA 26:169-71. [8]Rom 7:19. [9]Mt 23:26. [10]Ps 69:24 (68:24 LXX). [11]NBA 19/1:43. [12]Zech 6:12. [13]See Mal 4:2 (3:20 LXX). [14]Mt 4:16; Is 9:1. [15]Wis 8:1. [16]Is 2:2. [17]CTP 157:20-21. [18]Rom 1:3. [19]Jn 1:3. [20]PL 40:296.

beings were made in the image of God,[21] fell through malicious envy into jealousy and, compelled by this envy, caused another to be lost, not hurling down another by the instinct of his jealousy before he himself was hurled down by his own jealousy. He was made a prisoner before he imprisoned another. He was lost before he caused another to be lost, when, compelled by envy, he took from human beings the grace of immortality that had been given to them. He himself had in fact first lost what he once was. Beloved brothers, how great is the evil into which the angel fell by which that sublime and splendid nobility was deceived and subverted, by which the deceiver himself was deceived! From then on envy raged throughout the earth, since the one who will perish through the devil's spite pays homage to the master of perdition, and the one who is jealous imitates the devil, as it is written, "Death entered the world through the envy of the devil." Consequently, "those who belong to his party imitate him." ON ENVY AND JEALOUSY 4.[22]

WE GAVE IN TO THE DEVIL'S ALLUREMENTS. AUGUSTINE: Christ descended and died and by his death freed us from death. Dying, he destroyed death.[23] And you, brothers, know that death entered the world through the envy of the devil. Scripture says that "God did not make death, nor does he rejoice in the death of the living. He created all things that they might exist. But, by the devil's envy, death entered the world." Human beings would not have died at the hands of the devil, had it been a matter of being compelled by force. The devil did not have the power to force them, only the shrewdness to seduce them. Without your consent the devil would have remained impotent. It was your consent, O man, that led you to death. Born mortal from a mortal, we became mortal from the immortals that we were. By their origin in Adam all human beings are mortal.[24] But Jesus, the Son of God, the Word of God through whom all things were made,[25] the only-begotten Son,

equal to the Father, became mortal. "The Word became flesh and dwelled among us."[26] TRACTATES ON THE GOSPEL OF JOHN 12.10.[27]

HEALING FROM ENVY IS A DIFFICULT MATTER. JOHN CASSIAN: We must be convinced that the evil of envy is healed with more difficulty than the other vices. In fact, I would dare to say that if someone allows himself to be taken in only once by the plague of that poison, he will be without remedy. Envy is the scourge of which the prophet said figuratively, "See, I will send you poisonous snakes, against which no charm will work, and they will bite you."[28] Rightly, therefore, the bite of envy was compared by the prophet with the fatal poison of the basilisk, from the effect of which the author and initiator of all poisons himself perished and caused others to perish. In fact, even before he poured forth the poison of death on the man, whom he envied, that murderer had already ruined himself. Indeed, "death entered the world through the devil's envy, and those who belong to him experience it." Just as he who was first corrupted by the plague of that same evil was unable to accept the remedy of penitence and the provision for the cure, so also those who offer themselves to be struck by the same poisonous bites preclude any help from the divine enchanter.[29] CONFERENCES 3.18.16.[30]

ENVY INFLICTS A SERIOUS WOUND. PSEUDO-AMBROSE: From envy comes hatred, grumbling, disparagement, joy over the difficulties of one's neighbor and affliction over his prosperity. O perverse progeny, which, if it penetrates the soul and begins to dominate it, destroys every bud of holiness. One who envies or hates kills no one before he kills himself. One who murmurs and disparages tears out his own roots before those of others. The one who exults in his neighbor's

---

[21]See Gen 1:26-27. [22]PL 4:641. [23]See Heb 2:14. [24]Rom 5:14. [25]See Jn 1:3. [26]Jn 1:14. [27]NBA 24:289. [28]Jer 8:17. [29]See Ps 58:5-6 (57:5-6 LXX). [30]CTP 156:255.

difficulties and is tormented by his success strikes himself first with a foreign sword. This second branch of pride was first born when the one about whom it is written, "Death entered the world through the devil's envy," convinced Cain to shed his brother's blood, moved by the hatred brought about by envy.[31] But certainly Cain, through his envy, killed his own soul before he killed the other's flesh. Indeed, it is written, "Whoever hates his brother is a murderer, and you know that no murderer has eternal life in him."[32] PRAYER 2.4.[33]

HUMAN ENVY IS SIMILAR TO THE DEVIL'S ENVY. PSEUDO-AMBROSE: Envy says, "In what way are you inferior to this one or that one? Why then aren't you equal or superior to them? How many things are you capable of that they aren't? So, they can be neither superior nor even equal to you." Fraternal love, however, responds, "O mortal, if you think yourself better than others because of your virtues, you would be more secure in the lowest place than in the highest. The worst ruin always comes from the highest place. If, as you say, some are superior and others equal to you, what harm is it to you? How does it hurt you? As you envy the lofty position of others, be careful rather that you do not imitate him of whom it is written, 'Death entered the world through the devil's envy. Those who belong to his party imitate him.'" THE CONTEST BETWEEN VICES AND VIRTUE 6.[34]

ENVY IS THE DEVIL'S WEAPON. PSEUDO-AMBROSE: Death is the sword of the devil. "Death entered the world through the devil's envy." This is the sword with which he killed the first man, and then the human race, until it was redeemed by Christ. When we sin, we fall under this sword. Christ, however, did not have this sword, because "he committed no sin, and no deceit was found in his mouth."[35] He was not subject to original sin, because he was not born of sexual intercourse involving a man—a man who necessarily could not be without sin.

ON THE BOOK OF REVELATION 6.7.[36]

WE ALL INHERITED DEATH FROM ADAM. PSEUDO-AMBROSE: The man, who was formed by the initiative of divine action, was made lord of this earthly creation, so that in observance of the divine order he would respect only the will of him who, from nothing, had made him lord of all things. And from the beginning—not out of ignorance but corrupted by envy and wanting the creature to surpass what had been granted by God—he lost what nature had not given him, that is, grace, which had been granted him by the benevolence of the Creator. From then on, the transgressor, having received the sentence of death through the jealousy of the devil's deception, passed this sentence on to the descendents who would originate from him in the future. SERMON 35.3.[37]

2:25[38] *Imitating the Devil*

WE CAN CHOOSE TO IMITATE GOOD OR EVIL. JULIAN OF ECLANUM (VIA AUGUSTINE): Generation is properly attributed to the sexes, whereas imitation is always carried out by souls. This inclination of the soul to imitate, if it can, what it wants to, at times accuses a person and at times is to his credit, depending on the situation. Thus, in the good, imitation is spoken of regarding God, the angels and the apostles. Of God, "Be perfect, as your heavenly Father is perfect."[39] Of the angels, "Your will be done, on earth as it is in heaven."[40] Of the apostles, "Be imitators of me, as I am of Christ."[41] In evil, by contrast, people imitate the devil, as it is written, "Those who belong to him imitate him."[42] People also imitate other people: "Do not assume a melancholy air, like the hypocrites who disfigure their faces."[43] They imitate animals, as is implied in the warning, "Do not be like the horse or the

---

[31]See Gen 4:8. [32]1 Jn 3:15. [33]PL 17:756. [34]PL 17:1061. [35]1 Pet 2:22; Is 53:9. [36]PL 17:834. [37]PL 17:673. [38]Vg. [39]Mt 5:48. [40]Mt 6:10. [41]1 Cor 11:1. [42]Wis 2:25 Vg. [43]Mt 6:16.

mule, without intelligence."[44] By these words, both of persuasion and dissuasion, the inclination to imitation is indicated. Surely, if this were not possible, it would not be suggested to avoid it. TRACTATE (VIA UNFINISHED TRACTATE AGAINST JULIAN[45] 2.52).[46]

BLESSEDNESS AND DAMNATION. FULGENTIUS OF RUSPE: Believe with the firmest faith, not doubting in any way, that Christ, the Son of God, will come to judge the living and the dead. With his coming he will raise, glorify and, according to his promise, make equal to the holy angels[47] those who in this life are freely justified by faith through the gift of his grace. To these same justified ones he gives perseverance until the end in the faith and love of holy mother church. He will lead them to the state in which they are perfectly good, in the measure in which God grants to each.

After this they will no longer be able to lose that perfection in which the glory of the saints will differ, but the eternal life of all will be the same. The devil and his angels, however, Christ will send into the eternal fire, where they will never be free of the punishment prepared for them by the divine justice[48] and with the devil godless and wicked people, of whom Scripture says, "Those who are of his party imitate him."[49] They have imitated him in evil actions and have not done adequate penance before the end of this life— those godless and wicked people who are destined to burn in the torment of the eternal flames, after reassuming their bodies. LETTER TO PETER ON THE FAITH 71.28.[50]

---

[44]Ps 32:9 (31:9 LXX). [45]Julian's tractate is lost, but some quotations from it survive in Augustine's refutation. [46]NBA 19/1:247. [47]See Mt 22:30 par. [48]See Mt 25:41. [49]Wis 2:25 Vg. [50]CTP 57:165-66.

3:1-13 THE DESTINY OF THE JUST AND THE IMPIOUS

[1]But the souls of the righteous are in the hand of God,
and no torment will ever touch them.
[2]In the eyes of the foolish they seemed to have died,
and their departure was thought to be an affliction,
[3]and their going from us to be their destruction;
but they are at peace.
[4]For though in the sight of men they were punished,
their hope is full of immortality.
[5]Having been disciplined a little, they will receive great good,
because God tested them and found them worthy of himself;
[6]like gold in the furnace he tried them,
and like a sacrificial burnt offering he accepted them.
[7]In the time of their visitation they will shine forth,
and will run like sparks through the stubble.
[8]They will govern nations and rule over peoples,
and the Lord will reign over them for ever.

⁹Those who trust in him will understand truth,
and the faithful will abide with him in love,
because grace and mercy are upon his elect,
and he watches over his holy ones.ᵍ

¹⁰But the ungodly will be punished as their reasoning deserves,
who disregarded the righteous manʰ and

rebelled against the Lord;
¹¹for whoever despises wisdom and instruction is miserable.
Their hope is vain, their labors are unprofitable,
and their works are useless.
¹²Their wives are foolish, and their children evil;
¹³their offspring are accursed

g The text of this line is uncertain, and it is omitted here by some ancient authorities. Compare 4.15.   h Or *what is right*

OVERVIEW: The just are always with God (AUGUSTINE, CASSIODORUS). God never forgets a just person (AUGUSTINE). He, for instance, received Mary's soul into his care (JOHN OF DAMASCUS). "Malice" is the scriptural name for the torments inflicted on the martyrs (AUGUSTINE), but hope in God enabled them to accept their afflictions (PSEUDO-AUGUSTINE). God, though, never approves of human sacrifice (AUGUSTINE). God gives us the martyrs' relics to help us in following the martyrs' example (CHRYSOSTOM). Faith enables us to know the reward of the just and the eternity and blessedness of life in God (AUGUSTINE): the good will go to rest, which is the happiness of paradise. The wicked will receive punishment (PSEUDO-AUGUSTINE), since God gives bad things to the wicked (AUGUSTINE). God tests us (VIGILIUS) and purifies us (ORIGEN), but we must distinguish between the fire of sacrifice and the fire of flattery (AUGUSTINE). The just enjoy a glorious condition; they are like stars, and their bodies will shine like the moon (CASSIODORUS). They will be showered by the divine light (PSEUDO-AUGUSTINE). Discipline leads to God (CYPRIAN), and without conversion there is no hope for the future (FULGENTIUS).

3:1 *In the Hand of God*

THE MARTYRS' RELICS. JOHN CHRYSOSTOM: The good God,[1] showing his great and varied providence, not only ordained all of creation, unfolded the heavens,[2] spread the seas, enkindled the sun, caused the moon to shine, gave the earth to be inhabited and offered all the resources of the earth for food and for the sustenance of our bodies, but he also gave us the relics of the holy martyrs. After taking their souls ("The souls of the righteous," it says, "are in the hand of God"), he left us their bodies in the meantime as an exhortation and a comfort, so that, drawing near to the graves of these saints, we might be moved to zeal and to imitation and that seeing them we might keep the memory of their good works and of the rewards associated with them. BAPTISMAL INSTRUCTIONS 7.1.[3]

GOD NEVER FORGETS A JUST PERSON. AUGUSTINE: To say that God remembers[4] is to say that he acts. Conversely, to say that he forgets is to say that he does not act: not because there is forgetfulness in God (given that he never changes) or remembrance (given that he never forgets). For those, then, who did not know what they were doing,[5] "I have become like a man without support," when I was "free among the dead."[6] And for those who did not know what they were doing, I have become "like the slain who sleep in the grave. And they are cast away from your hand."[7] That is, when they reduced me to such a condition, "they were cast away from your hand." They thought I was a man without support;

[1] Literally, "lover of men."   [2] See Is 44:24.   [3] CTP 31:183-84.   [4] See Ps 88:6 (87:6 LXX).   [5] See Lk 23:34.   [6] Ps 88:5-6 (87:5 LXX), variant.   [7] Ps 88:6 (87:6 LXX), variant.

rather, it was they who were without the support of your hand. In fact, as it says in another psalm, "they dug a ditch before me, but they fell in it themselves."[8] I think that the words "and I have been cast away from your hand" are best interpreted in this way, rather than referring to those who sleep in the grave, whom God does not remember. In fact, there are some righteous people among these latter, of whom it is true that he has not remembered them yet, so as to raise them. Nevertheless, of these it is also said, "The souls of the righteous are in the hand of God." That is, they enjoy the support of the Most High, and they dwell in the protection of the God of heaven.[9] As for the others, however, they were cast away from the hand of God, since they thought that the Lord Jesus Christ was rejected by his hand, so much so that they could number him among the evildoers and kill him.[10] EXPOSITIONS OF THE PSALMS 87.5.[11]

GOD RECEIVED MARY'S SOUL. JOHN OF DAMASCUS: The Word of God, who out of mercy condescended to become her son, serves with his sovereign hands this most holy and most divine woman as is fitting toward a mother and receives her holy soul. What a good legislator! Not being subject to the law, he keeps the law that he decreed. It is he, in fact, who established the duty of children toward their parents. "Honor," he says, "your father and your mother."[12] I believe this is a truth that is obvious to anyone who is at least a little familiar with the divine revelation of sacred Scripture. If, as sacred Scripture says, "the souls of the righteous are in the hands of the Lord," how much more should she not entrust her soul to her Son and her God? HOMILY ON THE DORMITION 1.4.[13]

THE SAINTS ARE WITH GOD. AUGUSTINE: Where do we think these saints are? In a place where they are doing well. What more do you want? You do not know the place, but consider what it truly is. Wherever they are, they are with God. "The souls of the righteous are in

the hands of God; no torment will touch them." They passed through torments to reach the place without torment. Through narrowness and constriction they reached the place of freedom. Therefore, those who are heading toward such a homeland should not be dismayed if the way is difficult. SERMON 298.3.3.[14]

GOD'S POWER IS ALWAYS WITH THE JUST. CASSIODORUS: "My life is always in your hands, but I do not forget your law."[15] Because the soul of the righteous is persecuted by the wickedness of thieves, who want to seduce it with various traps, it very wisely says that it is placed "in the hands" of God. No violence of its adversaries can reach there, as it says, "The souls of the righteous are in the hands of God, and no fatal torment will touch them." And also, "My sheep listen to my voice," and a little later, "No one will steal them from my hand."[16] He added "ever," so that it would be understood that at no time is the soul left to the mercy of its foes. When it then says "in the hands," it means that God acts with power, since he keeps safe those who show themselves to have acted according to his judgments. Why then does he say that his soul is placed "in the hands" of the Lord? Because his law is not taught to someone who forgets. Therefore, we are under his protection if we do not stray in anything from the saving precepts. This is what is asked of us at all times and what we are commanded in particular here: to return to the law, and not to stray from the law. EXPLANATION OF THE PSALMS 118.109.[17]

3:2 Their Death Deemed a Disgrace[18]

FAITH KNOWS THE REWARD OF THE JUST. AUGUSTINE: "The sufferings of the present time cannot be compared with the future glory that

---

[8]Ps 57:7 (56:7 LXX). [9]See Ps 91:1 (90:1 LXX). [10]See Lk 22:37. [11]NBA 27:33. [12]Ex 20:12. [13]CTP 25:148-49. [14]NBA 33:365. [15]Ps 119:109 (118:109 LXX). [16]Jn 10:27-28. [17]PL 70:873. [18]Wis 3:2b Vg.

will be revealed in us."[19] But it remains hidden until it is revealed. And precisely because it is hidden, "in the eyes of the foolish they seemed to have died." But, by the fact that it is concealed, does it thus also remain hidden to God, before whom it is precious? "Precious in the eyes of the Lord is the death of his saints."[20] Consequently, in the face of this hidden mystery we need eyes of faith, so as to believe what we do not see and to suffer courageously, resolutely accepting unjust evils. SERMON 306.1.1.[21]

THE WORD MALICE HAS A SPECIAL MEANING. AUGUSTINE: "In the eyes of the foolish they seemed to have died, and their end was thought to be a punishment." "Malice," in Latin,[22] does not ordinarily have the same meaning that it has in the language used in sacred Scripture. In fact, in Latin one usually calls "malice" that which makes human beings wicked. In the language of the Scripture, however, by "malice" is also meant the evil suffered by human beings. In this passage, therefore, the term should be understood in the sense of "punishment." SERMON 306.1.1.[23]

GOD GIVES BAD THINGS TO THE WICKED. AUGUSTINE: "The Lord abandoned the evil he intended to inflict on his people."[24] God wanted it to be understood that this evil was a punishment, as is said, "Their end was thought to be an evil." Similarly, it is said that good and evil come from God,[25] but not according to the evil by which human beings are evil. God in fact is not evil, but he gives bad things to evil people, because he is just. QUESTIONS ON THE HEPTATEUCH 2.143.[26]

3:3 At Peace

IN THE JUDGMENT. PELAGIUS (?) (VIA PSEUDO-AUGUSTINE): But someone will ask, "Why do we see that the good die along with the bad?" The former do not perish but escape, because they are freed from commerce with the wicked and from persecution, and they are brought to rest.

The others die and truly perish, because what awaits them when they depart from this world is the torment and punishment of a terrible judgment. The good are called before their time, so that the perverse will torment them no more. The wicked and godless are taken away so that they would no longer persecute the good. The righteous are called from difficulties, tribulations and anguish into rest. The godless are dragged from luxury, abundance and pleasures to punishment. The former go to judge, the latter to be judged. The former, to receive their due, the latter to receive their punishment, as it is written, "The righteous, even if he dies prematurely, will find rest."[27] And also, "Because he lived among sinners, he was taken away."[28] And also, "His soul was pleasing to the Lord. Therefore God took him quickly from the wickedness around him."[29] And still, "They go to death together with the godless, but they are in peace."[30] You see therefore that this disintegration of the body is rest, not punishment, for the righteous and for those who worship God. In decay, rather than perishing, they are freed. Thus the faithful do not fear decay, nor are they overawed by it, but they desire and long for its coming. They understand that through it they will arrive at rest, not punishment. The perverse, the godless and those who are conscious of their crimes rightly fear decay, because of a natural disposition by which they cannot fail to judge themselves. Consequently, having received and understood this explanation, we must not sin at all, especially because we are not unaware that there is a judgment of sinners in this world, which remains in the future one. ON THE CHRISTIAN LIFE 5.[31]

3:4 Punished in the Sight of People

---

[19]Rom 8:18. [20]Ps 116:15 (115:6 LXX). [21]NBA 33:549. [22]Augustine explains the word *malitia*, used by the Vetus Latina in this verse, which usually means "wickedness" and is a literal translation of the Septuagint. [23]NBA 33:549. [24]Ex 32:14, variant. [25]See Sir 11:14. [26]PL 34:644. [27]Wis 4:7. [28]Wis 4:10. [29]Wis 4:14. [30]Wis 3:3, variant. [31]PL 40:1036.

HOPE IN GOD. PSEUDO-AUGUSTINE: How great is the constancy of the martyrs! How excellent is the faith of the saints who willingly accepted many torments for the name of Christ and who, nevertheless, despising these torments, defeated the devil who was in their persecutors! Indeed, Solomon said of them, "Even if to human eyes they suffer punishments, their hope is full of immortality." Therefore the saints had a great hope, because they believed that, enduring a temporary passion, they would receive in the resurrection what they hoped for. And what did they hope for in suffering these things? It is easier to speak of what they suffered, because who can speak of what they hoped for? Listen to the apostle Paul: "The sufferings of the present moment cannot be compared with the future glory that will be revealed in us."[32] SERMON 316.1.[33]

3:6 Tried Like Gold in a Furnace

GOD PURIFIES US WITH SPIRIT AND WITH FIRE. ORIGEN: God removes evil from us in two ways, by "wind" and by "fire."[34] If we are good and obedient to his teachings and allow ourselves to be instructed by his Word, the "wind" sweeps away our evils, according to what is written, "If by the Spirit you mortify the deeds of the flesh, you will live."[35] But if the Spirit has not taken away our evils, there is need of purification by fire. Observe closely, however, each combination of terms. The first is "wind" and "cloud," the second "fire" and "light," the third "electrum" and "splendor."[36] Each of these, as though it were sad, is paired with something more cheerful. Indeed, if the wind dies down, immediately a cloud appears. If fire appears, there is light. If one speaks of electrum, there is brightness all around. We must, "like gold in the furnace" and electrum, be fused by an extremely hot fire. You will find, in the prophet we are commenting on, the Lord who sits in the middle of Jerusalem, fanning those who are a heap of silver, tin, iron and lead.[37] With laments, he reproaches those who bear within themselves the

dross of more base material. He says, "You have become the dross of silver, silver that is no longer pure like the grape."[38] When we superimpose on God's creature, which at the beginning is good, the vices and passions that come from our wrongs, then we mix iron, tin and lead with gold and silver. To be purified, fire is necessary. As early as possible, then, we must act in such a way so as, when we arrive at this fire, to pass through it peacefully, like gold and silver and precious stones, which have no blemish of adultery. Not that we would be defeated by the fire, but that we might emerge from it approved. HOMILIES ON EZEKIEL 1.13.[39]

THE FIRE OF SACRIFICE AND THE FIRE OF FLATTERY. AUGUSTINE: There are two kinds of persecutors: those who insult and those who flatter. The tongue of the flatterer does more damage than the hand of the murderer, and Scripture calls such a tongue a furnace. Speaking of persecution, it says, "He tried them like gold in the crucible" (referring to the martyrs who had been killed), "and they pleased him like a sacrifice." Listen how the tongue of the flatterer is no different: "Fire puts gold and silver to the test, and a person is tested by the mouth that praises him."[40] Both the one and the other are fire. You must emerge unscathed from both. The one who insults you breaks you to pieces, and you are shattered in the furnace like a clay vase. The word of God formed you; then came the test of suffering. Indeed, it is necessary that what has been formed also be baked. If the vase was well formed, fire is welcome! It will serve to harden it. EXPOSITIONS OF THE PSALMS 69.5.[41]

TESTED BY THE TRINITY. VIGILIUS OF THAPSUS: The Father tests us, the Son tests us, the Holy Spirit tests us. He says of the Father to the Thessalonians, "Thus we preach, not seeking

---

[32]Rom 8:18. [33]PL 39:2351. [34]See Ezek 1:4. [35]Rom 8:13. [36]See Ezek 1:4. [37]See Ezek 22:18. [38]Ezek 22:18. [39]CTP 67:50-51. [40]Prov 27:21, variant. [41]NBA 26:707.

to please human beings but God, who tests our hearts."[42] Solomon says of the Son, "He tried them like gold in the crucible and found them worthy of himself." Of the Holy Spirit, Solomon says, "He who tests hearts is the Spirit of the Lord,"[43] and he will wipe out the wicked from the earth.[44] AGAINST VARIMADUS 3.64.[45]

3:6 Like a Sacrificial Offering

GOD DOES NOT APPROVE OF HUMAN SACRIFICE. AUGUSTINE: The nations "did for their gods what is abominable to the Lord and what he detests. They even burned their sons and daughters in the fire, in homage to their gods."[46] In what other way can it be more clearly shown than with these testimonies of sacred Scripture (and I have omitted others that are similar) that God, who gave these Scriptures to the human race, was not only not pleased but indeed detested sacrifices in which human beings were immolated? God loves and rewards fully those sacrifices in which a righteous person who suffers iniquity fights for the truth even to the point of death or is killed by enemies that he has offended for the sake of justice, repaying them good for evil, love for hatred. The Lord calls this righteous blood, from the blood of Abel until the blood of Zechariah.[47] And especially, because he poured out his blood for us and offered himself in sacrifice to God. This surely was an offering, as much as it was also his being killed by his enemies for the sake of justice. Imitating him, the army of the martyrs fought until death for the truth and was immolated by ruthless enemies. Scripture says of the martyrs, "He tried them like gold in the crucible, and he was pleased with them as with a holocaust." Thus the apostle says, "Indeed, I am already being sacrificed."[48] QUESTIONS ON THE HEPTATEUCH 7.49.[49]

3:7 Shining Like Stars

THE JUST SHINE LIKE STARS. CASSIODORUS: God said earlier that those who sincerely repent will be saved[50] and that after they have received the remedy of forgiveness, we must think of them as stars.[51] Indeed, those who have merited to be numbered among the saints shine like the nighttime stars of this creation. But as much as it might seem to us that there are many, many of these in the church, God has counted every one of those who will have the joy of participating in his kingdom. The fact that we can think of the stars as holy people is attested to in the passage of Genesis that says, "I will make your descendents as numerous as the stars of heaven."[52] And Solomon says, "The righteous will shine like the stars of heaven." EXPLANATION OF THE PSALMS 146.4.[53]

THE BODIES OF THE JUST. CASSIODORUS: "Like the moon, eternally perfect and a faithful witness in the sky."[54] First he spoke of the sun,[55] and we said that this referred to the soul of the righteous. Now he speaks of the moon, which is here appropriately compared with the human body, because it waxes and wanes with time. But he adds that it is "perfect" so that, by referring to that spiritual body,[56] you would understand that he is not speaking of something temporal but only of that eternity that will never fail. Our very body, in fact, will be filled with light "forever," like "the perfect moon." And this moon, that is, the structure of our body, will be a "faithful witness," because in it the promises will have been fulfilled. And see that he has placed it "in the heavens," that is, in a holy person. The bodies of those whose souls shine with divine light will shine in the same way, as Solomon says, "The righteous will shine forth and, like sparks in the stubble, run here and there."[57] EXPLANATION OF THE PSALMS 88.37.[58]

---

[42]1 Thess 2:4. [43]Prov 17:3 Vg. [44]See Prov 2:22. [45]PL 62:425. [46]Deut 12:31. [47]See Mt 23:35. [48]2 Tim 4:6. [49]PL 34:811. [50]See Ps 147:3 (146:3 LXX). [51]See Ps 147:4 (146:4 LXX). [52]Gen 22:17. [53]CCL 98:1306. [54]Ps 89:37 (88:37 LXX), variant. [55]See Ps 89:36 (88:36 LXX). [56]The moon, which in antiquity was often considered to be immaterial. [57]Wis 3:7, variant of Vg. [58]PL 70:638-39.

THE DIVINE LIGHT WILL COVER THE JUST.
PSEUDO-AUGUSTINE: Will it perhaps be that one who is cold must clothe himself, there where it will not even be necessary to cover the body, in the presence of that cold of which the prophet says, "Who can withstand his cold?"[59] Or, where the one who has lost his wedding garment will be naked forever?[60] Where the wicked person with a stained conscience will be clothed with darkness, and the good person with a mantle of immortality and blessedness. Where our merits will be our dress, as the Lord says, "The righteous will shine like the sun."[61] And the prophet, "Your priests are clothed with righteousness,"[62] or, "The queen is at your right hand, in a gown of spun gold."[63] Where an eternal light will shine that will replace the tunics of holy bodies. Where a garment that will never be removed will be changed into a body. Where the garment will be the prize and the angelic clothing will no longer be a covering or a garment but nature? SERMON 262.4.[64]

THE HAPPINESS OF PARADISE. PSEUDO-AUGUSTINE: As fellow citizens of the saints and members of God's family[65] and as heirs of God and coheirs with Christ,[66] let us examine, to the extent possible, the renowned happiness of our city. Let us say with the prophet, "Oh, wonderful things are said of you, city of God,[67] the home of all who rejoice in you!"[68] You are the sum of all the joys of earth. In you there is no old age or the misery of old age. In you there are no cripples, or lame, or hunchbacks or deformed,[69] but all "arrive at the stature of the perfect person, to the measure of the full maturity of Christ."[70] What can be more beautiful than this life in which there is no fear of poverty or the sadness of disability; where no one is hurt or angry or envious; where no concupiscence flares up, nor is there desire for food, and where we are not agitated by ambition for honor or power? There is no fear of the devil there or of the snares of demons, and the fear of hell is long gone. There is death neither of the body nor of the soul but a life made

joyous by the gift of immortality. There will be no more discord; rather, everything will be harmonious, of one heart, because there will be one unanimity among all the saints. Everything will be peaceful and joyful, calm and serene. There will be a perpetual splendor, not the one we see now but a greater brightness to match the greater happiness. Therefore, as we read, that "city will have no need of the light of the sun," but the almighty Lord will enlighten it, "and its lamp is the Lamb,"[71] where the saints will shine like stars forever, and those who teach many, like the splendor of the firmament.[72] Thus, there will never be night or any darkness. Clouds will not gather, nor will there be cold or heat or bitterness. Rather, everything will be such that "eye has not seen, nor ear heard, nor has it entered into the heart of man,"[73] except those found worthy to enjoy it, "whose names are written in the book of life."[74] MANUAL 17.[75]

3:8 The Lord Will Reign Forever

LIFE IN GOD IS ETERNAL AND BLESSED. AUGUSTINE: "If you want to enter into life, keep the commandments."[76] But, when we have arrived at life, what need is there for me to add "eternal"? And why add "happy"? Life, plain and simple, because that which is both eternal and happy is life. When we have arrived at life, we will have the certainty that we will live in it forever. In fact, if we find ourselves there and do not have the certainty of remaining there forever, even there we would be in fear. And if there is fear, there would be suffering, not of the body but of the soul, which is worse. But what kind of happiness is it where there is suffering? Thus, we will have the assurance of always being in that life, unable to see its end, because we will be in the kingdom of him about whom it was said, "And

---

[59]Ps 147:17. [60]See Mt 22:11. [61]Mt 13:43. [62]Ps 132:9 (131:9 LXX). [63]Ps 45:10 (44:10 LXX). [64]PL 39:2231. [65]See Eph 2:19. [66]See Rom 8:17. [67]Ps 87:3 (86:3 LXX). [68]Ps 87:7 (86:7 LXX, variant). [69]See Lev 21:18-19. [70]Eph 4:13. [71]Rev 21:23. [72]See Dan 12:3. [73]1 Cor 2:9; cf. Is 64:3. [74]Phil 4:3. [75]PL 40:958-59. [76]Mt 19:17.

his kingdom will have no end."[77] The book of Wisdom, making known to us the glory of God's saints, whose death is precious in his sight,[78] says, as you heard at the end of the reading, "And the Lord will reign over them forever."[79] We will therefore be in that great kingdom that endures forever, precisely because it is just, great and eternal. SERMON 306.8-9.7.[80]

3:11[81] *Despising Wisdom and Discipline*

DISCIPLINE LEADS TO GOD. CYPRIAN OF CARTHAGE: Discipline is the guardian of hope, the bond of faith, the guide on the way of salvation, the stimulus and nourishment of a good nature, the teacher of virtue. It makes one remain always in Christ and live unceasingly in God, allowing one to attain the heavenly promises and the divine rewards. THE DRESS OF VIRGINS 1.1.[82]

WITHOUT CONVERSION, THERE IS NO HOPE. FULGENTIUS OF RUSPE: What person, might I ask, who is living badly and hears the apostle say, "If anyone destroys God's temple, God will destroy him,"[83] if he is not converted in this life, could dare to assure himself of a hope of future pardon? Who would not fall trembling to the ground? Who would not hasten to penitence with a humble spirit, before the end of this present life? The apostle cries out, "If someone destroys God's temple, God will destroy him,"

and the vain person seduces himself with an extremely perverse thought, saying, "Even if I violate God's temple and live badly until the end, I will be saved." Is not the apostle speaking of such people when he says, "Let us do evil that good may result (and their condemnation is just)"[84]? It is not these that sacred Scripture calls unhappy and their hope completely vain when it says, "The one who disdains wisdom and discipline is unhappy. Their hope is vain, and their labor without fruit." Salvation will not be given, therefore, to the wicked but to the righteous, that is, to those who have corrected themselves and converted before the end of this life. Salvation will be given to the good who, by conversion, have pursued friendship with God. It will not be given to the bad who, remaining friends of the world, rightly deserve to be called enemies of God, in the words of the apostle's reproach. Blessed James in fact rebukes them, saying, "Adulterers, do you not know that friendship with this world is enmity with God? If, therefore, one wants to be a friend of this world, he makes himself an enemy of God."[85] ON THE FORGIVENESS OF SINS 2.3.4–4.1.[86]

---

[77]Lk 1:33. [78]Ps 116:15 (115:6 LXX). [79]Wis 3:8; this is one of the earliest instances of a liturgical use of Wisdom. [80]NBA 33:557-59. [81]Vg. [82]PL 4:440-41. [83]1 Cor 3:17. [84]Rom 3:8. [85]Jas 4:4. [86]CTP 57:69-70.

3:13–4:6 BARRENNESS IS BETTER THAN IMPIOUS OFFSPRING

For blessed is the barren woman who is undefiled,
who has not entered into a sinful union;
she will have fruit when God examines souls.

¹⁴*Blessed also is the eunuch whose hands have done no lawless deed,*
and who has not devised wicked things against the Lord;
for special favor will be shown him for his faithfulness,
and a place of great delight in the temple of the Lord.
¹⁵*For the fruit of good labors is renowned,*
and the root of understanding does not fail.
¹⁶*But children of adulterers will not come to maturity,*
and the offspring of an unlawful union will perish.
¹⁷*Even if they live long they will be held of no account,*
and finally their old age will be without honor.
¹⁸*If they die young, they will have no hope*
and no consolation in the day of decision.
¹⁹*For the end of an unrighteous generation is grievous.*

4 *Better than this is childlessness with virtue,*
for in the memory of virtue^i is immortality,
because it is known both by God and by men.
²*When it is present, men imitate^j it,*
and they long for it when it has gone;
and throughout all time it marches crowned in triumph,
victor in the contest for prizes that are undefiled.
³*But the prolific brood of the ungodly will be of no use,*
and none of their illegitimate seedlings will strike a deep root
or take a firm hold.
⁴*For even if they put forth boughs for a while,*
standing insecurely they will be shaken by the wind,
and by the violence of the winds they will be uprooted.
⁵*The branches will be broken off before they come to maturity,*
and their fruit will be useless,
not ripe enough to eat, and good for nothing.
⁶*For children born of unlawful unions*
are witnesses of evil against their parents when God examines them.^k

i Gk *it*   j Other ancient authorities read *honor*   k Gk *at their examination*

OVERVIEW: It would be better for a heretic to be sterile in every sense of the word (JEROME), and a long life brings no profit to the wicked (FULGENTIUS); heretics are doomed to disappear (OPTATUS). A soul that surrenders to vice is like an adulteress (ORIGEN). Refuse to seek what is temporary (AMBROSE), although this makes no sense to the wicked, who do not think in such terms and do not ultimately benefit from long life (FULGENTIUS).

3:13 The Barren, Undefiled Woman

THE BARRENNESS OF THE HERETIC. JEROME: The prophet entreats the Lord and says, "Give them, Lord." He responds, "What shall I give them?" And immediately he replies, "Give them a barren womb and withered breasts,"[1] so that they would not have prideful thoughts

[1] Hos 9:14.

and would be ashamed of what they are accustomed to glory in. It is clear that this can also be understood regarding teachers of heretical doctrines, who glory in the great numbers of children whom they have raised to perdition, drawing them out of the church and leading them on to homicide.[2] Indeed, as many children as the heretics have generated in error, the devil has butchered. Of such a soul it is said, "Blessed is the barren woman who is undefiled, who has not known a sinful bed." And, in fact, blessed is the person of the church who, as opposed to the heretic, has not generated children in error. And in another passage we read, "Better is childlessness with virtue, for the offspring of an illegitimate union will come to nothing. Even if they live a long life, they will be held of no account, and finally, their old age will be without honor." Indeed, the fertile host of the godless is good for nothing.[3] COMMENTARY ON HOSEA 2.10.14.[4]

3:16 Children of Adulterers

A SOUL THAT SURRENDERS TO VICE. ORIGEN: If the soul, joined to the spirit and, so to speak, conjugally united with it, now turns to the pleasures of the body, bending its senses to carnal enjoyments, then seems to obey the salutary admonitions of the spirit, only to again yield to the vices of the flesh—such a soul, contaminated by the body's adultery, cannot say that it would increase and multiply legitimately, because Scripture calls the children of adulterers imperfect. Such a soul, which sets aside its union with the Holy Spirit and entirely prostrates itself to the senses of the flesh and the desires of the body, shamelessly withdrawing from God, will hear the words, "Your face has become that of a prostitute, entirely without shame."[5] It will be punished like a prostitute, with the command that its children be readied for slaughter. HOMILIES ON GENESIS 1.15.[6]

REFUSE TO SEEK WHAT IS TEMPORARY. AMBROSE: For this reason it is written, "The children of adulterers will not reach maturity." Therefore, one who follows not the Father in heaven[7] but the one who lives in earthly squalor becomes part of the progeny of the earthly father. "As is the earthly person, so are those who are of the earth."[8] His life is earthly, and he will not have rest after death. He will not see the light for eternity, because he sought what is temporary. The one, rather, who follows the glory of Christ, who desires that "light that enlightens every person who comes into this world,"[9] will find and will see the eternal light, because Christ redeemed him from death. EXPOSITIONS ON THE PSALMS 48.26.[10]

3:17 Of No Account

A LONG LIFE IS USELESS FOR THE WICKED. FULGENTIUS OF RUSPE: Far be it from us to think or to say, according to the error of those without faith, that the young Christian "stole the black day and overpowered bitter death."[11] In fact, according to the words of the apostle John, the black day sweeps away those who "are in darkness and walk in darkness, not knowing where they are going, because the darkness has blinded their eyes."[12] The black day carried away those whom the true light himself[13] judges severely. "This is the judgment," he says, "because the light came into the world, and people preferred darkness to the light: their works in fact were evil."[14] Those who live in this way are in such a state that when they hear the voice of the Son of God, they will not be called to life but to judgment. The Lord says, "The hour will come when all those who are in their graves will hear his voice. Those who did good will go to the resurrection of life, and those who have done evil to the resurrection of judgment."[15] And because neither a brief nor a long life is of any use to

---

[2]The devil; cf. Jn 8:44. [3]Wis 4:3. [4]CTP 190:205. [5]Jer 3:3. [6]CTP 14:58. [7]See Mt 6:9. [8]1 Cor 15:48. [9]Jn 1:9. [10]PL 14:1166. [11]Virgil *Aeneid* 6:429. [12]1 Jn 2:11. [13]See Jn 1:9. [14]Jn 3:19. [15]Jn 3:28-29.

them, the book of Wisdom says of such persons, "Even if they have a long life, they will be held of no account, and in the end their old age will be without honor. If they die young, they will have neither hope nor comfort in the day of judgment." LETTERS 2.5.3.[16]

4:3 The Ungodly Will Be of No Use

HERETICS WILL FINALLY DISAPPEAR. OPTATUS: What you have mentioned is found in the prophet Solomon, "The children of adulterers will not reach maturity, and illegitimate plants cannot strike deep roots," can also be interpreted literally, because whatever you might mean figuratively is borne out by real adulterers. But let us suppose that this could also be understood figuratively. In this case, the passage must be referred to heretics, who make illicit unions of the sacraments and in whose beds is found iniquity. Among them the seeds of faith have been corrupted and now tend to destruction. When Valentinus[17] wanted to assert that the Son of God appeared in the form of a ghost[18] and not in real flesh, he corrupted his own faith and that of his followers. Thus the seed of their origin was destroyed, because they did not believe that the Son of God was born of the virgin Mary with a true body and suffered the passion in his real body. AGAINST THE DONATISTS 4.8.[19]

---

[16]CTP 149:57. [17]Valentinus was the founder of a Gnostic sect; he died in Rome toward the year 160. [18]See Mt 14:26; Mk 6:49; Lk 24:38. [19]CTP 71:176-77.

4:7-19 THE UNTIMELY DEATH OF THE JUST

[7]*But the righteous man, though he die early, will be at rest.*
[8]*For old age is not honored for length of time,*
nor measured by number of years;
[9]*but understanding is gray hair for men,*
and a blameless life is ripe old age.

[10]*There was one who pleased God and was loved by him,*
and while living among sinners he was taken up.
[11]*He was caught up lest evil change his understanding*
or guile deceive his soul.
[12]*For the fascination of wickedness obscures what is good,*
and roving desire perverts the innocent mind.
[13]*Being perfected in a short time, he fulfilled long years;*
[14]*for his soul was pleasing to the Lord,*
therefore he took him quickly from the midst of wickedness.
[15]*Yet the peoples saw and did not understand,*
nor take such a thing to heart,

that God's grace and mercy are with his elect,
and he watches over his holy ones.

¹⁶The righteous man who has died will condemn the ungodly who are living,
and youth that is quickly perfected[1] will condemn the prolonged old age of the unrighteous man.
¹⁷For they will see the end of the wise man,
and will not understand what the Lord purposed for him,
and for what he kept him safe.
¹⁸They will see, and will have contempt for him,
but the Lord will laugh them to scorn.
After this they will become dishonored corpses,
and an outrage among the dead for ever;
¹⁹because he will dash them speechless to the ground,
and shake them from the foundations;
they will be left utterly dry and barren,
and they will suffer anguish,
and the memory of them will perish.

1 Or ended

OVERVIEW: The destiny of human beings should remind us that a good life is better than a long life, since one may accomplish many things in a short time, and the genuine Christian always dies at what can be considered a mature age, measured not in fullness of years but in fullness of life (FULGENTIUS). With such a perspective, our physical appearance too is of little importance in the grand scheme of things (JEROME). Age calms the passions, and wisdom is the true old age (AMBROSE). However, true rest arrives only with death (AUGUSTINE), but only for the just; for the wicked, death is a punishment (PSEUDO-AUGUSTINE). Enoch did not experience death; he was taken by God (CYPRIAN), who knows the destiny of every human being (AUGUSTINE). Grace and faith are inseparable (PSEUDO-AUGUSTINE).

4:7 The Righteous Will Be at Rest

BEFORE DEATH, THERE IS NO REST. AUGUSTINE: "The righteous one, even if he dies prematurely, will find rest." For whom, or from whom, is there in fact rest in this world, if there

are trials on every side and, when we are spared these, temptations are everywhere? Indeed, this world should be feared, whether it threatens or seduces. But if one fears both God and the world, he will despise the latter, so as to better guard himself against it. Therefore, if we want to be at rest when death comes to surprise us, let us be righteous. SERMON 335M.[1]

4:8-9 Old Age Not Honored for Length of Time

CHRISTIANS ALWAYS DIE AT A MATURE AGE. FULGENTIUS OF RUSPE: The Christian who has lived in the fear of God, at whatever age he dies, is not swept away by a bitter and untimely death[2] but crosses over supported by a maturity approved by God. Indeed, in the book of Wisdom we read, "Old age is not honored for length of time or measured by number of years. Wisdom, rather, is a person's gray hair, and a blameless life

---

[1]NBA 33:945. [2]Fulgentius makes a wordplay of *acerbus*, which originally means "sour" but can also mean "bitter" and "precocious, unripe, immature."

is old age. Having become dear to God, this one was loved by him." LETTERS 2.7.4.[3]

WISDOM IS THE TRUE OLD AGE. AMBROSE: The righteous person lives a happy old age. It does not say "long" but "happy,"[4] because the righteous person grows old happily. This is not the case, however, for any of the godless, even if they were to live longer than the oldest stag. In fact, long life is common to both the wise and fools. To live well, however, belongs to the wise person, whose "old age is venerated and for whom advanced age is a blameless life." It also says that "it is not calculated by the number of years" or by gray hair but by wisdom. Therefore, one who has been wise ages well. ON ABRAHAM 2.9.64.[5]

PHYSICAL APPEARANCE IS OF LITTLE IMPORTANCE. JEROME: If it is said of the righteous person and of the member of the church, "Gray hair is a person's wisdom,"[6] why is it not said of the heretic's iniquity, "A person's gray hair is his folly"? Of this old age Daniel said to the old man, "You have grown old in evil."[7] Therefore, in the book of the Shepherd (if anyone is willing to accept that it be read), the church appears to Hermas first with gray hair, then as a young woman and a bride, with ornate hair.[8] COMMENTARY ON HOSEA 2.7.8.10.[9]

PASSIONS CALM WITH AGE. AMBROSE: Who would deny that adolescence and, in the beginning, youth itself, churn under the delusion of the various passions? Or that when a more mature age arrives, inasmuch as the season of youthful lusts fades away, it gives way to tranquility, and the boat of the exhausted soul arrives at quiet ports? The violent movements of our adolescence, therefore, are calmed in the tranquil season of old age. CAIN AND ABEL 1.3.11.[10]

4:11 Enoch Was Caught Up

ENOCH TAKEN AWAY BY GOD. CYPRIAN OF CARTHAGE: We see also that Enoch was taken away, because he was pleasing to God, as the divine Scriptures attest in Genesis: "Then Enoch walked with God and was no longer, because God had taken him."[11] Because he was pleasing before God, he was worthy to be taken away from the evil of this world. But the Holy Spirit also teaches through Solomon that those who are pleasing to God are taken first and freed from here earlier, so they would not be tainted by too long a sojourn in this world. ON MORTALITY 23.[12]

GOD KNOWS EVERY HUMAN DESTINY. AUGUSTINE: You will say, How much and how often have I prayed, and I have not been answered! But what did you ask for? Perhaps you asked for the death of your enemy. And . . . what if he asked for yours, as well? The one who created you also created him. You are a human being, and he is too, but God is the judge. He has listened to both of you and answered neither. Are you sad because your prayer against your enemy has not been granted? Rejoice, rather, that your enemy's prayer has not been granted, to your harm. But, you say, I did not ask for this. I did not ask for the death of my enemy but the life of my son. What evil is there in that? You asked for nothing evil, in your opinion. But what would you say if he was taken so that wickedness would not corrupt his soul? But, you object, he was a sinner! And this is why I wanted him to live, so that he would amend his life. You wanted him to live so that he would become better. And what would you say if someone told you that God knew that he would have become worse if he had lived? How do you know which would have been better

---

[3]CTP 149:58-59. [4]See Gen 15:15. [5]PL 14:487. [6]Wis 4:9, variant. [7]Sus 52 (Dan 13:52 LXX). [8]The *Shepherd* of Hermas was written in Rome toward the middle of the second century. This treatise was so highly appreciated during the first Christian centuries that sometimes it was quoted as Scripture and transmitted with the New Testament (e.g., in the Codex Sinaiticus of the Bible). Its author narrates visions in which the church is revealed to him under different forms: as an old and a young woman (chaps. 18–21) but also as a virgin dressed for marriage (chap. 23). [9]CTP 190:166. [10]PL 14:321. [11]Gen 5:24. [12]PL 4:598-99.

for him, to die or to live? If, then, you do not know, return to your heart, and leave every decision to God. You will say to me, "But, then, what should I do? What should I ask for in prayer?" What should you ask for? What the Lord, the heavenly teacher, taught us. Invoke God as God, love God as God. There is nothing better than him. Desire him, long for him! EXPOSITIONS OF THE PSALMS 85.8.[13]

4:13 Perfected in a Short Time

WE MAY ACCOMPLISH MANY THINGS IN A SHORT TIME. FULGENTIUS OF RUSPE: We should not think that your bishop, our brother, has departed here early and that he lived only a little while. It is right to say that he did not live only a little while if we realize that, as much as we may say of him, there is still more to say (even if, being finite, what is much here will be judged as though it were nothing). And he has not lived so little, if, instead of counting the years, we think of his works. Who knows how many people, though living many years, have not done even half of what he did in a few years? To want to keep him here, then, is nothing other than to envy him his happiness. Now, as human beings, we are saddened for the man. What would we do if we did not act like human beings? We are sad in a human way, therefore, for a man's departure. But as we heard in the divine lesson, "In a short time, he fulfilled a long career." But, then, let us count those times as one counts a day. All that he did among you, exhorting, speaking, offering himself for your imitation—preserve it so as to praise and adore God, and you will be his most splendid memorial. Indeed, what matters for him is not that he be hidden in a marble tomb but that he be built up in your hearts—that he who has been buried would live in living sepul-

chers. Indeed, your memory is his tomb. He lives near to God, to be happy. He lives near to you, so that you would be happy. SERMON 79.[14]

4:14-15 A Soul Pleasing to the Lord

A GOOD LIFE IS BETTER THAN A LONG LIFE. FULGENTIUS OF RUSPE: "His soul in fact was pleasing to God, because he hastened to take him away from iniquity." Precisely with these words the sacred Scripture teaches us that in this world, it is not a long life that matters but a good life. To know the merits, as much as we can, of a deceased person, you must closely observe not how long he lived but how he lived. In fact, just as in a wicked life, the longer one lives the more punishments are multiplied for the one who lives in sin, so in a good life, though it is over in a brief period of time, a great, unending glory is gained for the one who lives well. A wicked life, then, leads to increasing ill temper in bitter, immature old people, whereas a good life leads young people, who die mature, to the kingdom of God. LETTERS 2.7.4.[15]

GRACE IS GIVEN THROUGH FAITH. PSEUDO-AUGUSTINE: Similarly, in the book of Wisdom it says, "Because the grace of God is in his saints." It is said as a general rule that no one has ever been or is holy without the grace of God. But so this grace might be in the saints, to confirm them, they receive it freely through the faith that comes from God. They did not have it prior to faith. As David says, "You will save them without price."[16] HYPOMNESTICON 3.12.27.[17]

---

[13]NBA 26:1257-59. [14]PL 79:951. [15]CTP 149:59. [16]Ps 56:8 (55:8 LXX, variant). [17]PL 45:1635.

4:20–5:14 THE JUDGMENT OF THE WICKED*

²⁰They will come with dread when their sins are reckoned up,
and their lawless deeds will convict them to their face.
5 Then the righteous man will stand with great confidence
in the presence of those who have afflicted him,
and those who make light of his labors.
²When they see him, they will be shaken with dreadful fear,
and they will be amazed at his unexpected salvation.
³They will speak to one another in repentance,
and in anguish of spirit they will groan, and say,
⁴"This is the man whom we once held in derision
and made a byword of reproach—we fools!
We thought that his life was madness
and that his end was without honor.
⁵Why has he been numbered among the sons of God?
And why is his lot among the saints?
⁶So it was we who strayed from the way of truth,
and the light of righteousness did not shine on us,
and the sun did not rise upon us.
⁷We took our fill of the paths of lawlessness and destruction,
and we journeyed through trackless deserts,
but the way of the Lord we have not known.
⁸What has our arrogance profited us?
And what good has our boasted wealth brought us?

⁹"All those things have vanished like a shadow,
and like a rumor that passes by;
¹⁰like a ship that sails through the billowy water,
and when it has passed no trace can be found,
nor track of its keel in the waves;
¹¹or as, when a bird flies through the air,
no evidence of its passage is found;
the light air, lashed by the beat of its pinions
and pierced by the force of its rushing flight,
is traversed by the movement of its wings,
and afterward no sign of its coming is found there;
¹²or as, when an arrow is shot at a target,
the air, thus divided, comes together at once,
so that no one knows its pathway.

¹³*So we also, as soon as we were born, ceased to be,*
and we had no sign of virtue to show,
but were consumed in our wickedness."
¹⁴*Because the hope of the ungodly man is like chaff*ᵐ *carried by the wind,*
*and like a light hoarfrost*ⁿ *driven away by a storm;*
it is dispersed like smoke before the wind,
and it passes like the remembrance of a guest who stays but a day.

m Or *dust* n Other authorities read *spider's web* * The Vulgate adds a verse between the end of Wis 5:13 and the beginning of Wis 5:14: "They said such things, and they sinned."

OVERVIEW: The main theme of this pericope is the future judgment of the wicked (FULGENTIUS). The wicked must account for their iniquities (AUGUSTINE), since there is no repentance possible after death (CASSIODORUS). The just should not be scandalized by the well-being of the impious in this present life (ORIGEN), since the evil will experience a bitter awakening (FULGENTIUS). Weeping and remorse will be useless in hell (PSEUDO-CYPRIAN), whereas salvation will be given only to the just (FULGENTIUS) who themselves have received baptismal regeneration, although this regeneration is invisible (BEDE).

The sun can be interpreted in various ways (GREGORY THE GREAT): some people worship the sun as a false god (AUGUSTINE), but it can also serve as an image of Christ (AUGUSTINE), who is the new sun who revives all things (MAXIMUS OF TURIN). In turn, the moon serves as an image of the church (CASSIODORUS).

We are prompted by God to conversion in Christ, and God's promises do not fail (AUGUSTINE). Everything the impious do, however, is ultimately useless (AUGUSTINE), as is their arrogance (CASSIODORUS); the rich, too, are called to a bitter awakening (PATERIUS).

The ship is a symbol of the church (CHROMATIUS) and of the goods of this world that disappear, leaving no trace (HESYCHIUS).

4:20 Convicted by Their Lawless Deeds

WE WILL ACCOUNT FOR OUR MISDEEDS.
AUGUSTINE: "In you, Lord, I have taken refuge. I

will never be put to shame."[1] I am terrified, you say, of that confusion that lasts forever. There is a certain temporal confusion that is useful: the disturbance of a soul that realizes its sins, is horrified by what it sees and in that horror is ashamed and corrects what it is ashamed of. For this reason the apostle says, "But what fruit did you reap then of the things of which you are now ashamed?"[2] He says, then, that those who are already believers should blush not for the gifts they have now but for the sins of the past. The Christian does not fear this confusion. Indeed, if he had not known this confusion, he would know the eternal confusion. What is the eternal confusion? When what is said will take place: "Their iniquities will rise up against them to accuse them." And the entire herd of the wicked, their accusing iniquities before them, will be on the left, as goats separated from the sheep. They will hear, "Be gone, into the eternal fire prepared for the devil and his angels."[3] They will ask, "Why?" "I was hungry, and you did not give me to eat."[4] They despised the hungry Christ when they did not feed him. They gave him no drink when he was thirsty or clothes when he was naked. They did not take him in when he was a traveler or visit him when he was sick. They thus despised him. When he begins to point out all these sins, they will be covered with confusion, and this confusion will be eternal. EXPOSITIONS OF THE PSALMS 30.2.1.5.[5]

[1]Ps 31:2 (30:2 LXX). [2]Rom 6:21. [3]Mt 25:41. [4]Mt 25:42. [5]NBA 25:447-49.

5:2 Shaken with Fear

NO HOPE OF SALVATION FOR THE IMPIOUS.
FULGENTIUS OF RUSPE: No one, when reading
that the wicked will marvel at the sudden appearance of an unexpected salvation, should think that
for those who end the present life in sin, salvation will sooner or later be conferred on them
by divine gift. It in fact calls the salvation of the
righteous unexpected,[6] because if the wicked do
not hope that it will be given to them, it nevertheless remains for the righteous, who do hope for it.
Thus blessed David, in a psalm, sang of the hope
and of the salvation of the righteous as a single
reality, saying, "The salvation of the righteous
comes from the Lord, their refuge in time of
distress. The Lord comes to their help and rescues
them. He frees them from the godless and saves
them, because they have taken refuge in him."[7]
ON THE FORGIVENESS OF SINS 2.3.1-2.[8]

5:3 Speaking in Repentance

REPENTANCE AFTER DEATH IMPOSSIBLE.
CASSIODORUS: After the light disappears, there
remains only the recompense for merits. "Who
in the underworld sings your praises?"[9] must be
understood to refer to forgiveness. As Solomon
says of the godless, "Repentant, they will say to
one another, groaning in anguish of spirit," etc.
In fact, it is clear that the rich man who saw
Lazarus at rest confessed his sins,[10] but his plea
was not granted. That is because confession is
to be made in this world, in which one also finds
forgiveness. EXPLANATION OF THE PSALMS 7.6.[11]

5:4 An End Without Honor

THE WELL-BEING OF THE IMPIOUS. ORIGEN:
First, the punishments and the torments of sinners are decreed. The righteous will see their
fate and understand the difference between a
good and a bad life and from how many evils
they have escaped by living well. And those condemned to punishment will see the righteous in

glory and exclaim, "And we fools thought their
life was madness!" After having thus seen the
end of sinners, the righteous will be exalted and
lifted up to heaven so as to inherit the earth.[12]
Now the psalm speaks and comforts us concerning the problem that almost constantly disturbs
the heart of every person. Because often, when
we suffer and see that the wicked and impious
live surrounded by good fortune in this life—
full of success, abounding in riches and honors,
having fruitful and numerous children—we are
scandalized and murmur in our hearts, Where
is God's justice? If human life were ruled by
divine providence, would God allow this wicked
and godless person to rise to such a degree of
prosperity? That is why the divine word, speaking through the mouth of the righteous, says, "I
have seen a godless person"—not merely exalted
but "exalted and raised beyond all measure,"
and not above any tree but "above the cedars of
Lebanon."[13] He speaks of an exceedingly tall tree
and a mountain above all, and yet, having seen
all this, he says, "I passed by, and look—he was
no more."[14] HOMILIES ON THE PSALMS, PSALM
36, HOMILY 5.5.[15]

THE BITTER AWAKENING OF THE IMPIOUS.
FULGENTIUS OF RUSPE: This is the unexpected
salvation: they considered the life of the righteous madness, and though insane, they believed
themselves to be sane and did not expect the
retribution of divine justice. They therefore
neglected to correct their lives. In fact, they
delighted to live here in luxury for a brief time,
not believing that after a little while they would
be tormented with eternal punishments. For this
reason, seeing the righteous in the glory of the
children of God, that glory about which blessed
Paul says, "We live in it, and we boast in the
hope of the glory of God,"[16] the wicked will be

---

[6]See Sir 5:2. [7]Ps 38:39-40 (37:39-40 LXX). [8]CTP 57:67. [9]Ps 6:6.
[10]See Lk 16:23. [11]PL 70:63. [12]See Ps 37:29 (36:29 LXX). [13]Ps
37:35 (36:35 LXX). [14]Ps 37:36 (36:36 LXX). [15]BP 18:229. [16]Rom
5:2.

amazed at the glory of the righteous, that is, of the children of God, because the righteous are children of God. ON THE FORGIVENESS OF SINS 3.2.2-3.[17]

5:5 Numbered Among the Children of God

ONLY THE JUST WILL BE GIVEN SALVATION. FULGENTIUS OF RUSPE: The unhoped-for salvation, that is, not hoped for by the wicked, will surely be given to the righteous, not to the wicked. Indeed, it will not be given to those who, not hoping for it, live badly, but to those who, justly hoping for it and abstaining from carnal desires, observe the salutary precepts of blessed Peter, who says, "Beloved, I exhort you, as strangers and pilgrims, to abstain from the desires of the flesh that war on the soul. Let your conduct among the pagans be irreproachable."[18] ON THE FORGIVENESS OF SINS 2.3.3.[19]

BAPTISMAL REGENERATION IS INVISIBLE. BEDE: "What is born of the flesh is flesh, and what is born of the Spirit is Spirit."[20] The nature of the Spirit is invisible, that of the flesh, visible. Thus generation according to the flesh occurs visibly, with visible growth—one born of the flesh grows with the passage of time. Generation according to the Spirit, by contrast, takes place completely invisibly. We see one who is baptized descend into the font, be immersed in the water and come out again, but we do not in any way see what effect the bath of regeneration has had.[21] Only the piety of the faithful knows that he descends into the water a sinner but comes out purified; he descends a child of death but comes out a child of the resurrection; he descends a child of transgression but comes out a child of reconciliation; he descends a child of wrath[22] but comes out a child of mercy; he descends a child of the devil but comes out a child of God. Only Mother Church, who generates him, knows this, but to the eyes of the foolish it seems that he comes out of the font just as he went in, and the whole thing is just a game. Consequently,

at the end, seeing the glory of the saints, groaning in torment they will say, "Here are the ones whom we once derided and who were the target of our insults. How is it that they are numbered among the children of God?" And the apostle John says, "Beloved, now we are the children of God, and it has not yet been revealed what we will be."[23] In fact, what is born of the Spirit is Spirit,[24] because the one who is regenerated by water and the Spirit[25] is invisibly changed into a new person, and from being carnal he becomes spiritual.[26] And he is rightly called not only spiritual but even spirit, because as the essence of the spirit is invisible to our senses, likewise one who is renewed by the grace of God, in a way invisible to our eyes, becomes spiritual and a child of God, though he seems to all to be visibly flesh and a child of human beings. HOMILIES ON THE GOSPELS 2.18.[27]

5:6 The Light of Righteousness

CHRIST IS THE NEW SUN WHO REVIVES ALL THINGS. MAXIMUS OF TURIN: I would call the old sun of this world the one that at times disappears, at times is blocked by walls, at times is hidden by clouds. I would call the old sun that which is subject to vanity, fears corruption, is afraid of judgment. Indeed, it is written, "The sun will be turned into darkness and the moon into blood."[28] I would call old, one who partakes in human crimes, who does not flee adultery, who does not refrain from homicide and, while no person wants to be mixed up in it when a crime comes to light, he alone is always involved. Since it is obvious that this is old, we do not find a new one other than Christ the Lord, of whom it is written, "The Sun of righteousness will rise for us."[29] The prophet also speaks of him, impersonating sinners, "The light of righteousness

---

[17]CTP 57:68. [18]1 Pet 2:11-12. [19]CTP 57:68. [20]Jn 3:6. [21]See Tit 3:5. [22]See Eph 2:3. [23]1 Jn 3:2. [24]See Jn 3:6. [25]See Jn 3:5. [26]See 1 Cor 3:3. [27]CTP 90:438-39. [28]Joel 3:4 (2:31 Vg). [29]Mal 4:2 (3:20 LXX).

did not shine for us, nor did the sun ever rise for us." In fact, when the entire world was oppressed by the darkness of the devil and a haze, full of crimes, covered the world, this Sun deigned in the last days, when the night was almost here, to bring about the dawn of his birth. Beforehand—before the light, before the Sun of righteousness would shine—he sent an oracle of the prophets, like an announcement of the morning, as it is written, "I sent my prophets before the light."[30] Then he himself shone with his rays, through the brightness of his apostles, bathing the world with a light of truth so great that no one would fall in the darkness of the devil. This is the new sun that penetrates closed places, reveals what is most intimate, searches hearts. This is the new sun that by its spirit gives life to the dead, restores the corrupt and raises what is already lost. By its warmth, it cleans what is filthy, strengthens what is weak, burns what is vicious. SERMONS 62.2.[31]

THE PHYSICAL SUN. AUGUSTINE: Those who worship the sun will say, "The sun has not risen for us." While they worship the sun that he makes rise on the good and the wicked,[32] the sun that enlightens only the good has not risen for them. Therefore, they fashion new gods,[33] each one as he wishes. Indeed, what would prevent the workshop of an erring heart from giving the form he likes to his own fantasies? EXPOSITIONS OF THE PSALMS 80.14.[34]

THE SUN AS SYMBOL. AUGUSTINE: One must not believe that we owe religious cult to the heavenly lights or must worship them because they are sometimes used as images to refer to the saints.[35] We will now explain this in the name of Christ, showing how illogical it would be to want to worship the sun or the moon or the stars or the sky, because an image has been derived from them to indicate the saints. Many objects have been chosen by the inspired authors to represent the saints, but no one worships them. If in fact you wanted to worship everything symbol-

izing the saints, you would have to worship the mountains and the hills, given that it is written, "The mountains will exult like rams and the hills like lambs."[36] You refer to the saints, but I will speak of Christ himself. If it is written, "The lion of the tribe of Judah has triumphed,"[37] why don't you worship the lion? And the rock as well, since it is written, "And the rock was Christ."[38] If, then, you do not worship these earthly beings that symbolize Christ, even if certain images have been derived from them, you must remember that any creature that has been used to symbolize the saints is just an image and reserve your adoration for the Creator. Our Lord Jesus Christ has been called the sun. But is he perhaps this sun that the least significant animals see along with us? He is the light of which it is written, "He was the true light who enlightens every person who comes into this world."[39] Material light enlightens not only people but also quadrupeds, herds and every kind of animal. The Light that enlightens all people shines in the heart and illumines only those having an intellect. EXPOSITIONS OF THE PSALMS 93.4.[40]

THE SUN IS CHRIST, THE MOON IS THE CHURCH. CASSIODORUS: "And he will remain with the sun, and before the moon, from age to age."[41] This speaks of the honor of the Incarnation, who remains united to the Word. He in fact sits at the right hand of the Father, reigning forever in glory. By "sun" is certainly meant the Word of the Father, the Son of God, who is God made man. Christ is one, out of two: two distinct natures, each perfect. Indeed, of him the godless will say, "For us the sun has not risen, and the light of righteousness did not shine on us." Then, "And before the moon, from age to age,"[42] and by this must also be understood what was said earlier, "He will remain." Christ in fact

---

[30]Jer 7:25. [31]CCL 23:262. [32]See Mt 5:45. [33]See Ps 81:10 (80:10 LXX, variant). [34]NBA 26:1135. [35]See Phil 2:15. [36]Ps 114:4 (113:4 LXX). [37]Rev 5:5. [38]1 Cor 10:4. [39]Jn 1:9-10. [40]NBA 27:245. [41]Ps 72:5 (71:5 LXX), according to Vg. [42]Ps 72:5 (71:5 LXX), according to Vg.

remains before the moon, which is to say before the church, which perceives him at all times thanks to the lights of the heart. Rightly the moon can be compared with the church, which does not have a splendor of its own but in some way receives the light of the sun. Astronomers accurately explain this, among other things. EXPLANATION OF THE PSALMS 71.5.[43]

VARIOUS MEANINGS OF THE WORD SUN. GREGORY THE GREAT: Readers must use great discernment, so as to recognize that in sacred Scripture, a particular word does not always have one and the same meaning. The sun, for example, at times has a positive meaning and at times negative. In fact, sometimes it refers to our Redeemer and sometimes to persecution. According to the testimony of the book of Wisdom, the godless in hell will say, "We strayed from the way of truth, and the sun of righteousness never rose for us." And of the seed that was sown, the Lord says, "The sun rose, and it was scorched,"[44] because, when persecution comes, the word that was preached dries up in the hearts of the wicked. HOMILIES ON EZEKIEL 2.7.1.[45]

5:7 Lawlessness and Destruction

REMORSE USELESS IN HELL. PSEUDO-CYPRIAN: Then the pain of punishment will come without the fruit of repentance, regret will be fruitless and prayer useless. Too late will those who did not want to believe in eternal life believe in eternal punishment. BOOK ON THE VANITY OF IDOLS 24.[46]

CHRIST IS THE TRUE WAY. AUGUSTINE: We must come to him who is the way, the truth and the life.[47] And it should not surprise us that we reach, by faith, him through whom we walk in faith.[48] Indeed, because he is the way, we run with him. And since he is our homeland, once we have finished the race[49] we arrive where he is. In fact, being the rest and homeland of the angels according to his divinity, he became the

way of pilgrims according to his humanity. As the rest and homeland of the angels, and indeed of all the faithful, "in the beginning was the Word, and the Word was with God, and the Word was God."[50] And as the way of pilgrims, "the Word became flesh and came to dwell among us."[51] When, after the sin of the first man, we were cast out of the earthly paradise[52] as into a valley of tears, losing both the way and the homeland, we walked in difficult and lonely places, not knowing the way of the Lord. But not only did the good and merciful king of our homeland take it on himself to frequently send us his servants, but also he himself deigned to come down and prepare the way by which we can return to our homeland. O mortal, if you were lazy in looking for the way, the way himself deigned to look for you. If you were lazy in coming to the way, the way himself has come to you. Rise and walk.[53] Flee the way of the world, wide and spacious,[54] which delights for a time and damns for eternity. Run by the way of Christ, on which you will suffer for a very brief time, then rejoice forever together with the angels. SERMON 67.3-4.[55]

5:8 No Profit in Arrogance

GOD'S PROMISES ARE UNFAILING. AUGUSTINE: They placed their hope in corruptible things, and therefore their hope will become vain, whereas our hope will then become reality. So that God's promise to us would remain whole, fixed and certain, let us say with hearts full of faith, "Do not destroy in the end."[56] Do not fear, therefore, that some power might ruin the promises of God. God will not spoil them, because he is true. And there is no one more powerful than him who could cause them to fail. EXPOSITIONS OF THE PSALMS 74.1.[57]

---

[43]PL 70:808. [44]Mt 13:6. [45]CTP 18:155. [46]PL 4:562. [47]See Jn 14:6. [48]See 2 Cor 5:7. [49]See 2 Tim 4:7. [50]Jn 1:1. [51]Jn 1:14. [52]See Gen 3:23-24. [53]Lk 17:19. [54]See Mt 7:14. [55]PL 39:1874. [56]Ps 75:1 (74:1 LXX). [57]NBA 26:909.

THE ARROGANCE OF THE IMPIOUS. CAS-
SIODORUS: The proud despise the humble when
they hear them speak of things that they reject.
Because the proud love the things of this world,
they do not concern themselves with future
things and, in their malicious wickedness, attack
with greater violence those who try to follow
the Lord's precepts. But at the future judgment
they will experience an exchange of roles. Those
who are rich and proud will be despised and the
object of reproaches, as Solomon says of them:
"What good has our pride done for us? What
has our wealth and its boasting brought us?"[58]
It is clear that normal human speech would
have required that it be said, "Our soul is full
of the reproaches of the rich and the despising
of the proud." But by saying, "Our soul is full.
It is a reproach to the rich and a despising of
the proud,"[59] this seems to be a way of speaking proper to the divine Scripture, which must
not be considered mistaken but as something
that has not yet been contemplated by human
thought. EXPLANATION OF THE PSALMS 122.4.[60]

5:9 Vanished Like a Shadow

THE TIME FOR CONVERSION. AUGUSTINE:
Now is the time of mercy, then will be the time
of judgment. Why is now the time of mercy?
Now he calls to the one who is far away and
forgives the sins of the one who returns. He is
patient with sinners, until they convert, and once
they convert, he forgets the past and promises
the future. He exhorts the lazy, consoles the
afflicted, teaches the zealous, helps those who
struggle. He abandons none of those who labor
and cry out to him. He gives to those who give
to him; he gives the means by which they might
please him. The great time of mercy should not
pass in vain, brothers and sisters—it should not
pass in vain for us! The judgment will come, and
then also there will be repentance, but by then it
will be fruitless. "Repentant, they will speak to
each other, groaning in anguish of spirit" (these
things are written in the book of Wisdom).

"What has our arrogance profited us? And what
good has our boasted wealth brought us? All
this has passed like a shadow." Let us say now,
"All these things pass like a shadow." Let us say
it now, fruitfully, "They will pass," so we will
not have to say then, without fruit, "They have
passed." This is therefore the time of mercy, but
there will also be the time of judgment. EXPOSI-
TION 2 OF THE PSALMS 32.1.10.[61]

THE DEEDS OF THE IMPIOUS. AUGUSTINE:
"The posterity of the godless will perish."[62] This
is because the posterity of the godless are their
works. But we again see that the child of the
godless prospers in the world and, at times, becomes righteous and prospers in Christ. Observe
therefore how you must understand this, so as
to open the roof and come to Christ.[63] Do not
understand this carnally, because you would fall
into error. But the seed of the godless, all the
works of the godless, will perish; they will not
bear fruit. For the time being, in fact, they will
have some value, but later they will look for what
they have done and not find it. EXPOSITIONS OF
THE PSALMS 36.3.10.[64]

THE DIRE AWAKENING OF THE RICH. PA-
TERIUS: The rich person dies and finds nothing[65]—certainly nothing of the things that he
had. In fact, the sin of those things is brought
with him, even if all of that for which the sins
were committed is left here. Consequently, now
one can boast in what he has received, exalt
himself over others, be proud of having what
his neighbor does not have. A time will come
when he will wake up, and then he will know
how empty were the things he had while he was
dreaming. It often happens that someone who
is poor sleeps and dreams of being rich and of
thus gaining a courageous soul, rejoicing over

---

[58]Speaking from experience—Cassiodorus had served in the highest echelons of Roman power. [59]Ps 123:4 (122:4 LXX): Cassiodorus
explains the literal meaning of the verse according to the Vulgate.
[60]CCL 98:1158-59. [61]NBA 25:575. [62]Ps 37:28 (36:28 LXX, variant). [63]Cf. Mk 2:4; Lk 5:19. [64]NBA 25:827. [65]See Job 27:19.

having what he did not have and seeking to despise those by whom he had the pain of being despised. But, suddenly waking, he bemoans the image of the riches he had while he slept. Indeed, he groans continually under the weight of poverty, oppressed by the anguish of his straits and, even worse, of having been rich for a brief and useless moment. The rich of this world, who boast of what they have received, are just like this. They are incapable of doing good with their abundance. The rich are like those who sleep, but it would be good for them to awake to their poverty, because they will take nothing with them to that lasting judgment. And the higher they are exalted now, for a brief time, the more bitterly they will weep over themselves for eternity. And, according to the testimony of Wisdom, they will say at their damnation, "What has our arrogance profited us? And what good has our boasted wealth brought us? All this has passed like a shadow, like a fleeting rumor." When they are already lost, they will know that the things they had were contemptible and fleeting, though when present, they seemed so great and permanent to their foolish hearts. The rich person opens his eyes too late, seeing Lazarus at rest, whom he had despised lying at his door.[66] Then he will understand what he did not want to do, and what he lost, when he did not recognize his neighbor in the poor man. In fact, when the body sleeps in death, the soul awakens to true knowledge, and when the flesh dies, the soul is forced to see all that it had disdained to foresee. Then it will see happen what it feared, and the one who rejoiced to have a greater abundance of things than everyone else will find himself empty. EXPOSITION ON THE OLD AND NEW TESTAMENT 156, ON PSALM 75.6.[67]

5:10 Like a Ship Sailing Through the Water

THE SHIP SERVES AS AN IMAGE OF THE CHURCH. CHROMATIUS OF AQUILEIA: There is no doubt that the boat symbolizes the church, bearing in mind what the Holy Spirit says, through Solomon: "She is like a merchant ship, securing her provisions from afar."[68] This can be speaking of nothing other than the church for these reasons: under the guidance of the Lord, with the apostles for its pilots, being blown by the Holy Spirit, this church, by the preaching of the Word, races through the whole world. At the same time, it carries with it a treasure of inestimable value, with which it has purchased the whole human race, and indeed the whole world: the price is the blood of Christ. Solomon also speaks of this price in another passage when he says, "You cannot trace the path of a ship that crosses the sea." What this means to say is that the manner of life of the church is not according to the principles of this world but according to the norms of the heavenly life, as the holy apostle reminds us: "But our homeland is in heaven."[69] TRACTATE ON MATTHEW 42.5.[70]

THE GOODS OF THIS WORLD. HESYCHIUS: "Can you find the tracks of a passing boat or of an eagle seeking its prey?"[71] As indeed the sea does not preserve the tracks of a boat, or the air, those of an eagle seeking its prey, in the same way that their tracks are not found,[72] so the abundance of this world, when it passes, leaves no trace of happiness. It is forgotten along with what caused it. Thus Job despised all the fragility of this life, and taught us to not linger over it. HOMILIES ON JOB 12.[73]

---

[66]See Lk 16:23. [67]PL 79:864-65. [68]Prov 31:14. [69]Phil 3:20. [70]CTP 47:59-60. [71]Job 9:26 LXX, variant. [72]See Wis 9:10. [73]PO 42(191):325.

5:15-23* GLORIOUS DESTINY OF THE JUST AND PUNISHMENT OF THE IMPIOUS

> ¹⁵*But the righteous live for ever,*
> *and their reward is with the Lord;*
> *the Most High takes care of them.*
> ¹⁶*Therefore they will receive a glorious crown*
> *and a beautiful diadem from the hand of the Lord,*
> *because with his right hand he will cover them,*
> *and with his arm he will shield them.*
> ¹⁷*The Lord° will take his zeal as his whole armor,*
> *and will arm all creation to repel^p his enemies;*
> ¹⁸*he will put on righteousness as a breastplate,*
> *and wear impartial justice as a helmet;*
> ¹⁹*he will take holiness as an invincible shield,*
> ²⁰*and sharpen stern wrath for a sword,*
> *and creation will join with him to fight against the madmen.*
> ²¹*Shafts of lightning will fly with true aim,*
> *and will leap to the target as from a well-drawn bow of clouds,*
> ²²*and hailstones full of wrath will be hurled as from a catapult;*
> *the water of the sea will rage against them,*
> *and rivers will relentlessly overwhelm them;*
> ²³*a mighty wind will rise against them,*
> *and like a tempest it will winnow them away.*
> *Lawlessness will lay waste the whole earth,*
> *and evil-doing will overturn the thrones of rulers.*

o Gk He   p Or *punish*   * Wis 5:16-24 Vg.

OVERVIEW: God's wisdom is the source of deep pleasure (PSEUDO-AUGUSTINE). All will be judged by the Holy Spirit (NICETAS) who is both God and Lord (VIGILIUS).

5:15 The Righteous Live Forever

THE CONDITION OF THE JUST. PSEUDO-AUGUSTINE: If wisdom is pleasant in the knowledge of created things, how much more pleasant will be the Wisdom that created all things from noth-ing?[1] If a great abundance of pleasures are found in pleasant things, what, and how great, will the pleasure be in him who made pleasant things? O, for the one who will enjoy this good! What will he have, and what won't he have? He will surely have everything he will want and nothing that he won't want. In that place there will truly be the goods of body and soul, "those things that eye has not seen or ear heard, nor have they

[1]See Prov 3:19.

even entered the human heart."[2] Poor person, why then do you wander here and there seeking what is good for your body and soul? Love the one good in which all good things are, and that is enough. Desire that simple good that is every good, and that is enough. What do you love, my flesh? What do you desire, my soul? Everything that you love is there. Everything you desire is there. If beauty delights you, "The righteous will shine like the sun."[3] If it is swiftness, strength or a freedom of the body that nothing can hinder, "They will be like the angels of God,"[4] since "a natural body is sown, and a spiritual body is raised"[5]—by his power, of course, and not by nature. A long, healthy life is already an object of delight. There, there will be an eternity without evils, and eternal health, since "the righteous will live forever" and "the salvation of the righteous comes from the Lord."[6] If one speaks of fullness, they will be filled when the glory of the Lord appears.[7] If of intoxication, "They will be filled with the abundance of the Lord's house."[8] If of melody, up there the choirs of angels sing endlessly to God in unison. If of any kind of pure desire, the Lord will give them to drink of the stream of the delights of his divinity.[9] If of wisdom, "They will all be taught by God"[10] in such a way that wisdom itself will teach them. If of friendship, they will love God more than themselves and one another as themselves.[11] And God will love them more than they love themselves, since they will love him, loving themselves and one another in him, and he will love them in himself. If one speaks of harmony, they will all have a single will, because they will have only the will of God. If of power, they will enter into the power of the Lord,[12] and their wills will be almighty, like that of God. BOOK ON THE SPIRIT AND THE SOUL 64.[13]

5:23 A Mighty Wind Will Rise

THE HOLY SPIRIT WILL JUDGE EVERY CREATURE. NICETAS OF REMESIANA: That there will be only one divine judgment through Christ, the apostle Paul explicitly states when he says, "God will judge people's secrets through our Lord Jesus Christ."[14] Moreover, the same apostle tells us that the Spirit will also judge the antichrist, saying specifically of this figure, "The Lord Jesus will destroy him with the Spirit of his mouth."[15] If the antichrist will be destroyed by the Spirit of the mouth of the Lord, then every created being will also be judged by the Spirit, something of which Solomon also speaks, saying, "The Spirit of power will break out against them, and a mighty wind will scatter them." INSTRUCTION ON THE FAITH OF THE TRINITY.[16]

THE HOLY SPIRIT IS GOD AND LORD. VIGILIUS OF THAPSUS: The Lord taught in the Gospel that the Holy Spirit is judge and can convict the entire world regarding sin, righteousness and judgment. It says, in fact, "The Holy Spirit, when he comes, will convict the world about sin, about righteousness and about judgment."[17] And Isaiah says, "The Lord will wash away the filth of the sons and daughters of Zion."[18] And in Solomon it is said, "The Spirit of God will break out against them and will scatter them like a whirlwind."[19] Again Isaiah says, "See that in my Spirit I carry out judgment, says the Lord."[20] Why then do you deny that people may ask pardon for their sins from their judge, so as to be more cleansed and more purified of sins, if they are successful in asking? And having done so, if they were to fall again into the evil of sin through rash words, that they could ask the Holy Spirit, directly and without difficulty, to grant them pardon and remission of their sins—to him, that is, who intercedes for us with the Father with inexpressible groanings?[21] Since you accuse us of sacrilege for asserting, in confessing the Trinity, that the Holy Spirit

---

[2]1 Cor 2:9. [3]Mt 13:43. [4]Mt 22:30. [5]1 Cor 15:44. [6]Ps 37:39 (36:39 LXX). [7]See Ps 17:15 (16:15 LXX). [8]Ps 36:9 (35:9 LXX). [9]See Ps 36:9 (LXX 35:9). [10]Jn 6:45; Is 54:13. [11]See Mt 5:43, etc. [12]See Ps 71:16 (70:16 LXX), variant. [13]PL 40:828. [14]Rom 2:16. [15]2 Thess 2:8. [16]CTP 53:62. [17]Jn 16:8. [18]Is 4:4, variant. [19]Wis 5:23, variant. [20]See Is 26:9. [21]See Rom 8:26.

is God and Lord, watch that you yourselves do not become more worthy of this charge. Indeed, you refuse to confess that Holy Spirit whom the Lord wanted the apostles to proclaim, without distinction, together with the Father and the Son, "Go therefore and teach all nations, baptizing them in the name of the Father and of the Son and of the Holy Spirit."[22] If, regarding the essence of the divinity, the Holy Spirit were not equal to the Father and the Son, how is it possible that in the sacrament of baptism nothing happens without him? AGAINST VARIMADUS 2.17.[23]

---

[22]Mt 28:19. [23]PL 62:410.

6:1-11* THE MIGHTY WILL UNDERGO A RIGOROUS JUDGMENT

[1]Listen therefore, O kings, and understand;
learn, O judges of the ends of the earth.
[2]Give ear, you that rule over multitudes,
and boast of many nations.
[3]For your dominion was given you from the Lord,
and your sovereignty from the Most High,
who will search out your works and inquire into your plans.
[4]Because as servants of his kingdom you did not rule rightly,
nor keep the law,
nor walk according to the purpose of God,
[5]he will come upon you terribly and swiftly,
because severe judgment falls on those in high places.
[6]For the lowliest man may be pardoned in mercy,
but mighty men will be mightily tested.
[7]For the Lord of all will not stand in awe of any one,
nor show deference to greatness;
because he himself made both small and great,
and he takes thought for all alike.
[8]But a strict inquiry is in store for the mighty.
[9]To you then, O monarchs, my words are directed,
that you may learn wisdom and not transgress.
[10]For they will be made holy who observe holy things in holiness,
and those who have been taught them will find a defense.
[11]Therefore set your desire on my words;
long for them, and you will be instructed

---

* Wis 6:1-12 Vg, because there is an additional verse at the beginning of the pericope: [Wis 6:1] "Wisdom is better than strength, and a wise man is better than a strong one" (cf. Prov 24:5; 16:32).

OVERVIEW: The Holy Spirit reigns with the Father and the Son (VIGILIUS). Duties vary according to the condition of each Christian (ORIGEN). Unworthy priests will be punished (JEROME), and the mighty will not escape judgment (PSEUDO-AMBROSE). God takes care of all (HILARY OF POITIERS). People of all conditions meet at Christ's unique Eucharistic table (QUODVULT-DEUS). We are all then responsible for what we have received from God (JOHN OF DAMASCUS).

6:3 Dominion Was Given from the Lord

THE HOLY SPIRIT REIGNS WITH THE FATHER AND THE SON. VIGILIUS OF THAPSUS: The Father reigns, the Son reigns, the Holy Spirit reigns. Of the Father the Gospel says, "If one is not reborn of water and the Holy Spirit, he cannot see the kingdom of God."[1] Of the Son it is said, "Say to the peoples, 'The Lord reigned from the wood.'"[2] In Solomon it is said of the Holy Spirit, "Your sovereignty comes from the Holy Spirit."[3] And then, "Though you are ministers of his kingdom, you have not judged rightly." AGAINST VARIMADUS 3.62.[4]

6:6 The Mighty Will Be Mightily Tested

THE DUTIES OF CHRISTIANS. ORIGEN: "Their destiny will be of no benefit to them,"[5] because what is of benefit is not the mere fact of sitting in the presbytery but living a life worthy of that position, as the Word demands. The Word requires a good life from both you and from us, but if it is true that "the mighty will be mightily tested," then more is demanded of me than of a deacon, more of a deacon than of a layperson, and of the one entrusted with ecclesial power, even more is demanded.[6] HOMILIES ON JEREMIAH 11.3.[7]

ON UNWORTHY PRIESTS. JEROME: "The powerful will be severely tormented"[8] and "To one whom much has been given, much will be required."[9] This refers in particular to priests.

If they do not want to listen, guarding their hearts so as to glorify the Lord's name by their good conduct, but instead people curse his name because of them,[10] God will deprive them of every good and turn their blessing into a curse.[11] Those who abuse their health in licentious behavior and corrupt their good name with sordid conduct change God's blessings into curses. COMMENTARY ON MALACHI 2.1-2.[12]

THE PUNISHMENT OF THE MIGHTY. PSEUDO-AMBROSE: Tell me: Where are the kings? Where are the princes? Where are the rich? Where is their gold and their splendor? "All has passed like a shadow."[13] Their gold, their silver and their pomp have remained in the world, while they are endlessly tormented in hell, where their worm will never die and their fire will never go out,[14] since it is written, "The powerful will be severely tormented."[15] Down there they will live forever in darkness, in a dwelling without light. Down there the miserable will be with the miserable, the proud with the proud, murderers with murderers, adulterers with adulterers, the impious with the impious, liars with liars, those who commit sacrilege with others like them— all will be tormented together, forever, in hell. SERMON 24.5.[16]

6:7 Taking Thought for All Alike

GOD TAKES CARE OF EVERYBODY. HILARY OF POITIERS: The rich person does not easily attain riches of the soul, that is, the virtues of this world. He who says, "It is more difficult for a rich person to enter the kingdom of heaven"[17] is clearly saying that it is easier for a poor person to

---

[1]Jn 3:5. [2]Ps 96:10 (95:10 LXX). Vigilius quotes a very old variant that appeared before the mid-second century. It was created with the purpose of transforming the psalm into a prophecy concerning Christ's crucifixion and kingship; cf. Justin Martyr *Dialogue with Trypho* 73.1.4, etc. [3]Wis 6:3, variant. [4]PL 62:425. [5]Jer 12:13, variant. [6]Origen makes reference to the bishop. [7]CTP 123:135. [8]Wis 6:6 Vg. [9]Lk 12:48. [10]See Is 52:5. [11]See Mal 2:2. [12]PL 25:1554. [13]Wis 5:9. [14]Mk 9:48; Is 66:24. [15]Wis 6:6 Vg. [16]PL 17:653. [17]Mt 19:24.

do so. So that the poor person does not imagine that he has been excluded from God's care because of his poverty,[18] the prophet testifies, saying, "I created the poor and the rich, and I care for all alike." "God does not make distinctions between persons."[19] And it does not say that he cares only for the rich with respect to worldly goods but for everyone. He cares for the poor as well, and he will reward anyone who has been humble in riches or patient in poverty. LETTER OR BOOKLET 10.[20]

PEOPLE OF ALL CONDITIONS MEET AT THE EUCHARIST. QUODVULTDEUS: The prophet Isaiah says, "Then the wolf and the lamb will pasture together. The leopard will lie down with the kid. The ox, the lion and the lamb will eat hay together. And a little child will guide them."[21] And David says, "See, the kings of the earth have assembled and joined together. They saw and were amazed."[22] And again he says, "Who is like the Lord our God, who lives on high and looks down on earthly things? Who raises the indigent from the earth and lifts the poor from the dust, to make them sit with princes, with the princes of his people?"[23] And also Solomon says, "He has made the small and the great, and he cares for all alike." And he says further, "Wisdom has built her house, with seven pillars as its foundation. She has sacrificed her victims, prepared her wine in its cup and spread her table. She has sent out her servants, calling out and saying, 'Come, eat my bread and drink the wine that I have prepared for you.' "[24] The Lord confirms this in the Gospel, with the parable of the banquet prepared by the powerful rich man for his son.[25] "He sent his servants to tell those who had been invited to come, and they excused themselves. One said, 'I have bought a field and I am going to see it, please excuse me.' Another said, 'I have bought five pairs of oxen.' And another, 'I have just taken a wife.' "[26] In these three excuses we have "the concupiscence of the flesh, the concupiscence of the eyes and worldly show,"[27] which detained the Jews and kept them from coming

to Christ's table, to which they had been invited. "Go," says the father, "into the plazas and the streets and bring to me those whom you find."[28] The pagans were thus brought in. "There is still room," says the servant. The father responds, "Go along the hedgerows and the byways, and force those you find to come in."[29] Among these are the rich, kings and certain heretics who have left the Lord's flock, who are constrained to come by him who says, "No one can come to me if the Father who sent me does not draw him."[30] And to those who come he says, "Whoever eats my flesh and drinks my blood has eternal life, and I will raise him on the last day."[31] The apostle Paul shows who these are when he says, "There is neither Jew nor Greek, nor slave nor free person, nor man nor woman. All of you, in fact, are one person in Christ Jesus."[32] The verses of the Sibyl, which we cited above, confirm this: "I will lower the hills and raise the valleys from their depths. There will no longer be anything sublime or exalted among what is human."[33] Maro,[34] in agreement with the Sibyl, says, "Nor will the herds fear the great lions."[35] THE BOOK OF PROMISES AND PREDICTIONS OF GOD 3.39.46.[36]

6:8 A Strict Examination

GOD'S GIFTS AND OUR RESPONSE. JOHN OF DAMASCUS: No one is entirely without the gifts of God, but one will be inclined to this virtue and another to that. One to more virtue, another to less. One to the more elevated and supereminent virtues, another to those that are humble and modest. God has distributed to each according to the measure of his faith. The powerful will therefore be examined severely, and "of the one to whom much has been entrusted,

---

[18]See Prov 22:2. [19]Acts 10:34. [20]PL 10:742. [21]Is 11:6. [22]Ps 48:5-6 (47:5-6 LXX). [23]Ps 113:5-8 (112:5-8 LXX). [24]Prov 9:1-3.5. [25]See Mt 22:2. [26]Lk 14:16-20. [27]1 Jn 2:16. [28]Mt 22:9. [29]Lk 14:22-23. [30]Jn 6:44. [31]Jn 6:54. [32]Gal 3:28. [33]Sibylline Oracles 8:234-35. [34]Virgil, whose complete name in Latin was Publius Vergilius Maro. [35]Virgil Bucolics 4:22. [36]CTP 82:263-65.

much will be required."[37] Of each person will be demanded, in fact, according to the measure in which he has been entrusted by God's power. And the benefactor knows his recipient: "Every-

thing is naked and exposed before his eyes."[38] HOMILY FOR HOLY SATURDAY 34.[39]

---

[37]Lk 12:48. [38]Heb 4:13. [39]CTP 25:115.

6:12-21* THE OPPORTUNITY OF FINDING WISDOM

[12]*Wisdom is radiant and unfading,*
and she is easily discerned by those who love her,
and is found by those who seek her.
[13]*She hastens to make herself known to those who desire her.*
[14]*He who rises early to seek her will have no difficulty,*
for he will find her sitting at his gates.
[15]*To fix one's thought on her is perfect understanding,*
and he who is vigilant on her account will soon be free from care,
[16]*because she goes about seeking those worthy of her,*
and she graciously appears to them in their paths,
and meets them in every thought.

[17]*The beginning of wisdom[q] is the most sincere desire for instruction,*
and concern for instruction is love of her,
[18]*and love of her is the keeping of her laws,*
and giving heed to her laws is assurance of immortality,
[19]*and immortality brings one near to God;*
[20]*so the desire for wisdom leads to a kingdom.*

[21]*Therefore if you delight in thrones and scepters, O monarchs over the peoples,*
honor wisdom, that you may reign for ever.

q Gk *Her beginning* * Wis 6:13-23 Vg, because of the addition of a final verse: [Wis 6:23] "Love the light of wisdom, all you who govern on nations."

OVERVIEW: We should love wisdom and seek it (PSEUDO-AUGUSTINE). Knowledge of God leads to peace, not persecution (AUGUSTINE). The Christian receives the Holy Spirit, who fights for us against the devils (CYRIL OF JERUSALEM). God's providence governs all creation (AUGUSTINE). Apart from God, we experience corrupt-

ibility (ATHANASIUS). The desires we experience may be good or bad (AUGUSTINE).

6:12 Wisdom Is Radiant and Unfading

WE SHOULD SEARCH FOR AND LOVE WISDOM. PSEUDO-AUGUSTINE: Do you want to love? Love

---

wisdom, desire fervently to acquire it. Put the inner person in order, so that its appearance will not horrify you. As lustful eyes seek the beauty of the body, so you should seek that of the heart. And this beauty will not come from your riches, because wisdom hates the proud and those who in some way or another want to boast of what they have. "What do you have that has not been given to you?"[1] Wisdom will give you what pleases her. Love her greatly, and she will care for you. "Hold her close and she will exalt you, honor her and she will embrace you. She will put a graceful crown on your head."[2] "Wisdom is radiant and unfading; she is easily contemplated by those who love her and found by those who seek her." SERMON 391.5.[3]

6:15 Perfect Understanding

PERFECT KNOWLEDGE OF THE FATHER. AUGUSTINE: The Lord adds, "Because they do not know the one who sent me."[4] These words are said concerning that knowledge about which it is written elsewhere, "To know you is perfect wisdom."[5] Those who have this knowledge of the Father, by whom Christ was sent, absolutely cannot persecute the ones whom Christ gathers, because they themselves, along with the others, have been gathered by Christ. TRACTATES ON THE GOSPEL OF JOHN 88.4.[6]

6:16 Wisdom Seeks the Worthy

OUR ALLY AGAINST THE DEVILS. CYRIL OF JERUSALEM: How truly precious is the Holy Spirit, the good sovereign! Thus we receive baptism in the Father, in the Son and in the Holy Spirit![7] He fights against many demons who attack those who are still burdened by the body with beastly ferocity. But that demon whom so many are unable to bind with iron chains has often been conquered by the recitation of a single prayer, through the power of the Holy Spirit who lives within: the mere breath of the exorcist, like a fire, puts him to flight,[8] and he disappears.

God, therefore, has given us a mighty ally for the battle, a true protector—a great Teacher for the church, a great defender for each of us. We need not fear demons or the devil, because the one who fights for us is stronger. Let us open the door that he would come to meet us, "seeking those who are worthy of him" and desiring to give us his gifts. CATECHETICAL LECTURES 16.19.[9]

GOD'S PROVIDENCE. AUGUSTINE: God, through his hidden power, impresses an impetus on the entire universe of his creatures. And it is precisely in virtue of this impetus that every creature is set in motion—when the angels carry out God's orders, when the stars complete their orbit; when the winds blow now in one direction, now in another, when the abyss is stirred up by rushing waters and by condensed, swirling vapors in the air; when the vegetable kingdom germinates and its seeds develop, when animals are born and pass their lives according to their proper instincts; and when the wicked are allowed to torment the righteous. Thus God unfurls the ages that he had rolled up, so to speak, in the primordial creation. Those ages would not have followed their course if he who created them were to cease his providential government over them. The beings that grow and are born in time should teach us how we are to think of these things. Not without reason, in fact, does Scripture say that Wisdom "benevolently appears" to those who love her, "in their ways, and meets them with her unfailing providence."[10] Moreover, we should not listen to those who think that divine providence governs only the highest regions of the world, those on the outer edge of (that is, above) our atmosphere, which is denser; but that the lowest part—the earth and the sea, and the earthly atmosphere that is closer

[1]1 Cor 4:7. [2]Prov 4:8-9. [3]PL 39:1708-9. [4]Jn 15:19. [5]Wis 6:15 (6:16 Vg); cf. Wis 15:3. [6]NBA 24:1287. [7]See Mt 27:19. [8]Cyril is talking about the exorcism that precedes baptism, when the exorcist blows on the face of the candidate for baptism. [9]CTP 103:363-64. [10]Wis 6:16 (6:17 Vg).

and thus permeated with humidity because of evaporation from the land and the sea (and in which winds and clouds are formed)—is rather ruled by chance, agitated by random movements. Against these the psalm speaks that, after having praised the heavenly beings, turns its attention to those of earth and says, "Praise the Lord of the earth, you sea monsters and all you deeps. Fire and hail, snow and ice, storm winds which fulfill his command."[11] ON GENESIS 5.20.41–21.42.[12]

6:18 *Assurance of Immortality*

SIN LEADS TO CORRUPTION. ATHANASIUS: God created human beings and wanted that they remain incorruptible. But people, becoming careless, abandoned the contemplation of God, imagining and inventing evil. . . . Thus they received the sentence of death, which had been threatened them beforehand.[13] Afterward, they were no longer in the state in which they had been created but were subject to corruption in conformity with their thoughts, and death dominated and reigned over them. In fact, the transgression of the precept returned them to their nature, and given that they came into existence out of nonexistence,[14] it makes sense that in the course of time they would be subject to a corruption that tends to nonexistence. Indeed, if at one time their nature was nonexistence, and they were called into existence thanks to the presence and the goodness of the Word, it follows that human beings, now deprived of the knowledge of God and tending toward nonexistence (evil, in fact, does not exist, whereas good does exist because it was created by God, who is), would also be deprived of external existence. This is what it means to remain in death and corruption after decomposition. Human beings are mortal by nature, because they were made from nothing. But if they had preserved their likeness to him who is, by contemplating him, they would have diminished their natural corruption and become

incorruptible, as Wisdom says: "Respect for laws is the guarantee of incorruptibility." Being incorruptible, they would have lived like God, as a passage of the divine Scripture declares: "I said, You are gods and all children of the Most High. But you will die like human beings and fall like one of the princes."[15] ON THE INCARNATION 4.[16]

6:20 *Desire for Wisdom*

GOOD AND BAD DESIRES. AUGUSTINE: "At all times my soul longed to desire the ways of your righteousness."[17] A commendable passion, this, not a blameworthy one. It is not of this desire that it is written, "Do not covet,"[18] a prohibition that regards the passions with which the flesh rises against the spirit. This, rather is a longing by which the spirit rises against the flesh.[19] If you wanted to find a scriptural passage on this, you would find, "The desire for wisdom leads to a kingdom." And there are many other testimonies concerning this concupiscence in a good sense. It is very interesting to note that when speaking of desire in a good sense, the object that is desired is always expressed. On the contrary, if only concupiscence is spoken of, without adding the object, it must be understood in a bad sense. Thus in the cited passage it says, "The desire for wisdom leads to a kingdom." If it had not specified, "for wisdom," it certainly would not have said, "Concupiscence leads to a kingdom." The apostle writes, "I would not have known concupiscence, if the law had not said, 'Do not covet.' "[20] It does not specify the object of that desire or what it is prohibited to desire, yet it is certain that, expressing himself in this way, he is referring to a disordered desire. EXPOSITIONS OF THE PSALMS 118.8.3.[21]

---

[11]Ps 148:7-8. [12]NBA 9/2:275-77. [13]See Gen 2:17. [14]See 2 Macc 7:28. [15]Ps 82:6-7 (81:6-7 LXX). [16]CTP 2:44-45. [17]Ps 119:20 (118:20 LXX). [18]Ex 20:17. [19]See Gal 5:17. [20]Rom 7:7. [21]NBA 27:1171.

6:22-25* WISDOM IS NOT FOR A FEW CHOSEN PEOPLE

²²*I will tell you what wisdom is and how she came to be,*
and I will hide no secrets from you,
but I will trace her course from the beginning of creation,
and make the knowledge of her clear,
and I will not pass by the truth;
²³*neither will I travel in the company of sickly envy,*
*for envy*ʳ *does not associate with wisdom.*
²⁴*A multitude of wise men is the salvation of the world,*
and a sensible king is the stability of his people.
²⁵*Therefore be instructed by my words, and you will profit.*

r Gk *this*   * Wis 6:24-27 Vg.

OVERVIEW: God is naturally wise; humans may participate in God's wisdom (DIDYMUS). The wisdom of the Scripture is higher than common eloquence (AUGUSTINE). Ezra was wise in his zeal for God's law (QUODVULTDEUS).

6:24 The Salvation of the World

GOD'S WISDOM AND HUMAN WISDOM.
DIDYMUS THE BLIND: Only God is declared to be wise. He is defined as wise because he does not receive wisdom from another, nor does he participate in the wisdom of another. Many in fact are called wise, not by their nature but by the fact that wisdom is communicated to them. God, by contrast, who did not become wise by participation in the wisdom of another or by having gotten it somewhere else, is called the only wise, who generates wisdom and makes others wise. This wisdom is our Lord Jesus Christ, who is called the power and the wisdom of God.[1] But the Holy Spirit is also proclaimed to be wisdom. In fact, even in the books of the Old Testament it is said that Joshua, son of Nun, was full of the spirit of wisdom.[2] Only God, therefore, is wise, in that he does not receive wisdom from another principle but makes wise and generates wisdom. He alone is wise, as opposed to the other beings who are considered wise by his gift ("An abundance of wise people is the salvation of the world," and, further, "Those who know themselves are wise"[3] and, finally, "If you walk with the wise, you will become wise"[4]). Likewise the Holy Spirit, because he does not receive wisdom from another principle, is called the Spirit of wisdom.[5] His very being is Spirit of wisdom, and his nature is none other than Spirit of truth[6] and Spirit of God. ON THE HOLY SPIRIT 1.21.[7]

THE HIGHER WISDOM OF SCRIPTURE. AUGUSTINE: One who must speak with wisdom, if he is unable to do so eloquently, must absolutely follow the word of the Scriptures closely. The

[1]See 1 Cor 1:24. [2]See Num 27:18; Deut 34:9. [3]Prov 13:10. [4]Prov 13:20. [5]See Is 11:2. [6]See Jn 14:17; 15:26; 16:13; 1 Jn 4:6. [7]CTP 89:93.

poorer he is in himself, the more necessary it is that he be rich in the Scriptures, so as to demonstrate, using them, what he says with his own words. And one who is inferior in speaking will in some way grow, thanks to the testimony of what is superior. In fact, the one less able to delight by speaking will delight by demonstrating. One who makes an effort to speak not only with wisdom but also with eloquence will be even more useful if he is skilled in both. Willingly would I allow that a person whom I counsel to follow the masters of rhetorical art read, listen to or practice imitating the eloquent, because those who are read or listened to are known for speaking or for having spoken not only eloquently but also wisely and truly. In fact, those who speak with eloquence do so attractively, whereas those who speak with wisdom are listened to for salvation. For this reason, Scripture does not say, "An abundance of those who are eloquent," but "An abundance of the wise is the salvation of the world." CHRISTIAN INSTRUCTION 4.5.8.[8]

PRAISE OF EZRA'S WISDOM. QUODVULTDEUS:

Having arrived at Jerusalem, Ezra, inflamed with zeal for the Law, decided first of all to purify the people of their vices, since, as the prophet said, "A wise king is the salvation of his people." Having found the book of Moses, he showed, among other things, that the wrath of God was kindled against the people because they had married foreign wives[9] against God's commandment. With severity, which was his strength, he convinced them to send back their wives and their children.[10] No longer held back by carnal delights and wanting to propitiate God, they did what was commanded of them without hesitation. In this way they symbolized the Christian people, whom the first among all priests admonishes, "If anyone leaves house, fields, wife or children because of my name, he will be repaid many times over here and will gain eternal life."[11] THE BOOK OF PROMISES AND PREDICTIONS OF GOD 2.37.83.[12]

---

[8]PL 34:92. [9]See Ezra 10:2. [10]See Ezra 10:3. [11]Mt 19:29. [12]CTP 82:213-14.

7:1-6 ALL PEOPLE ARE EQUAL

[1]*I also am mortal, like all men,*
a descendant of the first-formed child of earth;
and in the womb of a mother I was molded into flesh,
[2]*within the period of ten months, compacted with blood,*
from the seed of a man and the pleasure of marriage.
[3]*And when I was born, I began to breathe the common air,*
and fell upon the kindred earth,
and my first sound was a cry, like that of all.
[4]*I was nursed with care in swaddling cloths.*
[5]*For no king has had a different beginning of existence;*
[6]*there is for all mankind one entrance into life, and a common departure.*

OVERVIEW: Christ was born as one of us (SEVERUS). In the waters of baptism, we are all born in the same way (PSEUDO-AUGUSTINE).

7:2 Becoming Flesh

CHRIST'S BIRTH. SEVERUS OF ANTIOCH: After the banishment from paradise and the loss of immortal life, Adam knew his wife,[1] and thus carnal relations were introduced, this mixture of emissions that is more appropriate to animals than to human beings endowed with intellect and that is the foreboding of corruption and death, though it assures the continuance of the race. Acting, then, with such wisdom and love toward humanity, what does Emanuel do?[2] He reunites both natures in one, that is, the creature that had been privileged with the grace of immortality (the soul) and that linked to corruption (the body) in a birth that comes from their union. He who in the beginning fashioned human beings from the earth[3] was fashioned from the Virgin, taking flesh from the Holy Spirit and from her. This flesh is consubstantial with ours, which is animated by a soul endowed with intellect. And this did not take place through sleep, by concupiscence or with the emission of human seed. What characterized our creation at the beginning was a coming in the flesh without seed.[4] But for us, what distinguishes this second way of coming into existence is to come entirely from the woman. (Likewise, the conception took place in time, because "the time came for her to have her child."[5]) The sacred Scriptures say on the one hand regarding the mother of God that this took place in a marriage but on the other hand that everything began without her having experienced carnal union and was accomplished in virginity, since, after the birth, the seal of her virginity remained intact. CATHEDRAL HOMILIES 7.10-12.[6]

7:6 Entrance and Departure

ALL BORN THE SAME WAY IN BAPTISM. PSEUDO-AUGUSTINE: Beloved, what has been celebrated in you? What has been accomplished this night in your regard that did not take place on previous nights? In what way have you been brought, each of you, from hidden places, to be shown before all the church? Down there, after bowing your head, which was wrongly exalted before, was your examination celebrated, with the humiliation of feet placed in sackcloth? Was the proud devil rooted out of you[7] when the humble and most high Christ was invoked over you? You were all, therefore, humble, and you implored humbly, praying, singing and saying, "Test me, Lord, and know my thoughts."[8] He has tested, he has examined, he has touched the hearts of his servants with fear. He has cast out the devil by his power and freed his family from his dominion. Here the poor and the rich have not been treated differently, or the master and the slave. In fact, "all enter life in the same way." If this is true for this fragile, fleeting life, how much more will it be true for the life that is immortal and eternal? SERMON ON THE CREED 1.1.[9]

---

[1]See Gen 4:1. [2]See Is 7:14. [3]See Gen 2:7. [4]Since the first human being was directly created by God. [5]Lk 2:6. [6]PO 38.2 (175):315-17 [71-73]. [7]A reference to the preparatory rite for baptism: bowing their heads, the candidates stand on a cilice during the recitation of the exorcisms. [8]Ps 139:23 (138:23 LXX). [9]PL 40:637.

7:7-14 WISDOM IS MORE PRECIOUS THAN ANY RICHES

⁷Therefore I prayed, and understanding was given me;
I called upon God, and the spirit of wisdom came to me.
⁸I preferred her to scepters and thrones,
and I accounted wealth as nothing in comparison with her.
⁹Neither did I liken to her any priceless gem,
because all gold is but a little sand in her sight,
and silver will be accounted as clay before her.
¹⁰I loved her more than health and beauty,
and I chose to have her rather than light,
because her radiance never ceases.
¹¹All good things came to me along with her,
and in her hands uncounted wealth.
¹²I rejoiced in them all, because wisdom leads them;
but I did not know that she was their mother.
¹³I learned without guile and I impart without grudging;
I do not hide her wealth,
¹⁴for it is an unfailing treasure for men;
those who get it obtain friendship with God,
commended for the gifts that come from instruction.

OVERVIEW: We should imitate Solomon and ask for wisdom (AMBROSE). Christ's wisdom is higher than Solomon's (PSEUDO-AMBROSE). The light of Christ the Son never goes out (VIGILIUS). God is the giver of every good gift (JOHN OF DAMASCUS).

7:7 The Spirit of Wisdom

WE SHOULD ASK FOR WISDOM. AMBROSE: God at times opens the heart through trials. Then the heart becomes so vast that, like the sands of the sea, it cannot be measured.[1] Listen to holy Solomon, who speaks to us of this openness: "Therefore I prayed, and in me prudence was increased. I implored, and the Spirit of wis-dom came to me." So as to receive wisdom from God, he did not ask for riches or noble descendants or power, but he asked for wisdom. And he obtained everything that he did not ask for.[2] For this reason Scripture says that the vastness of his heart was so great that, like the sand of the sea, it could not be measured.[3] So that you would understand this greatness, he consciously says of himself, "Write it in the vastness of your heart."[4] Therefore, one who has wisdom should not keep it hidden, not even for an instant, but should celebrate it in public. He should proclaim every-where, with authority, what prudence inspires in

---

[1]1 Kings 2:35 (3 Kings 2:35 LXX). [2]See 1 Kings 3:9-13 (3 Kings 3:9-13 LXX). [3]1 Kings 2:35 (3 Kings 2:35 LXX). [4]Prov 7:3, variant.

him. EXPOSITIONS ON THE PSALMS 43.93.[5]

CHRIST'S WISDOM IS HIGHER THAN SOLO-MON'S. PSEUDO-AMBROSE: Beloved brothers and sisters, how is it that Solomon, though possessing wisdom in such great abundance and knowing all those things hidden in the secrets of mysterious providence,[6] says that some things are impossible to know? He clearly received wisdom from God. He knew the beginnings of the ordering of the world[7] and about the heavens that all see, suspended at an unreachable height. He knew how the world is surrounded and covered by air, balanced in equilibrium in its midst and attracted downward by its inert weight. He knew the reasons why the eager course of the waves of the liquid element roils within the limits fixed by the shores. He knew the principles and ends of things and the relationship between the two.[8] Nor were the divisions and changes of times unknown to him. He understood how the years succeed one another, as the world completes its cycle, and why the stars followed their course, sometimes unexpectedly going ahead or remaining behind, as well as the place of their rising and setting. And he knew many other things, because he was told them by wisdom. It is surprising that he would say that some things were beyond his reach or that he could not know or see them. But, because everything collected in the divine books by the proclamation of the prophets had its preordained time, it is right that Solomon could not know, prior to the coming of our Lord Jesus Christ, about the flight of an eagle, or a serpent on the rock, or a boat that ploughs the waves or the way of a young man in his youth.[9] It was not yet the time in which the reality would emerge from shadows or the truth from the image.[10] To us, however, our Lord Jesus Christ has shown that everything concerning him was written in the Law[11] and that, for us, nothing is hidden that will not be revealed.[12] And after that book sealed with seven seals, which no one could open except Christ,[13] it was permitted and granted to us to see. We know all things, as the Lord says, "I bless you, Father,

Lord of heaven and earth, because you kept these things hidden to the wise and have revealed them to the simple."[14] Furthermore, "To you it has been given to know this mystery."[15] And I have said all this, not as a reproach to Solomon because he did not know things that he could not have known but to indicate that it was not yet the time to know them. SERMON 42.2.[16]

7:10 Wisdom's Radiance Never Ceases

THE LIGHT OF THE SON NEVER GOES OUT. VIGILIUS OF THAPSUS: The Son was in the bosom of the Father from the beginning,[17] and from the Father's heart he has poured forth a good word.[18] And how can one fail to believe that he who is in the Father's heart, together with him, dwells in inaccessible light?[19] Could the Father have remained in the Son without light or rest without light in the tabernacle of the Son, given that the Son is the radiance of the eternal light[20] and the spotless mirror of the divinity?[21] Solomon says to have preferred this light to his health, wanting always to delight in its beauty. Does he not say, "I loved her more than health and beauty, I preferred the possession of her to light itself, because the splendor that comes from her never sets"? For this reason, having desired this light, in his distress the prophet David proclaimed, "Send forth your light and your truth."[22] And also, "In your light we see light."[23] In the splendor of this light the Son anticipated his manifestation on the mountain to the three disciples. They prostrated themselves, deathly afraid, convinced that their lives were about to end.[24] In fact, the Son proclaimed this light by showing it in himself, admonishing his disciples that they should walk in it: "Walk while you have the light."[25] And

---

[5]PL 14:1133. [6]See Wis 7:17. [7]See Wis 7:17. [8]See Wis 7:18. [9]See Prov 30:19. [10]See Heb 10:1. [11]See Lk 24:44. [12]See Mt 10:26. [13]See Rev 5:1, etc. [14]Mt 11:25. [15]Lk 8:10. [16]PL 17:693-94. [17]See Jn 1:18. [18]See Ps 45:2 (44:2 LXX). [19]See 1 Tim 6:16. [20]See Heb 1:3. [21]See Wis 7:26. [22]Ps 43:3 (42:3 LXX). [23]Ps 36:10 (35:10 LXX). [24]See Mt 17:2-6 par. [25]Jn 12:35.

further, "I am the light of the world. Whoever follows me will not walk in darkness but will have the light of life."[26] And the Evangelist also says, "He was the true light, which enlightens every person who comes into this world."[27] If it has been shown that this light that is promised to the faithful is in the Son and is eternal along with him who is eternal, how is it that you separate the Son from the Father's inaccessible light?[28] AGAINST VARIMADUS 1.66.[29]

7:13 Learning and Imparting Wisdom

ALL GOOD THINGS COME FROM GOD. JOHN OF DAMASCUS: Everything that exists must give thanks to God, rendering him perpetual venera-tion, since all things have being from him[30] and subsist in him.[31] Without stint he gives a share of his gifts to all without being asked, and he wants everyone to be saved[32] and to partake of his goodness. He is patient[33] toward us sinners. He makes the sun rise on the righteous and the unrighteous and makes it rain on the bad and the good,[34] also because for our sake the Son of God became like us, making us partakers of his divine nature,[35] since we will be like him, as John the theologian says in the catholic epistle.[36] THREE TREATISES ON DIVINE IMAGES 3.30.[37]

---

[26]Jn 8:12. [27]Jn 1:9. [28]See 1 Tim 6:16. [29]PL 62:395. [30]See Rom 11:36. [31]See Col 1:17. [32]See 1 Tim 2:4. [33]See 2 Pet 3:9. [34]See Mt 5:45. [35]See 2 Pet 1:4. [36]See 1 Jn 3:2. [37]CTP 36:136-37.

7:15-22* WISDOM IS THE DIVINE MAKER
OF EVERYTHING

[15]May God grant that I speak with judgment
and have thoughts worthy of what I have received,
for he is the guide even of wisdom
and the corrector of the wise.
[16]For both we and our words are in his hand,
as are all understanding and skill in crafts.
[17]For it is he who gave me unerring knowledge of what exists,
to know the structure of the world and the activity of the elements;
[18]the beginning and end and middle of times,
the alternations of the solstices and the changes of the seasons,
[19]the cycles of the year and the constellations of the stars,
[20]the natures of animals and the tempers of wild beasts,
the powers of spirits[s] and the reasonings of men,
the varieties of plants and the virtues of roots;
[21]I learned both what is secret and what is manifest,
[22]for wisdom, the fashioner of all things, taught me.

s Or winds   * According to some versions, Wis 7:21 ends with "for wisdom, the fashioner of all things, taught me," a phrase that belongs to Wis 7:22, according to the RSV.

OVERVIEW: We can teach because the Spirit empowers us to teach (AUGUSTINE). The highest knowledge we could teach is knowledge of the Trinity (ORIGEN). The primary wisdom the heart seeks is God's wisdom (ORIGEN). Through what is visible we attain the knowledge of what is invisible (ORIGEN).

7:16 *In God's Hand*

THE SPIRIT TEACHES US HOW TO TEACH.
AUGUSTINE: Since concerning everything that must be explained in the light of faith and love, there are many things to say and many ways in which experts can speak about them, who knows, at the present moment, what would be useful for us to say or to hear, except the one who sees the hearts of all? And who makes us say what should be said, in the right way, if not him in whose hands are both we and all of our words? Therefore, even if one learns everything there is to teach, all that he ever wanted to know and teach, and acquires the ability to speak, as is appropriate to a church leader—when the moment comes to speak, he should remember that what the Lord says is more fitting than all his valid arguments. "Do not worry about how and what you are to say, because what you are to say will be given you in that moment. Indeed, it will not be you who are speaking but the Spirit of your Father who speaks in you."[1] If, then, the Holy Spirit speaks in those who have been handed over to persecution for Christ, why would he not also do so in those who hand over doctrine to those who want to know Christ? CHRISTIAN INSTRUCTION 4.15.32.[2]

7:17 *Knowledge of What Exists*

THERE IS NO HIGHER KNOWLEDGE. ORIGEN: In John it is written, "As the Father knows me, so I know the Father."[3] And in Psalm 45 it is written, "Be still and you will know that I am God."[4] Therefore the principal end of knowledge is to know the Trinity, and secondly to know

what has been created by him, after the one who said, "Indeed, he gave me true knowledge of what exists." COMMENTARY ON THE SONG OF SONGS 1.8.[5]

THE HEART UNDERSTANDS MANY THINGS.
ORIGEN: You see that the human heart is not small, because it understands many things. And you must not suppose that human greatness is in the size of the body but in the capacity of the senses, which can grasp so effectively the knowledge of the truth. And so that you might believe concerning the greatness of the human heart, I will offer some simple examples drawn from everyday life, such as the following. If we pass through a city, we preserve it in our spirit. In our heart are present the characteristics and locations of its squares, its walls and its buildings. We remember, both as an image and as a description, the street by which we entered and the sea we crossed to get there. As I said, the human heart is not small, which can understand so many things. Since it understands many things (and therefore is not small), in it the way of the Lord is prepared and the path straightened,[6] so that the word and the wisdom of God might walk on them. Prepare the way of the Lord by good behavior, and level the path with excellent works, so that the Word of God might walk in you without encountering obstacles, making you know his mysteries and his coming. HOMILIES ON THE GOSPEL OF LUKE 21.6-7.[7]

7:21 *What Is Secret and What Is Manifest*

WHAT IS VISIBLE TEACHES INVISIBLE THINGS. ORIGEN: The writer of divine wisdom, after having listed everything one by one, concludes by saying that he has acquired knowledge of what is hidden and what is manifest. By this he showed that each of the things that are manifest has a relation with something hidden—that

---

[1]Mt 10:19-20. [2]PL 34:103. [3]Jn 10:15. [4]Ps 46:11 (45:11 LXX). [5]CTP 1:150. [6]Is 40:3; Mt 3:3 par. [7]GCS Origenes 9:131.

every visible thing, that is, has a likeness and a formal relationship with invisible things. Given, then, that it is not possible for a person who lives in the flesh to know anything about hidden and invisible realities unless he receives some image and likeness of it from visible things, for this reason I think that the one who created everything in wisdom[8] created all the species of visible things on earth in such a way as to bear within them a principle of the knowledge of invisible and heavenly realities. Through them, therefore, the human mind can raise itself to spiritual understanding and seek in heavenly re-

alities the principles and causes of things. Thus, instructed by the wisdom of God, it also can say, "I have known everything that is hidden and manifest." In this sense it also knows the essence of the world, not only the visible and corporeal world that is before the eyes of all but also that incorporeal and invisible world that is hidden. It knows the elements not only of the visible world but also of the invisible world, and the properties of the one and the other. COMMENTARY ON THE SONG OF SONGS 2.9.[9]

---

[8]See Ps 104:24 (103:24 LXX). [9]CTP 1:232.

7:22–8:1* IN PRAISE OF WISDOM

For in her there is a spirit that is intelligent, holy,
unique, manifold, subtle,
mobile, clear, unpolluted,
distinct, invulnerable, loving the good, keen,
irresistible,[23]beneficent, humane,
steadfast, sure, free from anxiety,
all-powerful, overseeing all,
and penetrating through all spirits
that are intelligent and pure and most subtle.
[24]For wisdom is more mobile than any motion;
because of her pureness she pervades and penetrates all things.
[25]For she is a breath of the power of God,
and a pure emanation of the glory of the Almighty;
therefore nothing defiled gains entrance into her.
[26]For she is a reflection of eternal light,
a spotless mirror of the working of God,
and an image of his goodness.
[27]Though she is but one, she can do all things,
and while remaining in herself, she renews all things;
in every generation she passes into holy souls
and makes them friends of God, and prophets;
[28]for God loves nothing so much as the man who lives with wisdom.

²⁹For she is more beautiful than the sun,
and excels every constellation of the stars.
Compared with the light she is found to be superior,
³⁰ for it is succeeded by the night,
but against wisdom evil does not prevail.
8 *She reaches mightily from one end of the earth to the other,*
and she orders all things well.

* Some versions join the first phrase of Wis 7:22 to Wis 7:21.

OVERVIEW: All knowledge comes from God (SEVERIAN). Adam knew everything (CASSIAN). The sinlessness of the Holy Spirit points to his divinity (AMBROSE). Both the Trinity and wisdom are present everywhere (AUGUSTINE, VIGILIUS). The Spirit is mobile (GREGORY THE GREAT), manifold (PSEUDO-AMBROSE) and incorporeal (AMBROSE). Christ the Son is equal to the Father (QUODVULTDEUS [?], FULGENTIUS). God is infinite and eternal (FULGENTIUS). The Father and the Son are both eternal (FULGENTIUS). Both the Father and the Son have always existed (DIONYSIUS); the Son is the Father's image (AMBROSE) and the reflection of his light (GREGORY OF ELVIRA). The Scripture proves the equality of the Father and the Son (AUGUSTINE). The Trinity can be compared with the sun (AUGUSTINE). The light and its reflection have one nature that admits no confusion (FULGENTIUS). The Son is God's wisdom (AMBROSE). Our being comes totally from God (AUGUSTINE). The Trinity renews us (VIGILIUS). There is also a spiritual light that is created (AUGUSTINE). We believe in God, thanks to the prophets (AUGUSTINE). Wisdom spoke to Adam (AUGUSTINE) even as he speaks to all his children whom he loves (AUGUSTINE). Wisdom is beautiful (AMBROSE), expressed in God's goodness that overcomes every sin (FULGENTIUS). The Word fills everything (AUGUSTINE). All the living, in fact, were created with wisdom (AUGUSTINE). When the Son was sent, it was not as though he moved from one place to another (FULGENTIUS). He, as the Word made flesh, healed humanity through his incarnation (PSEUDO-AUGUSTINE).

7:22 Wisdom Taught Me

ALL WISDOM AND KNOWLEDGE COME FROM GOD. SEVERIAN OF GABALA: The image[1] has come into the world and investigates nature. He looks for plants and finds them—investigating their roots, he understands. He becomes an artisan and the inventor of all things. But so that he does not think to have found these things by himself and not thanks to the power of him who gave this capacity to his nature, by a single discourse it is indicated that God is the teacher of all of these things to our nature. Blessed Solomon came, saying, "He has given me an unerring knowledge of all that exists, to understand the structure of the world and the power of the elements, the beginning, the end and the middle of times, the cycle of the years and the position of the stars, the nature of animals and the instincts of wild beasts, the various plants and the properties of roots. All that is hidden and all that is clear, I know." And how did the image know this? "Wisdom, the fashioner of all things, taught me." ON THE VERSE "PUT YOUR HAND" 4.[2]

ADAM KNEW EVERYTHING. JOHN CASSIAN: "I said, 'You are gods, and all children of the Most High.' And yet you will die like human beings and fall like one of the mighty."[3] Thus they fell from the true discipline dictated by the knowledge of nature, that which was passed down to them by their ancestors and that the first man, he who appeared just after the creation of the

---

[1]See Gen 1:26-27. [2]PG 56:558. [3]Ps 82:6-7 (81:6-7 LXX).

universe, could obviously perceive directly and pass on to his posterity with his certain reason. That first man saw the very infancy of the world, when it was still young and, in a certain way, throbbing and uncultivated. The fullness of wisdom, however, dwelled in him to such a high degree, along with the grace of being able to see the future, given him by divine infusion, that he was able to name all the living creatures, though he was still only a rude inhabitant of this world. And he not only knew how to distinguish all the species of beasts and the fury of serpents but also the virtues of herbs and plants, as well as the qualities of minerals. He also knew the changes of the seasons, even when they had not yet occurred, such that he could say of himself, "He has given me the knowledge of what exists, to understand the structure of the world and the power of the elements, the alternations of times and the succession of the seasons, the cycle of the years and the position of the stars, the nature of animals and the ferocious instincts of wild beasts, the power of spirits and the thoughts of human beings, the variety of plants and the properties of roots. All that is hidden and all that is clear, I know." CONFERENCES 1.8.21.[4]

THE HOLY SPIRIT IS SINLESS. AMBROSE: We will now speak of the fact that no one is without sin, except God. We ask of our adversaries to teach that there is sin in the Holy Spirit. They cannot teach this, however, instead demanding an authoritative testimony showing why we teach from the Scriptures that the Holy Spirit has not sinned, as one reads of the Son that he has not committed sin.[5] And they would accept that we teach with the authority of Scripture, since it is written, "Because in wisdom there is a spirit intelligent, holy, unique, manifold, subtle, mobile, penetrating, without blemish." The Scripture calls him "without blemish." But has it perhaps lied regarding the Son, so you might believe it has also lied regarding the Spirit? In fact, the prophet said in the same passage of the book of Wisdom that "nothing defiled gains

entrance into her." Wisdom is without blemish, and its Spirit is without blemish. If, therefore, there is no sin in the Spirit, he is God. But how could the one who forgives sins be guilty of sin? Therefore he has not committed sin. And since there is no sin in him, he is not a creature. Every creature is in fact subject to sin. Only the eternal divinity is exempt from sin and without blemish. ON THE HOLY SPIRIT 3.18.134-36.[6]

WISDOM IS EVERYWHERE. AUGUSTINE: After many descriptive phrases it says of the Spirit of wisdom, "Acute, mobile, certain, immaculate." Thus the Wisdom of God is also mobile. Now, if it is mobile, when it dwells in one place, does it perhaps not dwell in another? Or if it is here, does it depart from there? What, then, about speed? Its speed derives from this: that it is always everywhere, and nothing can contain it. But we are incapable of thinking of such things—we are slow. Who could ever think of them? In fact, brothers and sisters, I have said something to you as best I can (if I have in fact understood something), and likewise you have understood as best you can. But what does the apostle say? "To him who can accomplish more than all we can ask or think."[7] What can we deduce from this? That even when we understand, we do not understand how things really are, objectively. Why is this? "The corruptible body weighs down the soul."[8] Therefore, as long as we are on earth we will be cold, whereas speed burns with heat—and all hot things are fast, but what is cold is slow. We are slow, and thus cold, while Wisdom runs at the maximum limit of speed. It is therefore exceedingly hot, and no one can escape its heat.[9] EXPOSITIONS OF THE PSALMS 147.22.[10]

THE MOBILITY OF THE SPIRIT. GREGORY THE GREAT: Because the Holy Spirit is God and co-eternal with the Father and the Son from before

---

[4]CTP 155:337. [5]See 1 Pet 2:22; Is 53:9. [6]PL 16:808. [7]Eph 3:20. [8]Wis 9:15. [9]Ps 19:7 (18:7 LXX). [10]NBA 28:849.

all time, we must ask ourselves why it is said that he moves. In fact, one who moves goes to a place were he was not and leaves a place where he was. Now, why do we say that the Holy Spirit moves, given that he contains everything and there is no place where he is not? As it is written, "The Spirit of the Lord fills the universe."[11] And yet, when Wisdom's praises are sung, it is added, "In her there is a spirit intelligent, holy, unique, manifold, subtle, mobile." And a little later, "friend of human beings, stable." These words raise a big problem for us. Why is it said that this Spirit who fills everything is simultaneously mobile and stable? If we recall, however, the usual way in which human beings express themselves, it will not be difficult for us to discover the writer's meaning. A person moves about freely in the area in which he lives—he might be found anywhere, and often he is in places we would hardly believe. Now, it says that the all-powerful Spirit is both mobile and stable, to indicate his universal presence. It says that he is stable, because by his essence he encompasses everything; that he is mobile, because he reaches even those who do not know it. He is called stable, because he holds all things together, mobile because he makes himself present to all. Thus the brightness of the fire moves in the midst of the living winged creatures, with its glow, because the Holy Spirit makes himself present simultaneously to each and to all. He enkindles those he reaches and enlightens those he enkindles, so that, after their former coldness, ablaze, they would burn, and with the fire of the love they have received, they would emit the flames of a good example. HOMILIES ON EZEKIEL 1.5.9-10.[12]

THE SPIRIT IS MANIFOLD. PSEUDO-AMBROSE: As light does not admit darkness, so the Holy Spirit is by nature incapable of all that is sordid. He departs from thoughts that are without God. He infuses himself into holy souls, transforming them into servants of God and prophets. Therefore, if someone does not have the Holy Spirit, neither the Father nor the Son—from whom he

is, and with whom he is one God—will come to him to make their dwelling in him.[13] This is the spirit of wisdom, who is consequently called manifold, since he has many things in himself and is what he has—and in everything he is still one. The things he does do not change him in any way, like the image of a ring left in wax, without leaving the ring. ON THE TRINITY 7.[14]

7:23 More Attributes of the Spirit

THE HOLY SPIRIT HAS NO BODY. AMBROSE: If the Spirit came from one place and went to another, then the Father would also be in a place, as well as the Son. If he were to leave a place when sent by the Father or the Son, it would certainly seem, as in godless interpretations, that the Spirit, moving and going to a place, would leave the Father and the Son, as with a body. I say this after the manner of those who say that the Spirit has a descending movement. But the Father is not circumscribed by a place, since he is above all things—not only those of a corporeal nature but also invisible creatures. Nor is the Son limited by the places and times of his works, because as the creator of every creature he is above every creature. And neither is the Spirit of truth,[15] being the Spirit of God, circumscribed by any kind of corporeal limit. Indeed, being incorporeal, he is higher than every intelligible created being, because of the unspeakable fullness of the divinity. He blows where he wills[16] and inspires whom he wills, endowed with power over all things. ON THE HOLY SPIRIT 1.10.117-18.[17]

7:24 Pervading and Penetrating All Things

CHRIST IS EQUAL TO THE FATHER. QUODVULTDEUS (?): For other heretics [the Arians], Christ, who is the very way by which one goes to the Father,[18] is not equal to the Father accord-

---

[11]Wis 1:7. [12]CTP 17:98-99. [13]See Jn 14:23. [14]PL 17:516. [15]See Jn 14:17; 15:26; 16:13; 1 Jn 4:6. [16]See Jn 3:8. [17]PL 16:732. [18]See Jn 14:6.

ing to his divinity. And even if he says, "I and the Father are one,"[19] they say, "If he was sent by the Father,[20] he is inferior. The one who sends is greater than the one who is sent." This is a human argument, not a divine testimony. O heretic, the Trinity's way of doing things is different from yours, and you do not understand it, because you understand it carnally. Your heart is not pure,[21] even regarding God. In fact, Christ is called "sent" in that he assumed human existence. As God, he is equal to the Father. Where did the Father send the Son that he himself would not be, together with him? Where did the Son go, that he would not be with the Father, as he says, "I am in the Father and the Father in me,"[22] and, "Philip, one who has seen me has seen the Father."[23] He is the one who says through the prophet, "I fill heaven and earth,"[24] and of whom Solomon says, "He reaches from one end of the earth to the other with power, governing all things well. By his purity he pervades and penetrates all things." But you, heretic, say that the one who sends is greater and the one who is sent less, because you think in terms of intervals of time. But you err greatly by placing within time the one who made time. If you profess that the Father is God and that the Son is God and believe that the Father and the Son are eternal, do not consider the Son inferior because he made you, just because he made himself inferior to redeem you. But, you reply, he said, "The Father is greater than I."[25] If you mean this phrase regarding the humanity he assumed, you err no longer. He says, "The Father is greater than I"[26] in the same way that the prophet said of him, "You have made him a little less than the angels."[27] Tell me, under what aspect do you consider him to be inferior? Power? "The Father judges no one, only the Son."[28] Works? "Everything was made through the Son."[29] If you believe, regarding time, that because you are older than your son, it is like this with God and his Son—may God keep the faithful from hearing these words! It is unworthy to believe such things of God. If in fact the

Son is the Word according to the divinity of God, as John the Evangelist says, "In the beginning was the Word, the Word was with God, and the Word was God,"[30] could there have been a time when the Father was without the Word, or was there a beginning before the beginning itself, given that the Son said that he was the beginning? Indeed, when the Jews asked him, "Who are you?" he replied, "The beginning."[31] Thus what is written in Genesis, "In the beginning God created the heavens and the earth,"[32] refers to the Son, who is the beginning. So, the Father is always God and the Son is always God, because the former has never not been Father and the latter has never not been Son. The Father did not diminish himself in generating the Son but generated from himself another like him, so that he would remain entirely in him. The Holy Spirit is not separated out as though he were a portion of that from which he proceeds; rather he is complete from another who is himself complete. And by proceeding from him, the Spirit does not diminish him, nor by being united to him does the Spirit make him any greater. And these three are one God, of whom the prophet says, "You are the only great God."[33] ON THE NEW SONG 7.1-17.[34]

GOD IS INFINITE AND ETERNAL. FULGENTIUS OF RUSPE: The psalm sings truthfully, "Great is the Lord our God, almighty, his wisdom has no limit."[35] And to show the limitless immensity of this infinite eternity, it says elsewhere, "Great is the Lord and worthy of all praise; his greatness cannot be measured."[36] Indeed, it is necessary that he who is by nature eternal also be proclaimed immeasurable by nature, since what always exists cannot be measured, and what is everywhere cannot be enclosed in a place. Thus finally another testimony of Scripture says, "By

---

[19]Jn 10:30. [20]See Jn 17:8, etc. [21]See Mt 5:8. [22]Jn 14:10. [23]Jn 14:9. [24]Jer 23:24. [25]Jn 14:28. [26]Jn 14:28. [27]Ps 8:6. [28]Jn 5:22. [29]Jn 1:3. [30]Jn 1:1. [31]Jn 8:25. [32]Gen 1:1. [33]Ps 86:10 (85:10 LXX). [34]CCL 60:388-89. [35]Ps 147:5 (146:5 LXX). [36]Ps 145:3 (144:3 LXX).

her purity she pervades all things." And a little later, "She reaches mightily from one end to the other, and governs all things well." And if now we hear that wisdom reaches from one end to the other, we must understand that if she reaches from one end to the other, she surpasses both ends by the immensity of her infinite nature. Indeed, only one who cannot be enclosed within creation can reach the entire creation, since, if in filling the heavens she is immeasurable, she is likewise infinite in reaching from one end to the other. THREE BOOKS TO TRASAMUNDUS 3.7.[37]

7:25 A Breath of the Power of God

FATHER AND SON ARE BOTH ETERNAL. DIONYSIUS OF ALEXANDRIA: Because the Father is eternal, the Son is eternal, since he is light from light. If there is a parent, there is also a Son. If there were not a son, how, and of whom, would there be a parent? But both exist, and exist always. Since God is light, Christ is radiance.[38] Since the spirit exists (in fact, "God is spirit"),[39] by analogy Christ is called emanation. Indeed, "he is an emanation of the power of God." To DIONYSIUS OF ROME 4.[40]

SIMILAR TO FIRE. FULGENTIUS OF RUSPE: Although it is said of Wisdom that it "is an emanation of the power of God," nevertheless the Holy Spirit also, whose nature is fire, can be correctly compared (to the extent that the knowledge of divine things requires it) with an emanation, according to the words of the apostle, "Be fervent in the Spirit."[41] AGAINST FABIANUS, FRAGMENT 22.[42]

7:26 A Reflection of Eternal Light

CHRIST IS THE FATHER'S IMAGE. AMBROSE: The apostle says that Christ is the image of the Father. He says in fact that he is the image of the invisible God, the firstborn of all creatures.[43] He speaks of the firstborn, and not of the first created, so that we would believe that by nature

he is generated, and first from all eternity. Elsewhere the apostle says, "He made him heir of all things, and through him he also made the world, the one who is the radiance of his glory and the imprint of his being."[44] The apostle says that he is an image, and Arius says that he is different. Why, then, speak of an image, if he were not the same? People ordinarily do not accept the image of a portrait as being different from the original, but Arius asserts that the Father is different from the Son. He maintains that the Father generated someone who is different from him, as though he were incapable of generating someone like himself. The prophets say, "In your light we see light."[45] They say, "He is a reflection of the eternal light, an unspotted mirror of the majesty of God and an image of his goodness." See in how many ways they speak. "Radiance," because the brightness of the Father's light is in the Son. "Unspotted mirror," since the Father is visible in the Son. "Image of his goodness," since it is not one body seen reflected in another but the whole power of the Godhead in the Son. "Image" teaches that here is no difference. "Imprint" indicates that he is the manifestation of the Father. "Splendor" bespeaks eternity. In fact, the "image" is not the bodily face, nor is it made with colors or from wax but is simply from God. He is from the Father, pouring forth from the spring. ON THE CHRISTIAN FAITH 1.7.48-49.[46]

A REFLECTION OF THE FATHER'S LIGHT. GREGORY OF ELVIRA: If, about what we all profess, you wanted to suggest some similitude in God, I am not sure if you could specify your comparison more clearly. For example, if you were to say "light from light" and had to explain it in detail, I would ask you how you conceive of this light from light. Perhaps like a lamp from a lamp, or a sun from the sun? Or would this example lead you to deduce that there are two lamps or two

---

[37]PL 65:254. [38]See Heb 1:3. [39]Jn 4:24. [40]PL 5:120. [41]Rom 12:11. [42]PL 65:777. [43]See Col 1:15. [44]Heb 1:2-3. [45]Ps 36:10 (35:10 LXX). [46]PL 16:539-40.

suns, as though there were two gods? Or would you understand the light from light as the effect of the light of the lamp itself or as the brilliance of the sun shining from the sun itself, comparing the figure of the Father with the source of the light and the Son with the brightness of its radiation? In fact, of this the prophet said, "In you is the source of life, and in your light we see light."[47] Or Solomon, when he says, "She is a reflection of the eternal light, a spotless mirror of the majesty of God and an image of his goodness." The apostle also preached that our Savior is the image of the invisible God,[48] because the image of the sun is its light, which proceeds from the sun itself. On the Faith 5.[49]

The Father and the Son Are Equal.

Augustine: The Son is sent, not because he is not equal to the Father but because he is "a pure emanation of the light of God" almighty. Here what is emanated and that from which it emanates are of one, identical being. It is not an emanation like that of water springing from a natural opening in the earth or in a rock but like that of light from light. When it says "splendor of the eternal light," what else can be meant but that it is the light of the eternal light? Light's splendor—what is it, except light? It is therefore coeternal with the light of which it is the light. Nevertheless, the Scripture preferred the expression "splendor of the light" to the other, "light of the light," so that no one would believe that the light that emanates is darker than that from which it emanates. Rather, hearing it called its splendor, it is easier to think that the one owes to the other its brilliance, rather than that one shines less brightly than the other. But because there was no chance that anyone would think the generating light to be inferior (no heretic has dared to assert this, nor does it seem believable that one would dare to do so), the Scripture anticipates the notion that the emanated light would be darker than the generating light. It eliminated this conjecture by saying, "It is the splendor of that light," that is, of the eternal

light, thus showing his equality. Indeed, if it were inferior, it would be the shadow, not the splendor. And if greater, it would not emanate, because it could not surpass that from which it was emanating. On the Trinity 4.20.27.[50]

The Son Is Equal to the Father.

Fulgentius of Ruspe: The Arians clearly show themselves to worship two gods when they deny that the Son is equal to the Father. And they declare him less, not regarding the assumption of the flesh (which the truth of the faith teaches) but with respect to the nature of the immeasurable divinity, even though it is said of him who is the wisdom of God[51] that he is "a reflection of the eternal light." It is also said of him, in the letter to the Hebrews, "that he is the radiance of his glory and the imprint of his being."[52] They should look at the "reflection of the eternal light" and recognize that, as that eternal light is infinite, so its reflection is in no way secondary or inferior by nature. Its eternity, rather, is identical to its infinity and its infinity to its eternity. Book to Victor Against the Sermon of Fastidiosus the Arian 6.3.[53]

The Trinity Compared with the Sun.

Augustine: Look at God, contemplate the Word, and unite yourself intimately to the Word who speaks. His word is not comprised of syllables; rather, his word is the resplendent brightness of wisdom. It is said of his wisdom that "it is the splendor of the eternal light." Observe the splendor of the sun. The sun is in the heavens and pours its splendor on all the earth and over all the seas, yet its light is only corporeal. If you could separate the sun's splendor from the sun itself, so also could you separate the Word from the Father. I have spoken of the sun. A weak little flame from a lamp, however, which can be blown out with a breath, also sheds its light all around. See the light given off by the flame.

---

[47]Ps 36:10 (35:10 lxx). [48]See Col 1:15. [49]PL 17:559. [50]NBA 4:221. [51]See 1 Cor 1:24. [52]Heb 1:3. [53]CCL 91:292.

See that it originates from the flame—you do not see the light without the flame. Convince yourselves, then, beloved brothers and sisters, that the Father, the Son and the Holy Spirit are inseparably united among themselves and that this Trinity is one God—and that all of the works of this one God are works of the Father, of the Son and of the Holy Spirit. TRACTATES ON THE GOSPEL OF JOHN 20.13.[54]

SHARING THE SAME NATURE. FULGENTIUS OF RUSPE: So as to show that the Son is infinite along with the Father, the sacred Scripture was careful to say of wisdom, "It is the reflection of the eternal light, a spotless mirror of the majesty of God and an image of his goodness." In this testimony are shown the oneness of nature, the distinction of persons and the infinite equality of the Father and the Son. No one can doubt that in this passage the Father is called the light and the Son the reflection. About this, the apostle also says authoritatively, "He is the radiance of his glory and the imprint of his being and sustains all things with the power of his word."[55] See that it is said that the Son is the reflection and governs all things. If someone thinks that the Father is infinite but that the Son has limits, let him show us in what way the light and its reflection could be different beings, when, even if they are differentiated by name, they are not distinct in kind, nor do they differ in extension. In fact, the light and its reflection do not have the same name, but neither do they have different natures. THREE BOOKS TO TRASAMUNDUS 2.9.[56]

7:27 Wisdom Can Do All Things

THE SON IS GOD'S WISDOM. AMBROSE: "O the depths of the riches, the wisdom and the knowledge of God! How inscrutable his judgments and unsearchable his ways! In fact, who has ever known the thoughts of the Lord? Or who has been his counselor? Or who has given him something, so as to receive something in

return? Since from him, because of him and for him all things are. To him be glory forever."[57] Of whom does this speak—the Father or the Son? Perhaps of the Father? But the Father is not the Wisdom of God, because the Wisdom of God is the Son.[58] And what can Wisdom not do, of whom it is written, "Though one, she can do all things; though remaining in herself, she renews all things"? Thus we read that Wisdom is not something temporary but permanent. According to Solomon, then, Wisdom is all-powerful and permanent. You will also read that it is good, because it is written, "Against wisdom, wickedness cannot prevail." ON THE CHRISTIAN FAITH 143-44.[59]

ALL BEING AND EXISTENCE COME FROM GOD. AUGUSTINE: Observing, then, all the other things put beneath you, I discovered that they neither wholly exist, nor do they wholly not exist. They exist, since they are from you, but they also do not exist because they are not what you are. For only what exists immutably, truly exists. It is good for me to be in union with God then,[60] since, if I do not remain in him, neither can I remain in myself. He, by contrast, "remaining stable in himself, renews all things." "You are my Lord, because you have no need of my goodness."[61] CONFESSIONS 7.11.17.[62]

THE SON IS EQUAL TO THE FATHER. AUGUSTINE: You believe in God, the Father almighty, invisible, immortal, king of the ages, creator of all things visible and invisible, and so on according to what is said of him, either by right reason or by the authority of sacred Scripture. From this greatness of the Father, then, you must not exclude the Son. Because these are things that are not said exclusively of the Father, as though he were unrelated to the one who said, "I and the Father are one,"[63] and of whom the apostle said, "Who,

---

[54]NBA 24:483. [55]Heb 1:3. [56]PL 65:255-56. [57]Rom 11:33-36. [58]See 1 Cor 1:24. [59]PL 16:644-45. [60]Ps 73:28 (72:28 LXX). [61]Ps 16:2 (15:2 LXX, variant). [62]NBA 1:201. [63]Jn 10:30.

being divine in nature, did not consider robbery his equality with God."[64] Robbery is the usurping of something that belongs to another, but this equality is his by nature. Consequently, how is the Son not almighty, through whom all things were made,[65] who is also the power and the wisdom of God,[66] that wisdom about which it is written, "Being one, she can do all things"? That nature is therefore also invisible,[67] by the very fact that he is equal to the Father. SERMON 212.1.[68]

THE TRINITY RENEWS US. VIGILIUS OF THAPSUS: The Father renews, the Son renews, and the Holy Spirit does the same. About the Father, we read in Jeremiah, "Make us return to you, Lord, and we will return. Renew our days as of old."[69] About the Son, in Solomon, "She reaches mightily from one end to the other and governs all things well." And also, "Though one, she renews all things." The Holy Spirit, in the letter to the Romans, "But now we are discharged from the law, dead to that which held us captive, so that we serve not under the old written code but in the new life of the Spirit."[70] AGAINST VARIMADUS 3.47.[71]

7:27 Friends of God and Prophets

THE SPIRITUAL LIGHT CREATED BY GOD. AUGUSTINE: If spiritual light was created when God said, "Let there be light,"[72] you must not think that this was the true light, coeternal with the Father, through whom all things were created[73] and who enlightens every person.[74] Rather, it was that light of which Scripture could say, "Among all things, Wisdom was created first."[75] In fact, when that eternal and immutable Wisdom, which is not created but generated, communicates itself to spiritual and rational creatures—as to holy souls so that, enlightened, they might shine—he constitutes in them, so to speak, a state of enlightened reason that can be understood as the creation of the light when God said, "Let there be light!"[76] If there already existed a spiritual creature called by the name

"heavens" in the passage where it is written, "In the beginning God created the heavens and the earth,"[77] these heavens are not the corporeal heavens but the incorporeal. They are superior to any body, not by the ordering of space into levels but because of the exceeding dignity of their nature. ON GENESIS 1.17.32.[78]

THANKS TO THE PROPHETS, WE BELIEVE IN GOD. AUGUSTINE: The world is the greatest of the visible beings. God is the greatest of the invisible beings. But we see that the world exists, and we believe that God exists. No one makes us believe with more certainty that God created the world than God himself. And when did we hear this? Nowhere better than in the holy Scriptures, where his prophet said, "In the beginning God created the heavens and the earth."[79] Was this prophet perhaps present when God created the heavens and the earth? No. But the Wisdom of God was there, through whom all things were made.[80] Entering holy souls, this Wisdom makes friends of God and prophets, silently making her works known in them. With them the angels of God also speak, who always see the face of the Father,[81] and communicate his will to those to whom it must be communicated. And one of these was this prophet who said and wrote, "In the beginning God created the heavens and the earth." And this is a text so trustworthy for belief in God that, thanks to the same Spirit of God through whom he knew these revealed things, he also predicted, long ago, the advent of our faith. CITY OF GOD 11.4.1.[82]

WISDOM SPOKE TO ADAM. AUGUSTINE: If Adam had been capable of understanding the word that God communicates to angelic spirits through his own essence, it cannot be doubted that God, without being moved himself through

---

[64]Phil 2:6. [65]Jn 1:3. [66]See 1 Cor 1:24. [67]See Col 1:15. [68]NBA 32/1:195. [69]Lam 5:21. [70]Rom 7:6. [71]PL 62:422. [72]Gen 1:3. [73]See Jn 1:3. [74]See Jn 1:9. [75]Sir 1:4. [76]Gen 1:3. [77]Gen 1:1. [78]NBA 9/2:47. [79]Gen 1:1. [80]See Jn 1:3. [81]Mt 18:10. [82]PL 41:319.

time, would have moved Adam's spirit in a mysterious and ineffable way. He would have taught him a useful and salutary precept of truth and, by the same Truth, what punishment awaited its transgressor. This is how all the salutary precepts of unchanging Wisdom that are communicated to holy souls at particular moments, at this or that time, should be seen and understood.[83] If, however, Adam was righteous only to the extent that he still needed another holier and wiser creature through whom he would come to know the will and command of God (as we have had need of the prophets, and they of the angels), why should we doubt that God would have spoken to him through such a creature, using a language that Adam could understand? ON GENESIS 8.27.50.[84]

7:28 God Loves One Who Lives with Wisdom

GOD ALSO LOVES BABIES. AUGUSTINE: In your opinion, even those who are born foolish—whom sacred Scripture says should be pitied more than the dead—receive their foolishness as fate from God their creator.[85] But even with these, God undoubtedly loves their souls in some way, because they exist, live and feel, and in any case they are greater than beasts, even if they are dull-minded souls. But that love is different, of which it is written, "God loves no one so much as the one who lives with wisdom." You, however, ask why God has more love for the souls of babies, for whom he provides the washing of regeneration,[86] sending them to the kingdom, and why would he not give this benefit to others, since babies have no merits of the will to distinguish them, nor is there preference of persons with God.[87] This is a completely stupid argument, which you are always bringing up to us. That where it was said, "You love souls,"[88] it did not say "all souls," there is no question. Perhaps it was said this way in the sense that God creates all souls but loves only those whom he distinguishes from the others, not based on their merits but by the generosity of his grace, so that they might live with wisdom, as it is written,

"God loves no one so much as the one who lives with wisdom—but the Lord gives the wisdom!"[89] UNFINISHED TRACTATE AGAINST JULIAN 4.125.[90]

7:29 More Beautiful Than the Sun

THE BEAUTY OF WISDOM. AMBROSE: Who would ever ruin the loveliness of a beautiful face by joining it with a beast-like body and claws? Indeed, the appearance of virtue is admirable and splendid, and especially the beauty of wisdom, as the succession of events narrated by Scripture demonstrates. Wisdom is more dazzling than the sun, and, compared with the light of the constellations, it surpasses them all. Indeed, whereas the night absorbs their light, wickedness cannot overcome wisdom. DUTIES OF THE CLERGY 2.13.64.[91]

7:30 Evil Does Not Prevail

GOD'S GOODNESS PREVAILS OVER ANY SIN. FULGENTIUS OF RUSPE: If our physician is an expert, he can heal every infirmity. If he is our merciful God, he can forgive every sin. A goodness that does not prevail over every evil is not perfect, nor is a medicine perfect if some disease cannot be cured by it. Indeed, it is written in the sacred texts, "Evil does not prevail over wisdom." Our physician's omnipotence is proclaimed in the psalm with these words, "Bless the Lord, my soul, and all my being bless his holy name. Bless the Lord, my soul, and do not forget all his benefits. It is he who pardons all your sins, who heals all your weakness, who rescues your life from the grave, who fulfills your desires with good things, who crowns you with mercy and goodness. Your youth will be renewed like the eagle's."[92] I ask you: What should we think cannot be forgiven us, since the Lord is kindly

---

[83]For Augustine, movement implies change. [84]NBA 9/2:447-49. [85]See Sir 22:11-12 (22:12-13 Vg). [86]See Tit 3:5. [87]See Rom 2:11; Eph 6:9. [88]Wis 11:26, variant. [89]Prov 2:6. [90]NBA 19/2:831-33. [91]SAEMO 13:219. [92]Ps 103:1-5 (102:1-5 LXX).

in all our misdeeds? Or what should we suppose cannot be healed in us, since the Lord heals all our weaknesses? Or how is it possible that one who is whole and righteous would still have some lack—one who is content to desire good things? Or up to what point do we think that one could not avail himself of the benefit of the full remission of sins—one who has been crowned with goodness and mercy? Let no one, therefore, remain in his infirmity, despairing of the physician. Let no one destroy himself in sins, belittling the mercy of God. The apostle declares that "Christ died for the godless."[93] And he likewise says, "Jesus Christ came into the world to save sinners."[94] Letters 7.4.3.[95]

8:1 Reaching the Ends of the Earth

The Word Fills Everything. Augustine: What is speed, brothers and sisters, essentially? It is everywhere and cannot be divided. Now this applies to the Word of God: not being divided in parts, being everywhere in its nature as Word, being the Power and Wisdom of God[96]—without, that is, considering the flesh he would assume. If we think of God in the form of God, of the Word equal to the Father, he is the Wisdom of God of which it was said, "She reaches mightily from one end of the earth to the other." What speed! "She reaches mightily from one end of the earth to the other." But perhaps these ends are reached by remaining immobile. If this occurs without motion, as when a boulder fills a space, so it is said of him that he reaches both ends of that space without any motion. Expositions of the Psalms 147.22.[97]

Living Beings Were Created with Wisdom. Augustine: There is a problem regarding certain very small animals, that is, whether they were created at the beginning of the creation or whether they derived later from the corruption of mortal beings. Most of these in fact come either from pathological mutations in living beings, or from their excrement or

fumes or from decayed cadavers. Some others come from rotten wood or grasses, and others from rotten fruit. Regarding all these animals, we nonetheless do not have the right to say that God did not create them, since they all have a certain natural beauty appropriate to their species. This beauty can provoke greater wonder in one who considers them closely, leading him to even greater praise of the almighty Artisan who made all of them in Wisdom,[98] which, extending from one end of the earth to the other and governing all things well, leaves not even the lowest creatures of nature without form. These creatures decay, as is appropriate to their species (something that horrifies us to see, recalling the punishment that made us mortal). He creates animals, however, having tiny bodies but acute senses. If we were to observe them more closely, we might be more amazed at the agility of a fly than at the power of a beast of burden that walks, and we might admire the works of ants more than the heavy loads carried by camels. On Genesis 3.14.22.[99]

The Trinity Is Omnipresent. Vigilius of Thapsus: The Father is everywhere, the Son everywhere, the Holy Spirit everywhere. About the Father it is said in Jeremiah, "The Word of the Lord of hosts, the God of Israel, 'Do not I fill the heavens and the earth?' "[100] and in Isaiah, "The heavens are my throne, the earth the footstool for my feet."[101] About the Son, in Solomon, "Against wisdom wickedness cannot prevail. She reaches mightily from one end of the earth to the other." And in Psalm 102, "In every place of his domain."[102] The Holy Spirit, in the psalm, "Where can I go from your spirit, where can I flee from your presence? If I descend to the netherworld, you are there," etc.[103] Against Varimadus 3.52.[104]

---

[93]Rom 5:6. [94]1 Tim 1:15. [95]CTP 149:161-62. [96]See 1 Cor 1:24. [97]NBA 28:849. [98]See Ps 104:24 (103:24 LXX). [99]NBA 9/2:137. [100]Zeph 2:9 and Jer 23:24. [101]Is 66:1. [102]Ps 103:22 (102:22 LXX). [103]Ps 139:7-8 (138:7-8 LXX). [104]PL 62:423.

THE MOVEMENT OF THE SON. FULGENTIUS OF RUSPE: The true Father sent the Truth[105] he had generated, he sent the Wisdom in which he had made everything,[106] he sent the Word that he had conceived in his heart.[107] In this mission, therefore, the coming must not be thought of as a change of place, as if the Son of God were sent from heaven to earth or that he was not on earth before taking flesh. Or, as if he abandoned heaven when he assumed flesh for our salvation, since he is the Wisdom of God of which it is said, "He extends powerfully from one end of the earth to the other, governing all things well." That divinity that by nature is one, of the Father, the Son and the Holy Spirit, is not in a place, just as it is not in time. It is not enclosed in a place, just as it does not change with time. That divinity that by nature is infinite and eternal had no beginning and is not contained in a place. Therefore the one God, Father, Son and Holy Spirit, fills all: he is entirely in everyone, entirely in all, entirely in small creatures, entirely in those that are bigger. This occurs by nature, not by grace. It happens when he creates human beings, not when he saves them; when he forms them, not when he restores them; when he makes this sun rise on the good and on the wicked,[108] and not when the Sun of righteousness[109] rises on those in whom life is infused—not that of the flesh, but of the heart—by the gift of his anticipatory mercy. ON THE INCARNATION 7.[110]

THE INCARNATION OF THE WORD HEALED HUMANKIND. PSEUDO-AUGUSTINE: Since the world was corrupted by original sin and actual sins, the Creator of the world wanted to heal its fall with a secret and wonderful plan, through the mystery of the incarnate Word.[111] By the same word through which he had created everything from nothing, he would restore what was lost. In fact, "he speaks and everything is made; he commands, and all exists."[112] Let us not think that this power is diminished or changed in him "in whom there is no altera-tion or shadow of change"[113] or that he is less powerful or wise in restoring than he was in creating. The hand of the all-powerful pot-ter, whose paths are all truth and mercy[114] and who, taking mud from the earth,[115] raised it to the dignity of a rational nature, wanted in this way to reconstruct in fragile vessels what had been ruined.[116] Thus the man's sin would not remain unpunished, since God is just, nor did it remain unhealed, since he is merciful. If the one whose wisdom "extends mightily from one end of the earth to the other and governs all things well" were only just, he could have fought by his power against the seducer of the human race, bringing the lost sheep back under his dominion in the flock.[117] But, by doing so, he would have only shown the excellence of his power and would not have exercised his healing mercy for the redeemed. Nor would it have become apparent with how much charity the Creator loved his creation—a creation he called to love him, offering in exchange con-siderable rewards—since miserable humanity, prior to receiving grace, would have obtained by merit what they otherwise would have received as a reward, even if they hardly deserved it. What the wisdom of God could have done with wisdom and power, he wanted to do with tenderness, uniting himself to the weakness of our flesh, which he had healed in the first place in himself. By this work, like a physician, he restored the human race to health. Not that it could not have been otherwise due to the skill and power of the Physician, but because an antidote corresponding to the illness could not have been more easily obtained. "The weakness of God is stronger than human beings, and the foolishness of God is wiser than human be-ings."[118] SERMON 247.1.[119]

[105]See Jn 14:6. [106]See Ps 104:24 (103:24 LXX). [107]See Ps 45:2 (44:2 LXX). [108]Mt 5:45. [109]See Mal 4:2 (3:20 LXX). [110]CCL 91A:317-18. [111]See Jn 1:14. [112]Ps 33:9 (32:9 LXX). [113]Jas 1:17. [114]See Ps 25:10 (24:10 LXX). [115]See Gen 2:7. [116]See 2 Cor 4:7. [117]See Mt 18:12-13 par. [118]1 Cor 1:25. [119]PL 39:2200-2201.

8:2-16 WISDOM THE IDEAL COMPANION OF LIFE

²I loved her and sought her from my youth,
and I desired to take her for my bride,
and I became enamored of her beauty.
³She glorifies her noble birth by living with God,
and the Lord of all loves her.
⁴For she is an initiate in the knowledge of God,
and an associate in his works.
⁵If riches are a desirable possession in life,
what is richer than wisdom who effects all things?
⁶And if understanding is effective,
who more than she is fashioner of what exists?
⁷And if any one loves righteousness,
her labors are virtues;
for she teaches self-control and prudence,
justice and courage;
nothing in life is more profitable for men than these.
⁸And if any one longs for wide experience,
she knows the things of old, and infers the things to come;
she understands turns of speech and the solutions of riddles;
she has foreknowledge of signs and wonders
and of the outcome of seasons and times.
⁹Therefore I determined to take her to live with me,
knowing that she would give me good counsel
and encouragement in cares and grief.
¹⁰Because of her I shall have glory among the multitudes
and honor in the presence of the elders, though I am young.
¹¹I shall be found keen in judgment,
and in the sight of rulers I shall be admired.
¹²When I am silent they will wait for me,
and when I speak they will give heed;
and when I speak at greater length
they will put their hands on their mouths.
¹³Because of her I shall have immortality,
and leave an everlasting remembrance to those who come after me.
¹⁴I shall govern peoples,
and nations will be subject to me;
¹⁵dread monarchs will be afraid of me when they hear of me;

among the people I shall show myself capable, and courageous in war.
¹⁶When I enter my house, I shall find rest with her,
for companionship with her has no bitterness,
and life with her has no pain, but gladness and joy.

OVERVIEW: Sarah is a figure of wisdom (ORIGEN). Desire and love are nearly synonymous (ORIGEN). Wisdom is the perfect and holy bride (HILARY OF POITIERS, CASSIODORUS). There are several kinds of wisdom (EPIPHANIUS). Mary is as beautiful as wisdom (ANDREW). Wisdom teaches the other virtues (AMBROSE, AUGUSTINE). In the Scripture something that is said hypothetically is totally sure (FULGENTIUS). God alone is truly immortal (AMBROSE). Wisdom teaches how to love wisdom (PSEUDO-AUGUSTINE).

8:2 Loved and Sought

SARAH AS A FIGURE OF WISDOM. ORIGEN: I think therefore that Sarah, which means "principal," or what has primacy,[1] is a figure of the *aretē* which is the virtue of the soul. This virtue is joined and clings to a wise and faithful husband, like that wise one who said of wisdom, "I sought to take her as my bride." For this reason God says to Abraham, "In everything that Sarah says to you, listen to her voice."[2] HOMILIES ON GENESIS 6.1.[3]

DESIRE AND LOVE ARE NEARLY SYNONYMOUS. ORIGEN: In many places the sacred Scripture has avoided the term "desire," replacing it with "love." At times, however, even if somewhat rarely, it uses precisely the term "desire" and invites and urges the soul to this, as in Proverbs when it says of wisdom, "Desire her, and she will serve you. Hold her close, and she will make you great. Honor her, that she would embrace you."[4] And in the book entitled the Wisdom of Solomon, it is further written of wisdom, "I desired her beauty."[5] Nevertheless, I think that the Scripture used the term "desire" only where there was no possibility of equivocation. Indeed, whatever is passionate or shameful can be found in the desire for wisdom or in the one who claims to desire wisdom. In fact, if the Scriptures had said that Isaac desired Rebecca or that Jacob desired Rachel, one could have thought of passion or of something shameful in the holy men of God because of these words, especially among those who do not know how to raise themselves from the letter to the spirit. And precisely in this book that we have before us, it is clear that the word *desire* has been replaced by "love," where it is said, "I implore you, daughters of Jerusalem: if you find my beloved, tell him that I am wounded by love."[6] It is as if she were to say, I have been pierced by an arrow of love. Therefore there is no difference if the sacred Scriptures speak of love or of desire, except that the term "love" is held in such high esteem that even God is personally called love, as John says, "Beloved, let us love one another, because love is from God, and everyone who loves is born of God and knows him. The one who does not love, however, does not know God, because God is love."[7] COMMENTARY ON THE SONG OF SONGS, PREFACE.[8]

WISDOM IS THE PERFECT BRIDE. HILARY OF POITIERS: Since, according to the Gospel, the Lord is the bridegroom[9] and, according to John, he has a bride,[10] must we think in terms of earthly, bodily spouses? Certainly not. But by this use of language we are taught that he is the one who has been promised to the nations. By

---

[1]This a traditional explanation of the name of Sarah. [2]Gen 21:12. [3]CTP 14:121. [4]Prov 4:6. 8. [5]The Greek text of the Septuagint says literally "the one who desires." [6]Song 5:8. [7]1 Jn 4:7-8. [8]CTP 1:44-45. [9]See Mt 9:15. [10]See Jn 3:29.

the Father's work, the inheritance of the church has been espoused to him, through the assumption of the body that he took from the Virgin. But, to learn what we should understand by the designation "bride," we must examine closely what is said elsewhere regarding the term. For example, Solomon says, "I sought to take wisdom as my bride." And because he seeks a bride, he wants her to be rich, and he recounts the benefits of his bride, saying, "She manifests her nobility in a life of communion with God, because the Lord of the universe loved her." And "if one desires wide experience, she knows what is past and infers what is to come." And further, "A strong woman, who can find? Her value is far beyond precious stones."[11] All of this was said in Proverbs, because a proverb does not explain what the words say but displays the power of what is said using ordinary words. In the Gospels, the Lord teaches how a proverb must be understood when he says, "The hour will come when I will no longer speak to you in proverbs, but I will speak openly to you of the Father."[12] Therefore, according to the rules governing proverbs, we must recognize that the strong woman is she whom Solomon desired to take as his bride. Of her he says further, "I therefore decided to take her as the companion of my life. I am enamored of her beauty." HOMILIES ON THE PSALMS 127.9.[13]

SEVERAL KINDS OF WISDOM. EPIPHANIUS OF SALAMIS: There is wisdom and there is wisdom. The apostle knew various kinds: that of which he spoke when he said, "The world does not know God with the wisdom of God."[14] And that which he spoke of saying, "God condemned as foolishness the wisdom of the world,"[15] or when he said that he spoke "not with the power of the flesh but by the power of God."[16] Solomon, by contrast, spoke of that wisdom of whose charm he was enamored and that he made his bride (Job asked himself, "Where can she be found, in what place of wisdom?"[17]). But did he speak of that "despised wisdom of the poor person,"[18] of the "wisdom guided by God"[19] or of the "Wisdom of the Father, the only-begotten"?[20] AN-CORATUS 42.7.[21]

THE TRUE BRIDE. CASSIODORUS: "Your wife like a fertile vine within your home, and your sons like olive plants around your table."[22] Once again the literal sense must be avoided here. We see in fact that many very holy men have neither wife nor sons and that the wicked have all that. How then can this part of the blessing be applied, which you know often does not pertain to the good but to the bad? "Wife" has the sense of sister. For this reason, as the wife of the blessed man one must understand wisdom, as Solomon says, "Who sought to take her as a wife." And elsewhere, "Love her, and she will watch over you. Do not abandon her, and she will care for you."[23] She is therefore the wife of the righteous, who captivates her husband with a chaste embrace. EXPLANATION OF THE PSALMS 127.3.[24]

Mary Is Beautiful Like Wisdom. Andrew of Crete: Foreseeing you, the prophet Isaiah exclaimed by divine inspiration, "See, the virgin will be with child."[25] And, "The root of Jesse will be raised."[26] And, "Blessed is the root of Jesse."[27] And, "A shoot shall sprout from the stump of Jesse, a shoot will grow from his roots."[28] Because of you the great Ezekiel proclaimed, "Here is the door toward the east. The door will be closed, and no one may enter by it. Only the Lord God will enter and leave by it, and the door will remain closed."[29] Prophesying of you, the beloved man[30] calls you a mountain, saying, "A stone taken from you, without human hands," hewn but not cut, removed but not split[31] by the assumption of our humanity. You are the greatness of that awesome economy "into which angels desire to look."[32] You are the beautiful dwelling of the descent of God, the land truly

---

[11]Prov 31:10, variant. [12]Jn 16:25. [13]PL 9:708. [14]1 Cor 1:21. [15]1 Cor 1:25. [16]See 2 Cor 1:12; 1 Cor 2:4. [17]Job 28:20. [18]See Eccles 9:16. [19]See Wis 7:15. [20]See 1 Cor 1:30. [21]CTP 9:105. [22]Ps 128:3 (127:3 LXX). [23]Prov 4:6. [24]CCL 98:1178-79. [25]Is 7:14. [26]Is 11:10. [27]Unidentified quotation. [28]Is 11:1. [29]Ezek 44:1-2. [30]See Dan 9:23. [31]See Dan 2:34. [32]1 Pet 1:12.

desired. In fact, "the king desired the glory of your beauty"[33] and was enamored with the riches of your virginity: he made his dwelling in you, "and dwelled among us"[34] and through you reconciled us with God the Father. You are the treasury of the "mystery hidden from ages past."[35] You are truly the living book of the spiritual Word, silently written in you with the life-giving pen of the Spirit. You alone are truly the book, written by God, of the new covenant that God once established with humanity. You are that "chariot of God in its tens of thousands,"[36] you who have led thousands of those gladdened by the incarnate one. You are Mount Zion, the fertile mountain, the rugged mountain,[37] "that God has chosen as his dwelling,"[38] from whom he who is above all being took shape and was formed in our flesh endowed with an intellectual soul. MARIAN HOMILY 8.[39]

8:7 Self-Control and Prudence, Justice and Courage

WISDOM IS AN ALLY OF ALL THE VIRTUES.
AMBROSE: Wisdom does not live with vice in any way but unites without conflict with the other virtues. Her spirit is intelligent, without blemish, trustworthy, holy, loving of the good, acute, not opposed to any good, beneficent, stable, sure, possessing all virtues and seeing all.[40] And then, "She teaches temperance and prudence, justice and fortitude." DUTIES OF THE CLERGY 2.13.65.[41]

WISDOM TEACHES THE FOUR VIRTUES.
AUGUSTINE: I have used a passage of the book of Wisdom according to the copy in our possession, where it is read, "Wisdom teaches sobriety, justice and virtue." Even using these words I have been able to speak of some truths, but, by chance, I became aware of their true meaning through an error. What is more true than the fact that Wisdom teaches the truth of contemplation, a concept that I had thought was expressed by the term "sobriety," or that it teaches uprightness of action, which I thought was indicated by the other two

terms, "justice and virtue"? But the best codices of that translation have, "It teaches sobriety and wisdom and justice and virtue." With these terms the Latin translator meant to designate the four virtues that pertain especially to philosophical language. He calls temperance sobriety, gives prudence the name of wisdom, names fortitude by the term "virtue," and has translated only justice by its own name. Much later, consulting the Greek copies, I noticed that in the book of Wisdom the four virtues are designated by the exact terms assigned them by the Greeks. RETRACTATIONS 1.7.3.[42]

8:8 Wisdom's Knowledge Is Ancient

FACT AND OPINION IN SCRIPTURE. FULGENTIUS OF RUSPE: The Scriptures are accustomed to speaking of opinion in two ways. They in fact speak of opinion both when someone thinks something that is not true and when he knows with all certainty that something is true. Blessed Stephen, in the Acts of the Apostles, speaks of an opinion concerning uncertain knowledge when he says of holy Moses, "He thought that his countrymen would have understood that God was offering them salvation through him." But, to show that this was an uncertain opinion, he adds, "But they did not understand."[43] Similarly, it is said in the same book when the angel brought blessed Peter out of the jail, "he still did not realize that what was happening through the angel was real: he thought he was having a vision."[44] In the book of Wisdom an utterly certain knowledge is given as an opinion, in the place where wisdom itself says, "And if one desires wide experience, she knows what is past and infers what is to come." What does it mean that wisdom infers, if not that it knows with all certainty? Thus also Paul, who had the mind of

[33]Ps 45:12 (44:12 LXX). [34]Jn 1:14. [35]Eph 3:9. [36]Ps 68:18 (67:18 LXX). [37]Ps 68:16 (67:16 LXX). [38]Ps 68:17 (67:17 LXX). [39]CTP 63:178-79. [40]See Wis 7:22-23. [41]PL 16:119-20. [42]NBA 2:34-37. [43]Acts 7:25. [44]Acts 12:9.

Christ,[45] spoke of thinking something that he knew with certainty, saying, "I consider, in fact, that the sufferings of the present moment are not to be compared with the future glory that will be revealed in us."[46] And neither in this case can it be said that Paul had an uncertain knowledge of these things. In fact, he had a certain knowledge of them. Similarly, blessed Jeremiah said of Christ, "He is our God, and he will not be compared with another."[47] Does "he will not be compared" perhaps not mean that another will not be known? Thus blessed Isaiah says, "Lord, beside you we have known no other. We have invoked your name."[48] AGAINST FABIANUS, FRAGMENT 11.[49]

8:13 Having Immortality

GOD ALONE IS IMMORTAL. AMBROSE: Who would dare deny the immortality of the Son, simply because he has given immortality also to others? Indeed, it is written of the wisdom of God, "Through her I will obtain immortality." But the immortality of his nature is one thing and the immortality of ours another. Perishable things must not be compared with divine things: the being of the divinity is one alone and cannot die. Thus the apostle, though knowing that the soul and the angels are immortal, preached that God alone is immortal.[50] In fact, even the soul dies: "The soul that sins will die."[51] And neither is an angel immortal by nature, because his immortality is dependent on the will of the Creator. ON THE CHRISTIAN FAITH 3.3.18-9.[52]

8:16 Companionship with No Bitterness

YEARN FOR WISDOM. PSEUDO-AUGUSTINE: Make it your purpose to possess [wisdom]. Yearn for her, burn with desire for her, be consumed by her. Deny yourself,[53] and do not deny her so as to please yourself. "In her company there is no bitterness." If you are lovers, love her. If you are beautiful, be pleasing to God. If you are young, conquer the devil. Daniel was called a man by the angel, on account of his desires.[54] What were his desires, if not those by which he fervently aspired to the beauty of wisdom? Indeed, at his young age he trampled lust underfoot, as a prisoner he crushed the pride of kings,[55] and, shut in, he shut the mouths of lions.[56] SERMON 391.5.[57]

---

[45]See 1 Cor 2:16. [46]Rom 8:18. [47]Bar 3:36. [48]Is 26:13, variant. [49]PL 65:763-64. [50]See 1 Tim 6:16. [51]Ezek 18:20, variant. [52]PL 16:593. [53]See Lk 9:23. [54]Dan 10:11, variant. [55]See Dan 6. [56]Cf. Dan 6:17-23; Bel 31-42 (Dan 14:31-42 LXX). [57]PL 39:1708-9.

8:17-21 PRAYER FOR ATTAINING WISDOM

[17]*When I considered these things inwardly,*
and thought upon them in my mind,
that in kinship with wisdom there is immortality,
[18]*and in friendship with her, pure delight,*
and in the labors of her hands, unfailing wealth,
and in the experience of her company, understanding,
and renown in sharing her words,

I went about seeking how to get her for myself.
[19]As a child I was by nature well endowed,
and a good soul fell to my lot;
[20]or rather, being good, I entered an undefiled body.
[21]But I perceived that I would not possess wisdom unless God gave her to me—
and it was a mark of insight to know whose gift she was—
so I appealed to the Lord and besought him,
and with my whole heart I said:

OVERVIEW: Perverse thoughts can lead to defiling the body and to death (FULGENTIUS). Some scriptural verses concerning the body may apply to Christ; others do not (ORIGEN, AUGUSTINE). A bodiless soul possesses no merit (AUGUSTINE). We should ask God for continence and patience (AUGUSTINE) and thank him when we receive them. Thanksgiving stems from knowledge (AUGUSTINE). Wisdom is a gift from the Son (VIGILIUS). God alone gives us continence, but we should act in accordance with the gift we receive (AUGUSTINE).

8:17 *Immortality in Wisdom*

AVOIDING PERVERSE THOUGHTS. FULGENTIUS OF RUSPE: What we think within ourselves we remember in our hearts, since mentioning both things, that is, a thought and a memory, has shown that they are not exterior but interior. It is said also in the book of Proverbs, "Son, do not let evil thoughts ensnare you, thoughts that abandon the teachings of youth and forget the divine covenant. Their dwelling is near death, and their paths with mortals, alongside the netherworld."[1] If evil thoughts, which have made their dwelling near death, are outside of death and not in it, they are certainly alive. And if they are near, but not in, the netherworld, the only remaining possibility is that what is not in death or in the netherworld would have life in heaven. For this reason it is said to God, "You have rescued my soul from death,"[2] because, through faith, he has given life to the soul, saying, "My righteous one, through faith, will live."[3] And thus it is also said to him, "From the depths

of the netherworld you have rescued my soul,"[4] since souls are rescued from the netherworld by the grace of God, so that they would live in heaven. Thus the apostle says, "Our homeland is in heaven."[5] Moreover, how was the soul, which was near death because of evil thoughts, freed from death, if it was not dead? And how was it taken from the netherworld, if it was near the netherworld but not in it? If in fact it was not in death, it was not dead. But who does not know that the soul dies through an evil will—that is, through sin—since God says, "The soul that sins will die."[6] It is therefore certain that the soul that thinks wickedly, being near death, is in death, and being near the netherworld is in the netherworld. And what does the Savior say? "What is impossible for human beings is possible for God."[7] LETTER TO MONIMUS 3.6.[8]

8:19-20 *Endowed Well by Nature*

THIS VERSE DOES NOT APPLY TO CHRIST. AUGUSTINE: After saying, "I was a child of a noble nature," explaining why he was good-natured, he immediately adds, "A good soul fell to my lot," receiving it, that is, from either the nature or the physical temperament of the father. He then says, "Being good beyond the usual, I entered an unsullied body." . . . If we wanted to understand these expressions as referring to the Lord with respect to the human nature assumed by the Word, in the same context there are

---

[1]Prov 2:17-18 LXX. [2]Ps 116:8 (114:8 LXX). [3]Rom 1:17; Hab 2:4. [4]Ps 86:13 (85:13 LXX). [5]Phil 3:20. [6]Ezek 18:20, variant. [7]Lk 18:27. [8]PL 65:203.

statements that cannot be applied to his sublime person, and especially the following. The same author, in the same book, a little above the passage we are now discussing, professes to have been formed from the blood that comes from the seed of a man.[9] This kind of birth, however, is absolutely different from the birth from the Virgin, since no Christian doubts that she conceived the flesh of Christ without the cooperation of male seed. On Genesis 10.17.31–18.32.[10]

A Verse That Applies to Christ. Origen: Do you not know that when the male child is forty days old, he is presented at the altar to be purified,[11] being impure from the conception itself, on account of both the paternal seed and the mother's womb? Thus every person is impure from his father and his mother,[12] but only my Lord Jesus entered this life purely and was not defiled in the mother. He in fact entered an undefiled body. It was he who once said through Solomon, "Or rather, being good, I entered an undefiled body." Consequently, he was not defiled in the mother, and certainly not in the father.[13] In his generation, Joseph offered nothing other than his service and affection. Thus Scripture, for his faithful service of a father, also gives him the name. Indeed, Mary says in the Gospel, "I and your father have been searching for you in sorrow."[14] Christ alone, therefore, is "the high priest who was not defiled in either the father or the mother."[15] Homilies on Leviticus 12.[16]

Souls Must Possess Bodies to Be Good. Augustine: A closer examination is needed of the passage in the book of Wisdom that says, "A good soul fell to my lot, and, because I was unusually good, I entered an undefiled body." This would in fact seem to support the opinion according to which it is believed that souls are not propagated from a single soul but enter bodies from on high. What, however, is the meaning of the phrase "a good soul fell to my lot"? One could imagine that in the creation of souls, if there is such a thing, some are good and oth-

ers not, and these are distributed on the basis of a kind of lottery, which would decide which type of soul would be infused in each individual person. Or, at the moment of conception or birth God makes some people good and others not, in such a way that each of them would receive the soul that had been assigned to them by the draw. It would be odd if the cited text were a convincing argument, at least for those who believe that souls are created in another place and sent by God, one by one, into each human body. Not so, however, for those who assert that souls are sent into bodies based on the merits from works done prior to being united to the body. Indeed, based on what criteria could it be thought that souls, some good and others not, enter bodies, except according to their actions? This is inconsistent, however, with a nature in which all souls are created by him who creates all natures good. Far be it from us, however, to contradict the apostle, who, when speaking of the twins who were still in Rachel's womb, says that, being as yet unborn, they had not done anything either good or evil. He thus concludes that, not based on works but by the grace of him who calls, Scripture says, "The older will serve the younger."[17] Let us therefore set aside for awhile the text being considered here from the book of Wisdom, because we must not ignore the opinion, correct or not, of those who believe that it especially and exclusively concerns the soul "of the mediator between God and humanity, the man Christ Jesus."[18] If necessary, we will examine the meaning of this text later in such a way that, if it cannot be applied to Christ, we will try to discover in what sense it must be understood so as to not contradict the doctrine of the apostle, starting from the hypothesis that souls have merits deriving from their actions prior to living in their bodies. On Genesis 10.7.12.[19]

---

[9]See Wis 7:2. [10]NBA 9/2:537. [11]See Lev 12:2-4. [12]See Lk 21:11. [13]See Lk 21:11. [14]Lk 2:48. [15]Lev 21:11. [16]CTP 51:258. [17]See Rom 9:10-12. [18]1 Tim 2:5. [19]NBA 9/2:511-13.

8:21 Wisdom Given by God

REQUEST CONTINENCE AND PATIENCE. AUGUSTINE: "I said, 'Have mercy on me, O Lord. Heal me, for I have sinned against you.' "[20] So— "I said." I do not, to excuse my sin, look for who sinned through me or who forced me to sin.[21] I do not say that it was by chance or that Fate wanted it. And finally, I do not say that it was the devil. Certainly the devil has power to suggest, even to cause fear and even, if he is allowed, to seriously harass. But we must ask the Lord for strength, so that the seductions do not captivate us and the difficulties do not break us. Against the seductions and threats of the enemy he gives us two virtues: continence and patience. To curb pleasures, so that prosperity does not seduce us, and to endure fears, so that difficulties do not break us. "But knowing," it is written, "that no one can be continent unless it is granted him by God," we see that he asked him, "Create a pure heart in me, O God."[22] And also, "Woe to those who have lost the strength to endure."[23] SERMON 20.2.[24]

8:21 Knowing Whose Gift Wisdom Is

KNOWLEDGE IS A SOURCE OF THANKSGIVING. AUGUSTINE: "And this also was wisdom: to know whose gift it was."[25] Therefore, if you have something from God and do not know from whom you have it, you will not receive a reward, since you will be ungrateful for it. If you do not know who gave it to you, you will not give thanks. And if you do not give thanks, you will also lose what you have. Indeed, "to him who has, more will be given." What is it to possess fully? To know from whom it comes. "But the one who does not have," that is, who does not know from whom it comes, "will lose even what he has."[26] Finally, as it also says, "And precisely this was wisdom: to know from whom the gift came."[27] The apostle Paul says this also when he exhorts us to give thanks to God in the Holy Spirit. And almost as if to respond to the ques-

tion, How will we know the difference? he adds, "that we may know all that has been given to us by God."[28] SERMON 283.2-3.[29]

WISDOM IS A GIFT FROM THE SON. VIGILIUS OF THAPSUS: There is a gift of God the Father, a gift of the Son and also a gift of the Holy Spirit. Concerning the Father the apostle says, "By grace you are saved through faith. And this is not from you, but it is the gift of God."[30] About the Son, in Solomon, "Because no one can be continent without the gift of God, and it was precisely intelligence to know from whom this gift comes." The Holy Spirit, in Acts, "Repent, and each of you be baptized in the name of Jesus Christ, for the remission of your sins. Then you will receive the gift of the Holy Spirit."[31] AGAINST VARIMADUS 3.86.[32]

ACT ACCORDING TO THE GIFT RECEIVED. AUGUSTINE: Continence is commanded of us. Where is this command? The apostle writes to Timothy, "Be continent!"[33] It is a command, a precept—we must listen to it and put it into practice. But if God does not help us, we are unable to. We try to do something about it with our will, and the will engages in the attempt. Do not presume to do it without someone to help you in your weakness! You have certainly been commanded to be continent, but listen now to another passage of Scripture: "Knowing that no one can be continent unless God grants it to him, and that it was a gift of wisdom itself to know who was the giver of this gift." So what did he do? He says, "I turned to the Lord and implored him." What need is there, my brothers and sisters, to cite many passages? Whatever command is given us, we must pray so as to be able to carry it out. Clearly not in the sense that we must go off and, as lazy people do, lay on the

---

[20]Ps 41:5 (40:5 LXX). [21]See Ps 141:4 (140:4 LXX). [22]Ps 51:12 (50:12 LXX). [23]Sir 2:14 (2:16 Vg). [24]NBA 29:373. [25]Wis 7:21. [26]Mt 13:12. [27]Wis 7:21. [28]1 Cor 2:12. [29]NBA 33:117. [30]Eph 2:8. [31]Acts 2:38. [32]PL 62:430. [33]1 Tim 5:22.

ground on our backs, saying, "God will rain food in our faces, so we'll have to do absolutely nothing." And then, when food falls in our mouths, we add, "God, stick it in our throats, as well!" We also must do something. We must apply ourselves, we must make an effort, and we must give thanks for what we have been able to do and pray for what we have been unable to do. By thanksgiving, you will avoid being condemned for ingratitude, by asking for what you do not yet have you will avoid being left empty-handed against the obstacles that hinder you. SERMONS 30.14.[34]

---

[34]NBA 35/2:805-7.

9:1-18 PRAYER FOR OBTAINING WISDOM

[1]*O God of my fathers and Lord of mercy,*
who hast made all things by thy word,
[2]*and by thy wisdom hast formed man,*
to have dominion over the creatures thou hast made,
[3]*and rule the world in holiness and righteousness,*
and pronounce judgment in uprightness of soul,
[4]*give me the wisdom that sits by thy throne,*
and do not reject me from among thy servants.
[5]*For I am thy slave and the son of thy maidservant,*
a man who is weak and short-lived,
with little understanding of judgment and laws;
[6]*for even if one is perfect among the sons of men,*
yet without the wisdom that comes from thee he will be regarded as nothing.
[7]*Thou hast chosen me to be king of thy people*
and to be judge over thy sons and daughters.
[8]*Thou hast given command to build a temple on thy holy mountain,*
and an altar in the city of thy habitation,
a copy of the holy tent which thou didst prepare from the beginning.
[9]*With thee is wisdom, who knows thy works*
and was present when thou didst make the world,
and who understands what is pleasing in thy sight
and what is right according to thy commandments.
[10]*Send her forth from the holy heavens,*
and from the throne of thy glory send her,
that she may be with me and toil,
and that I may learn what is pleasing to thee.

¹¹*For she knows and understands all things,*
and she will guide me wisely in my actions
and guard me with her glory.
¹²*Then my works will be acceptable,*
and I shall judge thy people justly,
and shall be worthy of the throne^t of my father.
¹³*For what man can learn the counsel of God?*
Or who can discern what the Lord wills?
¹⁴*For the reasoning of mortals is worthless,*
and our designs are likely to fail,
¹⁵*for a perishable body weighs down the soul,*
and this earthy tent burdens the thoughtful^u mind.
¹⁶*We can hardly guess at what is on earth,*
and what is at hand we find with labor;
but who has traced out what is in the heavens?
¹⁷*Who has learned thy counsel, unless thou hast given wisdom*
and sent thy holy Spirit from on high?
¹⁸*And thus the paths of those on earth were set right,*
and men were taught what pleases thee,
and were saved by wisdom.

t Gk *thrones*   u Or *anxious*

OVERVIEW: Wisdom is a cause of happiness (DHUODA). When we are freed from vice, we reach the condition of a king (CASSIODORUS). The Son always sees the Father (VIGILIUS). In the incarnation, the Son is sent by the Father to humankind and to specific individuals. We do not know how the resurrection of the body will occur (AUGUSTINE). Because of Christ, we no longer need to be shy before God (FULGENTIUS). Our life unfolds in uncertainty (FULGENTIUS). Human beings and angels know in different ways. Human beings are mortal. The flesh is weak when it attempts to praise God (AUGUSTINE). All human beings desire incorruption (CYRIL OF ALEXANDRIA). Praise and fasting go together (CHRYSOLOGUS). Resurrection and humility are linked (LEO). We should weep over our sins (FULGENTIUS). The just are torn between hope and temptation (PATERIUS). Everything in this life happens amidst pains and hardships (AUGUSTINE). We are called to believe with faith and not to investigate what is higher than us (CYRIL OF ALEXANDRIA). Without the Spirit, we do not understand what is spiritual (FULGENTIUS).

9:4 Give Me Wisdom

WISDOM GIVES HAPPINESS. DHUODA OF SEPTIMANIA: Therefore, son, pray, ask, as a certain author says in his verses, and repeat with him, "To you be praise, honor and power. You who are rich in all things, give me wisdom."[1] And further, "Give me wisdom, who is enthroned beside you, and do not exclude me from the number of your children. Send her from your holy heavens, send her from your glorious throne, so that she would help me and be with me in my labors, so that I may distinguish good from evil and choose what is best."[2] Love her from your youth, seek her un-

[1]Quotation made up from allusions to Ps 65:2 (64:2 LXX), Rev 4:11 and 2 Chron 1:10 (2 Par 1:10 LXX). Perhaps this phrase shows some influence from a liturgical text.   [2]See Is 7:16 and 1 Kings 3:5 (3 Kings 3:5 LXX).

ceasingly, invoking God. If God in his goodness grants her to you, love her, and she will embrace you, and you will be happier if she remains in your possession. MANUAL 3.5.[3]

9:7 Chosen to Be King of Your People

FREEDOM FROM VICE IS GENUINE KING-SHIP. CASSIODORUS: "You who give salvation to kings, who redeemed David your servant from the sword of the wicked."[4] He calls kings those righteous and true individuals who, as we have said, rule[5] their bodies with the Lord's help. The Lord gives salvation to these kings, since he has freed them from the vices of the flesh. Of them it is said in Wisdom, "He gives kings their rule."[6] EXPLANATION OF THE PSALMS 143.10.[7]

9:9 With God Is Wisdom

THE SON ALWAYS SEES THE FATHER. VIGILIUS OF THAPSUS: *Question:* Someone might say that the Son cannot, in a strict sense, see the Father, because it is written, "No one has ever seen God."[8]

Response: Let us now return to the origin of the source, by which we are taught, through the writings of both the Old and New Testaments, that the Son has always been able to see the Father, since Solomon says, "With you is wisdom, who knows your works, who was present when you created the world. She knows what is pleasing in your eyes." And the Lord, in the Gospel, said, "No one knows the Son except the Father, and no one knows the Father except the Son and the one to whom the Son wishes to reveal him."[9] And further, "No one has ever seen God; only the only-begotten Son, who is in the bosom of the Father, has revealed him."[10] And to the Jews he says further, "You do not know him. I, how-ever, know him. And if I were to say that I do not know him, I would be like you, a liar."[11] And in the same passage, "The one who is from God listens to the words of God."[12] And still, "I know him, because I come from him."[13] Therefore, we

have taught that the Son always sees the Father. How is it that you hold that he cannot see him? AGAINST VARIMADUS 1.18.[14]

9:10 Send Wisdom from Heaven

THE MISSIONS OF THE SON. AUGUSTINE: The Son is not properly said to have been "sent" by the simple fact that he was born of the Father. But he could be said to have been sent either when the Word made flesh was manifested in this world[15]—and thus he says, "I was born of the Father and have come into this world"[16]—or when in the course of time he is perceived by someone in their spirit, in the sense in which it is said, "Send her, that she might assist me and share in my labors." Now, what was born from Eternity exists eternally, for it is "the splendor of the eternal light,"[17] whereas what is sent in time is known by someone. But when the Son of God was manifest in the flesh, it is into this world that he was sent, in the fullness of time, through his birth of a woman.[18] "For, since in the wisdom of God the world, by its own wisdom, could not know God—given that the light shines in the darkness, but the darkness has not understood it—it pleased God to save those who firmly believe through the foolishness of what is preached."[19] That is, it pleased him that the Word would become flesh and dwell among us.[20] But, when in the course of time he comes forth and is perceived in the mind of someone, it is rightly said that the Word is sent, but not into this world,[21] because he clearly does not appear sensibly, that is, he is not perceived by the senses of the body. Nor are we in this world when, according to our capacity, we attain some-thing eternal with our spirit. ON THE TRINITY 4.20.28.[22]

---

[3]SC 225:156. [4]Ps 144:10 (143:10 LXX), variant. [5]This is a wordplay between *rex* ("king") and *rego* ("to govern"). [6]Wis 9:7, variant. [7]PL 70:1019. [8]Jn 1:18. [9]Lk 10:22. [10]Jn 1:18. [11]Jn 8:55. [12]Jn 8:47. [13]Jn 7:29. [14]PL 62:366. [15]See Jn 1:14. [16]Jn 16:28. [17]Wis 7:26. [18]See Gal 4:4. [19]1 Cor 1:21 and Jn 1:5. [20]See Jn 1:14. [21]See Jn 3:17. [22]NBA 4:223.

9:14 *Timid and Uncertain Reflections*

IGNORANT OF THE TIME OF THE RESURRECTION. AUGUSTINE: "And in my flesh I will see God"[23] unquestionably foretells the resurrection of the flesh. It did not say, however, "through my flesh." If it had said this, it would still be possible that Christ was meant by "God," for Christ will be seen by our flesh in the flesh. But, even understanding it of God, it is only equivalent to saying, "I will be in my flesh when I see God." And the apostle's phrase, "face to face"[24] does not lead us to believe that we will see God with the face of this body, in which we have our bodily eyes. Rather, we will see him continuously with the mind. If the face were not also that of the interior person, the apostle would not say, "And we, with unveiled faces, seeing as in a mirror the glory of the Lord, will be transformed into the same image, from glory to glory, as by the action of the Spirit of the Lord."[25] Nor do we interpret differently what is proclaimed in a psalm, "Draw near to him, and you will be enlightened, and your faces will not blush with shame."[26] One draws near to God by faith, which is certainly of the heart, not the body. But we are not unaware of the valid reasons that the spiritual body[27] has for drawing near to the Lord, since we speak of a reality outside our experience, and because in this matter an authoritative passage of sacred Scripture that can be interpreted unequivocally does not come to mind or help us. Thus, necessarily, what we read in the book of Wisdom is also true of us: "The reasonings of mortals are timid and our reflections uncertain." CITY OF GOD 22.29.4.[28]

NO LONGER TIMID BEFORE GOD. FULGENTIUS OF RUSPE: "The reasonings of mortals are timid," not with a praiseworthy fear but blamable, a fear that is not good but evil. We have been freed from such fear by the one who "through death destroyed him who has the power of death, that is, the devil, thus freeing those who, through fear of death, were held in bondage all their life long."[29] Our Redeemer clearly manifested this bondage from which he freed us and the freedom that he freely gave us, saying "If you remain faithful to my word, you will truly be my disciples. You will know the truth, and the truth will make you free."[30] To the response of the Jews, who were descendents of Abraham and had never been slaves to anyone,[31] by his response he showed at one and the same time both the condition, portending death, of their bondage, and the truth of the freedom that he had brought to his own, saying, "Truly, truly I say to you, whoever commits sin is a slave of sin. Now the slave does not remain in the house forever, but the son remains there forever. If, therefore, the Son frees you, you will be free indeed."[32] Thus, those thoughts are called "timid" by which sin is served, in those who are subject to bondage their entire lives. Paul teaches us that we have been set free from this bondage by the grace of God. "When in fact you were in bondage to sin, you were free with respect to righteousness. But what fruit did you harvest then, from things that you are now ashamed of? In fact, they lead to death. Now, however, freed from sin and made servants of God, you gather fruit leading to sanctification, with eternal life as your end."[33] See what the grace of God has given us! It has freed the timid, of whom Scripture says, "The reasonings of mortals are timid."[34] ON THE TRUTH OF PREDESTINATION 2.11.18–12.20.[35]

WE LIVE AMID UNCERTAINTY. FULGENTIUS OF RUSPE: "And our reflections are uncertain." Foresight is uncertain with regard to things that are uncertain, and those things of which we do not have secure possession are uncertain. Every day, without wanting to, we can lose what we cannot possess forever. Thus the reflections of mortals are uncertain when their souls remain

---

[23]Job 19:26 Vg, variant. [24]1 Cor 13:12. [25]2 Cor 3:18. [26]Ps 34:6 (33:6 LXX). [27]See 1 Cor 15:44. [28]NBA 5/3:411. [29]Heb 2:14-15. [30]Jn 8:31-32. [31]See Jn 8:33. [32]Jn 8:34-36. [33]Rom 6:20-22. [34]Wis 7:14. [35]CCL 91A:501-2.

enthralled by things, the possession of which can be taken from the possessor without his consent or from which the possessor can be deprived without him wishing it. ON THE TRUTH OF PREDESTINATION 2.12.20.[36]

9:15 The Soul Weighed Down

HUMAN KNOWLEDGE AND ANGELIC KNOWLEDGE DIFFER. AUGUSTINE: No knowledge can occur if there are not already objects to be known, and these objects exist in the Word, through whom all things were created,[37] prior to their existing in all the beings that have been made. Human intelligence thus first perceives creatures with the senses of the body, forming a concept of them according to the capacity of human weakness. It then looks for causes, through which it can arrive at what resides originally and immutably in the Word of God, in this way coming to see with the intellect the invisible perfections of God in the works he has made.[38] With what slowness and difficulty this happens, and how long it takes, on account of the corruptible body that weighs down the soul—even when the one who is ignorant is captivated by a most fervent desire to pursue it with insistence and perseverance! Angelic intelligence, by contrast, is united to the Word of God through pure charity. After being created according to the hierarchy from which all other creatures would proceed, it saw in the Word of God the things that would be created, before they were created. Thus things were originally made in angelic knowledge when God ordained that they exist, before they were constituted in their own nature.[39] ON GENESIS 4.32.49.[40]

THE MORTALITY OF THE HUMAN CONDITION. AUGUSTINE: We are human beings who carry the weight of the flesh along the paths of this life and who, though we are reborn from the seed of the Word of God, have nonetheless been renewed in Christ[41] in such a way as to not yet be entirely stripped of Adam.[42] In fact, it seems clear and evident that what is mortal and corruptible in us, weighing down the soul, comes from Adam. What is spiritual in us, lifting the soul, is the gift and mercy of God. He sent his only Son so that he might share with us in our death[43] and lead us to his immortality. TRACTATES ON THE GOSPEL OF JOHN 21.1.[44]

THE FLESH IS WEAK IN ITS PRAISE OF GOD. AUGUSTINE: "Praise the Lord, my soul."[45] Your soul will answer you, I will praise him as best I can, poorly, feebly, weakly. Why? Because as long as we are united to the body we are in exile, far from the Lord.[46] Why do you praise the Lord in this manner, not giving him a perfect and continuous praise? Ask the Scriptures. It is because "the corruptible body weighs down the soul, and the earthly dwelling burdens the mind with many thoughts." Take from me this body that weighs down the soul, and I will praise the Lord. Free me from this dwelling that pushes the mind downward with its many thoughts. From a multitude of things I will recollect myself into unity—then I will praise the Lord. But, as long as I am as I am, I cannot praise him. I am too weighed down. And what then? Will you remain silent and refuse to praise the Lord perfectly? "I will praise the Lord in my life."[47] EXPOSITIONS OF THE PSALMS 145.6.[48]

THE DESIRE FOR INCORRUPTION. CYRIL OF ALEXANDRIA: "Therefore we groan in our present state, desirous to be clothed with our heavenly body."[49] Thus we groan, as those weighed down by corruption. We long to put on the dwelling that is on high and that comes from heaven, which is to say immortality.[50] We groan, not seeking freedom from what now exists but rather asking that it be clothed with incorruptibility, which is a dwelling not made by human

---

[36]CCL 91A:502. [37]See Jn 1:3. [38]See Rom 1:20. [39]See Gen 1:3, etc. [40]NBA 9/2:217-19. [41]See 2 Cor 5:17. [42]See Col 3:9. [43]See 2 Cor 4:11. [44]NBA 24:485. [45]Ps 146:1 (145:1 LXX). [46]See 2 Cor 5:6. [47]Ps 146:2 (145:2 LXX). [48]NBA 28:737. [49]2 Cor 5:2. [50]See 1 Cor 15:53-54.

hands.[51] "And if we have clothed ourselves with it, we will not be found naked."[52] It is indeed true that "a corruptible body weighs down the soul." Let us make the oppression of this corruption an occasion for groaning. Let us long to put on the dwelling that is above and comes from heaven, that is, immortality.[53] What, then, does "to put on" mean, if not that incorruptibility will encompass the present body? FRAGMENT ON 2 CORINTHIANS 5.2.[54]

PRAISE OF FASTING. PETER CHRYSOLOGUS: "How many of my father's servants have bread in abundance, while here I am dying of hunger!"[55] Hunger calls back those whom surfeit had scattered. Hunger made him recognize the father, whom abundance had led to see only the parent. And if involuntary hunger bore such fruit, find out for yourselves what voluntary fasting can produce. A full belly spurs the heart to vice, oppressing the mind so that it cannot taste heavenly piety. "The body," it says, "which decays, weighs down the soul and burdens the mind, which harbors many thoughts." Thus also the Lord says, "Do not let your hearts be weighed down with carousing and drunkenness."[56] The stomach must therefore be kept empty with the temperance of fasting. The lightened soul can then tend upward, rising to virtues and freeing itself, winging toward the author of piety. This is confirmed by Elijah, who, purified by continual fasting,[57] rose from the weight of the flesh toward heaven, conquering death.[58] SERMONS 2.1.[59]

HUMILITY IS A CAUSE OF RESURRECTION. LEO THE GREAT: Then the Lord says, "Blessed are the meek, for they shall inherit the earth."[60] The earth has been promised to the gentle and the meek, the humble and the modest, those willing to put up with every kind of injury. And one should not think that this inheritance is small or to be disdained, as if it were something distinct from our heavenly dwelling, given that it is not said that anyone else will enter the kingdom of heaven. Therefore, the earth promised to the meek, and as a possession to the gentle, is the flesh of the saints, which will be transformed by a joyous resurrection on account of their humility and clothed with the glory of immortality. And it will no longer be opposed to the spirit in anything,[61] finding the harmony of a perfect unity with the will of the soul. Then the exterior person will be the tranquil and uncontested possession of the interior.[62] Then the mind that seeks to see God will no longer be impeded by human weakness. And it will no longer be necessary to say, "A corruptible body weighs down the soul, and the earthy tent burdens the mind with many thoughts," since the earth will no longer oppose itself to its inhabitant, nor will it try to do anything not under the control of the one who governs it. "The meek will inherit it" with an endless peace, and their title will never in any way fail, since "this corruptible body will be clothed with incorruptibility, and this mortal body will be clothed with immortality."[63] What was a danger will be changed into a reward, and what was a burden will become an honor.[64] SERMONS 95.5.[65]

WEEPING OVER OUR SINS. FULGENTIUS OF RUSPE: Tears that spring from compunction of heart defeat the enemy and gain for us the gift of a victorious happiness. In fact, those who "go out weeping, scattering their seeds, will return rejoicing, carrying their sheaves."[66] How wisely the holy prophet teaches that the seeds of good works must be watered with rivers of tears! And in fact, no seed germinates without being watered. Nor does a seed bear fruit if it has been without the benefit of water. Thus we also, if we wish to harvest the fruits of our seeds, should not cease watering them with tears, which should spring from the heart rather

---

[51]See 2 Cor 5:1. [52]2 Cor 5:3, variant. [53]See 1 Cor 15:53-54. [54]Pusey 350. [55]Lk 15:17. [56]Lk 21:34. [57]See 1 Kings 19:5-8 (3 Kings 19:5-8 LXX). [58]See 2 Kings 2:11 (4 Kings 2:11 LXX). [59]CTP 12:71-72. [60]Mt 5:5. [61]See Gal 5:17. [62]See 2 Cor 4:16. [63]1 Cor 15:53. [64]This is a common Latin wordplay between *onus* ("burden") and *honor* ("honor"). [65]CCL 138A:586-87. [66]Ps 126:6 (125:6 LXX).

than the body. This, in fact, is why we are told through the prophet to rend our hearts, not our garments.[67] And we can do this only if we recall that we often sin, if not in deeds, at least in our thoughts. Since "the earthly tabernacle oppresses the mind, which stirs up many thoughts," and our earth does not cease to germinate thorns and difficulties for us,[68] in the end we cannot eat our bread if we have not endured the sweat of our brow and hard work.[69] LETTERS 4.9.5.[70]

CHOOSE BETWEEN HOPE AND TEMPTATIONS.

PATERIUS: The saints are certain of their hope, even if, as the Psalmist gives them voice, they always fear temptation. "Let my heart rejoice that it may fear your name."[71] Note that it does not say, "Let my heart rejoice because it feels secure," but "Let it rejoice that it may fear." They remember, in fact, that though their works may have been successful, they are still in this life, about which Job says, "Life on earth is a trial."[72] They have also remembered what is written, "A corruptible body weighs down the soul, and the earthy tent burdens the mind with many thoughts." They have remembered and they fear, and they don't dare convince themselves they are secure. Rather, poised between the joy of hope and the fear of temptation, they trust and they fear, they feel comforted and they hesitate, they are certain and uncertain. EXPOSITION ON THE OLD AND NEW TESTAMENT 179, ON PSALM 85:11.[73]

9:16 What Is on Earth

THE PRESENT LIFE IS FULL OF HARDSHIP.

AUGUSTINE: Precisely by the name of sweat[74] the sacred Scripture has called suffering in general, from which no one is exempt, because, whereas some suffer from difficult operations, others do so from excruciating cures. The studies of all those wishing to learn partake of these same sufferings. And what earth gives birth to thorns[75] if not this one, which was not made burdensome by its maker when he created the first man?

Now, however, according to what was written, "a corruptible body weighs down the soul, and the tent of clay burdens the mind with many thoughts. We barely grasp earthly things and laboriously discover what is at hand." Whether or not, then, the doctrines that a person studies are useful, it is necessary that he suffer, since a corruptible body weighs down the soul. For him too, this earth gives birth to thorns. Nor can one say that the rich are exempt from these thorns, especially since in the Gospel the thorns that suffocate the seeds that were sown, so they do not reach fruitfulness, were explained by the teacher-God as the cares of this life and anxiety over riches.[76] UNFINISHED TRACTATE AGAINST JULIAN 6.29.[77]

WE SHOULD NOT PRY. CYRIL OF ALEXANDRIA:

Is it not perhaps superfluous and extremely dangerous to have to inquire into what is beyond our logical capacities and exceeds our intelligence? How can what God works, mysteriously, be clear to us? Moreover, what eye of the heart can be so acute as to be able to gaze on God? And, indeed, who could understand things that are far superior to us, even if someone were to speak about and explain them? In fact, our Lord Jesus Christ once spoke to Nicodemus of spiritual rebirth, saying, "Truly, truly I say to you, if a person is not born again, he cannot enter the kingdom of God,"[78] etc. But because he understood nothing, in the end Christ, revealing the coarseness of human intelligence and how far it is below the subtlety of certain concepts, says, "If you do not believe when I spoke to you of earthly things, how will you believe if I speak to you of heavenly things?"[79] Then he adds, "Truly, truly I say to you: we speak of what we know and testify to what we have seen, but no one accepts our testimony."[80] As you can see, what is above us remains inscrutable. If it is true, as it is written,

---

[67]See Joel 2:13. [68]See Gen 3:18. [69]See Gen 3:19. [70]CTP 149:126. [71]Ps 86:11 (85:11 LXX), variant. [72]Job 7:1, variant. [73]PL 79:871. [74]See Gen 3:19. [75]See Gen 3:18. [76]See Mt 13:22 par. [77]NBA 19/2:1185. [78]Jn 3:3, 5. [79]Jn 3:12. [80]Jn 3:11, 32.

that "only with difficulty do we know the things at hand," should we not think, without making further inquiries or vain research, that faith is indispensable for everything that surpasses our logical capacities? In this area, the most splendid ornament is prudence. COMMENTARY ON ROMANS 10.[81]

9:17 Who Has Learned Your Counsel?

SPIRITUAL THINGS ARE KNOWN ONLY IN THE SPIRIT. FULGENTIUS OF RUSPE: We must think that in any case heretics are carnal and earthly and therefore incapable of spiritual things. The apostle says of them, "The animal person, however, does not understand the things of the Spirit of God. They are foolishness to him, and he is not able to understand them, because they can be judged only through the Spirit."[82] Thus the apostle's authority affirms that heretics are above all carnal and earthly. In fact, blessed Paul also numbers heresy among the works of the flesh.[83] And the blessed apostle Jude also calls those who separate from the church earthly, saying, "These are those who provoke divisions, natural people, devoid of the Spirit."[84] This is precisely what we saw the apostle Paul say: "The animal person, however, does not understand the things of the Spirit of God."[85] We must not be surprised, then, that those who do not have the Spirit of God are incapable of comprehending divine things. In fact, it is written in the book of Wisdom, "Who has known your thoughts, if you have not granted him wisdom and sent him your holy spirit from on high?" Therefore the holy apostle further states that the things of God are revealed only by the Holy Spirit when he says, "But God revealed these to us by his Spirit."[86] And a little later he continues, "Now, we have not received the spirit of the world but the Spirit of God, to know all that God has given to us."[87] BOOK TO VICTOR AGAINST THE SERMON OF FASTIDIOSUS THE ARIAN 18.2-3.[88]

---

[81]CTP 95:110. [82]1 Cor 2:14. In the Latin version, the word *psychikos* ("animated") is translated as *animal* ("an animal"), but Paul's text designates the "natural" human being, that is, the one whose soul has not been illuminated by the Spirit. [83]See Gal 5:19-20. [84]Jude 19. [85]1 Cor 2:14. [86]1 Cor 2:10. [87]1 Cor 2:12. [88]CCL 91:303.

10:1-14 WISDOM IN HISTORY: FROM ADAM UNTIL JOSEPH

¹Wisdom[v] protected the first-formed father of the world, when he alone had been created;
she delivered him from his transgression,
²and gave him strength to rule all things.
³But when an unrighteous man departed from her in his anger,
he perished because in rage he slew his brother.
⁴When the earth was flooded because of him, wisdom again saved it,
steering the righteous man by a paltry piece of wood.

⁵Wisdom[w] also, when the nations in wicked agreement had been confounded,

recognized the righteous man and preserved him blameless before God,
and kept him strong in the face of his compassion for his child.

⁶Wisdom*w* rescued a righteous man when the ungodly were perishing;
he escaped the fire that descended on the Five Cities.*x*
⁷Evidence of their wickedness still remains:
a continually smoking wasteland,
plants bearing fruit that does not ripen,
and a pillar of salt standing as a monument to an unbelieving soul.
⁸For because they passed wisdom by,
they not only were hindered from recognizing the good,
but also left for mankind a reminder of their folly,
so that their failures could never go unnoticed.

⁹Wisdom rescued from troubles those who served her.
¹⁰When a righteous man fled from his brother's wrath,
she guided him on straight paths;
she showed him the kingdom of God,
and gave him knowledge of angels;*y*
she prospered him in his labors,
and increased the fruit of his toil.
¹¹When his oppressors were covetous,
she stood by him and made him rich.
¹²She protected him from his enemies,
and kept him safe from those who lay in wait for him;
in his arduous contest she gave him the victory,
so that he might learn that godliness is more powerful than anything.

¹³When a righteous man was sold, wisdom*z* did not desert him,
but delivered him from sin.
She descended with him into the dungeon,
¹⁴and when he was in prison she did not leave him,
until she brought him the scepter of a kingdom
and authority over his masters.
Those who accused him she showed to be false,
and she gave him everlasting honor.

v Gk She   w Gk She   x Or Pentapolis   y Or of holy things   z Gk she

OVERVIEW: Adam, too, was freed by Christ. The book of Wisdom professed that Adam would be pardoned. Human beings exercise dominion over creation (AUGUSTINE). Pagan wisdom and the riches of this world are useless (CASSIODORUS). The patriarch Joseph prefigures Christ's passion (QUODVULTDEUS).

10:1 Delivered from Transgression

ADAM WAS LIBERATED BY CHRIST. AUGUSTINE: The Christ, who died for us, descended into the realms of death, not of necessity but by power, and loosed the pains of hell.[1] In this way it must be understood that Wisdom released Adam from his crime. Not without reason does the church believe that he was released from those bonds by the holy flesh of the only Son of God—of whom Adam was the progenitor, being the father of the human race and thus also the father of the Christ, who was made man for the salvation of human beings—not by his own merit but by the grace of God in Jesus Christ our Lord. UNFINISHED TRACTATE AGAINST JULIAN 6.22.[2]

WISDOM PROPHESIED PARDON. AUGUSTINE: It must be understood that, according to the book of Wisdom, Adam was released from his crime. That book does not say this as an accomplished fact, but predicted it as future, though using the past tense. It says, "He freed him from his fall," just as it was said, "They have pierced my hands,"[3] and all the other events that are said there of the future using the verbal form of the past tense. UNFINISHED TRACTATE AGAINST JULIAN 6.30.[4]

10:2 Strength to Rule All Things

HUMANS RULE OVER CREATION. AUGUSTINE: There is no doubt that the man was made in the image of God[5] and that God, as is written in another text, "gave him power to rule all things." Yes, all things were under him, but above him was the One who created all. And the man had responsibility for everything that was under him, but even more so, he had to attend to the One above him. Keeping in mind the One who was above him, he would have peacefully dominated what was below him. Separating himself from the One who was above him, he came to be dominated by what was below. Take the example of three people. One of them has a servant and also a master (it often happens that wealthy servants have servants under them). Note well: such a person has a servant and a master. He

is subject to the one and commands the other. With respect to the servant he is superior, with respect to the master he is inferior. In the third position we place the one who is the servant of the servant, and in the first position the one who is the master of the master. In the middle is the one who is servant and master—the master of his servant and the servant of his master. The third is therefore only a servant, the first only a master, whereas the one in the middle is both servant and master. He will possess his servant peacefully if he is not in conflict with his master. And yet we have spoken of three persons, all three of the same race, all three of the same essence, all three of the same nature. The same cannot be said of the following three: God, human beings and creatures inferior to human beings. Of an entirely different condition and of a very different substance are the maker and what is made, the producer and the product, the craftsman and his work, the creator and his creature. As for created things, by a generic term they are all called creatures, but they differ between them in nature, dignity, merits and condition. NEWLY DISCOVERED SERMONS 21.5.[6]

10:8 Failures Could Not Go Unnoticed

THE VANITY OF WORLDLY RICHES AND WISDOM. CASSIODORUS: "They will see the death of the wise. The foolish and the senseless will perish as well, and they will leave their riches to others."[7] He thus arrives at the second way of teaching when he says that the sinners of this world will die along with the wise and that their riches, which they loved exceedingly, will be given as an inheritance not to their own but to strangers, which hurts even more. Not even their own heirs would enjoy the possession of those things for which they committed every kind of sin, as Solomon says: "Not even in the things in

---

[1]See Acts 2:24. [2]NBA 19/2:1129. [3]Ps 22:17 (21:17 LXX). [4]NBA 19/2:1195. [5]See Gen 1:26-27. [6]NBA 35/2:407-9. [7]Ps 49:11 (48:11 LXX).

which they sinned were they able to rejoice."[8] The sinner sees that the wise of this world, like, for example, Solon of Athens, Philo of Lacedemonia, Aristippus, and all the others who were highly praised for worldly wisdom, are not free from death. Rather, he sees that they die, like all those whom he considered to be partakers of divine Wisdom. It then says that "the foolish and the senseless will perish together." It is indeed necessary that the foolish and the senseless perish in desperation, knowing that their wise ones die. Nevertheless, these things must be understood in a more spiritual way. The senseless are those who did not want to listen to the proclamations of the prophets. Rightly called foolish are those who did not want to receive Christ the Lord, even when he came in person. They will perish together, because they will be condemned in the future judgment. The Jews left their riches to strangers, since, having despised the Lord and Savior, the rewards of their salvation passed to other peoples. Explanation of the Psalms 48.11.[9]

10:14 Joseph in Prison

Joseph Prefigures Christ. Quodvultdeus: Joseph is put in prison.[10] Our Joseph, the Christ, as Isaiah says, "was numbered among the wicked."[11] The innocent man is led among the guilty by the wisdom of God, which "de-scended with him," as it was written, "into the pit and did not abandon him in chains." Our Joseph, Christ, exclaims, "I have become like a man without strength, free among the dead."[12] What follows—that is, that the chief jailer saw how full of grace Joseph was and gave all of the keys and all oversight into his hands[13]—had to happen in the sense that, to him before whom the heavens bowed down in the figures of the sun, the stars and the moon, and the earth in the figure of the sheaves,[14] would also submit the subterranean creatures of the prison, so that before our Joseph, Christ, "every knee would bow, of heavenly beings, of earthly beings and of those under the earth."[15] Nor do I find it incompatible with the mystery of our Lord's passion that two of Pharaoh's eunuchs were thrown into prison with him,[16] so that in a certain sense the number of the three crucified would be fulfilled. Our Joseph, Christ, revealing the mysteries, had to punish the one with a merited punishment and save the other by a gratuitous grace.[17] These sacred acts were done then under the veil of allegory, so that the full revelation would be reserved to us. The Book of Promises and Predictions of God 1.28.40.[18]

---

[8]Wis 10:8, variant. [9]CCL 97:435. [10]See Gen 39:20. [11]Is 53:12. [12]Ps 88:5 (87:5 lxx). [13]See Gen 39:21-23. [14]See Gen 37:7. [15]Phil 2:10. [16]See Gen 40:3. [17]See Lk 23:33, 39-43; Gen 40:21-22. [18]CTP 82:96.

10:15–11:3 MOSES AND EXODUS

¹⁵*A holy people and blameless race*
wisdom^a delivered from a nation of oppressors.
¹⁶*She entered the soul of a servant of the Lord,*
and withstood dread kings with wonders and signs.
¹⁷*She gave holy men the reward of their labors;*
she guided them along a marvelous way,
and became a shelter to them by day,
and a starry flame through the night.
¹⁸*She brought them over the Red Sea,*
and led them through deep waters;
¹⁹*but she drowned their enemies,*
and cast them up from the depth of the sea.
²⁰*Therefore the righteous plundered the ungodly;*
they sang hymns, O Lord, to thy holy name,
and praised with one accord thy defending hand,
²¹*because wisdom opened the mouth of the dumb,*
and made the tongues of babes speak clearly.

11 *Wisdom^a prospered their works by the hand of a holy prophet.*
²*They journeyed through an uninhabited wilderness,*
and pitched their tents in untrodden places.
³*They withstood their enemies and fought off their foes.*

a Gk *she*

OVERVIEW: Wisdom enters the souls of human beings (FULGENTIUS). The exodus from Egypt is a mystical figure of the Eucharist (QUODVULTDEUS). Wisdom leads to eternal life (DHUODA). Faith is wisdom's gift (FULGENTIUS). God's greatness calls forth our praise (PSEUDO-AUGUSTINE).

10:16 Wisdom Enters the Soul

WISDOM IS INTERIOR. FULGENTIUS OF RUSPE: We read that it is written of wisdom, "Its memory is immortal, by the fact that it is recognized by God and by human beings."[1] How can it be recognized by human beings if it is not interior to them, but exterior? It cannot be recognized if it does not enter the soul of the person. It is said of wisdom, "Though remaining in itself, it renews all, and through the ages it enters holy souls."[2] And so that we should not think that to move into souls is something different than to enter them, the text of Scripture refers to it again with these words, "It freed a holy people and a blameless race from

---

[1]Wis 4:1. [2]Wis 7:27.

a nation of oppressors. It entered the soul of a servant of the Lord and withstood fearsome kings with wonders and signs." This entry into souls is also proclaimed in the Apocalypse of John: "See, I stand at the door and knock. If anyone listens to my voice and opens to me, I will come to him, I will sup with him, and he with me."[3] By this same movement the Father and the Son enter the one who loves them, and they establish their dwelling in him, as the Son says: "If anyone loves me, he will keep my word, and the Father will love him, and we will come to him and make our dwelling with him."[4] And if this coming of the Father and the Son to the one with whom they make their dwelling were exterior and not interior, we would then like to know: where will they come to, and where will they make their dwelling with him? Moreover, we have seen that Christ dwells interiorly in his faithful ones, as Paul proclaims, saying, "That Christ would dwell in your hearts through faith."[5] Letter to Monimus 3.5.[6]

10:17 The Reward of One's Labors

The Exodus from Egypt. Quodvultdeus: God gives to Moses the following instructions for the celebration of the Passover—that is, of that passage that represents all of the action of our faith and the mystery of the passion of the Lord. The Jews were to ask the Egyptians for gold and silver objects and clothing and, carrying them away, to despoil the Egyptians of what they had given them under the devastating shock of the loss of the firstborn.[7] Fearing also for themselves, the Egyptians sent the Jews away with all they had given them,[8] so that "to the just," as the prophet says, would be restored "the reward of their labors." Considering the two cities they built for the Egyptians,[9] the spoils the Jews carried away in no way constitute a theft but only the restitution of what was owed them. In fact, this passage had a mystical sense. According to the divine command, they must slay an unblemished year-old lamb under the tent,[10]

bathing the doorposts of the house with its blood.[11] None of its bones are to be broken.[12] It must be eaten with bitter herbs and unleavened bread,[13] with loins girded, in all haste.[14] Nothing must be left for the next day.[15] The authority of the Gospel tells how all of these instructions, which had a symbolic sense, are to be fulfilled. It commands us to eat the flesh of lambs until that day that will have no sunset—that is, until the resurrection—"not with the old yeast but with the unleavened bread of purity and truth."[16] We are to eat after marking with his blood the doorposts[17] of those on whose foreheads his cross will shine, eating "with bitter herbs,"[18] it says, that is, with those who pass a bitter life in grief. But these latter are blessed, because they will be consoled.[19] The Book of Promises and Predictions of God 1.37.53.[20]

A Well of Eternal Life. Dhuoda of Septimania: If you love God with your whole heart[21] and meditate on the books of the Scriptures of the Old and New Testaments, committing yourself to doing what you have read, then the spirit of wisdom will rest on you.[22] Indeed, "all wisdom comes from the Lord" (and it could not be otherwise), since, "it has always been with him and exists from before time."[23] If you seek it and keep it once you find it, you will be blessed and can be called wise. Moreover, "it will guide you on a marvelous way," sustaining and protecting you with its holy right hand. It will bring you to eternal life, which gives happiness, and will let you feel its embrace, and on you will rest the spirit of wisdom.[24] Manual 4.4.[25]

10:21 Wisdom Opens the Mouth of the Speechless

---

[3]Rev 3:20. [4]Jn 14:23. [5]Eph 3:17. [6]PL 65:200. [7]See Ex 12:35-36. [8]See Ex 12:31-33. [9]See Ex 1:11. [10]See Ex 12:5. [11]See Ex 12:7. [12]See Ex 12:10. [13]See Ex 12:8. [14]See Ex 12:11. [15]See Ex 12:10. [16]1 Cor 5:8. [17]See Ex 12:7. [18]See Ex 12:8. [19]See Mt 5:4. [20]CTP 82:113-14. [21]See Mt 22:37 par. [22]See Is 11:2. [23]Sir 1:1. [24]See Is 11:2. [25]SC 225:214.

FAITH IS A GIFT FROM WISDOM. FULGENTIUS OF RUSPE: It is written that "wisdom opened the mouth of the mute and loosed the tongues of infants." Wisdom indeed opened the mouths of the mute, so the incredulous might believe, and loosed the tongues of infants, so that they might preach what they believed. Therefore, not without reason does Paul attribute his faith and his ability to speak to the gift of the Holy Spirit, saying, "Moved by that same spirit of faith of which it is written, 'I believed, therefore I spoke,' we also believe, and therefore we speak."[26] A person believes with the will, and with the will speaks. The human will, however, cannot possess these things of its own if they are not given by God, "because wisdom opens the mouth of the mute and loosens the tongue of infants." ON THE TRUTH OF PREDESTINATION 2.6.9.[27]

WE MUST PRAISE GOD. PSEUDO-AUGUSTINE: If only I could sing like the choirs of angels! Oh, with what devotion I would pour myself out in your praises, reciting unceasingly and most excellently the hymn of your glory in the middle of the assembly! Will I perhaps keep silent because I cannot sing like them? Lord, woe to those who keep silent on your account, because "you open the mouth of the mute and loosen the tongue of infants." Since infants can only babble your praises, I ask you to accept the sacrifice from the tip of my tongue, from the love of my heart. MIRROR 23.[28]

---

[26]2 Cor 4:13. [27]PL 65:632. [28]PL 40:983-84.

11:4-14* THE MIRACLE OF WATER

[4]*When they thirsted they called upon thee,*
and water was given them out of flinty rock,
and slaking of thirst from hard stone.
[5]*For through the very things by which their enemies were punished,*
they themselves received benefit in their need.
[6]*Instead of the fountain of an ever-flowing river,*
stirred up and defiled with blood
[7]*in rebuke for the decree to slay the infants,*
thou gavest them abundant water unexpectedly,
[8]*showing by their thirst at that time*
how thou didst punish their enemies.
[9]*For when they were tried, though they were being disciplined in mercy,*
they learned how the ungodly were tormented when judged in wrath.
[10]*For thou didst test them as a father does in warning,*
but thou didst examine the ungodly[b] as a stern king does in condemnation.
[11]*Whether absent or present, they were equally distressed,*
[12]*for a twofold grief possessed them,*
and a groaning at the memory of what had occurred.

13For when they heard that through their own punishments
the righteous[c] had received benefit, they perceived it was the Lord's doing.
14For though they had mockingly rejected him who long before had been cast out and exposed,
at the end of the events they marveled at him,
for their thirst was not like that of the righteous.

b Gk *those*   c Gk *they*   * Wis 11:4-15 Vg, since it divides Wis 11:5 into two verses.

OVERVIEW: The rock is Christ. He gives us the water of salvation announced by Scripture (RABANUS MAURUS).

11:4 Water from the Rock

THE ROCK IS CHRIST. RABANUS MAURUS: What that rock from which the Israelites drank was to signify is attested to by Paul with these words, "They drank from a spiritual rock that accompanied them, and that rock was the Christ."[1] This rock, struck by the wood of the cross and announced by the spirits (that is, by the writings) of the prophets, poured forth the living water that fills all of the elect, restoring and satisfying them for all eternity.[2] For this reason the Truth says, "Whoever thirsts, let him come to me and drink, and rivers of living water will flow from his heart."[3] And elsewhere, "Whoever drinks of the water that I will give him, the water that I will give him will become in him a spring of water, welling up for eternal life."[4] This rock is also called most high,[5] because in it is contained the immense grace of the Spirit. And also hard rock, since it is firm and stable, and whoever is wise builds his house on it in such a way that no storm can shake it.[6] ON ECCLESIASTICUS 2.8.[7]

11:7 Abundant Water Given Unexpectedly

THE CUP OF SALVATION. RABANUS MAURUS: It indicates in a mysterious way that the people of God and the sheep of his pasture,[8] whom the great Shepherd[9] rescued with the price of his blood,[10] will have their thirst quenched with the fountain of living water[11] and that their persecu-

tors, falling into eternal destitution, will be given over to everlasting death. Similar to this passage is the one pronounced by the Lord through Isaiah against his adversaries: "See, my servants will eat, and you will be hungry. See, my servants will drink and you will be thirsty. See, my servants will rejoice and you will be downcast. See, my servants will shout for joy of heart, but you will cry out for sorrow of heart and howl for anguish of spirit."[12] One must therefore receive that drink that rises from the springs of Israel, and the one who drinks it will have in himself a "spring of water that wells up for eternal life,"[13] that drink that the Savior promises he will drink together with the apostles in the kingdom of the Father.[14] It gladdens the hearts of human beings,[15] so that those who drink it can say, "Blessed are they who hunger and thirst for righteousness."[16] And, full of the Holy Spirit, the mother of the Lord prophesied, "He has filled the hungry with good things," those who previously did not have the food of the Lord, and "he has sent the rich away empty,"[17] those who did everything they could to do away with him, rejecting the one whom they recognized to be a prophet. Of them, that is, of the Jewish people, the psalmist elsewhere sings, "The rich grow poor and are hungry." "But those who seek the Lord," that is, the multitude of the peoples, "lack nothing."[18] ON ECCLESIASTICUS 2.8.[19]

---

[1]1 Cor 10:4. [2]See Jn 4:10. [3]Jn 7:37-38. [4]Jn 4:14. [5]Rabanus Maurus explains literally the text of the Vulgate. [6]See Mt 7:24-25; Lk 6:48. [7]PL 109:719. [8]See Jn 10:16. [9]See 1 Pet 5:4. [10]See 1 Cor 6:20; 7:23. [11]See Jn 4:11. [12]Is 65:13-14. [13]Jn 4:14. [14]See Mt 26:29; Mk 14:25; Lk 22:18. [15]See Ps 104:15 (103:15 LXX). [16]Mt 5:6. [17]Lk 1:53. [18]Ps 34:11 (33:11 LXX). [19]PL 109:720.

11:15-20* DIVINE MODERATION TOWARD EGYPT

¹⁵*In return for their foolish and wicked thoughts,*
which led them astray to worship irrational serpents and worthless animals,
thou didst send upon them a multitude of irrational creatures to punish them,
¹⁶*that they might learn that one is punished by the very things by which he sins.*
¹⁷*For thy all-powerful hand,*
which created the world out of formless matter,
did not lack the means to send upon them a multitude of bears, or bold lions,
¹⁸*or newly created unknown beasts full of rage,*
or such as breathe out fiery breath,
or belch forth a thick pall of smoke,
or flash terrible sparks from their eyes;
¹⁹*not only could their damage exterminate men,*^d
but the mere sight of them could kill by fright.
²⁰*Even apart from these, men*^e *could fall at a single breath*
when pursued by justice
and scattered by the breath of thy power.
But thou hast arranged all things by measure and number and weight.

d Gk *them*   e Gk *they*   * Wis 11:16 21 Vg.

OVERVIEW: Riches and goods can lead to torment from the devil (CASSIAN). Zachariah, the father of John the Baptist, was punished for his foolish words (SOPHRONIUS). The wonders of creation elicit our amazement. God also created formless matter (AUGUSTINE). He created the world and transforms it (HESYCHIUS). According to the Scripture, the Son created everything (VIGILIUS). He created all the elements at once (PSEUDO-AUGUSTINE). Everything was made in the Word and disposed by God. God reveals himself to the creatures (AUGUSTINE). What is visible and what is invisible bears the image of God (FULGENTIUS). The order of the world was recognized also by the pagan philosophers (CASSIODORUS).

11:16 Punished by One's Sins

TIED TO THE DEVIL BY OUR RICHES AND GOODS. JOHN CASSIAN: If it happens that the yoke of Christ seems to us neither light nor sweet,[1] this must be attributed to our obstinacy. Affected as we are by diffidence and by lack of faith regarding his precept, indeed his counsel, which says, "If you want to be perfect, go, sell (that is, abandon) all of your belongings, then come and follow me,"[2] we rebel with a futile perverseness, turning again to the pursuit of earthly goods. And then, once the devil has our soul bound by these chains, what else does he need to do, when he wants to remove our spiritual joy, than to sadden us by the decrease or the total loss of earthly goods? He seeks a very precise goal with his clever deceptions. Indeed, once the

[1]See Mt 11:30. [2]Mt 19:21.

sweetness of the Savior's yoke and the lightness of his burden become heavy (through the perversity of our vicious longing), once we are trapped by the snares of those riches we have acquired in view of our rest and tranquility, will he not continuously torment us with the lash of worldly cares, drawing from our very selves the reasons for tearing us to bits? "Everyone is caught in the snares of his sins."[3] The prophet also says, "Look, all you who light the fire and surround yourselves with flames: walk by the heat of your fire, in the midst of the flames you have ignited."[4] Solomon also testifies to this: "Everyone will be punished through that by which he has sinned." The pleasures that we enjoy end in torments, and the delights and pleasures of the body will turn against their author like executioners. CONFERENCES 3.24.24.[5]

THE SILENCE OF ZECHARIAH. SOPHRONIUS OF JERUSALEM: Silence was imposed on Zechariah, symbolizing the silence of the Mosaic law. Having appeared to us in the flesh,[6] Christ, like a great legislator, rendered the law mute, wanting to himself be the model of the law. Zechariah, in fact, put his faith in the angel who purified his silence: "I am Gabriel, who stands before the face of God, and I have been sent to speak with you and to bring you this joyful news. And see, you will be mute and unable to talk until the day on which these things take place, because you have not believed my words, which will be fulfilled at their proper time."[7] Very fittingly was he punished by the loss of his voice, since the Creator of voices was to be born. Not only did he have to endure being the symbol of those who do not believe in the law, but he also did not believe that the voice that was commanded to announce these things had come by the work of the Creator, and, not believing the angel's words, rightly was he deprived of his voice. In fact, as the wise Solomon says, "By those very things through which one sins, he is later punished," so that he might learn to believe in the voice that comes from the wilderness.[8] HOMILY 6.8.[9]

11:17 God Created the World Out of Formless Matter

AMAZEMENT PROVOKED BY THE WONDERS OF CREATION. AUGUSTINE: But the "heaven of the heavens" belongs to you, Lord. And the earth that you assigned "to the children of mortals,"[10] for them to see and to touch, was not the one that we now see and touch. "It was invisible and confused," an abyss, on which no light shone. In other words, "darkness ruled over the abyss,"[11] that is, a darkness greater than that in the abyss. The abyss today, of visible waters, even in their depths have a semblance of light, perceivable in any case by fish and by the animals that crawl on the ocean floor. That other, rather, was altogether virtually nothing, because it was still absolutely without form. It was, however, such as could assume a form. You, Lord, brought forth "the world from unformed matter"—what was almost nothing, drawn by you out of nothing, to bring forth the great things that we human beings admire. This is truly the marvel of these corporeal heavens, that is, of the firmament, which you created between the waters on the second day, after the light was created, saying, "Let it be so. And so it was."[12] CONFESSIONS 12.8.8.[13]

GOD ALSO CREATED PRIMORDIAL MATTER. AUGUSTINE: We can ask ourselves if the Scripture calls "heaven and earth"[14] all the things already distinguished and arranged in their order. Or if, by the term "heaven and earth," it means the matter itself of the universe, originally unformed, which by the ineffable command of God was differentiated and arranged in the formed and magnificent natures that we now admire.[15] Although we in fact read in Scripture, "You who made the world, drawing it from formless mat-

---

[3]Prov 5:22. [4]Is 50:11. [5]CTP 156:446-47. [6]See 1 Tim 3:16. [7]Lk 1:19-20. [8]See Mt 3:3; Mk 1:3; Lk 3:4; Is 40:3. [9]CTP 92:169. [10]Ps 115:16 (113:24 LXX). [11]Gen 1:2. [12]See Gen 1:6-7. [13]NBA 1:413. [14]See Gen 1:1. [15]Augustine refers to his previous explanation on the same topic.

ter," we nevertheless cannot say that the matter itself (of whatever kind it may be) was not made by him from whom we declare and profess by faith that all things come. Consequently, we also call "world" the ordered arrangement of all the formed and distinct things, whatever they may be, while on the contrary, we call "heaven and earth" the matter itself, as if the latter were the primordial germ of the heaven and the earth. So "heaven and earth," something confused and mixed, is capable of receiving forms from God the creator. UNFINISHED LITERAL COMMENTARY ON GENESIS 1.3.10.[16]

GOD CREATED THE WORLD AND TRANSFORMS IT. HESYCHIUS: "Over time, in fact, the sea diminishes."[17] Perhaps this alludes to him who, threatening the sea, dries it up.[18] "And a desolate river is dried up."[19] It does not say "rivers" but "a river," since all rivers are a single river, as the accounts in the book of Genesis tell us: "A spring rose from the ground."[20] The one who created that river now dries it up, and, according to his will, he will render it invisible, when by his will he exhausts the sea and puts an end to the other elements of visible creatures. There is nothing surprising in the fact that Job spoke of what happened in the past and of what must take place in the future. Indeed, he speaks from the point of view of God, for whom future events, decided once and for all, are seen as having happened and passed. Thus it is not possible that events arranged by the creating hand would oppose his order. And therefore Job rightly recalled it, to indicate that when the visible elements are gone[21] and creatures have been renewed,[22] the ruler[23] given by God to this dwelling will also be renewed. HOMILIES ON JOB 17.[24]

THE SON CREATED EVERYTHING. VIGILIUS OF THAPSUS: *Question:* If you would say that the Son made what was made by command of the Father. *Response:* It is not as you claim, that the Son made what was made under the Father's orders.[25] Rather, by his will he created everything that he deemed in his providence should

be created, since the prophet Isaiah says, "Thus says the Lord, 'I made the earth by my word, and on it I created human beings. With my hand I spread out the heavens, giving order to all their ranks, that they might shine in the sky.' "[26] And, "My plan shall stand as valid, and I have fulfilled my entire purpose."[27] And still, "Thus says the Lord, who created the heavens and the earth. He made it and rendered it stable."[28] And further, "I am the first, and I am eternal. My hand laid the foundations of the earth, my right hand spread the heavens."[29] And still, "I made the earth with great power and with a mighty arm."[30] And in Jeremiah, "He formed the earth by his power; he established the world with his wisdom; with his intelligence he spread the heavens and made the waters in heaven roar."[31] And further, "Lord, you made the heaven and the earth with great power and a strong arm. You make their children after them suffer the punishment for the iniquity of their ancestors."[32] And in Solomon, "It was not difficult for your almighty hand, which created the world from invisible matter." And in Psalm 134, "Everything he wanted, the Lord has done, in heaven and on earth, in the seas and in the abyss."[33] And in Psalm 113, "Our God is in the heavens."[34] And again, "In heaven and on earth he made all that he willed."[35] And in Psalm 64, "You make the mountains firm by your strength, robed in power."[36] Since it is written that he did all these things, not under the command of the Father but by his power, how is it that you consider him to be inferior to the Father? AGAINST VARIMADUS 1.11.[37]

GOD CREATED ALL THE ELEMENTS AT ONCE. PSEUDO-AUGUSTINE: In Wisdom it says, "He who created the world from formless matter," and the opposite, "We were made from noth-

[16]NBA 9/1:207. [17]Job 14:11 LXX. [18]See Ex 14:21. [19]Job 14:11 LXX. [20]Gen 2:6 LXX. [21]See Mt 24:35. [22]Ps 104:30 (103:30 LXX). [23]See 1 Cor 15:51-52. Hesychius is talking about the human being. [24]PO 42.2:435. [25]See Jn 1:3. [26]Is 45:12, variant. [27]Is 46:10. [28]Is 45:18. [29]Is 48:12-13. [30]Jer 27:5 (34:5 LXX). [31]Jer 51:15-16. [32]Jer 32:17-18. [33]Ps 135:6 (134:6 LXX). [34]Ps 115:3 (114:11 LXX). [35]Ps 115:3 (114:11 LXX), variant. [36]Ps 65:7 (64:7 LXX). [37]PL 62:361-62.

ing."[38] The sense of Scripture affirms that God created the elements all at once, with darkness also mixed in with them. And God called this confusion of elements (that is, air, fire, water, land[39] and darkness) formless matter, as it says in Genesis: "The earth, moreover, was invisible and formless."[40] And from this confusion he then created the world, also establishing the firmament, so that, once the waters were gathered in a single place,[41] it might be the dwelling of the human race. Having distinguished and separated the elements, he made an inhabitable dwelling in the cavity that remained. QUESTIONS FROM THE OLD TESTAMENT 2.20.[42]

11:20 All Things Arranged by Measure, Number and Weight

EVERYTHING WAS MADE THROUGH THE WORD. AUGUSTINE: Everything was made through the Word, from the angels to the smallest worm. What among creatures is more exalted than an angel? What is easier to overlook than a worm? Well, he who made the angel also made the worm. The angel, however, was made for heaven, the worm for the earth. This was how the one who created them arranged it. If God had put the worm in heaven, you might criticize him. Likewise, if he had wanted the angel to be born of corruptible flesh. And yet God does something similar to this, and there is nothing to reproach him for. What, in fact, are human beings born of the flesh, if not worms? And God makes these worms into angels. If the Lord does not hesitate to say, "I am a worm and not a man,"[43] who would hesitate to say what is written in the book of Job, "How much more are human beings rot, and their children worms?"[44] First he says, "human beings are rot," and then, "their children are worms." The man is rot and his child a worm, because worms are born of decay. See what he who in the beginning was the Word wanted to do for you—the Word who was with God, the Word who was God.[45] And why did he lower himself like this for you? So that

you might feed on milk, given that you were still unable to nourish yourself on solid food.[46] And therefore, brothers and sisters, it is in this sense that you must understand the words, "Everything was made through him, and without him nothing was made."[47] Every creature, without exception, was made through him, the smallest just as the greatest, things above us just as things below us, things spiritual just as things corporeal—everything was made through him. There is no form, no cohesion or harmony of parts, no substance that can be measured by weight, number or height—nothing exists except through that Word and originates from that creator Word, to whom the word of Scripture refers, "You have arranged all things in number, weight and measure." TRACTATES ON THE GOSPEL OF JOHN 1.13.[48]

EVERYTHING WAS ARRANGED BY GOD. AUGUSTINE: When we read that God brought all his works to completion in six days and, in considering the number six, discover that it is a perfect number[49] and that the order of the creatures that were made is arranged in such a way as to appear to be the progressive distinction of the very divisors that comprise this number, the expression addressed to God in another passage of the Scriptures should come to mind: "You have arranged all things with measure, number and weight." We must further ask ourselves (and we can if we invoke God's help, which will allow us to do so, infusing in us the strength) if these three properties—measure, number and weight, according to which the Scripture says that God has arranged all things—in some way existed before the universe was created, or were they also created and, if they already existed, where were

---

[38]Wis 2:2, variant. [39]The text enumerates the four basic elements. According to classical cosmology, they were shaped from an original formless matter. [40]Gen 1:2. [41]See Gen 1:9. [42]PL 35:2392. [43]Ps 22:7 (21:7 LXX). [44]Job 25:6. [45]See Jn 1:1. [46]See Heb 5:12, 14. [47]Jn 1:3. [48]NBA 24:17. [49]In ancient computation, number 6 was deemed perfect because it is both the sum and the product of the first three numbers: $1 \times 2 \times 3 = 1 + 2 + 3 = 6$.

they. In fact, before the creation nothing existed besides the Creator. They were therefore in him—but how? In fact, we read that these things also, which are created, were in him.[50] Should we perhaps identify these properties with God, or should we perhaps instead say that the works of the creation are, so to speak, in him who guides and governs them? But how can these properties be identified with God? He is in fact neither measure nor number nor weight, nor all of these properties taken together. Or should we perhaps think that God is to be identified with these properties as we know them in creatures and therefore limit in things we measure, number in things we count and weight in things we touch? Or should we alternatively think that, in the sense that measure assigns to each thing its limit, number gives to each its specific form, and weight draws everything to its rest and stability, it is God who is identified with these three perfections in a fundamental, true and unique sense, since it is he who limits and he who gives specific form and order to all things? That is why the phrase, "You have arranged all things by measure, number and weight," according to the way that human intelligence and language could express itself, means nothing other than, "You have arranged all things in yourself." ON GENESIS 4.3.7.[51]

GOD MAKES HIMSELF KNOWN IN THE CREATURES. AUGUSTINE: I must confess that I do not know why mice and frogs were created, but I nonetheless understand that all things are beautiful in their kind, even if, because of our sins, they seem otherwise to us. Truthfully, I cannot consider the body and limbs of a living being without finding a measure, a proportion and an order that contribute to a harmonious unity. I do not understand where all these properties come from except from that supreme measure and proportion, and that supreme order, that exist in the absolutely perfect, unchanging and eternal essence of God. . . . When you see in all these beings their measure, their proportion and their order, look for the Creator in them, since you will find none other than the One in whom is supreme measure, supreme proportion and supreme order, that is, God, of whom Scripture says with absolute truth, "You have arranged all things with measure, number and weight." In this way, in the smallness of an ant you may find more reason to praise God than in crossing a river astride a tall beast of burden. ON GENESIS, AGAINST THE MANICHAEANS 1.16.26.[52]

WE FIND GOD'S IMAGE EVERYWHERE. FULGENTIUS OF RUSPE: This uncreated Trinity put some indications of the Trinity in its creation. As it is written, "You arranged all things with measure, number and weight." In fact, any body, small or large, can be quantified according to the number of its parts, can be measured and has weight. And quantity cannot exist without weight, nor measure without weight and quantity. None of these properties can exist without the other two. It is easy, however, to observe weight, quantity and measure in material objects; let us see if they can be found in incorporeal objects. In the human soul one finds memory, thought and will. In fact, you think what you want, and this is what your memory contains. Your will is your love. That is, you remember what you bear with love in your thoughts. Memory, intellect and will (which we have said is love) are three inseparable aspects—one of these cannot exist without the others. A certain Father once elegantly mentioned how all three are in the soul when praying to God: your memory, your intellect and your desire, and in this the image of God has been shown.[53] The human soul is therefore an image of God: not born but created, not equal but similar. ON THE TRINITY, TO FELIX 7.[54]

THE PHILOSOPHERS DISCERNED THE ORDER PRESENT IN THE WORLD. CASSIODORUS: The

---

[50]See Rom 11:36. [51]NBA 9/2:167-69. [52]NBA 9/1:93-95. [53]See Gen 1:26-27. [54]PL 65:504.

writers of secular letters held that arithmetic was the first among the disciplines, given that music, geometry and astronomy, which follow it, have need of arithmetic for the explanation of their laws. For example, the relationship between simple and double, which is proper to music, has need of arithmetic. Geometry, since it has the triangle, the rectangle and other similar figures for its object, needs arithmetic. Astronomy as well, since it calculates the positions and movement of the stars, needs arithmetic. However, no one would affirm that music, geometry and astronomy need to exist for there to be arithmetic. One therefore concludes that arithmetic is the source and mother of the other sciences. We know that Pythagoras celebrated this to the point of recalling that everything was created by God under the laws of number and of measure, also saying that some things were created in motion, others at rest, though in such a way that nothing has substance except the things mentioned above.[55] I think that Pythagoras, like many philosophers, took his cue from the prophetic saying that[56] "God arranged all things by measure, number and weight." THE INSTITUTES 2.4.1.[57]

[55]According to the Pythagoreans, numbers are the foundations of everything that exists. [56]Cassiodorus alludes to a theory of Jewish origin of the "Greeks' theft." It affirms that the pagans had known the Old Testament and used it as a doctrinal source. Indeed, some classical authors around the beginning of the Christian era were familiar with biblical themes, but no such influence is known to have happened in Pythagoras's time (sixth to fifth century B.C.). [57]FMTM 23:162-63.

11:21–12:2* GOD IS CAPABLE OF COMPASSION FOR ALL

[21]*For it is always in thy power to show great strength,*
and who can withstand the might of thy arm?
[22]*Because the whole world before thee is like a speck that tips the scales,*
and like a drop of morning dew that falls upon the ground.
[23]*But thou art merciful to all, for thou canst do all things,*
and thou dost overlook men's sins, that they may repent.
[24]*For thou lovest all things that exist,*
and hast loathing for none of the things which thou hast made,
for thou wouldst not have made anything if thou hadst hated it.
[25]*How would anything have endured if thou hadst not willed it?*
Or how would anything not called forth by thee have been preserved?
[26]*Thou sparest all things, for they are thine, O Lord who lovest the living.*
12 *For thy immortal spirit is in all things.*
[2]*Therefore thou dost correct little by little those who trespass,*
and dost remind and warn them of the things wherein they sin,
that they may be freed from wickedness and put their trust in thee, O Lord.

* Wis 11:22–12:1 Vg.

Overview: From the perspective of the Trinity, the world is a grain of sand (Vigilius). The Lord calls us to penance through Scripture (Pseudo-Augustine). Let us repent and trust the Lord in this life (Victor of Cartenna). God does not love all in the same way (Origen). God loves all he has done and hates only sin (Augustine). God does not desire the death of human beings (Pseudo-Augustine), but in his love sent his Son to save us (Didymus). The Trinity is infinitely good (Vigilius).

11:22 The Whole World Like a Speck

Like a Speck of Dust. Vigilius of Thapsus: Who can hide or flee before the unique divinity of the Trinity?[1] To the Trinity, the entire globe of the earth seems as a raindrop,[2] or a bit of foam[3] or a drop of morning dew that descends from heaven. As it is written, "He sits above the vault of the earth, from where its inhabitants seem like grasshoppers."[4] And, "He has measured the waters in the hollow of his hand and held the whole earth in his palm."[5] And further, "The heavens are my throne, the earth the footstool for my feet."[6] Notice that the power of the one divinity is incomprehensible, since the heavens, which he holds in his palm, are also his throne, and the earth, which is enclosed in his fist, is in turn the footstool for his feet. In fact, the whole of the heavens is contained in his palm, and the entire earth is enclosed in his hand. It is also the throne and footstool for his feet, as it is written, "To whom the whole world is like dust on the scales." And thus he fills all things, containing all things from within and without, since this eternal, undivided Trinity is present everywhere and possesses the invisible fullness of the divinity.[7] On the Trinity 5.[8]

11:23 Merciful to All

The Lord Invites Sinners to Penance. Pseudo-Augustine: Let us hear what the Lord says to the prophet Jeremiah concerning idola-

ters: "Go and say, 'Return, house of Israel, says the Lord. I will not show you an indignant face, because I am compassionate, says the Lord. I will not maintain my anger forever. Rise, acknowledge your guilt. You have been godless and followed strangers under every green tree.'"[9] See what God promises to those who return after they fall: to forgive their sins, once they have turned from their apostasy. And the Lord says further by the mouth of Jeremiah, "My pampered children have had to trod bitter paths, pushed along like a flock kidnapped by the enemy. Have courage, children, cry out to God, because he who has tested you will remember you. Just as you thought to separate yourselves from God, return to him, seeking him with ten times the zeal, since the one who afflicted you with so many calamities will also give you, with salvation, everlasting joy."[10] O the mercy of God! How he calls to those who have fallen, that they might rise again! How he exhorts them so that, after their errors with idols, they would return to him! Like a benevolent Father he promises the eternal joy of salvation to his children if they mend their ways. Among other things, he says further by the same prophet, "I will lead them back to this country. I will firmly reestablish them and will not destroy them. I will plant them, and never again will I uproot them."[11] In fact, since he had threatened, "The one who sacrifices to the gods will be uprooted,"[12] so that those who had sinned would not despair (as though, having been uprooted for having sacrificed to idols, they could not be replanted), he exhorts them, since if they repent they can be restored to their prior state. If they do not correct their crime, however, the sentence will be carried out. Moreover, it was preached to the Ninevites that their city would be destroyed after three days.[13] Why after three days, if not

---

[1]See Ps 139:7-8 (138:7-8 LXX). [2]See Sir 18:10 LXX. [3]See Wis 5:14 (5:15 Vg). [4]Is 40:22. [5]Is 40:12, variant. [6]Is 66:1. [7]See Col 2:9. [8]PL 62:275-76. [9]Jer 3:12-13, variant. [10]Bar 4:26-29. [11]Jer 24:6. [12]Cf. Ex 22:20. [13]See Jon 3:4 and Mt 12:40 par; Jon 2:1.

that they might repent and the sentence be cancelled, or that they might remain in their sin and have even greater reason to perish? This is as he said through the prophet, "I do not desire the death of the one who dies, but that he would return to me and live."[14] And thus it happened that the Ninevites, destined to die for their sins, were pardoned because of their repentance.[15] And why did the construction of the ark by Noah take a hundred years,[16] if not so that those who saw and heard what was threatened would correct themselves? Indeed, God wants no one to perish. This is why we read in Solomon, "The Lord had mercy on sinners."[17] And further, "You have compassion on all, because you can do all things. You overlook people's sins, that they might repent." It is in this sense that the Lord, deploring the faithlessness of the Jews, says, "Jerusalem, Jerusalem, you who kill the prophets and stone those who are sent to you, how often have I wanted to gather your children, like a hen gathers her chicks under her wings, but you were unwilling!"[18] Everywhere in the Law, then, the Lord exhorts sinners to conversion, not wanting that his creatures fall into perdition. And the Law that was given had no other purpose than that men and women would turn from error to the truth. Nonetheless, in the New Testament the author of the Law reveals himself as being more merciful, since he wanted to be more generous and rich in mercy[19] at that time when he deigned to manifest the sacrament of his Son our Lord, so that grace would be more abundant through the preaching of the Son than through the preaching of the servants. QUESTIONS FROM BOTH TESTAMENTS 102.[20]

LET US REPENT AND TRUST THE LORD. VICTOR OF CARTENNA: Let us turn and trust in the Lord while we live the season of this life, and let us prepare the viaticum of penance before our judge. Let us not fill our time with futile engagements or say that we are born to sin, but let us live to act well. And even if we fall into sin, since, given the setting of this world,[21] it is unavoidable

that we sin, let us come to our senses, desiring to flee the abyss of Gehenna. Therefore let us repent with faith, pray with the heart, weep from our very depths. ON PENANCE 27.[22]

11:24 God Loves All Things That Exist

GOD DOES NOT LOVE ALL IN THE SAME WAY. ORIGEN: Let us take an example from God. In fact, "he loves everything that exists" equally, "and he hates nothing that he has made: in fact, he created nothing that should be hated." Nonetheless, this did not mean that he loved Jews and Egyptians in the same way, or Pharaoh as Moses and Aaron. At the same time, he did not love the other children of Israel as he loved Moses and Aaron and Miriam, and further, he did not love Aaron and Miriam as he loved Moses. Although what is said is true, "You have mercy on all, because all is yours, Lord and lover of souls. In fact, a spirit of incorruptibility is in all," nevertheless the one who arranged all "with measure, number and weight" unquestionably also proportions his love to the measure of each one's merits. Do we perhaps think that Paul, when he persecuted the church of God, was loved in the same way as when he underwent persecutions and torments for it[23] and when he said that he bore within himself concern for all the churches?[24] COMMENTARY ON THE SONG OF SONGS 2.4.[25]

GOD LOVES EVERYTHING HE HAS CREATED. AUGUSTINE: The love with which God loves is incomprehensible and must not be thought of as subject to change. He did not begin to love us only when we were reconciled to him through the blood of his Son.[26] Rather, he loved us before the foundation of the world,[27] calling us to be his children together with the Only-Begotten,

---

[14]See Ezek 33:11. [15]See Jon 3:10. [16]See Gen 5-7. [17]Sir 12:3 Vg. [18]Mt 23:37. [19]See Eph 2:4. [20]PL 35:2305-6. [21]See 1 Cor 7:31. [22]PL 17:1000. [23]See 2 Cor 11:28. [24]See 2 Cor 4:9. [25]CTP 1:207. [26]See Rom 5:9. [27]See Eph 1:4.

when we were as yet absolutely nothing. The fact, then, that we "have been reconciled to God through the death of his Son"[28] should not be heard and understood in the sense that he began to love what he had previously hated, as when an enemy reconciles with his enemy and the two become friends and begin to mutually love one another just as they once hated one another. We have been reconciled with one who already loved us, one with whom, due to sin, we had become enemies. The apostle will show whether or not I speak the truth. He says, "God shows his love toward us because, while we were still sinners, Christ died for us."[29] God felt love for us even when, behaving as his enemies, we committed sin. And yet with all truth it was said of him, "Lord, you detest all who do evil."[30] Therefore, in a way both wonderful and divine, he loved us even when he hated us. He hated that in us that he did not make, but since our iniquity had not completely destroyed his work, he knew how to hate in each of us what was our own work and at the same time to love what was his work. And this can be applied to everything else, given that this was said to him in all truth, "You despise nothing that you have created."[31] If in fact he had hated something he would not have willed it, nor could something exist that the Almighty had not called into existence—and he would not have called it if, in the thing he hates, there were not at least something that he could love. Rightly he hates and condemns evil, because it is contrary to the principle of how he does things. Nevertheless, even in what is contaminated by evil, he loves either the love with which he heals it or his judgment with which he condemns it. Therefore God hates nothing that he has created, since as the author of nature, and not of sin, he hates only the evil that he did not create. And he is moreover the author of the good[32] that he draws from evil, whether healing it by his mercy or making it serve his secret plans. Granted therefore that God hates nothing of what he has made, who can speak adequately of the love that he feels for the members of his Only-Begotten? And, above all, who can speak worthily of the love that he bears for his Only-Begotten, in whom all things visible and invisible were made,[33] things that he loves in a way that corresponds perfectly to the place each one occupies in the plan of creation? TRACTATES ON THE GOSPEL OF JOHN 110.6.[34]

GOD HATES SIN. AUGUSTINE: We must try, with God's help, to reconcile the truth of this text, "You despise nothing that you have made," with that other, "I loved Jacob and hated Esau."[35] If, in fact, God hated Esau, because he was made as a vessel for common use, and the same potter made a vessel for noble use and another for common use,[36] how can it be that "you despise nothing that you have created"? He in fact hates Esau, whom he himself made for common use. This difficulty is resolved bearing in mind that God is the creator of all creatures. Now, every one of God's creatures is good,[37] and every person is a creature—as a person, not as a sinner. God is therefore the creator of the body and the soul of the person. Neither of these two realities is evil, and God does not hate them, since he hates nothing that he has created. Now the soul is superior to the body. But God, author and creator of both, hates only sin in human beings. A person's sin is disorder and perversion, that is, separation from the supreme Creator and attachment to inferior creatures. Therefore God does not hate Esau the man but Esau the sinner. ON VARIOUS QUESTIONS TO SIMPLICIANUS 1.2.18.[38]

GOD DESIRES DEATH FOR NO ONE. PSEUDO-AUGUSTINE: The Lord is true and merciful, and he does not delight in the destruction of the living.[39] What is the ruin of the living if not death? But the death of the living who live badly, who will perish in the second death,[40] not that of the

---

[28]Rom 5:10. [29]Rom 5:9. [30]Ps 5:6 (5:7 Vg). [31]Wis 11:24 (11:25 Vg). [32]See Gen 1:13. [33]See Col 1:16. [34]NBA 24:1477-79. [35]Rom 9:12; Mal 1:2-3. [36]See Rom 9:21. [37]See 1 Tim 4:4. [38]NBA 6/2:331. [39]See Wis 1:13. [40]See Rev 2:11, etc.

living who are righteous, that is, who seek God and are not subject to the second death but only to the first, which is a result of the sin of Adam with which they were born. If then God were the author of death, he should rejoice in the destruction of the living as though it were one of his good works, since it is written, "The Lord will rejoice in his works,"[41] and he made nothing out of hate, but everything that he made was very good,[42] as it is written, "Since you love everything that exists, and you despise nothing that you have created. If you had hated something, you would not have created it." HYPOMNESTICON I.I.[43]

11:26 God Spares All Things

GOD'S LOVE SAVES US IN THE SON. DIDYMUS THE BLIND: It is written, "Not a messenger or an angel but the Lord himself saved them."[44] He forgave them, for no other reason than that he loved them. Indeed, it says "forgive," as with his own children, according to that verse that is referred to in another book, "You have compassion on all things, Lord, lover of souls, because they are yours, nor do you nourish hatred toward the beings you have created." For their salvation, therefore, the Father, not sparing his own Son, gave him over to death,[45] so that by the death of his own Son, having reduced to powerlessness him who had power over death, that is, the devil,

he would free all those who were subject to him through the bonds of slavery.[46] For this reason it is added, "He himself rescued them, he comforted them and raised them up."[47] He in fact comforts and exalts those who are saved and lifts the redeemed on wings of virtue toward the most sublime heights. He dwells in them and with them, through both instruction and knowledge of the truth, not only for a day or two but for all the days of eternity, communicating life to them "until the end of the world,"[48] because he is the cause of salvation. ON THE HOLY SPIRIT 2.46.[49]

12:1 God's Immortal Spirit Is in All Things

THE TRINITY IS INFINITELY GOOD. VIGILIUS OF THAPSUS: The Father is good, the Son is good, the Holy Spirit is good. About the Father it is written in Psalm 72, "How good is the God of Israel toward those who are pure of heart!"[50] About the Son, "I am the good shepherd"[51] and "Good Teacher, what good must I do to gain eternal life?"[52] About the Holy Spirit, in Ezra, "You bestowed on them your good Spirit."[53] AGAINST VARIMADUS 3.19.[54]

---

[41]Ps 104:31 (103:31 LXX). [42]See Gen 1:13. [43]PL 45:1614. [44]Is 63:9. [45]See Rom 8:32. [46]See Heb 2:14-15. [47]Is 63:9. [48]Mt 28:20. [49]CTP 89:134-35. [50]Ps 73:1 (72:1 LXX), variant. [51]Jn 10:11. [52]Mt 19:16, variant. [53]Neh 9:20 (2 Ezra 19:20 LXX). [54]PL 62:416.

12:3-11 GOD ALSO TAKES CARE OF THE CANAANITES

[3]*Those who dwelt of old in thy holy land*
[4]*thou didst hate for their detestable practices,*
their works of sorcery and unholy rites,
[5]*their merciless slaughter* *of children,*
and their sacrificial feasting on human flesh and blood.

These initiates from the midst of a heathen cult,^g
⁶these parents who murder helpless lives,
thou didst will to destroy by the hands of our fathers,
⁷that the land most precious of all to thee
might receive a worthy colony of the servants^h *of God.*
⁸But even these thou didst spare, since they were but men,
*and didst send wasps*ⁱ *as forerunners of thy army,*
to destroy them little by little,
⁹though thou wast not unable to give the ungodly into the hands of the righteous in battle,
or to destroy them at one blow by dread wild beasts or thy stern word.
¹⁰But judging them little by little thou gavest them a chance to repent,
though thou wast not unaware that their origin^j *was evil*
and their wickedness inborn,
and that their way of thinking would never change.
¹¹For they were an accursed race from the beginning,
and it was not through fear of any one that thou didst leave them unpunished for their sins.

f Cn: Gk *slaughterers* g The Greek text of this line is uncertain h Or *children* i Or *hornets* j Or *nature*

OVERVIEW: Scripture speaks truth through the images it employs (AUGUSTINE). God has always called people to repentance (CLEMENT OF ROME). God is patient with sinners (ORIGEN) and gives us time to repent (DIDYMUS). Human beings are wicked because they are Adam's descendants (AUGUSTINE).

12:8 Spared by God

THE SCRIPTURE AT TIMES SPEAKS FIGU-RATIVELY. AUGUSTINE: "I will send hornets ahead of you, and they will drive out from your presence the Hivites, the Canaanites and the Hittites."[1] We ask ourselves what these hornets might mean. God in fact makes this promise, and the book of Wisdom affirms that it occurred, saying, "And he sent them wasps as the vanguard of his army." But we do not find it written that this took place, neither in the time of Moses, nor under Joshua, nor under the judges nor under the kings. But perhaps these wasps indicate the sting of the fear of understanding that prodded the peoples mentioned so that they would leave their land to the children of Israel. God in fact speaks, and if something is

said figuratively in his words that did not take place in the proper sense, this does not preclude putting faith in the account, from which one perceives the truth of the narration. Likewise, neither does the Gospel account lose its historicity if something is said there about Christ in a figurative sense. QUESTIONS ON THE HEPTA-TEUCH 2.93.[2]

12:10 A Chance to Repent

GOD CALLS US TO REPENTANCE. CLEMENT OF ROME: We look over all the generations, and we note that from generation to generation the Master "gave room for repentance" for all those who wanted to turn to him. Noah preached repentance, and all who listened to him were saved.[3] Jonah predicted the destruction of the Ninevites, but, repentant for their sins, God looked favorably on them, and they received salvation, though they were foreigners to God.[4] 1 CLEMENT 7.5-7.[5]

---

[1]Ex 23:28. [2]PL 34:630-31. [3]See 2 Pet 2:5. [4]See Jon 3:4-10. [5]CTP 5:53-54.

GOD IS PATIENT WITH SINNERS. ORIGEN: The God who "judges little by little" those he punishes "gives space for repentance." By not punishing all at once for the sin, he delays the consummation of the punishment for the sinner.[6] He thus punishes, "judging little by little." We have an example of this in Leviticus. In the curses against those who transgress the Law, after the first punishments it is written, "The Lord says, if you do not repent after these things, I will multiply my blows sevenfold."[7] And again he sets forth another punishment, "And if, despite these punishments, you do not want to correct yourselves and turn to me but oppose yourselves to me, I will also oppose you with fury."[8] You will note that God metes out punishments stingily, as it were, since he wants to lead the sinner to conversion instead of making him pay for everything all at once. With respect to the text, then, these are the things that befell the people. And threatening them with how much they might have suffered afterward, the Word says, "And yet in those days, I will not wholly destroy you."[9] HOMILIES ON JEREMIAH 7.1.[10]

GOD ALLOWS TIME FOR PENANCE. DIDYMUS THE BLIND: In the time of judgment, which is to say always, he judges everyone, sometimes calling this time the "time of judgment,"[11] sometimes "the day of wrath"[12] and "the day of rendering account."[13] "Until" this "punishment arrives," while "the punishment has not yet come,"[14] repent. There is "room for repentance." "The Lord does not delay in fulfilling his promise, as some believe, but is patient toward you, not wanting that anyone should perish but that all should come to repentance."[15] Since therefore an extension is given to you for repentance, repent before "the punishment comes."[16] ON ECCLESIASTES 12.1C.[17]

12:11 Accursed from the Beginning

ADAM'S WICKED DESCENDANTS. AUGUSTINE: Why would it have been written, "Their offspring was accursed from the beginning"? In fact, it was not said in the same sense in which we read, "offspring of Canaan and not of Judah,"[18] where it was shown to what persons they had become similar and from what persons they had degenerated. Rather, it called accursed the offspring of those very people whom it wanted us to understand to be naturally evil, as are all of the children of Adam. From among these, by grace, children of God are made.[19] UNFINISHED TRACTATE AGAINST JULIAN 3.11.[20]

---

[6]See Jer 5:18. [7]Ps 7:13 LXX and Lev 26:21. [8]Lev 26:23-24. [9]Jer 5:18. [10]CTP 123:97. [11]See Eccles 5:8. [12]See Rom 2:5, etc. [13]See Is 63:4. [14]See Eccles 12:1. [15]2 Pet 3:9. [16]See Eccles 12:1. [17]PTA 9:122. [18]Sus 56. [19]See Jn 1:12-14. [20]NBA 19/1:443.

12:12-18 GOD'S POWER AND MODERATION

[12]For who will say, "What hast thou done?"
Or who will resist thy judgment?
Who will accuse thee for the destruction of nations which thou didst make?
Or who will come before thee to plead as an advocate for unrighteous men?

*13For neither is there any god besides thee, whose care is for all men,[k]
to whom thou shouldst prove that thou hast not judged unjustly;
14nor can any king or monarch confront thee about those whom thou hast punished.
15Thou art righteous and rulest all things righteously,
deeming it alien to thy power
to condemn him who does not deserve to be punished.
16For thy strength is the source of righteousness,
and thy sovereignty over all causes thee to spare all.
17For thou dost show thy strength when men doubt the completeness of thy power,
and dost rebuke any insolence among those who know it.[l]
18Thou who art sovereign in strength dost judge with mildness,
and with great forbearance thou dost govern us;
for thou hast power to act whenever thou dost choose.*

k Or *all things* l The Greek text of this line is uncertain

OVERVIEW: Everything is possible for the mercy of God (EPIPHANIUS, AUGUSTINE), but God's wrath will judge the unrepentant. God creates in time but exists eternally outside time (AUGUSTINE). The Trinity omnipotently governs all things. God's promises always come true because in God will and power are one (FULGENTIUS).

12:12 Who Will Resist God's Judgment?

GOD'S OMNIPOTENCE. EPIPHANIUS OF SALAMIS: We are all descendants of Adam, according to an order of succession that has reached to us. Nor are the works of God to be understood allegorically: Adam did exist, the fig leaves existed, the fig tree,[1] the tree of the knowledge of good and evil, the tree set in the middle of the garden,[2] the serpent,[3] the disobedience, the obedience.[4] The rivers existed,[5] as did Eve. And everything was truly made by God, because "to him all things are possible,"[6] he who can make corruptible things incorruptible and earthly things perfect in incorruptibility. No one should wonder at this. Indeed, he gave us proof of this when he clothed his divinity with corruptible flesh, to offer us a model of incorruptibility in the flesh he assumed. "Who will oppose what he has done?" Let us now examine another exegetical aspect. The Scripture says that God cast

them out of the garden, placing two cherubim with flaming swords to guard the entrance to the tree of life, so that Adam and Eve took up their dwelling opposite the garden, barred from Paradise.[7] But this notwithstanding—let no one deceive you with empty words—"God, who can raise up his children from stones,"[8] was able to change corruptible beings into incorruptible, and he can do so at any time that he wants to make of the earth a place of peace, a paradise. In fact, earth and heaven do not have a different God, but everything is his, and he lavishes the gift of incorruptibility on every being as he wishes. ANCORATUS 61.1-7.[9]

GOD'S MERCY. AUGUSTINE: The liberating grace of God appeals to us on every page of Scripture, so that we would entrust ourselves to it. And this psalm, of which we have begun to speak, by your leave, sings of it. May the Lord help us, so that grace would be given us to understand it as we should and to describe it according to your needs. In this, the love and the fear of God greatly urge us on. The fear of God, because he is just. The love of God, because he is merciful. "Who, in fact, could remonstrate with him" if he

[1]See Gen 3:7. [2]See Gen 2:9. [3]See Gen 3:1. [4]See Rom 5:19. [5]See Gen 2:10-14. [6]Mt 19:26. [7]See Gen 3:24. [8]Mt 3:9. [9]CTP 9:130.

were to condemn the godless? How great, then, is his mercy when he justifies the godless! EXPOSITIONS OF THE PSALMS 70.1.1.[10]

12:18 Sovereign in Strength, Judging with Mildness

GOD WILL JUDGE THE UNREPENTANT. AUGUSTINE: Why did he not say "in wrath" but "as in wrath"?[11] Because God does everything with absolute tranquility. Indeed, it is also written, "You, master of strength, judge with gentleness." Therefore, even when he threatens he does not become angry, nor is he disturbed in any way. It calls him angry because he punishes and does justice. Similarly, people who do not want to amend their lives are as though they were alive, but they do not live, because vengeance for the first sin, and for those that they have added, hangs over them. This vengeance is called the wrath of God, because it proceeds from God's judgment. Thus the Lord says of the one who does not believe, "but the wrath of God hangs over him."[12] We also, being born mortal, were under the wrath of God. Therefore the apostle says, "We were once by nature deserving of wrath, like the others."[13] What does "by nature deserving of wrath" mean, if not that we carry with us the wrath of the first sin? But if we convert, wrath ceases, and grace is offered to us. If, however, you do not want to convert, you add other offenses to the ones you were born with. And, "as in wrath," you will be devoured even in the present time. EXPOSITIONS OF THE PSALMS 57.20.[14]

GOD CREATES WITHIN TIME. AUGUSTINE: How is it that it is written, "Power is in your hands whenever you want," as if God needs a period of time to carry out some work? Or, rather, are all things accomplished by God (as we say) like an artist thinks out a design—not over an extended period of time—but by that power that accomplishes in an enduring way even those things that we see are not enduring but

passing? Even with our own speech, when some words pass away while others follow, we should not think that the same thing happens with the thought that gave rise to the expression we just finished.[15] Consequently, although God, who exercises power when he wishes, accomplishes his works without the passage of time, nonetheless temporal natures themselves carry out their movements within time. UNFINISHED LITERAL COMMENTARY ON GENESIS 1.7.28.[16]

THE TRINITY IS ALMIGHTY. FULGENTIUS OF RUSPE: With respect to existence and power, the Trinity is everywhere, wholly one God, filling all things with his power, not by his mass but wholly in each creature, and simultaneously wholly in all creatures. Regarding our thoughts, it is said that God descends to our level when he divinely moderates his word in such a way that he condescends to communicate his knowledge and love to us, speaking to us in a human way. Conversely, he rises in us when we ascend in charity and knowledge of the divinity, learning not to look for anything local in him who is infinite, or think that there is anything lowly in him who is sublime, or believe that there is anything changeable in God or think that there is anything temporary in him who is eternal.

This is the way we are to understand the manifestation of the Father and of the Son and of the Holy Spirit. Indeed, it is said that God rested in the beginning after having finished the creation of the world,[17] although he was not fatigued by his work, because he accomplished everything solely by his will. To him it was said, "You exercise power when you wish," as we hear

---

[10]NBA 26:719. [11]Ps 58:10 (57:10 LXX), variant. [12]Jn 3:36. [13]Eph 2:3. [14]NBA 26:235-37. [15]In other words, our thoughts that give rise to our speech do not pass out of existence like the expressions they produced. The thoughts remain even as the words disappear. Augustine is trying to communicate the fact that God timelessly and creatively speaks his creative design through the Word and these things come to exist, then, in time even as God and the Word remain timeless, outside of time in their creative action. See his fuller discussion of this concept in *On The Literal Interpretation of Genesis* 2.8.19; 4.22.39–23.40. [16]NBA 9/1:229. [17]See Gen 2:2-3.

in the psalm, "Whatever the Lord wishes he does, in heaven and on earth, in the seas and in all the depths."[18] THREE BOOKS TO TRASAMUNDUS 2.11-12.[19]

GOD'S PROMISES ALWAYS COME TRUE. FULGENTIUS OF RUSPE: Abraham, "father of us all," as the apostle says,[20] "did not doubt God's promise in unbelief but was strengthened in faith and gave glory to God, fully convinced that what he had promised, he was also able to do."[21] There is therefore no falsehood whatsoever in God's promises,[22] since no obstacle can stand before the action of the Almighty. And consequently, the effect of his will can ever fail, since we discover that his will itself is nothing other than his power. He who can do whatever he wants

can want anything. Only of him, then, can it be truly said, "Whatever he wanted, he did."[23] And further, "You exercise power when you wish." For this reason we said that in him there is as much power of the will as there is the will itself of the power. Since "power always accompanies his will," in him will and power are one. In fact, just as God is not constrained by any necessity to promise what he does not want to do, so he is not impeded by anything in doing what he has promised to a lesser degree than he wants to or to delay its realization. LETTER TO MONIMUS 1.12.4–13.1.[24]

---

[18]Ps 135:6 (134:6 LXX). [19]PL 65:258. [20]Rom 4:16. [21]Rom 4:20-21. [22]Cf. Tit 1:2. [23]Ps 115:3 (113:11 lxx). [24]CCL 91:12-13.

12:19-22 GOD TEACHES MERCY AND JUSTICE

[19]*Through such works thou has taught thy people*
that the righteous man must be kind,
and thou hast filled thy sons with good hope,
because thou givest repentance for sins.
[20]*For if thou didst punish with such great care and indulgence[m]*
the enemies of thy servants[n] and those deserving of death,
granting them time and opportunity to give up their wickedness,
[21]*with what strictness thou hast judged thy sons,*
to whose fathers thou gavest oaths and covenants full of good promises!
[22]*So while chastening us thou scourgest our enemies ten thousand times more,*
so that we may meditate upon thy goodness when we judge,
and when we are judged we may expect mercy.

m Some ancient authorities omit *and indulgence; others read and entreaty* **n** Or *children*

OVERVIEW: Mercy was taught to Israel through the sufferings it endured in Egypt (PELAGIUS [?]).

12:19 *The Righteous Must Be Kind*

SUFFERING TEACHES MERCY. PELAGIUS (?)

(VIA PSEUDO-AUGUSTINE):[1] Their just God, teacher of mercy and compassion—who would later bestow the Law (by which he would give his people the precepts that would enable them to act with mercy and compassion and to do good works)—wanted them to first suffer every kind of affliction, tribulation and anguish in a foreign land. This was so they would more easily pity those who suffer these same things and so respect his commandments. Imagine a wise farmer who, before sowing the seed, takes time to soften the land with plow and rake, so that the seed that he entrusts to it will not be lost. Likewise God soaks and softens his people for a long time before bestowing on them the salutary seeds of the commandments. Finally, so that it would be even more evident that this was why he inflicted these things on his people, we see that the Lord says in his commandments, "Do not molest or oppress the alien, because you were aliens yourselves in the land of Egypt."[2] We also read, "The great God, who shows no partiality and accepts no bribes, who renders justice to the alien, the orphan and the widow. Delight in giving them bread and clothing, because you were like them in the land of Egypt."[3] And elsewhere it says, "When harvesting your fields, if you miss a sheaf, do not go back to get it. It will be for the alien, the orphan and the widow, that the Lord your God may bless you in all the works of your hands. You will remember that you were a slave in the land of Egypt. Therefore I command you to do this."[4] It is easy, then, to recognize that this is why he afflicted his people with every kind of misery, so that from what happened to them they would learn to be merciful toward others, as it is written, "In this way you taught your people that the righteous must love." In my opinion, it is very clear how God wants his people to be and how he shows, with many examples, the works by which they can gain his kindness. ON THE CHRISTIAN LIFE 8.[5]

---

[1]According to some sources the author is Fastidius of Britain. [2]Ex 22:20. [3]Deut 10:17-19, variant. [4]Deut 24:19, 22. [5]PL 40:391.

12:23-27 THE PUNISHMENT OF THE EGYPTIANS AS AN EXAMPLE

²³*Therefore those who in folly of life lived unrighteously*
thou didst torment through their own abominations.
²⁴*For they went far astray on the paths of error,*
accepting as gods those animals which even their enemies° despised;
they were deceived like foolish babes.
²⁵*Therefore, as to thoughtless children,*
thou didst send thy judgment to mock them.
²⁶*But those who have not heeded the warning of light rebukes*
will experience the deserved judgment of God.

*[27]For when in their suffering they became incensed
at those creatures which they had thought to be gods, being punished by means of them,
they saw and recognized as the true God him whom they had before refused to know.
Therefore the utmost condemnation came upon them.*

o Gk *they*

OVERVIEW: Pagans created their gods in the image of their passions (EPIPHANIUS). In the present time, God judges in a hidden fashion. God will judge in a visible fashion at the last day (AUGUSTINE). Scripture proclaims that the Son is truly God (VIGILIUS).

12:24 Astray on the Paths of Error

PAGANS PROJECT THEIR EVIL PASSIONS ONTO THEIR GODS. EPIPHANIUS OF SALAMIS: The Greeks did nothing other than design in the images of the gods their peculiar passions, almost so as to be able to contemplate them with their eyes. The bloodthirsty person called his passion Ares. The adulterer and the adulteress, promiscuous Aphrodite. The tyrant, winged Victory. The squalid person, entirely caught up in lust for possessions, designed Cronus as his archetype. The effeminate, Cybele, also known as Rhea, I believe because of the flowing moods of sexual contact.[1] Those who are always breathlessly moving about portrayed as their type Artemis the hunter. The drunkard, Dionysus. The one who faced many difficulties, Heracles. One who had sexual intercourse with anyone, Zeus and Apollo. But it is pointless to enumerate all the passions that agitate human beings. Indeed, the Egyptians deviated from the truth more than anyone, not only worshiping their passions but also exchanging the supreme Orderer[2] for winged creatures and four-legged animals, for wild and ferocious animals of land and sea—in short, with the beasts that the God of holiness had given them to serve them. They deviated more than others because, in a completely irrational way, they divinized the animals of their region. Even now they are not ashamed to worship the barking dog or the pole-

cat who eats reptiles, the goat, symbol of incontinence, and the sheep, symbol of weakness, or the huge, terribly sad crocodile, or the ibis that feeds on poison, the kite and the sparrow hawk, or the crow, which seems the most despicable of all animals, and the serpent, who deviously slithers and is totally disgusting. ANCORATUS 103.1-5.[3]

12:26 Heed Rebukes

GOD'S VISIBLE AND INVISIBLE JUDGMENT.
AUGUSTINE: For the one who does good, there are two judgments referred to in the Scriptures, one secret and the other manifest. The secret one takes place now, and the apostle Peter says of it, "It is time for judgment to begin with the household of the Lord."[4] It follows that the secret judgment is the pain by which each person is tormented now, so that he purifies himself, or by which he is admonished so that he converts or, if he has despised God's calling and his teachings, he remains blind to damnation. The manifest judgment is rather that by which the Lord, when he comes, will judge the living and the dead,[5] when all will know that it is he who assigns rewards to the good and torments to the wicked. But then, such a confession will not be a remedy for evils but a storing up of condemnation. It seems to me that the Lord spoke of these two judgments when he said, "The one who believes in me will pass from death to life and will not be judged,"[6] that is, in the manifest judgment. In fact, the passing from death to life by

---

1The explanation derives the Greek name of the goddess Rhea from the verb *rheō* ("to flow, to stream"). [2]See Rom 1:25. [3]CTP 9:200-201. [4]1 Pet 4:17. [5]See Mt 25:31-46, an allusion to the creed. [6]Jn 5:24.

means of the various sufferings with which God chastises every child he receives[7] is precisely the secret judgment. "The one who does not believe," rather, "is already judged,"[8] that is, in this secret judgment he has already made himself ready to undergo the manifest one. We also read of these two judgments in Wisdom, where it is written, "As to reckless young people, therefore, you sent them a judgment to mock them. But those who were not corrected by this judgment experienced the just judgment of God." Therefore, those who do not correct themselves following this secret judgment of God will be punished as they deserve in the manifest one. EXPOSITIONS OF THE PSALMS 9.1.[9]

12:27 Recognizing the True God

THE SON IS TRULY GOD. VIGILIUS OF THAPSUS: And if they were to repeat what the Son said? "Those who know you, the one true God, and the one whom you have sent, Jesus Christ."[10] Response: That the Son is true, just as the Father is, we demonstrate with the words of the prophets and the Gospels, since Isaiah says, "But my servants will be called by another name, which will be blessed on the earth, and they will bless the true God. And those who swear on earth will swear by the true God."[11] And in Solomon, "They will be ashamed of those who believed that it was the gods who punished them. Seeing him whom they had previously denied, they recognized the true God."[12] And in the psalm, "Truth sprung up from the earth, and justice looked down from heaven."[13] And the Lord in the Gospel, "I am the way, the truth and the life."[14] And in the same place, written of the Father, "Your word is truth."[15] Then in the letter of John the apostle, "We know that the Son of God has come, and God has given us understanding to know what is true, and so that we would be in his true Son, Jesus Christ. He is the true God and eternal life."[16] You must therefore acknowledge the unity of the Father and the Son, since the divine Scripture never fails to proclaim that, like the Father, the Son is true God. AGAINST VARIMADUS 1.34.[17]

---

[7]See Prov 3:12. [8]Jn 3:18. [9]NBA 25:131-33. [10]Jn 17:3. [11]Is 65:15-16. [12]Wis 12:27, variant. [13]Ps 85:12 (84:12 LXX). [14]Jn 14:6. [15]Jn 17:17. [16]1 Jn 5:20. [17]PL 62:375.

13:1-9 IDOLATRY DEIFIES NATURE

[1]For all men who were ignorant of God were foolish by nature;
and they were unable from the good things that are seen to know him who exists,
nor did they recognize the craftsman while paying heed to his works;
[2]but they supposed that either fire or wind or swift air,
or the circle of the stars, or turbulent water,
or the luminaries of heaven were the gods that rule the world.
[3]If through delight in the beauty of these things men[p] assumed them to be gods,
let them know how much better than these is their Lord,

for the author of beauty created them.
⁴And if men^p were amazed at their power and working,
let them perceive from them
how much more powerful is he who formed them.
⁵For from the greatness and beauty of created things
comes a corresponding perception of their Creator.
⁶Yet these men are little to be blamed,
for perhaps they go astray
while seeking God and desiring to find him.
⁷For as they live among his works they keep searching,
and they trust in what they see, because the things that are seen are beautiful.
⁸Yet again, not even they are to be excused;
⁹for if they had the power to know so much
that they could investigate the world,
how did they fail to find sooner the Lord of these things?

p Gk *they*

OVERVIEW: God's power affects every creature (HESYCHIUS), because he is superior to them in everything (AUGUSTINE). As we contemplate the creation we see the wonder of God's work (CYRIL OF JERUSALEM), and through the creation we can get a glimpse of God (DIDYMUS). Creatures are not to be adored (CYRIL OF ALEXANDRIA). God makes us know everything that is useful and what we can bear (JOHN OF DAMASCUS). Creatures reveal God, but the pagan sciences do not discern him in the creatures (AUGUSTINE).

13:3 Mistaking Things for the Real Thing

GOD'S POWER OPERATES IN EVERY CREATURE. HESYCHIUS: "He could not answer God one time in a thousand,"[1] because in fact he is incapable of it. Not only does God speak innumerable words for the good of every person, but, indeed, with his powerful wisdom and his immeasurable greatness, he is above all creatures. "He is wise of heart, powerful and great."[2] Beyond any doubt, the splendor of his creatures, their harmony and order, manifest his wisdom. But God did not acquire this by learning, because he is wisdom in his essence. Job called him "wise in heart," however, to make

us understand the true wisdom and intelligence of God. He mentioned his "greatness," thinking of the elements of visible creatures (and above all of invisible) that, though so great and numerous, hang "like a drop of water in a bucket"[3] from the power of his right hand. And his "power" is manifest by the fact that they remain within the limits that he set out for them.[4] HOMILIES ON JOB 12.[5]

13:4 The Power of the Creator

GOD IS SUPERIOR TO CREATURES IN EVERY WAY. AUGUSTINE: The prophet says, "I will be filled with the revelation of his glory."[6] We can sing of the glory that awaits us, of the goods that will accompany it, of the splendor with which it will shine, but we are incapable of expressing all of this in words. Paul explains the reason for this when he writes, "Those things that eye has not seen, that ear has not heard and that have never entered the heart of human beings, God has prepared for those who love him."[7] These many eternal, heavenly gifts have been prepared

---

[1]Job 9:3. [2]Job 9:4. [3]Is 40:15. [4]See Prov 8:29; Ps 104:9 (103:9 LXX). [5]PO 42.2(191):305. [6]Ps 17:15 (16:15 LXX), variant. [7]1 Cor 2:9.

by the almighty Lord for his faithful, holy people throughout the world. But who is God, who has arranged all these things for us? Of him we say only that we do not know how to measure or express or understand him, that he is beyond all, outside of all, above all. He surpasses all his creatures; he is beyond his works, above all of them. I could try to express his greatness, but he is greater, or his beauty, but he is more beautiful. He is sweeter than every sweetness, brighter than every splendor, more just than all justice, stronger than all strength, gentler than all gentleness. Reason does not admit of the creature claiming equality with its Creator, nor that something produced is put on the level of the one who produced it. Precisely thus we read in the prophet, "The one who made powerful things is more powerful than they are. And the one who made beautiful things is more beautiful than they." SERMON 384.1.1.[8]

13:5 Greatness of Created Things Corresponds to Their Creator

CREATURES MAKE GOD KNOWN. CYRIL OF JERUSALEM: If it is not possible to see the divine nature with eyes of flesh, it is possible to gain an image of the divine power of the Creator from his works. Solomon says this: "In fact, one knows the author by analogy from the greatness and beauty of creatures." He does not say simply that one knows the author from creatures but adds "by analogy." The more we consider his creatures in a contemplative way, in fact, the more God will show himself to be great. And the more our heart is raised in contemplation, the higher will be the image that we have of God. CATECHETICAL LECTURES 9.2.[9]

CREATION REVEALS GOD. DIDYMUS THE BLIND: God has a face that shows itself through his creatures. It is said, in fact, "one knows the author by analogy from the greatness and beauty of creatures." One knows him by the analogy of faith.[10] Just as, looking at a boat, we imagine

its maker even if he is not present, or spotting an approaching ship, we immediately think that there is someone who steers it, or seeing a coach driven well, even if we cannot make out the coachman, we imagine him—in the same way, faced with the fact that the world moves in an orderly way and with the beauty of nature, we derive an image of the beauty and greatness of God. If present things are great, how much greater will the one who made them be! Thus, if one gains an image of God from the world, from the order and arrangements of providence, then the hidden side of his face is no longer hidden. The Greek philosophers also reasoned in this way, deducing an image of God from creatures and their beauty. ON THE PSALM 30.21.[11]

GOD REVEALS HIMSELF. JOHN OF DAMASCUS: No one has ever known God, except the one to whom God has revealed himself.[12] This is true not only for human beings but also among the supracosmic powers and, I would say, even among the cherubim and seraphim. Nevertheless, God did not abandon us in total ignorance. In fact, knowledge of God exists and has been implanted naturally by him in everyone. The creation itself, its preservation and its regulation, proclaim the greatness of the divine nature. And he also revealed knowledge of himself, to the extent it can be attained, first through the Law and the prophets and then through his only-begotten Son, our Lord God and Savior Jesus Christ. For this reason we receive, acknowledge and reverence what has been passed down to us through the Law, the prophets, the apostles and the Evangelists, not seeking anything beyond these things. Indeed, God, being good, is the author of every good and is subject to neither envy or passion. "Envy is far from the divine nature, which is impassive and only good."[13] Therefore, knowing all things

---

[8]NBA 34:603. [9]CTP 103:169. [10]See Rom 12:6. [11]PTA 8:112. [12]Cf. Jn 1:18. [13]Gregory of Nazianzus *Theological Oration* 2 (28).11.

and concerned for what is useful for each, he revealed what is good for us to know, passing over in silence what we could not bear. ORTHO-DOX FAITH 1.1.[14]

13:9 How Did They Fail to Find the Lord?

PAGAN WISDOM DID NOT DISCOVER GOD IN HIS CREATURES. AUGUSTINE: "If they were capable of sufficient knowledge to account for the universe, how is it that they did not more easily find its Lord?" They are blamed for having spent their time, their activity and their discussions scrutinizing, and in a certain way measuring, what is created. They investigated the movement of the planets, the distance between the stars, the course of the heavenly bodies. Through these studies, they arrived at such a scientific knowledge as to be able to predict eclipses of the sun and the moon, which then occurred on the day and hour predicted, for the length of time and at the exact point in space they had said. What ability! What capacity! But when they were at the point of seeking to know the Creator—who was not far from them—they were unable to find him. If they had found him, they would have had him in themselves. SERMON 68.4.[15]

---

[14]CTP 142:47-48. [15]NBA 30/1:365.

13:10–14:11 AN IDOL IS A DEAD OBJECT

[10]*But miserable, with their hopes set on dead things, are the men*
who give the name "gods" to the works of men's hands,
gold and silver fashioned with skill,
and likenesses of animals,
or a useless stone, the work of an ancient hand.
[11]*A skilled woodcutter may saw down a tree easy to handle*
and skilfully strip off all its bark,
and then with pleasing workmanship
make a useful vessel that serves life's needs,
[12]*and burn the castoff pieces of his work*
to prepare his food, and eat his fill.
[13]*But a castoff piece from among them, useful for nothing,*
a stick crooked and full of knots,
he takes and carves with care in his leisure,
and shapes it with skill gained in idleness;[q]
he forms it like the image of a man,
[14]*or makes it like some worthless animal,*

giving it a coat of red paint and coloring its surface red
and covering every blemish in it with paint;
[15]then he makes for it a niche that befits it,
and sets it in the wall, and fastens it there with iron.
[16]So he takes thought for it, that it may not fall,
because he knows that it cannot help itself,
for it is only an image and has need of help.
[17]When he prays about possessions and his marriage and children,
he is not ashamed to address a lifeless thing.
[18]For health he appeals to a thing that is weak;
for life he prays to a thing that is dead;
for aid he entreats a thing that is utterly inexperienced;
for a prosperous journey, a thing that cannot take a step;
[19]for money-making and work and success with his hands
he asks strength of a thing whose hands have no strength.

14 Again, one preparing to sail and about to voyage over raging waves
calls upon a piece of wood more fragile than the ship which carries him.
[2]For it was desire for gain that planned that vessel,
and wisdom was the craftsman who built it;
[3]but it is thy providence, O Father, that steers its course,
because thou hast given it a path in the sea,
and a safe way through the waves,
[4]showing that thou canst save from every danger,
so that even if a man lacks skill, he may put to sea.
[5]It is thy will that works of thy wisdom should not be without effect;
therefore men trust their lives even to the smallest piece of wood,
and passing through the billows on a raft they come safely to land.
[6]For even in the beginning, when arrogant giants were perishing,
the hope of the world took refuge on a raft,
and guided by thy hand left to the world the seed of a new generation.
[7]For blessed is the wood by which righteousness comes.

[8]But the idol made with hands is accursed, and so is he who made it;
because he did the work, and the perishable thing was named a god.
[9]For equally hateful to God are the ungodly man and his ungodliness,
[10]for what was done will be punished together with him who did it.
[11]Therefore there will be a visitation also upon the heathen idols,
because, though part of what God created, they became an abomination,
and became traps for the souls of men
and a snare to the feet of the foolish.

q Other authorities read *with intelligent skill*

OVERVIEW: God uses many means to accomplish miracles (JOHN OF DAMASCUS). Angels mourn when we sin (ORIGEN). God's wrath is provoked by unbelieving idolatry (AUGUSTINE).

14:7 The Wood by Which Righteousness Comes

MANY KINDS OF MIRACLES. JOHN OF DAMASCUS: If the bones of the righteous are impure, how is it that the bones of Jacob and Joseph were carried out of Egypt with every honor?[1] Or how is it that a dead man was raised after coming in contact with the bones of Elisha?[2] If God works miracles through bones, it is clear that he can also do so through images, stones and many other things. This also happened with Elisha, who gave his staff to his servant and ordered him to go and raise the son of the Shunammite woman with it.[3] Moses too, with a staff, not only punished Pharaoh[4] but also divided the sea,[5] sweetened waters[6] and opened the rock and made water flow out.[7] Solomon says, "Blessed is the wood from which salvation comes." Elisha made a piece of iron float after throwing a stick in the Jordan,[8] and it is also written that "the tree of life"[9] and "the plant of Sabek"[10] lead to forgiveness. Moses lifted up the serpent on a stick, saving the lives of the people,[11] and confirmed the priesthood in the tent with a blooming branch.[12] THREE TREATISES ON DIVINE IMAGES 1.56.[13]

14:8 An Accursed Idol

ANGELS MOURN WHEN WE SIN. ORIGEN: By the disposition of the universe you find an angel appointed for the earth and another appointed for the waters, another appointed for the air and a fourth appointed for fire.[14] Arise, then—I beg of you—with your reason, and consider the disposition of the animals, the plants and the stars of heaven. There is an angel appointed for the sun, another of the moon and others of the stars. These angels, who accompany us during our time on earth, either rejoice or mourn over us when we sin. "Grieve," it says, "over the earth because of its inhabitants."[15] It calls the angel for the earth using the same name as the earth itself, "earth," as when it says, "The work of human hands and the one who has done it are accursed." It is not that the inanimate thing itself is accursed, but what resides in the inanimate statue is indicated by the expression "human hands," and from this it receives its name.[16] In this way I would say that the angel appointed for the earth is designated also by the name "earth," and the angel appointed for the water is designated by the name "water," as when it is said, "The waters saw you, O God, the waters saw you and feared. The abyss trembled, a great crash of waters, and the clouds sent out their voice. Behold, your arrows pass."[17] HOMILIES ON JEREMIAH 10.6.[18]

14:11 A Visitation on Idols

IDOLATRY ANGERS GOD. AUGUSTINE: In the book of Wisdom it is written, "For this reason there will also be an inquiry into the idols of the peoples." It could seem as though for a long time God did not consider that idols were worshiped and sacrifices offered to them. Then he who always watches finally made inquiry. He watched in tolerance, he inquired so as to punish. "Into the idols of the peoples," the book says, "there will be an inquiry, because God's creatures have become detestable." The pagans in fact provoke God through his creatures. How do they provoke God through his creatures? Because the carpenter shaped an idol, whereas God had created the wood. The goldsmith shaped an

---

[1]See Gen 50:13, 25. [2]See 2 Kings 13:21. [3]See 2 Kings 4:29. [4]See Ex 7–10. [5]See Ex 14:16. [6]See Ex 15:25. [7]See Ex 17:6. [8]See 2 Kings 6:6. [9]See Gen 2:9. [10]See Gen 22:13 LXX. The Septuagint and Hebrew refer to the plant by name rather than using the more generic description of bush or thicket. Melito of Sardis, in *Fragments on Genesis*, viewed it as a prototype of the cross. See G. W. Lampe, *A Patristic Greek Lexicon* (Oxford: Clarendon Press, 1961), 1220. [11]See Num 21:8-9. [12]See Num 17:8. [13]CTP 36:77-78. [14]Origen mentions the four elements of ancient cosmology. [15]Jer 12:3. [16]See Is 19:3. [17]Ps 77:17-18. [18]CTP 123:129-30.

idol, whereas God had created the gold. From an object of yours, do you form something that he might detest? Why, from a creature of God, do you wickedly mold something that he should find detestable? You must form yourself well, so that he will love you. You want to impress your image in wood. Rather, receive within you the image of God. What do you destroy inwardly, and what do you sculpt outwardly? "God's creatures," the book says, "have become detestable. They have become a scandal for the souls of human beings and a snare for the feet of fools.

Indeed, the beginning of fornication is the love of idols." If a woman who has many husbands were to merit praise, then let someone who worships many gods also be praised. If a woman who offers herself to men is an adulteress, how much more a soul that worships gods that do not exist? "The beginning of fornication is the love of idols, and their invention a corruption of life."[19] NEWLY DISCOVERED SERMONS 24.6.[20]

---

[19]Wis 14:12. [20]NBA 35/2.553-55.

14:12-21 THE BIRTH OF AN IDOLATROUS CULT

[12]For the idea of making idols was the beginning of fornication,
and the invention of them was the corruption of life,
[13]for neither have they existed from the beginning
nor will they exist for ever.
[14]For through the vanity of men they entered the world,
and therefore their speedy end has been planned.
[15]For a father, consumed with grief at an untimely bereavement,
made an image of his child, who had been suddenly taken from him;
and he now honored as a god what was once a dead human being,
and handed on to his dependents secret rites and initiations.
[16]Then the ungodly custom, grown strong with time, was kept as a law,
and at the command of monarchs graven images were worshiped.
[17]When men could not honor monarchs[r] in their presence, since they lived at a distance,
they imagined their appearance far away,
and made a visible image of the king whom they honored,
so that by their zeal they might flatter the absent one as though present.
[18]Then the ambition of the craftsman impelled
even those who did not know the king to intensify their worship.
[19]For he, perhaps wishing to please his ruler,
skilfully forced the likeness to take more beautiful form,

*²⁰and the multitude, attracted by the charm of his work,
now regarded as an object of worship the one whom shortly before they had honored as a man.
²¹And this became a hidden trap for mankind,
because men, in bondage to misfortune or to royal authority,
bestowed on objects of stone or wood the name that ought not to be shared.*

r Gk *them*

OVERVIEW: Idols are products of the devils and of the human mind (EPIPHANIUS). The idea of idolatry is demonically inspired (AUGUSTINE).

14:12 Idolatry the Beginning of Fornication

THE ORIGIN OF IDOLS. EPIPHANIUS OF SALAMIS: Condemn idols, openly denouncing their error. Indeed, do not even consider them to be dead, because they were never alive. Teach clearly everywhere and to all that these are vain and foolish things. Not existing and never having existed, there is no possibility of their being what they are said to be. They are the products of wicked demons and of the human mind full of impulses to pleasure, since each of us is led to make his own passion an object of veneration. Thus in the beginning idolatry was born of the wicked work of demons and by human conception, through a commingling that was called "the first fornication." At first they designed the figures of the idols, then they began to give gods to their own children as objects of veneration, made of various materials according to the art that each one possessed for providing for his needs

with his own hands: the potter with clay, the carpenter with wood, the goldsmith with gold, the silversmith with silver. ANCORATUS 102.5-7.[1]

14:20 Worshiping One Previously Honored as a Man

IDOLS ARE DEMONICALLY INSPIRED. AUGUSTINE: Human beings seek purification, but the devil, proud spirit, seeing that they sought this out of pride and boasted of it, anticipated them and presented himself as a mediator, capable of giving a semblance of purity to their souls. In this, hinting at his pride, he led people to think that he was necessary, that is, to show them that a soul desirous to reach God could purify itself through recourse to magic arts. He thus instituted in the temples those sacrilegious rites that assure purification to those who perform them. Many of those images were in fact suggested, as the Scripture says, by the desire to honor certain people held to be great, people not present or dead people. SERMONS 26.28.[2]

---

[1]CTP 9:199-200. [2]NBA 35/2:661-63.

14:22-31 THE CONSEQUENCES
OF THE IDOLATROUS CULT

²²*Afterward it was not enough for them to err about the knowledge of God,*
but they live in great strife due to ignorance,
and they call such great evils peace.
²³*For whether they kill children in their initiations, or celebrate secret mysteries,*
or hold frenzied revels with strange customs,
²⁴*they no longer keep either their lives or their marriages pure,*
but they either treacherously kill one another, or grieve one another by adultery,
²⁵*and all is a raging riot of blood and murder, theft and deceit, corruption, faithlessness, tumult,*
     perjury,
²⁶*confusion over what is good, forgetfulness of favors,*
pollution of souls, sex perversion,
disorder in marriage, adultery, and debauchery.
²⁷*For the worship of idols not to be named*
is the beginning and cause and end of every evil.
²⁸*For their worshipers^s either rave in exultation, or prophesy lies,*
or live unrighteously, or readily commit perjury;
²⁹*for because they trust in lifeless idols*
they swear wicked oaths and expect to suffer no harm.
³⁰*But just penalties will overtake them on two counts:*
because they thought wickedly of God in devoting themselves to idols,
and because in deceit they swore unrighteously through contempt for holiness.
³¹*For it is not the power of the things by which men swear,^t*
but the just penalty for those who sin,
that always pursues the transgression of the unrighteous.

s Gk *they*   t Or *of the oaths men swear*

OVERVIEW: Serving sin and serving an idol are the same thing (ORIGEN). We should not picture God according to the limitations of our intelligence (AUGUSTINE).

14:29-30 *Trusting in Lifeless Idols*

TO SERVE SIN IS TO SERVE AN IDOL. ORIGEN: Unquestionably, at the time when the early Israelites fell into sin, religion languished. Judah made for themselves "statues in Jerusalem," as well as in that part that came to be called Israel, "in Samaria."[1] But even now, if one considers the mass of sinners taken together, it would not be hard to say that everyone who, serving sin, makes a god out of what seems good to him—making a statue, casting the work of an artisan, setting it up in secret—is under the curse. It is precisely in the secret of the heart that we fabricate many idols when we sin. Therefore the

---

[1]See Is 10:10.

Word admonishes us to do penance and to "cry out in lamentation over the statues" and the idols that are "in Jerusalem and in Samaria."[2] Truly, if we who desire to be of the church commit sin, we fabricate "statues in Jerusalem." If those who are outside of the church sin, as heretics, they make "idols in Samaria." Nevertheless God, in conformity with his goodness, calls all to repentance, saying, "Cry out in lamentation, statues, in Jerusalem and in Samaria, since as I have acted toward Samaria and the works of their hands, so also will I act toward Jerusalem and its idols."[3] The threat will be carried out toward those who are in the church just as it was with the Samaritans. HOMILIES ON ISAIAH 8.1.[4]

THREE FALSE IDEAS ABOUT GOD. AUGUSTINE: Some attempt to apply to incorporeal and spiritual beings what they have perceived of corporeal beings through sensible experience or what they have learned about them thanks to the very nature of human intelligence, to keen reflection and with the aid of science. They want to measure and represent the former based on the latter. Others have an idea about God, if you can call this having an idea, consistent with the nature and affections of the human soul. From

this error it follows that they discuss God based on incorrect and false principles. There are still others who attempt to transcend the created universe, which is obviously changeable, and to raise their vision to that unchanging being that is God. But, weighed down by their mortal nature and wanting to appear wise in what they do not know, and incapable of knowing what they want to know,[5] they insist too boldly on conjectures. They thus preclude the ways of understanding, preferring to persist in their mistaken opinions rather than changing the opinion they once defended. This is the true evil of the three categories of persons we have just spoken of: those who think of God after the manner of bodily beings, those who conceive of him in a way consistent with spiritual creatures, like the soul, and finally those who, though keeping well away from corporeal and spiritual things, "thought erroneously about God," distancing themselves even more from the truth in that their idea of God is drawn neither from sensible experience, nor from spiritual creatures nor from the Creator himself. ON THE TRINITY 1.1.1.[6]

---

[2]Is 10:10. [3]Is 10:10-11. [4]CTP 132:160-61. [5]See Wis 9:13-16. [6]NBA 4:7.

15:1-6 ISRAEL DOES NOT ADORE IDOLS

[1]But thou, our God, art kind and true,
patient, and ruling all things[u] in mercy.
[2]For even if we sin we are thine, knowing thy power;
but we will not sin, because we know that we are accounted thine.
[3]For to know thee is complete righteousness,
and to know thy power is the root of immortality.

⁴For neither has the evil intent of human art misled us,
nor the fruitless toil of painters,
a figure stained with varied colors,
⁵whose appearance arouses yearning in fools,
so that they desire[v] the lifeless form of a dead image.
⁶Lovers of evil things and fit for such objects of hope[w]
are those who either make or desire or worship them

---

u Or *ruling the universe*   **v** Gk *and he desires*   **w** Gk *such hopes*

OVERVIEW: God's goodness and omnipotence are wonderful to contemplate. Idolaters and heretics are both criminals (RABANUS MAURUS).

15:1 God Rules All Things in Mercy

GOD'S GOODNESS AND OMNIPOTENCE.
RABANUS MAURUS: Our God is good, because love is ineffable. He is true because he deceives no one, and he is not deceived by anyone. He is patient, ordering all with mercy. In his goodness he waits patiently for us to turn to the good, because he wants no one to perish but all to be saved and to come to the knowledge of the truth.[1] It is he who says through the prophet, "I do not delight in the death of the wicked."[2] If we sin, we cannot flee from his hand, since we are his creatures. If we cease from sin and persist in good works, we will receive a sure reward from him in whom the essence of every good act remains whole and entire. He knows everyone, and no secret is hidden from him.[3] ON ECCLESIASTICUS 3.4.[4]

15:6 Lovers of Evil Things

IDOLATERS AND HERETICS ARE ALIKE. RABANUS MAURUS: Not only those who fabricate idols are criminals and traitors, but also those who love and worship them, putting their hope in them, since not only those who do evil deserve death but also those who agree with them.[5] The psalmist shows the condition of those who put their hope in idols, "The idols of the nations are of silver and gold, the work of human hands. They have mouths and do not speak, eyes and do not see, ears and do not hear, noses and do not smell. They have hands and do not feel, feet and do not walk. No sounds issue from their throats. Those who make them and trust in them will be like them."[6] Indeed, with wicked hands a mortal shapes something dead, and a fool worships what is beyond foolish. Speaking allegorically, this treats first of heretics, who devise and give shape to perverse opinions, while those who love and worship them are their followers and disciples. And all of them are condemned and destined to be lost. In fact, "they will all be amazed and confused together."[7] "The Lord will disperse the one who has acted thusly, the master and his disciple."[8] "Woe to the godless! He will be repaid according to the misdeeds of his hands."[9] ON ECCLESIASTICUS 3.5.[10]

---

[1]See 1 Tim 2:4. [2]Ezek 33:11. [3]See Heb 4:13. [4]PL 109:741-42. [5]See Rom 1:32. [6]Ps 115:4-8 (113:12-16 LXX). [7]Is 44:11. [8]Mal 2:12. [9]Is 3:11. [10]PL 109:742-43.

15:7-13 THE FOLLY OF THE POTTER WHO SHAPES IDOLS

⁷For when a potter kneads the soft earth
and laboriously molds each vessel for our service,
he fashions out of the same clay
both the vessels that serve clean uses
and those for contrary uses, making all in like manner;
but which shall be the use of each of these
the worker in clay decides.
⁸With misspent toil, he forms a futile god from the same clay—
this man who was made of earth a short time before
and after a little while goes to the earth from which he was taken,
when he is required to return the soul that was lent him.
⁹But he is not concerned that he is destined to die
or that his life is brief,
but he competes with workers in gold and silver,
and imitates workers in copper;
and he counts it his glory that he molds counterfeit gods.
¹⁰His heart is ashes, his hope is cheaper than dirt,
and his life is of less worth than clay,
¹¹because he failed to know the one who formed him
and inspired him with an active soul
and breathed into him a living spirit.
¹²But heˣ considered our existence an idle game,
and life a festival held for profit,
for he says one must get money however one can, even by base means.
¹³For this man, more than all others, knows that he sins
when he makes from earthy matter fragile vessels and graven images.

x Other authorities read *they*

OVERVIEW: God created both the body and soul (METHODIUS).

15:11 *The One Who Formed and Inspired Him*

HUMANITY WAS CREATED BY GOD ALONE.
METHODIUS: Perhaps someone among people, having little discernment and lacking in wisdom, might be able to convince them that the garment of the soul, that is, this body of flesh generated by human beings, is formed on its own impetus, outside of God's decision. He will certainly not be believed if he teaches that the substance of the soul is sown together with the mortal body. In fact, only the Almighty breathes into human

beings what is immortal and what does not decay, since he alone is Creator of all invisible and imperishable things. It says, "He breathed on his face a spirit of life, and the man became a living being."[1] Moreover, the Word, accusing precisely those artists who, to people's hurt, make statues of human features while not acknowledging the Creator, says in Wisdom, full of virtue, "Their heart is ashes, their wisdom more vain than the earth and their life more vile than mud, because they did not recognize the One who made them, who inspired in them the soul that acts and blew into them the spirit of life." The Creator of all people is therefore God. For this reason, according to the saying of the apostle, "He wants all people to be saved and to come to a knowledge of the truth."[2] SYMPOSIUM OR BANQUET OF THE TEN VIRGINS 2.7.[3]

---

[1]Gen 2:7. [2]1 Tim 2:4. [3]CTP 152:53-54.

15:14-19 THE ALL-ENCOMPASSING IDOLATRY OF THE EGYPTIANS

[14]But most foolish, and more miserable than an infant,
are all the enemies who oppressed thy people.
[15]For they thought that all their heathen idols were gods,
though these have neither the use of their eyes to see with,
nor nostrils with which to draw breath,
nor ears with which to hear,
nor fingers to feel with,
and their feet are of no use for walking.
[16]For a man made them,
and one whose spirit is borrowed formed them;
for no man can form a god which is like himself.
[17]He is mortal, and what he makes with lawless hands is dead,
for he is better than the objects he worships,
since[y] he has life, but they never have.

[18]The enemies of thy people[z] worship even the most hateful animals,
which are worse than all others, when judged by their lack of intelligence;
[19]and even as animals they are not so beautiful in appearance that one would desire them,
but they have escaped both the praise of God and his blessing.

y Other authorities read of which   z Gk They

OVERVIEW: To adore a human being is similar to offering worship to a corpse (AMBROSIASTER), even though humans are superior to the idols they fashion (AUGUSTINE). Pagans have distanced themselves so much from God that they adore disgusting animals (RABANUS MAURUS).

15:17 A Lifeless Image

DO NOT ADORE IMAGES OF HUMAN BEINGS.
AMBROSIASTER: "And they exchanged the glory of the incorruptible God for the likeness of the image of corruptible human beings."[1] Their heart was darkened to such a degree that they transferred the majesty of the invisible God, whom they knew from these works, not to human beings but, a worse and unpardonable crime, to the likeness of human beings. They thus call the image of the corruptible human being—the likeness of a person—god. In this way they attribute the glory that belongs to God to images of dead people,[2] to whom they would not dare to give this name while they were alive. What dullness, what foolishness, calling themselves wise to their own condemnation. In their eyes, the image is more powerful than truth, and the dead are better than the living! Indeed, separating themselves from the living God, they serve the dead. In this category are those of whom it is written in the Wisdom of Solomon, "The dead person forms a dead work with his wicked hands." The Wisdom of Solomon says this about this kind of person. COMMENTARY ON THE LETTER TO THE ROMANS 1.22-23.[3]

HUMANS ADORE IDOLS THAT THEY FORMED.
AUGUSTINE: You say that your god lies, but that that object that you have made convinces you of the truth. By the fact, however, that it convinces you of the truth, it does not follow that it is superior to you. Even if you say what is false and he what is true, even if you say that it is a god and he a piece of wood, it is not for that reason superior to you. You have no reason, therefore, to worship it, almost as though it were superior to you. You in fact have sensible faculties, whereas he does not. You hear, whereas he does not hear. You see, whereas he does not see. You walk, whereas he does not walk. You live, whereas of him, I cannot even say that he is dead, since he has never been alive. You, therefore, are superior to the image you have made. Well then, worship one who is superior to you, that is, the One who created you! It would be an insult to you if someone considered you as equal to that object you have made. You ask what the one you worship is like? If someone were to say to you out of ill will, "If only you were like that thing there," you would be beside yourself with rage. And yet you adore what you would abhor to be, and adoring it you become in some way similar to that object, not, of course, changing into wood and ceasing to be a person but rendering your interior person almost similar to the bodily effigy you have made. NEWLY DISCOVERED SERMONS 6.5.[4]

15:18 Worshiping Animals

PAGANS ADORE DISGUSTING ANIMALS.
RABANUS MAURUS: Paganism was so disgusting that it not only worshiped as gods the image of human beings shaped in insensible material, but it also gave perverse cult to the images of other animals, being entirely without discretion in this regard. Indeed, according to the sense of the truth, the living are prior to the dead, and sensible things prior to inanimate and rational animals prior to the other animals. But it stands to reason that someone who ignored the Creator would be unable to adequately distinguish his creatures. He who neglected to bear within himself the praise and blessing of God showed himself capable of erring with respect to the nature and differences between animals. ON ECCLESIASTICUS 3.6.[5]

---

[1]Rom 1:23. [2]See Wis 14:15. [3]CTP 43:61-62. [4]NBA 35/1.133. [5]PL 109:744-45.

16:1-4 FROGS AND QUAILS

[1]Therefore those men were deservedly punished through such creatures,
and were tormented by a multitude of animals.
[2]Instead of this punishment thou didst show kindness to thy people,
and thou didst prepare quails to eat,
a delicacy to satisfy the desire of appetite;
[3]in order that those men, when they desired food,
might lose the least remnant of appetite[a]
because of the odious creatures sent to them,
while thy people,[b] after suffering want a short time,
might partake of delicacies.
[4]For it was necessary that upon those oppressors inexorable want should come,
while to these it was merely shown how their enemies were being tormented.

a Gk *loathe the necessary appetite*   **b** Gk *they*

OVERVIEW: The plagues were aimed at the Egyptians but symbolize the heretics (Rabanus Maurus).

16:1 *Tormented by a Multitude of Animals*

THE PLAGUES OF EGYPT. RABANUS MAURUS: These words refer to the Egyptians who, being idolaters and given over to various kinds of errors, also unjustly persecuted the people of God. And the Lord punished them with ten plagues, because they did not want to free his people. They thus experienced the cruelty of the beasts: it is described how flies of various types[1] and grasshoppers[2] ravaged them. And also frogs[3] and poisonous toads and other animals that covered the earth, of which it is said in the psalm, "He sent horseflies to ravage them and frogs to molest them. He gave their harvests to the flames and the fruit of their labor to locusts."[4] One understands further that heretics and schismatics are torn to pieces, scattered and destroyed by the beasts (that is, by evil spirits). The former in fact are subject to the will of the latter (and thus also to the righteous judgment of God) and are tormented and scattered by them. ON ECCLESIASTICUS 3.6.[5]

[1]See Ex 8:16-19. [2]See Ex 10:1-7. [3]See Ex 8:1-5 (7:26–8:1 LXX).
[4]Ps 78:45-46 (77:45-46 LXX). [5]PL 109:745.

16:5-14 THE LOCUSTS AND THE BRONZE SERPENT

⁵For when the terrible rage of wild beasts came upon thy people^c
and they were being destroyed by the bites of writhing serpents,
thy wrath did not continue to the end;
⁶they were troubled for a little while as a warning,
and received a token of deliverance to remind them of thy law's command.
⁷For he who turned toward it was saved, not by what he saw,
but by thee, the Savior of all.
⁸And by this also thou didst convince our enemies
that it is thou who deliverest from every evil.
⁹For they were killed by the bites of locusts and flies,
and no healing was found for them,
because they deserved to be punished by such things;
¹⁰but thy sons were not conquered even by the teeth of venomous serpents,
for thy mercy came to their help and healed them.
¹¹To remind them of thy oracles they were bitten,
and then were quickly delivered,
lest they should fall into deep forgetfulness
and become unresponsive^d to thy kindness.
¹²For neither herb nor poultice cured them,
but it was thy word, O Lord, which heals all men.
¹³For thou hast power over life and death;
thou dost lead men down to the gates of Hades and back again.
¹⁴A man in his wickedness kills another,
but he cannot bring back the departed spirit,
nor set free the imprisoned soul.

c Gk *them*   d The meaning of the Greek is obscure

OVERVIEW: Levites led the people of Israel. The bronze serpent was an image of Christ, who heals the ills of the soul (ORIGEN, CHROMATIUS). The impious and the wicked will not see God; their fate is like the devil after his fall (ANONYMOUS ANOMOEAN).

16:7 Saved by Looking on the Bronze Serpent

THE SIGNIFICANCE OF THE LEVITES AND THE BRONZE SERPENT. ORIGEN: In the meantime, the priestly Levitical order must show the way to the people of God—who are leaving Egypt! It is they, in fact, who teach the people to flee Egypt, which is to say from the errors of the world, and to pass through the immense desert, that is, to pass through various kinds of temptations without being harmed by the serpents, which are the bites of demons, and to avoid the poison of perverse counsel. And if it happens that someone is bitten by a serpent in the desert, they also show him the bronze serpent[1] hanging on the cross. The one who sees it, who believes, that is, in him whom the serpent symbolized,[2] by this very fact will escape the devil's poison. HOMILIES ON JOSHUA 4.2.[3]

16:12 God's Word Heals All People

THE LORD HEALS THE ILLS OF THE SOUL. CHROMATIUS OF AQUILEIA: Illness of the soul is much more serious than that of the body. Bodily ills cause temporal death, but illness of the spirit brings eternal death. Indeed, when in paradise Adam transgressed the divine commandment, he did not contract an illness of the body but an illness of the soul, by which he would have perished eternally if the grace of Christ had not rescued him from death. Listen to the prophet who proclaims this, when he says, "By his wounds we have all been healed."[4] The wounds and the passion of the Lord were the remedy that healed humanity. In fact, illnesses of the soul are not healed by the medical arts but only by the grace of Christ. The fever of sin and the wounds of guilt are sicknesses of the soul, which do not enter the body from the outside but from within the soul. These wounds of the soul are not healed by human beings but by God—not by the incision of an earthly knife but by the sword of the divine Word that penetrates into the depths of the soul.[5] Listen to the prophet declare that "it was not an herb or an ointment that cured them but your word, O Lord, which heals everyone." And the words of David, "He sent his word to heal them."[6] And rightly the prophet prays to the Lord about the iniquity of the Jewish people in these terms, "Is there no balm in Gilead, no physician there? Why therefore does not the health of your people recover?"[7] The prophet does not speak of just any balm but of a heavenly remedy, nor of a human physician but of a physician who is God. SERMONS 31.2.[8]

16:14 A Mortal Cannot Free the Imprisoned Soul

THE DEVIL AND THE IMPIOUS DO NOT SEE GOD. ANONYMOUS ANOMOEAN: How could he again come before the face of God,[9] he who was not permitted to draw near the holy soul of Job or even to touch it?[10] How could he reach heaven who was not permitted to enter paradise?[11] Indeed, a cherubim with a flaming sword was posted to guard the gate of paradise, so that the one who had fallen in the past—that is, Adam—could not enter again.[12] Now, what must the holy virtues of the angels be who guard the gates of heaven, those of whom it was said, "Lift up the gates, you princes, that the king of glory may come in"?[13] It is not possible that the supremely perverse devil ever passed through or could pass through these gates or go over them to arrive in heaven. Indeed, having fallen from heaven because of his iniquity,[14] he would never again enter heaven, never again return. If God says to the godless and the wicked, "Do not trample my courts,"[15] how much more will the devil, author of all impiety and father and author of every crime, ever go up again to the heavenly court from which he fell by his own will, never returning there? Indeed, if the spirit that leaves does not return, nor is the soul recalled once it has gone, is it not even more true that he who left heaven by his own iniquity will never return there and he who by his obstinate wickedness was expelled from the chorus of the saints will never be recalled to repentance? COMMENTARY ON JOB 1.40.[16]

---

[1]See Num 21:6-9. [2]See Jn 3:14. [3]CTP 108:88. [4]Is 53:5. [5]See Heb 4:12. [6]Ps 107:20 (106:20 LXX). [7]Jer 8:22, variant. [8]CTP 20:198-99. [9]See Job 1:6; 2:2. [10]See Job 2:6. [11]Many fathers of the church distinguish paradise—which they often locate on the earth—from the kingdom of heaven. [12]See Gen 3:24. [13]Ps 24:7 (23:7 LXX). [14]See Is 14:12; Ezek 28:15-17; Lk 10:18; Rev 12:9. [15]Is 1:12. [16]CSEL 96:150-51.

16:15-29 HAIL AND MANNA

¹⁵To escape from thy hand is impossible;
¹⁶for the ungodly, refusing to know thee,
were scourged by the strength of thy arm,
pursued by unusual rains and hail and relentless storms,
and utterly consumed by fire.
¹⁷For—most incredible of all—in the water, which quenches all things,
the fire had still greater effect,
for the universe defends the righteous.
¹⁸At one time the flame was restrained,
so that it might not consume the creatures sent against the ungodly,
but that seeing this they might know
that they were being pursued by the judgment of God;
¹⁹and at another time even in the midst of water it burned more intensely than fire,
to destroy the crops of the unrighteous land.
²⁰Instead of these things thou didst give thy people food of angels,
and without their toil thou didst supply them from heaven with bread ready to eat,
providing every pleasure and suited to every taste.
²¹For thy sustenance manifested thy sweetness toward thy children;
and the bread, ministeringᵉ to the desire of the one who took it,
was changed to suit every one's liking.
²²Snow and ice withstood fire without melting,
so that they might know that the crops of their enemies
were being destroyed by the fire that blazed in the hail
and flashed in the showers of rain;
²³whereas the fire,ᶠ in order that the righteous might be fed,
even forgot its native power.

²⁴For the creation, serving thee who hast made it,
exerts itself to punish the unrighteous,
and in kindness relaxes on behalf of those who trust in thee.
²⁵Therefore at that time also, changed into all forms,
it served thy all-nourishing bounty,
according to the desire of those who had need,ᵍ
²⁶so that thy sons, whom thou didst love, O Lord, might learn
that it is not the production of crops that feeds man,
but that thy word preserves those who trust in thee.
²⁷For what was not destroyed by fire

was melted when simply warmed by a fleeting ray of the sun,
[28]to make it known that one must rise before the sun to give thee thanks,
and must pray to thee at the dawning of the light;
[29] for the hope of an ungrateful man will melt like wintry frost,
and flow away like waste water.

e Gk and it, ministering **f** Gk this **g** Or who made supplication

OVERVIEW: We must believe that the Son has the same substance as his Father (VICTOR OF VITA). There is a difference between the incarnation of the Word and the apparitions of the Holy Spirit (AUGUSTINE). God acts through the angels, and they accomplish his will (AUGUSTINE). We must choose the place, the orientation, the attitude, the dispositions and the time of prayer (ORIGEN). Let us be grateful for God's care for us (CHRYSOSTOM).

16:21 God's Sweetness Toward His Children

THE SON IS CONSUBSTANTIAL WITH THE FATHER. VICTOR OF VITA: That the Son is from the Father—that is, that he is of the same being as the Father—is proven by the following testimonies. The apostle says, "He is the splendor of his glory and the imprint of his being, sustaining all things by his powerful word."[1] And God the Father, reproaching the bad faith of unbelievers who did not want to listen to the voice of the Son who, while remaining in his being, had spoken through the prophets,[2] said, "They did not listen to the voice of my being."[3] And reproaching with fearsome words because the voice of his being had been despised, he speaks again to the same prophet, saying, "Weeping on the high mountains and grief on the desert roads, because they have failed, no longer being human. They did not listen to the voice of my being, from the birds of the air to the beasts."[4] And again reproaching those who, deviating from the profession of one being, did not want to remain in the being itself of faith, he says, "If they had remained in my being, I would have brought them back from their evil ways and their

wicked thoughts."[5] And it is again stated clearly that the Son must not be professed as being other than the being of the Father but that, with faith, he must be contemplated in his very being with the eyes of the intellect, when the prophet says, "Who has been in the being of the Lord and has seen his word?"[6] Thus, that the being of the Father is the Son was already clearly proclaimed by the oracles of the prophets, Solomon saying, "You in fact showed us your being and your sweetness that you have toward your children."[7] The Lord showed that these were poured out from heaven on the people of Israel in the figure and semblance of heavenly bread,[8] saying in the Gospel, "It was not Moses who gave you the bread from heaven, but it is my Father who gives you the bread from heaven."[9] He declares himself to be the bread when he says, "I am the living bread, who came down from heaven."[10] Of him the prophet David also says, "Human beings ate the bread of angels."[11] BOOK OF THE CATHOLIC FAITH 58–59.[12]

16:24 Creation Punishes the Unrighteous

THE HOLY SPIRIT DOES NOT BECOME INCARNATE. AUGUSTINE: The Holy Spirit did not beatify the dove[13] or the wind[14] or the fire,[15] nor did he unite them to himself and to his own person so as to remain in that state forever. Otherwise the nature of the Holy Spirit would be variable and convertible, if those phenomena had not hap-

---

[1]Heb 1:3. [2]See Heb 1:1. [3]See Jer 7:26. [4]Jer 9:9. [5]Jer 23:22. [6]Jer 23:18. [7]Wis 16:21 Vg. [8]See Ex 16. [9]Jn 6:32. [10]Jn 6:35, 41. [11]Ps 78:25 (77:25 LXX). [12]CTP 29:80-81. [13]See Mt 3:16; Mk 1:10; Lk 3:22; Jn 1:32. [14]See Acts 2:2. [15]See Acts 2:3.

pened by a change in the creatures, but the Holy Spirit was mutably changed from one thing into another, as water changes into ice. Rather, those creatures appeared when it was fitting that they appear, because the creature serves the Creator[16] and was changed and transformed according to the will of him who remains immutable in himself, so as to signify and reveal himself as it was necessary to signify and reveal himself to mortals. Thus, though the Scripture would call the dove the Holy Spirit[17] and would say of the fire, "And tongues as of fire appeared, which parted and came to rest on each of them, and they began to speak in different tongues as the Spirit gave them utterance"[18]—thus indicating that the Spirit was manifested through the fire just as through the dove—we can nevertheless not say that the Holy Spirit is God and dove or God and fire in the same way that we say that the Son is God and man. ON THE TRINITY 2.6.11.[19]

16:25 Serving God's All-Nourishing Bounty

ANGELS ARE GOD'S INSTRUMENTS. AUGUSTINE: Was it the work of angels when sensible creatures, docile to the will of the Creator, took forms adapted to the circumstances—bodily forms appearing to the eyes of human beings and voices resounding in their ears? Of such docility it is written in the book of Wisdom, "In fact, the creature that obeys you who made it, exerts itself to punish the unrighteous and restrains itself to benefit those who trust in you. At that time, then, adapting itself to all these changes, it served your goodness that nourishes all, according to the desire of those who aspired to you." The power of the divine will reaches, by means of spiritual creatures, even to the visible and sensible effects of bodily creatures. Indeed, where is the will of the Wisdom of almighty God[20] not effective, whose power extends from one end of the earth to the other and governs all with goodness?[21] ON THE TRINITY 3.1.6.[22]

16:28 To Give God Thanks

ATTITUDES AND DISPOSITIONS FOR PRAYING. ORIGEN: It seems to me that, to complete the argument of the prayer, it would not be out of place after this to discuss briefly the disposition and the attitude that one who prays must have, as well as the place where one should pray and the direction he should face[23] (if circumstances permit) and the choice of the appropriate time for praying, and topics of this kind. Disposition refers to the soul, attitude to the body. Thus Paul says . . . one must pray "without anger or dissension."[24] The attitude consists in "raising pure hands,"[25] expressions that seem to me to be derived from the psalms, which say, "May the raising of my hands be like the evening sacrifice."[26] Regarding the place, "I want therefore that people pray in every place."[27] Regarding the orientation, the Wisdom of Solomon says, "To make it known that one must rise before the sun to give you thanks and worship you before the dawning of the light." ON PRAYER 31.1.[28]

16:29 The Hope the Ungrateful Will Melt

LET US GIVE THANKS FOR GOD'S CARE. JOHN CHRYSOSTOM: No one has done more so that we might be good, great and thankful in everything than God who created us. Thus he often lavishes blessings on us beyond our will, blessings that we are for the most part unaware of. If this surprises you, let me point out that this happened, not just to anyone, but to blessed Paul. That blessed one, in fact, being in many dangers and trials, often begged God that temptations would depart from him. God nevertheless did not respond to his request, except to the extent that it was advantageous for him, and to show this he said, "My grace is enough for you. Indeed, my power is fully manifested in weakness."[29] Thus,

---

[16]See Rom 1:25; Job 26:11. [17]See Mt 3:16; Mk 1:10; Lk 3:22; Jn 1:32. [18]Acts 2:3-4. [19]NBA 4:85. [20]See 1 Cor 1:2; Sir 1:3-4. [21]Wis 8:1. [22]NBA 4:135. [23]Most probably Origen alludes to the fact that it was customary in early Christianity to pray toward the east. [24]1 Tim 2:8. [25]1 Tim 2:8. [26]Ps 141:2 (140:2 LXX). [27]1 Tim 2:8. [28]CTP 138:178-79. [29]2 Cor 12:9.

before telling him the reason why, he pours out blessings without Paul wanting or knowing about it. What is so unusual, then, if he commands us to be grateful in return for such tender care? So let us obey him, having this attitude always. In fact, nothing ruined the Jews more than their ingratitude, and this behavior alone brought on all those misfortunes, one after the other. Indeed, even prior to those misfortunes, it ruined and corrupted their souls. "The hope of the ingrate is like winter frost," it says. It dulls the soul and makes it die, just like the body.

This is born of arrogance and from believing oneself to be deserving of something. The contrite person, however, will give thanks to God not only for blessings but also for what seems to be against him, and, when he suffers, he will not think himself to have suffered unjustly. We too, then, the more we embrace virtue, the more we will humble ourselves, because virtue consists above all in this. HOMILIES ON THE GOSPEL OF MATTHEW 25.4-5.[30]

---

[30]CTP 170:466-67.

17:1–18:4 DARKNESS AND THE PILLAR OF FIRE

¹Great are thy judgments and hard to describe;
therefore uninstructed souls have gone astray.
²For when lawless men supposed that they held the holy nation in their power,
they themselves lay as captives of darkness and prisoners of long night,
shut in under their roofs, exiles from eternal providence.
³For thinking that in their secret sins they were unobserved
behind a dark curtain of forgetfulness,
they were scattered, terribly[b] alarmed,
and appalled by specters.
⁴For not even the inner chamber that held them protected them from fear,
but terrifying sounds rang out around them,
and dismal phantoms with gloomy faces appeared.
⁵And no power of fire was able to give light,
nor did the brilliant flames of the stars
avail to illumine that hateful night.
⁶Nothing was shining through to them
except a dreadful, self-kindled fire,
and in terror they deemed the things which they saw
to be worse than that unseen appearance.
⁷The delusions of their magic art lay humbled,

and their boasted wisdom was scornfully rebuked.
^{8}For those who promised to drive off the fears and disorders of a sick soul
were sick themselves with ridiculous fear.
^{9}For even if nothing disturbing frightened them,
yet, scared by the passing of beasts and the hissing of serpents,
^{10}they perished in trembling fear,
refusing to look even at the air, though it nowhere could be avoided.
^{11}For wickedness is a cowardly thing, condemned by its own testimony;^{i}
distressed by conscience, it has always exaggerated^j the difficulties.
^{12}For fear is nothing but surrender of the helps that come from reason;
^{13}and the inner expectation of help, being weak,
prefers ignorance of what causes the torment.
^{14}But throughout the night, which was really powerless,
and which beset them from the recesses of powerless Hades,
they all slept the same sleep,
^{15}and now were driven by monstrous specters,
and now were paralyzed by their souls' surrender,
for sudden and unexpected fear overwhelmed them.
^{16}And whoever was there fell down,
and thus was kept shut up in a prison not made of iron;
^{17}for whether he was a farmer or a shepherd
or a workman who toiled in the wilderness,
he was seized, and endured the inescapable fate;
for with one chain of darkness they all were bound.
^{18}Whether there came a whistling wind,
or a melodious sound of birds in wide-spreading branches,
or the rhythm of violently rushing water,
^{19}or the harsh crash of rocks hurled down,
or the unseen running of leaping animals,
or the sound of the most savage roaring beasts,
or an echo thrown back from a hollow of the mountains,
it paralyzed them with terror.
^{20}For the whole world was illumined with brilliant light,
and was engaged in unhindered work,
^{21}while over those men alone heavy night was spread,
an image of the darkness that was destined to receive them;
but still heavier than darkness were they to themselves.

18 But for thy holy ones there was very great light.
Their enemies^k heard their voices but did not see their forms,
and counted them happy for not having suffered,
^{2}and were thankful that thy holy ones, though previously wronged, were doing them no injury;
and they begged their pardon for having been at variance with them.^{l}
^{3}Therefore thou didst provide a flaming pillar of fire
as a guide for thy people's^m unknown journey,

167

and a harmless sun for their glorious wandering.
[4]For their enemies[n] deserved to be deprived of light and imprisoned in darkness,
those who had kept thy sons imprisoned,
through whom the imperishable light of the law was to be given to the world.

h Or, with other authorities, *unobserved, they were darkened behind a dark curtain of forgetfulness, terribly*   i The Greek text of this line is uncertain and probably corrupt   j Other ancient authorities read *anticipated*   k Gk they   l The meaning of the Greek of this line is uncertain   m Gk *their*   n Gk *those men*

OVERVIEW: The bloody sacrifices in the Scripture and martyrdom are both connected with Christ's passion (ORIGEN). We cannot know God's judgment unless he reveals it to us (HILARY OF POITIERS).

17:1 God's Judgments Hard to Describe

THE BLOODY SACRIFICE OF CHRIST AND MARTYRDOM. ORIGEN: In the Apocalypse we see "a Lamb, as though sacrificed."[1] This is the Lamb that, for certain ineffable reasons, became the sacrifice of expiation for the entire world, having accepted even to be sacrificed, according to the measure of the Father's love for humanity. By his blood he bought us back[2] from him who had bought us, in that we were corrupted by sins. Leading this lamb to the sacrifice was the God who was in the man, the great high priest,[3] as he himself attests, saying, "No one takes my life from me, but I myself give it. I have the power to give it and the power to take it up again."[4] All of the other sacrifices are related to this sacrifice by affinity, the sacrifices prescribed by the Law being a symbol of it. And in my opinion, the shedding of blood on the part of the noble martyrs are sacrifices similar to this one; not without reason does John the disciple contemplate them as surrounding the heavenly altar.[5] "Who is wise enough to understand these things, intelligent enough to know them?"[6] To grasp somewhat more contemplatively the reason for these sacrifices, which purify those for whom they are offered, we must understand the significance of the sacrifice of the daughter of Jephthah. Jephthah had defeated the Ammo-nites because of a vow, to which she who was to be sacrificed adhered, responding to her father's words, "I have given my word to the Lord against you," by saying, "Even if it is against me that you have given your word to the Lord, fulfill your vow."[7] In considering such events one could be led to attribute an element of great cruelty to God, to whom such sacrifices are offered for the salvation of human beings. One needs a more open and farsighted mind to reconcile this in light of the designs of providence, so as to be able to justify these things as both ineffable and beyond human nature, saying, "The judgments of God are great and difficult to tell. For this reason, ignorant souls fell into error." Moreover, it is also attested among the pagans that in times of pestilence, many were given over to sacrifice for the common salvation. The faithful Roman Clement also admits that this occurred, basing himself on history;[8] Paul testifies of him saying, "Together with Clement and my other coworkers, whose names are in the book of life."[9] Someone wanting to insult mysteries that escape the comprehension of the many finds the precepts regarding martyrs[10] similarly absurd. God, however, considers that it would be better for us to confess his divinity at the price of the most atrocious sufferings than to free ourselves for a brief time from apparent evils, declaring our acquiescence to the will of the enemies of truth. COMMENTARY ON THE GOSPEL OF JOHN 6.53-54.[11]

---

[1]Rev 5:6.   [2]See Rev 5:9.   [3]See Heb 8:1.   [4]Jn 10:18.   [5]See Rev 6:9.   [6]Hos 14:9 (14:10 LXX).   [7]Judg 11:35.   [8]See Clement of Rome *1 Clement* 55.1.   [9]Phil 4:3.   [10]See Mt 10:17-23.   [11]Trad. Corsini 369-70.

GOD'S JUDGMENTS ARE UNKNOWN. HILARY OF POITIERS: In the book of the psalms we read, "Your judgments, like the great abyss."[12] The apostle Paul says, "The judgments of God are inscrutable,"[13] and the prophet, "Your judgments are great and beyond number." In what sense, then, does the prophet dare to say, "With my lips I recited all the judgments of your mouth"?[14] And yet he is not saying here anything that contradicts himself or anyone else who is similarly inspired. In fact, he does not say, "With my lips I have recited all your judgments," but, "All the judgments of your mouth," knowing that there is a difference between the judgments of God and the judgments of the mouth of God. When he said, "Your judgments like the great abyss,"[15] did he in fact use the expression, "The judgments of your mouth like the great abyss"? Here, rather, he says, "I have announced the judgments of your mouth." The prophet, therefore, did not remain silent about those judgments that he knew from the prophets or from the word of God, and if he proclaimed them it is precisely so that they would be taught. HOMILIES ON THE PSALMS 118. BETH.8.[16]

---

[12]Ps 36:7 (35:7 LXX). [13]Rom 11:13. [14]Ps 119:13 (118:13 LXX). [15]Ps 36:7 (35:7 LXX). [16]CTP 186:33-34.

18:5-19 A NIGHT OF TRAGEDY AND FREEDOM

[5]*When they had resolved to kill the babes of thy holy ones,*
and one child had been exposed and rescued,
thou didst in punishment take away a multitude of their children;
and thou didst destroy them all together by a mighty flood.
[6]*That night was made known beforehand to our fathers,*
so that they might rejoice in sure knowledge of the oaths in which they trusted.
[7]*The deliverance of the righteous and the destruction of their enemies*
were expected by thy people.
[8]*For by the same means by which thou didst punish our enemies*
thou didst call us to thyself and glorify us.
[9]*For in secret the holy children of good men offered sacrifices,*
and with one accord agreed to the divine law,
that the saints would share alike the same things,
both blessings and dangers;
and already they were singing the praises of the fathers.°
[10]*But the discordant cry of their enemies echoed back,*
and their piteous lament for their children was spread abroad.

¹¹The slave was punished with the same penalty as the master,
and the common man suffered the same loss as the king;
¹²and they all together, by the one form of death,
had corpses too many to count.
For the living were not sufficient even to bury them,
since in one instant their most valued children had been destroyed.
¹³For though they had disbelieved everything because of their magic arts,
yet, when their first-born were destroyed, they acknowledged thy people to be God's son.
¹⁴For while gentle silence enveloped all things,
and night in its swift course was now half gone,
¹⁵thy all-powerful word leaped from heaven, from the royal throne,
into the midst of the land that was doomed,
a stern warrior ¹⁶carrying the sharp sword of thy authentic command,
and stood and filled all things with death,
and touched heaven while standing on the earth.
¹⁷Then at once apparitions in dreadful dreams greatly troubled them,
and unexpected fears assailed them;
¹⁸and one here and another there, hurled down half dead,
made known why they were dying;
¹⁹for the dreams which disturbed them forewarned them of this,
so that they might not perish without knowing why they suffered.

o Other authorities read *dangers, the fathers already leading the songs of praise*

OVERVIEW: The liberation of Israel was made possible by the killing of the Egyptian firstborn. God's word that arrives at midnight is God's Son who acts in Egypt and at the present hour (RABANUS MAURUS).

18:10 *The Discordant Cry of Their Enemies*

THE KILLING OF THE EGYPTIAN FIRST-BORN. RABANUS MAURUS: Recall what the book of Exodus recounts concerning the death of the firstborn, when God "at midnight struck every firstborn in the land of Egypt, from the firstborn of Pharaoh who sits on the throne, to the firstborn of the prisoner in the dungeon, and all the firstborn of the beasts."[1] At that point they did not feign to want to allow the Israelites to leave, as they had before, but openly asked the people of God to leave Egypt quickly, saying, "We are all going to die."[2] ON ECCLESIASTICUS.[3]

18:14 *Night Half Gone*

THE SON OF GOD ACTED IN EGYPT AND ACTS NOW. RABANUS MAURUS: It says that at midnight, almighty God made his word descend from heaven, from the royal throne, like a ruthless champion in the middle of the land of slaughter, to powerfully carry out the judgment of death on the godless.[4] What is the word of the Lord if not the Son of God, of whom John says, "In the beginning was the Word, the Word was with God, and the Word was God,"[5] through whom everything was made?[6] Elsewhere he is called the arm of God, as Isaiah says, "To whom has the arm of the Lord been revealed?"[7] He is also called the right hand of the Lord, in that he is the power that brings into effect the divine power. It must be understood, then, that

---

[1]Ex 12:29. [2]Ex 12:33. [3]PL 109:756. [4]Cf. Ex 12:29. [5]Jn 1:1. [6]See Jn 1:3. [7]Is 53:1.

this word, in virtue of the evangelical ministry, carried out at that time the judgment on the firstborn of the Egyptians and then consecrated the firstborn of the Israelites to himself.[8] He now saves the multitude of believers through the waters of baptism, at the same time destroying the huge army of spiritual enemies. ON ECCLESIASTICUS 3.15.[9]

---

[8]See Ex 13:1. [9]PL 109:756.

18:20-25 EXTERMINATION WAS THREATENED IN THE DESERT

[20]*The experience of death touched also the righteous,*
and a plague came upon the multitude in the desert,
but the wrath did not long continue.
[21]*For a blameless man was quick to act as their champion;*
he brought forward the shield of his ministry,
prayer and propitiation by incense;
he withstood the anger and put an end to the disaster,
showing that he was thy servant.
[22]*He conquered the wrath[p] not by strength of body,*
and not by force of arms,
but by his word he subdued the punisher,
appealing to the oaths and covenants given to our fathers.
[23]*For when the dead had already fallen on one another in heaps,*
he intervened and held back the wrath,
and cut off its way to the living.
[24]*For upon his long robe the whole world was depicted,*
and the glories of the fathers were engraved on the four rows of stones,
and thy majesty on the diadem upon his head.
[25]*To these the destroyer yielded, these he[q] feared;*
for merely to test the wrath was enough.

p Cn: Gk *multitude*   **q** Other authorities read *they*

OVERVIEW: The Greek word *kosmos* ("world") has a range of meanings in the Scripture (ORIGEN).

18:24 *The Whole World Was Depicted*

THE MANIFOLD MEANINGS OF THE WORD KOSMOS. ORIGEN: The name "world" is often used in the Scriptures with different meanings. What in Latin[1] we call "world," the Greeks call *kosmos*, and *kosmos* not only means "world" but also "ornament." In fact, in Isaiah, when a reproach is made against the powerful children of Zion, it is said, "Instead of golden ornaments you will be bald, because of your works,"[2] where "ornament" is indicated with the word that means "world," that is, *kosmos*. And it is also said that the explanation of the world was contained in the pontifical vestment, as we find in the Wisdom of Solomon, where it says, "The entire world was in the priestly vestment." Our earth with its inhabitants is also called world, as when the Scripture says that "the whole world is in the possession of the evil one."[3] And Clement, disciple of the apostles,[4] refers to those places that the Greeks called *antipodes* and to the other parts of the earth where no one can reach (just as none of the people there can reach us), and he calls them "world," saying, "The ocean cannot be crossed by people, nor the worlds that are beyond them, which are governed by the very dispositions of the Lord God."[5] We also call world this universe that is formed by the heavens and the earth, as Paul says, "The form of this world is passing away."[6] And our Lord and Savior also speaks of another beyond this visible world, which is difficult to describe and define in its reality. He says, "I do not come from this world."[7] As though he came from another world, he said, "I do not come from this world." We said that it is difficult to describe this world, so as to not provide anyone with occasion to claim that we assert the existence of the images that the Greeks call ideas. In fact, it is foreign to our way of thinking to assert the existence of an incorporeal world, consisting solely in the fantasy of the mind and fallacious thoughts.[8] ON FIRST PRINCIPLES 2.3.6.[9]

---

[1]The Greek word *kosmos* ("world") does not entirely overlap with the meaning of the Latin word *mundus*. This is why Rufinus somewhat adapts his translation of Origen. [2]Is 3:17, 24. [3]1 Jn 5:19. [4]Allusion to Clement of Rome. [5]Clement of Rome *1 Clement* 20.8. [6]1 Cor 7:31. [7]Jn 17:14. [8]Here Origen attacks Plato's philosophy. [9]Simonetti UTET 256-57.

19:1-12 THE RED SEA

[1]*But the ungodly were assailed to the end by pitiless anger,*
for God[r] knew in advance even their future actions,
[2]*that, though they themselves had permitted[s] thy people to depart*
and hastily sent them forth,
they would change their minds and pursue them.
[3]*For while they were still busy at mourning,*
and were lamenting at the graves of their dead,

they reached another foolish decision,
and pursued as fugitives those whom they had begged and compelled to depart.
⁴For the fate they deserved drew them on to this end,
and made them forget what had happened,
in order that they might fill up the punishment which their torments still lacked,
⁵and that thy people might experience[t] an incredible journey,
but they themselves might meet a strange death.

⁶For the whole creation in its nature was fashioned anew,
complying with thy commands,
that thy children[u] might be kept unharmed.
⁷The cloud was seen overshadowing the camp,
and dry land emerging where water had stood before,
an unhindered way out of the Red Sea,
and a grassy plain out of the raging waves,
⁸where those protected by thy hand passed through as one nation,
after gazing on marvelous wonders.
⁹For they ranged like horses,
and leaped like lambs,
praising thee, O Lord, who didst deliver them.
¹⁰For they still recalled the events of their sojourn,
how instead of producing animals the earth brought forth gnats,
and instead of fish the river spewed out vast numbers of frogs.
¹¹Afterward they saw also a new kind[v] of birds,
when desire led them to ask for luxurious food;
¹²for, to give them relief, quails came up from the sea.

r Gk he   s Other authorities read *had changed their minds to permit*   t Other authorities read *accomplish*   u Or *servants*   v Or *production*

OVERVIEW: The Red Sea prefigures baptism. The prophet and the apostle enjoin us to praise God in every circumstance (RABANUS MAURUS).

19:7 An Unhindered Way

AN IMAGE OF BAPTISM. RABANUS MAURUS: The Red Sea represents the sacrament of baptism, in which the faithful are saved and the powers that oppose them are drowned. ON ECCLESIASTICUS 3.17.[1]

19:9 The Lord Delivered Them

CONTINUOUS PRAISE. RABANUS MAURUS: It is fitting that we, too, give thanks at all times to our Creator for our liberation, saying with the prophet, "Bless the Lord, my soul, and all that is within me bless his holy name. Bless the Lord, my soul, and do not forget all his benefits."[2] And we see that the apostle also teaches us, "Pray constantly, in all things give thanks. This is the will of God for you in Christ Jesus."[3] ON ECCLESIASTICUS 3.17.[4]

---

[1]PL 109:760. [2]Ps 103:1-2 (102:1-2 LXX). [3]1 Thess 5:17-18. [4]PL 109:761.

19:13-17 EGYPT IS MORE GUILTY THAN SODOM

¹³*The punishments did not come upon the sinners*
without prior signs in the violence of thunder,
for they justly suffered because of their wicked acts;
for they practiced a more bitter hatred of strangers.
¹⁴*Others had refused to receive strangers when they came to them,*
but these made slaves of guests who were their benefactors.
¹⁵*And not only so, but punishment of some sort will come upon the former*
for their hostile reception of the aliens;
¹⁶*but the latter, after receiving them with festal celebrations,*
afflicted with terrible sufferings
those who had already shared the same rights.
¹⁷*They were stricken also with loss of sight—*
just as were those at the door of the righteous man—
when, surrounded by yawning darkness,
each tried to find the way through his own door.

OVERVIEW: The blindness of our errors makes it difficult for us to find the door which is Christ (RABANUS MAURUS).

19:17 Loss of Sight

ERROR PREVENTS ONE FROM FINDING CHRIST. RABANUS MAURUS: It rightly says that they were stricken with blindness, like those who were blinded by the darkness and wandered before the door of the righteous one—that is, of Lot—looking for the door's opening without finding it.[1] In fact, whoever suffers interiorly because of the darkness of error is surrounded on all sides by extremely grave dangers, since he does not know the way to life. And nor can one who errs find that door who says in the Gospel, "I am the door. If someone enters through me, he will be saved. He will come in and go out and find pasture."[2] ON ECCLESIASTICUS 3.18.[3]

---

[1]See Gen 19:11. [2]Jn 10:10. [3]PL 109:761-62.

19:18-22 THE UPSETTING OF THE NATURAL ORDER

¹⁸*For the elements changed*ʷ *places with one another,*
as on a harp the notes vary the nature of the rhythm,
*while each note remains the same.*ˣ

This may be clearly inferred from the sight of what took place.
¹⁹For land animals were transformed into water creatures,
and creatures that swim moved over to the land.
²⁰Fire even in water retained its normal power,
and water forgot its fire-quenching nature.
²¹Flames, on the contrary, failed to consume
the flesh of perishable creatures that walked among them,
nor did they melt^y the crystalline, easily melted kind of heavenly food.

²²For in everything, O Lord, thou hast exalted and glorified thy people;
and thou hast not neglected to help them at all times and in all places.

w Gk *changing*   x The meaning of this verse is uncertain   y Cn: Gk *nor could be melted*

OVERVIEW: Elements accomplish wonders because of the command of the Lord. Martyrs are tested by their trials (RABANUS MAURUS).

19:18 The Elements Changed Places

THE ELEMENTS OBEY THE LORD. RABANUS MAURUS: People and herds crossed the depths of the Red Sea dry-shod,[1] and frogs from the river filled the houses of the Egyptians.[2] Fire rained from heaven mixed with hail, and neither the fire opposed itself to the water nor the water to the fire, but falling together they struck the land of the Egyptians.[3] Where the children of Israel were, they hurt no one,[4] to show that all the elements of the world are subject not only to their proper condition but also to the service of the will of the Creator. ON ECCLESIASTICUS 3.18.[5]

19:22 Help at All Times

THE TRIALS OF THE MARTYRS. RABANUS MAURUS: We must not object that the bodies of the holy martyrs are given over to the hands of their persecutors, since this is not allowed for their condemnation but to try them. As gold does not burn in the furnace but is tested, so the souls of the elect, tried by the fire of tribulation, are made purer before their Creator, since it is written, "The furnace tries the objects of the potter, the temptation of tribulation tests the righteous."[6] "Many are the misfortunes of the righteous, but the Lord delivers him from them all. He preserves all his bones; not one of them will be broken. He rescues the lives of his servants. The one who trusts in him will not be condemned."[7] ON ECCLESIASTICUS 3.18.[8]

---

[1]See Ex 14:22, 29. [2]See Ex 8:3 (7:28 LXX). [3]See Ex 9:23. [4]See Ex 9:26. [5]PL 109:762. [6]Sir 27:5 Vg. [7]Ps 34:19-20, 22 (34:20-21, 23 MT; 33:20-21, 23 LXX). [8]PL 109:762.

ECCLESIASTICUS, OR THE WISDOM OF JESUS THE SON OF SIRACH

PROLOGUE*

Whereas many great teachings have been given to us through the law and the prophets and the others that followed them, on account of which we should praise Israel for instruction and wisdom; and since it is necessary not only that the readers themselves should acquire understanding but also that those who love learning should be able to help the outsiders by both speaking and writing, my grandfather Jesus, after devoting himself especially to the reading of the law and the prophets and the other books of our fathers, and after acquiring considerable proficiency in them, was himself also led to write something pertaining to instruction and wisdom, in order that, by becoming conversant with this also, those who love learning should make even greater progress in living according to the law.

You are urged therefore to read with good will and attention, and to be indulgent[a] in cases where, despite our diligent labor in translating, we may seem to have rendered some phrases imperfectly. For what was originally expressed in Hebrew does not have exactly the same sense when translated into another language. Not only this work, but even the law itself, the prophecies, and the rest of the books differ not a little as originally expressed.

When I came to Egypt in the thirty-eighth year of the reign of Euergetes and stayed for some time, I found opportunity for no little instruction.[b] It seemed highly necessary that I should myself devote some pains and labor to the translation of the following book, using in that period of time great watchfulness and skill in order to complete and publish the book for those living abroad who wished to gain learning, being prepared in character to live according to the law.

a Or *Please read therefore with good will and attention, and be indulgent*   b Other authorities read *a copy affording no little instruction*   * Conventionally this prologue is known as chapter 0, since it does not belong to the text proper but narrates the circumstances of its translation. The numbering of verses varies slightly in ancient and in modern translations. The RSV presents the text here without verse numbers. Euergetes is Ptolemy VII Euergetes. His thirty-eighth year is 132 B.C.

OVERVIEW: Sirach takes Solomon as his model in his way of writing and in the scope of material that he covers (THEODORE).

THE SCOPE OF SIRACH'S TEACHING. THEO-

DORE BAR KONI: His scope is the same as that which Solomon wrote. Forcing himself to imitate him, he has filled his book with characters, with personages, with fictitious speeches and with numerous allegories; basically, he has given his own, contemporary exposition. He, as well, presents wisdom and folly in the appearances of two women, in the way such as painters often represent greed and justice as female figures, placing them beside the images of the judges. Greed is usually depicted while swallowing large amounts of coins; the other, justice, is depicted while she is holding scales and weighing the rewards with justice. In a similar manner, these wise men have compared wisdom and folly with women. The author has also put his words in verse, indicating moreover that he has not received a grace such as that of Solomon's but that he has composed his work in virtue of his natural wisdom and of the culture that he had acquired.[1] His era is that in which the high priest Simon, son of Nathan, exercised his princely rule over the people, during the reign of Ptolemy. He has taken the nickname of Bar Sira as a reference to a despicable name, as David had spoken: "I am a worm and no man." *Sira*, in fact, denotes the dust that comes off the plaster of walls. BOOK OF SCHOLIA (SEERT) 5.5.[2]

---

[1]Theodore affirms a position which is shared by several ancient authors—especially in the East—namely, that the composition of Sirach is the result of a purely human wisdom and its author lacks Solomon's inspiration. [2]CSCO 431:279.

1:1-10* THE ORIGIN OF WISDOM

[1]*All wisdom comes from the Lord
    and is with him for ever.*
[2]*The sand of the sea, the drops of rain,
    and the days of eternity—who can count them?*
[3]*The height of heaven, the breadth of the earth,
    the abyss, and wisdom—who can search them out?*
[4]*Wisdom was created before all things,
    and prudent understanding from eternity.*[c]
[6]*The root of wisdom—to whom has it been revealed?
    Her clever devices—who knows them?*[d]
[8]*There is One who is wise, greatly to be feared,
    sitting upon his throne.*
[9]*The Lord himself created wisdom;*[e]
    *he saw her and apportioned her,
    he poured her out upon all his works.*
[10]*She dwells with all flesh according to his gift,
    and he supplied her to those who love him.*

c Other authorities add as verse 5, *The source of wisdom is God's word in the highest heaven, and her ways are the eternal commandments.*   d Other authorities add as verse 7, *The knowledge of wisdom—to whom was it manifested? And her abundant experience—who has understood it?*   e Gk her   * This pericope is also numbered Sir 1:1-8, since some witnesses omit two verses, which are supplied in the RSV notes.

OVERVIEW: Wisdom is the Son of God who was begotten from all eternity (FULGENTIUS). This generation of the Son must be numbered among the many things we do not understand about the world in which we live (THEODORET). When speaking about Wisdom in general, we should distinguish between created wisdom and the eternal Wisdom, who is the Son (AUGUSTINE).

1:1 All Wisdom Comes from the Lord

THE ETERNAL WISDOM IS THE SON. FULGENTIUS OF RUSPE: If the Arians say that God the Father is not created and God the Son is, then, as the natural creation of the innate Father makes known the unity of nature in the Father and in the Son, so eternity by nature of the Father does not allow one to attribute a beginning to divine creation. Therefore, the Father and the Son are without beginning, and the Father and the Son are one single and true beginning. For this reason God the Father speaks to his Son in the psalm: "With you the beginning, on the day of your power, among the splendors of the saints; from the womb I have created you before the dawn."[1] What is "with you the beginning," if not that which is said elsewhere of wisdom, "It comes forth from the Lord our God and has always been with him and is before the beginning of time"?[2] Therefore, rightly so, the Son affirms himself to be the beginning since he knows that he is coeternal with the Father from the beginning, just as he knows that he by nature is one single beginning with the same Father. And affirming himself to be the alpha and the omega,[3] that is, the beginning and the end, the Son confirms himself to be without beginning and without end. Just as, in fact, no letter exists before the alpha, in the same way no nature could possibly exist before the Son. Therefore, the Son says he is the alpha in order to demonstrate that he is the beginning of all things, before which there can be no other beginning. This is the reason why the Evangelist, wanting to express the eternity of the Word without beginning, through the inspiration of the Holy Spirit has found nothing more suitable or more congruous to say than, "In the beginning was the Word."[4] AGAINST FABIANUS, FRAGMENT 19.2-3.[5]

1:2 Who Can Count Them?

WE, TOO, CANNOT COMPREHEND MANY THINGS. THEODORET OF CYR: The ineffable personality of the only-begotten God is beyond the most perceptive conception of the Evangelists and perhaps even of the angels. Therefore, I do not think anyone should be considered pious who presumes to investigate this subject, in direct contradiction to the injunction, "Do not seek what is too difficult for you or inquire into what is too high for you."[6] For the knowledge of numerous other things incomparably inferior is beyond the capacity of the human mind and cannot therefore be attained, as has been said by Paul: "Eye has not seen, nor ear heard, neither have entered into the heart of people, the things that God has prepared for those who love him."[7] God also told Abraham that the stars could not be numbered by him[8] and asked, "Who shall number the grains of sand by the seashore, or the drops of rain?" If all this is so, how then can anyone but a madman presume to inquire into the nature of the Word of God? It is said by the Spirit of prophecy, "Who shall declare his generation?"[9] And, therefore, our Savior, in his kindness to those who were the pillars of the whole world[10]—and since he wanted to relieve them of the burden of striving after this knowledge—told them that it was beyond their natural comprehension and that the Father alone could discern this most divine mystery. "No one," he says, "knows the Son but the Father, and no one knows the Father except the Son."[11] It was, I think, concerning this same subject that the Father said, "My secret is for me and for

---

[1]Ps 110:3 (109:3 LXX). [2]Sir 1:1 Vg. [3]See Rev 1:6. [4]Jn 1:1. [5]CCL 91A:794-95. [6]Sir 3:21. [7]1 Cor 2:9. [8]Gen 15:5. [9]Is 53:8. [10]Namely, the Apostles; see Gal 2:9. [11]Mt 11:27.

mine."[12] ECCLESIASTICAL HISTORY 1.3.[13]

1:4 Wisdom Created Before All Things

A CREATED WISDOM EXISTS. AUGUSTINE: Wisdom was created before all things—not certainly that Wisdom that is clearly coeternal and equal to you, our God, his Father, and by whom all things were created[14] and in whom, as the Beginning, you created heaven and earth.[15] Rather, truly, it was that wisdom that has been created, namely, the intellectual nature that, in the contemplation of light, is light. For this is called wisdom, although it is created. But as great as the difference is between the Light that enlightens and that which is enlightened,[16] so great is the difference between the Wisdom that creates and that which has been created. It is just as great as the difference between the Righteousness that justifies and the righteousness that has been made by justification. CONFESSIONS 12.15.20.[17]

---

[12]Is 24:16, *Secretum meum mihi* (Vg.). [13]CTP 154:63-64; NPNF 2 3:36-37**. [14]Jn 1:3. [15]See Gen 1:1. [16]See Ps 36:10 (35:10 LXX). [17]NBA 1:421; NPNF 1 1:180-81**.

1:11-20* FEAR OF GOD

[11]The fear of the Lord is glory and exultation,
   and gladness and a crown of rejoicing.
[12]The fear of the Lord delights the heart,
   and gives gladness and joy and long life.
[13]With him who fears the Lord it will go well at the end;
   on the day of his death he will be blessed.

[14]To fear the Lord is the beginning of wisdom;
   she is created with the faithful in the womb.
[15]She made[f] among men an eternal foundation,
   and among their descendants she will be trusted.
[16]To fear the Lord is wisdom's full measure;
   she satisfies[g] men with her fruits;
[17]she fills their whole house with desirable goods,
   and their storehouses with her produce.
[18]The fear of the Lord is the crown of wisdom,
   making peace and perfect health to flourish.
[19]He saw her and apportioned her;

he rained down knowledge and discerning comprehension,
and he exalted the glory of those who held her fast.
²⁰*To fear the Lord is the root of wisdom,*
*and her branches are long life.*ᵇ

f Gk *made as nest* g Gk *intoxicates* h Other authorities add as verse 21, *The fear of the Lord drives away sins; and where it abides, it will turn away all anger.* * Sometimes numbered as Sir 1:9-20. Sir 1:11-27 in the Vulgate demonstrates a number of differences from the Septuagint. The most important is the addition of two verses: [Sir 1:14] "The love of God is a wisdom worthy of honor" and [Sir 1:15] "He will share it to those to whom he will reveal himself and in the recognition of his great works." Also, Sir 1:14-15 are sometimes numbered as Sir 1:16. Furthermore, there is the addition of three other verses—[Sir 1:17] "Fear of God is the piety of wisdom," [Sir 1:18] "Piety will guard and justify the heart; it will give joy and happiness," and [Sir 1:19] "One who fears God will be in good shape and will be blessed at the moment of his end." Then, Sirach 1:19 becomes Sir 1:23-24. Finally, there is the addition of yet another two verses—[Sir 1:26; cf. Sir 1:25 ʟxx] "In the treasures of wisdom intelligence and the piety of knowledge are to be found. Wisdom horrifies sinners instead" and [Sir 1:27] "The fear of the Lord drives away sins." This last verse [Sir 1:21 ʟxx] takes the form found in note **h** of the ʀsv text in some Greek manuscripts.

OVERVIEW: God's ministers should approach him with fear (CYRIL OF ALEXANDRIA). Fear is the beginning of our journey toward the knowledge of God (GREGORY OF NAZIANZUS) and toward wisdom (AUGUSTINE). God's threats recall us to conversion (CLEMENT OF ALEXANDRIA).

1:13 Blessed on the Day of His Death

GOD'S FEAR AND HOLINESS. CYRIL OF ALEXANDRIA: "I have acted thus so that he would be full of fear toward me; I have acted in such a way that he would cringe before my name."[1] Conveniently he enumerates all the splendid ornaments of the priesthood, obtained by means of the mystagogy of the Law. He inspired, first of all, the fear of God in the ministers of the divine worship, making them withdraw before his name, that is, making them fear and tremble when they hear the name of the Lord and driving them to experience a sentiment of reverence toward him that is not superficial but diligent, and next to which nothing is more precious. It is written, in fact, that he "who fears the Lord fares well." And again: "The fear of the Lord is glory and exultation." He has, therefore, guaranteed security to the one who fulfills the priesthood with sanctity and in truth. He does not simply say that they have been nourished with fear but that they were absolutely filled with fear, that is, the fear of God occupies their entire heart and

soul. In this verse, the emphasis and the repetition of the words indicate to the audience the steadfastness in virtue of those who are praised. COMMENTARY ON MALACHI 2.19.[2]

1:14 The Beginning of Wisdom

FROM FEAR TO HOLINESS. GREGORY OF NAZIANZUS: Since grace has been given to us to flee from superstitious error and to be joined to the truth and to serve the living and true God and to rise above creation—passing by all that is subject to time and motion—let us look at and reason on God and divine things in a way that corresponds to this grace given us. But let us begin our discussion of them from the most fitting point. And the most fitting is what Solomon laid down for us: The beginning of wisdom, he says, is to get wisdom.[3] And what this is he tells us: The beginning of wisdom is fear. For we must not begin with contemplation and leave off with fear—for an unbridled contemplation would perhaps push us over a precipice. Rather, we must be grounded and purified and so to say made light by fear, and thus we may be raised to the height. For where fear is there is keeping of commandments, and where there is keeping of commandments there is purifying of the flesh, that cloud that covers the soul and does not al-

---

[1]Mal 2:5. [2]CTP 60:305. [3]Prov 4:7.

low it to see the divine Ray. And where there is purifying there is illumination, and illumination is the satisfying of desire to those who long for the greatest things, or the greatest Thing or that which surpasses all greatness. ON THE HOLY LIGHTS, ORATION 39.8.[4]

FROM FEAR OF GOD TO WISDOM. AUGUSTINE: Isaiah the prophet presents us with those seven well-known spiritual gifts. He begins with wisdom and ends with the fear of God, as though he were coming down from the heights to our level. He does this to teach us to climb back up again. Thus, he began from where we want to finish, and he arrived at the point where we should begin. "Here will rest on him," he says, "the Spirit of God, the Spirit of wisdom and understanding, the Spirit of counsel and courage, the Spirit of knowledge and piety, the Spirit of the fear of the Lord."[5] Therefore, just as he descended from wisdom to fear—not because he was slipping back but in order to teach—we in the same way must climb from fear to wisdom. We do this not as a matter of pride but in order to progress. "For the fear of the Lord is the beginning of wisdom."[6] SERMON 347.2.[7]

1:21 *Fear of the Lord Drives Away Sins*

GOD THREATENS FOR OUR GOOD. CLEMENT OF ALEXANDRIA: The Lord often frequently speaks before he proceeds to act. "For my arrows," he says, "will make an end of them. They shall be consumed with hunger and be eaten by birds; and they will suffer incurable convulsions. I will send the teeth of wild beasts on them, with the rage of serpents creeping on the earth. Out in the open, the sword will make them childless, and in their chambers shall be fear."[8] This does not mean the divine Spirit gets angry, as some believe. He often shows restraint and provides encouragement while showing us what ought to be done. But he also employs this effective method that consists in producing fear in us so that we do not sin. "For the fear of the Lord drives away sins, and he who is without fear cannot be justified,"[9] the Scripture says. CHRIST THE EDUCATOR 1.8.68.3.[10]

---

[4]CTP 39:75-76; cf. NPNF 2 7:354. [5]Is 11:2-3. [6]See also Ps 111:10 (110:10 LXX); Prov 1:7. [7]NBA 34:115. [8]Deut 32:23-25. [9]Sir 1:21, variant. [10]CTP 181:97; ANF 2:226.

1:22-24 PATIENCE AND SELF-CONTROL

²²*Unrighteous anger cannot be justified,*
for a man's anger tips the scale to his ruin.
²³*A patient man will endure until the right moment,*
and then joy will burst forth for him.
²⁴*He will hide his words until the right moment,*
and the lips of many will tell of his good sense.

* Sir 1:28-30 Vg.

OVERVIEW: Fear of God keeps us away from sin (JULIAN POMERIUS). Anger and passion are like a drunkenness that darkens the soul more than wine (CHRYSOSTOM).

1:22 Unrighteous Anger

FEAR OF GOD LEADS AWAY FROM SIN. JULIAN POMERIUS: Regarding fear, our Scripture expresses itself in these terms: "Holy is the fear of the Lord, which lasts forever and ever."[1] But we should really clarify that this fear is to be distinguished from that other fear about which the apostle says, "In love there is no fear, but perfect love banishes fear."[2] The apostle is referring here to a fear that prevents one from sinning when one would otherwise be inclined to sin. This fear keeps a person righteous against his will. Then, there is the other kind of fear that the prophet speaks about: "The one who is without fear cannot be justified."[3] This refers to the person who is constantly increasing in love. So, on the one hand, there are those who fear to do evil when they know they will be punished, and there are those on the other hand who do not want to lose the righteousness that brings them such joy. Therefore, where sin is concerned, one should not nourish both fears but only that one of which it is written: "Fear has to do with punishment."[4] For the other situations—for instance, where it is said, "The fear of God banishes sin,"[5] and, "The one who is without fear cannot be justified,"[6] and, "Holy is the fear of the Lord, which lasts forever and ever"[7]—fear should not to be counted among the vices but should above all be regarded as the opponent of vices. ON THE CONTEMPLATIVE LIFE 3.31.3.[8]

DRUNK WITH ANGER AND PASSIONS. JOHN CHRYSOSTOM: Do not be misled. What I am about to tell you is that it is possible to become drunk even without wine. So that you understand that this is possible, listen to what the prophet says: "Woe to those who are drunk, but not with wine."[9] How then can someone get drunk without wine? There are any number of different ways: anger, conceit and foolishness provoke drunkenness. In fact, any one of the destructive passions born inside of us can arouse in us a sort of drunkenness and satisfaction that obscures our reason. Drunkenness, in fact, is nothing other than the alienation of our natural sentiments, the diversion of our thoughts and the loss of consciousness. In what way, then, tell me, are those who lose their temper any different from those who get drunk through wine? They get so drunk with anger and demonstrate such intemperance to the point where they throw themselves against everyone, no matter who it is, and they have no control over their words, nor do they distinguish one person from another.

In fact, just as madmen and lunatics do not notice it when they are throwing themselves into the abyss, so it is with those who lose their temper and are struck with anger. That is why a wise man who wanted to demonstrate the devastation such drunkenness can bring says, "A man's anger tips the scale to his ruin." Notice how succinctly he captures the enormity of this destructive passion. Now, conceit and foolishness are another form of drunkenness—and in fact even more disastrous than drunkenness. Whoever is in the grip of these passions loses, so to speak, the faculty of his senses and is not all that different from a madman. Tormented each and every day by these passions, he does not notice it until he is dragged into the very abyss of sin, taken over by evils that seem incurable. Let us therefore escape, I beg you, both the drunkenness that comes from wine and the clouding of our thoughts brought about in us through absurd passions. Let us instead listen to our common master of the universe, who says, "Do not get drunk with wine, for that is debauchery."[10] Do you see how clear this expression is about the possibility of getting drunk in other

---

[1]Ps 19:10 (18:10 LXX). [2]1 Jn 4:18. [3]Sir 1:22 (1:28 Vg), variant. [4]1 Jn 4:18. [5]Sir 1:21, variant. [6]Sir 1:21, variant. [7]Ps 19:10 (18:10 LXX). [8]CTP 64:299. [9]Is 29:9. [10]Eph 5:18.

ways besides drinking too much? If there were no other kind of drunkenness, why then, after having told us not to get drunk he added "with wine"? Do you see the exceeding wisdom and precision evident in his teaching through this additional phrase? After having affirmed that we should "not get drunk with wine," he adds, "for that is debauchery," almost seeming to indicate that this kind of excess is the root of all evils. "For that is debauchery," he says, that is, this is the reason we lose the wealth of virtue. BAPTISMAL INSTRUCTIONS 5.4-7.[11]

[11]CTP 31:159-160.

1:25-30* WISDOM AND PROBITY

[25]In the treasuries of wisdom are wise sayings,
    but godliness is an abomination to a sinner.
[26]If you desire wisdom, keep the commandments,
    and the Lord will supply it for you.
[27]For the fear of the Lord is wisdom and instruction,
    and he delights in fidelity and meekness.
[28]Do not disobey the fear of the Lord;
    do not approach him with a divided mind.
[29]Be not a hypocrite in men's sight,[i]
    and keep watch over your lips.
[30]Do not exalt yourself lest you fall,
    and thus bring dishonor upon yourself.
The Lord will reveal your secrets
    and cast you down in the midst of the congregation,
because you did not come in the fear of the Lord,
    and your heart was full of deceit.

i Syr: Gk *in the mouths of men*   * Sir 1:33-40 Vg; Sir 1:31-40 in Douay-Rheims translation of the Vulgate.

OVERVIEW: Wisdom begins from moral instruction (ORIGEN). One who does not seek justice cannot reach wisdom (AUGUSTINE). Let us follow God without hesitation with all of our being, body and soul (ISAAC).

1:26 Keep the Commandments

WISDOM BEGINS FROM THE COMMANDMENTS. ORIGEN: "I stretched out my words, and you did not listen."[1] It is reasonable that he said he stretched out words in his heart because . . . God granted him a large heart.[2] For one who

[1]Prov 1:24. [2]See 1 Kings 4:25.

can explain what is briefly said in mysteries in conjunction with the larger teachings asserted in Scripture has an enlarged heart. Therefore, it is necessary, in agreement with the teaching of the wise Solomon, for the person who desires to know wisdom to begin with moral training and to understand what is written: "You have desired wisdom; keep the commandments, and it will be given to you by God." COMMENTARY ON THE SONG OF SONGS, PREFACE.[3]

NO WISDOM IF JUSTICE IS LACKING. AUGUSTINE: Wisdom is a good that fills those with joy who possess it but weighs down those who do not. But what does Scripture say? "The fear of the Lord is the beginning of wisdom."[4] Who would not love to reign, and yet in the Psalms the Spirit admonishes, "And now, O kings, understand; be instructed, you who judge the earth; serve the Lord in fear, and exult before him with trembling."[5] This is also why Paul says, "Work out your salvation with fear and trembling."[6] And still we read, "If you desire wisdom, observe justice, and the Lord will grant it to you." Since many, as you can readily observe, do not observe justice even though they ardently aspire to wisdom, the Scripture admonishes them that they cannot arrive at what they desire if they do not observe what they are neglecting. Observe justice, it says, and the Lord will grant you the wisdom that you desire. But only one who fears God can observe justice. "The one who is without fear cannot be justified."[7] Therefore, if the Lord grants wisdom to the one who observes justice, the one who is without fear will not be found just. We thus return to the affirmation that I have cited at the beginning: "The fear of the Lord is the beginning of wisdom."[8] SERMON 347.1.[9]

1:28 An Undivided Mind

FOLLOWING GOD WITH ALL OUR BEING. ISAAC OF NINEVEH: How should we deal with the body when it is encircled in misery when the will, which is joined together with the body, is diminished in its desire for the good and loses the strength it had at the beginning? This happens generally to those who follow God but have only partially escaped from the world while they also remain partially in it. Therefore their heart is not cut off from things here. Instead, they are divided within themselves, sometimes looking ahead, sometimes looking back. I believe that the sage exhorted such divided individuals as these who come near to the way of God when he says, "Do not come to the Lord with two hearts" but approach his way as one who sows and one who reaps. Our Lord—seeing that among those who want to totally renounce the things of this world there are some whose wills are prepared to do so but whose thoughts are still turned back because they fear tribulation and because they have not left behind the love of their bodies—nonetheless spoke definitively to them in a desire to disperse the hesitancy in their minds when he said, "If anyone would come after me, let him deny himself."[10] ASCETICAL HOMILIES 37.[11]

---

[3]CTP 1:56. [4]Sir 1:12; Ps 111:10 (110:10 LXX); Prov 1:7. [5]Phil 2:12. [6]Sir 1:26 (1:33 Vg). [7]Sir 1:22 (1:28 Vg), variant. [8]See also Ps 111:10 (110:10 LXX); Prov 1:7. [9]NBA 34:115. [10]Mt 16:24. [11]CTP 44:269.

2:1-18* FEAR OF GOD IN TIME OF TESTING

¹My son, if you come forward to serve the Lord,
  prepare yourself for temptation.ʲ
²Set your heart right and be steadfast,
  and do not be hasty in time of calamity.
³Cleave to him and do not depart,
  that you may be honored at the end of your
  life.
⁴Accept whatever is brought upon you,
  and in changes that humble you be patient.
⁵For gold is tested in the fire,
  and acceptable men in the furnace of
  humiliation.
⁶Trust in him, and he will help you;
  make your ways straight, and hope in him.

⁷You who fear the Lord, wait for his mercy;
  and turn not aside, lest you fall.
  ⁸You who fear the Lord, trust in him,
    and your reward will not fail;
  ⁹you who fear the Lord, hope for good things,
    for everlasting joy and mercy.
¹⁰Consider the ancient generations and see:
  who ever trusted in the Lord and was put
  to shame?
Or who ever persevered in the fear of the
Lordᵏ and was forsaken?

Or who ever called upon him and was
  overlooked?
¹¹For the Lord is compassionate and merciful;
  he forgives sins and saves in time of affliction.

¹²Woe to timid hearts and to slack hands,
  and to the sinner who walks along two ways!
¹³Woe to the faint heart, for it has no trust!
  Therefore it will not be sheltered.
¹⁴Woe to you who have lost your endurance!
  What will you do when the Lord punishes
  you?
¹⁵Those who fear the Lord will not disobey his
  words,
  and those who love him will keep his ways.
¹⁶Those who fear the Lord will seek his
  approval,
  and those who love him will be filled with
  the law.
¹⁷Those who fear the Lord will prepare their
  hearts,
  and will humble themselves before him.
¹⁸Let us fallˡ into the hands of the Lord,
  but not into the hands of men;
for as his majesty is,
  so also is his mercy.

j Or *trials*   k Gk *of him*   l Gk *We shall fall*   * Sir 2:1-23 Vg, because of a different subdivision of some verses and the addition of others. In detail, one verse is added after Sir 2:9: "You that fear God, love him and your hearts will be enlightened," and another after Sir 2:17 (2:20 Vg): "Those who fear the Lord keep his commandments and will be patient until his visit." Sir 2:18 (2:22-23 Vg) is different: "Saying that if we do not lack penance we shall fall into God's hands and not into the hands of people. According to his greatness is his mercy before him."

OVERVIEW: Temptations and tribulations are prepared by providence for the good of the soul (DOROTHEUS, CHRYSOSTOM) and for our purification (GAUDENTIUS). Temptations become harder when the soul resists them (GREGORY THE GREAT). Persecutions were foretold by the

Lord (BEDE). God wants to purify us even from our smallest faults (CASSIAN). Their death notwithstanding, the requests of the martyrs were answered (AUGUSTINE). God neither forsakes nor disappoints those who trust him (THEODORET, FULGENTIUS). Let us follow and love God without hesitation (ORIGEN). Superstition is incompatible with faith. God protects believers and does not permit them to be tempted beyond what they can handle (AUGUSTINE). Faith leads to blessedness; its absence produces unhappiness (FULGENTIUS). Patience is necessary amid the adversities of life (AUGUSTINE).

2:1 Prepare for Temptation

TEMPTATIONS ARE FOR THE GOOD OF THE SOUL. DOROTHEUS OF GAZA: A monk who truly sets out to serve God, according to Wisdom, must prepare his soul against temptation lest he might at any time become separated from God or be overwhelmed by what happens to him. He must also believe that nothing happens without the providence of God. And since, in the providence of God, everything that happens is surely good and for the advantage of the soul, everything that happens is for our good and happens because God loves us and protects us. And we should, as the apostle says, "give thanks in all things for his goodness to us"[1] and not drag ourselves down or lose heart about what happens to us but accept the events convinced, as I have said, that all those things that God does to us, he always does out of goodness because he loves us. And what he does is always right. Indeed, it would be impossible for things to go well otherwise except for this mercy of God. SPIRITUAL INSTRUCTIONS 13.138.[2]

TEMPTATIONS INCREASE IF THE SOUL OPPOSES THEM. GREGORY THE GREAT: As soon as the soul starts to love the heavenly realities, as soon as it concentrates with full intensity in view of that intimate peace, then that ancient adversary that was hurled down from heaven[3] senses envy and begins to multiply the pitfalls. He advances temptations more relentless than normally, so that most of all he tempts the soul that resists, as he had never tempted it before when he possessed it. Therefore it is written: "My son, if you present yourself to serve the Lord, stand

firm in justice and in fear, and prepare yourself for temptations." And so also the possessed, who is cured by the Lord, is strongly shaken by the demon that leaves him, as it is written: "Screaming and shaking strongly, he leaves."[4] What does it mean that when the old enemy leaves, he strongly shakes the possessed who before had not shaken when he possessed him, if not that when he is expelled from the heart, he provokes in him temptations that are much more relentless than before when he possessed him peacefully? Therefore also the Israelites say to Moses and to Aaron: "The Lord proceeds against you and judges you, because you have raised us abhorrent in the eyes of Pharaoh and in the eyes of his ministers, giving them the sword in their hand to kill us."[5] Moses and Aaron represented the Law and the Prophets. And often the bad soul mutters within itself against the divine oracles, because after having begun to listen to and follow the heavenly words, the opposition of the king of Egypt, that is to say, the temptation of the malign spirit, grows. HOMILIES ON EZEKIEL 1.12.24.[6]

THE LORD PREDICTED PERSECUTIONS. BEDE: When the merits of the elect increase, the envy of the ancient enemy also immediately increases. It seeks either imperceptibly by himself, or openly through people who are subjected to his wickedness, to suffocate the incipient seeds of piety. Therefore, after having promised to the disciples the courage to preach, the Lord reveals the persecutions that would come on the part of those who would resist their preaching. In fact, he adds, "I have said this so you will not be shocked. They will chase you out of the synagogues."[7] Their loving Master wanted his disciples to know in advance the future hostility of the wicked, so that when it appeared it would cause them less harm, given that usually we more easily endure the adversities that

---

[1] 1 Thess 5:18. [2] CTP 21:193; cf. CS 33:192. [3] See Lk 10:18. [4] Mk 9:25. [5] Ex 5:21. [6] CTP 17:280-81. [7] Jn 16:2.

we can foresee. The evils that happen to one who is not prepared and does not know what is coming often cause a more precipitous fall from their state of security. Here is the warning Solomon provides: "Son, when you come to the service of God, stand firm in justice and in fear, and prepare your soul for temptations." And our Savior reminds his disciples that not only will they be cast out from fellowship with their fellow citizens but also they will be confronted with mortal peril. In fact, he continues, "But the hour has come in which anyone who kills you will think he is doing something in service to God."[8] The Jews believed they were doing something in service to God when they, full of hatred, were persecuting the ministers of the New Testament to the death, according to the testimony of the apostle: "They desire to please God, but not in an illuminated way."[9] And, he says about himself: "I myself believed it was my duty to do many things contrary to the name of Jesus of Nazareth, as I did in Jerusalem."[10] Therefore, after predicting the torments they would experience from their adversaries, in order to console his disciples, the Lord immediately adds, "But the hour has come in which each one who kills you will think he is doing something in service to God,"[11] as if he were saying: accept the tribulations brought on you by your fellow citizens, but accept them even more so knowing that they are not so much inflicted on you out of hatred against you as out of zeal for the law of God. HOMILIES ON THE GOSPELS 2.16.[12]

2:2 Be Steadfast

TRIBULATIONS ARE FOR OUR BENEFIT. JOHN CHRYSOSTOM: God often holds some kind of threat over our heads—not so that he may inflict it on us but so that he can draw us to himself. When we return to him, the fear quickly dissipates. Certainly, if we were the same person in temptations that we are when at ease, there would be no need for temptations. But why do I speak of us? Since even those

saints of old learned a great lesson, as the prophet says, "It was good for me that you humbled me."[13] And Jesus likewise said to the apostles, "In the world you will have tribulation."[14] And Paul alludes to just this when he says, "A thorn in the flesh was given to me; the messenger of Satan to buffet me."[15] Therefore when he looked for deliverance from temptation, he did not obtain it, because of the greater benefit that would follow from it. And if we should rehearse the whole life of David, we would find him more glorious when he was in danger—both he and everyone else who was like him. For such was the case with Job, who shined more brightly during his troubles, and Joseph too in this way became the more approved, and Jacob also, and his father likewise and his father's father. For all those who ever donned such crowns of peculiar glory, it was by tribulations and temptations that they first won their crowns. Only then did they have their names recited.

Being conscious of all these things, according to the wise saying, let us "not be hasty in time of calamity." Rather, let us teach ourselves only one thing: how to bear all nobly and not to be curious or inquisitive about any of the things that are happening. For to know when our tribulations will be over and done with belongs to God who permits them to happen to us. But to bear what is brought on us, with all thankfulness, is all the work of a good disposition on our part. And if this is the case, then all our blessings will follow. HOMILIES ON THE GOSPEL OF MATTHEW 10.8.[16]

2:5 Gold Tested in the Fire

AFFLICTIONS AIM AT OUR PURIFICATION. GAUDENTIUS OF BRESCIA: Regarding the punishment God inflicts on us, we hear, "When we are judged by the Lord, we are chastened so that we

---

[8]Jn 16:2. [9]Rom 10:2. [10]Acts 26:9-10. [11]Jn 16:2. [12]CTP 90:411-12. [13]Ps 119:71 (118:71 LXX). [14]Jn 16:33. [15]2 Cor 12:7. [16]CTP 170:200-201; NPNF 1 10:67**.

may not be condemned along with the world."[17] Regarding the just, however, he says, "We are afflicted in every way, but not crushed; perplexed, but not driven to despair; persecuted, but not forsaken; struck down, but not destroyed; always carrying in the body the death of Jesus, so that the life of Jesus may also be manifested in our bodies."[18] In yet again in another place, the blessed apostle Paul—after having mentioned that he had been taken up to the third heaven and to paradise where he had heard ineffable words[19]—adds immediately, "And to keep me from being too elated by the abundance of revelations, a thorn was given me in the flesh, a messenger of Satan, to harass me, to keep me from being too elated. Three times I besought the Lord about this, that it should leave me; but he said to me, 'My grace is sufficient for you, for my power is made perfect in weakness.' "[20] With even greater clarity another passage of the Scriptures that sounds quite similar says, "Gold and silver are refined in the fire, the just, however, in the furnace of humiliation." This is because, after the just have felt the heat of temptation and been weighed down by the burden of tribulations, there will be not even the slightest rise in them of pride over the merits of the justice they have received for their past actions, knowing that they will soon be rewarded with the very price of immortality. Indeed, the just become even more commendable in Christ when in good will they persevere in humility as those who are rich in sacred virtue and humble in heart. To BENIVOLUS 51–53.[21]

GOD CLEANSES US THOROUGHLY. JOHN CASSIAN: We know that even the saints have been given over in the flesh to Satan and to great afflictions for some very slight faults, since the divine mercy will not suffer the very least spot or stain[22] to be found in them on the day of judgment. He purges every spot of filth they have while in this world as the prophet, or rather God himself says, in order that he may commit them to eternity as gold or silver refined and needing

no punishment for purification. "And," he says, "I will entirely purge your dross, and I will take away all your tin. And after this you will be called the city of the just, a faithful city."[23] And again: "Just as silver and gold are tried in the furnace, so the Lord chooses the hearts."[24] And again, "The fire tries gold and silver, but human beings are tried in the furnace of humiliation."[25] And this also, "For whom the Lord loves he chastens, and scourges every child whom he receives."[26] CONFERENCES 1.7.25.[27]

2:10 Those Who Trust the Lord Are Not Put to Shame

MARTYRS WERE FREED THROUGH THEIR DEATHS. AUGUSTINE: "Listen, O God, to my prayer, while I am troubled; from fear of the enemy deliver my soul."[28] Enemies have raged against the martyrs. For what was that voice of Christ's body praying? It was praying for this: to be delivered from enemies and praying that enemies might not have power to kill them. Were they not therefore listened to because they were killed, and has God forsaken his servants who have contrite hearts and despised those who hope in him? Certainly not. For "who has called on God and been forsaken; who has hoped in him and been deserted by him?" Therefore, they were heard, and they were killed—and yet, they were delivered from their enemies. Others who were afraid gave in and lived, and yet these same people were swallowed up by their enemies. The slain were delivered, the living were swallowed up. This is what that recognizable voice of the psalmist is referring to when it says, "Perhaps they would have devoured us alive."[29] Many, in fact, were devoured alive, but many others were devoured dead. The ones who considered Christianity as foolish were already dead, in fact,

---

[17]1 Cor 11:32. [18]2 Cor 4:8-10. [19]See 2 Cor 12:2-4. [20]2 Cor 12:7-9. [21]CTP 129:32-33. [22]Eph 5:27. [23]Is 1:25-26. [24]Prov 17:3. [25]Sir 2:5, variant. [26]Heb 12:6. [27]CTP 155:298-99; NPNF 2 11:371**. [28]Ps 64:2 (LXX 63:2). [29]Ps 124:3 (LXX 123:3).

by the time they came to devour them. EXPOSITIONS OF THE PSALMS 63.2.[30]

GOD DOES NOT FORSAKE US IF WE TRUST HIM. THEODORET OF CYR: "And God conceded to Daniel to find compassion and mercy in the presence of the chief eunuch."[31] Divine providence is, in fact, a consequence of our free will. Thus, as soon as I choose the divine will, I will enjoy divine help. The same thing also happened in the life of Joseph, as it is said, "But the Lord was with Joseph. He was a successful man, and the Lord poured mercy on him, and he found favor in the eyes of the jailer."[32] And thus it is also taught in this case that God never abandons or neglects even one of those who confide in him. For this reason also another prophet cries out: "Consider the past generations, and reflect: who ever trusted in the Lord and was put to shame?" COMMENTARY ON DANIEL 1.9.[33]

TRUST GOD IN DIFFICULTIES. FULGENTIUS OF RUSPE: Know that God is working in you both to will and to do, according to a good will.[34] Therefore, attend to your salvation with fear and trembling.[35] Humble yourself before the Lord so that he may exalt you.[36] Ask him for the beginning of a good will, seek from him the effects of good works, ask him for the gift of perseverance. Do not believe that when his support has stopped you can want or do anything good. Ask him to turn your eyes somewhere else so that they do not see vanity;[37] beseech him to show you the way you should go,[38] pray, so that he may direct your steps according to his Word and so that you will not be dominated by sins;[39] call on him so that he can direct the work of your hands for you.[40] Therefore, "be strong and take heart."[41] "Entrust your concerns to the Lord, and he will provide for them."[42]

As he told you, you must not ascribe anything to your own strength, for you must not distrust divine power and devotion in anything. For, "The Lord is faithful in his words and holy in all his works." He will not deny you his help

in this world, nor will he withhold your reward in that life which is to come. He has shown you the right way and is himself the guide that will lead you to your heavenly home. "Trust, therefore, in the Lord, and do good."[43] Do not believe you will fail if he has agreed to have you under his protection. It is indeed written, "Has anyone trusted in the Lord and been put to shame? Or, has anyone persevered in the Lord and been abandoned? Or, has anyone called upon him and been neglected by him?" Therefore, do not lose your confidence which will have a great reward. Be strong and steadfast, knowing that your work shall not prove fruitless in the Lord. LETTERS 2.36.20–37.21.[44]

2:12 Walking Along Two Ways

LET US LOVE GOD WITHOUT HESITATION. ORIGEN: When we come to the grace of baptism, renouncing all the other gods and masters, we confess one God: Father, Son and Holy Spirit. But confessing this, if "we do not love the Lord our God with all our heart and all our soul" and do not adhere to him "with all our strength,"[45] we have not become the Lord's portion.[46] Rather, like those who sit on the fence, on the one side we allow to continue the very offenses we were fleeing to remain in our lives, while on the other we do not appease the Lord to whom we fled because we do not love him with a complete and honest heart.[47] The prophet cries over us because of this, because he sees a similar fickleness in our fluctuating when he says, "Woe to the double-minded," and again: "How long will you limp on both of your knees?"[48] But the apostle James also says, "The double-minded person is inconsistent in all his ways."[49] So, we who do not

---

[30]NBA 26:425; NPNF 1 8:263**. [31]Dan 1:9. [32]Gen 39:21. [33]CTP 188:68-69. [34]See Phil 2:13. [35]See Phil 2:12. [36]See Jas 4:10. [37]See Ps 119:37 (118:37 LXX). [38]See Ps 143:8 (142:8 LXX). [39]See Ps 119:133 (118:133 LXX). [40]See Ps 90:17 (89:17 LXX). [41]Ps 27:14 (26:14 LXX). [42]Ps 55:23 (54:23 LXX). [43]Ps 37:3 (36:3 LXX). [44]CTP 149:80-81. [45]Mk 12:30; Deut 6:5. [46]See Deut 32:9. [47]See Mk 12:30. [48]1 Kings 18:21. [49]Jas 1:8.

follow our Lord with an upright and perfect soul and who are removed from foreign gods stand, as it were, on the fence. On the one hand, we are treated like deserters by those foreign gods who cut us down, on the other, we are not defended by our Lord because we are unstable and hesitant. HOMILIES ON EXODUS 8.4.[50]

DO NOT GIVE IN TO SUPERSTITION. AUGUSTINE: If . . . one dies to whom one of these superstitious remedies[51] has been given—and how many have died with remedies, and how many have lived without them!—with what confidence does his spirit go forth to God? He has lost the sign of Christ, receiving instead the sign of the devil. Perhaps he may say that he has not lost the sign of Christ. Can you have, then, the sign of Christ along with the sign of the devil? Christ does not want cooperative ownership. He desires to have sole possession of what he has purchased. He bought it at such a high price[52] in order that he alone may possess it. Would you make him the partner of that devil to whom you have sold yourself by your sin? "Woe to the double-hearted," to those who in their hearts give a portion to God and a portion to the devil. Angered that the devil has a portion there, God leaves and the devil takes possession of the whole. There is a reason why the Apostle admonishes, "Allow no place for the devil."[53] TRACTATES ON THE GOSPEL OF JOHN 7.7.[54]

2:13 Lacking Trust in God

GOD PROTECTS BELIEVERS. AUGUSTINE: The one whose spirit has been entrusted to God clings to God. God is faithful and will not allow him to be tempted above that which he is able but will make with the temptation a way of escape also, so that he may be able to endure and not be turned back in the day of battle.[55] The one who, instead, glories in himself and not in God—even though he might make a big spectacle out of stretching and bending his bow—is the one who is destined to turn and run

in the day of battle. His spirit is not faithful to God, and therefore the Spirit of God is not with him. And, as it is written, "Anyone who has not believed in God will not be protected."[56] EXPOSITIONS OF THE PSALMS 77.10.[57]

GOD PROTECTS THE FAITHFUL. FULGENTIUS OF RUSPE: Faith competes with human nature—something for which the Creator has taken a great deal of care in ensuring that even the very hairs on our head are counted[58]—such that it is obvious that only when human nature senses that it is loved by God does it love God who loves it and then binds itself to him by means of pure-hearted faith. Faith is the way that carries us to blessedness; lack of faith brings great misery. Because of this you will be rightly punished when you do not believe in the Son of God, because your infidelity is your vice, just as faith is your strength—although it not the kind of strength one discovers in evil spirits but the kind God gives to his saints that triumphs over their wickedness. It is the same "faith that works through love."[59] In fact, "the evil spirits believe and tremble,"[60] but they do not love him from whom they are far removed because of pride. The first man was made to fall in pride through the counsel of the devil, through which he lost humility, through which he lost faith. And when he lost his faith, he lost divine protection. It is in fact written, "The one who does not believe in God will not be protected by God."[61] From that moment the one who was earth and ashes began to be proud because he threw away what was innermost in his life.[62] The Word of the Lord, thus, does not stop calling humanity to return to its most intimate longing, saying: "Return, you rebels, to the heart."[63] LETTERS 17.44.[64]

---

[50]CTP 27:156. [51]Augustine criticizes the use of amulets and the consultation of sorcerers. [52]See 1 Cor 6:20. [53]Eph 4:27. [54]NBA 24:165; NPNF 1 7:50-51**. [55]See 1 Cor 10:13. [56]Sir 2:15 Vg. [57]NBA 26:1017; NPNF 1 8:370**. [58]See Mt 10:3. [59]Gal 5:6. [60]Jas 2:19. [61]Sir 2:15 Vg. [62]Sir 10:9, variant of Vg. [63]Is 46:8. [64]CTP 149:444.

2:14 Woe to Those Who Lose Endurance

IN PRAISE OF PATIENCE. AUGUSTINE: One can read somewhere in the Gospel the following words of our Lord Jesus Christ: "With your patience you will save your souls."[65] And in another passage of the Scriptures it is said, "Woe to those who have lost patience."[66] Whether you call it patience or endurance or tolerance, the various terms allude to the same thing. Let us anchor in our hearts not so much the diversity of the words but the unique substance of the concept, and let us try to possess deep down what we express in words. The person who is conscious of the fact that the life he leads in this world is far away from his real home lives here in patience wherever he finds himself in the body, here on earth. He lives in patience when he knows that he possesses an eternal home in heaven, trusting that that place is where happiness is found that he cannot find here but can only long for here, and he burns with a such a good, holy and chaste desire for it. It is evident that patience is not necessary in prosperity but in adversity. One cannot say that one tolerates with patience that which is pleasing. That which we tolerate, that which we support patiently, is something hard, something bitter. Therefore, patience is not necessary in happiness but in unhappiness. SERMON 359/A.2.[67]

---

[65]Lk 21:19. [66]Sir 2:14 (2:16 Vg). [67]NBA 34:321.

3:1-16* DUTIES TOWARD PARENTS

¹Listen to me your father, O children;
    and act accordingly, that you may be kept in safety.
²For the Lord honored the father above the children,
    and he confirmed the right of the mother over her sons.
³Whoever honors his father atones for sins,
    ⁴and whoever glorifies his mother is like one who lays up treasure.
⁵Whoever honors his father will be gladdened by his own children,
    and when he prays he will be heard.
⁶Whoever glorifies his father will have long life,
    and whoever obeys the Lord will refresh his mother;
    ⁷he will serve his parents as his masters.m
⁸Honor your father by word and deed,
    that a blessing from him may come upon you.
⁹For a father's blessing strengthens the houses of the children,
    but a mother's curse uproots their foundations.

¹⁰*Do not glorify yourself by dishonoring your father,*
  for your father's dishonor is no glory to you.
¹¹*For a man's glory comes from honoring his father,*
  and it is a disgrace for children not to respect their mother.
¹²*O son, help your father in his old age,*
  and do not grieve him as long as he lives;
¹³*even if he is lacking in understanding, show forbearance;*
  in all your strength do not despise him.
¹⁴*For kindness to a father will not be forgotten,*
  and against your sins it will be credited to you;
¹⁵*in the day of your affliction it will be remembered in your favor;*
  as frost in fair weather, your sins will melt away.
¹⁶*Whoever forsakes his father is like a blasphemer,*
  and whoever angers his mother is cursed by the Lord.

m In other authorities this line is preceded by *Whoever fears the Lord will honor his father,*   * Sir 3:1-18 Vg.

OVERVIEW: God's pardon results in our gratitude (AUGUSTINE).

3:15 Sins Will Melt Away

THANKSGIVING TO GOD FOR PARDON. AUGUSTINE: "What shall I render to the Lord,"[1] that while my memory recalls these things my soul is not appalled at them? I will love you, O Lord, and thank you and confess your name,[2] because you have removed from me these terribly wicked and nefarious acts of mine. I attribute it to your grace and to your mercy that you have melted away my sin as if it were ice. I also attribute whatever of evil I have not committed to your grace—for what sin is there that I would not have committed, loving as I did the sin for the sin's sake? Yes, all my sins I confess to have been granted pardon to me, including those sins that I committed by my own perversity and those which, by your guidance, I did not commit.

Where is the person who, reflecting on his own infirmity, dares to ascribe his chastity and innocence to his own strength? To do so would mean loving you less, as though he were in less need of your mercy by which you forgive the transgressions of those who turn to you. Whoever, therefore, has responded to your call and followed your voice—avoiding those things that he reads me recalling and confessing of myself—should not despise me, who, being sick, was healed by that same Physician[3] who helped him not get sick, or at least less sick than he would have been. This is why he should love you as much, yes, even more than I do since once he sees how I have been restored by you from such a great enfeeblement of sin, he will see that he himself also has been preserved by you from a similar enfeeblement of sins. CONFESSIONS 2.7.15.[4]

---

[1]See Ps 116:12 (115:3 LXX). [2]See Ps 54:6 (53:8 LXX). [3]Lk 4:23.
[4]NBA 1:51; NPNF 1 1:59**.

3:17-29* DO NOT LOOK FOR
WHAT IS TOO DIFFICULT FOR YOU

¹⁷*My son, perform your tasks in meekness;*
   then you will be loved by those whom God accepts.
¹⁸*The greater you are, the more you must humble yourself;*
   *so you will find favor in the sight of the Lord.*ⁿ
²⁰*For great is the might of the Lord;*
   he is glorified by the humble.
²¹*Seek not what is too difficult for you,*
   nor investigate what is beyond your power.
²²*Reflect upon what has been assigned to you,*
   for you do not need what is hidden.
²³*Do not meddle in what is beyond your tasks,*
   for matters too great for human understanding have been shown you.
²⁴*For their hasty judgment has led many astray,*
   and wrong opinion has caused their thoughts to slip.^o

²⁶*A stubborn mind will be afflicted at the end,*
   and whoever loves danger will perish by it.
²⁷*A stubborn mind will be burdened by troubles,*
   and the sinner will heap sin upon sin.
²⁸*The affliction of the proud has no healing,*
   for a plant of wickedness has taken root in him.
²⁹*The mind of the intelligent man will ponder a parable,*
   and an attentive ear is the wise man's desire.

n Other authorities add as verse 19, *Many are lofty and renowned, but to the meek he reveals his secrets.*   **o** Other authorities add as verse 25, *If you have no eyes you will be without light; if you lack knowledge do not profess to have it.*   * Sir 3:19-32 Vg.

OVERVIEW: Do not confuse spiritual peacefulness with sluggishness (AUGUSTINE). Those who minister in the church need humility (ORIGEN), just as John the Baptist demonstrated when he humbly pointed toward the Christ (AUGUSTINE). Mary, too, was always humble despite the gifts God had given her (BEDE) and her descent from King David (ANDREW). The Spirit exhibits this same humility, even as he also delves into the nature of God, a nature that he shares as God (EPIPHANIUS). The Lord will make known his mysteries when we become capable of understanding them (AUGUSTINE), although at the moment, Christ's generation surpasses the understanding of humans and angels (CYRIL OF ALEXANDRIA). Heretics have no understanding of this, but rather than despairing, they should convert (FULGENTIUS).

3:17 Performing Tasks in Meekness

Gentleness Need Not Mean Laziness.
Augustine: The activity of a soul that aspires
to rest in quietness must be humble and gentle,[1]
which is appropriate for the follower of Christ
the Way.[2] It also should not be lazy or less than
fully committed but should instead be committed to running the race to its end.[3] It is, in fact,
written, "Do your work thoroughly in a spirit
of meekness,"[4] where the admonition, "Do your
work thoroughly" is aimed at preventing you
from allowing your meekness to degenerate into
laziness. Expositions of the Psalms 114.6.[5]

3:18 Humble Yourself

**Ministers of the Church Should Be
Humble.** Origen: Very often the priestly order
and the Levitical office are a cause of pride to
one who forgets that he holds such dignity in the
bosom of the church. How many priests, placed
at the head, have forgotten to be humble! As if
their ordination has given them a dispensation
from humility! On the contrary, they should
observe humility precisely because they have
been invested with such great dignity, according to the words of Scripture: "The greater you
are, the humbler." The assembly chooses you:
bow your head even more humbly. They have
elected you as a leader of others: do not feel as
though you are exalted. Be among them as one
of them.[6] You must be humble and modest. Flee
from pride, the source of all evil.[7] Homilies on
Ezekiel 9.2.[8]

**John the Baptist as an Example of Hu-
mility.** Augustine: You should listen to John,
you heretic. You should listen to the one who
runs forward as you run backwards. You should
listen to the humble, you who are proud. You
should listen to the burning oil lamp, you unlit
lamp. Listen to what John said when people
came to him. "I baptize you with water." You
too, if you would only acknowledge what you

really are, are a minister of water. "I," he says,
"baptize you with water; but he who shall come
is far greater than I." How much greater than
you is he? "I am not worthy to undo the lace of
his sandal."[9] How much would he have humiliated himself had he said he was worthy of this?
In reality, he said he was not even worthy to do
this—to undo the lace of his sandal. "It is he
who baptizes you with the Holy Spirit."[10] . . .
Repeat what the friend of the Bridegroom says[11]
instead of drawing attention to yourself and
away from the Bridegroom. "Neither is he that
plants anything, nor he that waters, but God
who lets it grow."[12]

Listen again to the one we are talking about,
the friend of the Bridegroom. It is true that
he had, it seems, his own disciples and that he
himself was not a disciple of Christ. Listen to
him though as he recognizes himself as a disciple
of Christ. See him there among the disciples of
Christ, both more true and more humble. The
humbler he was, the greater he was. Notice how
he behaves himself according to what is written:
"The greater you are, the more you must humble
yourself; so you will find favor in the sight of
the Lord." He rightly says, "I am not worthy to
loosen the lace of his sandals,"[13] but this was
not how he showed himself to be a disciple.
"He who comes from above," he says, "is above
everyone,"[14] "but we all have received from his
fullness."[15] Therefore, he too was among the
disciples who had disciples around him, just as
Christ did. Listen to him admitting with utmost
clarity to being a disciple: "The one who possesses the bride is the bridegroom, but the friend
of the bridegroom stands there and listens."[16]
Sermon 292.8.[17]

Mary's Humility. Bede: After the Virgin

---

[1]See Mt 11:29-30. [2]See Jn 14:6. [3]See 2 Tim 4:7. [4]Sir 3:17 (3:19
Vg). Augustine understands the Latin version literally: "Do your
works with meekness." [5]NBA 27:1071. [6]See Lk 22:27. [7]See Sir
10:12, variant. [8]CTP 67:155. [9]Lk 3:16; Jn 1:26-27. [10]Jn 1:33; Lk
3:16. [11]Cf. Jn 3:29. [12]1 Cor 3:7. [13]Jn 1:27. [14]Jn 3:31. [15]Jn 1:16.
[16]Jn 3:29. [17]NBA 33:219-21.

was found worthy to be exalted by seeing and hearing the angel, and after she had learned that she was to be honored by a divine birth,[18] she did not become proud because of these heavenly gifts as though she deserved them. In order that she might become more and more worthy of these gifts, however, she kept her mind focused on the custody of humility and thus responded to the angel who had brought her the annunciation: "Behold the handmaid of the Lord, let it be to me according to your word."[19] As we have learned subsequently from the reading of today, she also demonstrated this same humility that she had shown the angel to humankind, and—which is even more significant—even to those who were inferior to her.

Who does not know that a virgin consecrated to God has greater dignity than a married woman? Who doubts that the mother of the eternal King is to be placed before the mother of one of his soldiers? She, however, is mindful of the Scriptures that prescribe "The greater you are, the more humbly you should act in all things." And as soon as the angel that had talked to her returned to heaven, she got up and headed for the hill country, and, carrying God in her womb, she turned to the dwelling places of the servants of God and asked to talk to them. After the visit of the angel she rightly headed towards the hill country,[20] she who, having tasted the sweetness of humble heavenly life, headed towards the apex of virtue with the steps of humility. She entered the house of Zachariah and Elizabeth and saluted her who had learned that she would give birth to the servant and precursor of the Lord,[21] not as if she was in doubt about the prophecy that she had received but in order to congratulate her on the gift that, as she had found out, she had received—she who was a servant of the Lord like her. She did this not to confirm the words of the angel through the testimony of a woman but for her, a young virgin, to commit herself to serve an elderly woman. Homilies on the Gospels 1.4.[22]

3:21 Do Not Seek What Is Too Difficult for You

The Spirit Delves into God. Epiphanius of Salamis: The same holy apostle had said in a similar way, "No one knows the thoughts of a person except the spirit of the person that is in him. So also no one comprehends the thoughts of God."[23] In this second expression he does not add "except the spirit of the person that is in him." He limits himself to adding "except the Spirit of God," because one does not think of the divine Being as though he were a composite of two parts put together. He says "except the Spirit of God" also because "it is the Spirit of God who probes everything, even the depths of God."[24] We therefore do not say that his Spirit, who also probes the depths of God, is a stranger to God. Holy Scripture cautions us, "Reflect on what has been assigned to you, for you do not need what is hidden," or, "Seek not what is too difficult for you; nor investigate what is beyond your power." Of course, we cannot apply words that condemn vain curiosity to the Holy Spirit. We should say only that it is part of his nature to investigate the hidden things of God. Ancoratus 12.1-4.[25]

The Lord Reveals the Mysteries. Augustine: Let us, therefore, listen together to the admonition and to the words of Scripture: "Do not seek out the things that are too high for you, neither search the things that are above your strength." Not that such things are forbidden to us, since the divine Master says, "There is nothing hidden that shall not be revealed."[26] But if we continue along the way we have undertaken, as the apostle tells us, God not only will reveal to us what we do not know and ought to know but also anything else we care to know about.[27] The way we have undertaken is the way of faith: let

---

[18]See Lk 1:26-37. [19]Lk 1:38. [20]See Lk 1:39. [21]See Lk 1:40. [22]CTP 90:53-54. [23]1 Cor 2:11. [24]1 Cor 2:10. [25]CTP 9:55. [26]Mt 10:26. [27]See Phil 3:15.

us keep to it without wavering. Let it introduce us to the secrets of the King in whom are hidden all the treasures of wisdom and knowledge.[28] For it was surely not out of envy that the Lord Jesus Christ acted toward those great and specially chosen disciples of his when he said, "I have many things to say to you, but you cannot bear them now."[29] We must be walking, making progress and growing so that our hearts may become fit to receive the things that we cannot receive at present. And if the last day shall find us sufficiently advanced, we shall then learn what here we were unable to know. TRACTATES ON THE GOSPEL OF JOHN 53.7.[30]

PROPHECY CONCERNING MARY. ANDREW OF CRETE: This most celebrated Virgin was of David's seed, from which her husband also drew his descent. In fact, according to the great apostle, "Man is the head of the woman,"[31] and, according to Moses' law, "The two shall become one flesh."[32] And if the married woman who has offended her husband pays the punishment for adultery according to the Law—as by now she has become the body of the husband and has chosen the man as her head—how, then, does it not follow that, once the genealogy of the head is traced, the body is also counted together with the head? As a consequence it was also necessary in this case that the Virgin, being united with Joseph, was conveniently included in his genealogy, just as we have demonstrated that she was born of the same tribe as he—yes, from the very clan and family of David. And therefore also Gabriel foretold in the prophecy addressed to her, among other things: "And the Lord God shall give him the throne of his father David."[33] And what did he teach through this? That David was the forefather of him who was to be born from her. And how would it have been possible that the angel conveniently manifested these things to the Virgin, if not with the clear recognition that she descended from David? Indeed, if she had not been a descendent of David, he would not have said, "God shall give him the throne

of his father David." And had it not been clear that what he said was addressed to a daughter of David's, the Virgin could have rightly asked, "Of which father?" since she knew that she had not known a man. She then learned that she would conceive through the Holy Spirit.[34] Therefore Luke rightly says, "Joseph also went up from Galilee, from the city of Nazareth, to Judaea, to the city of David, which is called Bethlehem, because he was of the house and lineage of David, to be enrolled with Mary, his betrothed, who was with child."[35] We, then, having this interpretation ever since it came to light, no longer read this discourse ambiguously, as if Mary had only come to be enrolled together with him. Rather, it was because she also was of the house and the family of David. I believe that it has been clearly demonstrated that the genealogy of Joseph has not been uselessly traced by the divine Evangelists, because as a consequence of this the Virgin has been recognized as a descendant of David's, and thus Christ Jesus, born of her through a supreme miracle, is the Son of God who precedes all ages. And whoever attempts to contradict these words attempts above all to point the sword of his tongue against himself. And he shall be thrown out of the sacred gates of our hall! And in our turn, to us, to whom the Word of God has been sent along with grace and truth, it shall not be justifiable to probe anything further than that which has been said, since the divine Scripture closes the search for more profound things! In fact, it says, "Take care of what has been commanded to you; do not probe the things that are too high for you!" MARIAN HOMILY 3.[36]

3:23 *What Is Beyond Your Tasks*

THE MYSTERY OF CHRIST'S GENERATION. CYRIL OF ALEXANDRIA: Somewhere in Isaiah we

---

[28]See Col 2:3. [29]Jn 6:12. [30]NBA 24:1049-51; NPNF 1 7:293**. [31]1 Cor 11:3. [32]Gen 2:24. [33]Lk 1:32. [34]Lk 1:34-35. [35]Lk 2:4-5. [36]CTP 63:88-89.

read thus concerning Christ: "Who will be able to declare his generation?"[37] And the blessed prophet, speaking about God the Word,[38] has used the word "generation" instead of speaking about Being. Who, in fact, will be able to declare the mode of being of the Only-Begotten? And what language will explain the ineffable generation of the Son from the Father? And what mind will not be powerless in the face of this concept? In fact, we know and believe that the Word was generated from God the Father. But we say that the concept is unattainable for any intelligence, and any inquiry into this line of argument is risky at best. We should not have to explore that which is too advanced for our abilities, nor must we inquire about what is too difficult. We must rather hold on to what we are commanded and believe firmly that God truly exists and rewards those who diligently seek him.[39] But we must not search into—as it is written—the things that surpass our mind and our knowledge, and not only ours but of every creature, including those who are spirits. COMMENTARY ON THE GOSPEL OF JOHN 5.7.27.[40]

3:26 A Stubborn Mind

HERETICS ARE CALLED TO CONVERSION.
FULGENTIUS OF RUSPE: He receives the never-ending share of the heavenly inheritance who, guarding the unity of brotherly love within the catholic church, before finishing the present life gives up the lethal hardness of the impenitent heart and does not despair that within the one and truly catholic church the remission of all sins will be given by the Holy Spirit to those who have converted. Our Savior demonstrates as

much. Indeed, after the resurrection, breathing on his disciples and giving them the gift of the Holy Spirit, he gave them the power to forgive sins, saying, "Receive the Holy Spirit. If you forgive the sins of anyone, they shall be forgiven; if you retain them, they will be retained."[41] Therefore, they do not close the door of mercy—an action that would create a desperation that leads to death—on those who, separated from the catholic church, are tied to the error of whatever heresy or schism. Those heretics or schismatics will give up their hard-heartedness if they do not want to be punished with evils that will have no end. It is indeed written that "the stubborn mind will be afflicted at the end, and whoever loves danger will perish by it." What is there that is more dangerous than not offering obedience to the divine Word and disdaining the will of God who calls? Therefore, in the book of holy Job, just as eternal glory is promised to those who convert, the impious are denied the gifts of salvation because they do not obey. If indeed it is written, "Those who return from iniquity, if they listen and obey, will fill their days with blessings and their years with honor. But he does not preserve the ungodly because they are not willing to know the Lord and because when reproved they were disobedient,"[42] they therefore ought not to disdain the time dedicated to obedience but ought to return to the catholic church in which alone, through the gift of the Holy Spirit, "love covers a multitude of sins."[43] ON THE FORGIVENESS OF SINS 1.25.2–26.1.[44]

---

[37]Cf. Is 53:8. [38]See Jn 1:1-14. [39]Heb 11:6. [40]CTP 112:11-12. [41]Jn 20:22-23. [42]Job 36:10-12 LXX. [43]1 Pet 4:8. [44]CTP 57:57-58.

3:30–4:10* CHARITY TOWARD THE POOR

³⁰*Water extinguishes a blazing fire:*
　so almsgiving atones for sin.
³¹*Whoever requites favors gives thought to*
　　the future;
　at the moment of his falling he will find
　　support.

4 *My son, deprive not the poor of his living,*
　and do not keep needy eyes waiting.
²*Do not grieve the one who is hungry,*
　nor anger a man in want.
³*Do not add to the troubles of an angry mind,*
　nor delay your gift to a beggar.
⁴*Do not reject an afflicted suppliant,*
　nor turn your face away from the poor.
⁵*Do not avert your eye from the needy,*
　nor give a man occasion to curse you;

⁶*for if in bitterness of soul he calls down a*
　　curse upon you,
　his Creator will hear his prayer.

⁷*Make yourself beloved in the congregation;*
　bow your head low to a great man.
⁸*Incline your ear to the poor,*
　and answer him peaceably and gently.
⁹*Deliver him who is wronged from the hand*
　　of the wrongdoer;
　and do not be fainthearted in judging a
　　case.
¹⁰*Be like a father to orphans,*
　and instead of a husband to their mother;
you will then be like a son of the Most High,
　and he will love you more than does your
　　mother.

---

* Sir 3:33–4:11 Vg. In the Vulgate, Sir 4:8 reads: "Incline your ear to the poor without taking offense, and pay your debt, and respond to him with words of peace in meekness."

OVERVIEW: Penance is visible in many ways (CASSIAN). One way may be in our attitude toward riches, which, for some of us, are like a fire we should get rid of (SALVIAN). Instead, we ought to treat the poor with sweetness (CHRYSOSTOM) and spend our riches for the good of all (SALVIAN).

3:30 Almsgiving Atones for Sin

VARIOUS WAYS OF DOING PENANCE. JOHN CASSIAN: Eternal salvation is promised not only under the particular name of repentance, of which the blessed apostle Peter says, "Repent and be converted that your sins may be forgiven."[1] John the Baptist and the Lord himself said, "Repent, for the kingdom of heaven is at hand."[2] The burden of our sins is also overwhelmed by the affection of love, for "love covers a multitude of sins."[3] In the same way, by the fruits of almsgiving a remedy is also provided for our wounds because "as water extinguishes fire, so does almsgiving extinguish sin."[4] So also the washing away of offenses is gained by the shedding of tears, for "every night I will wash my bed; I will water my couch with tears."[5] Finally, to show that they are not shed in vain, he adds, "Depart from me all you who work iniquity, for the Lord has heard the voice of my weeping."[6] Moreover, by means of confession of sins, their absolution is granted, for "I said, I will confess

---

[1]Acts 3:19. [2]Mt 3:2; 4:17. [3]1 Pet 4:8. [4]Sir 3:30 (3:33 Vg). [5]Ps 6:7. [6]Ps 6:9.

against myself my sin to the Lord, and you forgave the iniquity of my heart,"[7] and again, "Declare your iniquities first, that you may be justified."[8] Forgiveness for crimes committed is obtained also by afflicting the heart and body, for he says, "Look on my humility and my labor, and forgive me all my sins."[9] This is especially true when considering the amendment of one's life. "Take away," he says, "the evil of your thoughts from my eyes. Stop doing evil; learn to do good. Seek judgment, relieve the oppressed, judge the orphan, defend the widow. And come, reason with me, says the Lord, and though your sins were as scarlet, yet they shall be as white as snow, though they were red as crimson, they shall be as white as wool."[10] CONFERENCES 3.20.8.[11]

RICHES BURN LIKE FIRE. SALVIAN THE PRESBYTER: The apostle calls people to contrition; I only to a cure. He affirms that riches are a fire;[12] I desire to extract from them water that helps to extinguish the blaze. This is precisely why it is written, "Water extinguishes a lit fire; alms extinguish sins." The apostle attests that damnation is the punishment for riches improperly packed away; I desire to obtain eternal life through these very riches that he says cause eternal damnation to all. Not that I believe that riches will enable anyone who has always lived among the pleasures of the flesh to obtain eternal life if he persists in such sin even up to death—even if he bequeaths all he has when he is at death's door—unless, in fact, he has previously bid farewell to his sins and taken off his filthy clothes, filled with the filth of his profligacy, and puts on the new robe of repentance, of holiness, from the hands of the apostle who admonishes him. AGAINST AVARICE 1.8.39-40.[13]

4:8 Answer the Poor Gently

SWEETNESS TOWARD THE POOR. JOHN CHRYSOSTOM: The wisest of people understands the avarice and pride of human nature. He consid-

ers the nature of poverty and its terrible power to depress even the most generous spirit and to induce it often to act without shame. And so, in order that a person should not be irritated when accosted or be provoked by the continual placing of demands on him so that he becomes an enemy when he ought to bring help, such a person is instructed to be affable and accessible to the one who is asking him for things by the words, "Incline your ear to the poor, and answer him peaceably and gently." And passing over the case of one who succeeds in exasperating—for what can one say to him who is overcome?—he addresses the person who is able to bear the other's infirmity, exhorting him before he bestows his gift to correct the suppliant by the gentleness of his countenance and the mildness of his words. ON THE PRIESTHOOD 3.16 (304).[14]

SPENDING WEALTH FOR DOING GOOD. SALVIAN THE PRESBYTER: The divine voice admonishes each one of us through the language of the holy Scriptures, "Honor the Lord with your belongings."[15] In another passage it says, "Pay your debt."[16] God is a tender and mild master. He invites us to spend the goods of our earthly belongings! He says, "Honor the Lord with your belongings."[17] Everything that is given to us is his, and yet, he affirms that it is ours so that we can give it away. Thus, he calls the ownership of these possessions ours so that there may be a greater reward for work since we spend more time and effort on possessions that belong to us, and in this way the worker necessarily receives a considerably greater reward for his labor.

The Lord has said that the ownership is ours. However, in order that our soul not become too proud, he adds, "Pay back your debt."[18] If a person is not induced to be generous from his devotion, however, he will be constrained to pay from necessity. If faith is of no help to persuade a saint

---

[7] Ps 32:5 (31:5 LXX). [8] Is 43:26. [9] Ps 25:18 (24:18 LXX). [10] Is 1:16-18. [11] CTP 156:292-93; NPNF 2 11:499-500. [12] See Rom 2:5. [13] CTP 10:39; cf. FC 3:283-84**. [14] CTP 24:85; NPNF 1 9:56**. [15] Prov 3:9. [16] Sir 4:8 Vg. [17] Prov 3:9. [18] Sir 4:8 Vg.

to operate, that which obliges him to satisfy his debt will motivate him. First he says, "Honor the Lord with your possessions,"[19] and then, "Pay your debt,"[20] so that, if you are devoted, you should give as though it belonged to you; if you are not, provide restitution as though it were not yours. Thus, God has rightly fixed in the law both the will to give and the necessity to pay.

He wants to say to everyone, "You are invited with persuasive words or constricted by contracted debt to do holy deeds. Give, if you want; provide restitution in the contrary case." The apostle also provided similar teaching when he ordered the rich not to be proud, not to put hope on the uncertainty of riches but on God, who, he says, "gives us everything in abundance, which we can enjoy in the will to do good works.' "[21] It is one phrase, but with this the apostle teaches us who is the benefactor and what is the reason for the possessions that have been given. AGAINST AVARICE 1.5.27–6.29.[22]

---

[19]Prov 3:9.　[20]Sir 4:8 Vg.　[21]1 Tim 6:17-18.　[22]CTP 10:34-35.

4:11-19* WISDOM THAT TEACHES

[11]Wisdom exalts her sons
　　and gives help to those who seek her.
[12]Whoever loves her loves life,
　　and those who seek her early will be filled
　　　with joy.
[13]Whoever holds her fast will obtain glory,
　　and the Lord will bless the place she[p]
　　　enters.
[14]Those who serve her will minister to the
　　　Holy One;[q]
　　the Lord loves those who love her.
[15]He who obeys her will judge the nations,
　　and whoever gives heed to her will dwell
　　　secure.

[16]If he has faith in her he will obtain her;
　　and his descendants will remain in
　　　possession of her.
[17]For at first she will walk with him on
　　　tortuous paths,
　　she will bring fear and cowardice upon him,
and will torment him by her discipline
　　until she trusts him,
and she will test him with her ordinances.
[18]Then she will come straight back to him and
　　　gladden him,
　　and will reveal her secrets to him.
[19]If he goes astray she will forsake him,
　　and hand him over to his ruin.

p Or he　q Or at the holy place　* Sir 4:12-22 Vg.

OVERVIEW: Life comes from Christ, who is Wisdom personified (RABANUS MAURUS).

4:12 Whoever Loves Wisdom Loves Life

WISDOM THAT GIVES LIFE IS CHRIST. RABANUS MAURUS: Let us understand that the divine wisdom, which is rightly praised, in some way, is the same wisdom of God, that is, nothing else than Christ, the Son of God, of whom the apostle says, I preach Christ, the power of God and wisdom of God."[1] That same wisdom "inspires the lives of his children"[2] when it gives to his disciples and to all the other faithful the knowledge of his mystery and reveals that of the gospel. It welcomes those who search for it, as it shall welcome the meek, and it shall precede them on the way of the justice of the Lord, who says, "I am the way, the truth and the life;[3] whoever follows me shall not walk in darkness but shall have the light of life."[4] Therefore, who loves him, loves life, for he, observing his command-

ments, shall obtain eternal life,[5] and "everyone who watches over it shall overflow with joy."[6] It is as promised in the book of Proverbs: "Blessed is the one who hears me, watching every day at my gates and looking toward my doorposts."[7] Call the holy Scriptures and their doctors the gates and the doorposts of the gate, without which we cannot enter into the promised life. ON ECCLESIASTICUS I.17.[8]

---

[1]1 Cor 1:24. [2]Sir 4:11 Vg, variant. [3]Jn 14:6. [4]Jn 8:12. [5]See Jn 12:50. [6]Sir 4:12 Vg. [7]Prov 8:34 Vg. [8]PL 109:785-86.

4:20-31* MODESTY AND RESPECT FOR PUBLIC OPINION

[20]Observe the right time, and beware of evil;[r]
and do not bring shame on yourself.
[21]For there is a shame which brings sin,
and there is a shame which is glory and favor.
[22]Do not show partiality, to your own harm,
or deference, to your downfall.
[23]Do not refrain from speaking at the crucial time,[s]
and do not hide your wisdom.[t]
[24]For wisdom is known through speech,
and education through the words of the tongue.
[25]Never speak against the truth,
but be mindful of your ignorance.

[26]Do not be ashamed to confess your sins,
and do not try to stop the current of a river.
[27]Do not subject yourself to a foolish fellow,
nor show partiality to a ruler.
[28]Strive even to death for the truth
and the Lord God will fight for you.

[29]Do not be reckless in your speech,
or sluggish and remiss in your deeds.
[30]Do not be like a lion in your home,
nor be a faultfinder with your servants.
[31]Let not your hand be extended to receive,
but withdrawn when it is time to repay.

---

r Or an evil man   s Cn: Gk at a time of salvation   t So some Gk Mss and Heb Syr Vg: other Gk Mss omit and do not hide your wisdom   * Sir 4:23-36 Vg.

OVERVIEW: We should ask to be purified with vigils and prayers (NICETAS) and not be ashamed of doing good (GREGORY THE GREAT). There are many ways of offering ourselves in

sacrifice (ORIGEN) and in witness to Christ (AUGUSTINE).

4:21 Two Kinds of Shame

VIGILS AND PRAYERS CLEANSE US. NICETAS OF REMESIANA: Surely it ought not to seem heavy or difficult, not even for a fragile body, to reserve a part of the week, the two nights of Saturday and Sunday, for the divine office. For with these two we can sanctify, so to speak, all the other five days or nights passed in the heavy sleep of the flesh and in the mud of mundane works. Nor should anyone blush at dedicating himself with holy fervor to the devout practices. No, the wicked do not blush in committing abominable works! The biblical proverbial expression is not put forward in vain: "There is a shame that leads to sin." It is a sin to feel ashamed for good works, while it is deadly not to be ashamed for this wickedness. If you are holy, then you love the vigils that enable you to so carefully guard your treasure and enable you to preserve yourself in holiness. If you are a sinner, you have all the more reason to keep watch and pray in order to obtain purification, beating yourself on your chest and begging even more often, "Cleanse me, Lord, from the sins that I do not see, and forgive your servant for the ones I ignore."[1] The one who, in fact, desires to purify himself from sins he does not see certainly cannot enjoy rolling around in the ones that defile him! PRAYER, VIGIL AND HYMNS OF PRAISE.[2]

DO NOT BE ASHAMED OF DOING THE GOOD. GREGORY THE GREAT: "Behold, I have made your face strong against their faces and your forehead hard against their forehead."[3] Just as shame is laudable when confronting evil, so it is reproachful in dealing with what is good. To blush because of evil is to act like a wise person; to blush because of good is a foolish thing. Therefore it is written, "There is the shame of one who confesses his sin, and there is the shame of one who boasts."[4] One who blushes, repenting of the evil he has committed, enjoys the freedom of life; one who is ashamed of doing good, however, falls from his upright state[5] and tends toward damnation, as the Redeemer says: "If someone is ashamed because of me and because of my words, the Son of man will be ashamed of him when he comes in his majesty."[6] And there are some who already conceive the good in their minds, but their word not being credible, they are not able to defend the truth. He is able to defend the truth who is neither afraid nor ashamed to say what he righteously thinks. HOMILIES ON EZEKIEL 1.10.17.[7]

4:28 Strive for the Truth

SACRIFICING THE BODY. ORIGEN: If the ancient use of the sacrifices is clear to you, we see what they furthermore contain according to the mystic sense. You have heard that there are two sanctuaries, one visible and open to the priests, the other invisible and inaccessible—except for the one high priest, all the rest of whom remain outside.[8] I think that this first sanctuary could be understood as this sanctuary we now occupy, which is our flesh: in this the priests serve at the altar of burnt offerings[9] on which that fire is lit of which Jesus has said, "I have come to cast the fire on the earth, and I wish that it were already kindled."[10] Do not marvel that this sanctuary is open only to priests since all those who have been united with the ointment of the holy chrism have become priests, as Peter also says to the entire church: "You are a chosen generation, a royal priesthood, a holy nation."[11] You are therefore of priestly descent, and thus you have access to the sanctuary. Furthermore, each one of us has in him his burnt offering and lights the altar with his sacrifice, so that it always burns. If I renounce all that I possess, I take up my cross and follow Christ,[12] I offer a burnt offering at the altar of God; or "if I give my body to be burnt, having charity"[13] and if I obtain the glory of martyrdom, I offer myself in a burnt offering at the altar of God. If I love my brothers, up to "giving my life for my brothers,"[14] if "I fight until

---

[1]Ps 19:13-14 (18:13-14 LXX). [2]CTP 53:74. [3]Ezek 3:8. [4]Sir 4:21, variant. [5]See 1 Cor 10:12. [6]Lk 9:26. [7]CTP 17:215. [8]See Heb 9:6-7. [9]See Lev 9. [10]Lk 12:49. [11]1 Pet 2:9. [12]See Lk 14:33; Mk 8:34. [13]1 Cor 13:3. [14]1 Jn 3:16.

death for justice, for the truth,"[15] I offer a burnt offering at the altar of God. If I let my limbs die at each temptation of the flesh,[16] if "the world is crucified for me and I for the world," [17] I offer a burnt offering at the altar of God, and I myself become the priest of my victim. HOMILIES ON LEVITICUS 11.[18]

STRONG AND WEAK WITNESSES. AUGUSTINE: "Martyrs" is a Greek word; however, tradition nowadays uses this name instead of the Latin one; in Latin, rather, one would say "witnesses." So, there are authentic martyrs, and there are false ones. There are, in fact, true witnesses and false witnesses. But the Scripture affirms, "The false witness will not remain unpunished."[19] If the false one does not remain unpunished, then the true witness will not remain without rewards. Certainly, it would be an easy thing to render testimony to the Lord Jesus Christ and to the truth of him being God; but it would be an assignment arduous enough to render it until death. There were some leaders of the Jews, cited in the Gospel, who believed in the Lord Jesus; but because of the Jews, it is said, they did not dare to recognize him publicly. And it is immediately noted down in the passage; in fact,

the Evangelist, continuing, affirms, "For they loved the glory of people more than the glory of God."[20] There were, then, those who, before people, were ashamed to recognize Christ; there were still others, certainly better, who were not ashamed to recognize Christ before people, but who were incapable of confessing him unto death. In fact, the gifts of God are such that sometimes they only gradually develop themselves in the soul. First pay attention, then confront among them these three categories of witnesses: the first includes he who believes in Christ and hardly manages to whisper his name; the next, he who believes in Christ and recognizes him openly; the third, he who believes in Christ and, in his confession, is ready to die for Christ. The first is so weak that his shame prevails over his fear; the second already puts on a brave face, but not yet until the blood; the third has everything, so there is nothing left to be desired. He meets in fact all that is written: "He fights until death for the truth."[21] SERMON 286.1.1–2.1.[22]

---

[15]Sir 4:28, variant. [16]See Col 3:5; 1 Jn 2:16. [17]Gal 6:14. [18]CTP 51:226-27. [19]Prov 19:5, 9. [20]Jn 12:43. [21]Sir 4:28 (4:33 Vg). [22]NBA 33:145.

5:1-8* WEALTH AND PRESUMPTUOUSNESS

[1]Do not set your heart on your wealth,
　nor say, "I have enough."
[2]Do not follow your inclination and strength,
　walking according to the desires of your
　heart.
[3]Do not say, "Who will have power over me?"
　for the Lord will surely punish you.

[4]Do not say, "I sinned, and what happened
　to me?"
　for the Lord is slow to anger.
[5]Do not be so confident of atonement
　that you add sin to sin.
[6]Do not say, "His mercy is great,
　he will forgive[u] the multitude of my sins,"

for both mercy and wrath are with him,
and his anger rests on sinners.
⁷Do not delay to turn to the Lord,
nor postpone it from day to day;
for suddenly the wrath of the Lord will go
forth,

and at the time of punishment you will
perish.

⁸Do not depend on dishonest wealth,
for it will not benefit you in the day of
calamity.

u Heb: Gk *he* (or *it*) *will atone for*   * Sir 5:1-10 Vg.

OVERVIEW: Sinners should not despise God's patience (FAUSTUS). The Lord admonishes the arrogant and consoles those who are in despair. The uncertainty of the date of our death dissuades us from sin (AUGUSTINE). No one knows the date of God's judgment. God's judgment is being delayed until the number of the elected is complete (FULGENTIUS).

5:4 The Lord Is Slow to Anger

GOD'S PATIENCE IS NOT TO BE DESPISED. FAUSTUS OF RIEZ: While punishment is reserved for the day of judgment and the long-suffering of the Lord invites correction, impunity nourishes disdain in a servant. God, "who shall render to each one according to his deeds,"[1] certainly does not impose on people the necessity to sin by virtue of predestination. One can read that he will ask a person to account for what he has done. "I have sinned," the prophet says, "and what has happened to me?" As if to say, God certainly must not know the sins if he does not punish and chastise immediately; and again, "He thinks: 'God has forgotten, he has hidden his face, he will never see it.' "[2] When he says, "God has forgotten," he is making a judgment that the patience of the forgiver is actually negligence. He considers it an omission when, in reality, it is what this magnanimous administrator of justice has reserved for later. ON GRACE 1.17.[3]

5:7 Turn to the Lord

PRESUMPTION AND DESPAIR. AUGUSTINE: The mind fluctuates between presumption and desperation. You must have fear, otherwise presumption will kill you; you must have fear, that is, rather than counting on the mercy of God, lest you fall into judgment. You also need to have fear so that desperation does not kill you when you begin to think that the horrible sins that you have committed cannot be forgiven you. In that case, you end up not repenting and incur instead the sentence of Wisdom, which says, "I also will laugh at your destruction."[4] How then does the Lord treat those who are in danger from both these maladies? To those who are in danger from presumption, he says, "Do not be slow in turning to the Lord. Do not put it off from day to day, for suddenly his anger will come and in the time of vengeance will utterly destroy you." To those who are in danger from despair, what does he say? "In whatever day the wicked person shall be converted, I will forget all his iniquities."[5] Accordingly, for the sake of those who are in danger because of despair, he has offered us a refuge of pardon. And for those who are in danger because of presumption and are deluded by delays, he has made the day of death uncertain. You do not know when your last day may come. You are an ingrate. Why not use the day today that God has given you to repent? TRACTATES ON THE GOSPEL OF JOHN 33.8.[6]

THE CERTITUDE OF DEATH DRIVES AWAY FROM SIN. AUGUSTINE: "Do you not know that God's kindness is meant to lead you to repen-

---

[1]Rom 2:6. [2]Ps 10:11 (9:32 LXX). [3]CTP 178:108. [4]Prov 1:26. [5]This quotation combines Ezek 18:21-22, 27. [6]NBA 24:713; NPNF 1 7:199-200.

tance? But by your hard and impenitent heart you are storing up wrath for yourself on the day of wrath when God's righteous judgment will be revealed. For he will render to everyone according to his works."[7] The fear of God must therefore take hold in your heart. If you do not want to sin, you should reflect on the fact that God is always present with you. This is the case not only in public but also in your own home, and not only in your home but in your own room, even at night in your very own bed, in your heart. If, then, you abolish the safe haven of penance and repentance, sins would increase out of desperation. As you see, those who think that the safe haven of repentance presented by the Christian faith is an occasion for sin have nothing more to say.

And what happens next? Shouldn't God have made provision for preventing sin from increasing since people would count on there being this hope of forgiveness? In other words, just as he has provided that sin would not be added to because of desperation, he should also make sure that sin also would not be added to because of hope. In reality, the person who despairs adds to his sins just as much as the one who counts on forgiveness. You might even say to yourself, "In the meantime, I will do what I want. Then, when I repent, God is good and will forgive me."

You certainly can say to yourself, "When I convert, he will forgive me"—if you know you will be alive tomorrow. Don't the Scriptures warn you, though, saying, "Do not delay turning back to the Lord or put it off from day to day; for suddenly his wrath will come, and in the time of vengeance he will destroy you." You see, divine Providence has kept watch over us, allowing us to avoid one or the other danger: in order to make sure we do not increase our sin out of despair, there is the safe haven of repentance; in order to make sure we do not increase them out of excessive hope of forgiveness, the day of our demise has been made unknown. SERMONS 352.9.[8]

WAITING FOR THE COMPLETE NUMBER OF THE ELECT. FULGENTIUS OF RUSPE: Therefore the Savior warns each one of us ahead of time, saying, "Make friends quickly with your adversary, while you are going with him to court, lest your adversary hand you over to the judge, and the judge to the guard, and you be put in prison; truly, I say to you, you will never get out till you have paid the last penny."[9] People turn the Word of God into their adversary when they do the very things that the word of God prohibits. In the Psalms they are told, "You hate discipline, and you cast my words behind you."[10] If someone will not consent to this divine Word until he is on his way, that is, if he does not consent soon in this life, then once he is thrown into prison, into the eternal fire, there will be no more peace. In fact, the best adversary is the one who is hostile toward us in keeping us away from the hostility of sin that is the bearer of death. We learn from another passage of Scripture that we should repent soon because the more we delay our repentance, the more chance death has to lead us to damnation instead of salvation. And so Scripture says, "Do not delay turning back to the Lord or put it off from day to day; for suddenly his wrath will come, and in the time of vengeance he will destroy you." The Word of God reveals that when the time of vengeance arrives, our repentance will certainly not deliver us from the pain of punishment; rather, God's vengeful wrath will give us the sentence we deserve. This, in fact, will not be a time of forgiveness or of indulgence but of vengeance. It is deferred due to the long-suffering of God as he waits for the full number of saints to be completed. The blessed John recalls in the Apocalypse that the saints have in fact asked for this vengeance when they cry out, "O sovereign Lord, holy and true, how long before you will judge and avenge our blood on those who dwell on the earth?"[11] And

---

[7]Rom 2:4-6. [8]NBA 34:222. [9]Mt 5:25-26. [10]Ps 50:17 (49:17 LXX). [11]Rev 6:10.

in order to teach that the time of vengeance is deferred, by divine disposition, because of those who still must join this gathering, John continues, "Then they were each given a white robe and told to rest a little longer, until the number of their fellow servants and their brethren should be complete."[12] ON THE FORGIVENESS OF SINS 2.5.1-3.[13]

---

[12]Rev 6:11. [13]CTP 57:70-72.

5:9–6:4* FIRMNESS AND SELF-CONTROL

[9]Do not winnow with every wind,
  nor follow every path:
  the double-tongued sinner does that.
[10]Be steadfast in your understanding,
  and let your speech be consistent.
[11]Be quick to hear,
  and be deliberate in answering.
[12]If you have understanding, answer your
    neighbor;
  but if not, put your hand on your mouth.
[13]Glory and dishonor come from speaking,
  and a man's tongue is his downfall.

[14]Do not be called a slanderer,
  and do not lie in ambush with your
    tongue;
for shame comes to the thief,

and severe condemnation to the double-
    tongued.
[15]In great or small matters do not act amiss,
6 and do not become an enemy instead of a
    friend;
for a bad name incurs shame and reproach:
  so fares the double-tongued sinner.

[2]Do not exalt yourself through your soul's
    counsel,
  lest your soul be torn in pieces like a bull.[v]
[3]You will devour your leaves and destroy your
    fruit,
  and will be left like a withered tree.
[4]An evil soul will destroy him who has it,
  and make him the laughingstock of his
    enemies.

v The meaning of the Greek of this verse is obscure   * Sir 5:11–6:4 Vg, with great differences.

OVERVIEW: Silence is to be preferred to idle questions (CYRIL OF ALEXANDRIA).

5:12 If You Have Understanding

DO NOT ASK IDLE QUESTIONS. CYRIL OF ALEXANDRIA: "When they found him on the other side of the sea, they said to him, 'Rabbi, when did you come here?' "[1] The episode has the aspects of a scene between friends and expresses something delicate. However, some elements seem rather senseless and childish. They should not, in fact, have followed such a great teacher only to talk about frivolous things instead of asking to learn something. What need was there to ask when he had arrived? Or what advantage

---

[1]Jn 6:25.

would have resulted from knowing? We must then seek wisdom from the wise and let a prudent silence be preferred over inept speeches. For the apostle exhorts us to flavor our speech with salt,[2] and another of the wise invites us with similar words: "If you have understanding, answer your neighbor; but if you do not, put your hand on your mouth." And we also learn from another place how evil it is to be condemned for any recklessness of language: "If any one thinks he is religious, and does not bridle his tongue, but deceives his heart, this man's religion is vain."[3] COMMENTARY ON THE GOSPEL OF JOHN 3.4.25.[4]

---

[2]See Col 4:6. [3]Jas 1:26. [4]CTP 111:419.

6:5-17 FRIENDSHIP

[5]*A pleasant voice multiplies friends,*
   and a gracious tongue multiplies courtesies.
[6]*Let those that are at peace with you be many,*
   but let your advisers be one in a thousand.
[7]*When you gain a friend, gain him through testing,*
   and do not trust him hastily.
[8]*For there is a friend who is such at his own convenience,*
   but will not stand by you in your day of trouble.
[9]*And there is a friend who changes into an enemy,*
   and will disclose a quarrel to your disgrace.
[10]*And there is a friend who is a table companion,*
   but will not stand by you in your day of trouble.
[11]*In your prosperity he will make himself your equal,*
   and be bold with your servants;
[12]*but if you are brought low he will turn against you,*
   and will hide himself from your presence.
[13]*Keep yourself far from your enemies,*
   and be on guard toward your friends.

[14]*A faithful friend is a sturdy shelter:*
   he that has found one has found a treasure.
[15]*There is nothing so precious as a faithful friend,*
   and no scales can measure his excellence.
[16]*A faithful friend is an elixir of life;*
   and those who fear the Lord will find him.
[17]*Whoever fears the Lord directs his friendship aright,*
   for as he is, so is his neighbor also.

OVERVIEW: True friendship requires much effort (RABANUS MAURUS).

6:17 Directing Friendship Properly

TRUE FRIENDSHIP. RABANUS MAURUS: The gift of a full and perfect friendship cannot last if it is not among people of similar virtue. And this is what the holy Fathers taught, establishing certain stages in order to arrive at a perfect and unchanging condition of friendship. They said that the first step of true friendship is to despise earthly things and all possessions. Second, everyone should put in check his own will in order to avoid thinking that he is the only wise and sensible person around, preferring his own opinions to those of his neighbor. Third, they said that he should know to defer everything, even the things that he considers useful and necessary, when it will benefit charity and peace. Fourth, he should be convinced that he must not anger himself for no reason at all, whether the anger is just or unjust. Fifth, he should desire that the anger of his brother be assuaged like his own, even if that anger rises against him without reason, knowing that the pain of the one is equally damaging to both; if he lashes out against someone else, he will make every effort to remove that offense of his brother as well. Finally, he should believe that every day might be his last, which sentiment undoubtedly brings about the death of any vice. This conviction not only leaves no place for any sadness in our heart but furthermore stops any movement of evil desire and impedes all sins. Whoever, then, respects these things cannot experience or carry out the bitterness of anger and discord. ON ECCLESIASTICUS 2.2.[1]

---

[1]PL 109:797-98.

6:18-37* THE SCHOOL OF WISDOM

[18]*My son, from your youth up choose instruction,*
 and until you are old you will keep finding wisdom.
[19]*Come to her like one who plows and sows,*
 and wait for her good harvest.
For in her service you will toil a little while,
 and soon you will eat of her produce.
[20]*She seems very harsh to the uninstructed;*
 a weakling will not remain with her.
[21]*She will weigh him down like a heavy testing stone,*
 and he will not be slow to cast her off.
[22]*For wisdom is like her name,*
 and is not manifest to many.

[23]*Listen, my son, and accept my judgment;*

do not reject my counsel.
²⁴*Put your feet into her fetters,*
and your neck into her collar.
²⁵*Put your shoulder under her and carry her,*
and do not fret under her bonds.
²⁶*Come to her with all your soul,*
and keep her ways with all your might.
²⁷*Search out and seek, and she will become known to you;*
and when you get hold of her, do not let her go.
²⁸*For at last you will find the rest she gives,*
and she will be changed into joy for you.
²⁹*Then her fetters will become for you a strong protection,*
and her collar a glorious robe.
³⁰*Her yoke*ʷ *is a golden ornament,*
and her bonds are a cord of blue.
³¹*You will wear her like a glorious robe,*
and put her on like a crown of gladness.

³²*If you are willing, my son, you will be taught,*
and if you apply yourself you will become clever.
³³*If you love to listen you will gain knowledge,*
and if you incline your ear you will become wise.
³⁴*Stand in the assembly of the elders.*
Who is wise? Cleave to him.
³⁵*Be ready to listen to every*ˣ *narrative,*
and do not let wise proverbs escape you.
³⁶*If you see an intelligent man, visit him early;*
let your foot wear out his doorstep.
³⁷*Reflect on the statutes of the Lord,*
and meditate at all times on his commandments.
*It is he who will give insight to*ʸ *your mind,*
and your desire for wisdom will be granted.

w Heb: Gk *Upon her*   **x** Heb: Gk adds *divine*   **y** Heb: Gk *will confirm*   * The Vulgate has a different distribution of verses.

OVERVIEW: There are two kinds of fetters: the weakness of the flesh and the discipline of wisdom (AUGUSTINE). Following the example of the saints, we should avoid the former, which is often found among those who exert bad influence on us (CALLINICUS). The apostles followed the latter, even as they followed Christ and his example (AUGUSTINE).

6:24 Wisdom's Fetters

THE DISCIPLINE OF WISDOM. AUGUSTINE: The weakness and the corruptibility of the body are truly fetters that weigh down the soul.[1] The body's fragility is like the material a persecutor could use for causing pain and suffering, thus forcing many of the saints into impiety. The apostle longed to be unbound from these fetters and to be with Christ, but to remain in the flesh

[1]See Wis 9:15.

was necessary for the sake of those to whom he was ministering the gospel.[2] Until, then, this corruptible puts on incorruption, and this mortal puts on immortality,[3] the weak flesh will imprison the willing spirit.[4] No one feels these fetters except those who groan inwardly, who are burdened[5] and wanting to be clothed with the tabernacle that is from heaven, because death is terrifying and mortal life brings sorrow. The prophet redoubles his own groaning in behalf of these individuals who are suffering so that their groaning may come before the sight of the Lord.

Those who are bound by the disciplines of wisdom may also be understood to be fettered. But these disciplines, if patiently endured, can be turned into adornments, which is why it is written, "Put your feet into [wisdom's] fetters."[6] EXPOSITIONS OF THE PSALMS 78.15.[7]

6:34 Cleave to the Wise One

FOLLOWING THE PATH OF THE SAINTS. CALLINICUS: If you find someone who zealously carries out the commandments of Christ and his actions agree with his words, then you will find him denying himself night and day with a heart that is always contrite. The person who acts like this remains in the truth,[8] and you should associate yourselves with such a person. Let us therefore admit him among us as a father, master and brother, as a member of the faith[9] related to us, as a faithful friend and a sincere advocate of our ideals, according to him who says, "Frequent the gatherings of the elders, and if one is wise, then join him," and, "If you see a wise person, go quickly to him." Indeed, one who associates himself with the saints will be sanctified. And again, "Make no friendship with a person given

to anger nor go with a wrathful person, lest you learn his ways and entangle yourself in a snare,"[10] since "evil companions corrupt good manners."[11] Therefore, if you want to make friends with someone, make friends with someone good and wise. "A good person, indeed, brings forth that what is good out of the treasure of his heart"[12] and shall always advise you that what is good, because he wants to you to be like him and wants to guide you to God, according to him who says, "I wish that all were as I myself am. But each has his own special gift from God."[13] LIFE OF HYPATIUS.[14]

6:36 Wear Out the Doorstep of the Wise

THE APOSTLE'S EXAMPLE. AUGUSTINE: Andrew was Peter's brother, and we know from the Gospel that the Lord called Peter and Andrew from the ship, saying, "Come, follow me, and I will make you fishers of men."[15] And from that time they joined him and did not leave him. On the present occasion these two followed him, however, not as those who were not again to leave him but to see where he was living and to fulfill the Scripture, "Let your foot wear out the threshold of his doors; get up and come to him continually and be instructed in his commandments." He showed them where he lived. They came and remained with him.[16] TRACTATES ON THE GOSPEL OF JOHN 7.9.[17]

---

[2]See Phil 1:23-24. [3]See 1 Cor 15:53. [4]See Mt 26:41; Mk 14:38. [5]See 2 Cor 5:3-4. [6]Sir 6:25Vg. [7]NBA 26:1089-91; NPNF 1 8:385**. [8]See Jn 8:44. [9]See Gal 6:10; Rom 12:5. [10]Prov 22:24-25. [11]1 Cor 15:33. [12]Lk 6:45. [13]1 Cor 7:7. [14]CTP 30:134-35. [15]Mt 4:19. [16]See Jn 1:38-39. [17]NBA 24:165-67; NPNF 1 7:51**.

7:1-21* VARIOUS ADVICE

¹Do no evil, and evil will never befall you.
  ²Stay away from wrong, and it will turn away from you.
³My son, do not sow the furrows of injustice,
  and you will not reap a sevenfold crop.

⁴Do not seek from the Lord the highest office,
  nor the seat of honor from the king.
⁵Do not assert your righteousness before the Lord,
  nor display your wisdom before the king.
⁶Do not seek to become a judge,
  lest you be unable to remove iniquity,
lest you be partial to a powerful man,
  and thus put a blot on your integrity.
⁷Do not offend against the public,
  and do not disgrace yourself among the people.

⁸Do not commit a sin twice;
  even for one you will not go unpunished.
⁹Do not say, "He will consider the multitude of my gifts,
  and when I make an offering to the Most High God he will accept it."
¹⁰Do not be fainthearted in your prayer,
  nor neglect to give alms.

¹¹Do not ridicule a man who is bitter in soul,
  for there is One who abases and exalts.
¹²Do not devise² a lie against your brother,
  nor do the like to a friend.
¹³Refuse to utter any lie,
  for the habit of lying serves no good.
¹⁴Do not prattle in the assembly of the elders,
  nor repeat yourself in your prayer.

¹⁵Do not hate toilsome labor,
  ⁻ or farm work, which were created by the Most High.
¹⁶Do not count yourself among the crowd of sinners;
  remember that wrath does not delay.
¹⁷Humble yourself greatly,
  for the punishment of the ungodly is fire and worms.ª

^{18}Do not exchange a friend for money,
    or a real brother for the gold of Ophir.
^{19}Do not deprive yourself of a wise and good wife,
    for her charm is worth more than gold.
^{20}Do not abuse a servant who performs his work faithfully,
    or a hired laborer who devotes himself to you.
^{21}Let your soul love[b] an intelligent servant;
    do not withhold from him his freedom

---

z Heb: Gk *plow*   a The Hebrew text reads *for the expectation of man is worms*   b The Hebrew text reads *Love like yourself*   * Sir 7:1-23 Vg.

OVERVIEW: Giving up wrongdoing is indispensable for our salvation (FULGENTIUS). The Lord justifies us if we recognize our faults (CHRYSOSTOM). Bishops are to be above fault and reproach (BARSANUPHIUS AND JOHN). Penance becomes useless if we sin afterwards (GREGORY THE GREAT) even as there is bitterness in the pleasures of the sinners (ATHANASIUS).

7:1 Do No Evil

NO SALVATION FOR THOSE WHO ACT WICKEDLY. FULGENTIUS OF RUSPE: If some people are in the catholic church but live badly, let them hurry to distance themselves from their evil life before concluding this life. Do not let them think that the catholic name is sufficient for their salvation if they do not do the will of God. In fact, our Savior says, "Not everyone who says to me, 'Lord, Lord,' shall enter into the kingdom of heaven, but he who does the will of my Father who is in heaven shall enter into the kingdom of heaven."[1] Indeed, also in the book of Psalms it is written that "the Lord is close to all who call on him in truth. He will fulfill the desire of those who fear him, and he will hear their prayers, and he will save them."[2] Therefore also in Proverbs each one of us is ordered both to fear the Lord and to distance ourselves from evil. There you can read, "Fear the Lord and turn away from all evil, and your body shall have peace and your bones rest."[3] In fact, also in Ecclesiasticus, all the faithful are warned not to do evil with these words: "Do not perform evil deeds, and they will not seize you. Distance yourself from evil, and evil will distance itself from you. Do not sow evil deeds in the furrows of injustice, and you will not harvest them multiplied seven times." In the same book again, because no one, adding sin to sin, wants to deceive himself with a vain thought regarding the mercy of God, the doctrine of salvation meets us with words of this kind: "Do not . . . add sin to sin. Do not say, 'His mercy is great, he will forgive the multitude of my sins,' for both mercy and wrath are with him, and his anger rests on sinners."[4] Again, saint Job says, "Does not calamity befall the unrighteous and disaster the workers of iniquity?"[5] It is written in Proverbs, "The iniquities of the wicked ensnare him, and he is caught in the toils of his sin. He dies for lack of discipline, and because of his great folly he is lost."[6] ON THE FORGIVENESS OF SINS 1.26.23.[7]

7:5 Do Not Assert Your Righteousness

LET US RECOGNIZE OUR FAULTS. JOHN CHRYSOSTOM: Nothing will generate presumptions so much as a good conscience, if we are not careful. Therefore, knowing that after we do something honest that this sentiment might arise in us, Jesus said to his disciples, "When you shall have done all those things you say: 'We are unprofitable servants.' "[8] When the evil beast is about to enter you, with these words, then,

---

[1]Mt 7:21. [2]Ps 145:18-19 (144:18-19 LXX). [3]Prov 3:7-8. [4]Sir 5:5-6. [5]Job 31:3. [6]Prov 5:22-23. [7]CTP 57:58-59. [8]Lk 17:10.

he says, close the door. Notice, he did not say, "When you shall have done all those things you are useless," but "say, 'We are useless.'" Tell him not to fear because I do not pass my sentence on the basis of your judgment. If you say you are useless, I shall crown you as useful. Elsewhere we read, "First declare your transgressions, so that you may be justified."[9] In other tribunals, the death of the culprit follows after the accusation; in the divine tribunal, the crown comes after the accusation of the trespasses. Therefore also Solomon said, "Do not justify yourself before the Lord." HOMILIES ON HOSEA 3.1.[10]

7:6 Partiality a Blot on Your Integrity

THE BEHAVIOR OF THE BISHOP. BARSANUPHIUS AND JOHN: We do not advise you to leave the one who entrusted you with the care of the holy churches of God,[11] but only to look after your own soul in the fear of God. Do not accept gifts from anyone,[12] do not waver in judgment,[13] do not be ashamed before a powerful person, do not declare innocent the guilty or condemn the innocent.[14] Keep away from avarice, which is the root of all evils;[15] in fact, it is called, and it is, a second kind of idolatry.[16] And do not pride yourself, so that you may be a disciple of the apostle who says, "Do not be haughty, but associate with the lowly."[17]

Do not try to please people, for you know what happens to people who do this. They become estranged from the service of Christ. In fact, the apostle says, "For if I were still pleasing people, I would not be the servant of Christ."[18] And submit to the Lord, who says, "Learn from me, for I am meek and humble in heart, and you will find rest for your souls."[19] Extinguish anger and chase it far from you, for it is the ruin of a person; do everything according to God and you will find him as your helper. Always fear death, for it is necessary that it comes to us all. Remember the hour of your departure, and do not sin against God. And if you arrive at the point of calmness, you

will find rest and grace wherever you decide to withdraw. BOOK OF LETTERS 789.[20]

7:14 Do Not Prattle

AVOIDING SIN. GREGORY THE GREAT: It is written, "The dog returns to his own vomit again, and the sow that was washed to her wallowing in the mire."[21] For the dog, when he vomits, certainly throws up the food that weighed on his stomach. But when he returns to his vomit, he is again loaded with what he had been relieved from. And those who mourn their transgressions certainly throw up by confession the wickedness that wickedly sated them and that oppressed the innermost parts of their soul. And yet, in going back to it again after confession, they take it in again. But the sow, by wallowing in the mire when washed, is made more filthy. And one who mourns past transgressions yet does not leave them behind subjects himself to the penalty of an even worse sin, since he both despises the very pardon that he might have won by his weeping and as it were rolls himself in the mire, because in withholding purity of life from his weeping he makes even his very tears filthy before the eyes of God. Thus again it is written, "Do not repeat a word in your prayer." For to repeat a word in prayer, after wailing about it, is to commit what again requires wailing. And so it is said through Isaiah, "Wash and be clean."[22] For whoever does not maintain an innocent life after his tears of repentance have been shed is neglecting the cleanliness he received after washing. They are indeed washed but are in no way clean when they are the ones who do not stop crying about the things they have committed but then go on to commit again the very things they were crying about. This is why a certain wise man said, "He that is cleansed from the touch of a dead body and touches it again—what good

---

[9]Is 43:26. [10]CTP 162:258. [11]See 2 Cor 11:28. [12]See Prov 15:27; Sir 20:29. [13]See Ex 23:2 par. [14]Sus 53 (Dan 13:53 LXX). [15]See 1 Tim 6:10. [16]See Eph 5:5. [17]Rom 12:16. [18]Gal 1:10. [19]Mt 11:29. [20]CTP 93:572-73; cf. FC 114:291. [21]2 Pet 2:22. [22]Is 1:16.

did his washing do?"[23] For indeed he is cleansed from the touch of a dead body who is cleansed from sin by weeping. But the one who, after his tears, repeats his sin touches a dead body after his cleansing. PASTORAL RULE 3.30.[24]

7:17 The Punishment of the Ungodly

THE PAINFUL PLEASURES OF THE SINNER.
ATHANASIUS: Sin possesses the very bread of his death, to which it invites those who love pleasures and the fools, saying, "Touch with pleasure the secret bread and the sweet stolen waters."[25] He who merely touches it "does not know that the children of the earth perish because of it."[26] When one thinks about tasting pleasure, the result that comes from this nourishment will not be sweet for him in the end, as again the Wisdom of God affirms: "Bread of deceit is pleasant to a person, but afterwards his mouth shall be full of sand,"[27] and, "Honey drips from the lips of a prostitute, which for a certain time is sweet to your palate. Afterwards you will find it more bitter than wormwood, sharper than a two-edged sword."[28] Thus, eating it and enjoying it a little, afterwards he is devoured by worms, while he renders his soul far away,[29] because the fool does not know that "they that are far from God perish."[30] FESTAL LETTERS 7.5.17.[31]

---

[23]Sir 34:25. [24]CTP 28:224-25; NPNF 2 12:62**. [25]Prov 9:17. [26]Prov 9:18. [27]Prov 20:17. [28]Prov 5:3-4. [29]See Prov 5:5. [30]Ps 73:27 (72:27 LXX). [31]LCPM 34:310-11.

7:22-28* CHILDREN AND PARENTS

[22]*Do you have cattle? Look after them;*
   if they are profitable to you, keep them.
[23]*Do you have children? Discipline them,*
   and make them obedient[c] from their youth.
[24]*Do you have daughters? Be concerned for their chastity,[d]*
   and do not show yourself too indulgent with them.
[25]*Give a daughter in marriage; you will have finished a great task.*
   But give her to a man of understanding.

[26]*If you have a wife who pleases you,[e] do not cast her out;*
   but do not trust yourself to one whom you detest.
[27]*With all your heart honor your father,*
   and do not forget the birth pangs of your mother.
[28]*Remember that through your parents[f] you were born;*
   and what can you give back to them that equals their gift to you?

c Gk *bend their necks*   d Gk *body*   e Heb Syr omit *who pleases you*   f Gk *them*   * Sir 7:24-30 Vg.

OVERVIEW: God admonishes us because we are his children (CLEMENT OF ALEXANDRIA). Without such severity the soul is in danger (GREGORY THE GREAT).

7:23-24 Discipline Your Children

GOD ADMONISHES US AS CHILDREN. CLEMENT OF ALEXANDRIA: Christ the educator of humanity, our divine Logos, with every effort and with every gift of wisdom, has offered to save his children, warning them, reproaching, punishing, accusing, threatening, curing, making promises and granting grace. "With various bridles he keeps within bounds"[1] the excessive outbursts of humanity. In short, the Lord conducts himself with us as we conduct ourselves with our children. "Do you have children? Discipline them," Wisdom exhorts, "and make them obedient from their youth. Do you have daughters? Be concerned for their chastity, and do not show yourself too indulgent with them." Yet, our children, male and female, are what we love the most above anything else. CHRIST THE EDUCATOR 1.11.75.1-2.[2]

BEING SEVERE WITH OUR SOUL. GREGORY THE GREAT: "Set your face toward it and let it be in a state of siege."[3] What does it mean to set the face toward Jerusalem that is portrayed on a brick,[4] except that the master should not reveal the vision of heavenly peace or show himself too forgiving or merciful toward a soul if he sees it still uncertain in its deeds? For thus it is written: "Do you have daughters? Be concerned for their chastity, and do not show yourself too indulgent with them." Evil souls that are inclined toward worldly desires are sometimes better served through severity. A fixed gaze accompanied by severe vigilance that offers no hope for any frivolous indulgence frightens the wayward soul and rigorously pulls it away from any enticement toward vice. But even as a master does this, he must always preserve in his heart tenderness and humility toward him in so far as he must have a great deal of love for the individual and should never use his position of authority against him through pride. Nevertheless, he still must refrain from revealing his love and tender regard for the individual's own good. HOMILIES ON EZEKIEL 1.12.30-31.[5]

---

[1]Plato *Laws* 7.808d. [2]CTP 181:103. [3]Ezek 4:3. [4]See Ezek 4:1. [5]CTP 17:286.

7:29-31* THE PRIEST

[29]With all your soul fear the Lord,
    and honor his priests.
[30]With all your might love your Maker,
    and do not forsake his ministers.
[31]Fear the Lord and honor the priest,
    and give him his portion, as is commanded you:
the first fruits, the guilt offering, the gift of the shoulders,
    the sacrifice of sanctification, and the first fruits of the holy things.

* Sir 7:31-35 Vg.

OVERVIEW: God does not look at the quantity of the offerings but at the spirit with which they are offered (RABANUS MAURUS).

7:34[1] *Purify Yourself from Your Carelessness*

A RIGHT SPIRIT. RABANUS MAURUS: It shows that the offering that one offers to God with a humble mind and pure love purifies him from many shortcomings and omissions, even if they are small. Concerning these matters it is writ-ten, "Love covers a multitude of sins."[2] And the psalmist writes, "A broken spirit is a sacrifice to God, a broken and contrite heart, O God, you will not despise."[3] And it is for this same reason that the Lord did not despise the two small coins from the poor widow but accepted them with joy.[4] ON ECCLESIASTICUS 2.10.[5]

---

[1]Vg. [2]1 Pet 4:8. [3]Ps 51:19 (50:19 LXX). [4]See Mk 12:42-43; Lk 21:2-3. [5]PL 109:810.

7:32-36[*] THE POOR AND THE AFFLICTED

[32]Stretch forth your hand to the poor,
 so that your blessing may be complete.
[33]Give graciously to all the living,
 and withhold not kindness from the dead.
[34]Do not fail those who weep,
 but mourn with those who mourn.
[35]Do not shrink from visiting a sick man,
 because for such deeds you will be loved.
[36]In all you do, remember the end of your life,
 and then you will never sin.

[*] Sir 7:36-40 Vg.

OVERVIEW: Job's friends assisted him in his suffering (ANONYMOUS ANOMOEAN).

7:34 *Mourn with Those Who Mourn*

JOB AND HIS FRIENDS. ANONYMOUS ANOMOEAN: These blessed men who went to Job, that is to say, his friends, being devoted faithfully to God and repelling all the execrable seductions of the demons, "sat down with him for seven days and seven nights."[1] They did not look for evil or try to predict the future. Instead, they limited themselves to lifting up their souls to God, moaning and sighing for the grief of Job. What did they do by sitting next to him? They fulfilled what the Scriptures tell us to do: "Do not deny consolation to the afflicted,"[2] and "Weep with them that weep,"[3] and, "It is better to go to a house of mourning than to go to a house of feasting."[4] They sat next to him keeping silent before his patience, his endurance and his steadfastness. COMMENTARY ON JOB 3.21.[5]

---

[1]Job 2:13. [2]Sir 7:34 (7:38 Vg), variant. [3]Rom 12:15. [4]Eccles 7:2. [5]CSEL 96:373.

8:1-7* PRUDENCE AND REFLECTION

¹*Do not contend with a powerful man,*
    lest you fall into his hands.
²*Do not quarrel with a rich man,*
    lest his resources outweigh yours;
for gold has ruined many,
    and has perverted the minds of kings.
³*Do not argue with a chatterer,*
    nor heap wood on his fire.

⁴*Do not jest with an ill-bred person,*
    lest your ancestors be disgraced.
⁵*Do not reproach a man who is turning away from sin;*
    remember that we all deserve punishment.
⁶*Do not disdain a man when he is old,*
    for some of us are growing old.
⁷*Do not rejoice over any one's death;*
    remember that we all must die.

* Sir 8:1-8 Vg.

OVERVIEW: Let us not despise the person who has converted and changed his ways (ORIGEN).

8:5 Do Not Reproach One Who Turns from Sin

DO NOT DESPISE ONE WHO HAS CONVERTED. ORIGEN: There is a person full of faith who comes forward in the assembly and accuses himself, making everyone aware of some sin he has committed. And yet, those who themselves have no fear of God's future judgment, on hearing his words, instead of suffering with him who suffers, instead of burning with him who is offended,[1] instead of falling with him who is fallen, say, Get away from me and don't come near me because I am pure! Then they begin to curse this person whom they previously admired and withdraw their friendship from this person who did not want to conceal his crime. Conveniently they say of those who make the confession, "My friends and companions stand aloof from my plague, and my kin stand afar off."[2] It is not the case, however, that he ought to be afraid of the behavior of others when, after having committed a sin, he desires to save himself, nor should he fear the reproaches of those who do not think about their own sins or recall the words of the divine Scriptures: "Do not insult a person converted from sin, remember that we all

---

[1]See 2 Cor 11:29. [2]Ps 38:11 (37:12 LXX).

deserve punishment." Do not worry about such things. Instead, worry about your soul, and pray to God that he may hear you and raise you after you fall so that you will be able to say also that which follows: "I confess my iniquity; I am sorry for my sin."[3] HOMILIES ON THE PSALMS, PSALM 37, HOMILY 2.1.[4]

---

[3]Ps 38:19 (37:19 LXX). [4]BP 18:293-95.

8:8-9* TRADITION

[8]*Do not slight the discourse of the sages,*
    but busy yourself with their maxims;
because from them you will gain instruction
    and learn how to serve great men.
[9]*Do not disregard the discourse of the aged,*
    for they themselves learned from their fathers;
because from them you will gain understanding
    and learn how to give an answer in time of need.

* Sir 8:9-12 Vg.

OVERVIEW: Anyone who is called to teach must learn with great care (RABANUS MAURUS).

8:9 Gaining Understanding

LEARN WITH DILIGENCE. RABANUS MAURUS: The apostle Peter recommends, "In your hearts reverence Christ as Lord. Always be prepared to make a defense to anyone who calls you to account for the hope that is in you."[1] It is good for a servant of God to learn from his masters with diligence and commitment what afterwards he must teach to others with prudence and for their benefit. Because if he does not and instead is lazy and indolent in applying himself, he will turn out to be useless in teaching others later. ON ECCLESIASTICUS 2.13.[2]

---

[1]1 Pet 3:15. [2]PL 109:816.

8:10-19* PRUDENCE

¹⁰*Do not kindle the coals of a sinner,*
    lest you be burned in his flaming fire.
¹¹*Do not get up and leave an insolent fellow,*
    lest he lie in ambush against your words.
¹²*Do not lend to a man who is stronger than you;*
    but if you do lend anything, be as one who has lost it.
¹³*Do not give surety beyond your means,*
    but if you give surety, be concerned as one who must pay.

¹⁴*Do not go to law against a judge,*
    for the decision will favor him because of his standing.
¹⁵*Do not travel on the road with a foolhardy fellow,*
    lest he be burdensome to you;
for he will act as he pleases,
    and through his folly you will perish with him.
¹⁶*Do not fight with a wrathful man,*
    and do not cross the wilderness with him;
because blood is as nothing in his sight,
    and where no help is at hand, he will strike you down.
¹⁷*Do not consult with a fool,*
    for he will not be able to keep a secret.
¹⁸*In the presence of a stranger do nothing that is to be kept secret,*
    for you do not know what he will divulge.[g]
¹⁹*Do not reveal your thoughts to every one,*
    lest you drive away your good luck.[h]

g Or *it will bring forth*   **h** Heb: Gk *let him not return a favor to you*   * Sir 8:13-22 Vg.

OVERVIEW: David was a model of behavior during persecution, realizing the importance of not stoking the anger of the one pursuing you (EUSEBIUS). Godparents have great responsibilities (CHRYSOSTOM).

8:10 Do Not Provoke a Sinner

DAVID IN THE PERSECUTION. EUSEBIUS: Saul chased David, who in fact carried out these words, "When they persecute you in this city, flee into another."[1] He fled in order not to irritate his enemy with his presence and to become for him a reason to spill blood. In fact, David grasped the saying, "Do not incite the arm of a sinner," better than anyone. This is why he withdrew and moved away, although he was loved

---

[1]Mt 10:23.

by all the people[2] and had many who shared his pains and his sorrow and who would have been able to receive him and hide him in their homes. But, in order not to become a cause of danger to others, he fled into the desert and preferred to live in caves. It seems to me that the holy apostle also alludes to him when he says, "They wandered in deserts, in the mountains, in dens and in caves of the earth."[3] COMMENTARY ON THE PSALMS 2.56.[4]

8:13 Giving Surety

BAPTISMAL GODPARENTS. JOHN CHRYSOSTOM: Consider, dearly beloved, those who vouch for someone concerning money, how they have to submit themselves to a greater risk than the one who is responsible for and receives the money. Indeed, if the person who has received the loan shows himself benevolent, he pays back what he owes to the person who has given the guarantee; but if he turns out to be bad, he prepares a much larger disaster for the person who has vouched for him. For this reason a wise man warned, "If you give surety, be concerned as one who must pay." Now then, if those who vouch for someone concerning money render themselves responsible for everything, how much more do those who vouch for someone relating to spiritual things and on the theme of virtue must demonstrate great vigilance, exhorting, advising, correcting and revealing paternal affection. And they should understand that what is happening should not be taken lightly but that their own reputation is at stake. There will be mutual benefit if through their personal admonition they lead them someone onto the road of virtue, while a grave condemnation will be incumbent on them if they neglect to do so. For this reason, it is customary to call these people spiritual parents, so that they may learn what affection they must demonstrate for them with their own deeds in the teaching of spiritual things. If it is good to push those to embrace virtue with whom we have no relationship, how much more must we carry out this command regarding someone whom we receive whom we call a spiritual son or daughter. BAPTISMAL INSTRUCTIONS 2.15-16.[5]

---

[2]See 1 Sam 18:16. [3]Heb 11:38. [4]PG 23:505. [5]CTP 31:118-19.

9:1-9* WOMEN

[1]Do not be jealous of the wife of your bosom,
   and do not teach her an evil lesson to your own hurt.
[2]Do not give yourself to a woman
   so that she gains mastery over your strength.
[3]Do not go to meet a loose woman,
   lest you fall into her snares.
[4]Do not associate with a woman singer,

lest you be caught in her intrigues.
⁵Do not look intently at a virgin,
  lest you stumble and incur penalties for her.
⁶Do not give yourself to harlots
  lest you lose your inheritance.
⁷Do not look around in the streets of a city,
  nor wander about in its deserted sections.
⁸Turn away your eyes from a shapely woman,
  and do not look intently at beauty belonging to another;
many have been misled by a woman's beauty,
  and by it passion is kindled like a fire.
⁹Never dine with another man's wife,
  nor revel with her at wine;
lest your heart turn aside to her,
  *and in blood*ⁱ *you be plunged into destruction.*

i Heb: Gk *by your spirit*   * Sir 9:1-13 Vg.

OVERVIEW: The causes of sin are not in God's creation but in the wicked heart (CHRYSOSTOM).

9:8 Turn Your Eyes Away

SIN COMES FROM A CORRUPT HEART. JOHN CHRYSOSTOM: Where is it that the Scriptures have spoken of sin and its causes? It accuses the people who lived before the flood for their illegitimate unions. Hear how it cites the cause: "The sons of God, having seen how the daughters of men were fair, took them as wives."[1] And so? Beauty was the cause of sin? It could never be so. In fact, beauty is the work of the wisdom of God. And a work of God could never become the cause of wickedness. Was it, then, a sin for having seen them? No, for this is also nature's work. What is it then? Having seen them with evil intentions—that, indeed, is very much the result of a corrupt will. Therefore also a wise man provided this exhortation: "Do not gaze on the beauty of others." He did not say, "Do not look," because it so happens that this occurs spontaneously; rather, he says, "Do not gaze on," excluding the intentional consideration, the importunate gaze, the prolonged contemplations that derive from a corrupt soul and are prey to desire. But what damage, if one objects, could derive from this? "Following this," it is said, "love lights up like fire." Like fire, indeed, after it has reached hay or straw does not waste time but simultaneously sticks to wood and ignites a splendid flame, so also the fire of desire that is within us, after it becomes glued to a beautiful and splendid image through the instrumentality of the eyes, immediately burns the souls of the one who watches. HOMILIES ON HOSEA 3.4.[2]

---

[1]Gen 6:2. [2]CTP 162:266-67.

9:10-18* RELATIONS WITH OTHERS

¹⁰*Forsake not an old friend,*
 for a new one does not compare with him.
A new friend is like new wine;
 when it has aged you will drink it with pleasure.

¹¹*Do not envy the honors of a sinner,*
 for you do not know what his end will be.
¹²*Do not delight in what pleases the ungodly;*
 remember that they will not be held guiltless as long as they live.

¹³*Keep far from a man who has the power to kill,*
 and you will not be worried by the fear of death.
But if you approach him, make no misstep,
 lest he rob you of your life.
Know that you are walking in the midst of snares,
 and that you are going about on the city battlements.

¹⁴*As much as you can, aim to know your neighbors,*
 and consult with the wise.
¹⁵*Let your conversation be with men of understanding,*
 and let all your discussion be about the law of the Most High.
¹⁶*Let righteous men be your dinner companions,*
 and let your glorying be in the fear of the Lord.
¹⁷*A work will be praised for the skill of the craftsmen;*
 so a people's leader is proved wise by his words.
¹⁸*A babbler is feared in his city,*
 and the man who is reckless in speech will be hated.

* Sir 9:14-25 Vg, with variants.

OVERVIEW: The Old Testament anticipates the New (FULGENTIUS), which tells us that only Christ frees us (ORIGEN). While enjoying this freedom, let us also restrain our tongue and not indulge in anger (CHRYSOSTOM).

9:10 Do Not Forsake an Old Friend

THE TWO TESTAMENTS. FULGENTIUS OF RUSPE: The New Testament must be held in veneration in such a way that the Old Testament not be neglected in any way. This is what Ecclesiasticus seems to me to recommend under the guise of old and new friends when it says, "Forsake not an old friend, for a new one does not compare with him."[1] From the mouth of Jeremiah, the divine Scripture anticipates the difference that is found in the mysteries of the two Testaments, saying, "The days are coming, says the Lord, when I will make a new testament with the house of Israel and the house of Judah, not according to the testament that I made with their ancestors."[2] For the other, that is, the New Testament comes, not like the Old Testament which was brought to an end by the Lord, but as the one in which the Lord has given the fulfillment of the commandments, and after he had removed the old mysteries, he instituted the different mysteries of the revealed truth. Therefore, what he promised in the Old he has brought to fulfillment in the New. Since therefore the knowledge of the mysteries of the New Testament can be truly salutary and joyful only if one acknowledges that the promise that went before in the mysteries of the Old Testament is true, when the Scriptures says, "Do not leave an old friend because the new one will not be like him," there is immediately added, "A new friend is like new wine; when it has aged, you will drink it with pleasure."[3] What does "aged" mean except that the type[4] of the New Testament appears in the Old Testament? This new wine is thus drunk with joy if its meaning and promise are acknowledged in the Old Testament. LETTERS 14.46.[5]

9:13 Walking Among Snares

CHRIST FREES US. ORIGEN: "Know that you are walking in the midst of snares and that you are going about on the city battlements." Everything is full of nets; the devil has filled up everything with snares. But if the Word of God comes to you and begins to appear through the nets,[6] you will say, "Our soul has been freed like a sparrow from the snare of the hunters; the snare has been broken, and we have been freed. We are blessed by the Lord who has made heaven and earth."[7] The bridegroom "appears" then "through the nets."[8] Jesus has prepared the

way for you. He descended to earth and submitted himself to the nets of the world. Seeing the great flock of humanity imprisoned in the nets and seeing that only he could tear them, he came to the nets and assumed a human body and subjected it to the snares of the powerful enemy and tore them apart for you.[9] Thus, you can say, "See. He is at the back, behind our wall, watching through the windows, appearing through the nets."[10] HOMILIES ON THE SONG OF SONGS 2.12.[11]

9:15 Converse with People of Understanding

DO NOT GIVE IN TO ANGER. JOHN CHRYSOSTOM: That you may therefore with confidence draw near to God, do not receive wrath when it comes in on you and desires to be with you. Drive it away, instead, like a mad dog. For this is also what Paul commanded. His phrase was, "lifting up holy hands without wrath and disputing."[12] Instead, adorn it with gentleness, with humility, make it worthy of the God who is entreated, fill it with blessing, with much almsgiving. For it is possible even with words to give alms. "For a word is a better thing than a gift," and "Answer the poor peaceably with meekness."[13] And all the rest of your time, too, adorn it with the rehearsing of the laws of God. "Yes, let all your communication be in the law of the Most High." Having thus adorned ourselves, let us come to our King and fall at his knees, not with the body only but also with the mind. Let us consider whom we are approaching and on whose behalf, and what we want to accomplish. HOMILIES ON THE GOSPEL OF MATTHEW 51.5.[14]

---

[1]Sir 9:14 Vg. [2]Jer 31:31-32 (38:31-32 LXX). [3]Sir 9:14-15 Vg. [4]Type is a technical term that indicates that the Old Testament already shows in some way the image of the New Testament. [5]CTP 149:344-45; FC 95:563-64**. [6]See Song 2:9. [7]Ps 124:7-8 (123:7-8 LXX). [8]Song 2:9. [9]See Acts 2:24; Ps 18:4 (17:4 LXX). [10]Song 2:9. [11]CTP 83:89-90; ACW 26:302**. [12]1 Tim 2:8. [13]Cf. Sir 4:8. [14]CTP 171:374; NPNF 1 10:319.

10:1-5 GOVERNMENT

[1]*A wise magistrate will educate his people,*
and the rule of an understanding man will be well ordered.
[2]*Like the magistrate of the people, so are his officials;*
and like the ruler of the city, so are all its inhabitants.
[3]*An undisciplined king will ruin his people,*
but a city will grow through the understanding of its rulers.
[4]*The government of the earth is in the hands of the Lord,*
and over it he will raise up the right man for the time.
[5]*The success of a man is in the hands of the Lord,*
and he confers his honor upon the person of the scribe.[j]

j Or *the official*

OVERVIEW: The city is the church, whose head is Christ (RABANUS MAURUS).

10:2 *Like the Magistrate*

THE CHURCH IS CHRIST'S CITY. RABANUS MAURUS: The city of Christ is the holy church, which follows his footsteps with the affection of a devoted heart and imitates him in the realization of good works. It is there where his ministers, that is, the leaders of the faithful, and the holy preachers observe his commandments and never cease in ordering others to do so as well. And Qoheleth[1] praises their conduct inspired by moderation: "Happy are you, O land, when your king is the son of free people, and your princes feast at the proper time, for strength, and not for drunkenness!"[2] Of another king he says quite the opposite: "Woe to you, O land, when your king is a child, and your princes feast in the morning!"[3] Woe, then, to the land whose king is the devil, always avid for new prey; as judges and princes he has those who love the pleasures of this world, those who say before their death arrives, "Let us eat and drink, for tomorrow we die."[4] Instead, blessed is the land of the church, for Christ is its king, the son of nobles, of Abraham, Isaac and Jacob, who descends from the lineage of the prophets and all the saints, from those who have not been dominated by sin and for that reason are free. His princes are the apostles and all the saints, whose king is the son of nobles, and they do not eat until the morning—or with voracious appetites. They do not indeed search for the pleasures of this world, but they will eat in their due time, when the moment of reward arrives: "Blessed is one who shall eat bread in the kingdom of God."[5] ON ECCLESIASTICUS 3.1.[6]

---

[1]The Hebrew designation for the author of Ecclesiastes, often translated "the Preacher." [2]Eccles 10:17. [3]Eccles 10:16. [4]1 Cor 15:32; Is 22:13. [5]Lk 14:15. [6]PL 109:825-26.

10:6-18* AGAINST ARROGANCE

⁶*Do not be angry with your neighbor for any injury,*
and do not attempt anything by acts of insolence.
⁷*Arrogance is hateful before the Lord and before men,*
and injustice is outrageous to both.
⁸*Sovereignty passes from nation to nation*
on account of injustice and insolence and wealth.
⁹*How can he who is dust and ashes be proud?*
for even in life his bowels decay.[k]
¹⁰*A long illness baffles the physician;*[l]
the king of today will die tomorrow.
¹¹*For when a man is dead,*
he will inherit creeping things, and wild beasts, and worms.
¹²*The beginning of man's pride is to depart from the Lord;*
his heart has forsaken his Maker.
¹³*For the beginning of pride is sin,*
and the man who clings to it pours out abominations.
Therefore the Lord brought upon them extraordinary afflictions,
and destroyed them utterly.
¹⁴*The Lord has cast down the thrones of rulers,*
and has seated the lowly in their place.
¹⁵*The Lord has plucked up the roots of the nations,*[m]
and has planted the humble in their place.
¹⁶*The Lord has overthrown the lands of the nations,*
and has destroyed them to the foundations of the earth.
¹⁷*He has removed some of them and destroyed them,*
and has extinguished the memory of them from the earth.
¹⁸*Pride was not created for men,*
nor fierce anger for those born of women.

k Heb: Gk is obscure   **l** Heb Vg: Gk is uncertain   **m** Some authorities read *proud nations*   * Sir 10:6-22 Vg, with differences and additions. After Sir 10:8 (10:9 Vg) it adds, "Nothing is more wicked than the avaricious; he has a greedy soul." Sir 10:9-10 (10:10 Vg) read: "Why does he who is dust and ashes take pride? Since in his life he has thrown out his intimate things. A long illness oppresses the physician; a short illness cheers up the doctor. Short is the life of every mighty one; the king of today tomorrow will be dead." It adds also a verse after Sir 10:17 (10:20 Vg): "God has deleted the memory of the proud and has kept the memory of those who have humble feelings." Often Sir 10:13 is found under this form: "The beginning of sin is pride."

OVERVIEW: This text condemns the greedy (SALVIAN). We should not think we need to be wealthy to know God. Even in our lowly condi-tion we are capable of knowing God (AUGUS-TINE). But the admonitions to the humble and to the proud are not the same (GREGORY THE

GREAT). Pride and arrogance belong to the devil (ORIGEN). The one who is humble looks within himself; the one who is arrogant throws everything out (AUGUSTINE). The ability of doing good comes from God alone; thus we should not be proud for what God has done in us (FULGENTIUS). Sins are punishments caused by arrogance. Arrogance is the cause of heresies (AUGUSTINE). Let us watch, therefore, lest arrogance spoil the fruit of good actions (GREGORY THE GREAT). Pride is the beginning of all sins (JULIAN POMERIUS).

10:8[1] *A Venal Soul*

LET US NOT BE GREEDY. SALVIAN THE PRESBYTER: People must aspire to wealth, procure it, hold in trust, increase it—only they should do so having in mind those we previously indicated. Otherwise, when one makes bad use of the assets he has, which are a gift from God, disastrous, irreparable damage occurs. As sacred Scripture says, "There is nothing more wicked than a miser."[2] Wealth kept from one's Lord does the worst and most deadly kind of damage.[3] This is an incontrovertible truth! What is worse or more horrible than for anyone to change the asset we enjoy in the world into disasters for the future? What is worse than the fact that death and damnation are pursued with these very things that have been given to us by the Lord for the purpose of obtaining a true eternally happy life from them? But we must also contemplate the fact that if wealth held in trust is a source of trouble for people, piling up more wealth without stopping to see what it is doing constitutes an even more serious calamity. Who among the rich, in fact, is equipped with the kind of temperament that can limit himself to conserve and not to increase his assets? Our present time is indeed wretched and deplorable in which people reduce themselves to this. Scripture asserts that it is a serious crime to even keep money. Today, people believe it is a virtue not only to keep but also to add to their wealth. Once again, therefore, we ask: How can someone think he or she is undamaged by guilt, if even at the moment of death, having no thought for salvation, people do not donate the assets they possess, since they have already committed a crime in keeping them until the moment they depart this life? How will these people not be guilty who, by a predilection toward vanity that is completely sacrilegious, leave their wealth to just anyone, especially since those who have not deprived themselves of at least a portion of their possessions for the worship of God will be found guilty in this life? The same Lord is our master in this matter as well. Through the apostle he says, "And now to you who are rich: weep over the disaster that will come on you! Your wealth is corrupted, and your gold and silver are consumed by rust; their rust will be raised in testimony against you and will devour your flesh like fire. You have accumulated treasures for the last days!"[4] AGAINST AVARICE 1.7.31-33.[5]

10:9 *Dust and Ashes*

WE CAN KNOW GOD. AUGUSTINE: "No one knows the things of a person except the spirit of man which is in him."[6] And yet, there is something of a person that "the spirit . . . in him" does not know. But you, Lord, who made him, you fully know him. I indeed, though in your sight I despise myself and consider "myself but dust and ashes"—I still know something concerning you that I do not know about myself. Most assuredly, "we see through a glass dimly," "not yet face to face."[7] As long as I am absent from you, I am more present with myself than with you. CONFESSIONS 10.5.7.[8]

ADMONITIONS TO THE HUMBLE AND THE PROUD. GREGORY THE GREAT: The humble and the proud are admonished differently. For the humble, it is to be insinuated how true that ex-

---

[1]Vg. [2]Sir 10:8, variant of Vg. [3]Eccles 5:12. [4]Jas 5:1-4. [5]CTP 10.36-37. [6]1 Cor 2:11. [7]See 1 Cor 13:12. [8]NBA 1:305.

cellence is that they hold in hoping for it. For the proud, it is to be intimated how that temporal glory is as nothing, that even when they embrace it they are not holding it. Let the humble hear how eternal the things are that they long for, how transitory the things are that they despise. Let the proud hear how transitory the things are that they court and how eternal the things are that they lose. Let the humble hear from the authoritative voice of the Truth, "Everyone who humbles himself shall be exalted."[9] Let the proud hear, "Everyone who exalts himself shall be humbled."[10] Let the humble hear, "Humility goes before glory";[11] let the proud hear, "The spirit is exalted before a fall."[12] Let the humble hear, "To whom shall I have respect, but to one who is humble and quiet and trembles at my words?"[13] Let the proud hear, "Why are earth and ashes proud?" Let the humble hear, "God respects the humble."[14] Let the proud hear, "And the proud he knows from afar."[15] Let the humble hear, "That the Son of man came not to be ministered to but to minister."[16] Let the proud hear that "the beginning of all sin is pride."[17] Let the humble hear that "our Redeemer humbled himself, being made obedient even to death."[18] Let the proud hear what is written concerning their head: "He is king over all the children of pride."[19] The pride, therefore, of the devil became the occasion of our perdition, and the humility of God has been found as the argument for our redemption. For our enemy, who is among the created beings, desired to appear exalted above all things. But our Redeemer, remaining great above all things, decided instead to become little among all things. Let the humble, then, be told that when they abase themselves, they ascend to the likeness of God. Let the proud be told that when they exalt themselves, they fall into imitation of the apostate angel. PASTORAL RULE 3.17.[20]

PRIDE, THE DEVIL'S SIN. ORIGEN: Pride, haughtiness and arrogance are the sins of the devil, and for these faults you must leave heaven for earth.[21] Thus, "God resists the proud and gives grace to the humble."[22] And "How can he make dust and ashes proud?" so that one becomes arrogant, forgetting what he will become, in which fragile casing he is contained, in which excrements he drowns and which garbage he continuously emits from his flesh? What do the Scriptures say? "How can he make dust and ashes proud?" And again: "During life, one ruins one's own entrails." Pride is the greatest of all sins and the principal fault of the devil. When sometimes the Scriptures list the sins of the devil, you will discover that these come forth from the source of pride. Indeed, it says, "I will act in strength, and in the wisdom of my understanding I will remove the boundaries of nations and will spoil their strength. And I will shake the inhabited cities: and I will take with my hand all the world as a nest: and I will even take them as eggs that have been left."[23] Observe how arrogant and haughty his words are and how he does not take anything into account. So are all those who are puffed up by boasting and by pride. Wealth, prestige and earthly glory are bait for pride. HOMILIES ON EZEKIEL 9.2.[24]

THE HUMBLE AND THE ARROGANT. AUGUSTINE: I am afraid that the reason why the soul went forth away from God is that it was proud. In fact, I have no doubt about it. For it is written, "Pride is the beginning of all sin,"[25] and "the beginning of human pride is a falling away from God." It is written, it is firm and sure, it is true. And so, what is said of proud mortal humanity, clad in the tattered rags of the flesh, weighed down with the weight of a corruptible body,[26] and all the while extolling himself, and forgetting the very skin he is clothed with— what, I ask, do the Scriptures say to him? "Why is dust and ashes proud?" Why proud! Let the

---

[9]Lk 18:14. [10]Lk 18:14. [11]Prov 15:33. [12]Prov 16:18. [13]Is 66:2. [14]Ps 138:6 (137:6 LXX). [15]Ps 138:6 (137:6 LXX). [16]Mt 20:28. [17]Variant of Vg. [18]Phil 2:8. [19]Job 41:25. [20]CTP 28:163-64; NPNF 2 12:41. [21]Origen alludes to the belief that the devil is a fallen angel. [22]Jas 4:6. [23]Is 10:13-14 LXX. [24]CTP 67:154. [25]Sir 10:13, variant of Vg. [26]See Wis 9:15.

Scriptures tell why. "Because in his life he put forth his inmost parts."[27] What does "put forth" mean except that he "threw it far away"? In other words, to send them out. For to enter within is to long after the inmost parts; to put forth the inmost parts is to send them out. The proud man gets rid of the inmost parts, the humble man earnestly desires the inmost parts. If we are cast out by pride, let us return by humility. TRACTATES ON THE GOSPEL OF JOHN 25.15.[28]

IN GOD WE CAN DO WHAT IS GOOD. FULGENTIUS OF RUSPE: We should not think of God as the author of good works as if only at the dawn of creation he provided human nature the possibility of doing good in such a way that, after his help was taken away, human nature on its own could want or do anything good on its own. In reality, on its own initiative, human nature could not have realized such a possibility, not even in the first man even while he was still not yet wounded by sin. Therefore, how can human nature restore its own health without the aid of a physician since, while it was healthy, it could not even succeed in safeguarding its health then? Therefore, earth and ash should not get puffed up because it has abandoned its most visceral thoughts in this life;[29] nor should the wounded act as if he were healthy because he thinks he has healed that part of himself. Rather, he should reflect with the humility of a wounded heart on the putridness of his wounds so that, proclaiming with the prophet, "My wounds grow foul and fester because of my foolishness,"[30] he can obtain healing not because of his own merit but because of the free gift of divine mercy. In fact, what does a person possess that he has not already received? But if he has received it, then why does he glory in himself as if he had not received it?[31] LETTERS 4.2.3-4.[32]

10:12 Forsaking One's Maker

SINS ARE ALSO PUNISHMENTS. AUGUSTINE: "Those who do such things deserve to die."[33]

Which things? Those he had previously listed as punishments. In fact, "God gave them up," he says, "in the lusts of their hearts to impurity,[34] because they do that which should not be done.[35] To be an adulterer is already a kind of punishment; to be a liar, a miser, a cheat, a murderer, these are already punishments. Punishments for which sin? Of the primordial apostasy, the supreme sin of pride. "The beginning of human sin is rebellion against God,"[36] and, "The beginning of every sin is pride."[37] For the apostle had spoken of this antecedent of sin: "Although they knew God, they neither gave him glory nor rendered thanks to him; instead, they have become futile in their reasonings, and their obtuse minds have become darkened."[38] A darkened heart is already a punishment. But from what does it derive? "While declaring themselves wise, they have become fools."[39] They said that what they had received from God derived from themselves; or, if they knew from whom they had received it, they still did not give the glory to the one from whom they received it. EXPOSITIONS OF THE PSALMS 57.18.[40]

10:13 The Beginning of Pride

HERESIES STEM FROM PRIDE. AUGUSTINE: "The gate of hell"[41] means the beginning of sin because it is written, "The wages of sin is death,"[42] and to say "death" is equivalent to saying "hell." The Scripture also explains what constitutes the beginning of sin: "The beginning of every sin is pride."[43] Therefore pride is the gate of hell. When one inquires concerning the causes that have produced heresies, one sees that they were born from pride because pride pushes people, in the end, toward heresies and schisms when they boast of their abilities and

---

[27]Sir 10:9, variant of Vg. [28]NBA 24:587. [29]See Sir 10:9, variant of Vg. [30]Ps 38:6 (LXX 37:6). [31]See 1 Cor 4:7. [32]CTP 149:122; FC 95:334-35**. [33]Rom 1:32. [34]Rom 1:24. [35]Cf. Rom 1:28. [36]Sir 10:12 (10:14 Vg), variant of Vg. [37]Sir 10:13 (10:15 Vg), variant of Vg. [38]Rom 1:21. [39]Rom 1:22. [40]NBA 26:231; WSA 3 17:141**. [41]Mt 16:18. [42]Rom 6:23. [43]Sir 10:13, variant of Vg.

their holiness with the goal of attracting people to themselves but with the result of detaching them from Christ. But all heresies and schisms derive from these children of pride who will not overcome the catholic church, as it was precisely foretold, "The gates of hell will not prevail against it."[44] SERMON 346/B.3.[45]

ARROGANCE MAY SPOIL GOOD WORKS.

GREGORY THE GREAT: A person looks around him with vigilance and care. He examines his thoughts; bringing back to mind the life of his audience, he humbles himself and does his best in every way because then pride does not pop up in the mind in order to dominate him with its deeds. That is why it is written, "The beginning of all sin is pride."[46] What, then, shall be the fruit of good work before the eyes of God, if it is corrupted from the root by pride? Often . . . his soul is tempted by anger, but looking around him, he immediately composes himself within and, submitting himself to discipline, acts thus so that the movement of the soul does not pass into words, does not explode into voice. And so it happens that the anger of the agitated soul dies, suffocated by reason, where it would otherwise rise through negligence. And so it happens that from a fault conceived, the soul gives birth to virtue, since although he did not know how to persistently keep watch so that the movement would not arise, he nevertheless vigorously conquered the agitation. HOMILIES ON EZEKIEL 2.6.7.[47]

PRIDE IS THE BEGINNING OF SIN.

JULIAN POMERIUS: Who could say anything clearer or of more value? "Pride is the beginning," it says, not simply of some but "of every sin,"[48] in order to emphasize how pride is, in itself, the cause of all sins. Not only is it in itself sin, but also no sin could have been, can be or ever will be committed without pride. Every sin, in effect, is nothing other than contempt of God, leading one to trample on his commandments. And what, other than pride, inspires people to this contempt? Indeed, in the devil it showed itself to be the cause of eternal damnation, and from the angel that he was he became (precisely) the devil.[49] And it was he who, knowing that he was cast out of heaven for the sin of pride and banished to this dark prison, and corrupting the one whom God had created innocent, with serpentine cunning he insinuated the vice of pride in humankind.[50] He was certain that once pride, the root of every evil, was accepted, the man would then easily commit all sins, which germinate only in the proud soul. ON THE CONTEMPLATIVE LIFE 3.2.1.[51]

---

[44]Mt 16:18. [45]NBA 34:105; *WSA* 3 10:82**. [46]Sir 10:13 (10:15 Vg), variant of Vg. [47]CTP 18:136. [48]Sir 10:13 (10:15 Vg), variant of Vg. [49]Allusion to the theory that the devils are fallen angels. [50]See Gen 3:5. [51]CTP 64:202-3.

10:19-25* PEOPLE WORTHY OF HONOR

^{19}*What race is worthy of honor? The human race.*
  What race is worthy of honor? Those who fear the Lord.
What race is unworthy of honor? The human race.
  What race is unworthy of honor? Those who transgress the commandments.
^{20}*Among brothers their leader is worthy of honor,*
  and those who fear the Lord are worthy of honor in his eyes."
^{22}*The rich, and the eminent, and the poor—*
  their glory is the fear of the Lord.
^{23}*It is not right to despise an intelligent poor man,*
  nor is it proper to honor a sinful man.
^{24}*The nobleman, and the judge, and the ruler will be honored,*
  but none of them is greater than the man who fears the Lord.
^{25}*Free men will be at the service of a wise servant,*
  and a man of understanding will not grumble.

n Other authorities add as verse 21, *The fear of the Lord is the beginning of acceptance; obduracy and pride are the beginning of rejection*   * Sir 10:23-28 Vg.

OVERVIEW: The saints are worthy of praise (STEPHEN) as those who lived out the freedom they received from the slavery of sin through the forgiveness granted to them by grace (AMBROSIASTER).

10:24 *None Greater Than One Who Fears the Lord*

LET US PRAISE THE SAINTS. STEPHEN OF HNES: You know the greatness of him whom we praise. You have now watched from the part of this spiritual tree[1] that blossoms over us on the waters of life,[2] that does not fear the heat of the drought of the heretics that come on him who gives his fruit in his season,[3] that is, in life. And even in death God has not ceased to give fruit through the grace of the good sower,[4] our Lord Jesus Christ. If he promises this to the sons of Jonadab, in the ancient Scriptures,[5] how much more will he do this to the sons of grace at his

coming into the world. Thus, therefore, even if we say absolutely nothing about the glory of our Father, the facts proclaim his greatness.[6] In fact, I have not written these things in order to tell you his life—I am not at that level yet to engage in such an enterprise—but I have at least obeyed the command of the apostle regarding this. He says, "Remember them that rule over you."[7] Truly great in heaven and on earth is he whom we praise. And indeed "who is greater than him who fears God in his heart?" according to that which is written? LIFE OF APOLLO THE ARCHIMANDRITE 18.[8]

10:25 *At the Service of a Wise Servant*

FORGIVENESS CANCELS THE SERFDOM OF SIN. AMBROSIASTER: "He who is called in the

---

[1]See Ps 1:3. [2]See Jn 4:10-11; 7:38. [3]See Ps 1:3. [4]See Ps 1:3. [5]See Jer 37:18 (42:18 LXX). [6]See Ps 145:6 (144:6 LXX). [7]Heb 13:7. [8]CTP 41:214-15.

Lord as a slave is a freedman of the Lord."[9] Someone who is rescued from sins, which are truly indicative of "slaves," becomes a freedman of the Lord. For he who behaves unwisely is a slave through and through. This was the opinion of the ancients too, who called wise people "free," and all the unwise, "slaves." Thus Solomon says, "Free people shall serve a slave who is wise." Therefore one who believes, even if he is a slave for a time, becomes a freedman

of the Lord because, in believing in Christ, he is doing a wise thing. For sins create slaves, as Ham the son of Noah was made a slave for his sin and lack of prudence,[10] for when someone receives remission of sins, he becomes a freedman. COMMENTARY ON THE FIRST LETTER TO THE CORINTHIANS 7.22.1.[11]

[9]1 Cor 7:22. [10]See Gen 9:22-24. [11]CTP 78:112.

10:26-31* HUMILITY AND TRUTH

[26]Do not make a display of your wisdom when you do your work,
  nor glorify yourself at a time when you are in want.
[27]Better is a man who works and has an abundance of everything,
  than one who goes about boasting, but lacks bread.
[28]My son, glorify yourself with humility,
  and ascribe to yourself honor according to your worth.
[29]Who will justify the man that sins against himself?
  And who will honor the man that dishonors his own life?
[30]A poor man is honored for his knowledge,
  while a rich man is honored for his wealth.
[31]A man honored in poverty, how much more in wealth!
  And a man dishonored in wealth, how much more in poverty!

* Sir 10:29-34 Vg.

OVERVIEW: Avoid vainglory and do what is good even in face of adversity. We should not forget that the present riches are perishable (RABANUS MAURUS).

10:26 Do Not Glorify Yourself

DO WHAT IS GOOD. RABANUS MAURUS: Avoid boasting about one's own good works, for ar-

rogance of this kind is an abomination before the eyes of God[1] and stops one from doing good in adversity, "because tribulation produces perseverance, and perseverance produces character, and character produces hope."[2] ON ECCLESIASTICUS 3.3.[3]

[1]See Lk 16:15. [2]Rom 5:3-5. [3]PL 109:837.

10:31[4] *Do Not Glory in Wealth*

Present Riches Are Perishable. Rabanus Maurus: This means that the one who places all of his trust in the abundance of earthly things must fear future poverty, always remembering that evangelical parable of the rich man dressed in purple and the poor Lazarus. The one clothed with temporary glory is thrown into eternal torments while the other clothed in the misery of the present life rises to eternal joy.[5] And James also says this: "Let the brother of low degree rejoice in that he is exalted and the rich in that he is made low."[6] For whoever humbly undergoes adversities for the Lord shall receive the highest rewards of the kingdom from him. In other words, the rich should boast in their humiliation—in an ironic twist—otherwise, they will see the "glory" that is due them for the pride they placed in their riches while disregarding the poor or even oppressing them—their end will be perpetual punishment. On Ecclesiasticus 3.3.[7]

---

[4]Vg. [5]See Lk 16:19-23. [6]Jas 1:9-10. [7]PL 109:838.

11:1-6 DO NOT TRUST APPEARANCES

[1]*The wisdom of a humble man will lift up his head,*
   and will seat him among the great.

[2]*Do not praise a man for his good looks,*
   nor loathe a man because of his appearance.
[3]*The bee is small among flying creatures,*
   but her product is the best of sweet things.
[4]*Do not boast about wearing fine clothes,*
   nor exalt yourself in the day that you are honored;
for the works of the Lord are wonderful,
   and his works are concealed from men.
[5]*Many kings have had to sit on the ground,*
   but one who was never thought of has worn a crown.
[6]*Many rulers have been greatly disgraced,*
   and illustrious men have been handed over to others.

Overview: Even animals can know God (Chrysostom).

11:3 *The Bee Is Small*

Animals Also Know God. John Chrysostom: God shows that the prescriptions of the Law are not arduous. His requests of humankind are not inordinate. In fact, those beings without reason, and even the most senseless among them, easily obey what he commands. Someone might allege, however, that they instinctually have the capacity to know. Therefore it is possible that what they rightly do by instinct we do through our own choice. "The ox knows his owner."[1] Not only does he place before them how exceptional his gift is, but he further intensifies his accusation against their inordinate wickedness by comparing them not with other human beings but with the elements of nature—those, in particular, who are without reason and are the most senseless among them. He says that they are even worse than these. This is also what Jeremiah does, bringing into play the turtledove and the swallow.[2] Solomon, too, does something similar, returning the one who lives an idle life to now face the ant,[3] now the bee. COMMENTARY ON ISAIAH 1.2-3.[4]

---

[1]Is 1:3. [2]See Jer 8:7. [3]See Prov 6:6-8. [4]CTP 162:56.

11:7-11 REFLECTION AND SLOWNESS

[7]Do not find fault before you investigate;
  first consider, and then reprove.
[8]Do not answer before you have heard,
  nor interrupt a speaker in the midst of his words.
[9]Do not argue about a matter which does not concern you,
  nor sit with sinners when they judge a case.

[10]My son, do not busy yourself with many matters;
  if you multiply activities you will not go unpunished,
and if you pursue you will not overtake,
  and by fleeing you will not escape.
[11]There is a man who works, and toils, and presses on,
  but is so much the more in want.

OVERVIEW: Avoid hasty judgments. The greedy search for riches brings about disgrace (Rabanus Maurus).

11:7 Consider, and Then Reprove

AVOID HASTY JUDGMENTS. RABANUS MAURUS: Avoid reckless judgments. This is why the Lord commands that the innocent, or the one against whom there is only one witness, should not be punished. Instead, "everything must be established by the testimony of two or three witnesses."[1] Likewise, the apostle orders Timothy to "not receive accusations against an elder without

---

[1]See Deut 19:15; Mt 18:16.

the deposition of two or three witnesses."[2] On Ecclesiasticus 3.4.[3]

11:10 Do Not Busy Yourself with Many Matters

LOOKING FOR RICHES. RABANUS MAURUS: Divine wisdom teaches its children not to overly struggle to obtain earthly profits, for otherwise you will not avoid such adversity as greed, envy and similar pains. Therefore it is written in the book of Proverbs, "The one with a covetous eye is impatient to enrich himself and does not consider that misery will fall on him."[4] And again, "He who is greedy of dishonest gain troubles his own house,"[5] and, "Better is little with the fear of the Lord than a great treasure with trouble,"[6] and, in Qoheleth, "He who loves silver shall not be satisfied with silver; nor he that loves abundance with profit."[7] On Ecclesiasticus 3.4.[8]

---

[2] 1 Tim 5:19. [3] PL 109:840. [4] Prov 28:22. [5] Prov 15:27. [6] Prov 15:16. [7] Eccles 5:9. [8] PL 109:840.

11:12-28* WE SHOULD TRUST GOD ALONE

[12] *There is another who is slow and needs help,*
    who lacks strength and abounds in poverty;
but the eyes of the Lord look upon him for his good;
    he lifts him out of his low estate
[13] *and raises up his head,*
    so that many are amazed at him.

[14] *Good things and bad, life and death,*
    poverty and wealth, come from the Lord.[o]
[17] *The gift of the Lord endures for those who are godly,*
    and what he approves will have lasting success.
[18] *There is a man who is rich through his diligence and self-denial,*
    and this is the reward allotted to him:
[19] *when he says, "I have found rest,*
    and now I shall enjoy[p] *my goods!"*
he does not know how much time will pass
    until he leaves them to others and dies.
[20] *Stand by your covenant*[q] *and attend to it,*
    and grow old in your work.

[21] *Do not wonder at the works of a sinner,*

234

but trust in the Lord and keep at your toil;
for it is easy in the sight of the Lord
  to enrich a poor man quickly and suddenly.
²²*The blessing of the Lord is*ʳ *the reward of the godly,*
  and quickly God causes his blessing to flourish.
²³*Do not say, "What do I need,*
  and what prosperity could be mine in the future?"
²⁴*Do not say, "I have enough,*
  and what calamity could happen to me in the future?"
²⁵*In the day of prosperity, adversity is forgotten,*
  and in the day of adversity, prosperity is not remembered.
²⁶*For it is easy in the sight of the Lord*
  to reward a man on the day of death according to his conduct.
²⁷*The misery of an hour makes one forget luxury,*
  and at the close of a man's life his deeds will be revealed.
²⁸*Call no one happy before his death;*
  a man will be known through his children.

o Other authorities add as verse 15 and 16, ¹⁵*Wisdom, understanding, and knowledge of the law come from the Lord; affection and the ways of good works come from him.* ¹⁶*Error and darkness were created with sinners; evil will grow old with those who take pride in malice.*   p Gk *eat of*   q Heb *task*   r Gk *is in*   * Sir 11:12-30 Vg.

OVERVIEW: Everything that happens depends on God's will and not on fate and the stars (PROSPER). The remembrance of good actions frees from desperation (GREGORY THE GREAT). God is immutable in his nature; we are not (CASSIAN). The destiny of the saints is called blessed (JOHN OF DAMASCUS). Like God's works, the actions of the saints are known through their fruits (STEPHEN).

11:14 *All Things Come from the Lord*

GOD'S WILL. PROSPER OF AQUITAINE: God in truth has created the body and the spirit of every single human being. Besides the diversity each person may choose to pursue, there is an infinite variety created by God beyond what could be voluntarily achieved by everyone in what each person receives at the beginning of his or her existence. But there are those who would upset us and many who would lead us astray with their vain sayings and false opinions among those who presume to be in the know about unknowable things, having attributed these original differences to fate (even if it does not exist) and to the stars. But we are firmly convinced that God the creator forms all the different types and models of things according to his will from the original elements, and although the nature of the spirit is of one kind and the body another, he deals with them according to the methods most agreeable to him. And surely these acts of God would not have been withdrawn from human knowing if there was a reason for them to be known; or it would be clearly revealed why everything happens the way it does, if it were not sufficient to know that it happens in this way. The Lord said to Moses, "Who has given speech to humankind and who has made the dumb and the deaf, the seeing and the blind? Is it not perhaps I the Lord God?"[1] And again in Isaiah, " 'Have I not made the sterile and the fecund?' says the Lord."[2] In the book of Ecclesiasticus there is the saying, "Good and evil, life and death, poverty and

---

[1]Ex 4:11. [2]Is 66:9.

riches come from the Lord." And Job says, "The tents of robbers are at peace, and with impudence they provoke God, even though he has given everything into their hands."[3] THE CALL OF ALL NATIONS 1.14.[4]

11:25 In Prosperity, Adversity Is Forgotten

DO NOT DESPAIR. GREGORY THE GREAT: Since Job was patient and was supported by the serenity of his soul in the midst of a malicious people, he said, "Did perhaps the men of my tent not say, 'To whom has he not given his flesh to be satisfied?' "[5] So, why, now, does a holy person list all of his merits in the midst of scourges? Why does he praise with his mouth the works he has done, if not because in the midst of the plagues and of the words that could otherwise drive him to despair, he leads his soul back to hope? He who was humble in prosperity remembers his merits and thus does not lose heart in his adversity. In the midst of many scourges, indeed, these words would have induced despair in the soul of anyone who could not have recalled to his own memory the good he had done. The holy person, therefore, having to listen to all these evil things, saw his mind driven to desperation. He did everything he could to anchor himself in the secure hope of his own good works. Thus is fulfilled what is written: "On good days remember the bad, on bad days remember the good." If, indeed, when we have good days we remember the bad ones that we have already suffered or that we may yet suffer, we do not think overly highly of ourselves for the good things that we have received because the fear that springs from the memory of the bad things we have experienced contains the joy we have over the good things that have happened to us. And the same holds true for when we are in trouble: if at those times we remember the good things we have received or that we still hope to receive, the burden of our trouble will not push our soul toward desperation because the memory of the good that has

happened to us lifts us toward hope. HOMILIES ON EZEKIEL 2.7.20.[6]

11:28 Call No One Happy Before His Death

GOD DOES NOT CHANGE. JOHN CASSIAN: But that even the powers above are, as we said, subject to change is shown by those who fell from their ranks through the fault of a corrupt will.[7] This is why we should not think that the nature of those who remain in the blessed condition in which they were created is unchangeable, simply because they were not similarly led astray to choose the worse part. For it is one thing to have a nature incapable of change and another thing for a person through the efforts of his virtue, and by guarding what is good through the grace of the unchangeable God, to be kept from change. For everything that is secured or preserved by care can also be lost by carelessness. And so we read, "Call no one happy before his death,"[8] because so long as an individual is still engaged in the struggle, and if I may use the expression, still wrestling—even though he generally conquers and carries off many prizes of victory—yet he can never be free from fear and from the suspicion of an uncertain outcome. And therefore God alone is called unchangeable and good because his goodness is not the result of effort, but he possesses it naturally, and so he cannot be anything but good. No virtue then can be acquired by an individual without the possibility of change. However, in order that when it once exists it may be continually preserved, it must be guarded with the same care and diligence with which it was acquired. CONFERENCES 1.6.16.[9]

THE DEATH OF THE SAINTS. JOHN OF DAMASCUS: Death, previously abhorred and hated, is now the object of praise and declared blessed. What at one time procured pain and sadness, tears and melancholy, now appears as a source of

---

[3]Job 12:6. [4]CTP 143:74-75; ACW 14:56-57**. [5]Job 31:31. [6]CTP 18:179. [7]Cassian alludes to the fall of the devil. [8]Sir 11:30 Vg. [9]CTP 155:266-67; NPNF 2 11:360-61.

joy and feasting. All the servants of God enjoy a blessed death because the end of their lives bears the security of being welcomed by God. In fact, they become perfect, and this perfection renders them blessed, giving them the solidity of virtue, as the oracle affirms, "Do not judge a person blessed before his death." HOMILY ON THE DORMITION 1.12.[10]

THE WORKS OF THE SAINTS REVEALED BY THEIR FRUITS. STEPHEN OF HNES: The one who desires to know the greatness of the deeds of our father Apollo in works and not only in words is able to know in part of his greatness from that which he sees. If "God is clearly known through his creatures,"[11] according to the words of the apostle, and if "the tree is known by its fruit,"[12] according to the words of God, and if, according to the words of another sage, "a man is known through his children,"[13] then you recognize the greatness of Apollo by the fruits of his justice. In fact, if our father had not suffered, the Lord would not have given him this congregation, worthy of his love, just as the fecundity of a livestock animal stands out most prominently in the place where his offspring abound. LIFE OF APOLLO THE ARCHIMANDRITE 17.[14]

---

[10]CTP 25:161. [11]Rom 1:20. [12]Mt 12:33. [13]Sir 11:28, variant of LXX. [14]CTP 41:213.

11:29-34* MISTRUST THE WICKED

> [9]Do not bring every man into your home,
>   for many are the wiles of the crafty.
> [30]Like a decoy partridge in a cage, so is the mind of a proud man,
>   and like a spy he observes your weakness;[s]
> [31]for he lies in wait, turning good into evil,
>   and to worthy actions he will attach blame.
> [32]From a spark of fire come many burning coals,
>   and a sinner lies in wait to shed blood.
> [33]Beware of a scoundrel, for he devises evil,
>   lest he give you a lasting blemish.
> [34]Receive a stranger into your home and he will upset you with commotion,
>   and will estrange you from your family.

s Heb: Gk *downfall*   * Sir 11:31-36 Vg.

OVERVIEW: The patriarchs practiced hospitality and were blessed (PALLADIUS).

11:29 The Wiles of the Crafty

ADVICE ON HOSPITALITY. PALLADIUS: I have not intended in the least to diminish the virtue of our ancestors, and above all the virtue of hospitality. In reality, among the virtues practiced by the most eminent of the patriarchs, this is the only one that tends toward piety. One of them had God the Savior at his own table; another had the angels as his guests; one received as a reward a son at his advanced age; the other his own salvation, fleeing from Sodom.[1] This is what the apostle is talking about when he exhorts us to imitate them: "Do not neglect to show hospitality; for thereby some have received angels without knowing it."[2] It happens, however, that the one who offers hospitality has the prudence of the serpent and the simplicity of the dove,[3] thus complying with the double precept of the Lord: "Give to every one who asks of you,"[4] and, "Do not bring such a person into your home." This is so that you do not run the danger of bringing a wolf to the place where the lamb dwells[5] or a bear to the place where the ox resides,[6] with the risk of turning your gain into a loss. It is first of all necessary to be aware of the place where you are—if it is deserted or has frequent visitors. Then, you must also be aware of your own ability to tolerate characters that are too difficult. Finally, you must well consider who

it is who is destined to receive your benefits—whether he is rich or poor, healthy or weak, in need of food or clothes. These are the areas where acts of mercy come into play. In reality, the blessed Abraham did not receive into his home consuls, captains, the important people of this temporary world like those who have horses with bridles and glittering stirrups and whose harnesses, burnished with bronze, belch forth from afar the resonance of their pride. On the contrary, Abraham lived in a deserted place and welcomed all who passed by. Those who traveled the desert went to the patriarch because they were attracted by his virtue and because they were reduced to being beggars, which is about as extreme a poverty as you can get. In a similar way Lot, who lived in the worst city of that same desert, rightly welcomed all who passed by, given the customs of those inhabitants. DIALOGUE ON THE LIFE OF SAINT JOHN CHRYSOSTOM 12.[7]

---

[1]See Gen 18-19. [2]Heb 13:2. [3]See Mt 10:16. [4]Lk 6:30. [5]See Mt 7:15. [6]See Is 11:7. [7]CTP 125:184-85.

12:1-7* BENEFITS

[1]*If you do a kindness, know to whom you do it,*
and you will be thanked for your good deeds.
[2]*Do good to a godly man, and you will be repaid—*
if not by him, certainly by the Most High.
[3]*No good will come to the man who persists in evil*
or to him who does not give alms.
[4]*Give to the godly man, but do not help the sinner.*
[5]*Do good to the humble, but do not give to the ungodly;*
hold back his bread, and do not give it to him,

lest by means of it he subdue you;
for you will receive twice as much evil
    for all the good which you do to him.
⁶For the Most High also hates sinners
    and will inflict punishment on the ungodly.ᵗ
⁷Give to the good man, but do not help the sinner.

---

t Other authorities add *and he is keeping them for the mighty day of their punishment*   * The Vulgate has a different verse distribution.

OVERVIEW: A good action toward a sinner does not necessarily imply approval of his sin (AUGUSTINE). Likewise, give alms with wisdom and without sinning (GREGORY THE GREAT). God punishes the wicked and the sinners (FULGENTIUS).

12:4 Give to the Godly

EVEN SINNERS DESERVE TO BE TREATED WITH GOODNESS. AUGUSTINE: Execute mercy to the wicked, but not because he is wicked. Do not receive the wicked, in so far as he is wicked, that is, do not receive him because you have an inclination and love toward for his iniquity. For it is forbidden to give to a sinner and to receive sinners. Yet how do we hear, "Give to every one that asks of you,"[1] and this, "If your enemy is hungry, feed him"?[2] This is seemingly contradictory, but it is opened to those who knock in the name of Christ and will be clear to those who seek.[3] "Do not help a sinner," and, "Do not give to the ungodly," and yet, "Give to every one who asks of you." But it is a sinner who asks of me. Give, not as though you were giving to a sinner. When do you give as though you were giving to a sinner? When that which makes him a sinner pleases you so that his sin becomes the reason that you give. EXPOSITIONS OF THE PSALMS 102.13.[4]

12:5 Do Good to the Humble

ALMS AND PRUDENCE. GREGORY THE GREAT: The mind should first be predisposed to patience, and then either much or all should be given bountifully, otherwise, when the inroad of want is borne with but little equanimity, then, both the reward of previous bounty could be lost and subsequent murmuring might bring even worse ruin on the soul. Just in case they should give nothing at all to those on whom they ought to bestow something, let them hear what is written: "Give to everyone who asks of you."[5] And, just in case they should give something, however little, to those on whom they ought to bestow nothing at all, let them hear what is also written: "Give to the good person, and do not receive a sinner; do well to the one who is lowly, and do not give to the ungodly." And again, "Set out your bread and wine on the burial of the just, but do not eat and drink with sinners."[6]

For the one who gives his bread and wine to sinners provides assistance to the wicked because they are wicked. This is also why some of the rich of this world nourish players with profuse bounties, while the poor of Christ are tormented with hunger. He, however, who gives his bread to one that is indigent, though he is a sinner, not because he is a sinner but because he is a human being, does not in truth nourish a sinner but a poor righteous person, because what he loves in him is not his sin but his nature. Those who already distribute compassionately what they possess are to be admonished also so that they might learn how to be vigilant, lest, when they redeem by alms the sins they have committed, they commit others that will still

---

[1]See Mt 5:42. [2]Rom 12:20. [3]See Mt 7:7. [4]NBA 27:609; NPNF 1 8:506**. [5]Lk 6:30. [6]Tob 4:18.

require redemption;[7] otherwise they might suppose that the righteousness of God is for sale, thinking that if they take care to give money for their sins, they can sin with impunity. PASTORAL RULE 3.20.[8]

12:6 God Will Punish the Ungodly

SINNERS WILL BE CONDEMNED. FULGENTIUS OF RUSPE: The impious and sinners who have no intention of repenting of their impiety or iniquity will be condemned at the end to eternal torments, while to those who have repented God will lavish his mercy. This is what is written in the book of Ecclesiasticus: "The Most High has mercy on the penitent and will inflict punishment on the impious and sinners."[9] Further, in the same book it is said, "Remember that wrath will not be late in coming. Humble yourself to the utmost, because fire and worms fill up the punishment of the ungodly."[10] Again, Isaiah says that "their fire shall not be quenched, and their worm shall not die."[11] It is also written in Ecclesiasticus, "A synagogue of sinners is like a bundle of oak, and their end will be the flame of fire. The way of sinners is full of offenses, and, at the end, there will be the fiery pit, darkness and pains."[12] ON THE FORGIVENESS OF SINS 1.27.2.[13]

---

[7]See Sir 3:29. [8]CTP 28:176-77; NPNF 2 12:45-46. [9]Sir 12:6 (12:7 Vg), variant of Vg. [10]Sir 7:16-17 (7:18-19 Vg). [11]Is 66:24; cf. Mk 9:48. [12]Sir 21:9-10 (21:9-11 Vg). [13]CTP 57:60-61; FC 95:144-45**.

12:8-18* TRUE AND FALSE FRIENDS

[8]*A friend will not be known[u] in prosperity,*
    nor will an enemy be hidden in adversity.
[9]*A man's enemies are grieved when he prospers,*
    and in his adversity even his friend will separate from him.
[10]*Never trust your enemy,*
    for like the rusting of copper, so is his wickedness.
[11]*Even if he humbles himself and goes about cringing,*
    watch yourself, and be on your guard against him;
and you will be to him like one who has polished a mirror,
    and you will know that it was not hopelessly tarnished.
[12]*Do not put him next to you,*
    lest he overthrow you and take your place;
do not have him sit at your right,
    lest he try to take your seat of honor,
and at last you will realize the truth of my words,
    and be stung by what I have said.

¹³*Who will pity a snake charmer bitten by a serpent,*
or any who go near wild beasts?
¹⁴*So no one will pity a man who associates with a sinner*
and becomes involved in his sins.
¹⁵*He will stay with you for a time,*
but if you falter, he will not stand by you.

¹⁶*An enemy will speak sweetly with his lips,*
but in his mind he will plan to throw you into a pit;
an enemy will weep with his eyes,
but if he finds an opportunity his thirst for blood will be insatiable.
¹⁷*If calamity befalls you, you will find him there ahead of you;*
and while pretending to help you, he will trip you by the heel;
¹⁸*he will shake his head, and clap his hands,*
and whisper much, and change his expression.

u Other authorities read *punished*   * Sir 12:8-19 Vg.

OVERVIEW: Let us refrain from vanity, which is like a wild beast (CHRYSOSTOM). The words of the sinners are untrue; in the just there is no duplicity (ANONYMOUS ANOMOEAN).

12:13 A Snake Charmer Bitten by a Serpent

VANITY IS LIKE A WILD BEAST. JOHN CHRYSOSTOM: Like a wild beast fallen onto a noble and delicate body incapable of defending itself, thus vanity has sunk its heavy teeth into you and injected its poison and diffused a great stench. It has thrown away some parts, after having mutilated them; other parts it has torn to pieces, again others devoured. And, if it were possible for someone to see vanity and the church in the same arena, the pitiful spectacle might have looked like this—although much more distressing than what happens in the arena—the body thrown away with the beast towering over it and watching over every part of it. The beast drives back anyone who assaults it and does not distance itself or abandon that body. Who then will chase this wild animal away? It is the duty of him who wages this battle to send his angels, invoked by us, and, after they have closed this beast's daring and impudent mouth as if with

braces, they will chase it away. But when he waged the battle it was under the condition that once it was chased away, we would not go after it. And so, after he sends it away, ordering that terrible beast to stay away from us, if we—even after we have been saved from its clutches and it has been chased into its cave—covered with a thousand wounds still go looking for it again and get it roused up and excited again, then he will not have further pity on us, and he will not save us: "Who, in fact, will have pity on a snake charmer bitten by a serpent and on those who get close to the wild beasts?" ON VAINGLORY AND THE RIGHT WAY FOR PARENTS TO BRING UP THEIR CHILDREN 1.[1]

12:16 An Enemy Will Speak Sweetly

THE WORDS OF THE JUST ARE TRUTHFUL. ANONYMOUS ANOMOEAN: "He was upright,"[2] truthful, pure, simple, without pretense. There was no duplicity in him. There was no hesitation in him. He did not say one thing with his mouth while thinking something else with his mind. He did not say one thing with words and think an-

---

[1]CTP 7:25-26. [2]Job 1:1.

other thing with his heart. His words were not sweet on the lips and daggers in secret.[3] Nowadays, there are many—even a great many—of whom it is said, "His words are more viscous than oil, yet they are unsheathed swords,"[4] and again, "Everyone speak peace to his neighbor while in his heart he hatches a trap,"[5] and again,

"An enemy will speak sweetly with his lips, but in his mind he will plan to throw you into a pit."[6] COMMENTARY ON JOB 1.10.[7]

---

[3]Cf. Prov 26:23. [4]Ps 55:22 (54:22 LXX). [5]Jer 9:7 (9:8 Vg). [6]Sir 12:15 Vg. [7]CSEL 96:102-3.

13:1-26* GO WITH YOUR PEERS

[1]*Whoever touches pitch will be defiled,*
and whoever associates with a proud man will become like him.
[2]*Do not lift a weight beyond your strength,*
nor associate with a man mightier and richer than you.
How can the clay pot associate with the iron kettle?
The pot will strike against it, and will itself be broken.
[3]*A rich man does wrong, and he even adds reproaches;*
a poor man suffers wrong, and he must add apologies.
[4]*A rich man[v] will exploit you if you can be of use to him,*
but if you are in need he will forsake you.
[5]*If you own something, he will live with you;*
he will drain your resources and he will not care.
[6]*When he needs you he will deceive you,*
he will smile at you and give you hope.
He will speak to you kindly and say, "What do you need?"
[7]*He will shame you with his foods,*
until he has drained you two or three times;
and finally he will deride you.
Should he see you afterwards, he will forsake you,
and shake his head at you.

[8]*Take care not to be led astray,*
and not to be humiliated in your feasting.[w]
[9]*When a powerful man invites you, be reserved;*
and he will invite you the more often.
[10]*Do not push forward, lest you be repulsed;*
and do not remain at a distance, lest you be forgotten.
[11]*Do not try to treat him as an equal,*

nor trust his abundance of words;
for he will test you through much talk,
    and while he smiles he will be examining you.
¹²*Cruel is he who does not keep words to himself;*
    he will not hesitate to injure or to imprison.
¹³*Keep words to yourself and be very watchful,*
    for you are walking about with your own downfall.^x

¹⁵*Every creature loves its like,*
    and every person his neighbor;
¹⁶*all living beings associate by species,*
    and a man clings to one like himself.
¹⁷*What fellowship has a wolf with a lamb?*
    No more has a sinner with a godly man.
¹⁸*What peace is there between a hyena and a dog?*
    And what peace between a rich man and a poor man?
¹⁹*Wild asses in the wilderness are the prey of lions;*
    likewise the poor are pastures for the rich.
²⁰*Humility is an abomination to a proud man;*
    likewise a poor man is an abomination to a rich one.

²¹*When a rich man totters, he is steadied by friends,*
    but when a humble man falls, he is even pushed away by friends.
²²*If a rich man slips, his helpers are many;*
    he speaks unseemly words, and they justify him.
If a humble man slips, they even reproach him;
    he speaks sensibly, and receives no attention.
²³*When the rich man speaks all are silent,*
    and they extol to the clouds what he says.
When the poor man speaks they say, "Who is this fellow?"
    And should he stumble, they even push him down.

²⁴*Riches are good if they are free from sin,*
    and poverty is evil in the opinion of the ungodly.
²⁵*A man's heart changes his countenance,*
    either for good or for evil.^y
²⁶*The mark of a happy heart is a cheerful face,*
    but to devise proverbs requires painful thinking.

v Gk He   w Other authorities read *folly*   x Other authorities add *When you hear these things in your sleep, wake up!* ¹⁴*During all your life love the Lord, and call on him for your salvation.*   y Other authorities add *and a glad heart makes a cheerful countenance*   * Sir 13:1-32 Vg.

OVERVIEW: The faithful should not mingle with those who do not believe rightly (CYRIL OF ALEXANDRIA), realizing that everyone will receive a punishment apportioned to his responsibilities (ORIGEN). God wants to live in those who love him (CYRIL OF ALEXANDRIA). He does not want to live in those who steal from the poor, which the rich do to an inordinate degree (SALVIAN). He rather seeks to live in the beautiful souls of his saints who build up the church (ORIGEN).

13:1 Being Defiled

AVOID HERETICS. CYRIL OF ALEXANDRIA: We who have been justified in Christ, who, through faith in him, have obtained communion with the Holy Spirit,[1] must be careful not to mix with those of perverse mind and impious spirit who do not have the true faith. They are in fact foreigners; they speak a different language and say perverse things[2]. If someone mixes with them, he too will be contaminated, since it is written, "One who handles pitch blackens his hand." Therefore, if it is possible to bear fruit in the churches of Christ, why would anyone want to associate with those on the fringe or have anything to do with the impure congregations, provoking against oneself the God of the universe? COMMENTARY ON MALACHI 2.[3]

13:2 A Weight Beyond Your Strength

PUNISHMENT KEEPS PROPORTION WITH RESPONSIBILITIES. ORIGEN: All in the church who are sinners, who "have tasted the word of God"[4] and transgress it, justly merit punishment, but each will be tormented according to his position. A leader of the church who sins will undergo greater punishment. Does not the faithful catechumen deserve more indulgence than a leader? Is not the lay person more worthy of pardon than a deacon, and the latter, in turn, more worthy of understanding than a priest? And even if I do not describe them, you know the other scenarios. Fearing God's judgment, then, and with my gaze always fixed on that series of judgments contained in the Scriptures, the phrase comes to mind, "Do not take on yourself a burden beyond your strength." And the other, "Do not seek to be a judge if you are

not capable of rooting out injustice."[5] What good would it be for me to sit on the cathedra, my head lifted high, receiving the homage of the great, but being unable to perform actions that are fully worthy of my charge? Would I not be afflicted by an even greater suffering because the honor due the just is given to me by all, though I am a sinner? HOMILIES ON EZEKIEL 5.4.[6]

13:15 Every Creature Loves Its Own Kind

GOD REMAINS IN THOSE WHO LOVE HIM. CYRIL OF ALEXANDRIA: When Jesus has shown in advance and rightly defined who those that love him are[7] and of what blessings they will partake, he at once proceeds to treat of others who have not yet chosen to love him. "For they will not keep my words," he says, for this is the meaning of the saying, "He will not keep my word,"[8] spoken as if it was about one man, even though it has a broad and generic signification. And what he says here has a very apt connection with what precedes. For, if the keeping of his commandments or his word is a clear proof of love toward him, surely the converse of this will be true. For treating his bidding as of no account and thrusting his commandment aside will be a sign that we refuse to love him, since these are the acts of people inured to evildoing. But just as he promised that together with God the Father he would abide with those who keep his laws,[9] for the same reason, I think, he will pass away from and wholly abandon those who do the reverse. For thus the truth of Solomon's saying will be seen: "Into the soul of the one who makes iniquity wisdom will not enter or dwell in the body given over to sin."[10] For in common life you can observe that a similar result follows: for does not a person gain a reputation by conversing with those who are like-minded and who choose the same path of life, rather than

---

[1]See 1 Cor 6:11; 2 Cor 4:13. [2]Cf. Acts 20:30. [3]CTP 60:313. [4]See Heb 6:5. [5]Sir 7:6. [6]CTP 67:105. [7]See Jn 14:15. [8]Cf. Jn 14:24. [9]See Jn 14:23. [10]See Wis 1:4.

with others? And "every creature loves his own," according to the saying, and "people will seek union with his own kind." And if it seems most desirable even among ourselves to live with those of similar habits to ourselves, how can we escape the reflection that this is still more the case with God? For as he is good by nature and the beginning and source of all virtue, he takes up his abode not in the lovers of wickedness but in the workers of virtue and disdains the impure. COMMENTARY ON THE GOSPEL OF JOHN 10.14.24.[11]

13:19 Pastures for the Rich

THE WEALTHY STEAL FROM THE POOR. SALVIAN THE PRESBYTER: Is there anyone who has been found to live next door to a rich person who has not been robbed or even reduced to a state of permanent poverty? This is because as the powerful continue to encroach, the weak lose their possessions, or even themselves along with their possessions. The Word of God traces the profile of both with this most appropriate phrase, "The wild ass is the lion's prey in the desert; so also the poor are devoured by the rich."[12] But it is also true that it is not only the poor who endure such tyranny but nearly the entire human race. What other dignity, after all, is there for those of high rank if not the power to confiscate the assets of the citizens? Concerning some, whose names I will not mention, what is a political position except a kind of plunder? For there is no worse pillaging of the poor than that which occurs among those in political power. Government positions are bought by the few and paid for by the ravaging of the rest of the citizenry. What can be more scandalous and evil than this? The poor pay the price for positions that are not for them. They do not know the meaning of buying, they only know the meaning of paying.[13] The world is turned upside down for just a few individuals. The elevation of one person brings about the general ruin of everyone else. THE GOVERNANCE OF GOD 4.4.20-21.[14]

13:26 The Mark of a Happy Heart

APPLICATION TO THE SOUL AND THE CHURCH. ORIGEN: He also says, "And your face is beautiful."[15] If it refers to that face of which Paul says, "We shall all then with unveiled face,"[16] and again, "But then face to face,"[17] then you will understand whether it is this or the face of the soul that is praised by the Word of God and is said to be beautiful. It is, without a doubt, the face that every day renews itself in the image of the one who created it, the one who in itself finds no spot or wrinkle but is holy and immaculate, which Christ has presented to himself as the church,[18] that is, the souls who have come to perfection who altogether form the body of the church. Such a body will appear beautiful if the souls who compose it remain in every grace of perfection. In fact, just as an angry soul distorts the face of the body and disturbs it but when it is found in a state of tranquility and peace renders a countenance that is peaceful and mild, so also the face of the church in relation to the attitudes and the feelings of believers is defined as graceful or ugly, according to what we read written: "A cheerful countenance is the token of a heart that is in prosperity," and again, "The face of the light hearted is filled with laughter, but it is morose if the heart is found in sadness."[19] Therefore the heart is happy when it has the Spirit of God in itself, whose firstfruit is love and whose second is joy.[20] Thus I believe that some sages of this world have formed the opinion that only the sage is beautiful, while all the fools are only ugly.[21] COMMENTARY ON THE SONG OF SONGS 2.13-14.[22]

---

[11]CTP 113:155. [12]Sir 13:23 Vg; cf. 13:19 LXX. [13]Salvian denounces the fact that many public positions were auctioned and those who obtained them oppressed the poor to get back their money. [14]CTP 114:112-13. [15]Song 2:14. [16]2 Cor 3:18. [17]1 Cor 13:12. [18]See 2 Cor 4:16; Col 3:10; Eph 5:27. [19]Prov 15:13. [20]See Gal 5:22. [21]Stoic phrase. [22]CTP 1:263-64; ACW 26:251-52**.

14:1-2 TRUE HAPPINESS

¹Blessed is the man who does not blunder with his lips
   and need not suffer grief for sin.
²Blessed is he whose heart does not condemn him,
   and who has not given up his hope.

OVERVIEW: The just do not sin with words, but even when they do sin, they can get up again (RABANUS MAURUS).

14:1 *One Who Does Not Blunder in Speech*

THE JUST PERSON WHO SINS CAN GET UP AGAIN. RABANUS MAURUS: Declare blessed one who is prudent in his words and tries not to say what he might regret. In fact, "one who guards his mouth and tongue keeps himself from trouble."[1] This also agrees with the words of James, "If one does not err in speech, he is a perfect person."[2] But you might ask us, how can he say that one who does not offend in speech is perfect, since the apostle had just said, "We all fall short in many respects"?[3] And Solomon says, "There is no one on earth so just that he does only good and never sins."[4] And the psalmist, "I said with dismay, 'Everyone is false.' "[5] And John the Evangelist, "If we say that we are without sin, we deceive ourselves, and the truth is not in us."[6] To which it can be replied that there are different kinds of falling short, since the elect fall short in a different way than reprobates, according to Solomon's testimony: "Because if the just person falls seven times, he gets up, but the impious succumb to disaster."[7] Indeed, if the just individual falls short through the weakness of the flesh or through ignorance, he does not cease to be just, since, as this type of failure is daily and inevitable, so also is the remedy of prayer and good works always at hand. This immediately raises up the just individual who sins, so that he does not end up staining or ruining the wedding garment[8] of charity and faith with the dirt of vice. ON ECCLESIASTICUS 3.9.[9]

---

[1]Prov 21:23. [2]Jas 3:2. [3]Jas 3:2. [4]Eccles 7:20. [5]Ps 116:11 (115:2 LXX). [6]1 Jn 1:8. [7]Prov 24:16. [8]Cf. Mt 22:11-12. [9]PL 109:854-55.

14:3-19* ENVY AND GREED

³Riches are not seemly for a stingy man;
   and of what use is property to an envious man?
⁴Whoever accumulates by depriving himself, accumulates for others;
   and others will live in luxury on his goods.
⁵If a man is mean to himself, to whom will he be generous?

He will not enjoy his own riches.
⁶*No one is meaner than the man who is grudging to himself,*
    and this is the retribution for his baseness;
⁷*even if he does good, he does it unintentionally,*
    and betrays his baseness in the end.
⁸*Evil is the man with a grudging eye;*
    he averts his face and disregards people.
⁹*A greedy man's eye is not satisfied with a portion,*
    and mean injustice withers the soul.
¹⁰*A stingy man's eye begrudges bread,*
    and it is lacking at his table.

¹¹*My son, treat yourself well, according to your means,*
    and present worthy offerings to the Lord.
¹²*Remember that death will not delay,*
    *and the decree*ᶻ *of Hades has not been shown to you.*
¹³*Do good to a friend before you die,*
    and reach out and give to him as much as you can.
¹⁴*Do not deprive yourself of a happy day;*
    let not your share of desired good pass by you.
¹⁵*Will you not leave the fruit of your labors to another,*
    and what you acquired by toil to be divided by lot?
¹⁶*Give, and take, and beguile yourself,*
    because in Hades one cannot look for luxury.
¹⁷*All living beings become old like a garment,*
    *for the decree*ᵃ *from of old is, "You must surely die!"*
¹⁸*Like flourishing leaves on a spreading tree*
    which sheds some and puts forth others,
so are the generations of flesh and blood:
    one dies and another is born.
¹⁹*Every product decays and ceases to exist,*
    and the man who made it will pass away with it.

z Gk *covenant*   a Gk *covenant*   * Sir 14:3-20 Vg.

OVERVIEW: Avarice is a source of pain (CHRYSOSTOM).

14:9 The Greedy Unsatisfied with a Portion

THE UNHAPPINESS OF THE GREEDY. JOHN CHRYSOSTOM: Someone once said, "Nothing is more wicked than a money-lover."[1] This is the kind of person who puts a price even on himself and goes around as a common enemy of the world, complaining that the earth does not bear gold instead of corn, or fountains instead of streams or mountains instead of stones. He complains about the fruitfulness of the seasons, troubled if everyone receives some common benefits from something. He shuns every means that does not yield a monetary reward, he puts up with anything from which he can scrape

---

[1]This form of the quotation seems to be exclusive to Chrysostom.

together even two farthings. He hates everyone, rich and poor alike. He hates the poor, lest they should come and beg from him. He hates the rich. because he does not have what they have. He considers everyone else to have what really should belong to him and thinks that everyone has wronged him, and so he is displeased with everyone. He does not know what it means to have plenty, nor does he have any experience with being satisfied. He is more wretched than anyone, even as the one who is freed from these things and practices self-restraint is the most enviable. For the virtuous individual, even though he might be a servant or a prisoner, is the most happy of all. HOMILIES ON THE GOSPEL OF MATTHEW 80.4.[2]

[2]CTP 172:263-64; NPNF 1 1:483-84**.

14:20–15:10* THE HAPPINESS OF THE WISE

20*Blessed is the man who meditates on[b] wisdom*
  and who reasons intelligently.
21*He who reflects in his mind on her ways*
  will also ponder her secrets.
22*Pursue wisdom[c] like a hunter,*
  and lie in wait on her paths.
23*He who peers through her windows*
  will also listen at her doors;
24*he who encamps near her house*
  will also fasten his tent peg to her walls;
25*he will pitch his tent near her,*
  and will lodge in an excellent lodging place;
26*he will place his children under her shelter,*
  and will camp under her boughs;
27*he will be sheltered by her from the heat,*
  and will dwell in the midst of her glory.

15 *The man who fears the Lord will do this,*
  and he who holds to the law will obtain wisdom.[d]
2*She will come to meet him like a mother,*
  and like the wife of his youth she will welcome him.
3*She will feed him with the bread of understanding,*
  and give him the water of wisdom to drink.

⁴He will lean on her and will not fall,
    and he will rely on her and will not be put to shame.
⁵She will exalt him above his neighbors,
    and will open his mouth in the midst of the assembly.
⁶He will find gladness and a crown of rejoicing,
    and will acquire an everlasting name.
⁷Foolish men will not obtain her,
    and sinful men will not see her.
⁸She is far from men of pride,
    and liars will never think of her.

⁹A hymn of praise is not fitting on the lips of a sinner,
    for it has not been sent from the Lord.
¹⁰For a hymn of praise should be uttered in wisdom,
    and the Lord will prosper it.

b Other authorities read *dies in*   c Gk *her*   d Gk *her*   * Sir 14:21–15:10 Vg.

OVERVIEW: Wisdom reveals the true meaning of Scripture (ORIGEN). Sinners, heretics and schismatics do not understand that meaning and are thus excluded from the celebration of Easter with the faithful (ATHANASIUS). Jesus did not accept the witness of those who opposed him, such as the devils (JEROME). Those who do not oppose him and are renewed in their faith sing a song of love to God (AUGUSTINE). But knowledge of God and of Scripture is useless if we are not virtuous (CASSIAN).

14:22 Pursue Wisdom

THE TRUE MEANING OF THE SCRIPTURES.
ORIGEN: The last story that is related in the book of Numbers is the one in which the Lord commands Moses "to give orders to the children of Israel,"[1] that when "they have entered the holy land" they may know how to take possession of its inheritance and that they should observe the boundaries of their limits in these things. And after this, with the Lord now describing this, it is said, "toward Africa," that is, toward the west, the boundary of that place should be observed, and of that place toward the east, and thus the Lord indicates through the four regions of the

sky certain names that the people of God ought to keep in that earthly Judea.

Thus one of the more simple hearers will say that here there are things that are necessary and useful even according to the letter, in that no one should go beyond the borders that have been appointed through the Lord's command and one tribe should not dare to violate the boundaries of another. And what will we do when no possibility remains for the Jews, not merely to invade the borders of another nation in these lands but even of possessing them at all? For they have been banished from that land, they are exiles and refugees, and those who now possess and guard the boundaries are not those whom the divine law appointed but those whom they have entrusted the rights of victors. What, I ask, will we do, who read these things in the church? If we read them according to the sense of the Jews, they will seem superfluous to us and pointless.

But I am one who reads what is written about Wisdom: "I went out after her as a tracker." I want to go out after her, and since I do not find her in the physical realities, I desire to pursue her tracks and investigate where she is going and to

[1]Num 34:2.

249

see into which rooms she leads my understanding. For I think that if I am able to follow her with care and to investigate her ways, she will give me some opportunities from the Scriptures to understand how it is, even in these passages we need to explain, if we believe what Paul says in a mystery, that those who serve through the law are serving "the shadow and image of heavenly things."[2] And if, no less in accordance with the judgment of that man, the law, of which this reading that we have in hand is a portion, "contains a shadow of the good things to come,"[3] it seems logical and necessary that everything that is described in the law, as it were concerning earthly things, is a shadow of the good things of heaven; and the whole inheritance of that land, which is called the "holy land"[4] and the "good land,"[5] is an image of the good things of heaven. These things, as we have said, that are mentioned as good things on earth contain a shadow and an image of these. HOMILIES ON NUMBERS 28.1.1-2.[6]

15:9 Hymns Not Appropriate from a Sinner

NO EASTER FEAST FOR SINNERS, HERETICS AND SCHISMATICS. ATHANASIUS: Therefore, although wicked people press forward to keep the feast and praise God as though they were at a feast and intrude into the church of the saints, yet God confutes them, saying to the sinner, "Why do you speak of my decrees?"[7] And the gentle Spirit rebukes them, saying, "Praise is not attractive in the mouth of sinners," neither does sin have anything in common with the praise of God; for the sinner has a mouth speaking perverse things, as the proverb says, "The mouth of the wicked answers evil."[8] For how is it possible for us to praise God with an impure mouth, since things that are contrary to each other cannot coexist? "For what communion has righteousness with iniquity, or what fellowship is there between light and darkness?"[9] So exclaims Paul, a minister of the gospel. Thus it is that sinners, and all those who have alienated themselves from the catholic church, heretics

and schismatics, since they are excluded from glorifying God with the saints, cannot properly even continue as observers of the feast. FESTAL LETTERS 7.4.13-14.[10]

JESUS REJECTED THE TESTIMONY OF DEVILS. JEROME: What did the Savior say to the devil? "And Jesus ordered him, 'Be silent, and come out of this man.'"[11] Truth does not need false confirmation. "I have not come to be recognized by your testimony but to cast you out of one of my creatures. 'A compliment from a sinner is unseemly.' I have no need of the testimony of one to whom I wish every kind of suffering. Be quiet. Your silence itself praises me. I do not want your voice to praise me, but your torment. Your every suffering honors me. Should I be happy that you praise me? No, I am happy that you go. 'Be silent, and come out of this man.'"[12] It is as though he said, "Get out of my house. What are you doing in my dwelling? I want to enter. You, be silent and leave this man, this rational being. Come out of this man: leave to me this dwelling prepared for me. The Lord wants his own dwelling: leave this man, therefore, this rational being." HOMILIES ON MARK 2.[13]

THE JUST PERSON SINGS TO GOD. AUGUSTINE: The old song sings about sexual lust, the new song sings of divine love.[14] If your song is moved by lust, then you are singing an old song. Let the words of the new song resonate in your mouth, but if you are sinner there is no such thing as beautiful praise on your lips. It is best to be renewed and chastened than to continue singing the same old song. If, in fact, you have become a new person, even if you remain silent and your singing never reaches human ears, your heart elevates the new inner song[15] so that it reaches

---

[2]Heb 8:5. [3]Heb 10:5. [4]See Ex 3:8. [5]See Deut 8:7. [6]CTP 76:401-2; ACTHN 183-84*. [7]Ps 50:16 (49:16 LXX). [8]Prov 15:28. [9]2 Cor 6:14. [10]LCPM 34:309; NPNF 2 4:524-25**. [11]Mk 1:25. [12]Mk 1:25. [13]CTP 88:59. [14]See Ps 96:1 (95:1 LXX). [15]See Ps 96:1 (95:1 LXX).

the ear of God who has restored you. You love, and, even if you are silent, your love is itself a voice that sings to God. EXPOSITIONS OF THE PSALMS 95.2.[16]

WITHOUT VIRTUE, KNOWLEDGE OF SCRIPTURE IS USELESS. JOHN CASSIAN: Of those then who seem to acquire some show of knowledge or of those who while they devote themselves diligently to reading the sacred volume and to committing the Scriptures to memory, yet do not leave behind carnal sins, it is well said in Proverbs: "As a golden ring in a swine's snout, so is the beauty of an evil-disposed woman."[17] For what does it profit someone to gain the ornaments of heavenly eloquence and the most precious beauty of the Scriptures if by clinging to filthy deeds and thoughts he destroys it by burying it in the foulest ground or defiles it by the dirty wallowing of his own lusts? For the result will be that which is an ornament to those who rightly use it is not only unable to adorn them but becomes dirty by the increased filth and mud. For "from the mouth of a sinner praise is not attractive." In fact, the prophet says about souls like this, "Why do you declare my righteous acts and take my covenant in your lips?"[18] They never possess in any lasting way the fear of the Lord of which it is said, "The fear of the Lord is instruction and wisdom."[19] And yet, they try to get at the meaning of Scripture by continual meditation on them. Thus, it is appropriately asked about them in Proverbs: "What use are riches to a fool? For a senseless person cannot possess wisdom."[20] CONFERENCES 2.14.16.[21]

---

[16]NBA 27:335. [17]Prov 11:22. [18]Ps 50:16 (49:16 LXX). [19]Prov 15:33. [20]Prov 17:16. [21]CTP 156:128; NPNF 2 11:443**.

15:11-20* HUMAN LIBERTY

[11]Do not say, "Because of the Lord I left the right way";
    for he[e] will not do what he hates.
[12]Do not say, "It was he who led me astray";
    for he has no need of a sinful man.
[13]The Lord hates all abominations,
    and they are not loved by those who fear him.
[14]It was he who created man in the beginning,
    and he left him in the power of his own inclination.
[15]If you will, you can keep the commandments,
    and to act faithfully is a matter of your own choice.
[16]He has placed before you fire and water:
    stretch out your hand for whichever you wish.
[17]Before a man[f] are life and death,
    and whichever he chooses will be given to him.
[18]For great is the wisdom of the Lord;

he is mighty in power and sees everything;
¹⁹*his eyes are on those who fear him,*
    and he knows every deed of man.
²⁰*He has not commanded any one to be ungodly,*
    and he has not given any one permission to sin.

e Heb: Gk *you*   f Gk *men*   * Sir 15:11-21 Vg.

OVERVIEW: God made human will capable of choosing what is good (FAUSTUS) so that we are endowed with free will (GAUDENTIUS). Death is an obstacle to faith and shall be annihilated by Christ, who is life (ORIGEN). Our present life is the premise for our future life (SALVIAN).

15:15 Keep the Commandments

WE CAN CHOOSE WHAT IS GOOD. FAUSTUS OF RIEZ: Scripture shows beyond a doubt that the seeds of a good will have been sown in human beings when it says, "If you want to, you will keep the commandments. Faithfulness depends on your good will," and, "Do not despise the Lord's instruction,"[1] and, "Do not withhold a benefit from one in need,"[2] and, "Do not plot evil against your neighbor,"[3] and, "Do not be like the horse and mule, without intelligence,"[4] and, "Do not despise your mother's teaching,"[5] and, "Do not listen to a deceitful woman,"[6] and, "He refuses to understand, to do good,"[7] and, "They do not want to be converted."[8] If someone is accused of not willing something, it is clearly demonstrated that it was in his power to do so. And there are many other similar examples in the Scriptures of the Old Testament, all of which blame and show as culpable especially the will itself. Even the new books of the gospel and of the apostles demonstrate nothing other than free will. ON GRACE 1.12.[9]

15:16 Fire and Water

FREE WILL. GAUDENTIUS OF BRESCIA: The Lord, who is truly a just judge,[10] wants that everyone be the cause of what he merits. He wants the just to suffer for justice alone, and the wicked person, if he persists in evil, to be judged as liable to death based on his free will. As Scripture attests, God formed human beings, making them in his image and likeness,[11] and left the faculty of decision in their hands. "He put before them fire and water, saying, 'Reach out your hand to what you will.' "[12] God "put before the man," it said, "water and fire," that is, rest and punishment, forgiveness and torment, life and death.[13] Who, I ask, would not flee torment, punishment and death and not choose rest, forgiveness and life? One flees death, however, who walks in the ways of the precepts that give life. One attains the gift of life who, through the effort of his commitment to spiritual things, avoids actions that bring death. This is why it was said, "Here is water and fire. Reach out your hand" (that is, your actions) "to what you will."[14] By the hand are meant actions, since we cannot be subjected to sufferings without offenses or merit the prize without a fight, since the apostle says, "Is God unjust in inflicting his wrath?"[15] And also, "Because no one who takes part in a contest is crowned unless he competes according to the rules."[16] SERMONS 13.16-18.[17]

15:17 Choosing Life or Death

CHRIST DESTROYED DEATH. ORIGEN: "He must reign until all things are placed under his feet,"[18] until "the last enemy to be destroyed

---

[1]Prov 3:11. [2]Prov 3:27. [3]Prov 3:29. [4]Ps 32:9 (31:9 LXX). [5]Prov 6:20. [6]Prov 5:3. [7]Ps 35:4 (34:4 LXX). [8]Jer 5:3. [9]CTP 178:87. [10]See 2 Tim 4:8; Ps 7:12. [11]See Gen 1:26-27. [12]Sir 15:16 (15:17 Vg). [13]See also Deut 30:15, 19; Jer 21:8. [14]Sir15:17 Vg. [15]Rom 3:5. [16]2 Tim 2:5. [17]CTP 129:124. [18]1 Cor 15:25.

will be death."[19] Once this is destroyed, there will be only the Life[20] in which we believe. And while death is present among people, those whom it holds prisoner do not believe in Life. But once death is done away with, then all will believe in Life. In the Law, however, you will find both the words, "I have placed before you life and death,"[21] and, "You will live in constant suspense. You will never be sure of your life."[22] COMMENTARY ON MATTHEW 15.23.[23]

PREPARATION FOR THE FUTURE LIFE. SAL-VIAN THE PRESBYTER: It is written that life and death both confront humankind and that he reaches out his hand toward what he wants. We draw from these words that everyone will possess for eternity those goods that they seized with their hand, so to speak, during this life. And whatever they became attached to, they will remain attached to, with his mind and will entirely fixated on it. AGAINST AVARICE 1.1.7.[24]

---

[19]1 Cor 15:26. [20]See Jn 11:25; 14:6, etc. [21]Deut 30:15. [22]Deut 28:66. [23]CTP 151:245-46. [24]CTP 10:26.

16:1-14* THE WICKED ARE CURSED

[1]Do not desire a multitude of useless children,
   nor rejoice in ungodly sons.
[2]If they multiply, do not rejoice in them,
   unless the fear of the Lord is in them.
[3]Do not trust in their survival,
   and do not rely on their multitude;
for one is better than a thousand,[g]
   and to die childless is better than to have ungodly children.
[4]For through one man of understanding a city will be filled with people,
   but through a tribe of lawless men it will be made desolate.
[5]Many such things my eye has seen,
   and my ear has heard things more striking than these.

[6]In an assembly of sinners a fire will be kindled,
   and in a disobedient nation wrath was kindled.
[7]He was not propitiated for the ancient giants
   who revolted in their might.
[8]He did not spare the neighbors of Lot,
   whom he loathed on account of their insolence.
[9]He showed no pity for a nation devoted to destruction,

for those destroyed in their sins;
¹⁰nor for the six hundred thousand men on foot,
*   who rebelliously assembled in their stubbornness.*
¹¹Even if there is only one stiff-necked person,
*   it will be a wonder if he remains unpunished.*
For mercy and wrath are with the Lord;ʰ
*   he is mighty to forgive, and he pours out wrath.*
¹²As great as his mercy, so great is also his reproof;
*   he judges a man according to his deeds.*
¹³The sinner will not escape with his plunder,
*   and the patience of the godly will not be frustrated.*
¹⁴He will make room for every act of mercy;
*   every one will receive in accordance with his deeds.ⁱ*

g The text of this line is uncertain   h Gk *him*   i Other authorities add ¹⁵*The Lord hardened Pharaoh so that he did not know him; in order that his works might be known under heaven.* ¹⁶*His mercy is manifest to the whole of creation, and he divided his light and darkness with a plumb line.*   * Sir 15:22–16:15 Vg.

OVERVIEW: One who does not care about the proper education of children is worse than a barbarian. The fall of the just is more momentous than the fall of a city (CHRYSOSTOM). One just person is worth the whole world; many wicked are reckoned as nothing by God (ORIGEN). God is good and wants all to be saved (CLEMENT OF ALEXANDRIA).

16:1-3 Godly or Ungodly Children

THE PROPER EDUCATION OF CHILDREN. JOHN CHRYSOSTOM: Is it not true that not only do we fail to take to heart the care of our children but insidiously target and oppose those who would do so and end by being more cruel toward our children than barbarians? The cruelty of barbarians amounts only to reducing their enemies to slavery, the destruction and subjugation of their country and the outrage of bodily torture. You, however, reduce their very souls to slavery, fastening them with fetters like slaves, giving them over as prey to wicked and ferocious demons and to their passions. Indeed, by the fact that you give them no spiritual counsel nor permit others who are disposed to carry out this duty to do so, your conduct is in no way different. And no one

should say to me that many who have ignored their children, even more than did Eli,[1] have not suffered anything of the kind. On the contrary, many, in quite a few cases and for similar faults, have had to undergo even worse punishments. Indeed, what was the origin of early death? What caused the damage, the calamities, the misfortunes, the innumerable evils? Is it not perhaps that we neglect the duty of correcting our children when they err? And that this conclusion is not mere conjecture is sufficiently demonstrated by the disgrace of the elderly Eli.[2] And I also refer you to the words that one of our wise men wrote on this theme. Speaking precisely of children, he says, "Do not delight in your children if they are godless. If they do not fear God, do not expect a long life for them." AGAINST THE OPPONENTS OF THE MONASTIC LIFE 3.3.[3]

ONE JUST PERSON. JOHN CHRYSOSTOM: "O that my head were water, and my eyes a fountain of tears!"[4] It is seasonable for me to utter these words now, yes, much more than for the prophet in his time. For although I am not about

---

[1]See 1 Sam 2:12-25; 3:12-14; 4:11. [2]See 1 Sam 4:18. [3]CTP 130:146-47. [4]Jer 9:1 (8:23 LXX).

to mourn over many cities or whole nations, yet shall I mourn over a soul that is of equal value with many such nations, yes, even more precious. For if one person who does the will of God is better than ten thousand transgressors,[5] then you were formerly better than ten thousand Jews. This is why no one would now blame me if I were to compose more lamentations than those that are contained in the prophet and to utter complaints yet more vehement. For it is not the overthrow of a city that I mourn, or the captivity of wicked people, but the desolation of a sacred soul, the destruction and effacement of a Christ-bearing temple.[6] LETTER TO THE FALLEN THEODORE 1.1.[7]

16:4 Through One Person of Understanding

ONE JUST PERSON COUNTS MORE THAN MANY WICKED. ORIGEN: Take the whole number of the human race and pick out those who are faithful from all the nations: doubtless they will be fewer than the whole. Then select the better ones from the number of the faithful: it is certain that the number will be far lower. And again, from those whom you have chosen, select the more perfect ones: you will find even fewer. And the more you continue to make choices, the more you will find them to be scanty and very few, until you finally come to a certain one who confidently says, "I labored more than all of them."[8] Thus, "those who are more" will receive more land and more of a physical inheritance, but the "few" will attain to a small amount of land, since they have more in the Lord; but some will receive no earthly inheritance, if they become worthy to be priests and ministers of God; for "of these" the Lord will be their whole inheritance.[9] And who is so blessed that among the few he receives either a small amount of land or that among the chosen priests and ministers he merits in the allotment of his inheritance to have room for the Lord alone? For granted they receive some land on account of their beasts of burden,[10] yet

it is from that land that borders on cities and is attached to cities.

Yet these words that say that the inheritance is multiplied to those who are more can be understood in still another way as well. For one just person is considered as "more" in accordance with the fact that "he is accepted by God."[11] After all, it is even written, "Through one wise person a city will be considered, but the tribes of the unjust will be desolated." And one just person is reckoned for the whole world, but the unjust, even if they are many, are considered by God as scanty and as nothing.

So there is a praiseworthy multitude, as we see was said to Abraham as well, when "he led him outside and said to him: look at the sky if you are able to number the stars; thus will be your seed."[12] Consider here how the just person is interior and always abides in what is interior, since it is "inside" that "he prays to the Father in secret,"[13] and "all the glory of the king's daughter," that is, of the royal soul, "is within."[14] Nevertheless, God "leads him outside," when circumstances demand it and the rational order of visible things demands it. Therefore, even in this way, to the many who are "as the stars of heaven in multitude,"[15] an inheritance is multiplied; and to the scanty few, namely, those who, even if they are many in number, nevertheless are considered scanty due to the unworthiness and commonness of their life, a scanty inheritance is appointed. HOMILIES ON NUMBERS 21.2.2-3.[16]

16:11 Mercy and Wrath Are with the Lord

GOD IS GOOD AND WANTS ALL TO BE SAVED. CLEMENT OF ALEXANDRIA: The book of Wisdom plainly says, "For mercy and wrath are with him, for he alone is Lord of both." He is

---

[5]Sir 6:3, variant. [6]See 1 Cor 3:16. [7]CTP 174:55; NPNF 1 9:91**. [8]1 Cor 15:10. [9]See Num 18:20. [10]See Josh 14:4. [11]Acts 10:35. [12]Gen 15:5. [13]See Mt 6:6. [14]Ps 45:13. [15]Heb 11:12. [16]CTP 76:296-98; ACTHN 133-34*.

Lord of propitiations and pours forth wrath according to the abundance of his mercy. It is the same with his reproof. For the aim of mercy and of reproof is the salvation of those who are reproved. Now, that the God and Father of our Lord Jesus is good,[17] the Word will again attest: "For he is kind to the unthankful and the evil,"[18] and further, when he says, "Be merciful, as your Father is merciful."[19] Still further also he plainly says, "None is good but my Father, who is in heaven."[20] In addition to these, again he says, "My Father makes his sun to shine on all."[21] CHRIST THE EDUCATOR 1.72.1-2.[22]

---

[17]2 Cor 1:3. [18]Lk 6:36. [19]Lk 6:35. [20]Lk 18:18, variant. [21]Mt 5:45. [22]CTP 178:100-101.

16:17-23 THE CERTITUDE OF REWARD

[17]Do not say, "I shall be hidden from the Lord,
  and who from on high will remember me?
Among so many people I shall not be known,
  for what is my soul in the boundless creation?
[18]Behold, heaven and the highest heaven,
  the abyss and the earth, will tremble at his visitation.
[19]The mountains also and the foundations of the earth
  shake with trembling when he looks upon them.
[20]And no mind will reflect on this.
  Who will ponder his ways?
[21]Like a tempest which no man can see,
  so most of his works are concealed.
[22]Who will announce his acts of justice?
  Or who will await them? For the covenant is far off."
[23]This is what one devoid of understanding thinks;
  a senseless and misguided man thinks foolishly.

OVERVIEW: God sends evils for reasons we do not know (ORIGEN).

16:21 Most of God's Works Are Concealed

WE DO NOT KNOW WHY GOD ALLOWS EVIL. ORIGEN: "And I will send hunger on them and will cause people and beast to die."[1] How can I proclaim publicly such profound truths? From where will I receive help that I might make you understand how the earth is touched by hunger and fruitfulness, by abundance and poverty? "O the depths of the riches, the wisdom and the knowledge of God!"[2] Hunger perhaps comes

---

[1]Ezek 14:13. [2]Rom 11:33.

because of people and because of the wickedness of souls. Or perhaps it is the fault of the angels to whom the things of the earth were entrusted[3] that the things we see happen take place, if they commit sin. If some are set up as instruments of heavenly providence, but they themselves become interested in the fruits, then the earth's sterility is probably also due to them. "The greater part of his works are hidden." We cannot speak of the greatness of wisdom. "Who has counted the sands of the sea, the raindrops, the days of the ages? The height of the heavens, the wideness of the earth, the depths of the wisdom of God."[4] Homilies on Ezekiel 4.2.[5]

---

[3]Cf. Deut 32:8. [4]Sir 1:2-3. [5]CTP 67:87-88.

16:24–17:14 HUMANITY IN THE CREATION

[24]Listen to me, my son, and acquire knowledge,
   and pay close attention to my words.
[25]I will impart instruction by weight,
   and declare knowledge accurately.

[26]The works of the Lord have existed from the beginning by his creation,[j]
   and when he made them, he determined their divisions.
[27]He arranged his works in an eternal order,
   and their dominion[k] for all[l] generations;
they neither hunger nor grow weary,
   and they do not cease from their labors.
[28]They do not crowd one another aside,
   and they will never disobey his word.
[29]After this the Lord looked upon the earth,
   and filled it with his good things;
[30]with all kinds of living beings he covered its surface,
   and to it they return.

17 The Lord created man out of earth,
   and turned him back to it again.
[2]He gave to men[m] few days, a limited time,
   but granted them authority over the things upon the earth.[n]
[3]He endowed them with strength like his own,[o]
   and made them in his own image.
[4]He placed the fear of them[p] in all living beings,
   and granted them dominion over beasts and birds.[q]
[6]He made for them[r] tongue and eyes;

he gave them ears and a mind for thinking.
⁷He filled them with knowledge and understanding,
and showed them good and evil.
⁸He set his eye upon their hearts
to show them the majesty of his works.ˢ
¹⁰And they will praise his holy name,
to proclaim the grandeur of his works.
¹¹He bestowed knowledge upon them,
and allotted to them the law of life.
¹²He established with them an eternal covenant,
and showed them his judgments.
¹³Their eyes saw his glorious majesty,
and their ears heard the glory of his voice.
¹⁴And he said to them, "Beware of all unrighteousness."ᵗ
And he gave commandment to each of them concerning his neighbor.

j Heb: Gk *judgment* k Or *elements* l Gk *their* m Gk *them* n Gk *it* o Cn: Gk *proper to them* p Syr: Gk *him* q Other authorities add ⁵*They obtained the use of the five operations of the Lord; as sixth he distributed to them the gift of mind, and as seventh reason, the interpreter of his operations.* r Syr: Gk *Inclination and* s Other authorities add ⁹*and he gave them to boast of his marvels for ever* t Or *every unrighteous man*

OVERVIEW: God created the desert so that Christians could make it fertile (EUCHERIUS). The soul was created according to the image of God (ANONYMOUS ANOMOEAN).

16:27 God Arranged His Works

IN THE DESERT WE MEET GOD. EUCHERIUS: There is the story of the man who asked another where he thought God could be found, and the other responded, "Run close behind me!" So he ran behind him, until they came to a wide desert. The guide then showed him the peace of that vast solitude[1] and said, "Here is where God is!" And indeed, is it not right to think that God would be more easily reachable there? Even at the beginning of time, when God made all things with wisdom, adapting them one by one for future needs,[2] he in no way left this part of the world useless and without importance. Indeed, since he created everything not only because he felt generous at that moment but especially because he already knew the future, he provided solitary places. I think he did this for the saints who would frequent them—this is how I see

it. God wanted to give the places that are rich in fruit to others and to the saints, instead of those more generous lands, this fruitful one. In this way the deserts would also become fertile, and the valleys would be covered with abundant crops,[3] while he "from on high would water the mountains,"[4] thus remedying the unproductiveness of those places, filling a barren place with inhabitants. IN PRAISE OF SOLITUDE 4-5.[5]

17:3 Endowed with Strength

IN PRAISE OF THE SOUL. ANONYMOUS ANOMOEAN: "Do not touch his soul,"[6] which was created in the image of God,[7] impregnated with incorruptible wisdom, crowned with speech and knowledge, clothed with the knowledge of God, receiving the honor of dominion over this corruptible world and attaining on earth "a glory a little less than the angels."[8] COMMENTARY ON JOB 2.21.[9]

---

[1]See Deut 32:10. [2]Sir 16:27 (16:26 Vg). [3]See Ps 65:12-13 (64:13-14 LXX). [4]Ps 104:13 (103:13 LXX). [5]CTP 139:72. [6]Job 2:6. [7]See Gen 1:26-27. [8]Ps 8:6. [9]CSEL 96:279.

17:15-24 THE DIVINE JUDGE

^{15}*Their ways are always before him,*
  they will not be hid from his eyes.^{u}
^{17}*He appointed a ruler for every nation,*
  but Israel is the Lord's own portion.^{v}
^{19}*All their works are as the sun before him,*
  and his eyes are continually upon their ways.
^{20}*Their iniquities are not hidden from him,*
  and all their sins are before the Lord.^{w}
^{22}*A man's almsgiving is like a signet with the Lord,*^{x}
  and he will keep a person's kindness like the apple of his eye.
^{23}*Afterward he will arise and requite them,*
  and he will bring their recompense on their heads.
^{24}*Yet to those who repent he grants a return,*
  and he encourages those whose endurance is failing.

u Other authorities add ^{16}*Their ways from youth tend toward evil, and they are unable to make for themselves hearts of flesh in place of their stony hearts.* ^{17}*For in the division of the nations of the whole earth*   v Other authorities add ^{18}*whom, being his first-born, he brings up with discipline, and allotting to him the light of his love, he does not neglect him.*   w Other authorities add ^{21}*But the Lord, who is gracious and knows his creatures, has neither left nor abandoned them, but spared them.*   x Gk *him*

OVERVIEW: The ways of people refers to their desires and actions. The rulers of the nations are their angels or their teachers (RABANUS MAURUS).

17:15 Their Ways Are Before God

THE WAYS OF HUMAN BEINGS. RABANUS MAURUS: The ways of human beings are their desires and their actions, which in any case do not escape God's knowledge, since "everything is naked and exposed before his eyes."[1] This is why the psalmist says, "The Lord knows a person's thoughts: they are but a breath."[2] But he has especially known the way of those whom he approves. Conversely, it is said that he does not know the ways of those whose actions he condemns. Thus it is written, "The Lord watches over the way of the just, but the way of the wicked ends in ruin."[3] ON ECCLESIASTICUS 4.5.[4]

17:17 A Ruler for Every Nation

ANGELS AND DOCTORS RULE THE NATIONS. RABANUS MAURUS: We may interpret that the rulers placed by God over every people are the angels to whom he entrusted the care of each people, according to that word of Deuteronomy, "He set the boundaries of the peoples according to the number of the angels of God."[5] And one reads in the book of Daniel that there is a head of the Greeks and a head of the Persians, besides

---

[1]Heb 4:13.   [2]Ps 94:15 (93:15 LXX).   [3]Ps 1:6.   [4]PL 109:878-79.   [5]Deut 32:8, variant.

Michael, who is the head of the people of God.[6] It also deals with the holy doctors, whom divine election established as those who would preach his word throughout the earth. Thus John was commanded in the Apocalypse to write to the angel of Ephesus and to the angel of Smyrna, and also to the angel of Pergamum and to the angels of the other churches.[7] ON ECCLESIASTICUS 4.5.[8]

---

[6]See Dan 10:13, 20-21; 12:1. [7]See Rev 2:1–3:22. [8]PL 109:879.

17:25-32* CALL TO PENANCE

[25]Turn to the Lord and forsake your sins;
    pray in his presence and lessen your offenses.
[26]Return to the Most High and turn away from iniquity,[y]
    and hate abominations intensely.
[27]Who will sing praises to the Most High in Hades,
    as do those who are alive and give thanks?
[28]From the dead, as from one who does not exist, thanksgiving has ceased;
    he who is alive and well sings the Lord's praises.
[29]How great is the mercy of the Lord,
    and his forgiveness for those who turn to him!
[30]For all things cannot be in men,[z]
    since a son of man is not immortal.
[31]What is brighter than the sun? Yet its light fails.[a]
    So flesh and blood devise evil.
[32]He marshals the host of the height of heaven;
    but all men are dust and ashes.

---

y Other authorities add *for he will lead you out of darkness to the light of health*   z The Greek text of this line is uncertain   a Or *suffers eclipse*   * Sir 17:21-31 Vg, with many differences.

OVERVIEW: God frees us from our faults when we acknowledge them (AUGUSTINE).

17:23 From the Dead, Thanksgiving Has Ceased

LET US ACKNOWLEDGE OUR FAULTS. AUGUS-TINE: "And do not let the abyss swallow me or the pit close its mouth around me."[1] What does this mean? What is he praying for? The abyss of human iniquity is a great pit, and anyone who falls into it will fall very far down. However, if

---

[1]Ps 69:16 (68:16 LXX).

the one who has fallen confesses his sins to God, then the pit will not close its mouth around him. As it is written in the Psalms, "Out of the depths have I cried to you, Lord. O Lord, listen to my voice."[2] But it is different if the disaster found in another Scripture has happened to the sinner: "One who is devoid of reverence sinks deep into sin and is defiant."[3] The pit has closed its mouth on him. In what sense does it mean that it closed its mouth? It has plugged the sinner's mouth shut. When the sinner refuses to confess his own guilt, then he is truly dead, and it has been fulfilled in him what is said elsewhere, "A confession coming from a dead person is like one who does not exist."[4] Brothers and sisters, we must greatly fear such a disaster. If you see someone commit a sin, consider that person as though he or she were sunk in the pit.

But if, at present, you point out the person's sin and he says to you, "I have sinned. I truly confess," the pit has not yet closed its mouth on him. If instead you hear that person saying, "Is what I have done that bad?" then he has become a defender of his sin and the pit has closed its mouth. There is no way for him to be pulled back outside. Clearly if there is no confession, there is no recourse to mercy. If you defend your sin, how can God free you from it? If therefore you want him as your liberator, you must be your own prosecutor. EXPOSITIONS OF THE PSALMS 68.1.19.[5]

---

[2]Ps 130:1-2 (129:1-2 LXX). [3]Prov 18:3. [4]Augustine follows the old Latin version (Vetus Latina), which translates literally the Septuagint. [5]NBA 26:663-65; WSA 3 17:382**.

18:1-7 GOD'S GREATNESS

[1]He who lives for ever created the whole universe;
   [2]the Lord alone will be declared righteous.[b]
[4]To none has he given power to proclaim his works;
   and who can search out his mighty deeds?
[5]Who can measure his majestic power?
   And who can fully recount his mercies?
[6]It is not possible to diminish or increase them,
   nor is it possible to trace the wonders of the Lord.
[7]When a man has finished, he is just beginning,
   and when he stops, he will be at a loss.

b Other authorities add *and there is no other beside him;* [3]*he steers the world with the span of his hand, and all things obey his will; for he is king of all things, by his power separating among them the holy things from the profane.*

OVERVIEW: God created everything at once, but the Bible narrates the creation in six days so that we may understand it better (AUGUSTINE). The example of John the Baptist shows that our understanding of Scripture is limited (ORIGEN). Ultimately, the search for God is endless (AUGUSTINE).

18:1 God Created the Whole Universe

THE BIBLE NARRATES THE CREATION IN SIX DAYS. AUGUSTINE: Scripture narrates the story of how the God who finished all his work in six days is the same one who it says elsewhere, and without any contradiction, that "he created everything at the same time."[1] Consequently, he who created all things at the same time simultaneously also simultaneously created these six or seven days, or, rather, this one day repeating the day six or seven times. What need was there to enumerate these six days in such a precise and ordered way? Surely it was necessary for those who cannot arrive at a comprehension that "God created everything at the same time," that Scripture accompanied them more slowly, step by step, to the final goal of the story to which it was leading them. ON THE LITERAL INTERPRETATION OF GENESIS 4.33.52.[2]

18:7 When a Mortal Has Finished

WE DO NOT ALWAYS UNDERSTAND THE SCRIPTURE. ORIGEN: In the three [Synoptic] Gospels, John the Baptist says he is not sufficient,[3] while in the Gospel of John[4] he says he is not worthy.[5] But it may be that the one who formerly declared that he was not sufficient became sufficient later, even though perhaps he was not worthy. Or it may have been that while he was saying he was not worthy, and was in fact not worthy, he came to be worthy—unless one would say that human nature can never arrive at performing this loosing or this bearing in a worthy manner and that John, therefore, speaks the truth when he says that he never became sufficient to loose the thongs of our Savior's sandals, nor was he worthy of doing so either. No matter how much we try to understand, there are still things left that we do not understand. This is what we read in the Wisdom of Jesus, Son of Sirach: "When a person has finished, he is just beginning, and when he stops, he will be at a loss." COMMENTARY ON THE GOSPEL OF JOHN 6.20.[6]

THE SEARCH FOR GOD HAS NO END. AUGUSTINE: The language of the divine hymn is, "Seek God, and your soul shall live."[7] Let us search for that which needs to be discovered, and into that which has been discovered. He whom we need to discover is concealed, in order to be sought after; and when found, is infinite, in order still to be the object of our search. Therefore it is said in another place, "Seek his face always."[8] For even as he satisfies the seeker to the utmost of his capacity, he makes the finder still more capable so that he may seek to be newly filled according to the growth of his ability to receive. Therefore it was not said, "Seek his face always,"[9] in the same sense as of certain others, who are "always learning and never coming to a knowledge of the truth."[10] Rather, as the preacher says, "When a person has finished, then he begins," till we reach that life where we shall be so filled that our natures shall attain their utmost capacity because we shall have arrived at perfection and will no longer be aiming at more. For then all that can satisfy us will be revealed to our eyes. But here let us always be seeking, and let our reward in finding put no end to our searching. For we do not say that it will not be so always, because it is only so here. Rather, here we say we must always be seeking, lest at any time we should imagine that here we can ever cease from seeking. TRACTATES ON THE GOSPEL OF JOHN 63.1.[11]

---

[1]Sir 18:1, variant of Vg. [2]NBA 9/2:223; WSA 1 13:273**. [3]See Mt 3:11; Mk 1:7; Lk 3:16. [4]Origen refers to John the Baptist's words in the three Synoptic Gospels (Matthew, Mark and Luke), then to his words in the Gospel of John. [5]See Jn 1:26. [6]Trad. Corsini 343. [7]Ps 69:3 (68:3 LXX). [8]Ps 105:4 (104:4 LXX). [9]Ps 105:4 (104:4 LXX). [10]2 Tim 3:7. [11]NBA 24/2:1129; NPNF 1 7:314**.

18:8-14 HUMAN BEINGS ARE NOTHING

⁸*What is man, and of what use is he?*
  What is his good and what is his evil?
⁹*The number of a man's days is great if he reaches a hundred years.*
¹⁰*Like a drop of water from the sea and a grain^c of sand*
  so are a few years in the day of eternity.
¹¹*Therefore the Lord is patient with them*
  and pours out his mercy upon them.
¹²*He sees and recognizes that their end will be evil;*
  therefore he grants them forgiveness in abundance.
¹³*The compassion of man is for his neighbor,*
  but the compassion of the Lord is for all living beings.
He rebukes and trains and teaches them,
  and turns them back, as a shepherd his flock.
¹⁴*He has compassion on those who accept his discipline*
  and who are eager for his judgments.

c Gk *pebble*

OVERVIEW: Before God, we are all unjust and in need of his mercy (EUSEBIUS).

18:13 Compassion for One's Neighbor

WE ALL NEED GOD'S MERCY. EUSEBIUS: "Salvation is far from sinners, since they have not sought your decrees. Many are your mercies, Lord. Give me life according to your judgment."[1] It is said, "The compassion of a person is toward his neighbor: but the mercy of God is on all flesh." As much as one might appear extremely just when compared with human beings, before God's severe judgment he has need of mercy. Even the very fact that he seems just is due to the mercy of God, since who has ever done anything worthy of eternal blessedness and the kingdom of heaven without God's help? COMMENTARY ON THE PSALMS 5.118.[2]

---

[1]Ps 119:155-56 (118:155-56 LXX). [2]CTP 177:438.

18:15-18 HOW TO MAKE A GIFT

15My son, do not mix reproach with your good deeds,
nor cause grief by your words when you present a gift.
16Does not the dew assuage the scorching heat?
So a word is better than a gift.
17Indeed, does not a word surpass a good gift?
Both are to be found in a gracious man.
18A fool is ungracious and abusive,
and the gift of a grudging man makes the eyes dim.

OVERVIEW: We never lack occasions to be merciful (DOROTHEUS). For instance, a gift is more precious if is accompanied by words of encouragement (CHRYSOSTOM).

18:15-17 A Word Is Better Than a Gift

WE CAN ALWAYS BE MERCIFUL. DOROTHEUS OF GAZA: No one can say, "I am poor, I do not have any way to show mercy." If you cannot give like those who are rich who throw their offering into the treasury box, then give two mites like the poor widow and God will consider this a greater gift than the offerings of the rich.[1] You do not have that much? But you do still have power to be merciful, and with this you can exercise mercy in the service of those who are sick. Can you not do even this? But you can console your brother with words. Therefore be merciful with him by your words, and listen to him who says, "A word is better than a gift." Suppose you cannot exercise mercy with words; still if your brother is mad at you, you can have mercy on him and support him in the midst of his turmoil, seeing that he is being mistreated by a common enemy,[2] and instead of responding with a sharp word and getting him even more upset, keep silent and have mercy on him and his soul, stealing it from the enemy. Even if your brother turns against you, you still can have mercy on him and forgive his sin against you in order also to receive forgiveness from God. God, in fact, has said, "Forgive and you will be forgiven,"[3] and thus you will have been found providing mercy for the soul of your brother by pardoning his sins against you. SPIRITUAL INSTRUCTIONS 14.158.[4]

GIVE A WORD OF CONSOLATION. JOHN CHRYSOSTOM: When, because of hunger, one is constrained to beg and because of his begging he is compelled to act shamefully, and then because of acting shamefully he endures reproach—then the weight of despondency becomes rather complex and is accompanied by a darkness that settles on the soul. The one who takes care of such people should do so in a way that is long-suffering, rather than in a way that will only increase their despondency with further irritations. But he should also mitigate the majority of

---

[1]See Mk 12:41-44; Lk 21:1-4. [2]Dorotheus refers to the devil. [3]Lk 6:37. [4]CTP 21:216-17; CS 33:210**.

his already despondent nature with encouragement. For just as the one who has been insulted, even though he may be enjoying great abundance does not feel the advantage of his wealth because of the blow that he has received from the insult, in the same way, one who has been addressed with kind words and for whom the gift has been accompanied with encouragement, exults and rejoices all the more. That which he has been given is doubled in value because of the way in which it was offered. ON THE PRIESTHOOD 3.306-7.[5]

18:19-29 REFLECTION AND CAUTION

[19]Before you speak, learn,
　and before you fall ill, take care of your health.
[20]Before judgment, examine yourself,
　and in the hour of visitation you will find forgiveness.
[21]Before falling ill, humble yourself,
　and when you are on the point of sinning, turn back.
[22]Let nothing hinder you from paying a vow promptly,
　and do not wait until death to be released from it.
[23]Before making a vow,[d] prepare yourself;
　and do not be like a man who tempts the Lord.
[24]Think of his wrath on the day of death,
　and of the moment of vengeance when he turns away his face.
[25]In the time of plenty think of the time of hunger;
　in the days of wealth think of poverty and need.
[26]From morning to evening conditions change,
　and all things move swiftly before the Lord.

[27]A wise man is cautious in everything,
　and in days of sin he guards against wrongdoing.
[28]Every intelligent man knows wisdom,
　and he praises the one who finds her.
[29]Those who understand sayings become skilled themselves,
　and pour forth apt proverbs

d Or offering a prayer

OVERVIEW: Let us practice temperance, justice and piety (FULGENTIUS).

18:20 Examine Yourself

TEMPERANCE, JUSTICE AND PIETY. FULGENTIUS OF RUSPE: Therefore, the blessed hope, the sure expectation, the future happiness is for those who, having rejected the secular ungodliness and desires, have lived soberly and with justice and piety in this world. Therefore, sobriety, justice and piety must be very carefully guarded by Christians. The one who guards his sobriety harmonizes his customs with his life. The one who lives with justice does not bring evil on his neighbor and, in so far as he can, offers aid with good works. The one who lives with piety neither believes or says anything perverse in regard to God. Whoever, therefore, wants to reach the kingdom of heaven must live soberly, practice justice with his neighbor and persevere in piety toward God.

These virtues then will be of help in the future life if they are a reality in the life of this present world. This in fact is what the blessed apostle knew and taught when he ordered us "to live soberly and with justice and piety in this world,"[1] teaching that those who before the judgment have led a just life in this world will receive mercy in the judgment. Therefore divine Scripture warns us in the book of Ecclesiasticus, "Procure justice before the judgment, and you will find propitiation in the presence of God."[2] Therefore, anyone who wants to find propitiation in the presence of God must prepare justice for himself here. In fact, whatever one has not begun to procure in the present world, he will not have at the time of future retribution. ON THE FORGIVENESS OF SINS 1.28.2-29.[3]

---

[1]Tit 2:12. [2]Sir 18:20, variant. [3]CTP 57:61-62; FC 95:145-46.

18:30–19:3 SELF-CONTROL

³⁰*Do not follow your base desires,*
   but restrain your appetites.
³¹*If you allow your soul to take pleasure in base desire,*
   it will make you the laughingstock of your enemies.
³²*Do not revel in great luxury,*
   lest you become impoverished by its expense.
³³*Do not become a beggar by feasting with borrowed money,*
   when you have nothing in your purse.

19 *A workman who is a drunkard will not become rich;*
   he who despises small things will fail little by little.
²*Wine and women lead intelligent men astray,*
   and the man who consorts with harlots is very reckless.
³*Decay and worms will inherit him,*
   and the reckless soul will be snatched away.

OVERVIEW: The throne of our desires is in our heart, not in our body (CHRYSOSTOM). We are free not to follow our passions (AUGUSTINE). Thus, with that freedom from following lustful desires, the polygamy of the Old Testament slowly fell out of favor and finally ended (METHODIUS). Those who cannot control their passions will fall because of their perversion, just as a certain city rotted from within (SALVIAN).

18:30 Restrain Your Appetites

DESIRES COME FROM THE SOUL. JOHN CHRYSOSTOM: "For the desires of the flesh are against the Spirit, and the desires of the Spirit are against the flesh; for these are opposed to each other, to prevent you from doing what you would."[1] Here some level the charge that the apostle has divided the human being into two parts, making it seem as though human beings are constituted from opposing substances and indicating the existence of a conflict between body and soul. But this is certainly not the case. For by "the flesh," he does not mean the body. If he did, what would be the sense of the clause immediately following, "For it lusts," he says, "against the Spirit"? And yet, the body does not move but is moved. It is not an agent but is acted on. How then does it lust, because lust belongs to the soul, not to the body? For in another place it is said, "My soul longs,"[2] and, "Whatever your soul desires, I will even do it for you,"[3] and, "Do not walk according to the desires of your soul," and, "My soul pants."[4] Why then does Paul say, "The flesh lusts against the Spirit"?[5] He usually refers to the flesh as the depraved will, not the natural body, as when he says, "But you are not in the flesh but in the Spirit,"[6] and again, "Those who are in the flesh cannot please God."[7] What then? Is the flesh to be destroyed? Was not he who thus spoke clothed with flesh? Such doctrines are not of the flesh but from the devil, for "he was a murderer from the beginning."[8] What then is his meaning? It is the earthly mind, slothful and careless, that he here calls the flesh,

and this is not an accusation of the body but a charge against the slothful soul. The flesh is an instrument, and no one feels aversion and hatred toward an instrument, but to him who abuses it. For it is not the instrument of iron but the murderer whom we hate and punish. COMMENTARY ON GALATIANS 5.17.[9]

LET US NOT ENCOURAGE OUR PASSIONS. AUGUSTINE: The perfection of the good consists in being totally free from lust because the elimination of evil consists in this. This is what the apostle asserts: "The perfect performance of good is not in my power."[10] It was not in his power not to feel lust. It was in his power to refrain from lust, however, in order not to give in to it and to refuse to offer his members to the service of lust. "To perfect that which is good is not in my power,"[11] since it is impossible for me to fulfill the commandment: "You shall not lust."[12] What is therefore necessary? That you put into practice, "Do not follow after your lusts." This is what you do so long as illicit lusts are present in your flesh: "Do not follow after your lusts." Remain faithful to the service of God, in the liberty of Christ. Serve the law of God with your mind. Do not yield to your lusts, because when you follow them, you add to their strength. By giving them strength, how can you hope to conquer them when you are nourishing these very enemies on your own strength? TRACTATES ON THE GOSPEL OF JOHN 41.12.[13]

19:2 Leading Intelligent Men Astray

POLYGAMY IN THE OLD TESTAMENT. METHODIUS: Now Abraham, when he first received the covenant of circumcision,[14] seems to signify, by receiving circumcision in a member of his own body, nothing else than this: that one should no

---

[1]Gal 5:17. [2]Ps 84:3 (83:3 LXX). [3]1 Sam 20:4. [4]Ps 42:2 (41:2 LXX). [5]Gal 5:17. [6]Rom 8:9. [7]Rom 8:8. [8]Jn 8:44. [9]CTP 35:154-55. [10]Rom 7:18. [11]Rom 7:18. [12]Ex 20:17. [13]NBA 24:837-39; NPNF 1 7:234**. [14]See Gen 17:9-27.

longer conceive children with one born of the same parent. In this way he shows that everyone should abstain from intercourse with his own sister, as his own flesh. And thus, from the time of Abraham, the custom of marrying with sisters has ceased. And from the times of the prophets the contracting of marriage with several wives has been done away with. For we read, "Do not go after your lusts, but refrain from satisfying your appetites," for "wine and women will make men of understanding fall away." And, in another place, "Let your fountain be blessed, and rejoice with the wife of your youth," [15] which clearly forbids a plurality of wives. And Jeremiah clearly gives the name of "fed horses" [16] to those who lust after other women. And we read, "The multiplying brood of the ungodly shall not thrive, nor will bastard plants take deep root or lay any firm foundation." [17] SYMPOSIUM OR BANQUET OF THE TEN VIRGINS 1.3. [18]

A CITY THAT FELL BECAUSE OF ITS WICKEDNESS. SALVIAN THE PRESBYTER: Everything was destroyed from two dominant common defects: avarice and drunkenness. For, unrestrained in their greed for drink, it came to the point where the city authorities could not even get up from the table—not even when the enemy had already penetrated into the city. I think that God intentionally wanted to show them the reason of their ruin: that at the moment when they were experiencing ruin, they continued to conduct themselves in the very thing that ultimately led to their ruin. I have seen with my own eyes

deplorable scenes in that city. [19] It mattered not whether they were boys or old men. It was the same scurrilous partying and levity. All kids of evil were going on at the same time: luxury, drinking, depravity. Everyone was doing the same thing: they amused themselves, got drunk and used prostitutes. Both old and young let themselves go during the banquets. Individuals who were already too weak to live were nonetheless daunting in their wine drinking; those nearly incapable of walking were still sturdy in their drinking; those otherwise uncertain in their steps were agile and lively in their dancing.

What is there left to say? Well, they were so filthy in all the evils of which I have spoken that the saying of the sacred text came true that says, "Wine and women make men fall away from God." And, in fact, while they were drinking, amusing themselves, having sex and going crazy, they did begin to deny Christ. And although this happened, we are still astonished that they lost their material assets, even though they had begun to unravel morally for quite some time! Therefore, let no one think that city perished only on the day in which it was destroyed! Where such things happen, the people were destroyed long before they were overwhelmed by their enemies. THE GOVERNANCE OF GOD 6.13.77-79. [20]

---

[15]Prov 5:18. [16]See Jer 5:8. [17]Wis 4:3. [18]CTP 152:41; ANF 6:312**. [19]Salvian perhaps has in mind Mainz and Cologne. [20]CTP 114:193-94.

19:4-12 AGAINST GOSSIP

⁴*One who trusts others too quickly is lightminded,*
 and one who sins does wrong to himself.
⁵*One who rejoices in wickednessᵉ will be condemned,ᶠ*
 ⁶*and for one who hates gossip evil is lessened.*
⁷*Never repeat a conversation,*
 and you will lose nothing at all.
⁸*With friend or foe do not report it,*
 and unless it would be a sin for you, do not disclose it;
⁹*for some one has heard you and watched you,*
 and when the time comes he will hate you.
¹⁰*Have you heard a word? Let it die with you.*
 Be brave! It will not make you burst!
¹¹*With such a word a fool will suffer pangs*
 like a woman in labor with a child.
¹²*Like an arrow stuck in the flesh of the thigh,*
 so is a word inside a fool.

e Other authorities read *heart*   f Other authorities add *but he who withstands pleasures crowns his life.* ⁶*He who controls his tongue will live without strife,*

OVERVIEW: Two things damage the soul: gullibility and the inability to make up one's mind. The fool wavers in between the two (RABANUS MAURUS). The dog may, according to the context, symbolize either good or bad (RABANUS MAURUS).

19:4 Being Light-Minded

CREDULITY AND MUTABILITY OF THOUGHT.
RABANUS MAURUS: "One who trusts lightly will be harmed, and one who sins against his own soul will suffer even worse harm."[1] Note that this statement does not contradict that of the apostle, who says regarding charity, "It bears all, believes all, hopes all. Charity will never end,"[2] since here the perfection of a good will is present, always ready for any good work. The other statement, rather, describes levity of soul, always changeable and lacking in stability. For this reason it is written elsewhere, "The fool changes like the moon."[3] One, therefore, who with itching ears lets himself be easily convinced, stops listening to the truth and turns to fables will suffer harm in both his intelligence and his virtue, and one who harms his own soul will be considered a fool. ON ECCLESIASTICUS 4.10.[4]

19:12 Like an Arrow Stuck in the Flesh

AN IMAGE OF GOOD AND BAD. RABANUS MAURUS: "Like an arrow stuck in a dog's leg are words in the heart of a fool."[5] The dog is at times explained in a good sense, at times in a bad.

[1]Sir 19:4 Vg. [2]1 Cor 13:7-8. [3]Sir 27:11. [4]PL 109:889. [5]Sir 19:12, variant. Rabanus explains a curious reading: instead of *femori carnis* ("in the flesh of the thigh"), he reads *femori canis* ("in the thigh of a dog").

The good sense one finds in the Psalter: "They return at evening, hungry as dogs, and roam about the city,"[6] which indicates the doctors of Judaism who hunger for the justice of God's law.[7] After the evening of Christ's passion, they went diligently about the city of the church, defending it with the barking of their preaching. We also read in the Gospel that the dogs licked the wounds of Lazarus the beggar.[8] The dog is understood in a negative sense, however, when it indicates the filthiness of sinners, as in this passage: "As the dog returns to its vomit, so the fool repeats his folly."[9] The arrow sticks in the dog's thigh when, under the devil's inspiration, perverse concupiscence lodges in the heart of a sinner. He is rightly called foolish, since like an ox he is led to the slaughter, neither thinking of himself nor keeping himself from ruin and eternal death. ON ECCLESIASTICUS 4.11.[10]

---

[6]Ps 59:7 (58:7 LXX). [7]See Mt 5:6. [8]See Lk 16:20-21. [9]Prov 26:11. [10]PL 109:890-91.

19:13-17* CHECKING HEARSAY

[13]Question a friend, perhaps he did not do it;
　but if he did anything, so that he may do it no more.
[14]Question a neighbor, perhaps he did not say it;
　but if he said it, so that he may not say it again.
[15]Question a friend, for often it is slander;
　so do not believe everything you hear.
[16]A person may make a slip without intending it.
　Who has never sinned with his tongue?
[17]Question your neighbor before you threaten him;
　and let the law of the Most High take its course.[g]

g Other authorities add *and do not be angry.* [18]*The fear of the Lord is the beginning of acceptance, and wisdom obtains his love.* [19]*The knowledge of the Lord's commandments is life-giving discipline; and those who do what is pleasing to him enjoy the fruit of the tree of immortality* * Sir 19:13-18a Vg. In the Vulgate, Sir 19:17-18 (19:18 Vg) are syntactically connected: "And call the law of the Most High, since every wisdom is fear of God, and in it there is the fear of God, and in every wisdom there is the practice of the law."

OVERVIEW: God teaches us to verify the facts before trusting slander (PSEUDO-CHRYSOSTOM).

19:15 *Question a Friend*

DO NOT TRUST GOSSIP. PSEUDO-CHRYSOSTOM: What does it mean when it says, "I want to go down and see if in fact they have done all the evil that has been cried out against them to me. I want to know!"?[1] That is, "A rumor has reached me." But I want to have a more precise knowledge by means of the facts themselves, not

---

[1]Gen 18:20.

because I do not know them but because I want to teach human beings not simply to put faith in words or to believe it if someone says something against another. Rather, one must first look into it and gain knowledge based on the facts, and only then believe. This is why another passage of Scripture says, "Do not believe every word." Nothing upsets human life like too hastily putting faith in what is said. This is what the prophet David prophesied: "Whoever slanders his neighbor in secret I will cause to perish."[2] Have you noted that it was not ignorance on the Savior's part when he said, "Where have you laid him?"[3] or when the Father said to Adam, "Where are you?"[4] or to Cain, "Where is Abel, your brother?" or also to Abraham, "I want to go down and see if in fact they have done all the evil that has been cried out against them to me. I want to know!"[5] ON LAZARUS DEAD SINCE FOUR DAYS.[6]

---

[2]Ps 101:5 (100:5 LXX). [3]Jn 11:34. [4]Gen 3:9. [5]Gen 18:20. [6]SC 396:218-20.

19:20-30* FALSE AND TRUE WISDOM

[20]*All wisdom is the fear of the Lord,*
and in all wisdom there is the fulfilment of the law.[h]
[22]*But the knowledge of wickedness is not wisdom,*
nor is there prudence where sinners take counsel.
[23]*There is a cleverness which is abominable,*
but there is a fool who merely lacks wisdom.
[24]*Better is the God-fearing man who lacks intelligence,*
than the highly prudent man who transgresses the law.
[25]*There is a cleverness which is scrupulous but unjust,*
and there are people who distort kindness to gain a verdict.
[26]*There is a rascal bowed down in mourning,*[i]
but inwardly he is full of deceit.
[27]*He hides his face and pretends not to hear;*
but where no one notices, he will forestall you.
[28]*And if by lack of strength he is prevented from sinning,*
he will do evil when he finds an opportunity.
[29]*A man is known by his appearance,*
and a sensible man is known by his face, when you meet him.
[30]*A man's attire and open-mouthed laughter,*
and a man's manner of walking, show what he is.

---

h Other authorities add *and the knowledge of his omnipotence.* [21]*When a servant says to his master, "I will not act as you wish," even if later he does it, he angers the one who supports him.* i Gk *blackness* * Sir 19:20-30 LXX (19:18b-28 Vg), with variants.

OVERVIEW: Wisdom has many faces, but it always comes from God (ORIGEN). It evidences itself, for instance, in the outward appearance of the Christian who is truly wise in faith (CHRYSOSTOM).

19:22 Knowledge of Wickedness Is Not Wisdom

MANIFOLD WISDOM ALWAYS COMES FROM GOD. ORIGEN: In the book that among us is usually considered to be among the books of Solomon and is called Ecclesiasticus but among the Greeks is called the Wisdom of Jesus, son of Sirach, it is written: "All wisdom is from God."[1] Possibly we could interpret this to mean that even that wisdom of this world, which is said to be destined for destruction,[2] is from God, and that of the rulers of this world, and if there is any other through which false wisdom is commended. However, in the same little book it was said later on: "For the wisdom of evil is not instruction." By this he surely shows that all instruction that asserts anything false, even if it seems vigorous and truthful and the kind that could scarcely be undermined, nevertheless we should by no means attach the name of wisdom to knowledge of this sort. Well then, what is the meaning of the statement "All wisdom is from God"?[3]

To me the following sense seems apparent: we may designate as wisdom given by the Lord either every skill that is considered necessary for human use in a craft or the knowledge of any matter may be called wisdom given by the Lord. After all, in Job it is written, "Who has given women the wisdom to weave and the knowledge of embroidery?"[4] HOMILIES ON NUMBERS 18.3.2.[5]

19:30 One's Outward Appearance

A CHRISTIAN'S BODY LANGUAGE. JOHN CHRYSOSTOM: Once we have been inscribed in this spiritual senate of the church, it is right that we not permit ourselves the same actions as others but always manifest control of our tongue and purity of mind, educating each of our members to undertake no action that is not very useful to the soul. What am I saying? To use the tongue only for hymns, for praise, for the reading of the divine judgments and for spiritual conversation. As it says, "Let there be speech that is good for edifying, conferring grace on the listeners. And do not grieve the spirit of God in whom you have been sealed."[6] Do you know that to fail to do this is to sadden the Holy Spirit? Therefore, I implore you, try to do nothing that saddens the Holy Spirit. If we must go out, let us not attend dangerous or unreasonable meetings, full of foolishness. Rather, prefer nothing to the church of God, to houses of prayer and to meetings where spiritual things are discussed. And let each of our actions be very dignified. As it says, "A person's attire, his laughter and his gait reveal who he is." The external posture can be a clear image of the condition of the soul; indeed, the movement of the members reveals its beauty in a particular way. If we go into the town square, let our gait, our serenity and our composure be such as to attract the notice of those we encounter, let our eye not roam or our feet walk in a disorderly manner, and let our tongue proffer words with tranquility and gentleness. In other words, let our entire exterior disposition indicate the interior beauty of the soul. Let our behavior be already as though foreign and transformed, because the things that we do are new and foreign, as the blessed Paul indicates when he says, "If anyone is in Christ, he is a new creature."[7] BAPTISMAL INSTRUCTIONS 4.24-26.[8]

---

[1]Sir 1:1. [2]See 1 Cor 2:6. [3]Sir 1:1. [4]See Job 38:36. [5]CTP 76:255; ACTHN 112*. [6]Eph 4:29-30. [7]2 Cor 5:17. [8]CTP 31:152-53.

20:1-8 SILENCE AND SPEECH

^{1}There is a reproof which is not timely;
  and there is a man who keeps silent but is wise.
^{2}How much better it is to reprove than to stay angry!
  And the one who confesses his fault will be kept from loss.^{j}
^{4}Like a eunuch's desire to violate a maiden
  is a man who executes judgments by violence.
^{5}There is one who by keeping silent is found wise,
  while another is detested for being too talkative.
^{6}There is one who keeps silent because he has no answer,
  while another keeps silent because he knows when to speak.
^{7}A wise man will be silent until the right moment,
  but a braggart and fool goes beyond the right moment.
^{8}Whoever uses too many words will be loathed,
  and whoever usurps the right to speak will be hated

j Other authorities add ^{3}How good it is to show repentance when you are reproved, for so you will escape deliberate sin!

OVERVIEW: There is a time for speaking and a time for being silent (GREGORY THE GREAT).

20:7 Silent Until the Right Moment

SPEAKING AT THE RIGHT MOMENT. GREGORY THE GREAT: Those who notice what is evil in their neighbors, and yet refrain their tongue in silence, withdraw, as it were, the aid of medicine from observed sores and become the cause of death because they would not cure the venom that they could have cured. The tongue, therefore, should be discreetly curbed, not tied up fast. For it is written, "A wise person will hold his tongue until the opportune time." He will do this in order that when he considers it opportune, he can with assurance relinquish the censorship of silence and apply himself to the helpful service by speaking such things as are appropriate. And again it is written, "There is a time to keep silence and a time to speak."^{1} For, indeed, the appropriate time for each should be discreetly weighed just in case, on the one hand, when the tongue should be restrained it is allowed to run loose to no profit in what is said, or, on the other hand, when it could say something profitably, it shirks its duty and restrains itself. The psalmist spoke of this well when he said, "Set a watch, O Lord, on my mouth, and guard the door of my lips."^{2} For he is not looking for a wall to set about his lips but a door—in other words, something that can be opened or shut. This is something we need to learn with discretion so that we use our voice in a discreet

^{1}Ps 141:3 (140:3 LXX). ^{2}Ps 140:3.

and fitting time to open the mouth, and at the appropriate time also let silence close it. But those who spend time in much speaking are to be admonished that they vigilantly note from what a state of being in the right they fall away when they flow forth in a multitude of words. For the human mind is just like water, which, when closed in is collected to higher levels because it seeks again the height from which it descended. By the same token, when that water is let loose, it falls away in that it disperses itself unprofitably through the lowest places. PASTORAL RULE 3.14.[3]

---

[3]CTP 28:153-54; NPNF 2 12:38**.

20:9-17* PARADOXES

⁹*There may be good fortune for a man in adversity,*
    and a windfall may result in a loss.
¹⁰*There is a gift that profits you nothing,*
    and there is a gift that brings a double return.
¹¹*There are losses because of glory,*
    and there are men who have raised their heads from humble circumstances.
¹²*There is a man who buys much for a little,*
    but pays for it seven times over.
¹³*The wise man makes himself beloved through his words,*
    but the courtesies of fools are wasted.
¹⁴*A fool's gift will profit you nothing,*
    for he has many eyes instead of one.
¹⁵*He gives little and upbraids much,*
    he opens his mouth like a herald;
today he lends and tomorrow he asks it back;
    such a one is a hateful man.
¹⁶*A fool will say, "I have no friend,*
    and there is no gratitude for my good deeds;
    those who eat my bread speak unkindly."
¹⁷*How many will ridicule him, and how often!*

* Sir 20:9-19 Vg.

OVERVIEW: The number seven can be a figure for the fullness of good or of evil (RABANUS MAURUS).

20:14 A Fool's Gift Will Profit Nothing

THE NUMBER SEVEN AS VIRTUOUS OR DE-

monic. Rabanus Maurus: The gift of a fool is useless, since the doctrine of heretics benefits no one. "It is as though he had seven eyes,"[1] because the intentions of his will are contaminated by various perversities, always ready to do harm. The number seven, which is identified with perfection by the divine charisms that the prophet Isaiah lists as gifts of the Holy Spirit,[2] can, conversely, sometimes indicate the fullness of wickedness, as in that Gospel passage where the Savior tells about the unclean spirit that for a time abandons a person. "When the unclean spirit leaves the person, it roams through arid places in search of repose, and, finding none, it says, 'I will return to my house where I left.' Returning, he finds it swept and clean. Then he goes and brings with him seven other spirits worse than himself, and they enter and dwell there, and the last condition of that person is worse than the first."[3] On Ecclesiasticus 4.13.[4]

---

[1]Sir 20:14 Vg. The Greek text, "He has many eyes instead of one," describes an avid look. [2]See Is 11:2. [3]Mt 12:43-45; Lk 11:24-26. [4]PL 109:896-97.

20:18-23* CLUMSY WORDS

¹⁸*A slip on the pavement is better than a slip of the tongue;*
 so the downfall of the wicked will occur speedily.
¹⁹*An ungracious man is like a story told at the wrong time,*
 which is continually on the lips of the ignorant.
²⁰*A proverb from a fool's lips will be rejected,*
 for he does not tell it at its proper time.

²¹*A man may be prevented from sinning by his poverty,*
 so when he rests he feels no remorse.
²²*A man may lose his life through shame,*
 or lose it because of his foolish look.
²³*A man may for shame make promises to a friend,*
 and needlessly make him an enemy.

* Sir 20:20-25 Vg.

Overview: The perils of the tongue are tremendous (Chrysostom).

20:18 A Slip of the Tongue

Circumspection Is Needed. John Chrysostom: A person once said,[1] indicating how easily one falls because of the tongue, "Many fall by

---

[1]Chrysostom recognizes Sirach as Scripture, but like other Antiochene authors, he has some reservations about it, since they believe that the wisdom it teaches is human and not revealed.

the sword, but not as many as by the tongue."
And revealing the seriousness of such a fall, the
same person again said, "A slip on the pavement
is preferable to a fall caused by the tongue." And
not only does he speak of falls, but also he urges
great vigilance against being made to fall when
he says, "Make gates and bars for your mouth,"[2]

not that we would set actual gates and bars
but that with great caution we would close our
mouths before what is unbecoming. BAPTISMAL
INSTRUCTIONS 1.17.[3]

---

[2]Sir 28:25. [3]CTP 31:52-53.

20:24-26* LIES

²⁴*A lie is an ugly blot on a man;*
it is continually on the lips of the ignorant.
²⁵*A thief is preferable to a habitual liar,*

but the lot of both is ruin.
²⁶*The disposition of a liar brings disgrace,*
and his shame is ever with him.

* Sir 20:26-28 Vg.

OVERVIEW: One sin may be worse than another,
but both are worthy of punishment (Rabanus
Maurus).

20:25 A Thief Preferable to a Habitual Liar

**GREAT OR SMALL, ALL SIN MERITS PUNISH-
MENT.** RABANUS MAURUS: The text was not
written to justify the thief as though he were not
guilty, but by using the comparison it indicates
that the habit of lying is worse. As is said in the
prophet Ezekiel, the fornication of Jerusalem is
worse if compared with that of Samaria,[1] though
both merit condemnation. And in the Gospel,
according to the word of the Lord, the sin of So-

dom will be judged with more forbearance than
that of Judea.[2] In a mysterious way the thieves
could indicate the Jews, of whom Paul says, "You
who preach against stealing, steal,"[3] and the
lying heretics, whose crime is more intolerable
than that of the Jews, since after receiving the
grace of baptism and putting on the garments of
Christ,[4] they have returned to apostasy, offending the grace of the Spirit—but both crimes will
be met with eternal perdition if repentance does
not intervene. ON ECCLESIASTICUS 4.14.[5]

---

[1]See Ezek 16:46-51. [2]See Mt 10:15; 11:23-24; Lk 10:12. [3]Rom
2:21. [4]See Gal 3:26. Rabanus alludes to the imposition of a white
robe after baptism. [5]PL 109:899-900.

20:27-31* ABOUT WISDOM

²⁷*He who speaks wisely will advance himself,*
and a sensible man will please great men.
²⁸*Whoever cultivates the soil will heap up his harvest,*
and whoever pleases great men will atone for injustice.
²⁹*Presents and gifts blind the eyes of the wise;*
like a muzzle on the mouth they avert reproofs.
³⁰*Hidden wisdom and unseen treasure,*
what advantage is there in either of them?
³¹*Better is the man who hides his folly*
than the man who hides his wisdom.ᵏ

k *Other authorities add* ³²*Unwearied patience in seeking the Lord is better than a masterless charioteer of one's own life.* * Sir 20:29-33 Vg.

OVERVIEW: The ability of preaching is a treasure to be shared (GREGORY THE GREAT).

20:30 Hidden Wisdom and Unseen Treasure

ONE WHO KNOWS HOW TO PREACH HAS A TREASURE. GREGORY THE GREAT: Differently to be admonished are those who, though able to preach worthily, are afraid by reason of excessive humility and those whom imperfection or age forbids to preach and yet precipitancy impels. For those who, though able to preach with profit, still shrink back through excessive humility are to be admonished to gather from consideration of a lesser matter how faulty they are in a greater one. For, if they were to hide from their indigent neighbors money that they possessed themselves, they would undoubtedly show themselves to be promoters of their calamity. Let them perceive, then, in what guilt those are implicated who, in withholding the word of preaching from their sinning brethren, hide away the remedies of life from dying souls. Concerning this, a certain wise man also well says, "Wisdom that is hid and treasure that is unseen—what profit is in them both?" If a famine were wasting away the people, and they themselves kept hidden corn, undoubtedly they would be the authors of death. Let them consider therefore with what punishment they must be visited who, when souls are perishing from famine of the Word, do not supply the bread of grace that they have themselves received. Solomon also had something good to say about this: "He who hides corn shall be cursed among the people."[1] For to hide corn is to retain for one's self the words of sacred preaching. And everyone who does so is cursed among the people, because through his fault of silence only he is condemned in the punishment of the many whom he might have corrected. PASTORAL RULE 3.25.[2]

[1]Prov 11:26. [2]CTP 28:198; NPNF 2 12:52-53**.

21:1-10* DIFFERENT SINS

¹*Have you sinned, my son? Do so no more,*
  but pray about your former sins.
²*Flee from sin as from a snake;*
  for if you approach sin, it will bite you.
Its teeth are lion's teeth,
  and destroy the souls of men.
³*All lawlessness is like a two-edged sword;*
  there is no healing for its wound.

⁴*Terror and violence will lay waste riches;*
  thus the house of the proud will be laid waste.
⁵*The prayer of a poor man goes from his lips to the ears of God,ˡ*
  and his judgment comes speedily.
⁶*Whoever hates reproof walks in the steps of the sinner,*
  but he that fears the Lord will repent in his heart.
⁷*He who is mighty in speech is known from afar;*
  but the sensible man, when he slips, is aware of it.

⁸*A man who builds his house with other people's money*
  is like one who gathers stones for his burial mound.ᵐ
⁹*An assembly of the wicked is like tow gathered together,*
  and their end is a flame of fire.
¹⁰*The way of sinners is smoothly paved with stones,*
  but at its end is the pit of Hades.

l Gk *his ears*   m Other authorities read *for the winter*   * Sir 21:1-11 Vg.

OVERVIEW: Penance and prayer are useless without works of mercy (AUGUSTINE), although the forgiveness of sins is always attainable through prayer (FULGENTIUS).

21:1 *Sin No More*

PENANCE, PRAYER AND WORKS OF MERCY.
AUGUSTINE: We know that repentance over one's sins renews a person, making him better, but it will result in nothing more if it does not result in works of mercy. Truth testifies the same thing through the mouth of John when against those who were approaching him he said, "Generation of vipers! Who made you to believe that you could escape from the coming wrath? Produce fruit therefore in keeping with repentance, and do not say to yourselves, 'We are descendants of Abraham,' because I assure you that God is able to raise up children of Abraham from these stones. The ax is already at the root of the trees, ready to cut; every tree that does not yield good

fruit will be cut down and thrown into the fire."[1] This is the fruit about which he had said in the preceding phrase, "Produce fruits in keeping with repentance."[2] Anyone who does not produce such fruits has no reason to believe that an unfruitful penance will merit the forgiveness of sins. And what these fruits are, the same John indicates, because after he had said these things, "The crowds questioned him, saying, 'What shall we do?'"[3] that is, what are these fruits that he was pressing them to produce. "And he answered, 'Whoever possesses two cloaks should give one to the person who has none, and he should do the same with his provisions.'"[4] It is an unambiguous, clear, explicit answer. So what is the meaning of what he said first, "Every tree that does not yield fruit will be cut down and thrown into the fire,"[5] except what those who are on his left are going to hear to whom he says, "Be gone into the eternal fire, for I was hungry and you gave me nothing to eat."[6] It is not enough therefore just to stop sinning if we neglect repairing the guilt of the past. In fact, Scripture says, "Son, have you sinned? Sin no more." However, if you think that this alone will make him safe, "and about the past" he quickly adds, "pray that the guilt of your transgressions may be pardoned."[7] But what good does such praying do for you if you do not become worthy to be heard by not yielding fruits worthy of repentance, so that you are not cut down like a barren tree and thrown into the fire?[8] If you want to be heard when you pray for your sins, "Forgive, and you will be forgiven; give, and it will be given to you."[9] SERMON 389.6.[10]

PRAYER BRINGS ABOUT THE FORGIVENESS OF SINS. FULGENTIUS OF RUSPE: Penance can be useful to every person in this life. Whenever one does it, however evil he was, however burdened with years of life, if with all his heart he has renounced the sins of his past and poured out tears in the presence of God, not only for the body but also for the soul, and he has taken care to wash the stains of his evil works with good works, he will receive the forgiveness of all his sins. This, in fact, is what the Lord promises to us with the words of the prophet, saying, "If you will be converted and weep, you will be saved."[11] Elsewhere it is also said, "My child, have you sinned? Sin no more, but ask forgiveness for your previous sins so that they may be forgiven."[12] Prayer for sins would not have been commanded of the sinner if forgiveness of sins would not have to be granted to the one praying. But penance is fruitful for the sinner if it takes place in the catholic church; to the church, God in the person of Peter granted the power to bind and to loose, saying, "Whatever you bind on earth will be bound in heaven; whatever you loose on earth will be loosed in heaven."[13] Therefore, at whatever age an individual makes true penance for his sins and corrects his life through the gift of illumination that God gives to him, he will not be deprived of the gift of forgiveness because God, as he asserts through the prophet, does not desire the death of one dying but rather that he be converted from his perverse way and that his soul live.[14] LETTER TO PETER ON THE FAITH 39.[15]

---

[1]Lk 3:7-9. [2]Lk 3:8. [3]Lk 3:10. [4]Lk 3:11. [5]Lk 3:9. [6]Mt 25:42. [7]Sir 21:1, variant. [8]See Lk 3:9. [9]Lk 6:37-38. [10]NBA 34:346-49; WSA 3 10:411**. [11]Is 30:15. [12]Sir 21:1, variant. [13]Mt 16:19. [14]See Ezek 33:11. [15]CTP 57:142-43; FC 95:84-85**

21:11-28* THE WISE AND THE FOOLISH

¹¹*Whoever keeps the law controls his thoughts,*
    and wisdom is the fulfilment of the fear of the Lord.
¹²*He who is not clever cannot be taught,*
    but there is a cleverness which increases bitterness.
¹³*The knowledge of a wise man will increase like a flood,*
    and his counsel like a flowing spring.
¹⁴*The mind of a fool is like a broken jar;*
    it will hold no knowledge.

¹⁵*When a man of understanding hears a wise saying,*
    he will praise it and add to it;
when a reveler hears it, he dislikes it
    and casts it behind his back.
¹⁶*A fool's narration is like a burden on a journey,*
    but delight will be found in the speech of the intelligent.
¹⁷*The utterance of a sensible man will be sought in the assembly,*
    and they will ponder his words in their minds.

¹⁸*Like a house that has vanished, so is wisdom to a fool;*
    and the knowledge of the ignorant is unexamined talk.
¹⁹*To a senseless man education is fetters on his feet,*
    and like manacles on his right hand.
²⁰*A fool raises his voice when he laughs,*
    but a clever man smiles quietly.
²¹*To a sensible man education is like a golden ornament,*
    and like a bracelet on the right arm.

²²*The foot of a fool rushes into a house,*
    but a man of experience stands respectfully before it.
²³*A boor peers into the house from the door,*
    but a cultivated man remains outside.
²⁴*It is ill-mannered for a man to listen at a door,*
    and a discreet man is grieved by the disgrace.
²⁵*The lips of strangers will speak of these things,*ⁿ
    but the words of the prudent will be weighed in the balance.

^{26}*The mind of fools is in their mouth,*
 but the mouth of wise men is in^o their mind.
^{27}*When an ungodly man curses his adversary,^{p}*
 he curses his own soul.
^{28}*A whisperer defiles his own soul*
 and is hated in his neighborhood.

---

n The Greek text of this line is uncertain   o Other authorities omit *in*   p Or *curses Satan*   * Sir 21:12-31 Vg.

OVERVIEW: Scripture may be interpreted in various ways (RUFINUS). Fear of God spares upheavals and brings peace (BARSANUPHIUS AND JOHN). The wise person thinks before speaking; the fool does not (HILARY OF POITIERS). Many devils accomplish the works of the devil (ORIGEN).

21:15 Hearing a Wise Saying

VARIOUS MEANINGS OF SCRIPTURE. RUFINUS OF AQUILEIA: "Benjamin, ravenous wolf, still eating by morning and by evening dividing the food. All these are the twelve sons of Jacob, and the words their father said to them as he blessed them. Each according to his blessing, he blessed them."[1] I wish that those who insist on the letter[2] would tell me what there could be in Benjamin of the ravenous wolf, or how, eating by morning, he could then divide the food in the evening. Even the coarse Jews reject the insult of the letter in this passage. Some refer it to the greediness of the altar, meaning that it was built on Benjamin's portion,[3] since what is offered in the morning is divided in the evening by the priests.[4] Others, with various stories, which are nonetheless fables, admit that these words can have no literal force. In the church, many hold the opinion that this passage refers to the apostle Paul.[5] I do not reject or question this interpretation but try to do what is written: "Hearing a wise word, he praises it and adds another."[6] And thus to the explanation that my predecessors have validly referred to Paul and that I do not deny, I nevertheless add another. Benjamin, it says, means "son of sorrow."[7] By lot he obtained as his inheritance the place in which the earthly Jerusalem was located,[8] which is the type and has the form of the heavenly.[9] When, therefore, the time will come for the heavenly Jerusalem and the church of the firstborn enrolled in heaven to be manifest,[10] this Jerusalem that at present has been cast out and driven away for its lack of faith, that for so long with its children has suffered hunger for the word of God[11] and thirst for spiritual drink[12]—when the fullness of the Gentiles has been reached, according to the apostle's promise, "then all Israel will be saved."[13] THE BLESSINGS OF THE PATRIARCHS 2.28-29.[14]

21:20 A Clever Person Smiles Quietly

PEACE OF MIND STEMS FROM THE FEAR OF GOD. BARSANUPHIUS AND JOHN: The fear of God is without turmoil, agitation or restlessness. If, therefore, before our encounter with others, we prepare our hearts with vigilance in the fear of God, why should there be any reason for us to become upset or laugh? There is, in fact, no laughter in the presence of godly fear. It is said of the fools that they raise their voice when they laugh and that the speech of the fool is agitated and results in unpleasantness. Of the righteous one, however, it is said that he only smiles. If, therefore, we bring to ourselves in a similar way the memory of God and fill our thoughts with

---

[1]Gen 49:27-28. [2]Rufinus polemicizes against those who maintain that Scripture always should be interpreted literally. [3]See Josh 18:1-28, etc. [4]This interpretation whose origin is unknown is to be found also in Jerome. [5]See Rom 11:1; Phil 3:5. [6]Sir 21:15 (21:18 Vg). [7]See Gen 35:18. [8]See Josh 18:1-28, etc. [9]See Heb 12:22. [10]See Heb 12:23. [11]See Deut 8:3; Mt 4:4 par. [12]See 1 Cor 10:4. [13]Rom 11:25-26. [14]CTP 120:106-7.

quiet humility when we are in the company of our friends, we love them in this way and hold before their eyes the tremendous judgment of God.[15] Such a disposition will drive away from our heart every evil thought. For where, in fact, there is quiet, gentleness and humility, this is where God dwells. BOOK OF LETTERS 454.[16]

21:26 The Mouth of the Wise

WISE PEOPLE REFLECT BEFORE SPEAKING. HILARY OF POITIERS: For what good reason would the prophet have said "the tongue meditates injustice,"[17] if meditation pertains to the living soul through its rational consciousness, whereas the tongue was not created according to a rational nature proper to it but to be at the service of the rational nature? And yet, another prophet also shows the authoritativeness of a similar inspired and perfect saying when he says, "The heart of fools is in their mouth," meaning that they randomly say things that have no foundation, accustomed as they are to not treating any argument with the deliberation of reason and after meditating on it in the heart but only by the imprudent movement of a rash tongue. If a fool's heart is in his mouth, it is because he does not say what he has thought but thinks afterwards about what he has said. This refers to the tongue of the fool. Of the tongue of the wise, rather, we read, "The tongue of the wise meditates wisdom."[18] And, "My tongue like the pen of a nimble scribe."[19] The tongue of the wise is born of meditation on wisdom, and therefore of itself, like the pen of a scribe, it does nothing disordered or uncertain. It submits itself, rather, to what has been thought and read, which make it flow nimbly according to the judgment of reason. HOMILIES ON THE PSALMS 51.7.[20]

21:27 Cursing One's Own Soul

THE DEVIL AND HIS MANY DEVILS. ORIGEN: Some may find it difficult or think it is a fable when we say there are many demons to take care

of each particular sinner. Let them return to the authority of the Gospel and find that man who lived in the tombs, possessed by the demons.[21] When the Savior asks it, "What is your name?" it answers, "Legion, for we are many."[22] Why therefore does it seem strange to attribute a demon to a particular kind of sin, since it is written that in a single man an entire legion of demons was found? But I remember saying similar things when we were expounding that verse in the psalms where it says, "In the mornings I wiped out all the sinners on the earth in order to disperse from the city of the Lord all those who do iniquity."[23] Thus it is also said that "in the hand of the just there are swords that cut in two,"[24] undoubtedly in order for them to destroy opposing powers. But I believe that, in order to bring even more force to these affirmations, we can cite the word of the apostle Paul: "May the God of peace swiftly grind Satan under your feet."[25] If, in fact, Satan is alone, can he be subjected under the feet of the servants of God and then take action again? If he has been subjected, and subjected by God, he surely can act no longer. Perhaps it will be necessary then to think that there are as many satans as there are those who complete his works. It seems to me that this is also what is indicated in the book of Wisdom[26] where it is said, "The impious who curse Satan are cursing their own soul." But we also find this kind of thinking in a booklet not even contained in the canon, entitled The Testament of the Twelve Patriarchs, that individual satans ought to be recognized in individual sinners.[27] The same idea seems to be expressed in a still more

---

[15]See Heb 10:27. [16]CTP 93:392-93; FC 114:68**. [17]Ps 52:4 (51:4 LXX). [18]Ps 37:30 (36:30 LXX). [19]Ps 45:2 (44:2 LXX). [20]CTP 185:204. [21]See Mk 5:2-3; Lk 8:27. [22]Mk 5:9; Lk 8:30. [23]Ps 101:8 (100:8 LXX). [24]Ps 149:6. [25]Cf. Rom 16:20. [26]Origen speaks about the Wisdom of Sirach, that is, another name of Sirach. [27]Testament of Reuben 2-3. In Greek, *diabolos* means originally "adversary, accuser"; later, in the Hellenistic epoch, it takes also the meaning of "devil." The Testaments of the Twelve Patriarchs were composed in Hebrew or Aramaic, but the original text is known only from fragments found in Qumran. The complete text exists only in an old Greek translation, which was partly rewritten by Christians.

illuminating way when looking at the meaning of its name, according to the instruction of erudite Hebrews: Satan means "adversary." All those, therefore, who oppose the will of God can be called satans.[28] HOMILIES ON JOSHUA 15.6.[29]

---

[28]See Mt 16:23. [29]CTP 108:221-22; FC 105:148-49**.

22:1-6 THE INDOLENT AND BAD CHILDREN

[1]*The indolent may be compared to a filthy stone,*
and every one hisses at his disgrace.
[2]*The indolent may be compared to the filth of dunghills;*
any one that picks it up will shake it off his hand.

[3]*It is a disgrace to be the father of an undisciplined son,*
and the birth of a daughter is a loss.
[4]*A sensible daughter obtains her husband,*
but one who acts shamefully brings grief to her father.
[5]*An impudent daughter disgraces father and husband,*
and will be despised by both.
[6]*Like music in mourning is a tale told at the wrong time,*
but chastising and discipline are wisdom at all times.

OVERVIEW: The call to conversion comes in many forms (CLEMENT OF ALEXANDRIA).

22:6 Chastising and Discipline

THE CALL TO CONVERSION. CLEMENT OF ALEXANDRIA: It is not out of hatred that the Lord chides human beings, for he suffered for us when he could have destroyed us because of our faults. For he is a good Teacher who has the consummate ability to censure with words of rebuke. His words of reproach are like a whip that scourges the sluggish mind of people. And then, once he scourges them, he can move on to exhorting them. For those who are not motivated by praise are spurred on by censure. And those whom censure cannot rouse to salvation, as if they were dead, are by denunciation roused to the truth. "For the whip and correction are suited in every circumstance to wisdom." CHRIST THE EDUCATOR 1.8.66.2-3.[1]

---

[1]CTP 181:95; ANF 2:226**.

22:7-18* WISDOM AND FOOLISHNESS

^{7}He who teaches a fool is like one who glues potsherds together,
  or who rouses a sleeper from deep slumber.
^{8}He who tells a story to a fool tells it to a drowsy man;
  and at the end he will say, "What is it?"^{q}
^{11}Weep for the dead, for he lacks the light;
  and weep for the fool, for he lacks intelligence;
weep less bitterly for the dead, for he has attained rest;
  but the life of the fool is worse than death.
^{12}Mourning for the dead lasts seven days,
  but for a fool or an ungodly man it lasts all his life.

^{13}Do not talk much with a foolish man,
  and do not visit an unintelligent man;
guard yourself from him to escape trouble,
  and you will not be soiled when he shakes himself off;
avoid him and you will find rest,
  and you will never be wearied by his madness.
^{14}What is heavier than lead?
  And what is its name except "Fool"?
^{15}Sand, salt, and a piece of iron
  are easier to bear than a stupid man.

^{16}A wooden beam firmly bonded into a building
  will not be torn loose by an earthquake;
so the mind firmly fixed on a reasonable counsel
  will not be afraid in a crisis.
^{17}A mind settled on an intelligent thought
  is like the stucco decoration on the wall of a colonnade.^{r}
^{18}Fences set on a high place
  will not stand firm against the wind;
so a timid heart with a fool's purpose
  will not stand firm against any fear.

q Other authorities add ^{9}Children who are brought up in a good life, conceal the lowly birth of their parents. ^{10}Children who are disdainfully and boorishly haughty stain the nobility of their kindred.   r Or on a smooth wall   * Sir 22:9-18 LXX (22:7-23 Vg).

OVERVIEW: Friends join in your sorrow, as Job's friends did (ANONYMOUS ANOMOEAN).

22:12 The Span of Mourning

JOB'S FRIENDS MOURNED HIM FOR SEVEN DAYS. ANONYMOUS ANOMOEAN: When these men arrived and saw Job, they were shocked and filled with an immense sorrow, sadness and groaning. "They sat by him on the ground for seven days and seven nights,"[1] drenched in sorrow, sated with groaning, drunk with tears. Evoking such things, the holy ones said in words what these men lived, "Tears are my bread day and night."[2] And, "I forget to eat my bread, for my long groaning."[3] And, "You make us drink tears in abundance."[4] Thus these men were filled with sadness, sorrow and groaning to the point of forgetting all carnal and present things, and they nourished themselves, and were filled and quenched their thirst precisely with sadness and grief. Indeed, as Job was filled with tremendous sorrow, likewise those blessed men were filled with an immense sadness and weeping. Therefore it says, "They sat by him on the ground for seven days and seven nights."[5] The dead mourned near Job, the living. In fact, "the dead are mourned for seven days." COMMENTARY ON JOB 3.13.[6]

---

[1]Job 2:13. [2]Ps 42:4 (41:4 LXX). [3]Ps 102:5-6 (101:5-6 LXX). [4]Ps 80:6 (79:6 LXX). [5]Job 2:13. [6]CSEL 96:361-62.

22:19-26* FRIENDSHIP

[19]*A man who pricks an eye will make tears fall,*
  and one who pricks the heart makes it show feeling.
[20]*One who throws a stone at birds scares them away,*
  and one who reviles a friend will break off the friendship.
[21]*Even if you have drawn your sword against a friend,*
  do not despair, for a renewal of friendship is possible.
[22]*If you have opened your mouth against your friend,*
  do not worry, for reconciliation is possible;
but as for reviling, arrogance, disclosure of secrets, or a treacherous blow—
  in these cases any friend will flee.

[23]*Gain the trust of your neighbor in his poverty,*
  that you may rejoice with him in his prosperity;
stand by him in time of affliction,
  that you may share with him in his inheritance.[s]
[24]*The vapor and smoke of the furnace precede the fire;*
  so insults precede bloodshed.

²⁵*I will not be ashamed to protect a friend,*
  and I will not hide from him;
²⁶*but if some harm should happen to me because of him,*
  whoever hears of it will beware of him.

---

s Other authorities add *For one should not always despise restricted circumstances, nor admire a rich man who is stupid.*   * Sir 22:24-32 Vg.

OVERVIEW: Intelligence is like water that flows in the soul. The gift of prophecy, too, is desirable (ORIGEN).

22:19 *The Heart Shows Feeling*

THE WATER OF UNDERSTANDING FLOWS IN THE SOUL. ORIGEN: Let us try to do what Wisdom admonishes us, saying, "Drink the waters from your own springs and pools, and let your spring be your own."[1] Make sure, O hearer, that you have your own well and spring, so that you, when you take in hand the book of the Scriptures, may also begin to express from your own learning some understanding of the text, and, in agreement with what you have learned in church, you too may also attempt to drink from the source of your own spirit. Within you is the source of living water,[2] perennial veins and abundant currents flowing with rational understanding if they have not been obstructed by earth and detritus. But get busy so that you can dig out your earth and purify it from the filth, that is, in order to remove laziness from your soul and throw out the inactivity of your heart. For listen to what the Scripture says: "Sting the eye, and it will bring forth a tear; sting the heart, and it will bring forth understanding." Therefore you too should purify your spirit so that you may drink from your own living springs[3] and may draw living water from your wells.[4] For, in fact, if you have received in yourself the Word of God, if you have received living water from Jesus and have received it with faith, it will become in you a "fountain of water that springs up to eternal life."[5] HOMILIES ON GENESIS 12.5.[6]

CRAVE THE GIFT OF PROPHECY. ORIGEN: Since the blessed apostle orders us to be imitators of this grace, that is, the gift of prophecy, although it is imperfect and in our power, saying, "Be zealous for the greater gifts, above all the gift of prophecy,"[7] let us also try to have a zeal for those good gifts and, so far as we are able, to ask for them and then await the fullness of the gift from the Lord. For this, in fact, is what the Lord says by means of the prophet: "Open your mouth, and I will fill it up."[8] This is also why another Scripture says, "Sting the eye, and it will bring forth a tear; sting the heart, and it will bring forth understanding." HOMILIES ON EXODUS 4.5.[9]

---

[1]Prov 5:15, 17. [2]See Gen 26:19. [3]See Prov 5:15. [4]See Gen 26:19; Prov 5:15. [5]Jn 4:14. [6]CTP 14:195-96; FC 71:183-84**. [7]1 Cor 12:31; 14:1. [8]Ps 81:11 (80:11 LXX). [9]CTP 27:87.

22:27–23:6* VIGILANCE

²⁷*O that a guard were set over my mouth,*
and a seal of prudence upon my lips,
that it may keep me from falling,
*so that my tongue may not destroy me!*ᵗ
23 *O Lord, Father and Ruler of my life,*
do not abandon me to their counsel,
and let me not fall because of them!
²*O that whips were set over my thoughts,*
*and the discipline of wisdom over my mind!*ᵘ
That they may not spare me in my errors,
*and that it may not pass by my*ᵛ *sins;*
³*in order that my mistakes may not be multiplied,*
and my sins may not abound;
then I will not fall before my adversaries,
and my enemy will not rejoice over me.
⁴*O Lord, Father and God of my life,*
do not give me haughty eyes,
⁵*and remove from me evil desire.*
⁶*Let neither gluttony nor lust overcome me,*
and do not surrender me to a shameless soul.

t *Or Who will set a guard . . . destroy me?*   u *Or Who will set whips . . . my mind?*   v *Gk their*   * Sir 22:33–23:6 Vg.

OVERVIEW: Calamities sent by God do not always elicit conversion (ORIGEN) since the ungodly always long for what is harmful for their soul (QUODVULTDEUS).

23:2 The Discipline of Wisdom

CALAMITIES MAY NOT BRING ABOUT CONVERSION. ORIGEN: It is said with regard to sinners, "You whipped them, but they did not suffer."[1] The perceived whips of this world, inflicted on living bodies, whether those whipped want them or not, produce pain. But God's whips are of a kind that to some of those who are whipped they cause pain but for others who are whipped, they do not. Let us see if we can explain what it means to suffer from the whips of God and what it means not to suffer: why those with evil natures do not suffer from the whips of God while those who do suffer from the whips of God are blessed. Wisdom says, "Who will apply whips to my thoughts and seals of prudence to my lips so that they[2] would not spare me in my errors and so that my sins will not lead me to perdition?"[3] Pay attention to the words "who will apply whips to my thoughts." There are, therefore, whips that whip the thought. They are the whips of God that whip thought because the

---

[1]Jer 5:3.   [2]The whips.   [3]Sir 23:2, 22:27 and 23:2-3.

Word, joining itself to the soul and guiding it to the knowledge of its sins, whips it. It whips the blessed soul so that it suffers under its whips because the Word comes and penetrates the soul at its core, but it does not drive away the one who is reproved. But if someone is found to be insensitive to this whip, so to speak, it will be said of him, "You have whipped them, but they did not suffer."[4] Although the same word of accusation is pronounced in order to penetrate the mind of the one who has a spotted conscience[5] from some sin, if one of the listeners suffers for this word to the point where it can be said of him, "You have seen that such a person was moved deeply"[6] while another who hears does not suffer but remains insensitive to the one who is accusing him, surely of the insensitive one it will be said, "You have whipped them, but they have not suffered."[7] HOMILIES ON JEREMIAH 6.2.[8]

23:6 Do Not Surrender Me to a Shameless Soul

THE WICKED WANT WHAT IS HARMFUL FOR THEM. QUODVULTDEUS: Forgetful of freedom and grace and desiring the Egyptian foods, the people were found guilty of murmuring against God and against Moses.[9] They say, "Who will give us meat to eat? We remember the fish that we ate freely in Egypt, the cucumbers, the leeks, the garlic and the onions. Now, however," they add, "our life has dried up, and we see nothing before us but this manna."[10] The sweet things are rejected, the bitter desired. A grave, debilitating illness leads the soul to want to take what is harmful and to despise and reject what is useful and good for salvation. Thus they refused the manna, that is, Christ, saying, "We know that God spoke to Moses, but we do not know where this one comes from."[11] Christ says in reproof, "If you believed Moses, you would also believe me, because it is of me that he wrote.[12] Indeed, I am the living bread come down from heaven."[13] Did they not reject the holy manna when they said to Pilate, who wanted to release Jesus, "Release not him but Barabbas"?[14] Barabbas was a notorious thief,[15] and by asking for his release they professed to have in a certain sense desired, from among the thief's crimes, the leeks, the onions and the garlic, those unpleasant Egyptian foods that make one cry. To those who murmured, in fact, the divine majesty offered meats that did not restore but instead ruined those who ate them.[16] It says in Scripture, "The natural person does not understand the things of the Spirit:[17] every sluggard lives in concupiscence."[18] It is right that the spiritual person asks that the desires of his flesh be taken from him.[19] All these things show that it is wicked to desire and to ask of God things that are harmful to the soul, and especially to ask for them with murmuring. If a soul desires to enter the promised land,[20] it must guard itself from offending God with such a desire. THE BOOK OF PROMISES AND PREDICTIONS OF GOD 2.8.14.[21]

---

[4]Jer 5:3. [5]See 1 Cor 8:7. [6]1 Kings 20:29 (3 Kings 20:29 LXX). [7]Jer 5:3. [8]CTP 123:92-93; FC 97:63-64**. [9]See Num 11:1. [10]Num 11:4-6. [11]Jn 9:29. [12]Jn 5:46. [13]Jn 6:51. [14]Jn 18:40. [15]Cf. Jn 18:40. Quodvultdeus uses the Vulgate, which translates the Greek word *lēstēs* ("bandit"—later also—"thief") as *latro* ("robber, thief"). [16]See Num 11:33-34; Ps 78:30-31 (77:30-31 LXX). [17]1 Cor 2:14. [18]See Prov 21:25. [19]Sir 23:6 Vg. [20]See Heb 11:9. [21]CTP 82.

23:7-11* OATHS

[7]*Listen, my children, to instruction concerning speech;*
  the one who observes it will never be caught.
[8]*The sinner is overtaken through his lips,*
  the reviler and the arrogant are tripped by them.
[9]*Do not accustom your mouth to oaths,*
  and do not habitually utter the name of the Holy One;
[10]*for as a servant who is continually examined under torture*
  will not lack bruises,
so also the man who always swears and utters the Name
  will not be cleansed from sin.
[11]*A man who swears many oaths will be filled with iniquity,*
  and the scourge will not leave his house;
if he offends, his sin remains on him,
  and if he disregards it, he sins doubly;
if he has sworn needlessly, he will not be justified,
  for his house will be filled with calamities.

---

* Sir 23:7-14 Vg, which replaces Sir 23:9 with: "Do not accustom your mouth to the oath, since in it are many fallings. God's name should not be often in your mouth, nor should you mingle it with the names of the holy things, since you shall not escape from them."

OVERVIEW: Do not swear even when you are speaking the truth (LEANDER).

23:9 Using Oaths

NEVER SWEAR. LEANDER OF SEVILLE: Seek with the same scrupulousness to never offer oaths but to always speak the truth. As oaths are permitted to worldly people out of fear of deception, so for one leading a religious life oaths are prohibited, even when he has a clear conscience. The Lord says, "Let your speech be yes, yes, and no, no. Anything more comes from the evil one."[1] Do not swear even when you speak the truth, because that comes from evil. It is said that it comes from evil because the need to swear comes from a bad conscience: one constrains a person to swear when he doubts his sincerity. You who should have the simplicity[2] of the heart on your lips, why would you spontaneously bind yourself with an oath? Do not make a habit of either swearing in the good or perjuring in the bad. Speak the truth with all your heart, and there will be no need for oaths, as we read: "Do not accustom yourself to oaths, because by swearing many have fallen."[3] LETTER TO HIS SISTER FLORENTINE 29.[4]

---

[1]Mt 5:37. [2]Cf. Eph 6:5; Col 3:22; where "singleness" can also be translated "simplicity." [3]Sir 23:9, variant of Vg. [4]CTP 66:106.

23:12-21* IMPURE WORDS

¹²There is an utterance which is comparable to death;ʷ
  may it never be found in the inheritance of Jacob!
For all these errors will be far from the godly,
  and they will not wallow in sins.
¹³Do not accustom your mouth to lewd vulgarity,
  for it involves sinful speech.
¹⁴Remember your father and mother
  whenˣ you sit among great men;
lest you be forgetful in their presence,
  and be deemed a fool on account of your habits;
then you will wish that you had never been born,
  and you will curse the day of your birth.
¹⁵A man accustomed to use insulting words
  will never become disciplined all his days.
¹⁶Two sorts of men multiply sins,
  and a third incurs wrath.
The soul heated like a burning fire
  will not be quenched until it is consumed;
a man who commits fornication with his near of kinʸ
  will never cease until the fire burns him up.
¹⁷To a fornicator all bread tastes sweet;
  he will never cease until he dies.
¹⁸A man who breaks his marriage vows
  says to himself, "Who sees me?
Darkness surrounds me, and the walls hide me,
  and no one sees me. Why should I fear?
The Most High will not take notice of my sins."
¹⁹His fear is confined to the eyes of men,
  and he does not realize that the eyes of the Lord
  are ten thousand times brighter than the sun;
they look upon all the ways of men,
  and perceive even the hidden places.
²⁰Before the universe was created, it was known to him;
  so it was also after it was finished.
²¹This man will be punished in the streets of the city,
  and where he least suspects it, he will be seized.

w Other authorities read *clothed about with death*   x Gk *for*   y Gk *in the body of his flesh*   * Sir 23:15-31 Vg, with many differences.

OVERVIEW: The body should be kept away from sin (CYRIL OF JERUSALEM), remembering that God sees even in the darkness (AMBROSE).

23:18 *Under Cover of Darkness*

STAYING AWAY FROM SIN. CYRIL OF JERUSALEM: Let us be careful about our bodies. Let us also not misuse them as though they were not our own. Let us not say, like the heretics do, that this vesture of the body does not belong to us. Instead, let us take care of it as our own, for we must give account to the Lord of all things done through the body.[1] Do not say, No one sees me. Do not think that there is no witness of what you did. More often than not, there is no human witness, but he who made us—an unerring witness—remains faithful in heaven,[2] and sees what you are doing. And the stains of sin also remain in the body. For as when a wound has gone deep into the body, even if there has been healing, the scar remains, so sin wounds soul and body, and the marks of its scars remain in all. And they are removed only from those who receive the washing of baptism. The past wounds therefore of soul and body God heals by baptism; against future ones let us one and all jointly guard ourselves, that we may keep this vestment of the body pure and may not, for practicing fornication and sensual indulgence or any other sin for a short season, lose the salvation of heaven but may inherit the eternal kingdom of God; of which may God, of his own grace, deem all of you worthy. CATECHETICAL LECTURES 18.20.[3]

GOD SEES THROUGH DARKNESS. AMBROSE: We are always to walk becomingly, as in the day, and reject the works of darkness.[4] We know that the night has been appointed for the rest of the body, not for carrying out some task or activity, and therefore it is at night that we pass into sleep and blissful oblivion. "We are not to be involved in feasting and drunkenness, in orgies and immodesty."[5] We should not say, "The darkness and the walls hide us, and goodness knows if the Most High will succeed in seeing us."[6] We are instead to love the light and be honest in our dealings, so that, like walking in the sunlight, we want our works to be resplendent in the presence of God.[7] HEXAMERON 2.10.38.[8]

---

[1]See 2 Cor 5:10. [2]Ps 89:38 (88:38 LXX). [3]CTP 103:422-23. [4]See Rom 13:12. [5]Rom 13:13. [6]Sir 23:18 (23:26 Vg). [7]See Mt 5:10. [8]CTP 164:61; FC 42:43-44**.

23:22-27* THE ADULTERESS

²²*So it is with a woman who leaves her husband*
    and provides an heir by a stranger.
²³*For first of all, she has disobeyed the law of the Most High;*
    second, she has committed an offense against her husband;
and third, she has committed adultery through harlotry
    and brought forth children by another man.
²⁴*She herself will be brought before the assembly,*

and punishment will fall on her children.
²⁵Her children will not take root,
and her branches will not bear fruit.
²⁶She will leave her memory for a curse,
and her disgrace will not be blotted out.
²⁷Those who survive her will recognize
that nothing is better than the fear of the Lord,
and nothing sweeter than to heed the commandments of the Lord.ᶻ

z Other authorities add ²⁸*It is a great honor to follow God, and to be received by him is long life.*   * Sir 23:32-38 Vg.

OVERVIEW: The souls that forsake the baptismal faith and join the heretics are adulterous (RABANUS MAURUS).

23:22 A Woman Who Leaves Her Husband

HERESY IS LIKE ADULTERY. RABANUS MAURUS: The divine judgment condemns the adultery of both the husband and the wife in the same way, and the fruit of such unions is not pleasing to the Lord, nor can what has clearly been born of the contamination of sin please him. According to allegorical interpretation, the assembly of the heretics, or any soul that is deceived by heretical perversity, ceases to please God, since she has abandoned her first husband, the guide of her youth,[1] who had united her to himself in the sacred bond of baptism and adorned her with the beauty of virtue. Ezekiel wrote very clearly on this: "She has united with another man," that is, with the devil, "who has contaminated her with various errors, making her completely guilty."[2] ON ECCLESIASTICUS 10.11.[3]

---

[1]Cf. Prov 2:17. [2]The origin of this quotation has not been identified, although it is attributed to Ezekiel. [3]PL 109:921-22.

24:1-22* WISDOM SPEAKS

¹Wisdom will praise herself,
and will glory in the midst of her people.ᵃ
²In the assembly of the Most High she will open her mouth,
and in the presence of his host she will glory:
³"I came forth from the mouth of the Most High,
and covered the earth like a mist.
⁴I dwelt in high places,
and my throne was in a pillar of cloud.
⁵Alone I have made the circuit of the vault of heaven

and have walked in the depths of the abyss.
⁶In the waves of the sea, in the whole earth,
   and in every people and nation I have gotten a possession.
⁷Among all these I sought a resting place;
   I sought in whose territory I might lodge.

⁸"Then the Creator of all things gave me a commandment,
   and the one who created me assigned a place for my tent.
And he said, 'Make your dwelling in Jacob,
   and in Israel receive your inheritance.'
⁹From eternity, in the beginning, he created me,
   and for eternity I shall not cease to exist.
¹⁰In the holy tabernacle I ministered before him,
   and so I was established in Zion.
¹¹In the beloved city likewise he gave me a resting place,
   and in Jerusalem was my dominion.
¹²So I took root in an honored people,
   in the portion of the Lord, who is their inheritance.

¹³"I grew tall like a cedar in Lebanon,
   and like a cypress on the heights of Hermon.
¹⁴I grew tall like a palm tree in En-gedi,ᵇ
   and like rose plants in Jericho;
like a beautiful olive tree in the field,
   and like a plane tree I grew tall.
¹⁵Like cassia and camel's thorn I gave forth the aroma of spices,
   and like choice myrrh I spread a pleasant odor,
like galbanum, onycha, and stacte,
   and like the fragrance of frankincense in the tabernacle.
¹⁶Like a terebinth I spread out my branches,
   and my branches are glorious and graceful.
¹⁷Like a vine I caused loveliness to bud,
   and my blossoms became glorious and abundant fruit.ᶜ

¹⁹"Come to me, you who desire me,
   and eat your fill of my produce.
²⁰For the remembrance of me is sweeter than honey,
   and my inheritance sweeter than the honeycomb.
²¹Those who eat me will hunger for more,
   and those who drink me will thirst for more.
²²Whoever obeys me will not be put to shame,
   and those who work with my help will not sin."

a Or will glorify herself in the midst of the people.   b Other authorities read on the beaches   c Other authorities add ¹⁸I am the mother of beautiful love, of fear, of knowledge, and of holy hope; being eternal, I therefore am given to all my children, to those who are named by him.   * Sir 24:1-31 Vg.

OVERVIEW: Scripture witnesses in many ways to the divinity of the Son (ILDEFONSUS) and of the Holy Spirit (VICTOR OF VITA). Those who say that the Father is immortal do not exclude the Son but speak about the Trinity (AUGUSTINE). Scripture is like a field where a treasure is hidden (ORIGEN). The palm is the symbol that wisdom gives to the martyrs (QUODVULTDEUS). Christ gives the commandments as true food (AUGUSTINE).

24:3 *From the Mouth of the Most High*

TESTIMONIES TO THE SON'S DIVINITY. ILDEFONSUS OF TOLEDO: Malachi says, "The Lord whom you seek will come to his holy temple, and the angel of the covenant whom you desire."[1] Similarly in Exodus, the Father says to the lawgiver, "See, I send my angel who goes before you, who guards you on your way and who brings you to the place I have prepared. Honor him, and listen to his voice, and do not disregard him, because he will not forgive you when you sin. My name is on him."[2] Perhaps because you hear "angel" you do not believe it is God the creator but some created angel? Impossible! You are confused by a tremendous folly if you believe that God would have given his power and his very name to some angel, and therefore (contrary to your word and mine) that it was not the only God who did everything. Why do you say the angel is equal to him when this cannot be so? Indeed, who above the clouds is equal to the Lord?[3] Or who among the children of God is like God?[4] That is, among the good angels and among the holy people whom, in adoptive love, the divine mercy calls children. From where did Christ come? Well, from where did he come? Clearly, he came from nowhere else than from God. Listen to Christ speak by the mouth of Solomon: "I came forth from the mouth of the Most High."[5] And to what the Father says of him in the Psalms: "From the womb before the dawn I begot you."[6] Here and elsewhere, Christ says through Solomon, "Before the hills I was brought into the world."[7] And Zechariah, "Thus says the Lord of hosts: after the glory he sent me to the peoples, to those who plundered you. Whoever strikes you strikes the apple of my eye, because, look, I will raise my hand over you, and they will be plunder for those who served them. And you will know that the Lord of hosts sent me."[8] ON MARY'S PERPETUAL VIRGINITY 5.[9]

THE NATURE OF THE HOLY SPIRIT. VICTOR OF VITA: From the books of the Old Testament and then also from those of the New, we are taught that the Father, the Son and the Holy Spirit are of a single substance. Indeed, the book of Genesis begins, "In the beginning God created the heavens and the earth. Now the earth was invisible and shapeless, and darkness was over the abyss, and the Spirit of God moved over the waters."[10] He was the beginning,[11] he who spoke to the Jews who had asked him who he was, saying, "The beginning, who speaks to you."[12] The Spirit of God, then, moved over the waters[13] as creator, sustaining the creation by the virtue of his power, so that, producing from them all the living species, he gave the heat of his own fire to the crude elements, and the nature of water (suggesting even then the mystery of baptism) received sanctifying power and for the first time brought forth animated bodies to life. David, inspired by God, testifies, "By the Word of the Lord the heavens were fixed, and by the Spirit of his mouth all of their power."[14] See how rich his brief words are, and how he clearly returns to the mystery of unity: by "Lord" indicating the Father, indicating the Son with the term "Word" and designating the Holy Spirit with the expression "from the mouth of the Most High."[15] And so the term "Word" would not be understood as the emanation of the voice, he says that the heavens were fixed through him.[16] And so the

---

[1]Mal 3:1. [2]Ex 23:20. [3]See Ps 89:7 (88:7 LXX). [4]See Ps 89:7 (88:7 LXX). [5]Sir 24:3 (24:5 Vg). [6]Ps 110:3 (109:3 LXX). [7]Prov 8:25. [8]Zech 2:12-13. [9]CTP 84:73-74. [10]Gen 1:1-2. [11]See Jn 1:1-2. [12]Jn 8:25. [13]See Gen 1:1-2. [14]Ps 33:6 (32:6 LXX). [15]Sir 24:3 (24:5 Vg).[16]See Ps 33:6 (32:6 LXX).

term "Spirit" would not be understood as breath, he showed in him the fullness of the power of heaven. In fact, where there is power, there must be a person. By saying "all" he means not a power taken from the Father or from the Son but a power perfect in the Holy Spirit, not in such a way that he alone would have that which is in the Father and in the Son, but that he would have it fully, together with them both. BOOK OF THE CATHOLIC FAITH 77-78.[17]

24:5 The Vault of Heaven

IMMORTALITY BELONGS TO THE WHOLE TRINITY. AUGUSTINE: The apostle Paul was not only referring to the Father when he said, "Who alone has immortality."[18] He was referring to the one and only God, which is the Trinity itself. For that which is itself eternal life is not mortal according to any changeableness. Therefore the Son of God, because "he is eternal life,"[19] is also himself understood with the Father, where it is said, "Who only has immortality."[20] For we, too, are made partakers[21] of this eternal life and become, in our own measure, immortal. But the eternal life itself, of which we are made partakers, is one thing; we ourselves, who, by partaking of it, shall live eternally, are another. For if he had said, "Whom in his own time the Father will show, who is the blessed and only potentate, the King of kings and Lord of lords; who only has immortality,"[22] not even then would it be necessarily understood that the Son is excluded. For neither has the Son separated the Father from himself, because he himself, speaking elsewhere with the voice of wisdom (for he himself is the Wisdom of God),[23] says, "I alone compassed the circuit of heaven."[24] And therefore it is even more unnecessary that the words "who has immortality" should be understood of the Father alone, omitting the Son, when they are said thus: "That you keep this commandment without spot, unrebukeable, until the appearing of our Lord Jesus Christ: whom in his own time he will show, who is the blessed and only potentate,

the King of kings and Lord of lords; who only has immortality, dwelling in the light that no one can approach; whom no one has seen or can see: to whom be honor and power everlasting. Amen."[25] In these words neither the Father, nor the Son nor the Holy Spirit is specially named, but the blessed and only potentate, the King of kings and Lord of lords; in other words, the one and only and true God, the Trinity itself. ON THE TRINITY 1.6.10.[26]

24:12 Taking Root in an Honored People

SCRIPTURE CONCEALS A TREASURE. ORIGEN: Here we must inquire separately as to the field and the treasure hidden in it, and in what sense the person who has found this hidden treasure goes away with joy and sells all that he has in order to buy that field.[27]. . . I believe, based on the context, that the field is the Scripture planted with what appears in the historical witnesses, the law and the prophets, and the rest of the thoughts. For the planting of the words in the whole of Scripture is great and varied. "The treasure hidden in the field," however, is the thoughts concealed and lying under that which is obvious, "of wisdom hidden in a mystery,"[28] "even Christ, in whom are all the treasures of wisdom and knowledge hidden."[29] COMMENTARY ON MATTHEW 10.5.[30]

24:14 Growing Tall Like a Palm Tree

THE SYMBOL OF MARTYRS. QUODVULTDEUS: The place that offered rest to this people, with its twelve springs and seventy palm trees,[31] has had a sacred meaning in our mysteries. In fact, after the baptism of the twelve apostles, who are our springs, spouts of pure doctrine overflow to fill hearts. The sacred psalm thus resounds,

---

[17]CTP 29:90-91. [18]1 Tim 6:16. [19]1 Jn 5:20. [20]1 Tim 6:16. [21]See Heb 12:8. [22]See 1 Tim 6:15-16. [23]1 Cor 1:24. [24]Sir 24:5 (24:8 Vg). [25]1 Tim 6:14-16. [26]NBA 4:21; NPNF 1 3:22**. [27]Mt 13:44. [28]See 1 Cor 2:7. [29]Col 2:3. [30]CTP 145:86-87; ANF 9:416**. [31]See Ex 15:27.

"In the churches, bless the Lord God from the springs of Israel."[32] By the seventy palm trees is symbolized the whole number of the thousands of martyrs who, fighting for the truth to death, receive the palm of the heavenly calling.[33] In the Apocalypse the apostle John speaks of them thusly: "I saw an enormous throng whom no one could count, from every tribe, people and tongue. They were clothed in white garments and had palms in their hands,"[34] palms that Wisdom, that palm that rises at Kadesh,[35] gave to the victors. THE BOOK OF PROMISES AND PREDICTIONS OF GOD 1.38.55.[36]

24:21 *Hungering and Thirsting for More*

THE TRUE FOOD GIVEN BY CHRIST. AUGUSTINE: Christ is for you both the shepherd and the door;[37] he is both the pasture and the provider. "I alone am the door of the sheep," I declare. "The one who enters through me I will accept. He will be able to come and go and to find the pastures."[38] The pastures the good Shepherd has prepared for you and where he has placed you are not those various sweet, mixed grasses that you love, which are here one minute and gone the next according to the changing of the seasons. The Word of God is your pasture, and its commandments are the sweet fields where you graze. Those pastures were savored by the one who sang to God, "How sweet are your words to my palate, more than honey in my mouth."[39] The same person refers to these pastures when addressing the sheep of the Lord: "Taste and see how sweet the Lord is."[40] Therefore, read the laws of the Decalogue of the Old Testament where they tell us "not to kill, not to steal, not to speak false testimony,"[41] and those that follow. Read the New Testament's praise of these commandments: "Blessed are the poor in spirit, for theirs is the kingdom of heaven. Blessed are the meek, for they shall inherit the earth,"[42] and those that follow, and still many more transmitted from the prophets and the apostles. These are the pastures referred to when the Shepherd turns and exclaims to the sheep, "Work for food that does not perish."[43] It does not perish because the Word of God remains forever.[44] The Word of the Lord is your food, indeed, not only food but also drink. Thus, through the prophet, he addresses the people of old: "However many partake of me will still be hungry, and however many drink of me will still have thirst."[45] And referring directly to himself he says the same thing: "My flesh is real food, my blood is real drink."[46] These pastures are found next to the water[47] that recreates, and these pastures and water are found only in the catholic church. Here your pastures are found in the commandments of life, here is found the fountain of water that flows to eternal life.[48] Those streams will renew you when you come to be baptized in order to be restored in Christ. This is the water that must water your pastures so that you can grow; only the baptism of Christ produces fruits from the commandments, and only these nourish us so that we may be satisfied. SERMON 366.3.[49]

---

[32]Ps 68:27 (67:27 LXX). [33]See Phil 3:14. [34]Rev 7:9. [35]Sir 24:14 (24:18 Vg). [36]CTP 82:116. [37]See Jn 10:7, 11, 14. [38]Jn 10:9. [39]Ps 119:103 (118:103 LXX). [40]Ps 34:9 (33:9 LXX). [41]Ex 20:13-16. [42]Mt 5:3-4. [43]Jn 6:27. [44]See Is 40:8. [45]Sir 24:21 (24:29 Vg). [46]Jn 6:56. [47]See Ps 23:2 (22:2 LXX). [48]See Jn 4:14. [49]NBA 34:455-57; WSA 3 10:289-90**.

24:23-34* WISDOM AND THE LAW

[23]*All this is the book of the covenant of the Most High God,*
    the law which Moses commanded us
    as an inheritance for the congregations of Jacob.[d]
[25]*It fills men with wisdom, like the Pishon,*
    and like the Tigris at the time of the first fruits.
[26]*It makes them full of understanding, like the Euphrates,*
    and like the Jordan at harvest time.
[27]*It makes instruction shine forth like light,*
    like the Gihon at the time of vintage.
[28]*Just as the first man did not know her perfectly,*
    the last one has not fathomed her;
[29]*for her thought is more abundant than the sea,*
    and her counsel deeper than the great abyss.

[30]*I went forth like a canal from a river*
    and like a water channel into a garden.
[31]*I said, "I will water my orchard*
    and drench my garden plot";
and lo, my canal became a river,
    and my river became a sea.
[32]*I will again make instruction shine forth like the dawn,*
    and I will make it shine afar;
[33]*I will again pour out teaching like prophecy,*
    and leave it to all future generations.
[34]*Observe that I have not labored for myself alone,*
    but for all who seek instruction.[e]

d Other authorities add [24]*"Do not cease to be strong in the Lord, cleave to him so that he may strengthen you; the Lord Almighty alone is God, and besides him there is no savior."* e Gk it * Sir 24:32-47 Vg.

OVERVIEW: The five rivers make the earth fruitful and cleanse it like the preaching of Christ's disciples (RABANUS MAURUS).

24:25-27 The Pishon, the Tigris, the Euphrates, the Jordan and the Gihon

THE FIVE RIVERS REPRESENT THE PREACHING OF THE GOSPEL. RABANUS MAURUS: We will first speak of the nature itself of the rivers, according to what we have learned from writers in the natural sciences, so as to then expound their allegories. The Pishon[1] is a river that is also called the Ganges,[2] which flows out of paradise

[1]See Gen 2:11. [2]The identification of the Pishon with the Ganges is very common and is already used by Flavius Josephus, who affirms also that its name means "multitude."

toward the regions of India. Pishon means "multitude," since the river is formed from the confluence of ten large rivers. The Ganges received its name from king Gangaro of India. It is also said that it has floods like those of the Nile, inundating the lands of the East. The Tigris is a river of Mesopotamia that flows out of paradise and runs toward Assyria,[3] and after many bends it empties into the Dead Sea. It received this name because of its velocity, which is like that beast called the tiger, which runs with great agility.[4] The Euphrates is a river of Mesopotamia, full of gems, that springs from paradise[5] and flows across Babylon. It receives its name from the harvests, that is, from its fruitfulness, since in Hebrew *Euphrata* means "fertility,"[6] and it irrigates some parts of Mesopotamia like the Nile does Alexandria. Sallust, a very reliable author, says that the Tigris and the Euphrates rise at the same source in Armenia and, following separate courses, move away from each other leaving a space of many miles, and that the land they embrace is called Mesopotamia.[7] The Jordan is a river of Judea that receives its name from two sources, one of which is called Ghor and the other Dan. These begin at a great distance from each other but then flow together into a single bed, called the Jordan from that point on.[8] It begins at the feet of Mount Lebanon and separates Judea from Arabia, and after a sinuous course it flows into the Dead Sea. The Gihon River flows out of paradise and encircles all of Ethiopia.[9] It was given this name because it irrigates the entire land of Egypt with its floods. *Ge* in Greek is the same as "earth" in Latin.[10] The Egyptians call it the Nile for the silt that it carries and that causes fertility: for this

reason the Nile is called *Niam ciaon*, and previously in Latin it was called *Melo*. It makes its appearance in the Nile lake, from which it enters Egypt from the south; there it encounters winds from the north that make the waters regress, swelling and flooding Egypt. The identification of the four rivers of paradise, which come from a single source,[11] with the wisdom of the king born of David, indicates that the four Gospels proceed from our Lord Jesus Christ, true Son of God and also true Son of man, that is, of David, since he took flesh from David's descendant. And the Gospels irrigate all the lands of the peoples with their preaching, so that Christ's faithful might cause many fruits of virtue to germinate. The course of the Jordan also comes from the same source, since the sacrament of baptism has come into the world that the offenses of the human race might be purified by its administration. It sends forth discipline as light, since its precepts give the light of eternal life to those who follow it faithfully. For this reason, when Christ sent his disciples to teach and baptize the nations after his resurrection, he said to them in the Gospel, "Go therefore and teach all nations, baptizing them in the name of the Father and of the Son and of the Holy Spirit, teaching them to observe all that I have commanded you. See, I am with you all days, to the end of the world."[12] ON ECCLESIASTICUS 6.2.[13]

---

[3]See Gen 2:14. [4]This etymology is traditional but false. [5]See Gen 2:14. [6]This interpretation is traditional and is used already by Philo of Alexandria. [7]Sallust *Histories* 4.77. [8]This interpretation is traditional, even if it is poorly attested. [9]See Gen 2:13. [10]This interpretation is possible only in Greek. Its origin is unknown. [11]See Gen 2:10. [12]Mt 28:19-20. [13]PL 109:942-43.

25:1-2* PROVERBS

¹*My soul takes pleasure in three things,*
   *and they are beautiful in the sight of the Lord and of men:*ᶠ
agreement between brothers, friendship between neighbors,
   and a wife and husband who live in harmony.
²*My soul hates three kinds of men,*
   and I am greatly offended at their life:
a beggar who is proud, a rich man who is a liar,
   and an adulterous old man who lacks good sense.

f Syr Vg: Gk *In three things I was beautified and I stood in beauty before the Lord and men*   * Sir 25:1-4 Vg.

OVERVIEW: Pride is an insidious danger, even for the ministers of the Lord (ORIGEN).

25:2 Pride, Deceit, Adultery

FEAR OF ARROGANCE. ORIGEN: Each of us, however small, however insignificant, even if he possesses no standing in the world, can be afflicted by the vice of pride. And nothing is as base and detestable, as Scripture says, as a proud poor person or a mendacious rich person. Sometimes this sickness of pride penetrates not only among the poor but assails even the very order of priests and Levites. At times we find it even among us, who are put forth as examples of humility and gathered around the altar as a mirror for those who watch, and yet among whom the vice of arrogance sends its stench. Thus it happens that from the altar of the Lord, which should burn with the sweet aroma of incense, emanates the pestilent odor of pride and self-importance. HOMILIES ON THE BOOK OF JUDGES 3.2.[1]

[1]CTP 101:83-84.

25:3-6* THE ELDERS

³*You have gathered nothing in your youth;*
   how then can you find anything in your old age?
⁴*What an attractive thing is judgment in gray-haired men,*

and for the aged to possess good counsel!
⁵How attractive is wisdom in the aged,
    and understanding and counsel in honorable men!
⁶Rich experience is the crown of the aged,
    and their boast is the fear of the Lord.

* Sir 25:5-8 Vg.

OVERVIEW: Not all elders are worth following (CASSIAN).

25:3 Gathering Nothing in Your Youth

WORTHY AND UNWORTHY ELDERS. JOHN CASSIAN: Just as young people are not all fervent in the Spirit in the same way and not all are completely formed in learning and good morals, so also old people are not always found equally perfect and exemplary. In fact, the wealth of old people is not to be measured by gray hairs but by their diligence in youth and the rewards of their past hard work. For, it says in Scripture, "How will you find in your old age the things you did not collect in your youth?" "For venerable old age is not longevity or counted by the number of years, but the understanding of a person is gray hairs, and a spotless life is old age."[1] Therefore, we are not to follow in the steps or embrace the traditions and advice of every old person whose head is covered with gray hairs and whose age is his sole claim to respect. Rather, we should only follow those whom we find to have distinguished themselves in youth in an approved and praiseworthy way—those who have been trained not in self-assurance but in the tradition of the elders. CONFERENCES 1.2.13.[2]

---

[1]Wis 4:9. [2]CTP 155:119-20; NPNF 2 11:313**.

25:7-11* BLESSEDNESS

⁷With nine thoughts I have gladdened my heart,
    and a tenth I shall tell with my tongue:
a man rejoicing in his children;
    a man who lives to see the downfall of his foes;
⁸happy is he who lives with an intelligent wife,
    and he who has not made a slip with his tongue,
    and he who has not served a man inferior to himself;
⁹happy is he who has gained good sense,
    and he who speaks to attentive listeners.
¹⁰How great is he who has gained wisdom!

> *But there is no one superior to him who fears the Lord.*
> [11] *The fear of the Lord surpasses everything;*
>   *to whom shall be likened the one who holds it fast?[g]*

g Other authorities add [12]*The fear of the Lord is the beginning of love for him, and faith is the beginning of clinging to him.*   * Sir 25:9-16 Vg.

OVERVIEW: Those who do not listen to the Word of God are likened to the poor (ORIGEN). The fear of God is a source of wisdom (PROSPER).

25:9 Speaking to Attentive Listeners

THOSE WHO DO NOT HEED THE WORD OF GOD. ORIGEN: "And I said, Perhaps they are poor since they have lost the capability, since they have not known the way of the Lord and the judgment of God. I will go to the strong, and I will speak to them."[1] Those who are strong in soul are objects of praise. This comes close to what the Greeks call the strength and the greatness of the rational soul. Thus, when anyone does something great and has worthwhile plans and always considers what is right and what must happen in order for him to live according to reason, without wanting to know anything abject and small, such a person has in the soul strength and greatness. But those others that the word disparaged at first since they were poor did not listen, the prophet says, they did not hear because they are poor, "I will go to the strong and I will speak to them,"[2] and if it is true that the blessed are meant when it says "the ears of those who listen," one is also blessed if he ever meets a strong and great listener. Therefore, after such things had been said in this way, knowing that with those who speak the damage is minor in comparison with those who although they listen do not receive admonition, seeing also that Jeremiah accused them of poverty of spirit and thoughts, let us ask to receive from God power and greatness as the word grows in us so that we are able to hear the sacred and holy words. HOMILIES ON JEREMIAH 6.3.[3]

25:11 The Fear of the Lord Surpasses Everything

FEAR OF GOD IS A SOURCE OF WISDOM. PROSPER OF AQUITAINE: "The fear of the Lord is the beginning of wisdom."[4] This fear, which results from some type of frightening experience, renders one willing who began by being previously afraid, and not only willing but also wise. For thus it is written, "Happy are those to whom it has been granted to have the fear of God."[5] What could possibly render the soul more blessed than this fear that is the parent and master of wisdom? The will is filled with the devotion that springs from wisdom and progresses from that same fear with which it began and that provoked grace. When, therefore, this fear becomes instilled in us with the force of great terror, this does not mean that it extinguishes reason or lessens our intelligence; rather, the haze that has hovered over our mind is removed, yes, and the will that was at first depraved and taken prisoner becomes right and free. For just as the spirit does not receive virtue if it has not received the beam of the true light, so grace does not confer anything to the one on whom it calls if the eyes of the will have not been opened. THE CALL OF ALL NATIONS 2.27.[6]

---

[1]Jer 5:4-5. [2]Jer 5:5. [3]CTP 123:95-96; FC 97:66-67**. [4]Prov 9:10. [5]Sir 25:11 (25:15 Vg). [6]CTP 143:160-61; ACW 14:136**.

25:13–26:18* WOMEN

¹³*Any wound, but not a wound of the heart!*
   Any wickedness, but not the wickedness of a wife!
¹⁴*Any attack, but not an attack from those who hate!*
   And any vengeance, but not the vengeance of enemies!
¹⁵*There is no venom^h worse than a snake's venom,^h*
   and no wrath worse than an enemy's wrath.

¹⁶*I would rather dwell with a lion and a dragon*
   than dwell with an evil wife.
¹⁷*The wickedness of a wife changes her appearance,*
   and darkens her face like that of a bear.
¹⁸*Her husband takes his meals among the neighbors,*
   and he cannot help sighingⁱ bitterly.
¹⁹*Any iniquity is insignificant compared to a wife's iniquity;*
   may a sinner's lot befall her!
²⁰*A sandy ascent for the feet of the aged—*
   such is a garrulous wife for a quiet husband.
²¹*Do not be ensnared by a woman's beauty,*
   and do not desire a woman for her possessions.^j
²²*There is wrath and impudence and great disgrace*
   when a wife supports her husband.
²³*A dejected mind, a gloomy face,*
   and a wounded heart are caused by an evil wife.
Drooping hands and weak knees
   are caused by the wife who does not make her husband happy.
²⁴*From a woman sin had its beginning,*
   and because of her we all die.
²⁵*Allow no outlet to water,*
   and no boldness of speech in an evil wife.
²⁶*If she does not go as you direct,*
   separate her from yourself.

26 *Happy is the husband of a good wife;*
   the number of his days will be doubled.
²*A loyal wife rejoices her husband,*
   and he will complete his years in peace.
³*A good wife is a great blessing;*

she will be granted among the blessings of the man who fears the Lord.
⁴Whether rich or poor, his heart is glad,
    and at all times his face is cheerful.
⁵Of three things my heart is afraid,
    and of a fourth I am frightened:ᵏ
The slander of a city, the gathering of a mob,
    and false accusation—all these are worse than death.
⁶There is grief of heart and sorrow when a wife is envious of a rival,
    and a tongue-lashing makes it known to all.
⁷An evil wife is an ox yoke which chafes;
    taking hold of her is like grasping a scorpion.
⁸There is great anger when a wife is drunken;
    she will not hide her shame.
⁹A wife's harlotry shows in her lustful eyes,
    and she is known by her eyelids.
¹⁰Keep strict watch over a headstrong daughter,
    lest, when she finds liberty, she use it to her hurt.
¹¹Be on guard against her impudent eye,
    and do not wonder if she sins against you.
¹²As a thirsty wayfarer opens his mouth
    and drinks from any water near him,
so will she sit in front of every post
    and open her quiver to the arrow.

¹³A wife's charm delights her husband,
    and her skill puts fat on his bones.
¹⁴A silent wife is a gift of the Lord,
    and there is nothing so precious as a disciplined soul.
¹⁵A modest wife adds charm to charm,
    and no balance can weigh the value of a chaste soul.
¹⁶Like the sun rising in the heights of the Lord,
    so is the beauty of a good wife in her well-ordered home.
¹⁷Like the shining lamp on the holy lampstand,
    so is a beautiful face on a stately figure.
¹⁸Like pillars of gold on a base of silver,
    so are beautiful feet with a steadfast heart.ˡ

h Cn: Gk *head* i Other authorities read *and listening he sighs* j Heb Syr: Some Gk authorities read *for her beauty* k The Greek of this line is uncertain l Other authorities add verses 19-27 * Sir 25:17–26:24 Vg.

OVERVIEW: Death is an inherited punishment that was abolished by Christ. The wound in Christ's side makes up for the sin of the one who was born from man's side (AUGUSTINE). Woman was created as a help to man (CHRYSOSTOM). A good wife is a gift from God (EUSEBIUS).

25:19 A Wife's Iniquity

CHRIST ABOLISHED DEATH AS A PUNISH-

ment. Augustine: Our death comes as a punishment we have been given to drink. We have received this from the stock of our origin as human branches spreading out from the root. The first Adam deserved this because of sin.[1] "Sin had its beginning from a woman," as it says in Scripture, "and because of her we all die."[2] And again: "Because of a single human being sin has entered into the world, and death through sin; thus death has caught up all of humanity because all have sinned."[3] Thus in our nature there is present both guilt and punishment. God created our nature immune from guilt, and, if it had persisted without guilt, it would not then have had to experience the punishment. From our origin we have contracted this, and many other evils are derived from it as well. Therefore guilt and punishment are present in our nature: in the flesh of Jesus there was punishment without guilt because he came and abolished the guilt and the punishment. Sermon 299.8.[4]

The Wound in Christ's Side. Augustine: Since it has been written, "Sin had its beginning from the woman, and this is why all die,"[5] remember from which member the woman was taken and notice where the Lord was hit by the spear. Remember, I say, our primitive condition because it was not in vain, in fact, that I previously mentioned, "Our old self has been crucified with him so that the body of sin might be destroyed and we would no longer be enslaved to sin."[6] Eve, from whom sin had its beginning, was formed by drawing her from the side of the man.[7] While she was drawn from his side, he lay there asleep; Christ was hanging and dead on the cross when he was wounded.[8] To sleep and to die are closely related, and thus so are these two sides, Adam's side and Christ's side; the Lord was wounded where our sins originated. But from that side Eve was formed who in her sinning procured death for us; from Christ's side, however, the church was formed that brought us back to life by giving us birth. Sermon 336.5.[9]

25:24 Sin's Beginning

Woman Created as a Helper for Man. John Chrysostom: "How is it," one could say, "that Scripture calls a helper she who was a hindrance? In fact it says, 'Let us make a helper like him.' "[10] And I would ask you: how can she be a helper who deprived the man of such security and drove him out of that wonderful existence in paradise, casting him into the tumult of the present life? A schemer does this, not a helper! "Woman," it says, "was the beginning of sin, and because of her we all die." And blessed Paul says, "Adam was not deceived. It was the woman who, being deceived, transgressed."[11] How, then, can she be a helper who put the man at the mercy of death? How could she be a helper who brought it about that the children of God, which is to say all of the inhabitants of the earth, are submerged in death together with the beasts, the birds and all the other animals?[12] Would not the woman have caused the ruin of righteous Job,[13] if he had not been truly a man?[14] Was it not the woman who brought about Sampson's ruin?[15] Was it not a woman who did her best that the whole Hebrew people take up the worship of Baal of Peor and was slaughtered at the hands of her brothers?[16] And who more than anyone else consigned Ahab to the devil,[17] and before him Solomon,[18] despite his wisdom and fame? Even now, do not women often lead their husbands to offend God? Did not the wise man say, perhaps for this reason, "Any kind of evil is small, compared with the evil of a woman"? "How is it then," you ask me, "that God said, 'Let us make a helper like him'?[19] God does not lie." Nor do I say so—never! She was made for that purpose and reason, but like her companion, she did not

---

[1]See 1 Cor 15:45. [2]Sir 25:24 (25:33 Vg). [3]Rom 5:12. [4]NBA 33:381; WSA 3 8:235-36**. [5]Sir 25:23 (25:33 Vg). [6]Rom 6:6. [7]Cf. Gen 2:21. [8]See Jn 19:33-34. [9]NBA 33:957; WSA 3 9:269-70**. [10]Gen 2:18. [11]1 Tim 2:14. [12]See Gen 7:21-22. [13]See Job 2:9-10. [14]See Job 1:1. [15]See Judg 16:17-21. [16]See Num 25:1-5, 18. [17]See 1 Kings 16:29-31 (3 Kings 16:29-31 lxx). [18]See 1 Kings 11:1-2 (3 Kings 11:1-2 lxx). [19]Gen 2:18.

want to remain in the dignity that was hers. The man was created by God in his image and likeness. Indeed, God said, "Let us make the man in our image and likeness,"[20] just as he said, "Let us make him a helper."[21] Once created however, the man immediately lost both of these prerogatives. He knew how to keep neither the image nor the likeness (and how could he have, if he gave himself over to absurd desire, was prey to deception and was unable to overcome pleasure?). To his disgrace, the image was taken from him for all time to come. ON VIRGINITY 46.1-3.[22]

26:3 A Good Wife Is a Great Blessing

A GOOD WIFE IS A GIFT FROM GOD. EUSEBIUS: "Your wife like a fruitful vine."[23] This is given to him who, though still imperfect, fears the Lord, but it does not hold for one who loves him with all his soul, all his heart and all his strength.[24] For him, there are "those things that eye has not seen," etc.[25] To one who fears the Lord is given a consort of whom it is said, "A good wife is good fate" and "A strong woman, who can find her?"[26] She is more precious than the most costly stones.[27] An evil consort is wrath that comes from God. COMMENTARY ON THE PSALMS 5.127.[28]

---

[20]Gen 1:26. [21]Gen 2:18. [22]CTP 4:213-215. [23]Ps 128:3 (127:3 LXX). [24]See Mk 12:30 par. [25]1 Cor 2:9. The meaning of this passage is that a woman, even when she is very good, is an imperfect gift compared with the gifts that God promises to his elected ones. [26]Prov 31:10. [27]See Prov 3:15. [28]CTP 177:452.

26:28* THINGS THAT GRIEVE

[28]*At two things my heart is grieved,
    and because of a third anger comes over me:
a warrior in want through poverty,
    and intelligent men who are treated contemptuously;
a man who turns back from righteousness to sin—
    the Lord will prepare him for the sword!*

* Sir 26:25-27 Vg.

OVERVIEW: The one who converts without any hope of leaving sin behind is left with the sin (CHRYSOSTOM).

WITHOUT HOPE, WE REMAIN IN OUR SIN. JOHN CHRYSOSTOM: For who would choose to fatigue himself if was not to gain any good from his labor? So then he also who sows words, and tears, and confession, unless he does this with a good hope, will not be able to desist from sinning, being still held down by the evil of despair. But just as that farmer who despairs of any crop of fruit will not in the future hinder any of those things that damage the seeds, so also he who sows his confession with tears but does not expect any advantage for this will not be able to overthrow those things that spoil repentance. And what does spoil repentance is being again entangled in the same evils. "For there is one," we read, "who builds, and one who pulls down; what have they gained more than toil? He who is dipped in water because of contact with a dead body and then touches it again, what has he gained by his washing?"[1] Even so if someone fasts because of his sins and goes his way again and does the same things, who will listen to his prayer? And again we read, "If someone goes back from righteousness to sin, the Lord will prepare him for the sword,"[2] and, "As a dog when he has returned to his vomit and become repugnant, so is a fool who by his wickedness has returned to his sin."[3] LETTER TO THE FALLEN THEODORE 1.20.[4]

---

[1]Sir 34:23-26; see Prov 18:17. [2]Sir 26:19. [3]Prov 26:11. [4]CTP 174:108; NPNF 1 9:108**.

26:29–27:3* COMMERCE

[29]*A merchant can hardly keep from wrongdoing,
  and a tradesman will not be declared innocent of sin.*
27 [1]*Many have committed sin for a trifle,[m]
  and whoever seeks to get rich will avert his eyes.*
[2]*As a stake is driven firmly into a fissure between stones,
  so sin is wedged in between selling and buying.*
[3]*If a man is not steadfast and zealous in the fear of the Lord,
  his house will be quickly overthrown*

m One ancient authority reads *gain*   * Sir 26:28–27:4 Vg.

OVERVIEW: Commerce and riches are not reproachful when they are not used in wicked ways (RABANUS MAURUS).

26:29 The Innocent Merchant

TRADE AND RICHES SHOULD BE USED FOR GOOD. RABANUS MAURUS: If we do not examine it closely, this passage seems contradictory and problematical. If in fact every merchant or shopkeeper merits condemnation, then no one who practices a trade can escape the same punishment. Is not a transaction the attempt to sell something at a higher price than what it cost? Elsewhere, we read in the *Lives of the Fathers*[1] that Paphnutius,[2] a very holy man, was compared by a divine revelation with a merchant, and even now we find some in the church who are dedicated to business but are very highly thought of. What is condemned is evil action, not honest activity, as when we read

---

[1]A collection of short stories about the monks of the Egyptian desert. [2]Of Thebes. Also known as Paphnutius the Confessor, who was a disciple of Saint Anthony.

that a rich person will not enter the kingdom of heaven,[3] though Job and the patriarchs Abraham, Isaac and Jacob were very rich.[4] Therefore, only those merchants are considered blameworthy who, corrupted by an immoderate desire for money, never think of the Lord's justice and fix their prices more to cheat people than to make an honest gain. Such were cast out of the temple by the Lord with the words, "Do not make of my Father's house a marketplace and a den of thieves."[5] ON ECCLESIASTICUS 6.5.[6]

---

[3]See Mt 19:23-24; Mk 10:25; Lk 18:24-25. [4]These Old Testament patriarchs are often quoted by the Fathers as examples of rich people who used properly their riches. [5]See Jn 2:16 and Mt 21:13; Mk 11:17; Lk 19:46. [6]PL 109:960.

27:4-7* THOUGHTS AND WORDS

[4]*When a sieve is shaken, the refuse remains;*
  so a man's filth remains in his thoughts.
[5]*The kiln tests the potter's vessels;*
  so the test of a man is in his reasoning.
[6]*The fruit discloses the cultivation of a tree;*
  so the expression of a thought discloses the cultivation of a man's mind.
[7]*Do not praise a man before you hear him reason,*
  for this is the test of men.

* Sir 27:5-8 Vg.

OVERVIEW: Christians do not complain when they are tested for their purification (CYPRIAN). Afflictions are a test for the just and a correction for sinners (GAUDENTIUS).

27:5 Testing the Potter's Vessels

CHRISTIANS DO NOT COMPLAIN WHEN THEY ARE TESTED. CYPRIAN OF CARTHAGE: After shipwrecks, after scourgings, after many and terrible tortures of the flesh and body,[1] the apostle Paul says that he is not hurt but benefited by his adversity because through such terrible affliction he might more truly be proved. "There was given to me," he says, "a thorn in the flesh, the messenger of Satan to buffet me, that I should not be lifted up. I sought the Lord three times about this so that it might leave me; and he said to me, My grace is sufficient for you, for strength is made perfect in weakness."[2] When, therefore, weakness and inefficiency and any destruction seize us, then our strength is made perfect. Then, if our faith is put to the test, it will stand fast and receive a crown, as it is written: "The furnace tries the vessels of the potter, and the trial of tribulation tests just people." This, in short, is the difference between us and others who do not know God, that in misfor-

---

[1]See 2 Cor 11:23-33. [2]2 Cor 12:7-10.

tune they complain and murmur, while adversity does not call us away from the truth of virtue and faith but strengthens us by its suffering. ON MORTALITY 13.[3]

AFFLICTIONS ARE FOR OUR GOOD. GAUDENTIUS OF BRESCIA: If you are a sinner, recognize that it is for your correction that you have been afflicted, or at least for your purification. . . . If, rather, you are righteous (but do not presume to attribute this title to yourself), then you will understand that your sufferings happen so that you might receive glory from the trial. It is written, "As the furnace tests what it receives from the potter, so the temptation of trials tests the righteous." Thus the apostle also says, "Trials lead to patience, patience produces perseverance, and perseverance, hope. And hope does not deceive."[4] In this world, therefore, various pains are inflicted to test the righteous, to correct sinners or to punish the impious. These blows bring death to some; to others, salvation. Precisely for this reason the following is written in the book of Psalms, with great acuity, "The death of sinners is miserable, and those who hate the righteous will be condemned."[5] Here it considers miserable the death of those sinners who, desiring to remain in the wickedness of their sins, hate the righteous One who afflicts them. Of those who can be corrected, it says, "There are many lashes for sinners."[6] Finally, of the saints it says, "Many are the trials of the righteous."[7] It is not at all difficult, for anyone who has the Spirit, to discern these differences based on the fruit of each, as the Lord says, "By their fruits you will know them."[8] TO BENIVOLUS 42–43.[9]

---

[3]CTP 42:30-31. [4]Rom 5:3-5. [5]Ps 34:22 (33:22 LXX). [6]Ps 32:10 (31:10 LXX). [7]Ps 34:20 (33:20 LXX). [8]Mt 7:16. [9]CTP 129:29-30.

27:8-15* JUSTICE

[8]*If you pursue justice, you will attain it*
   and wear it as a glorious robe.
[9]*Birds flock with their kind;*
   so truth returns to those who practice it.
[10]*A lion lies in wait for prey;*
   so does sin for the workers of iniquity.

[11]*The talk of the godly man is always wise,*
   but the fool changes like the moon.
[12]*Among stupid people watch for a chance to leave,*
   but among thoughtful people stay on.
[13]*The talk of fools is offensive,*
   and their laughter is wantonly sinful.

[14]The talk of men given to swearing makes one's hair stand on end,
    and their quarrels make a man stop his ears.
[15]The strife of the proud leads to bloodshed,
    and their abuse is grievous to hear.

* Sir 27:9-16 Vg.

OVERVIEW: Inconstancy of the soul is like epilepsy (ORIGEN), but God never forsakes anyone, not even the fool (AUGUSTINE).

27:11 Changing Like the Moon

SPIRITUAL EPILEPSY. ORIGEN: Epilepsy attacks the sufferers at considerable intervals, during which he who suffers from it seems in no way different from the person in good health, at the season when the epilepsy is not working on him. Similar disorders you may find in certain souls that are often supposed to be healthy in point of temperance and the other virtues—but then, sometimes, as if they were seized with a kind of epilepsy arising from their passions, they fall down from the position in which they seemed to stand[1] and are drawn away by the deceit of this world and other lusts.[2] Perhaps, therefore, you would not be in error if you said that such persons, so to speak, are epileptic spiritually, having been cast down by "the spiritual hosts of wickedness in the heavenly places."[3] They are often ill at the time when the passions attack their soul; at one time falling into the fire of burnings,[4] when, according to what is said in Hosea, they become adulterers, like a pan heated for the cooking from the burning flame;[5] and, at another time, into the water,[6] when the king of all the dragons in the waters[7] casts them down from the sphere where they appeared to breathe freely, so that they come into the depths of the waves of the sea of human life. This interpretation of ours in regard to the lunatic will be supported by him who says in the book of Wisdom with reference to the even temperament of the just person, "The discourse of a pious person is always wisdom," but, in regard to what we have said, "the fool changes as the moon." COMMENTARY ON MATTHEW 13.4.[8]

GOD DOES NOT ABANDON ANYONE. AUGUSTINE: "You have made perfect sun and moon."[9] The sun indicates spiritual people; the moon, carnal ones. As carnal as one is, may he not be forsaken and may he too be made perfect. The sun, as it were, is a wise person; the moon, as it were, is an unwise person. You have not however forsaken either one. For thus it is written, "A wise person endures as the sun, but a foolish person as the moon is changed."[10] What then? Because the sun endures, that is, because the wise person endures as the sun, a foolish person is changed like the moon. Is one who is still carnal, still unwise, to be forsaken? And where is that which has been said by the apostle, "To the wise and unwise a debtor I am"?[11] EXPOSITIONS OF THE PSALMS 73.19.[12]

---

[1]See 1 Cor 10:12. [2]See Mk 4:19. [3]See Eph 6:12. [4]See Mt 17:15. [5]Hos 7:4. [6]See Mt 17:15. [7]See Job 41:26. [8]CTP 151:26-28. [9]Ps 74:16. Augustine explains the Latin word *perfecisti* as "you have made perfect," whereas the normal meaning of the word is "you have accomplished, modeled." [10]Sir 27:11 (27:12 Vg). [11]Rom 1:14. [12]NBA 26:893.

27:16-21* SECRETS

¹⁶*Whoever betrays secrets destroys confidence,*
and he will never find a congenial friend.
¹⁷*Love your friend and keep faith with him;*
but if you betray his secrets, do not run after him.
¹⁸*For as a man destroys his enemy,*
so you have destroyed the friendship of your neighbor.
¹⁹*And as you allow a bird to escape from your hand,*
so you have let your neighbor go, and will not catch him again.
²⁰*Do not go after him, for he is too far off,*
and has escaped like a gazelle from a snare.
²¹*For a wound may be bandaged,*
and there is reconciliation after abuse,
but whoever has betrayed secrets is without hope.

* Sir 27:17-24 Vg.

OVERVIEW: Treason is a cause of despair, as we can see from Judas (Rabanus Maurus).

27:21 Without Hope

JUDAS'S DESPAIR. RABANUS MAURUS: Treachery is the worst evil, and of difficult remedy. This was shown by the example of Judas the traitor, of whom it was said through the prophet in the psalm, "Even the friend in whom I trusted, even he, who ate my bread, raises his heel against me."[1] One who despairs in horror at the consciousness of his own sin thinks more of the noose[2] than of the salutary medicine of repentance. This is why it is written about him, "He loved cursing: may it fall on him! He did not want blessing: may it be far from him!"[3] ON ECCLESIASTICUS 6.7.[4]

[1]Ps 41:10 (40:10 LXX). [2]Rabanus makes a word play on the word *laqueus*, which evokes both a trapped animal and Judas's suicide (see Mt 27:5). [3]Ps 109:17 (108:17 LXX). [4]PL 109:965.

27:22-29* HYPOCRISY

²²Whoever winks his eye plans evil deeds,
   and no one can keep him from them.
²³In your presence his mouth is all sweetness,
   and he admires your words;
but later he will twist his speech
   and with your own words he will give offense.
²⁴I have hated many things, but none to be compared to him;
   even the Lord will hate him.
²⁵Whoever throws a stone straight up throws it on his own head;
   and a treacherous blow opens up wounds.
²⁶He who digs a pit will fall into it,
   and he who sets a snare will be caught in it.
²⁷If a man does evil, it will roll back upon him,
   and he will not know where it came from.
²⁸Mockery and abuse issue from the proud man,ⁿ
   but vengeance lies in wait for him like a lion.
²⁹Those who rejoice in the fall of the godly will be caught in a snare,
   and pain will consume them before their death.

n Other authorities read *proud men*   * Sir 27:25-32 Vg.

OVERVIEW: The leaders of the Jews were punished for having killed Jesus (ORIGEN). Daniel is an image of Jesus since there were those who plotted for his death as well (QUODVULTDEUS).

27:25 Throwing Stones on One's Own Head

THE FATE OF THOSE WHO KILLED JESUS.
ORIGEN: Those who handed Jesus over were forsaken. The high priests ceased to exist, with no others coming after them. The scribes who condemned Jesus to death, their intelligence darkened and their minds blinded, were no longer able to see the meaning of the sacred text. All those who condemned Jesus to death were handed over to Christ's enemy, death. Those who mocked him in turn became the object of mockery when "Jerusalem was surrounded by armies" and its desolation drew near.[1] Those who scourged Jesus were themselves scourged and continue to be so, until "the fullness of the nations has come in."[2] In fact, "one who throws a rock in the air hits himself on the head." And all of this happened so that God's vigilance over them would cease and would be transferred to those who have been saved from among the nations, along with the "chosen remnant."[3] Indeed, "if the Lord of hosts had not left a remnant," they would already be "like Sodom," and they would have become like Gomorrah.[4] COMMENTARY ON MATTHEW 16.3.[5]

---

[1]See Lk 21:20. [2]Rom 11:25. [3]Rom 11:5. [4]See Is 1:9. [5]CTP 157:16-18.

27:26 Falling into a Pit

APPLICATION TO DANIEL AND JESUS. QUOD-
VULTDEUS: In the ninth vision[6] Darius the Mede
took the throne.[7] He set up 120 satraps in his
kingdom, commanded by three leaders, one
of whom was Daniel,[8] who had found favor in
the king's sight. Envious men, plotting a trick
against the servant of God, convinced the king
to command that for thirty days no prayer could
be offered to a god or a person but only to the
king, with the penalty that if someone transgressed the king's order he would be thrown
into the pit as food for the lions.[9] Although he
saw the posted decree, the prophet continued
to pray to his Lord three times a day, as was his
custom.[10] They arrested him as a rebel and took
him to the king, who, unable to save him from
their envy, entrusted the prophet to his God,
confessing that he only could save him from
death,[11] which is exactly what happened. In his
distress, the king would not eat, taking neither
food nor sleep, and at dawn he went in haste to
see Daniel.[12] Finding him alive and unhurt and
glorifying the true God, he ordered Daniel to be
taken from the pit and those who accused him to
be thrown in instead, and they were immediately
devoured in his presence.[13] In these events also
the prophecy was fulfilled: "One who digs a pit
for his neighbor will fall into it. And one who
lays a snare for his neighbor will perish in it."
And our Lord Jesus, in whom all of these figures
appeared, says by the mouth of the prophet,
"They have dug a pit before me and have fallen in
it themselves,"[14] and, "The Lord sent his mercy
and his truth and has freed my life from the
lions."[15] THE BOOK OF PROMISES AND PREDIC-
TIONS OF GOD 2.35.77.[16]

---

[6]See Dan 5:1-29. [7]See Dan 5:30. [8]See Dan 6:1-2. [9]See Dan
6:4-8. [10]See Dan 6:11. [11]See Dan 6:15-17. [12]See Dan 6:19-20.
[13]See Dan 6:21-25. [14]Ps 57:7 (56:7 LXX). [15]Ps 57:4-5 (56:4-5 LXX).
[16]CTP 82:208-9.

27:30–28:7* RESENTMENT

³⁰*Anger and wrath, these also are abominations,*
    and the sinful man will possess them.
28 *He that takes vengeance will suffer vengeance from the Lord,*
    and he will firmly establishᵒ his sins.
²*Forgive your neighbor the wrong he has done,*
    and then your sins will be pardoned when you pray.
³*Does a man harbor anger against another,*
    and yet seek for healing from the Lord?
⁴*Does he have no mercy toward a man like himself,*
    and yet pray for his own sins?
⁵*If he himself, being flesh, maintains wrath,*
    who will make expiation for his sins?

⁶Remember the end of your life, and cease from enmity,
    remember destruction and death, and be true to the commandments.
⁷Remember the commandments, and do not be angry with your neighbor;
    remember the covenant of the Most High, and overlook ignorance.

---

o Other authorities read *closely observe*   * Sir 27:33–28:9 Vg.

OVERVIEW: God urges us to reconciliation (CHRYSOSTOM) before we die, reminding us that there is no chance to be reconciled once death comes (BARSANUPHIUS AND JOHN).

28:3 Harboring Anger, Seeking Healing

RECONCILIATION IS URGED BY GOD. JOHN CHRYSOSTOM: If it is not right to trample on those who are chastised by God but to grieve with them, much more is it the case with those who have sinned against us. For this is love's sign; God prefers love to all things. For as in making the royal purple, the flowers and dyes that make up the color of the robe are considered the most precious, so here too, those virtues are the most precious that preserve love. But nothing maintains love so much as when we do not remember those who have sinned against us. But why? Did he not guard the other side as well? Why? Did he not drive the one that has done the wrong to the person who is wronged? Does he not send him from the altar to go and meet the other person, and after the reconciliation then invite him to the table?[1] But do not, therefore, wait for the other to come, since if you do so, you have lost everything. For to this intent most especially does he appoint to you an unspeakable reward, that you be the first to act before the other, since, if you are reconciled by his entreaties, the love is no longer the result of the divine command but of the other party's diligence. This is why you go away uncrowned while he receives the rewards.

What are you saying? Do you have an enemy and you are not ashamed? Why, isn't the devil enough of an enemy for us that we have to bring on ourselves those of our own race as well? Would that not even he had been minded to wage war against us! Would that not even he were a devil! Don't you know how great the pleasure is after reconciliation? For it does not appear great at all when we are at enmity. But it is sweeter to love someone who does us wrong than to hate him. That is what we learn after the enmity is done away with. Why then do we imitate the mad, devouring one another, warring against our own flesh? Hear even under the Old Testament how great regard there was for this: "The ways of vengeful people lead to death."[2] One person keeps his anger against another, and does he seek the healing of God? And yet God allowed an "eye for an eye" and a "tooth for a tooth,"[3] so how then does he find fault?" Because he allowed even those things, not that we should do them to one another, but so that through the fear of suffering we might abstain from the commission of a crime. And besides, those acts are the fruits of a short lived anger, but to remember injuries is the part of a soul that exercises itself in evil. But have you suffered evil? And yet, it was nothing so great as you will do to yourself by remembering injuries. HOMILIES ON THE GOSPEL OF MATTHEW 79.4-5.[4]

28:6 Remember the End of Your Life

IT IS USEFUL TO REMEMBER DEATH. BARSANUPHIUS AND JOHN: If one reminds himself that his soul is mortal and therefore strives to do good, is this not a voluntary gain? It is good to remind oneself of death, for thus one recognizes his own mortality and comes to realize that mor-

---

[1]See Mt 5:23-24. [2]Prov 12:28 LXX. [3]See Ex 21:24. [4]CTP 172:250-52; NPNF 1 10:478-79**.

tals will not live forever. For someone who is not eternal must surely abandon this world, even if by force. Therefore by continually remembering one's mortality the individual learns to do good according to his own free will. Thus, when one sees mortality before his eyes and does what is good, this is not the same as the one who is con-

tinually meditating on it and chooses to do good; rather, if it is out of impending fear of death, then what one does is out of necessity. BOOK OF LETTERS 639.[5]

---

[5]CTP 93:514; FC 114:218-19**.

28:8-12* STRIFE

[8]*Refrain from strife, and you will lessen sins;*
  for a man given to anger will kindle strife,
[9]*and a sinful man will disturb friends*
  and inject enmity among those who are at peace.
[10]*In proportion to the fuel for the fire, so will be the burning,*
  and in proportion to the obstinacy of strife will be the burning;[p]
in proportion to the strength of the man will be his anger,
  and in proportion to his wealth he will heighten his wrath.
[11]*A hasty quarrel kindles fire,*
  and urgent strife sheds blood.
[12]*If you blow on a spark, it will glow;*
  if you spit on it, it will be put out;
and both come out of your mouth.

---

p Other authorities place this line at the end of the verse, or omit it   * Sir 28:10-14 Vg.

OVERVIEW: Heretics and schismatics bring about quarrels and trouble on the church (RABANUS MAURUS).

28:9 Disturbing Friends, Ruining the Peace

HERETICS AND SCHISMATICS DISTURB THE CHURCH. RABANUS MAURUS: If we consider what a good peace is, it is easy to understand the evil of discord. If, in fact, "blessed are the peacemakers, for they will be called children of God,"[1]

there is no doubt that the contentious are evil and children of the devil, since, giving birth to enmities, they sow discord among those who are at peace. Principal among these are the heretics and schismatics who, defending their pernicious sects, are not afraid to provoke arguments and scandals. For this reason the apostle Paul exhorted Timothy with these words: "Avoid vain discussions, which are good for nothing but the

---

[1]Mt 5:8.

destruction of those who listen."[2] And, "Avoid
foolish and ignorant debates, knowing that
they breed quarrels. A servant of the Lord must
not be quarrelsome but meek toward all, apt to

teach, patient, gentle in reproof of those who oppose the truth."[3] ON ECCLESIASTICUS 6.8.[4]

[2]2 Tim 2:14. [3]2 Tim 2:23-25. [4]PL 109:970.

28:13-26* THE TONGUE

[13]Curse the whisperer and deceiver,
   for he has destroyed many who were at peace.
[14]Slander[q] has shaken many,
   and scattered them from nation to nation,
and destroyed strong cities,
   and overturned the houses of great men.
[15]Slander[q] has driven away courageous women,
   and deprived them of the fruit of their toil.
[16]Whoever pays heed to slander[r] will not find rest,
   nor will he settle down in peace.
[17]The blow of a whip raises a welt,
   but a blow of the tongue crushes the bones.
[18]Many have fallen by the edge of the sword,
   but not so many as have fallen because of the tongue.
[19]Happy is the man who is protected from it,
   who has not been exposed to its anger,
who has not borne its yoke,
   and has not been bound with its fetters;
[20]for its yoke is a yoke of iron,
   and its fetters are fetters of bronze;
[21]its death is an evil death,
   and Hades is preferable to it.
[22]It will not be master over the godly,
   and they will not be burned in its flame.
[23]Those who forsake the Lord will fall into its power;
   it will burn among them and will not be put out.
It will be sent out against them like a lion;
   like a leopard it will mangle them.

^{24}See that you fence in your property with thorns,
  lock up your silver and gold,
^{25}make balances and scales for your words,
  and make a door and a bolt for your mouth.
^{26}Beware lest you err with your tongue,^{s}
  lest you fall before him who lies in wait.

q Gk *a third tongue* r Gk *it* s Gk *with it* * Sir 28:15-30 Vg.

OVERVIEW: The tongue is more dangerous than weapons and poison (VALERIAN). There is a healing for the wounds of the body and a healing for the wounds of the soul (ORIGEN). We should cherish with humility and patience the gifts given by God (BARSANUPHIUS AND JOHN). It is not what he eats but what he says that makes a person impure (ORIGEN). There is hope for those who have malice toward another as long as it is not uttered (VALERIAN).

28:14 Slander

DANGERS OF THE TONGUE. VALERIAN OF CIMIEZ: The tongue, by nature restless, does no small amount of harm among mortals so that either it squanders an opportunity by saying too much or wreaks havoc by not saying anything for long periods of silence. But when do quarrels ignite, if the tongue is checked? Or what space is there for enmities where the poison of words has ceased? Indeed, the malicious tongue always acts in this way: it sows quarrels, incites hatreds and leads to death, as Solomon says on the matter: "The tongue has upset the peace of many. It has destroyed cities and ruined families."[1] They certainly are mistaken who think that there is nothing stronger than iron, or more deadly than poison: although these things by their nature would have a particular inclination to cause death, they nonetheless give way when compared with words. Indeed, nothing that is within one's power is more harmful or malicious than the tongue, once it is aroused. HOMILY 5.1.[2]

28:18 The Sword and the Tongue

BODILY WOUNDS AND SPIRITUAL WOUNDS. ORIGEN: If a wound is inflicted on the body or a bone is broken or a nerve center ruptured, wounds of this sort usually happen to bodies in the space of one hour and then are barely healed with great pain and suffering over a long period of time. For how much swelling and what great agony arises from the wounded spot? But now, if it happens that someone is repeatedly wounded in the same place or the same bone is broken more than once, by what tremendous pain and agony can this be healed and cured? And by what length of time is this brought to healing, if indeed it is even possible? And scarcely ever will one be cured in such a way that he avoids a physical infirmity or a nasty scar.

Pass now from the example of the body to the wounds of the soul. However often the soul sins, just that often it is wounded. And lest you be in doubt that it is wounded by sins, as if by arrows and swords, listen to the apostle when he admonishes us to take up "the shield of faith by which," he says, "you can extinguish all the flaming arrows of the evil one."[3] So you see that sins are the "arrows of the evil one," which are aimed at the soul. But not only does the soul suffer the wounds of arrows, but it also experiences fractures of its feet when "snares are prepared for its feet"[4] and when its "steps are made to trip."[5] So, by what length of time do you think that these wounds and others like them can be cured? O, if we could only see how with each sin our inner person is wounded, how bad words

[1]Sir 28:14 (28:16-17 Vg). [2]CTP 122:68-69. [3]Eph 6:16. [4]Ps 57:6. [5]Ps 37:31.

inflict a wound! Have you not read, they say, that "swords inflict wounds, but not as much as the tongue." The soul is wounded, then, even by the tongue; it is also wounded by evil thoughts and desires; but it is fractured and shattered by the works of sin. If we could see all this and feel the scars of a soul that has been wounded, we would certainly resist sin to death.[6] But now, just as those who are filled with a demon or the mentally insane do not perceive it when they are wounded, because they lack natural senses, so is it with us. Since we have become crazed by the desires of the world[7] or intoxicated with vices, we cannot feel the extent of the wounds or the extent of the grief we are bringing on our soul by sinning. And therefore it is perfectly consistent that the reckoning of the punishment, that is, of the medical treatment and cure, is extended over time and that for each wound the length of healing be prolonged as well, according to the nature of the wound.[8]

So then, the justice and kindness of God will also become evident in those very penalties of the soul. Let the one who hears this and has committed sin come to his senses and sin no more.[9] For conversion in the present life and a penance having been carried out fruitfully will bring swift medicine to wounds of this sort, since penance not only heals a past wound, but it does not allow the soul to be wounded further by sin. HOMILIES ON NUMBERS 8.1.6-8.[10]

28:24 Lock Up Your Silver and Gold

CHERISHING THE GIFTS GIVEN BY GOD.
BARSANUPHIUS AND JOHN: If those who receive silver coins from the king conserve them with zeal and care, they will remain shiny and clean. If instead they neglect them, they will not only rust but also may soon be lost. For the wise man has said, "Lock up your gold and your silver." And I am not only telling you to bind it with a firm faith but also to seal it with humility and the patience of perseverance by which the one who perseveres is saved.[11] What I am saying to

you, by God's permission, is an audacious thing. For the great mediator Jesus,[12] Son of the blessed Father, distributor of the holy and life-giving Spirit says to you through me, who am least of all, "Your many sins are forgiven you,"[13] from birth up until this very minute. In receiving this great and inexpressible joy,[14] you then love him with all your might,[15] displaying fruit worthy of repentance,[16] proclaiming with Saint Paul those melodious words, "Who will separate us from the love of Christ? Shall tribulation or distress, or hunger, or persecution, or nakedness, or danger, or fear or the sword?"[17] And again, "Because of you we are being put to death all day long; we are counted as sheep for the slaughterhouse. But in all these things we are more than conquerors through him who loved us. I am confident that neither death, nor life, neither angels, nor principalities, nor authorities, nor things present or things future, neither powers, nor height, nor depth nor anything else in all of creation will be able to separate us from the love of God that is in Christ Jesus our Lord."[18] Make sure you not only meditate on these things in what you say but also in what you do. For Jesus says, "By your patience your soul is acquired."[19] You have become worthy of a great dignity: perform great and worthy works of patience and thanksgiving through which come the expectation of perfection, in the name of the Father and of the Son and of the Holy Spirit. Amen. Think about these things continually and conscientiously, and you will taste their sweetness, as they become fragrant to your soul and the souls of those who are able to choose them. BOOK OF LETTERS 115.[20]

28:25 Balances and Scales for Your Words

[6]See Heb 12:4. [7]See 1 Jn 2:16. [8]Origen's purgatorial understanding of divine punishment is revealed here. See his *Commentary on Romans* 2.2.2; 7.5.10; 8.12.8; *On First Principles* 2.5.3; 2.10.6; *Homilies on Ezekiel* 1.2. [9]See Jn 8:11. [10]CTP 76:102-3; ACTHN 34*. [11]See Mt 10:22; Mk 13:13; Lk 21:19. [12]See Heb 8:6. [13]Lk 7:47-48; 5:20. [14]See 1 Pet 1:8. [15]See Mt 22:37; Mk 12:30; Lk 10:27; Deut 6:5. [16]See Mt 3:8. [17]Rom 8:35. [18]Rom 8:36-39. [19]Lk 21:19. [20]CTP 93:182-83; FC 113:134-35**.

ONE IS DEFILED BY HIS WORDS. ORIGEN: We are clearly taught by the Savior that when we read in Leviticus[21] and in Deuteronomy[22] concerning the precepts about clean and unclean meat—the carnal Jews[23] and the Ebionites,[24] who differ little from them, accuse us of disobeying these precepts—we are not to think that the scope of the Scripture is to be found in any superficial material understanding of them. If, in fact, it is not what enters the mouth that renders one unclean but what comes out of the mouth,[25] especially when the Savior in the Gospel of Mark said that "he makes all food clean,"[26] it is clear that we do not contaminate ourselves if we eat things that the Jews, wanting to be enslaved by the letter of the Law,[27] say are impure. But it is clear that we do contaminate ourselves when, although our lips should be bound with intelligence[28] and we ought to make for them what we call a balance and weight, we speak whatever comes to mind and talk about things that we should not discuss, which then become the source of sins. COMMENTARY ON MATTHEW 11.12.[29]

MALICE IN THOUGHT AND WORD. VALERIAN OF CIMIEZ: All evil certainly issues from the heart. However harmful in itself, though, this can easily be tolerated if what has been fed by wicked counsel has not led to quarrels. In such a case one suffers silently or simply closes himself in his house and remains quiet. In fact, the infirmity of evil thoughts can be healed to the same degree that what is conceived in the heart is restrained by a taciturn mouth. But once the tongue is loosed and it bursts forth, it is useless to seek a doctor. Indeed, there is no remedy for a misdeed in words, because no amount of tears can eliminate an injury that has entered through the ears and had its effect. Listen to the Lord, who says, "Make gates and bolts for your mouths, and a balance to weigh your words."[30] HOMILY 5.4.[31]

---

[21]See Lev 11. [22]See Deut 14. [23]See 1 Cor 10:18. [24]The Ebionites were an ancient Christian sect that kept the Jewish prescriptions. [25]Mt 5:11. [26]Mk 7:19. [27]See Rom 7:6. [28]See Prov 15:7. [29]CTP 145:215-17. [30]Sir 28:25 (28:28 Vg), variant. [31]CTP 122:72.

29:1-7* LENDING

[1]He that shows mercy will lend to his neighbor,
 and he that strengthens him with his hand keeps the commandments.
[2]Lend to your neighbor in the time of his need;
 and in turn, repay your neighbor promptly.
[3]Confirm your word and keep faith with him,
 and on every occasion you will find what you need.
[4]Many persons regard a loan as a windfall,
 and cause trouble to those who help them.
[5]A man will kiss another's hands until he gets a loan,
 and will lower his voice in speaking of his neighbor's money;
 but at the time for repayment he will delay,

and will pay in words of unconcern,
    and will find fault with the time.
[6]*If the lender[t] exerts pressure, he will hardly get back half,*
    and will regard that as a windfall.
If he does not, the borrower[u] has robbed him of his money,
    and he has needlessly made him his enemy;
he will repay him with curses and reproaches,
    and instead of glory will repay him with dishonor.
[7]*Because of such wickedness, therefore,[v] many have refused to lend;*
    they have been afraid of being defrauded needlessly.

t Gk he u Gk he v Other authorities read *It is not because of wickedness that* * Sir 29:1-10 Vg.

OVERVIEW: Those who do not accomplish bad actions are nevertheless worthy of reproach unless they have mercy (RABANUS MAURUS).

29:7 Afraid of Fraud

MERCY IS NECESSARY. RABANUS MAURUS: This statement refers to the attitude of those who do not desire to do evil with ill will but are reprehensible for the fact that they do not want to help others, out of fear of losing perishable things. To this sickness one must apply the remedy of mercy and charity and the recollection of that saying of the Lord that says, "Do not store up for yourselves treasure on earth, where moth and rust consume and where thieves break in and steal. Rather, store up for yourselves treasure in heaven, where neither moth nor rust consume, where thieves do not break in and steal."[1] And elsewhere one reads regarding riches what comes from the same charity, "To one who has will be given more, and he will have in abundance. But to one who has not, even what he has will be taken away."[2] ON ECCLESIASTICUS 6.10.[3]

[1]Mt 6:19-20. [2]Mt 25:29. [3]PL 109:974.

29:8-13* ALMS

[8]*Nevertheless, be patient with a man in humble circumstances,*
    and do not make him wait for your alms.
[9]*Help a poor man for the commandment's sake,*
    and because of his need do not send him away empty.
[10]*Lose your silver for the sake of a brother or a friend,*
    and do not let it rust under a stone and be lost.
[11]*Lay up your treasure according to the commandments of the Most High,*

and it will profit you more than gold.
[12]Store up almsgiving in your treasury,
*   and it will rescue you from all affliction;*
[13]more than a mighty shield and more than a heavy spear,
*   it will fight on your behalf against your enemy.*

* Sir 29:11-18 Vg, with many differences.

OVERVIEW: The other virtues are vain without almsgiving (AUGUSTINE). Almsgiving is indispensable for receiving forgiveness from the Lord (GAUDENTIUS). We are the beneficiaries of the alms we give (VALERIAN).

29:12 Almsgiving Will Rescue You from Affliction

VIRTUES ARE BARREN WITHOUT ALMS.
AUGUSTINE: Those who are going to receive the kingdom have given aid to the poor like good, faithful Christians, following the words of the Lord and confidently hoping in his promises. This is how they conducted themselves, because if they had not, their lives that were otherwise suited to holiness would have remained sterile, limiting themselves to abstaining from sins, not violating chastity or abandoning themselves to drunkenness, not stealing or doing anything bad. If they had not added charitable actions, they would remain sterile, only observing the first part of the commandment, "Stay far away from evil," and not the other part, "and do good."[1] Thus, when it says, "Come, receive your kingdom,"[2] this call is not motivated by the fact that they have lived in chastity, refrained from stealing, or that they have not taken advantage of the poor, or robbed other people's possessions or perjured themselves. Rather, it says, "Because I was hungry and you gave me something to eat."[3] This fact is recognized as all the more important if the Lord was silent about the rest and only focused on this merit. In an analogous way, when he says to others, "Go into the eternal fire prepared for the devil and his angels,"[4] he does not introduce any of the other causes that could have

been adduced for their sentences because they were adulterers, murderers, liars, sacrilegious, blasphemers, unbelievers; instead he only says, "I was hungry, and you gave me nothing to eat."[5] I see that this has made an impression on you and astonishes you; this is truly amazing what he is saying. I will try to sort out for you the meaning and communicate it to you. It is written, "As water extinguishes a blazing fire, so aid given to the poor cancels one's sins."[6] And still, "Visit mercy on the heart of the poor, and the same will pray to the Lord for you."[7] We have already cited the passage, "Listen, my king, and redeem your sins with mercy."[8] These are some of the many passages from the Word of God that demonstrate the importance of mercy in order to extinguish and to cancel sins. Or, there are also those whom the Lord condemns—or no, rather, those whom he is going to reward with crowns, as we have heard, for their acts of charity, as though he were saying, It would be difficult when weighing and examining carefully your actions to find a reason not to condemn you. Instead, he says, "Enter into the kingdom because I was hungry and you gave me something to eat."[9] Therefore, they will be saved, not because they have not sinned but because they have redeemed their sins with their good works. SERMON 389.5.[10]

IF WE GIVE ALMS. GAUDENTIUS OF BRESCIA: The rapacity of the one who grasps does not reduce avarice but provokes it. Indeed, it is written, "One who loves money will not be satisfied

---

[1]Ps 37:27 (36:27 LXX). [2]Mt 25:34. [3]Mt 25:35. [4]Mt 25:41. [5]Mt 25:42. [6]Sir 3:30 (3:33 Vg). [7]Sir 29:12 (29:15 Vg), variant. [8]Dan 4:27 (4:24 Vg). [9]Mt 25:34-35. [10]NBA 34:645; WSA 3 10:409-10**.

by money."[11] Nor does one love God who does not pity the poor, in whom Christ asks us to recognize that he is either helped or neglected. "When you did not do this to one of these least," he says, "you did not do it to me."[12] And the apostle John says in his epistle, "If someone sees his brother or sister in need and closes his heart to them, the love of God is not in him."[13] One falsely says that he loves Christ if he does not love the poor person, if he denies in his actions the love that he professes with his words. Let everyone therefore make an effort to give proof by their actions that they love God, because the love of God will purify them from all sin. Do you want, then, to know to what a great extent alms lighten the weight of sins? Listen to the counsel the prophet Daniel offers to the rich sinner: "Now, O king," he said, "may my advice please you: redeem your evil actions with alms and your sins with acts of mercy to the poor."[14] But perhaps you are thinking of keeping for yourself and your children what you do not want to give to the poor? I do not want you to worry yourself so dangerously, since "you do not know what tomorrow will bring."[15] Our God is powerful enough to give to them and to you. Indeed, everything that you give to the poor as alms you have put to your account and to that of your children. Nothing can be lacking to those whom you have joined to Christ. The one who assures us that he receives through the poor knows how to

repay. Give without worries. He is a trustworthy borrower,[16] the one who promises the kingdom of heaven. The divine Scripture says, "Hide your alms in the bosom of the poor person, and he will pray to God for you."[17] It is as though it said, "Sell your inheritance and acquire a surety, by which you can look with an unveiled face[18] on the judge who is coming, certain of having obtained pardon." Then in the Gospel it says, "If you want to be perfect, sell what you have, give to the poor, and you will have treasure in heaven, and come, follow me."[19] SERMONS 13:29-32.[20]

OUR ALMS ADVANTAGEOUS FOR OURSELVES. VALERIAN OF CIMIEZ: Listen to Solomon, who says, "Do something good for yourself; give alms to the poor."[21] Whoever, then, desires to look out for his own advantage willingly sustains the poor. There is no lack of opportunities by which, every day, you may acquire gain if you pay attention to the needs of the poverty of others. In fact, the Scripture says, "Sins are cleansed by alms and by faith."[22] Look, this one seeks a meal with a famished mouth. And that one, by his nakedness, says that he lacks even the scantiest of clothing. HOMILY 8.3.[23]

---

[11]Eccles 5:9. [12]Mt 25:45. [13]1 Jn 2:17. [14]Dan 4:24. [15]Prov 27:1. [16]See Prov 19:17. [17]Sir 29:12 (29:15 Vg), variant. [18]See 2 Cor 3:18. [19]Mt 19:21. [20]CTP 129:127-28. [21]Sir 29:12 (29:15 Vg), variant. [22]Prov 15:27. [23]CTP 122:93.

29:14-20* GUARANTEES

[14]*A good man will be surety for his neighbor,*
     but a man who has lost his sense of shame will fail him.
[15]*Do not forget all the kindness of your surety,*

for he has given his life for you.
¹⁶A sinner will overthrow the prosperity of his surety,
  ¹⁷and one who does not feel grateful will abandon his rescuer.
¹⁸Being surety has ruined many men who were prosperous,
  and has shaken them like a wave of the sea;
it has driven men of power into exile,
  and they have wandered among foreign nations.
¹⁹The sinner who has fallen into suretyship
  and pursues gain will fall into lawsuits.
²⁰Assist your neighbor according to your ability,
  but take heed to yourself lest you fall.

* Sir 29:19-27 Vg, with many differences.

OVERVIEW: There is no free will before grace (RABANUS MAURUS).

29:16 Overthrow the Prosperity of One's Surety

PELAGIUS IS DISPROVED BY SCRIPTURE.
RABANUS MAURUS: This passage opposes Pelagius, who puts free will before grace, even though the elect are freed from every stain only by the grace of Christ. Thus the apostle says, "By grace we have been saved."[1] And, "Who will free me from this body given over to death? The grace of God through Christ our Lord."[2] And again, "By the grace of God I am what I am, and his grace in me has not been in vain."[3] ON ECCLESIASTICUS 7.2.[4]

---

[1]Eph 3:5. [2]Rom 7:24-25, variant. [3]1 Cor 15:10. [4]PL 109:977.

29:21-28* HOSPITALITY

²¹The essentials for life are water and bread
  and clothing and a house to cover one's nakedness.
²²Better is the life of a poor man under the shelter of his roof
  than sumptuous food in another man's house.
²³Be content with little or much.^w
²⁴It is a miserable life to go from house to house,
  and where you are a stranger you may not open your mouth;
²⁵you will play the host and provide drink without being thanked,
  and besides this you will hear bitter words:

²⁶"Come here, stranger, prepare the table,
  and if you have anything at hand, let me have it to eat."
²⁷"Give place, stranger, to an honored person;
  my brother has come to stay with me; I need my house."
²⁸These things are hard to bear for a man who has feeling:
  scolding about lodgingˣ and the reproach of the moneylender.

---

w Other authorities add *and you will not hear reproach for your sojourning.*   **x** Or *from the household,* or (Syr) *from the host*   * Sir 29:28-35 Vg.

OVERVIEW: The modest food of Scripture is better than the speculations of pagans and heretics (RABANUS MAURUS).

29:22 Under the Shelter of One's Roof

SCRIPTURE IS THE BEST FOOD FOR THE SOUL. RABANUS MAURUS: According to the literal sense it is more agreeable to take a frugal but secure meal under the roof of a shack than to seek splendid banquets but in uncertain circumstances and at the price of enormous effort and excessive worry. Allegorically, the food of the spiritual sense that the poor people of the church obtain under the humble roof of the letters of catholic unity is better than the ambitious delicacies of philosophical dogmas, enclosed as they are by philosophers or heretics in the various books of the rhetoricians in the form of errors or hypotheses, instead of in respect for the truth. These latter involve huge labors and excessive worries and are of little use. Paul says on this theme, "They are always learning, without ever arriving at a knowledge of the truth."[1] In fact, "God has shown the wisdom of this world to be foolish,"[2] and "the kingdom of God does not consist in words but in virtue."[3] ON ECCLESIASTICUS 7.3.[4]

---

[1]2 Tim 3:7. [2]1 Cor 1:20. [3]1 Cor 4:20. The Latin word *virtus* is ambiguous, since it can mean "power" but also "virtue." The context seems to indicate that Rabanus is using it in the second meaning. [4]PL 109:979.

30:1-13 EDUCATION

¹He who loves his son will whip him often,
  in order that he may rejoice at the way he turns out.
²He who disciplines his son will profit by him,
  and will boast of him among acquaintances.
³He who teaches his son will make his enemies envious,
  and will glory in him in the presence of friends.
⁴Theʸ father may die, and yet he is not dead,

for he has left behind him one like himself;
[5]*while alive he saw and rejoiced,*
and when he died he was not grieved;
[6]*he has left behind him an avenger against his enemies,*
and one to repay the kindness of his friends.

[7]*He who spoils his son will bind up his wounds,*
and his feelings will be troubled at every cry.
[8]*A horse that is untamed turns out to be stubborn,*
and a son unrestrained turns out to be wilful.
[9]*Pamper a child, and he will frighten you;*
play with him, and he will give you grief.
[10]*Do not laugh with him, lest you have sorrow with him,*
and in the end you will gnash your teeth.
[11]*Give him no authority in his youth,*
and do not ignore his errors.
[12]*Bow down his neck in his youth,[z]*
and beat his sides while he is young,
lest he become stubborn and disobey you,
and you have sorrow of soul from him.[a]
[13]*Discipline your son and take pains with him,*
that you may not be offended by his shamelessness.

y Gk *His*   z Other authorities omit this line and the preceding line   a Other authorities omit this line

OVERVIEW: If you care too much, you may bring your children to ruin (CHRYSOSTOM).

30:7 Spoiling One's Children

TOO MUCH CARE BRINGS ABOUT RUIN.
JOHN CHRYSOSTOM: "Because the one who would save his life will lose it," he says, "but the one who loses his life for my sake will find it. Indeed, what advantage would it be to gain the whole world and lose one's soul? Or what can a person give in exchange for his soul?"[1] This means: I ordain these things, not because I am not concerned for you but because I am very concerned for you. In fact, one who is always helping his child ruins him, while the one who does not always help saves him. A wise man said the same thing: "If you beat your child with the rod, he will not die. Rather, you will free his soul from death."[2] And, "One who spoils his child will bind up his wounds." This is also the case in the army. If the general, in his concern for the soldiers, orders that they always stay inside the city, he will cause not only the soldiers to die, but the others in the city as well. So that this would not also happen to you, he says, You must be ready for a continual death. Indeed, even now a difficult battle breaks out. Do not remain inside, therefore, but go out and fight. Even if you fall in battle, you will have lived. If, in earthly wars, one who is ready to be killed is held in more esteem than the others and is more invincible and fearsome to the enemy—even if, after his death, the king for whom he has taken up arms cannot bring him back to life—how much more in these

[1]Mt 16:25-26. [2]Prov 23:13-14.

battles, with such a great hope of resurrection, will the one who exposes his life to death find it,[3] first because he will not be taken quickly, and second, because even if he falls, it will bring

him to a higher life. HOMILIES ON THE GOSPEL OF MATTHEW 55.2.[4]

[3]Mt 16:25. [4]CTP 171:424-25.

30:14-20* HEALTH

[14]*Better off is a poor man who is well and strong in constitution*
   than a rich man who is severely afflicted in body.
[15]*Health and soundness are better than all gold,*
   and a robust body than countless riches.
[16]*There is no wealth better than health of body,*
   and there is no gladness above joy of heart.
[17]*Death is better than a miserable life,*
   and eternal rest[b] than chronic sickness.

[18]*Good things poured out upon a mouth that is closed*
   are like offerings of food placed upon a grave.
[19]*Of what use to an idol is an offering of fruit?*
   For it can neither eat nor smell.
So is he who is afflicted by the Lord;
[20]*he sees with his eyes and groans,*
   like a eunuch who embraces a maiden and groans.

b Some authorities omit *eternal rest*   * Sir 30:14-21 Vg.

OVERVIEW: Pagan funerals do not help the dead (AUGUSTINE). A hundred people together cannot despoil one who is poor and naked. Eliminate occasions by which others can harm you (CHRYSOSTOM).

30:18 Offerings Placed on Graves

PAGAN FUNERALS. AUGUSTINE: So now that he is buried, I want to see if I can hear his voice. Or if I cannot hear his, I'll try to hear my father's voice, or my grandfather's or my great-grandfather's. But in fact no one has ever risen from the grave, no one has ever told us what is done in the beyond. Let us enjoy life while we live, and if our loved ones—our parents, or relatives or friends—bring remembrances to our grave after we are dead, this can only satisfy them; it has nothing to do with us! The Scripture also criticized this practice when, speaking about those who do not recognize the good things they have, it says, "As though making offerings of food at a grave."[1] It is obvious that this can be of no use to the one who is dead. It is in fact a pagan custom and not part of the tradition that conforms to the truth of the Patriarchs. Of them, one reads that they did solemnly celebrate the funeral rites but not that they carried sacrificial offerings to the tombs. This can also be seen in the practice of the Jews who, even if they did not preserve the fruit of the virtues of the ancestors, nevertheless did maintain the ancient custom with much solemnity. SERMON 361.6.6.[2]

30:20 *Seeing and Groaning*

THE MISER IS INSATIABLE. JOHN CHRYSOSTOM: Why, O mortal, do you pile up gold? Why acquire for yourself a more bitter slavery? A harsher imprisonment? Why create for yourself a more piercing anxiety? You think that the veins of gold in the mines or the gold in palaces could be yours. In fact, even if you had that pile of wealth, you would only hoard it. It would not serve you, because if you do not make use even now of your goods, not touching them as though they belonged to someone else, how much more would you do so if you had more? Usually, for the avaricious, the more abundant the wealth they surround themselves with, the more they save. "But," you could reply, "I know that it's mine." In that case, the possession is only in your thoughts and not in enjoyment. But, you could object, I will be formidable before others. Actually, you would be more vulnerable before the rich, the poor, thieves, calumniators, servants— in effect, before all those who might plot against

you. If you want to be formidable, eliminate the occasions by which all those who do this kind of thing might take advantage of and harm you. Have you never heard the proverb that says that not even a hundred people together could ever despoil a poor, naked person?[3] In fact, he has the greatest defender, poverty, one that not even the king could subjugate and conquer. Instead, all these things create anguish for the avaricious person. And why speak of people, given that moths and worms war against such an individual? But why even speak of moths? A long period of time is sufficient, even with no one to bother them, for riches to undergo major damage. What, therefore, is the pleasure of riches? I see the unpleasant aspects, whereas you speak to me of the pleasure you derive from them. What, you might reply, are the unpleasant aspects? Worries, plots, hostilities, hatred, fear, endless thirst after riches and anxiety over them. If someone embraces the girl he loves but cannot satisfy his desire, he suffers an even greater torment. This also happens to the rich person. He certainly has riches and is with them, but he cannot satisfy all his desire. The same happens with all rich people as what is spoken of by a wise man: "Like the desire of a eunuch to deflower a maiden,"[4] and, "Like a eunuch who embraces a virgin and groans." HOMILIES ON THE GOSPEL OF MATTHEW 83.2-3.[5]

---

[1]Sir 30:18 (30:19 Vg). [2]NBA 34:351-53. [3]Although this proverb seems to be of Stoic origin, it is not attested by other sources. [4]Sir 20:4. [5]CTP 172:302-3.

30:21-25* JOY

^{21}Do not give yourself over to sorrow,
 and do not afflict yourself deliberately.
^{22}Gladness of heart is the life of man,
 and the rejoicing of a man is length of days.
^{23}Delight your soul and comfort your heart,
 and remove sorrow far from you,
for sorrow has destroyed many,
 and there is no profit in it.
^{24}Jealousy and anger shorten life,
 and anxiety brings on old age too soon.
^{25}A man of cheerful and good heart
 will give heed to the food he eats.

* Sir 30:22-27 Vg.

OVERVIEW: The Lord exhorts us to have mercy toward ourselves (SALVIAN).

30:23 Delight Your Soul

MERCY TOWARD OURSELVES. SALVIAN THE PRESBYTER: "Have compassion on your own soul."[1] Great is the mercy of God our Lord, who invites us to be charitable toward ourselves. He says, "Have compassion on your own soul," that is, "you also should have compassion on yourself, you for whom I feel an aching commiseration, for whom I experience an infinite compassion. If you see me so moved over the soul of another, you at least should have mercy on your own soul." O extremely wretched person, God acts toward you in this way, and you do not put faith in him. He beckons you to be charitable toward yourself, and you do not want to be so? He pleads your case with you, and he cannot win the decision from you? AGAINST AVARICE 3.19.86.[2]

---

[1]Sir 30:23 (30:24 Vg). The Vulgate translates a variant of the Septuagint. [2]CTP 10:120-21.

31:1-11 RICHES

[1]*Wakefulness over wealth wastes away one's flesh,*
  and anxiety about it removes sleep.
[2]*Wakeful anxiety prevents slumber,*
  and a severe illness carries off sleep.[c]
[3]*The rich man toils as his wealth accumulates,*
  and when he rests he fills himself with his dainties.
[4]*The poor man toils as his livelihood diminishes,*
  and when he rests he becomes needy.

[5]*He who loves gold will not be justified,*
  and he who pursues money will be led astray[d] by it.
[6]*Many have come to ruin because of gold,*
  and their destruction has met them face to face.
[7]*It is a stumbling block to those who are devoted to it,*
  and every fool will be taken captive by it.
[8]*Blessed is the rich man who is found blameless,*
  and who does not go after gold.
[9]*Who is he? And we will call him blessed,*
  for he has done wonderful things among his people.
[10]*Who has been tested by it and been found perfect?*
  Let it be for him a ground for boasting.
Who has had the power to transgress and did not transgress,
  and to do evil and did not do it?
[11]*His prosperity will be established,*
  and the assembly will relate his acts of charity.

c Other authorities read *sleep carries off a severe illness*   d Heb Syr: Gk *will be filled*

OVERVIEW: Riches should not prevail on us, but we must use them for good aims (AUGUSTINE). The people of Israel voluntarily forsook God (PROSPER).

31:8 Blessed Are the Rich Who Are Blameless

USING RICHES FOR A GOOD PURPOSE. AUGUSTINE: How can one approve those who seem to dominate in this world, if they do less than they can? The Scripture praises precisely the one "who could have sinned but did not, who did not run after gold." Gold must follow you, and not you gold. In fact, gold is a good thing—certainly God created nothing evil.[1] Don't you be evil, then, and the gold good. See here, I place some gold between an upright person and a dishonest

---

[1]See Gen 1:31, etc.; Wis 11:24.

one. If the dishonest person takes it, the poor are oppressed, magistrates corrupted, laws broken, social life upset. Why? Because a dishonest person took the gold. If the upright person were to have it, the poor would be sustained, the naked clothed, the oppressed liberated, prisoners redeemed.[2] How much good is derived from the gold the honest person has, and how many evils from the gold of the dishonest person! To what end, therefore, do you say in disgust, "And what if gold did not exist at all?" You should not love gold. If you are dishonest, you will follow gold. If you are upright, it will follow you. What does "it will follow you" mean? That you will rule it and not be made its servant, because you will possess it, rather than being possessed by it. SERMON 311.9.9.[3]

31:10 The Power to Do Evil

ISRAEL FORSOOK GOD. PROSPER OF AQUI-TAINE: If we go back to the beginnings of the world, we find that the Spirit of God guided all of the saints before the flood, and for this reason they are also called children of God, since, as the apostle says, "All those who are guided by the Spirit of God are children of God."[4] And because, neglecting to obey the ancestors, they became involved in illicit and reprobate marriages, and because of this wicked communion were judged worthy of extermination, the Lord said, "My Spirit will not remain forever with these people, for they are flesh."[5] From this it is clear that this people, whose history is narrated year by year in an orderly manner, was first spiritual, that is, having a will that was guided by the Holy Spirit, in such a way however that this government and guidance did not take away their freedom to turn toward sin. If the people had not exercised this freedom, they would not have abandoned God. Nor would they have been abandoned by God, and they would rather have been that of which it is written, "Happy the one who could have sinned but did not." Therefore, as long as they remained with God, they remained in the will that God inspired in them and by which he would have governed them. "The will," as it is written, "is predisposed by the Lord."[6] THE CALL OF ALL NATIONS 2.10.[7]

---

[2]See Is 61:1; Lk 4:18. [3]NBA 33:643. [4]Rom 8:14. [5]Gen 6:3. [6]Prov 8:35. [7]CTP 143:127-28.

31:12-24* BANQUETS

[12]Are you seated at the table of a great man?[e]
  Do not be greedy[f] at it,
  and do not say, "There is certainly much upon it!"
[13]Remember that a greedy[g] eye is a bad thing.
  What has been created more greedy[g] than the eye?
  Therefore it sheds tears from every face.
[14]Do not reach out your hand for everything you see,
  and do not crowd your neighbor[h] at the dish.
[15]Judge your neighbor's feelings by your own,

and in every matter be thoughtful.
¹⁶*Eat like a human being what is set before you,*
and do not chew greedily, lest you be hated.
¹⁷*Be the first to stop eating, for the sake of good manners,*
and do not be insatiable, lest you give offense.
¹⁸*If you are seated among many persons,*
do not reach out your hand before they do.

¹⁹*How ample a little is for a well-disciplined man!*
He does not breathe heavily upon his bed.
²⁰*Healthy sleep depends on moderate eating;*
he rises early, and feels fit.[i]
The distress of sleeplessness and of nausea
and colic are with the glutton.
²¹*If you are overstuffed with food,*
get up in the middle of the meal, and you will have relief.
²²*Listen to me, my son, and do not disregard me,*
and in the end you will appreciate my words.
In all your work be industrious,
and no sickness will overtake you.

²³*Men will praise the one who is liberal with food,*
and their testimony to his excellence is trustworthy.
²⁴*The city will complain of the one who is niggardly with food,*
and their testimony to his niggardliness is accurate.

e Heb Syr: Gk *at a great table*   f Gk *open your throat*   g Gk *evil*   h Gk *him*   i Gk *his soul is with him*   * Sir 31:12-29 Vg.

OVERVIEW: The pleasure of eating is ephemeral and full of affliction (CHRYSOSTOM).

31:20 *Healthy Sleep Depends on Moderate Eating*

THE EPHEMERAL PLEASURE OF EATING. JOHN CHRYSOSTOM: Let us first examine the vice considered the most attractive, that of a fine table. Tell me, then, of its time and for what part of the day it detains us: such a small part, in fact, that it is difficult even to calculate. From the moment one begins to feel full, pleasure ceases. And not only that, it ceases even earlier, passing more swiftly than a running stream, even while the food is still between the teeth, and cannot last beyond the swallowing of the food itself. As soon as food passes the teeth, it loses all of its attractiveness. I will not go on about the evils that follow or how great is the storm that derives from the pleasures of the table. In fact, the one who abstains not only feels more at ease but also feels lighter and rests more easily than the one who lies down on his bed oppressed by a full stomach. "Healthy sleep with moderate eating," the Scripture says. Is there perhaps need to recall the illnesses, the disgust, the calamities, the wasted expense? From such meals, how many arguments, what envy, what calumnies result? AGAINST THE OPPONENTS OF THE MONASTIC LIFE 2.10.[1]

---

[1]CTP 130:130-31.

31:25-31* WINE

^{25}Do not aim to be valiant over wine,
  for wine has destroyed many.
^{26}Fire and water prove^j the temper of steel,
  so wine tests hearts in the strife of the proud.
^{27}Wine is like life to men,
  if you drink it in moderation.
What is life to a man who is without wine?
  It has been created to make men glad.
^{28}Wine drunk in season and temperately
  is rejoicing of heart and gladness of soul.
^{29}Wine drunk to excess is bitterness of soul,
  with provocation and stumbling.
^{30}Drunkenness increases the anger of a fool to his injury,
  reducing his strength and adding wounds.
^{31}Do not reprove your neighbor at a banquet of wine,
  and do not despise him in his merrymaking;
speak no word of reproach to him,
  and do not afflict him by making demands of him.

j Gk *The furnace by dipping proves*   * Sir 31:30-42 Vg.

OVERVIEW: Wine is a symbol of the Word and the Holy Spirit (ORIGEN). When taken with moderation, wine is a gift from God (AMBROSE).

31:27-28 *Wine Is Like Life*

SPIRITUAL WINE. ORIGEN: "Bring me into the wine cellar."[1] The Bridegroom had stopped outside and was welcomed by the bride. Truly he had rested on her bosom.[2] Many young maidens[3] are not such as to be worthy of having the Bridegroom as their guest: "to the crowds" outside, he "speaks in parables."[4] How I fear that many of us are maidens! "Bring me into the wine cellar."[5] Why do I wait outside for so long? "See, I stand at the door and knock. If someone opens to me, I will come in to him, and sup with him, and he with me."[6] "Bring me in." Even now the divine Word says the same words: see that the Christ says, "Let me in." He speaks also to you, catechumens, "Let me in," not simply into the house but "into the wine cellar,"[7] that your soul might be filled with the "wine of delight,"[8] the wine of the Holy Spirit. Thus, "bring into" your "house" the Bridegroom, the Word, Wisdom, the Truth.[9] Thus it can also be said of those who are not yet perfect, "Bring me into the wine cellar."[10] HOMILIES ON THE SONG OF SONGS 2.7.[11]

WINE IS GOD'S GIFT. AMBROSE: God, knowing

---

[1]Song 2:4. [2]See Song 1:13. [3]See Song 1:3. [4]Mk 4:11. [5]Song 2:4. [6]Rev 3:20. [7]Song 2:4. [8]See Sir 31:27; 40:20; Ps 104:15 (103:15 LXX). [9]See Jn 14:6. [10]Song 2:4. [11]CTP 83:77-78.

well that wine drunk in moderation contributes to health and increases discernment, whereas gulped without measure, it gives birth to vices,[12] gave us this creature. He left to human freedom, however, the possibility of using it abundantly, so that the frugality of nature might be a lesson in sobriety and the human condition would impute to itself the damage of abuse and the guilt of drunkenness. Noah became drunk and, groggy from wine, fell into a deep sleep.[13] In this way he who gained glory through the flood was disgraced by wine. But the Lord also preserved in wine the good qualities of his creature, to the extent of making its fruit contribute to our salvation, making the forgiveness of our sins derive from it.[14] HEXAMERON 5.17.72.[15]

---

[12]Sir 31:28-29 (31:37-38 Vg). [13]See Gen 9:21. [14]See Mt 26:28. [15]CTP 164:138.

32:1-13* FEASTS

[1]*If they make you master of the feast, do not exalt yourself;*
  be among them as one of them;
take good care of them and then be seated;
  [2]*when you have fulfilled your duties, take your place,*
that you may be merry on their account
  and receive a wreath for your excellent leadership.

[3]*Speak, you who are older, for it is fitting that you should,*
  but with accurate knowledge, and do not interrupt the music.
[4]*Where there is entertainment, do not pour out talk;*
  do not display your cleverness out of season.
[5]*A ruby seal in a setting of gold*
  is a concert of music at a banquet of wine.
[6]*A seal of emerald in a rich setting of gold*
  is the melody of music with good wine.

[7]*Speak, young man, if there is need of you,*
  but no more than twice, and only if asked.
[8]*Speak concisely, say much in few words;*
  be as one who knows and yet holds his tongue.
[9]*Among the great do not act as their equal;*
  and when another is speaking, do not babble.

[10]*Lightning speeds before the thunder,*

and approval precedes a modest man.
¹¹*Leave in good time and do not be the last;*
go home quickly and do not linger.
¹²*Amuse yourself there, and do what you have in mind,*
but do not sin through proud speech.
¹³*And for these things bless him who made you*
and satisfies you with his good gifts.

* Sir 32:1-17 Vg.

OVERVIEW: Joshua's humility is an image of Jesus (ORIGEN). Humbleness, rather than love of power, is necessary to guide the soul (GREGORY THE GREAT). Rising has a negative and a positive meaning (AUGUSTINE). Humility is the source of other virtues (CHRYSOSTOM).

32:1 Do Not Exalt Yourself

JOSHUA IS AN IMAGE OF JESUS. ORIGEN: Joshua[1] gave the inheritance to all of the children of Judah. He who gave it to Ephraim and to the half-tribe of Manasseh.[2] He gave the inheritance to the glorious Caleb, son of Jephunneh,[3] having sent three men from each tribe to go through the country and describe it in a book[4] and return to show it to them. He himself drew the lots for all[5] and reserved the last place for himself. Why do you think he wanted to be last? Certainly to be the first of all.[6] He did not take this part of himself but received it from the people, who gave the inheritance to the one from whom they had received it. In fact, it is written, "The children of Israel gave the part to Joshua, son of Nun."[7] "But this happened to them as a sign,"[8] that it might be proposed as a model for us and that we in turn might observe the precept he practiced, which says, "The greater you are, the more humble you will be, and thus you will find grace with the Lord,"[9] and also that which is written, "If they have made you the head, do not exalt yourself but be among them as one of them."[10] HOMILIES ON JOSHUA 24.2.[11]

HUMILITY IN GUIDING SOULS. GREGORY THE

GREAT: Directors of souls should remain firm in that exterior attitude they assume in view of the good of others, while preserving in their heart that disposition that makes them fear nothing so much as a high estimation of themselves. Those under them, however, should be able to perceive, from certain indications of a sober spontaneity, that they are humble, and in this way see both what they must fear of their authority and what they must imitate of their humility. For this reason, the greater their power appears outwardly to others, the more superiors must not cease to ensure that they inwardly keep it under control. They cannot let it overcome their thoughts or let their hearts be carried away by its delights, lest the mind prove unable to control the very thing it submits itself to, due to a lust for domination. In fact, so that the heart of the superior not be carried away to the point of exaltation over pleasure in his power, a wise man rightly said, "They have made you a leader. Do not exalt yourself but be among them as one of them." For this reason Peter also says, "Not as masters over those assigned to you, but be an example to the flock."[12] The Truth, therefore, inviting us to the highest merits of virtue, says, "Know that the rulers of the Gentiles lord it over them, and those who are greater make their power felt. It shall not be this way among you, but the one who wants to be the greatest will be your servant, and the one who wants to be first among you will be your slave—

---

[1]The explanation is based on the homonimity between Jesus and Joshua in Greek. [2]See Josh 16–17. [3]See Josh 15:13. [4]See Josh 18:4, 9. [5]See Josh 13:7. [6]See Mt 19:30. [7]Josh 19:49. [8]1 Cor 10:11. [9]Sir 3:18. [10]Sir 32:1. [11]CTP 108:299-300. [12]1 Pet 5:3.

like the Son of man, who did not come to be served but to serve."[13] This is the meaning of the words referring to that servant who was exalted by the power he had received, but afterward punishments await him, "And if that wicked servant says in his heart, 'My master is delayed in coming,' and begins to beat his fellow servants, and to eat and drink with drunkards, then the master of that servant will come on a day that he does not expect and an hour he does not know, and he will cut him off, and his fate will be that of the hypocrites."[14] And one is rightly considered a hypocrite who, under the pretext of discipline, turns the ministry of governance into an exercise of power. PASTORAL RULE 2.6.[15]

32:4 Do Not Display Your Cleverness

RISING AND ITS MEANINGS. AUGUSTINE: "May it be exalted"[16] means nothing other than that the thing in question be raised on high. When this expression is used in a bad sense, it usually means pride, as when the Scripture says, "Do not exalt yourself in your wisdom,"[17] whereas if it is understood in a good sense, the expression supposes a greater honor, as if the thing really were raised on high. In this sense it is written, "In the nights, lift your hands toward the holy, and bless the Lord."[18] EXPOSITIONS OF THE PSALMS 71.10.[19]

32:10 Approval Precedes a Modest Person

IN PRAISE OF HUMILITY. JOHN CHRYSOSTOM: What is the head of the virtues? Humility. He therefore begins with it, saying, "Blessed are the poor."[20] This head has neither tresses nor curls but a beauty such as to attract God to itself. "On whom," he says, "will I turn my gaze but on the meek, humble one who fears my words?"[21] And, "My eyes are on the meek of the earth."[22] And, "The Lord is near to the contrite of heart."[23] This head, instead of having hair and tresses, offers sacrifices pleasing to God. It is an altar of gold, a spiritual altar. "A contrite spirit, in fact, is a sacrifice to God."[24] This is the mother of wisdom. If someone has this, he will have the rest as well. Have you seen a head that you have never seen before? Do you want to see, indeed to know, the face as well? Observe first its red, blooming color, with many graces, and learn where these come from. Well, where do they come from? From decency and from blushing. For this reason someone said, "Grace precedes a modest person." It sheds a great beauty even on the other members. Even if one mixes colors beyond number, they will not attain such beauty. If you want to see the eyes as well, observe that they are precisely delineated by modesty and temperance. They become so beautiful and perceptive that they are able to see even the Lord. Indeed, he says, "Blessed are the pure in heart, for they shall see God."[25] HOMILIES ON THE GOSPEL OF MATTHEW 47.4.[26]

---

[13]Mt 20:25. [14]Mt 24:48-51. [15]CTP 28:85-86. [16]Ps 72:7 (71:7 LXX). [17]Sir 32:4 (32:6 Vg). [18]Ps 134:1-2 (133:1-2 LXX). [19]NBA 26:805. [20]Mt 5:3; Lk 6:20. [21]Is 66:2. [22]Ps 76:10 (75:10 LXX); 101:6 (100:6 LXX). [23]Ps 34:19 (33:19 LXX). [24]Ps 51:19 (50:19 LXX). [25]Mt 5:8. [26]CTP 171:310-11.

32:14–33:6* FEAR OF GOD

¹⁴He who fears the Lord will accept his discipline,
  and those who rise early to seek him[k] will find favor.
¹⁵He who seeks the law will be filled with it,
  but the hypocrite will stumble at it.
¹⁶Those who fear the Lord will form true judgments,
  and like a light they will kindle righteous deeds.
¹⁷A sinful man will shun reproof,
  and will find a decision according to his liking.

¹⁸A man of judgment will not overlook an idea,
  and an insolent[l] and proud man will not cower in fear.[m]
¹⁹Do nothing without deliberation;
  and when you have acted, do not regret it.
²⁰Do not go on a path full of hazards,
  and do not stumble over stony ground.
²¹Do not be overconfident on a smooth[n] way,
  ²²and give good heed to your paths.[o]
²³Guard[p] yourself in every act,
  for this is the keeping of the commandments.

²⁴He who believes the law gives heed to the commandments,
  and he who trusts the Lord will not suffer loss.
33 No evil will befall the man who fears the Lord,
  but in trial he will deliver him again and again.
²A wise man will not hate the law,
  but he who is hypocritical about it is like a boat in a storm.
³A man of understanding will trust in the law;
  for him the law is as dependable as an inquiry by means of Urim.

⁴Prepare what to say, and thus you will be heard;
  bind together your instruction, and make your answer.
⁵The heart of a fool is like a cart wheel,
  and his thoughts like a turning axle.
⁶A stallion is like a mocking friend;
  he neighs under every one who sits on him.

k Other authorities omit *to seek him*   **l** Heb: Gk *alien*   **m** The meaning of this line is uncertain. Other authorities add the phrases *and after acting, with him, without deliberation*   **n** Or *an unexplored*   **o** Syr Vg: Gk *and beware of your children*   **p** Heb Syr: Gk *Trust*   * Sir 32:18–33:6 Vg, with a different distribution of the verses.

OVERVIEW: God treats the just and sinners differently (CLEMENT OF ALEXANDRIA). The Lord asks from us to judge with honesty and truth (ORIGEN). Avoid hurriedness and act wisely (GREGORY THE GREAT). The horsemen are wicked spirits, and the horses are the wicked on which they ride (ANONYMOUS ANOMOEAN).

32:17 A Sinful Person Will Shun Reproof

JUST AND SINNER BEFORE GOD. CLEMENT OF ALEXANDRIA: In Jeremiah it says, "Jerusalem has committed a great sin, and it has thus fallen into turmoil. All those who honored it now despise it, because they have seen its abomination."[1] Through Solomon, however, he attenuates the severity and harshness of the accusation and shows the sweetness of his pedagogy, saying, "My son, do not despise the Lord's corrections, and do not spurn his reproofs. In fact, the one whom the Lord loves, he corrects, and he always scourges the one he accepts,"[2] whereas "the sinner shuns reproof." Therefore "let the just one accuse me," says the Scripture, "and correct me, but let not the oil of sinners anoint my head."[3] CHRIST THE EDUCATOR 1.9.78.3-4.[4]

32:19 Do Nothing Without Deliberation

HONESTY AND TRUTH IN JUDGING. ORIGEN: "Because the Lord loves judgment and will not abandon his holy ones."[5] In what sense does the Lord love judgment? Because nothing in him is not weighed thoroughly, nothing happens without a reason. Consequently you also, knowing that the Lord loves judgment, do everything with an honest and truthful judgment. Thus you will listen to the admonition of him who says, "Do everything sensibly, drink wine with prudence."[6] HOMILIES ON THE PSALMS 4.7 (PSALM 36).[7]

ACTING AT THE RIGHT MOMENT. GREGORY THE GREAT: Through Solomon it is rightly said, "One who minds the wind will never sow, and one who watches the clouds will never reap."[8] What is expressed by the wind but the temptation of evil spirits? And what are the clouds, which are moved by the wind, if not the hostility of evil people? Clearly, the clouds are blown by the wind because evil people are excited by the breath of unclean spirits. Consequently, the one who pays attention to the wind will not sow, and one who watches the clouds will never reap, because the one who fears the temptation of evil spirits and the persecution of human beings will neither sow the grain of good works nor cut the sheaves of holy retribution. The precipitous, who anticipate the time for good actions, pervert their merit and frequently fall into evil, because they have no discernment of the good. They do not inquire into what would be the right moment to do something but for the most part only think of this once they have done it, with an awareness that it should have been done differently. To these, under the guise of speaking to a pupil, Solomon says, "Do nothing without counsel, and after you have done it you will not regret it."[9] And further, "Let your eyelids precede your steps."[10] Our eyelids precede our steps when good counsel precedes our action. The one who neglects to consider in advance what he expects to do straightens his steps, closes his eyes and arrives at the end of his way but does not precede his steps with foresight. Consequently, he more quickly stumbles, because he does not pay attention, with the eyelids of counsel, to where to plant the foot of his works. PASTORAL RULE 3.15.[11]

33:6 Like a Mocking Friend

WICKED HORSEMEN AND WICKED HORSES. ANONYMOUS ANOMOEAN: Who were the horsemen who formed three bands, that is, who armed themselves in three ways and surrounded the camels in a threefold war?[12] These were spiritual horsemen, that is, spirits of the air, who

---

[1]Lam 1:8. [2]Prov 3:11-12. [3]Ps 141:5 (140:5 LXX). [4]CTP 181:106. [5]Ps 37:28 (36:28 LXX). [6]Sir 31:27-28 and Eccles 9:7. [7]BP 18:207. [8]Eccles 11:4. [9]Sir 32:24 Vg. [10]Prov 4:25. [11]CTP 28:158-59. [12]See Job 1:17.

in their aerial wickedness roam the earth, plow the sea, rush through the air, stronger and faster than any wind, water or storm. It is right to also call them horsemen, because they sit on all lustful and indecent people as on horses, stoking their desires and hounding them until they carry out their iniquity and their desires—those about whom it is said that the adulterer "neighs like a stallion under whoever rides him." And, "Do not be like the horse or the mule, without intelligence."[13] And further, "They are like stallions, each one neighing after the wife of his neighbor."[14] These, therefore, are the horses of the devil, these are the evil horses—these, and all those who are in the service of his iniquity, those "whose feet run to evil," because the feet of these horses "hasten to shed blood,"[15] and their utterly perverse riders are the demons and spirits of the air. COMMENTARY ON JOB 1.72.[16]

---

[13]Ps 32:9 (31:9 LXX). [14]Jer 5:8. [15]Is 59:7. [16]CSEL 96:200-201.

33:7-18* UNEQUAL CONDITIONS

[7]*Why is any day better than another,*
    when all the daylight in the year is from the sun?
[8]*By the Lord's decision they were distinguished,*
    and he appointed the different seasons and feasts;
[9]*some of them he exalted and hallowed,*
    and some of them he made ordinary days.
[10]*All men are from the ground,*
    and Adam was created of the dust.
[11]*In the fulness of his knowledge the Lord distinguished them*
    and appointed their different ways;
[12]*some of them he blessed and exalted,*
    and some of them he made holy and brought near to himself;
but some of them he cursed and brought low,
    and he turned them out of their place.
[13]*As clay in the hand of the potter—*
    for all his ways are as he pleases—
so men are in the hand of him who made them,
    to give them as he decides.

[14]*Good is the opposite of evil,*
    and life the opposite of death;
    so the sinner is the opposite of the godly.

¹⁵*Look upon all the works of the Most High;*
they likewise are in pairs, one the opposite of the other.

¹⁶*I was the last on watch;*
I was like one who gleans after the grape-gatherers;
by the blessing of the Lord I excelled,
and like a grape-gatherer I filled my wine press.
¹⁷*Consider that I have not labored for myself alone,*
but for all who seek instruction.
¹⁸*Hear me, you who are great among the people,*
and you leaders of the congregation, hearken.

* Sir 33:7-19 LXX.

OVERVIEW: This verse occasions discussion about the day and light (ANONYMOUS ANOMOEAN) and the nature of the earth, which can be considered a name for all human beings since they derive from it (HILARY OF POITIERS).

33:7 Any Day Better Than Another?

DAY AND LIGHT. ANONYMOUS ANOMOEAN: The day does not exist as a nature or as a substance or by its own power. You see the light but not a substance. Its nature, for its part, cannot be touched or grasped, because the day has neither nature nor substance. It has a name but not a nature. Just as an hour has a name but not a substance, in the same way the day has a name but not a substance or a nature. What, then, is a day? The time of light, the trajectory of the light, the rising of the sun and its path from the east, until it sets. The light of the sun is thus called day; the course of the sun is considered to be a day. And this is exactly how it is: the course of the sun measures the time of the day, bringing the day to an end, making it longer or shorter. That it is this way, the Scripture shows when it says, "All the light of the day comes from the sun," as if to say, all the time of the day comes from the sun. COMMENTARY ON JOB 3.25.[1]

33:10 Created of the Dust

"EARTH" MEANS ALL OF HUMANKIND. HI-LARY OF POITIERS: So as not to refer these words to the lifeless mass of this earth, the totality of all of us who are generated from the earth in Adam, our progenitor, is designated in the plural, when it says, "Cry out to God in joy, all the earth."[2] In fact, in this verse both our duty and the origin of all people are recalled at the same time. HOMILIES ON THE PSALMS 65.4.[3]

---

[1]CSEL 96:379-80. [2]Ps 66:1 (65:1 LXX). The plural of this imperative verb ("to cry out") is not reflected in English translations. [3]CTP 185:362.

33:19-23* INDEPENDENCE

¹⁹*To son or wife, to brother or friend,*
do not give power over yourself, as long as you live;
and do not give your property to another,
lest you change your mind and must ask for it.
²⁰*While you are still alive and have breath in you,*
do not let any one take your place.
²¹*For it is better that your children should ask from you*
than that you should look to the hand of your sons.
²²*Excel in all that you do;*
bring no stain upon your honor.
²³*At the time when you end the days of your life,*
in the hour of death, distribute your inheritance.

* Sir 33:20-24 LXX.

OVERVIEW: The leaders of the church should nurture their disciples as parents do their children (Rabanus Maurus).

33:19 Do Not Give Anyone Power Over Yourself

LIKE EDUCATING ONE'S CHILDREN. RABANUS MAURUS: Reason teaches the immediate sense of these things to parents, concerning the right way to rule over their children and to raise them strictly until they have reached maturity, so that they will be worthy heirs of their parents after they are gone. Moreover, according to the spiritual sense it instructs the leaders of the church, so that they might preserve the dignity of their order until death, with a deliberate authority and right guidance. In this way they will leave disciples who have been raised well and who will be useful heirs of their works. ON ECCLESIASTICUS 7.11.[1]

[1]PL 109:1003.

33:24-31* SLAVES

²⁴*Fodder and a stick and burdens for an ass;*
  bread and discipline and work for a servant.
²⁵*Set your slave to work, and you will find rest;*
  leave his hands idle, and he will seek liberty.
²⁶*Yoke and thong will bow the neck,*
  and for a wicked servant there are racks and tortures.
²⁷*Put him to work, that he may not be idle,*
  for idleness teaches much evil.
²⁸*Set him to work, as is fitting for him,*
  and if he does not obey, make his fetters heavy.
²⁹*Do not act immoderately toward anybody,*
  and do nothing without discretion.

³⁰*If you have a servant, let him be as yourself,*
  because you have bought him with blood.
³¹*If you have a servant, treat him as a brother,*
  for as your own soul you will need him.
If you ill-treat him, and he leaves and runs away,
  which way will you go to seek him?

* Sir 33:25-33 LXX.

OVERVIEW: God punishes us so as to drive us away from sin (CHRYSOSTOM).

33:27 Idleness Teaches Evil

GOD'S PUNISHMENT KEEPS US FROM SIN.
JOHN CHRYSOSTOM: If, following the devil's promise that after the transgression he would be seen as equal to God,[1] the man actually enjoyed such an honor, then he would have fallen into three extreme evils. First of all, he would have thought that God was jealous, a deceiver and a liar. Second, that the real deceiver and the father of lies[2] and envy was in fact a benefactor and a friend. And third, he would have continued to sin for all eternity. But God kept all this far from the man by casting him out of paradise.[3] In the same way a doctor who ignores a wound produces a worse inflammation. But if he resorts to an incision, he prevents the infection from spreading. Nor did God stop there, but he also added sweat and toil,[4] because it is the nature of human beings to not be made for relaxation. And if, though being inflicted with these punishments, we persist in sin, what would we have not dared to do if God had moved us toward softness and idleness? "Idleness teaches many evils," it is said. Both what happens every day and the things that happened to those who came before us testify

---

[1]See Gen 3:5. [2]See Jn 8:44. [3]See Gen 3:23. [4]See Gen 3:17-19.

to this. It is written, in fact, that "the people sat down to eat, then rose up to revel."[5] And, "you became fat, gross and bloated, and the one who was beloved has rejected God."[6] To STAGIRIUS

WHO WAS TORMENTED BY A DEVIL 1.3.[7]

[5]Ex 32:6; cf. 1 Cor 10:7. [6]Deut 32:15. [7]CTP 163:49-50.

34:1-8 DREAMS

[1]*A man of no understanding has vain and false hopes,*
  and dreams give wings to fools.
[2]*As one who catches at a shadow and pursues the wind,*
  so is he who gives heed to dreams.
[3]*The vision of dreams is this against that,*
  the likeness of a face confronting a face.
[4]*From an unclean thing what will be made clean?*
  And from something false what will be true?
[5]*Divinations and omens and dreams are folly,*
  and like a woman in travail the mind has fancies.
[6]*Unless they are sent from the Most High as a visitation,*
  do not give your mind to them.
[7]*For dreams have deceived many,*
  and those who put their hope in them have failed.
[8]*Without such deceptions the law will be fulfilled,*
  and wisdom is made perfect in truthful lips.

OVERVIEW: Dreams require discernment, since some are natural, some come from the devil, and some come from God (GREGORY THE GREAT).

34:7 Dreams Have Deceived Many

DISCERNING DREAMS. GREGORY THE GREAT: Know that the images that occur in dreams can be impressed on the soul in six different ways. Sometimes, in fact, dreams are caused by bad digestion or by fasting, at times they are the fruit of an illusion, at other times of reflection and illusion together, at still other times of revelation, and, finally, at times of reflection and revelation together. Everyone experiences the first two types. The other four, rather, we find in the pages of sacred Scripture. If, in fact, dreams were not for the most part provoked by the hidden enemy through an illusion, the wise man would not have put us on guard, saying, "Dreams have led many into error, and those who put their hope in them have gone astray."

Nor would he exhort us, "Do not practice any sort of divination or magic."[1] These words show unequivocally how one must flee from everything having anything to do with the divining arts. Furthermore, if dreams did not at times proceed from reflection joined to illusion, the wise man would never had said, "From many cares come dreams."[2] And if, at times, the mystery of a revelation did not give origin to dreams, Joseph would not have been revered by his brothers in a dream,[3] nor would an angel have said to the husband of Mary in a dream to take the baby and flee to Egypt.[4] Moreover, if dreams did not proceed from reflection together with a revelation, the prophet Daniel, when he interpreted the dream of Nebuchadnezzar, would not have begun by referring to a reflection, saying, "O king, the thoughts that came to you while you were in bed concern the future. He who reveals mysteries wanted to reveal to you what will take place."[5] And then, "As you watched, O king, you saw a statue, an enormous statue of extraordinary splendor, rising before you with a terrifying appearance."[6] Thus Daniel, while he cautiously allows it to be understood that the dream will become reality and shows from what reflection it was produced, clearly shows that at times a dream is born simultaneously from reflection and from a revelation. Clearly, precisely because dreams have such different characteristics and origins, the more difficult it is to discern what their source is, the less should one be inclined to put faith in them. The saints, however, by a special sensibility they possess, are able to distinguish between illusions and revelations and to penetrate the meaning of the words and images in visions. Thus they know either what they have received from the good spirit or what illusion they have been victimized by. But if a soul is not prudent regarding dreams, it will find itself lost in a forest of vanity through the work of the deceiving spirit, whose art it is at times to predict many true things, so as to then imprison the soul in the snare of a single lie. DIALOGUES 4.50.2-6.[7]

---

[1]Lev 19:26. [2]Eccles 5:2. [3]See Gen 37:5-10. [4]See Mt 2:13. [5]Dan 2:29. [6]Dan 2:31. [7]GMO 4:433-35.

34:9-17* JOURNEYS

[9]An educated[q] man knows many things,
   and one with much experience will speak with understanding.
[10]He that is inexperienced knows few things,
   but he that has traveled acquires much cleverness.
[11]I have seen many things in my travels,
   and I understand more than I can express.
[12]I have often been in danger of death,
   but have escaped because of these experiences.

[13]The spirit of those who fear the Lord will live,

for their hope is in him who saves them.
¹⁴He who fears the Lord will not be timid,
 nor play the coward, for he is his hope.
¹⁵Blessed is the soul of the man who fears the Lord!
 To whom does he look? And who is his support?
¹⁶The eyes of the Lord are upon those who love him,
 a mighty protection and strong support,
a shelter from the hot wind and a shade from noonday sun,
 a guard against stumbling and a defense against falling.
¹⁷He lifts up the soul and gives light to the eyes;
 he grants healing, life, and blessing.

---

q Other authorities read *A traveled* * Sir 34:9-20 Vg, with many differences.

OVERVIEW: Temptations are tests we can overcome (CYRIL/JOHN OF JERUSALEM).

34:10 *The Inexperienced Know Few Things*

TEMPTATION. CYRIL/JOHN OF JERUSALEM: "And lead us not into temptation,"[1] Lord. Does the Lord perhaps teach us to pray that we will never be tempted? Why does he say elsewhere, "The person who has not been tempted is not proven,"[2] and again, "Consider it supreme joy, brothers and sisters, when you fall into various temptations."[3] But to enter into temptation is not to let oneself be overwhelmed by temptation. In fact, temptation seems like a stream of difficult passage. Some, who do not let themselves be submerged by temptation, make it across. They are good swimmers who do not allow themselves to be carried away by the stream. Others, who are not good swimmers, are submerged when they enter the stream. Thus, for example, Judas, having entered into the temptation of avarice,[4] did not overcome it but hanged himself,[5] being materially and spiritually submerged. Peter entered into the temptation of denial[6] but, overcoming it, was not submerged by it. He crossed the stream with courage and was not carried away. In yet another passage, listen to the chorus of the perfect saints, who give thanks for having escaped temptation. "You tried us, O God. Like silver you passed us through the fire. You pushed us into the snare, you laid sufferings on our backs. You made people pass over our heads. We passed through fire and water, and you have brought us to refreshment."[7] MYSTAGOGICAL LECTURES 5.17.[8]

---

[1]Mt 6:13. [2]Sir 34:10, variant. [3]Jas 1:2. [4]See Jn 12:6. [5]See Mt 27:5; Acts 1:18. [6]See Mt 26:69-75; Mk 14:66-72; Lk 22:56-62; Jn 18:25-27. [7]Ps 66:10-12 (65:10-12 LXX). [8]CTP 8:87.

34:18-26* SACRIFICES

¹⁸*If one sacrifices from what has been wrongfully obtained, the offering is blemished;*^r
  the gifts^s *of the lawless are not acceptable.*
¹⁹*The Most High is not pleased with the offerings of the ungodly;*
  and he is not propitiated for sins by a multitude of sacrifices.
²⁰*Like one who kills a son before his father's eyes*
  is the man who offers a sacrifice from the property of the poor.
²¹*The bread of the needy is the life of the poor;*
  whoever deprives them of it is a man of blood.
²²*To take away a neighbor's living is to murder him;*
  to deprive an employee of his wages is to shed blood.

²³*When one builds and another tears down,*
  what do they gain but toil?
²⁴*When one prays and another curses,*
  to whose voice will the Lord listen?
²⁵*If a man washes after touching a dead body, and touches it again,*
  what has he gained by his washing?
²⁶*So if a man fasts for his sins,*
  and goes again and does the same things,
who will listen to his prayer?
  And what has he gained by humbling himself?

r Other authorities read *is made in mockery*   s Other authorities read *mockeries*   * Sir 34:21-31 Vg.

OVERVIEW: Almsgiving is necessary to heal avarice (GREGORY THE GREAT), even as the prayer of the saints is useless without an effort from the sinner (BARSANUPHIUS AND JOHN). Tears, too, are useless if we persevere in evil (FULGENTIUS). We also include here a brief discussion about a textual variant (AUGUSTINE).

34:20 Sacrificing the Poor

HEALING FROM AVARICE TO GIVE ALMS.
GREGORY THE GREAT: If the fault is not burned at the roots right as it begins to spread, the thorn of avarice, spreading through the branches, will never dry up. The occasion for stealing is removed, therefore, if the limits of the right of possession are clearly established beforehand. Only those who have been admonished in this way should then hear how they should mercifully distribute what they possess. That is, when they have learned to not mix the good of mercy with the wickedness of theft, since they will later seek, with violence, what they had earlier bestowed in mercy. It is one thing to be merciful toward sins and another to sin so as to be merciful—which, besides, can no longer be called

mercy, because the tree that has become bitter[1] cannot yield sweet fruit, due to the poison of a diseased root. For this reason the Lord reproves the sacrifices themselves through the prophet, saying, "I the Lord love justice and hate thievery in sacrifices."[2] He also says, "The sacrifices of the impious are an abomination, issuing from crimes."[3] This is because they often take what they offer to God from the poor. But the Lord shows with what blame he rejects them, saying through a wise man, "One sacrifices a son before his own father who offers a sacrifice with the goods of the poor." What could be more unbearable than the death of a son before his father's eyes? In this way it shows the wrath with which this sacrifice is regarded, which is compared with the sorrow of a father deprived of his son. And yet, they frequently weigh up what they give but fail to consider what they steal. They count what they give as though it were wages due but refuse to attentively weigh their wrongs. Listen, then, to what is written: "The one who gathered wages put them in a sack with a hole in it,"[4] since one sees when he puts the money into such a sack, but he does not see when he loses it. PASTORAL RULE 3.21.[5]

34:23 Gaining Only Toil

CONVERSION AND THE PRAYER OF THE SAINTS. BARSANUPHIUS AND JOHN: If a person does not do what he can, uniting himself to the prayers of the saints, neither does he derive any benefit if the saints pray for him. If they abstain and intercede for him but he abandons himself to dissoluteness and pleasure, what good is their prayer for him? The word is thus fulfilled, "If one builds and another destroys, what good is further labor?" If this could in fact occur, that the one for whom the saints prayed would be saved without him making even a minimum of effort, nothing would stop them from doing this for all the sinners in the world. The sinner, moreover, if he does make a bit of effort, also has need of the prayers of the righteous. As the

apostle says, "The intense prayer of the righteous can do much."[6] This happens when a holy and righteous person intercedes and the sinner cooperates with the saints' prayers, to the extent possible for him, by penance, being unable to pay his debt by himself. His contribution is small, but that of the prayer of the saints is great. It is as though someone needed to carry ten sacks of grain and was unable to carry even two but finds a God-fearing person who takes nine of them, leaving him with just one. And he is protected in this way until he arrives safe and sound, unharmed by robbers. This also is the same thing. BOOK OF LETTERS 616.[7]

34:25 What Has Been Gained by Washing?

TEXTUAL DISCUSSION. AUGUSTINE: It was not Donatus of Carthage who established that Christians had to be rebaptized, as I thought when I responded to his letter. Nor is it true that he drew the words necessary for his purpose directly from an expression of Ecclesiasticus, where it is written, "If a person is baptized after touching a dead person and touches him again, what good was it for him to wash."[8] He claims it reads, "If someone is baptized by a dead person, what good was it for him to wash?"[9] We later ascertained that even before the Donatist party existed, many codices—mostly, to be honest, African—did not have in this context the words "and touches him again." RETRACTATIONS 1.21.3.[10]

34:26 Who Will Listen to His Prayer?

TEARS AND CONVERSION. FULGENTIUS OF RUSPE: When it is said to a sinner who desires to receive the benefit of salvation that if he converts

---

[1]See Mt 7:17-18; 12:32-33; Lk 6:43-44. [2]Cf. Is 61:8. [3]Prov 21:27. [4]Hag 1:6. [5]CTP 28:183-84. [6]Jas 5:16. [7]CTP 93:503-4; cf. FC 114:205-6. [8]Sir 34:25 (34:30 Vg). [9]This is a variant to the Latin biblical text that was used by the Donatists and before them by Cyprian and other African authors to justify rebaptism. [10]NBA 2:117.

and groans he will be saved,[11] one must also understand that if he groans but is not converted, he will not be saved. Indeed, not in vain did the Word of God unite both these elements, that we might know that both are necessary, conversion and groaning, to attain salvation. Some, in fact, humiliated by the consideration of their offenses, groan in prayer over their iniquities, but, this notwithstanding, they do not distance themselves from their bad actions. They recognize they have behaved badly but do not want to put an end to their wicked actions. They humbly denounce before God the sins that oppress them but obstinately pile up in their perverse heart the same sins they denounce with their humble speech. The indulgence that they ask for with tearful groanings, they take away by their bad actions. They ask the doctor for medicine and give sustenance to the sickness, to their ruin. And thus vainly they seek by their words to placate the just judge,[12] who they incite to greater fury by wicked actions. Such people will never purify their sins with groanings, because they do not stop sinning after their groaning. They groan for their misdeeds, and after they groan, they return to them. In Ecclesiasticus, the sacred Scripture speaks of such persons thusly: "The one who purifies himself after having touched a dead person and touches him again, what good did it do him to have been purified? Likewise, the person who fasts for his sins and again does the same actions, what advantage does he gain from humiliating himself? Who will listen to his prayers?" Fine, says God to such a person, "If you convert and groan, you will be saved."[13] With the severe and good God, when one has turned to God with the humility of a contrite heart,[14] then the prayer of the one who groans will be heard, the request made with tears will be attended to, salvation will be granted to the one who weeps. Certainly God will pardon the sinner and have mercy on him if the sinner acknowledges his iniquity by conversion. ON THE FORGIVENESS OF SINS 1.12.1-2.[15]

---

[11]Cf. Is 30:15. [12]See 2 Tim 4:8. [13]Is 30:15. [14]See Ps 51:19 (50:19 LXX). [15]CTP 57:34-35.

35:1-11* LAW AND SACRIFICES

[1]*He who keeps the law makes many offerings;*
* he who heeds the commandments sacrifices a peace offering.*
[2]*He who returns a kindness offers fine flour,*
* and he who gives alms sacrifices a thank offering.*
[3]*To keep from wickedness is pleasing to the Lord,*
* and to forsake unrighteousness is atonement.*
[4]*Do not appear before the Lord empty-handed,*
[5]*for all these things are to be done because of the commandment.*
[6]*The offering of a righteous man anoints the altar,*
* and its pleasing odor rises before the Most High.*

⁷*The sacrifice of a righteous man is acceptable,*
    and the memory of it will not be forgotten.
⁸*Glorify the Lord generously,*
    and do not stint the first fruits of your hands.
⁹*With every gift show a cheerful face,*
    and dedicate your tithe with gladness.
¹⁰*Give to the Most High as he has given,*
    and as generously as your hand has found.
¹¹*For the Lord is the one who repays,*
    and he will repay you sevenfold.

* Sir 35:1-10 LXX (35:1-13 Vg).

OVERVIEW: The faithful celebrate the memory of the saints and of their death, looking toward eternal life (ANONYMOUS ANOMOEAN).

35:6 The Offering of the Righteous

MEMORIALIZING THE SAINTS AND THE DEAD.
ANONYMOUS ANOMOEAN: We remember the saints, and we celebrate with devotion the memory of our parents and friends who have died in the faith, rejoicing together over their freedom and asking a pious end in faith for ourselves as well. And it is thus that we do not celebrate the birth, as do those who have no hope,[1] but we celebrate the day of their death,[2] since those who die live forever. We celebrate, remembering believers as well as priests, inviting the faithful together with the clergy and satisfying the miserable and the poor, orphans and widows,[3] so that our feast would be a memorial of rest for the deceased souls whose memory we celebrate and for us would be transformed into a pleasing fragrance before the face of the eternal God.[4] COMMENTARY ON JOB 3.34.[5]

[1]See Eph 2:12; 1 Thess 4:13. [2]The author probably has in mind the Latin phrase *dies natalis* ("day of birth") used by Christians to talk about death (especially of the martyrs) as the beginning of a new life. [3]See Deut 16:11. [4]Sir 35:5 (35:8 Vg). [5]CSEL 96:392-393.

35:12-20* DIVINE JUSTICE

¹²*Do not offer him a bribe, for he will not accept it;*
    and do not trust to an unrighteous sacrifice;
for the Lord is the judge,
    and with him is no partiality.
¹³*He will not show partiality in the case of a poor man;*
    and he will listen to the prayer of one who is wronged.

¹⁴He will not ignore the supplication of the fatherless,
  nor the widow when she pours out her story.
¹⁵Do not the tears of the widow run down her cheek
  as she cries out against him who has caused them to fall?
¹⁶He whose service is pleasing to the Lord will be accepted,
  and his prayer will reach to the clouds.
¹⁷The prayer of the humble pierces the clouds,
  and he will not be consoled until it reaches the Lord;^t
he will not desist until the Most High visits him,
  and does justice for the righteous, and executes judgment.
¹⁸And the Lord will not delay,
  neither will he be patient with them,
till he crushes the loins of the unmerciful
  and repays vengeance on the nations;
till he takes away the multitude of the insolent,
  and breaks the scepters of the unrighteous;
¹⁹till he repays man according to his deeds,
  and the works of men according to their devices;
till he judges the case of his people
  and makes them rejoice in his mercy.
²⁰Mercy is as welcome when he afflicts them
  as clouds of rain in the time of drought.

t Or *until the Lord draws near* * Sir 35:11-24 LXX (35:14-26 Vg).

OVERVIEW: Through prayer we become capable of winning over the enemy (ORIGEN). Tears and prayers defeat the enemy (FULGENTIUS). God sends his mercy in time of tribulation (AUGUSTINE).

35:17 The Prayer of the Humble

FIGHTING THE DEVIL WITH PRAYER. ORIGEN: The soul should attend not only to the hearing of the words but to the understanding of the realities. Recall the past, understand the present, attend to the future. Compare events in their succession, and contemplate the magnificence of the divine powers. Earlier, six hundred thousand[1] armed sons of Israel advanced against Midian, and they were all defeated because of the sin that was in them. Now, however, the victorious Midianites, who had routed six hundred thousand men, are beaten by twelve thousand, so that you would know that Israel does not win by the multitude or number of its soldiers but by the justice and piety that are in them. Thus also in their blessings it is said that if they observe the law of the Lord, one of them will pursue a thousand, and two will cause ten thousand to flee.[2] See, then, that a single saint who prays is worth much more than innumerable sinners in battle. "The prayer of the Holy One pierces heaven."[3] How will it not also defeat earthly enemies? For this reason, in every way you must make an effort to "seek" first and to preserve "the righteousness of God."[4] If you attain it and keep it, it will subject all of your enemies to you: if, as the apostle says, you are "clothed with the breastplate of righteousness and the belt of truth, if you take up the helmet of salvation

---

[1]See Num 11:21. [2]See Lev 26:8. [3]Sir 35:17 (35:21 Vg). [4]See Mt 6:33.

and the sword of the Spirit" and, above all, the "shield of faith, with which you will be able to extinguish all the fiery darts of the evil one."[5] Equipped with these weapons, you will put to flight all of the camps of the devil and his whole army, and you will faithfully sing, "If they encamp against me, my heart will not fear. If they raise a battle against me, even then will I hope."[6] HOMILIES ON NUMBERS 25.2.1-2.[7]

TEARS AND PRAYERS DEFEAT THE ADVERSARY. FULGENTIUS OF RUSPE: We defeat the adversary only if we fight with tears and with prayers, in continual humility of heart. It is written, in fact, that "the prayer of the humble penetrates the clouds and is not withdrawn from God until it is answered."[8] The weeping of the humble is therefore a great antidote against carnal concupiscence. Tears that spring from compunction of heart defeat the enemy and gain for us the gift of a victorious happiness. In fact, those who "go out weeping, scattering their seeds, will return rejoicing, carrying their sheaves."[9] How wisely the holy prophet teaches that the seeds of good works must be watered with rivers of tears! Indeed, no seed germinates without being watered. Nor does a seed bear fruit if it has been without the benefit of water. We also, therefore, if we wish to harvest the fruits of our seeds, should not cease watering them with tears, which should spring from the heart more than from the body. This is why we are told through the prophet to rend our hearts, not our garments.[10] LETTERS 4.9.5.[11]

35:20 *Mercy Is Welcome*

GOD'S MERCY IN TRIBULATION. AUGUSTINE: When tribulation comes, you will not be without help. This will show you that what he sent you during the day was true. In a certain passage it is written, "Mercy is as wonderful in time of affliction as clouds that bear rain in time of drought." "By day the Lord sent his mercy, and by night I will tell of it."[12] At no time does he show you his help more than when tribulation comes, in such a way that he who had promised by day that he would do so, frees you from it. EXPOSITIONS OF THE PSALMS 41.16.[13]

---

[5]Eph 6:14-17. [6]Ps 27:3 (26:3 LXX). [7]CTP 76:341; ACTHN 154-55*. [8]Sir 35:17-18 (35:21 Vg). [9]Ps 126:6 (125:6 LXX). [10]See Joel 2:13. [11]CTP 149:126. [12]Ps 42:9 (41:9 LXX), variant. [13]NBA 25:1027.

36:1-17* PRAYER FOR ISRAEL'S LIBERATION AND REBIRTH

[1]*Have mercy upon us, O Lord, the God of all, and look upon us,*
   [2]*and cause the fear of thee to fall upon all the nations.*
[3]*Lift up thy hand against foreign nations*
   and let them see thy might.
[4]*As in us thou hast been sanctified before them,*

so in them be thou magnified before us;
⁵*and let them know thee, as we have known*
   that there is no God but thee, O Lord.
⁶*Show signs anew, and work further wonders;*
   make thy hand and thy right arm glorious.
⁷*Rouse thy anger and pour out thy wrath;*
   destroy the adversary and wipe out the enemy.
⁸*Hasten the day, and remember the appointed time,ᵘ*
   and let people recount thy mighty deeds.
⁹*Let him who survives be consumed in the fiery wrath,*
   and may those who harm thy people meet destruction.
¹⁰*Crush the heads of the rulers of the enemy,*
   who say, "There is no one but ourselves."
¹¹*Gather all the tribes of Jacob,*
   and giveᵛ them their inheritance, as at the beginning.
¹²*Have mercy, O Lord, upon the people called by thy name,*
   upon Israel, whom thou hast likened to aʷ first-born son.
¹³*Have pity on the city of thy sanctuary,ˣ*
   Jerusalem, the place of thy rest.
¹⁴*Fill Zion with the celebration of thy wondrous deeds,*
   and thy templeʸ with thy glory.
¹⁵*Bear witness to those whom thou didst create in the beginning,*
   and fulfil the prophecies spoken in thy name.
¹⁶*Reward those who wait for thee,*
   and let thy prophets be found trustworthy.
¹⁷*Hearken, O Lord, to the prayer of thy servants,*
   according to the blessing of Aaron for thy people,
and all who are on the earth will know
   that thou art the Lord, the God of the ages

---

u Other authorities read *remember thy oath*   **v** Other authorities read *I gave*   **w** Other authorities read *hast named thy*   **x** Or *on thy holy city*   **y** Heb Syr: Gk Vg *people*   * Sir 36:1-19 Vg.

OVERVIEW: The church is the new Zion, where the power of the Lord becomes visible (RABANUS MAURUS).

36:14 Zion Celebrates God's Deeds

THE CHURCH IS THE NEW ZION. RABANUS MAURUS: Zion is translated as "contemplation."[1] And the holy church is rightly called "contemplation," because it is from there that the hearts of the faithful contemplate the joys of the heavenly kingdom. The Lord fills them with his unspeakable words and instructs them with knowledge of the divine books, in which are proclaimed the inexpressible power of God and the incomparable glory of his majesty. Moreover, by the signs of miracles he manifests his power among all peoples, so that, for this reason, it will be a motive for terror and for honor among all the surrounding nations. Thus we read in the Acts of the Apostles that while Paul preached and performed miracles in the city of Ephesus,

---

[1] Traditional etymology.

"all were filled with fear," that is, the Jews and the Gentiles who lived there, "and they glorified the name of the Lord Jesus. Many who had embraced the faith came to confess their actions in public. And many who had followed magic arts brought their books and burned them before all. The value of all of these was calculated, and they found it to be fifty thousand drachmas of silver. In this way the word of God grew and was strengthened."[2] ON ECCLESIASTICUS 8.7.[3]

---

[2]Acts 19:17-20. [3]PL 109:1019.

36:18-20* DISCERNMENT

^{8}The stomach will take any food,
    yet one food is better than another.
^{19}As the palate tastes the kinds of game,
    so an intelligent mind detects false words.
^{20}A perverse mind will cause grief,
    but a man of experience will pay him back.

---

* Sir 36:20-22 Vg.

OVERVIEW: The true believer rejects heretical deception with true faith and God's Word (RABANUS MAURUS).

36:20 A Perverse Mind

REJECTING SNARES FROM THE HERETICS. RABANUS MAURUS: The perverse heart of heretics contemplates injustice[1] all day long, and their tongue prepares to deceive.[2] The expert in right doctrine resists them with the shield of the true faith and with "the sword of the Spirit, which is the word of God."[3] ON ECCLESIASTICUS 8.7.[4]

---

[1]See Ps 140:3 (139:3 LXX), variant. [2]See Ps 5:10. [3]Eph 6:17. [4]PL 109:1021.

36:21-26* CHOOSING A WIFE

²¹*A woman will accept any man,*
but one daughter is better than another.
²²*A woman's beauty gladdens the countenance,*
and surpasses every human desire.
²³*If kindness and humility mark her speech,*
her husband is not like other men.
²⁴*He who acquires a wife gets his best possession,^z*
a helper fit for him and a pillar of support.^a
²⁵*Where there is no fence, the property will be plundered;*
and where there is no wife, a man will wander about and sigh.
²⁶*For who will trust a nimble robber*
that skips from city to city?
So who will trust a man that has no home,
and lodges wherever night finds him?

z Heb: Gk *enters upon a possession*   a Heb: Gk *rest*   * Sir 36:21-27 LXX (36:23-28 Vg).

OVERVIEW: The devil laid snares to Job using his wife (ANONYMOUS ANOMOEAN).

36:24 A Man's Best Possession

JOB'S WIFE LAID TRAPS FOR HIM. ANONYMOUS ANOMOEAN: "Job watched her."[1] What did he watch? He watched his wife—the plots, the trap, the destruction, the ruin. In fact, she who should have been wife and counselor and helper in all the good things of his life[2] had become a snare for him, a net, a fraud and counselor and promoter of every sort of impiety—although the righteous Job did not listen to her. But in the meantime, having become a servant of the evil one, she sought to deceive and ruin blessed Job, and the just one, "watching her," rightly saw the one who principally spoke through her. He understood that the devil, the first enemy, threatened him by her words, and so he resisted her malice. And, through her who had spoken to him, he confounded and rejected the wickedness of the devil. COMMENTARY ON JOB 2.52.[3]

---

[1]Job 2:10. [2]Sir 36:24 (36:26 Vg). [3]CSEL 96:328.

37:1-6 FALSE FRIENDS

^{1}*Every friend will say, "I too am a friend";*
   but some friends are friends only in name.
^{2}*Is it not a grief to the death*
   when a companion and friend turns to enmity?
^{3}*O evil imagination, why were you formed*
   to cover the land with deceit?
^{4}*Some companions rejoice in the happiness of a friend,*
   but in time of trouble are against him.
^{5}*Some companions help a friend for their stomach's sake,*
   and in the face of battle take up the shield.
^{6}*Do not forget a friend in your heart,*
   and be not unmindful of him in your wealth.

OVERVIEW: Job's friends were sympathetic with him, even if they criticized him (ANONYMOUS ANOMOEAN).

37:5 Helping a Friend

IN PRAISE OF JOB'S FRIENDS. ANONYMOUS ANOMOEAN: When they saw Job in such misery and in such a pitiful condition, they did not despise or disdain him but showed complete sincerity. Those blessed men were not ungrateful like the people of today, who distance themselves or are ill-willed. When someone is doing well, they are friends and appear sincere and pure, but if tribulation strikes, they distance themselves, they despise their friend, they forget and abandon him, thus showing the emptiness of everything that went before and their ingratitude for it. But those men were not like that, maintaining sincerity and affection for one another until death, as is clearly shown by the one who says, "A companion sympathizes with his friend until death and in time of war takes up arms." Those sincere men were like this, friends to Job without wavering, not changing their opinion so as to become his enemies or deny or abandon him, though they did contradict him with words and in their discussions, because they were convinced they were defending the righteousness of God. COMMENTARY ON JOB 3.11.[1]

---

[1]CSEL 96:358-59.

37:7-15* COUNSELORS

⁷Every counselor praises counsel,
   but some give counsel in their own interest.
⁸Be wary of a counselor,
   and learn first what is his interest—
   for he will take thought for himself—
lest he cast the lot against you
   ⁹and tell you, "Your way is good,"
   and then stand aloof to see what will happen to you.
¹⁰Do not consult with one who looks at you suspiciously;
   hide your counsel from those who are jealous of you.
¹¹Do not consult with a woman about her rival
   or with a coward about war,
with a merchant about barter
   or with a buyer about selling,
with a grudging man about gratitude
   or with a merciless man about kindness,
with an idler about any work
   or with a man hired for a year about completing his work,
with a lazy servant about a big task—
   pay no attention to these in any matter of counsel.
¹²But stay constantly with a godly man
   whom you know to be a keeper of the commandments,
whose soul is in accord with your soul,
   and who will sorrow with you if you fail.
¹³And establish the counsel of your own heart,
   for no one is more faithful to you than it is.
¹⁴For a man's soul sometimes keeps him better informed
   than seven watchmen sitting high on a watchtower.
¹⁵And besides all this pray to the Most High
   that he may direct your way in truth

* Sir 37:7-19 Vg.

OVERVIEW: The science of the faithful is superior to the wisdom of philosophers (RABANUS MAURUS).

37:14 Informed by One's Soul

THE BELIEVER IS SUPERIOR TO THE PHILOSOPHER. RABANUS MAURUS: Having first discussed the differences between counselors, here he adds how human wisdom is surpassed by the knowledge of the holy person, infused in him by the gift of the Holy Spirit. The seven counselors are the philosophers that teach the liberal arts (which they have divided into seven parts).[1] It is clear, however, that in every way the modest doctrine of a person having right faith, which is found in the divine books, is more true than the manifold intelligence of the philosophers in discussion and argumentation. In the one, the truth shines without blemish by means of a few pure words. In the other, in babbling on about abstruse questions, erroneous opinions emerge, or even obvious falsehoods. ON ECCLESIASTICUS 8.11.[2]

---

[1]Rabanus mentions the classical and mediaeval educational system, which divided science into seven parts: grammar, dialectic, rhetoric, arithmetic, music, geometry and astronomy. [2]PL 109:1026-27.

37:16-26* TRUE AND FALSE WISDOM

[16]*Reason is the beginning of every work,*
and counsel precedes every undertaking.
[17]*As a clue to changes of heart*
[18]*four turns of fortune appear,*
good and evil, life and death;
and it is the tongue that continually rules them.
[19]*A man may be shrewd and the teacher of many,*
and yet be unprofitable to himself.
[20]*A man skilled in words may be hated;*
he will be destitute of all food,
[21]*for grace was not given him by the Lord,*
since he is lacking in all wisdom.
[22]*A man may be wise to his own advantage,*
and the fruits of his understanding may be trustworthy on his lips.
[23]*A wise man will instruct his own people,*
and the fruits of his understanding will be trustworthy.
[24]*A wise man will have praise heaped upon him,*
and all who see him will call him happy.
[25]*The life of a man is numbered by days,*
but the days of Israel are without number.
[26]*He who is wise among his people will inherit confidence,*[b]
and his name will live for ever.

b Other authorities read *honor* * Sir 37:20-29 Vg.

Overview: The words of the heretics are captious and deceptive (Rabanus Maurus).

37:20 One Skilled in Words

Avoid the Speeches of Heretics. Rabanus Maurus: With this statement, malicious discourse is reproved and the malice of heretics condemned. In fact, the arts of debate and calculation are not referred to the senses of the body but to the rational faculty of the soul. Through these arts the truth is piously sought by those who fear God, who find it with profit, but the art of debate is useful for deepening and resolving every sort of question found in the holy Scriptures. One must merely avoid the desire to argue and the puerile ostentation of deceiving one's adversary. There are many arguments called sophisms,[1] that is, deductions based on false reasoning, that so closely imitate true reasoning that they deceive not only the obtuse but also those who, gifted with intelligence, do not give them the necessary attention. Someone, for example, says to another, "You are not what I am." And he responds that he agrees (which is in part true). But since the one was treacherous and the other a simpleton, the first added, "I am a man." And when the second said that he agreed, the first added, "Then you are not a man." I think that the Scripture condemns this kind of captious conclusion when it says, "One who has recourse to sophisms in discourse is hated,"[2] but also discourse that, though not being deceptive, is contorted by making use of more twists and turns of words than is appropriate to seriousness. This way of speaking by sophisms is characteristic of heretics, who do everything so as to seduce others with captiousness and malice. They are detestable to God and to all virtuous people. On Ecclesiasticus 8.12.[3]

---

[1]Rabanus alludes to the text of the Vulgate, which has literally "he who speaks using sophisms." [2]Sir 37:20 Vg. [3]PL 109:1028.

37:27-31* RESTRAINT

[27]My son, test your soul while you live;
    see what is bad for it and do not give it that.
[28]For not everything is good for every one,
    and not every person enjoys everything.
[29]Do not have an insatiable appetite for any luxury,
    and do not give yourself up to food;
[30]for overeating brings sickness,
    and gluttony leads to nausea.
[31]Many have died of gluttony,
    but he who is careful to avoid it prolongs his life.

* Sir 37:30-34 Vg.

OVERVIEW: Restraint and fast are good for health (ANONYMOUS ANOMOEAN).

37:30 Overeating and Gluttony

IN PRAISE OF MODERATION. ANONYMOUS ANOMOEAN: When some people eat or drink without restraint, their intestines, which were fine before, become upset, and they begin to be in pain or to become ill, as it is said, "The abuse of food causes illness."[1] Fools then say the person is bewitched. O people, when we fast and abstain from the enjoyment of meats, wine and superfluous foods, why are we not bewitched then? Rather, as soon as we begin to eat and drink again, we can count on upsetting the stomach and a disturbance of the intestines, which is avoided only by one who makes an effort not to eat anything superfluous. Thus it is not witchcraft that prevails but people's moderation. COMMENTARY ON JOB 3.17.[2]

---

[1]Sir 37:30 (37:33 Vg). [2]CSEL 96:368.

38:1-15 MEDICINE AND ILLNESS

[1]Honor the physician with the honor due him,[c] according to your need of him,
    for the Lord created him;
[2]for healing comes from the Most High,
    and he will receive a gift from the king.
[3]The skill of the physician lifts up his head,
    and in the presence of great men he is admired.
[4]The Lord created medicines from the earth,
    and a sensible man will not despise them.
[5]Was not water made sweet with a tree
    in order that his[d] power might be known?
[6]And he gave skill to men
    that he[e] might be glorified in his marvelous works.
[7]By them he heals and takes away pain;
    [8]the pharmacist makes of them a compound.
His works will never be finished;
    and from him health[f] is upon the face of the earth.

[9]My son, when you are sick do not be negligent,
    but pray to the Lord, and he will heal you.
[10]Give up your faults and direct your hands aright,
    and cleanse your heart from all sin.

^{11}*Offer a sweet-smelling sacrifice, and a memorial portion of fine flour,*
   and pour oil on your offering, as much as you can afford.^{g}
^{12}*And give the physician his place, for the Lord created him;*
   let him not leave you, for there is need of him.
^{13}*There is a time when success lies in the hands of physicians,^{h}*
      ^{14}*for they too will pray to the Lord*
that he should grant them success in diagnosis^i
   and in healing, for the sake of preserving life.
^{15}*He who sins before his Maker,*
   may he fall into the care^j of a physician

c Other authorities omit *with the honor due him*   d Or *its*   e Or *they*   f Or *peace*   g Heb: Vulgate omits *as much as you can afford;* Greek is obscure   h Gk *in their hands*   i Heb: Gk *rest*   j Gk *hands*

OVERVIEW: The episode of Marah is an image of the cross of Christ (RABANUS MAURUS).

38:5 *Water Made Sweet by Wood*

A FIGURE OF CHRIST'S CROSS. RABANUS MAURUS: The passage records an ancient episode, when the children of Israel "walked three days in the desert of Shur and did not find water. They arrived" finally "at Marah, but they could not drink the waters of Marah, because they were bitter." But the Lord "pointed out a piece of wood" to Moses, and when he "threw it into the water, it became sweet."[1] According to the account, the power of God was manifested there through his medical science,[2] in the waters made sweet by the wood. And the mystery of this event is obvious. The people grumble, seeing the waters and being unable to drink. Moses throws the wood into the waters, and they become sweet. Understand that the bitter waters represent the letter that kills[3] and the Law. If one throws on this the confession of the cross and adds the mystery of the passion of the Lord, then the bitter water becomes sweet, and the bitterness of the letter is transformed into the sweetness of spiritual knowledge. For this reason it is written, "The Lord established a law and judgments for his people, and he tested them."[4] According to another sense, the bitter waters that become sweet by receiving the wood are an image of the bitterness of the nations over the wood of the cross of Christ, which at a certain point is destined to become sweet. ON ECCLESIASTICUS 8.13.[5]

---

[1]Ex 15:22-25.   [2]God "healed" the water, restoring its natural condition, as a physician does with health.   [3]See 2 Cor 6:3.   [4]Unidentified quotation.   [5]PL 109:1030-31.

38:16-23* BEREAVEMENT

^{16}My son, let your tears fall for the dead,
  and as one who is suffering grievously begin the lament.
Lay out his body with the honor due him,
  and do not neglect his burial.
^{17}Let your weeping be bitter and your wailing fervent;
  observe the mourning according to his merit,
for one day, or two, to avoid criticism;
  then be comforted for your sorrow.
^{18}For sorrow results in death,
  and sorrow of heart saps one's strength.
^{19}In calamity sorrow continues,
  and the life of the poor man weighs down his heart.
^{20}Do not give your heart to sorrow;
  drive it away, remembering the end of life.
^{21}Do not forget, there is no coming back;
  you do the dead[k] no good, and you injure yourself.
^{22}"Remember my doom, for yours is like it:
  yesterday it was mine, and today it is yours."
^{23}When the dead is at rest, let his remembrance cease,
  and be comforted for him when his spirit has departed.

k Gk *him*   * Sir 38:15-24 Vg.

OVERVIEW: Scripture teaches us to honor and mourn the dead (PAULINUS).

38:16 *Begin the Lament*

BURYING AND MOURNING THE DEAD. PAULINUS OF NOLA: Before all else, I will praise in you the fruitful work of your Christian piety. In fact, the sacred Scripture shows that your behavior is also pleasing to God when it says, "Shed tears over the dead. As one who suffers grievously, begin the lament, and do not neglect his tomb." Our patriarchs are also examples of the performance of this ritual. Abraham, the father of our faith, wept over Sarah, the mother of our vocation,[1] not because he doubted ever seeing her again but out of sorrow for having lost her. How could the father of our faith have had doubts about the resurrection, he who was the first to hear the divine promise?[2] Mindful of her human condition, however, he did not despise care for the body in view of eternal salvation, but after acquiring a field suited for the burial, he interred his dead wife in an honorable grave.[3] In this way he wanted to show what people should do for the dying, since he, immediately after leaving the land of his ancestors at the call of God,[4] and though acquiring no land among the

[1]See Gen 23:2. [2]See Gen 12:1-3. [3]See Gen 23:9. [4]See Gen 12:1.

fertile plots of the various countries, nevertheless wanted to buy—he, the pilgrim of every nation[5]—a small fistful of dirt for the burial,[6] that is, a perennial and permanent possession, a field not for profit but for eternal rest. Jacob also honored his beloved and awaited Rachel, not only with a famous mausoleum but also with an epitaph that was a religious comfort in his suffering and at the same time a testimony to posterity.[7] Although he marked that grave with a mournful epitaph about his dead wife, with a prophetic spirit he foresaw that whereas the law was passing away, the gospel was coming into force. In the folds of this mystery, in many places the wife of the patriarch represented the image of the church. Nevertheless, as I believe, she dies as a symbol of the synagogue and in her delivery generates the son of pain,[8] whereas the Virgin, also by childbirth, generates the end of the law: the end of the law is Christ.[9] Tobias also suggests to us a holy and sanctified hope through his care for burial, and in a special way he was justified by the Lord for taking the initiative in this task, and indeed he was praised by the word of the archangel because he preferred the burial of a poor person to his own nourishment.[10] Ignoring his stomach because he was famished in soul, he preferred to die of bodily

hunger than of spiritual, so that he would be an example to us to prefer physical fasting at any cost, so as to secure for ourselves the salvation of our souls. See the goodness of care for the dead, see the goodness of the tears of love with which father Abraham desired to bury the mother of the ancient promises.[11] Good also were the pious tears that Joseph the righteous shed for his dead father[12] and the prayerful tears with which David bathed his bed almost every night.[13] But why recall the grief of the holy patriarchs? Jesus mourned his friend,[14] condescending to assume even this passion of our human condition, to the point of shedding tears for the dead and acting like a weak human person toward him whom he was going to raise by divine power. In that single man, however, the merciful and compassionate Lord also grieved over the condition of the human race, and in those tears with which he grieved our sins, he also cleansed them. LETTER 13, TO PAMMACHIUS.[15]

---

[5]See Gen 14:13. [6]See Gen 23:4. [7]See Gen 35:19-20. [8]See Gen 35:19. The text alludes to the name Rachel gave to Benjamin when she was dying: Ben-Oni, which means "son of pain." [9]See Rom 10:4. [10]See Tob 12:12-13. [11]See Gen 23:2. [12]See Gen 50:1. [13]See Ps 6:7. [14]See Jn 11:35. [15]CTP 42:83-85.

38:24-34* THE WORKS OF ARTISANS

[24]*The wisdom of the scribe depends on the opportunity of leisure;*
and he who has little business may become wise.
[25]*How can he become wise who handles the plow,*
and who glories in the shaft of a goad,
who drives oxen and is occupied with their work,
and whose talk is about[l] bulls?

^{26}He sets his heart on plowing furrows,
   and he is careful about fodder for the heifers.
^{27}So too is every craftsman and master workman
   who labors by night as well as by day;
those who cut the signets of seals,
   each is diligent in making a great variety;
he sets his heart on painting a lifelike image,
   and he is careful to finish his work.
^{28}So too is the smith sitting by the anvil,
   intent upon his handiwork in iron;
the breath of the fire melts his flesh,
   and he wastes away in^m the heat of the furnace;
he inclines his ear to the sound of the hammer,^{n}
   and his eyes are on the pattern of the object.
He sets his heart on finishing his handiwork,
   and he is careful to complete its decoration.
^{29}So too is the potter sitting at his work
   and turning the wheel with his feet;
he is always deeply concerned over his work,
   and all his output is by number.
^{30}He moulds the clay with his arm
   and makes it pliable with his feet;
he sets his heart to finish the glazing,
   and he is careful to clean the furnace.

^{31}All these rely upon their hands,
   and each is skilful in his own work.
^{32}Without them a city cannot be established,
   and men can neither sojourn nor live there.
^{33}Yet they are not sought out for the council of the people,
   nor do they attain eminence in the public assembly.
They do not sit in the judge's seat,
   nor do they understand the sentence of judgment;
they cannot expound discipline or judgment,
   and they are not found using proverbs.
^{34}But they keep stable the fabric of the world,
   and their prayer is in the practice of their trade.

l Or *among*   m Cn Compare Syr: Gk *contends with*   n Cn: Gk *the sound of the hammer renews his ear*   * Sir 38:25-39a Vg.

OVERVIEW: Every craft is a symbol of the activity deployed by the preacher who is committed to ministry (RABANUS MAURUS).

38:29 The Potter

THE PREACHER AS A ZEALOUS ARTISAN.
RABANUS MAURUS: And what is meant by this potter if not the holy preachers that we have spoken of already? Through various activities they worthily exercise the degrees of their

ministry, adapting their doctrine according to the condition of their hearers. The wise, in fact, must be admonished in a way different from the ignorant, the strong different from the weak, the young different from the old and men different from women. With the plow of the gospel they cultivate the field of the Lord. They pasture the sheep and animals of the Lord with the fodder of the Word. They engrave the seals of the new person in human hearts, producing the weapons of the virtues by the ministry of their tongue. They give an example, consoling by their words and behavior those who are fragile and sickly, until they are transformed into honorable vessels, fully fit for God's ministry.[1] This is why this potter works, turning the wheel with his feet, transforming the changeable situations of this life into an example for his disciples through the signs of good works. He watches what he does so that he might persevere in good actions, and by his own actions he invigorates the activity of the sick, giving them an example of humility and meekness and setting his whole heart on the smoothing of all that is bitter in the habits of those under him by the sweetness of his example. In addition, he spends all of his solicitude cooking every action of the disciples in the fire of the furnace of the heart, so as to render them firmer by the flame of love. He does this because all of his work could be damaged by a fall if it is not held together by the bond of charity. On Ecclesiasticus 8.16.[2]

---

[1]See also 2 Tim 2:21. [2]PL 109:1037.

39:1-11* THE SCRIBE

[1]*On the other hand he who devotes himself*
to the study of the law of the Most High
will seek out the wisdom of all the ancients,
and will be concerned with prophecies;
[2]*he will preserve the discourse of notable men*
and penetrate the subtleties of parables;
[3]*he will seek out the hidden meanings of proverbs*
and be at home with the obscurities of parables.
[4]*He will serve among great men*
and appear before rulers;
he will travel through the lands of foreign nations,
for he tests the good and the evil among men.
[5]*He will set his heart to rise early*
to seek the Lord who made him,
and will make supplication before the Most High;

he will open his mouth in prayer
and make supplication for his sins.

⁶If the great Lord is willing,
he will be filled with the spirit of understanding;
he will pour forth words° of wisdom
and give thanks to the Lord in prayer.
⁷He will direct his counsel and knowledge aright,
and meditate on his secrets.
⁸He will reveal instruction in his teaching,
and will glory in the law of the Lord's covenant.
⁹Many will praise his understanding,
and it will never be blotted out;
his memory will not disappear,
and his name will live through all generations.
¹⁰Nations will declare his wisdom,
and the congregation will proclaim his praise;
¹¹if he lives long, he will leave a name greater than a thousand,
and if he goes to rest, it is enough^p for him.

o Other authorities read *his words*   p Cn: the meaning of the Greek is uncertain   * Sir 38:39b–39:15 Vg, with many differences.

OVERVIEW: God governs everything for our salvation (SALVIAN).

39:7 Meditating on God's Secrets

GOD GUIDES EVERYTHING. SALVIAN THE PRESBYTER: The holy book says that everything, day after day, is ruled by the divine will and that God governs all things unceasingly. It says, "The Lord loves wisdom and an ordered life,"[1] and "There is no other God who cares for all."[2] And still, "Since you are just, you guide all things with equity, and you govern us with great respect."[3] So then, it speaks to you of God who guides and governs without interruption, but in this passage of Scripture not only is the government of God set forth but the dignity of human beings as well, since by saying "he governs us,"

it wants to convey the power of the divine rule, and by saying "with great respect," it allows us to understand how high is human dignity. Elsewhere in a prophet, it is written, "Do I not fill heaven and earth?"[4] God declares the reason why he fills all things: "Because I am with you to save you."[5] And with these words the Lord makes us understand not only that he governs and fills the universe but also the power and fruits of his presence. The divine presence, of itself, produces this fruit: the salvation of what it fills. And this is why saint Paul says in the Acts of the Apostles, "In him we have life, movement and being."[6] THE GOVERNANCE OF GOD 2.2.8-9.[7]

---

[1]Sir 39:7 (Vg 39:10), variant. [2]Wis 12:13. [3]Wis 12:15, 18. [4]Jer 23:24. [5]Jer 42:11. [6]Acts 17:28. [7]CTP 114:70-71.

39:12-35* A CALL TO PRAISE GOD

2 I have yet more to say, which I have thought upon,
and I am filled, like the moon at the full.
13 Listen to me, O you holy sons,
and bud like a rose growing by a stream of water;
14 send forth fragrance like frankincense,
and put forth blossoms like a lily.
Scatter the fragrance, and sing a hymn of praise;
bless the Lord for all his works;
15 ascribe majesty to his name
and give thanks to him with praise,
with songs on your lips, and with lyres;
and this you shall say in thanksgiving:
16 "All things are the works of the Lord, for they are very good,
and whatever he commands will be done in his time."

17 No one can say, "What is this?" "Why is that?"
for in God's[q] time all things will be sought after.
At his word the waters stood in a heap,
and the reservoirs of water at the word of his mouth.
18 At his command whatever pleases him is done,
and none can limit his saving power.
19 The works of all flesh are before him,
and nothing can be hid from his eyes.
20 From everlasting to everlasting he beholds them,
and nothing is marvelous to him.
21 No one can say, "What is this?" "Why is that?"
for everything has been created for its use.
22 His blessing covers the dry land like a river,
and drenches it like a flood.
23 The nations will incur his wrath,
just as he turns fresh water into salt.
24 To the holy his ways are straight,
just as they are obstacles to the wicked.
25 From the beginning good things were created for good people,
just as evil things for sinners.
26 Basic to all the needs of man's life
are water and fire and iron and salt
and wheat flour and milk and honey,

the blood of the grape, and oil and clothing.
²⁷*All these are for good to the godly,*
    just as they turn into evils for sinners.

²⁸*There are winds that have been created for vengeance,*
    and in their anger they scourge heavily;
in the time of consummation they will pour out their strength
    and calm the anger of their Maker.
²⁹*Fire and hail and famine and pestilence,*
    all these have been created for vengeance;
³⁰*the teeth of wild beasts, and scorpions and vipers,*
    and the sword that punishes the ungodly with destruction;
³¹*they will rejoice in his commands,*
    and be made ready on earth for their service,
    and when their times come they will not transgress his word.
³²*Therefore from the beginning I have been convinced,*
    and have thought this out and left it in writing:
³³*The works of the Lord are all good,*
    and he will supply every need in its hour.
³⁴*And no one can say, "This is worse than that,"*
    for all things will prove good in their season.
³⁵*So now sing praise with all your heart and voice,*
    and bless the name of the Lord.

q Gk *his*   * Sir 39:16-41 Vg.

OVERVIEW: Confession can also mean praising God (AUGUSTINE). Creation is good, but nothing is better than contemplating God, all things being good in their season (CASSIAN). What is good is good because of God the creator's goodness (AUGUSTINE).

39:15 Ascribe Majesty to God's Name

CONFESSION IN PRAISE OF GOD. AUGUSTINE: The confession of sins is that ordinary confession that is known to you. It is therefore unnecessary to speak of the reasons for its use. We must rather look into confession in praise of God and the proofs that demonstrate it. People are so habituated to calling "confession" the confession of sins that every time they hear the reader say the words, "Confess yourselves," they beat their breasts, and a kind of noisy buzz arises in their consciences as they are reminded of their duty. This almost always happens, and yet one is not always speaking of the confession of sins. At times, in fact, one speaks of the confession of praise, as in that passage of Scripture where it says, "Confess to the Lord, and in your confession you will say, 'All the works of the Lord are very good.'"[1] When you hear, "In your confession you will say, 'All the works of the Lord are very good,'" it is clear that this is a confession of praise to God and not of your guilt. In this case, you confess that all the works of the Lord are good, not that your actions are bad. And here is another passage about which, as with the

---

[1]Sir 39:15-16 (39:20-21 Vg). Augustine explains literally the Latin version: "In your confession."

previous one, there can be no doubt. The Lord Jesus certainly committed no sin,[2] yet in the Gospel it says, "I confess to you, Father, Lord of heaven and earth." And he continues with praise: "Because you have hidden these things from the wise and the intelligent and have revealed them to the little ones. Yes, Father, because that is what it pleased you to do."[3] This is the confession of one who praises God, not of one who accuses himself. Since, therefore, one who confesses either accuses himself or praises God, you should reflect a bit about the advantages of each type of confession. SERMONS 8.2.[4]

39:16 Everything Is the Work of the Lord

ALL THINGS ARE GOOD IN THEIR SEASON. JOHN CASSIAN: All the merits of holiness, though good and useful not only for the present life but also in view of gaining eternity, when compared with the merits of divine contemplation must nevertheless be considered vile and, so to speak, of little worth. And so that this comparison would be confirmed by the authority of the Scriptures, is it not true that the Scripture states comprehensively concerning all the things created by God, "And all the things that God created were very good,"[5] and, "All the things created by God are good in their time"? So then, the things of the present world are not simply called good but superlatively good. For us who live in this world, they serve for the needs of life, of bodily health, or some other useful reason unknown to us. Or, they are even "very good" in that they enable us "to see the invisible things of God from the creatures of the world, being understood by the things that are made, even his eternal power and Godhead,"[6] through such a great and ordered disposition of the created

universe and of all the things existing in it. Yet all of these things will not be deemed worth being called good once they are compared with the future age, in which there will be no alteration of good things and where no interruption of the true blessedness is to be feared. CONFERENCES 3.23.3.[7]

39:33 The Works of the Lord

THE GOODNESS OF CREATED THINGS. AUGUSTINE: Your creature had existence from the fullness of your goodness, so that a good that was entirely useless to you and, though it was from you and not equal to you,[8] because it could be created by you, would not fail to exist. What value did the heavens and the earth, which you created in the beginning, have for you?[9] And spiritual and bodily natures, created by you in your Wisdom[10]—let them too declare what they deserve from you, because even the inchoate and the formless beings depend on your Word. In their element, whether spiritual or corporeal, they tend away from you toward disorder and degeneration—although a formless spiritual being is superior to a formed bodily being and a formless corporeal being in turn superior to what is absolutely nothing. Thus they would have remained suspended in your word, formless, if this same word had not called them to your unity, endowed them with form and made all of them very good[11] thanks to you, the One and highest Good. CONFESSIONS 13.2.2.[12]

---

[2]See 2 Cor 5:21; 1 Pet 2:22. [3]Mt 11:25-26. [4]NBA 35/1:157-59. [5]Gen 1:31. [6]Rom 1:20. [7]CTP 156:382-83. [8]See Phil 2:6. [9]Gen 1:1. [10]Ps 104:24 (103:24 LXX). [11]See also Gen 1:31. [12]NBA 1:451-53.

40:1-11 HUMAN MISERY

¹*Much labor was created for every man,*
and a heavy yoke is upon the sons of Adam,
from the day they come forth from their mother's womb
*till the day they return to*ʳ *the mother of all.*
²*Their perplexities and fear of heart—*
their anxious thought is the day of death,
³*from the man who sits on a splendid throne*
to the one who is humbled in dust and ashes,
⁴*from the man who wears purple and a crown*
to the one who is clothed in burlap;
⁵*there is anger and envy and trouble and unrest,*
and fear of death, and fury and strife.
And when one rests upon his bed,
his sleep at night confuses his mind.
⁶*He gets little or no rest,*
and afterward in his sleep, as though he were on watch,
he is troubled by the visions of his mind
like one who has escaped from the battle-front;
⁷*at the moment of his rescue he wakes up,*
and wonders that his fear came to nothing.
⁸*With all flesh, both man and beast,*
and upon sinners seven times more,
⁹*are death and bloodshed and strife and sword,*
calamities, famine and affliction and plague.
¹⁰*All these were created for the wicked,*
and on their account the flood came.
¹¹*All things that are from the earth turn back to the earth,*
and what is from the waters returns to the sea.

r Other authorities read *are buried in*

OVERVIEW: We are all subject to suffering and death (PROSPER). No one is free from original sin (QUODVULTDEUS).

40:1 *A Heavy Yoke*

SUFFERING AND DEATH ARE OUR DESTINY.

PROSPER OF AQUITAINE: At no time does our corruptibility participate in incorruptibility, given that, our nature being destined to die, it is at all times subject to death. The beginning of this life is the beginning of death, and no sooner does our age begin to increase than our life begins to decrease. And if a stretch of time is added to it, it is not added in a permanent way but transitorily, always moving toward death. Thus a person, mortal from the beginning, who one day dies, does not die in violation of the law of mortality, and the possibility of dying is always greater for him than that of living. And although the mortality of all people derives from a single cause, nevertheless many are the weaknesses that lacerate corruptible human nature. And not only the years or the months or days of human life but every hour and each individual moment are subject to illness, depression and injuries. And there is no manner of dying that does not happen to at least someone among mortals. There hangs "a severe yoke over the children of Adam, from the day they come forth from their mother's womb until the day of their burial in the mother of all, the earth." THE CALL OF ALL NATIONS 2.21.[1]

OUR COMMON ORIGIN. QUODVULTDEUS: God said to the woman, "Multiplying, I will multiply your groaning and your pain."[2] The prophet David confirms that the children of transgressors are born in this way. "I was conceived," he says, "in iniquity, and in the midst of sins my mother fed me at her breast."[3] Solomon also attests to the same thing. "Heavy," he says, "is the yoke on the children of Adam, from the day they come forth from their mother's womb until the day of their burial in the mother of all." And similarly, "And I, when born, inhaled the common air and fell on the same earth, and like everyone else I emitted my first sound with tears. I was raised in swaddling clothes, with great care. No king, in fact, has begun existence differently, because there is only one entrance into life for all and only one exit."[4] And a little later, "They were an accursed race from the beginning."[5] And Isaiah, "Evil race, wicked children, you have abandoned the Lord."[6] Job also says, "No one is immune from defilement, not even a baby whose life on earth has been but a single day."[7] And again, "No one can make pure what has been conceived of an impure seed, except you alone, who are pure."[8] To expiate the curse of this seed and to purify the impurity of both the woman who has given birth and the child, the Law instituted sacrifices until the kingdom of Christ, who, his body offered in sacrifice,[9] saves the small and the great. THE BOOK OF PROMISES AND PREDICTIONS OF GOD 1.4.6.[10]

---

[1]CTP 143:152-53. [2]Gen 3:16. [3]Ps 51:7 (50:7 LXX). [4]Wis 7:3-6. [5]Wis 12:11. [6]Is 1:4. [7]Job 14:4. [8]Job 14:4 Vg. [9]See Eph 5:2. [10]CTP 82:57-58.

40:12-27* VARIOUS SAYINGS

12All bribery and injustice will be blotted out,
    but good faith will stand for ever.
13The wealth of the unjust will dry up like a torrent,
    and crash like a loud clap of thunder in a rain.
14A generous man will be made glad;
    likewise transgressors will utterly fail.

¹⁵*The children of the ungodly will not put forth many branches;*
  they are unhealthy roots upon sheer rock.
¹⁶*The reeds by any water or river bank*
  will be plucked up before any grass.
¹⁷*Kindness is like a garden of blessings,*
  and almsgiving endures for ever.
¹⁸*Life is sweet for the self-reliant and the worker,^s*
  but he who finds treasure is better off than both.
¹⁹*Children and the building of a city establish a man's name,*
  but a blameless wife is accounted better than both.
²⁰*Wine and music gladden the heart,*
  but the love of wisdom is better than both.
²¹*The flute and the harp make pleasant melody,*
  but a pleasant voice is better than both.
²²*The eye desires grace and beauty,*
  but the green shoots of grain more than both.
²³*A friend or a companion never meets one amiss,*
  but a wife with her husband is better than both.
²⁴*Brothers and help are for a time of trouble,*
  but almsgiving rescues better than both.
²⁵*Gold and silver make the foot stand sure,*
  but good counsel is esteemed more than both.
²⁶*Riches and strength lift up the heart,*
  but the fear of the Lord is better than both.
There is no loss in the fear of the Lord,
  and with it there is no need to seek for help.
²⁷*The fear of the Lord is like a garden of blessing,*
  and covers a man^t better than any glory.

s Cn: Gk *self-reliant worker*   t Gk *him*   * Sir 40:12-28 Vg.

OVERVIEW: Any time and place is fitting for prayer (BASIL). The saints accept God's will and are rewarded (CYRIL OF ALEXANDRIA). The church is like paradise, since it is filled with virtue and joy (AUGUSTINE).

40:20 Wine and Music Gladden the Heart

TIMES FOR PRAYING. BASIL THE GREAT: Prayer is the request for good made to God by pious persons. In no way do we limit such requests merely to words. We do not believe that God needs to be reminded of things with words. He already knows the things that are good for us, even when we do not ask for them.[1] So, what are we saying? That our prayer should not consist in syllables but in the soul's purpose and in virtuous actions that spread throughout our entire life. "Whether you eat," says the apostle, "or drink or do any other thing, do everything to the glory of God."[2] Seated at table, pray. Taking your bread, thank him who gave it to you. Fortifying the weakness of the body with wine, remember him who offers you this gift for the

---

[1]Cf. Mt 6:8, 32; Lk 12:30. [2]1 Cor 10:31.

gladness of your heart[3] and comfort in illness.[4] Do you no longer feel the need for food? Do not allow the memory of the Benefactor to fade! If you put on your tunic, give thanks to him who gave it to you. If you wrap yourself in your cloak, let your love for God grow, who has given you suitable clothing in both winter and summer, to care for your life and to cover what is shameful. Has the day ended? Give thanks to him who lavished sunlight in service of the affairs of the day and fire to illuminate the night, for dealing with what is left to be done. ON THE MARTYR JULITTA.[5]

IN PRAISE OF SAINTS. CYRIL OF ALEXANDRIA: We say that the saints who have arisen in the churches—mystagogues and teachers—are called holy stones that roll on the earth.[6] They were similar in appearance "to the precious, chosen cornerstone, placed by the God and Father in the foundation of Zion."[7] And if the foundation is of stones, compacted and joined to him and raised to God as a holy temple, these also are rightly called stones. It is very well said that they roll,[8] thus in some way indicating the agility and velocity with which they move toward every aspect of holiness. Round or spherical stones, in fact, overcome any obstacle and move with great facility, if one wants to move them. The mind of the saints, in turn, willingly adapts to the will of God. Since we are such "stones," it is clear that we should be righteous and blameless. But if there is some good, it is his, if there is something beautiful, it comes from him,[9] because God lavishes on us everything related to piety. What things? "Grain for the youths, sweet-smelling wine to the virgins."[10] One who

. . . is disposed to follow God's will with youthful boldness, wanting to do good, will receive from him even greater strength, symbolized by grain, since "bread strengthens the heart."[11] Another, who has been purified and has a pure mind and may justly be compared with the venerable and holy virgins, will receive like intelligible wine the clear and secure knowledge of God "that gladdens hearts."[12] Young people and virgins, therefore, as we have just explained, will rightly be called to participate to a high degree in the goods of heaven, and they will hear God say, "Eat and drink, become inebriated, you who are near me."[13] These are close to God, not with respect to place—it is stupid to think or imagine this—but in relation to an incontestable firmness of intellect and the aspiration to every virtue and to love for Him. COMMENTARY ON ZECHARIAH 9.64.[14]

40:27 A Garden of Blessing

THE CHURCH RESEMBLES PARADISE. AUGUSTINE: The church, for the faithful servants of God who live in temperance, justice and love for God, is rightly called paradise, rich as it is with abundant graces and chaste delights.[15] Even in tribulation, such a servant glories in his patience and is filled with great joy because the consolations of God gladden his soul in proportion to the many sufferings he experiences in his heart.[16] SERMONS 12.34.65.[17]

---

[3]See Sir 40:20; 31:27; Ps 104:15 (103:15 LXX). [4]See 1 Tim 5:23. [5]CTP 147:54-55. [6]See Zech 9:16. [7]Is 28:16. [8]See Zech 9:16. [9]See Zech 9:17. [10]Zech 9:17. [11]Ps 104:15 (103:15 LXX). [12]Zech 9:17. [13]Song 5:1. [14]CTP 60:165-66. [15]See Song 8:5. [16]See Ps 94:19 (93:19 LXX). [17]NBA 9/2:721.

40:28-30* BEGGING

^{28}My son, do not lead the life of a beggar;
  it is better to die than to beg.
^{29}When a man looks to the table of another,
  his existence cannot be considered as life.
He pollutes himself with another man's food,
  but a man who is intelligent and well instructed guards against that.
^{30}In the mouth of the shameless begging is sweet,
  but in his stomach a fire is kindled.

* Sir 40:29-32 Vg.

OVERVIEW: There are both material and spiritual beggars (ORIGEN).

40:28 Better to Die Than to Beg

MATERIAL AND SPIRITUAL MENDICANCY.
ORIGEN: The beggar begs because he lacks what is necessary and because he finds it impossible to procure these things in a dignified way. You might find in such a condition those who, so to speak, beg for saving remedies from the Greeks or from the barbarians who promise truth; they lack a dignified means, suitable for a being endowed with *logos*, of procuring without danger the abundant contemplation of the truth. But the Logos forbids this manner of seeking, saying somewhere, "Do not lead the life of a beggar. It is better to die than to beg." The unfaithful administrator in the Gospel was ashamed to beg, and therefore he says to the one who owes a hundred measures of wheat, "Take your note and write fifty," and to the one who owes a hundred barrels of oil, "Take your note and write eighty,"[1] preferring to decrease what is owed to his master than to shamefully beg, and for this he is praised.[2] Jesus, therefore, not only freed the blind man of the blindness that had afflicted him from birth[3] but also from begging,[4] because together with his sight he also gave him the possibility of finding a way to procure for himself what was necessary for the salvation of his soul.[5] In this case, the reason for begging was blindness, whereas in the Acts it was being lame:[6] one who is freed from these things will no longer beg. COMMENTARY ON THE GOSPEL OF JOHN, FRAGMENT 64.[7]

---

[1]Lk 16:6-7. [2]See Lk 16:8. [3]See Jn 9:1. [4]See Jn 9:8. [5]See Jn 9:35-38. [6]See Acts 3:2. [7]Trad. Corsini 869.

41:1-4* DEATH

¹O death, how bitter is the reminder of you
    to one who lives at peace among his possessions,
to a man without distractions, who is prosperous in everything,
    and who still has the vigor to enjoy his food!
²O death, how welcome is your sentence
    to one who is in need and is failing in strength,
very old and distracted over everything;
    to one who is contrary, and has lost his patience!
³Do not fear the sentence of death;
    remember your former days and the end of life;
this is the decree from the Lord for all flesh,
    ⁴and how can you reject the good pleasure of the Most High?
Whether life is for ten or a hundred or a thousand years,
    there is no inquiry about it in Hades.

* Sir 41:1-7 Vg.

OVERVIEW: Bitter is the death of someone who thinks only about the goods of this world (Rabanus Maurus).

41:1 The Bitter Reminder of Death

TRUSTING THE GOODS OF THIS WORLD. RABANUS MAURUS: The death of the flesh, which is the end of bodily life, is bitter for one who trusts in the prosperity of this world and the pursuit of riches, since he has not learned to love the joys of the future life. But since "the world and its disordered desires are passing away,"[1] all those who love it will weep when it is no more. ON ECCLESIASTICUS 9.2.[2]

[1] Jn 2:17. [2] PL 109:1056.

41:5-13* THE DESTINY OF THE UNGODLY

⁵*The children of sinners are abominable children,*
  and they frequent the haunts of the ungodly.
⁶*The inheritance of the children of sinners will perish,*
  and on their posterity will be a perpetual reproach.
⁷*Children will blame an ungodly father,*
  for they suffer reproach because of him.
⁸*Woe to you, ungodly men,*
  who have forsaken the law of the Most High God!
⁹*When you are born, you are born to a curse;*
  and when you die, a curse is your lot.
¹⁰*Whatever is from the dust returns to dust;*
  so the ungodly go from curse to destruction.

¹¹*The mourning of men is about their bodies,*
  but the evil name of sinners will be blotted out.
¹²*Have regard for your name, since it will remain for you*
  longer than a thousand great stores of gold.
¹³*The days of a good life are numbered,*
  but a good name endures for ever.

* Sir 41:8-16 Vg.

OVERVIEW: The descendants of sinners inherit their blame if they imitate them (RABANUS MAURUS).

41:5 The Children of Sinners

THOSE WHO IMITATE SINNERS. RABANUS MAURUS: The children of sinners are detestable in the eyes of the Lord, not because they are born of sinful parents (since many righteous people had wicked fathers, like Hezekiah son of Ahaz[1] and Josiah son of Amon),[2] but because they imitated the wicked actions of their fathers. For this reason he added, "One who stays in the dwelling of the ungodly,"[3] speaking of those who imitated the crimes of their reprobate parents, whose conduct was wicked and who consequently will miss the inheritance of the heavenly homeland, forever ashamed.[4] ON ECCLESIASTICUS 9.2.[5]

---

[1]See 2 Kings 18:1 (4 Kings 18:1 LXX). [2]The text, which is probably defective, reads, "Josiah son of Joram." [3]Sir 41:5 (41:8 Vg), variant. [4]See Ps 31:2 (30:2 LXX). [5]PL 109:1057.

41:14–42:8* SHAME

¹⁴My children, observe instruction and be at peace;
hidden wisdom and unseen treasure,
    what advantage is there in either of them?
¹⁵Better is the man who hides his folly
    than the man who hides his wisdom.
¹⁶Therefore show respect for my words:
For it is not good to retain every kind of shame,
    and not everything is confidently esteemed by every one.

¹⁷Be ashamed of immorality, before your father or mother;
    and of a lie, before a prince or a ruler;
¹⁸of a transgression, before a judge or magistrate;
    and of iniquity, before a congregation or the people;
of unjust dealing, before your partner or friend;
    ¹⁹and of theft, in the place where you live.
Be ashamed before the truth of God and his covenant.
    Be ashamed of selfish behavior at meals,^u
of surliness in receiving and giving,
    ²⁰and of silence, before those who greet you;
of looking at a woman who is a harlot,
    ²¹and of rejecting the appeal of a kinsman;
of taking away some one's portion or gift,
    and of gazing at another man's wife;
²²of meddling with his maidservant—
    and do not approach her bed;
of abusive words, before friends—
    and do not upbraid after making a gift;
²³of repeating and telling what you hear,
    and of revealing secrets.
Then you will show proper shame,
    and will find favor with every man.
42 Of the following things do not be ashamed,
    and do not let partiality lead you to sin:
²of the law of the Most High and his covenant,
    and of rendering judgment to acquit the ungodly;
³of keeping accounts with a partner or with traveling companions,
    and of dividing the inheritance of friends;
⁴of accuracy with scales and weights,

and of acquiring much or little;
[5]of profit from dealing with merchants,
    and of much discipline of children,
    and of whipping a wicked servant severely.[v]
[6]Where there is an evil wife, a seal is a good thing;
    and where there are many hands, lock things up.
[7]Whatever you deal out, let it be by number and weight,
    and make a record of all that you give out or take in.
[8]Do not be ashamed to instruct the stupid or foolish
    or the aged man who quarrels with the young.
Then you will be truly instructed,
    and will be approved before all men.

---

u Gk *of fixing the elbow on the bread*   **v** Gk *making the side of a wicked servant bleed*   ***** Sir 41:17–42:8 Vg; the Septuagint has a different distribution of verses.

OVERVIEW: Let us avoid heretics and carnal delights (RABANUS MAURUS).

41:21-22 Do Not Gaze at Another Man's Wife

HERETICS AND THE DELIGHTS OF THE FLESH. RABANUS MAURUS: The wife of another man is the perverse doctrine of the heretic, who is estranged from faith and from religion, from the company of God and from association with the faithful. For this reason wisdom forbids turning one's gaze toward her, that is, to love her captivating speech. The maidservant is rather his carnal desire, which must be subjected to the dominion of the spirit, according to the words of the Lord to Cain, "Your instinct is toward you, but you can dominate it,"[1] but which nonetheless prevails in the life of reprobates. For this reason we are forbidden to look toward this maidservant, that is, to give in to her suggestions or to enter her bed, that is, to lie down in her delights. And it is for this reason that in Proverbs, wisdom reproaches this lustful woman in her bed and forbids us to follow her ways, saying, "Now, my son, listen to me, pay attention to the words of my mouth. Let not your heart turn toward her ways, do not lose yourself on her paths, because she has caused many to fall, pierced through, and every one of her victims was vigorous. Her house is a road to the netherworld, leading down to the chambers of death."[2] ON ECCLESIASTICUS 9.3.[3]

---

[1]Gen 4:7. [2]Prov 7:24-27. [3]PL 109:1062.

42:9-14 ANXIETY CONCERNING A DAUGHTER

[9]*A daughter keeps her father secretly wakeful,*
and worry over her robs him of sleep;
when she is young, lest she do not marry,
or if married, lest she be hated;
[10]*while a virgin, lest she be defiled*
or become pregnant in her father's house;
or having a husband, lest she prove unfaithful,
or, though married, lest she be barren.
[11]*Keep strict watch over a headstrong daughter,*
lest she make you a laughingstock to your enemies,
a byword in the city and notorious[w] among the people,
and put you to shame before the great multitude.

[12]*Do not look upon any one for beauty,*
and do not sit in the midst of women;
[13]*for from garments comes the moth,*
and from a woman comes woman's wickedness.
[14]*Better is the wickedness of a man than a woman who does good;*
and it is a woman who brings shame and disgrace.

w Gk *called out*

OVERVIEW: Virgins require more care than daughters (CHRYSOSTOM).

42:9 Care for a Daughter

PROTECTING A VIRGIN. JOHN CHRYSOSTOM: The enemy of holiness always presses virgins and troubles them, ready to devour them if someone wavers and falls. There are many insidious men, and beyond all this there is the fury of nature. She must prepare for a twofold war: one that attacks from the outside, and the other that disturbs within. Thus great is the fear of one who protects them, greater the danger and the anguish if something unwanted happens. If an enclosed daughter robs her father of sleep and anxiety for her keeps him awake over fear that she will be sterile or that she would age or no longer be loved, what would the suffering be of one who is worried not for these reasons but for other, much more serious ones? Here one does not refuse a man but Christ himself. Here sterility does not end in ignominy but in harm, in the ruin of the soul. "Every tree," says the Scripture, "that does not produce good fruit will be cut down and thrown in the fire."[1] ON THE PRIESTHOOD 3.317-18.[2]

_____

[1]Mt 3:10. [2]CTP 24:88.

42:15-25* GOD'S GLORY IN NATURE

¹⁵*I will now call to mind the works of the Lord,*
  and will declare what I have seen.
By the words of the Lord his works are done.
¹⁶*The sun looks down on everything with its light,*
  and the work of the Lord is full of his glory.
¹⁷*The Lord has not enabled his holy ones*
  to recount all his marvelous works,
which the Lord the Almighty has established
  that the universe may stand firm in his glory.
¹⁸*He searches out the abyss, and the hearts of men,^x*
  and considers their crafty devices.
For the Most High knows all that may be known,
  and he looks into the signs^y of the age.
¹⁹*He declares what has been and what is to be,*
  and he reveals the tracks of hidden things.
²⁰*No thought escapes him,*
  and not one word is hidden from him.
²¹*He has ordained the splendors of his wisdom,*
  and he is from everlasting and to everlasting.
Nothing can be added or taken away,
  and he needs no one to be his counselor.
²²*How greatly to be desired are all his works,*
  and how sparkling they are to see!^z
²³*All these things live and remain for ever*
  for every need, and are all obedient.
²⁴*All things are twofold, one opposite the other,*
  and he has made nothing incomplete.
²⁵*One confirms the good things of the other,*
  and who can have enough of beholding his glory?

x Gk *and the heart*   y Gk *sign*   z The Greek of this line is uncertain   * Sir 42:15-26 Vg.

OVERVIEW: Whatever was created is known through the Word (VIGILIUS). God created things in pairs. This is evident even in spiritual matters (EVAGRIUS).

42:15 By the Words of the Lord

THE WORD INSTRUCTS US ABOUT THE

CREATION. VIGILIUS OF THAPSUS: The apostle Paul, writing to the Hebrews about the Son, says, "Because he is the image of the invisible God and bears the seal of his being."[1] And also Jeremiah, the wisest of the prophets, speaks of the person of God the Father and says, "If

[1]Heb 1:3; cf. Col 1:15.

they had remained in my being and listened to my word, I would have turned them from their wicked desires."[2] To make it understood that he had said this in reference to the Son, he adds, "Who has been in my being and has seen my word?"[3] In fact, that the Word was the Son is affirmed by the prophet David, who said regarding the person of the Father, "My heart has spoken the good word."[4] And John the Evangelist, knowing that the Word was with the Father, that is, that from the beginning the Son was with the Father and that the Word has never been separated from the Father, put this at the beginning of his Gospel, his pronouncement, saying, "In the beginning was the Word, and the Word was with God, and God was the Word."[5] In another passage the Scripture passed all of this down to us, saying, "The Word as the beginning of the work," not because in the creation of the Word (that is, beginning from the creation of the Son) God began to make the other creatures, but because through the Word of God (that is, through the Son) all created things are known. It is for this reason that the prophet David sings, saying,

"By the Word of the Lord the heavens were made,"[6] and, to show that the Holy Spirit participated in this, he continued, "And from the Spirit of his mouth derived their every virtue."[7] AGAINST THE ARIANS 2.19.[8]

42:24 *Nothing Incomplete*

ACTIVE PRAYER AND CONTEMPLATIVE PRAYER. EVAGRIUS OF PONTUS: Given that "all things are in pairs, the one opposite the other," as Jesus the wise man says,[9] receive what I send you according to the letter and according to the spirit, and consider that in every case the letter presupposes the intellect: without this, not even the letter would exist.[10] Thus prayer also involves two ways, active and contemplative. And the same for numbers, which in an immediate way express quantity and in their deeper meaning quality. CHAPTERS ON PRAYER, PROLOGUE.[11]

---

[2]Jer 23:22 LXX. [3]Jer 23:18 LXX. [4]Ps 45:2 (44:2 LXX). [5]Jn 1:1. [6]Ps 33:6 (32:6 LXX). [7]Ps 33:6 (32:6 LXX). [8]CTP 184:134-35. [9]The author of Sirach. [10]See 2 Cor 3:6. [11]CTP 117:68.

43:1-5 THE SUN

[1]*The pride of the heavenly heights is the clear firmament,*
   the appearance of heaven in a spectacle of glory.
[2]*The sun, when it appears, making proclamation as it goes forth,*
   is a marvelous instrument, the work of the Most High.
[3]*At noon it parches the land;*
   and who can withstand its burning heat?
[4]*A man tending[a] a furnace works in burning heat,*
   but the sun burns the mountains three times as much;
it breathes out fiery vapors,

and with bright beams it blinds the eyes.
⁵Great is the Lord who made it;
 and at his command it hastens on its course.

---

a Other authorities read *blowing*

OVERVIEW: The sun reveals its Creator, who establishes its course (CYRIL OF JERUSALEM).

43:2 The Sun Proclaims

THE SUN REVEALS ITS CREATOR. CYRIL OF JERUSALEM: How could anyone who lifts his eyes to the sun not admire the way in which it is regulated? When it first appears, it could in fact seem to be something of little account, whereas in reality it has a truly great power. It gives us light from its rising in the east until it sets in the west. When the psalmist says that it rises in the morning "like a bridegroom from his chamber,"[1] he gives an image of its temperate rays that do not bother the eyes at its rising, because at its appearance "like a bridegroom," we find it pleasant. Only when it directs its horses[2] toward midday do we for the most part shelter ourselves from its burning rays. Note above all how it regulates itself, although it is not the sun itself that appoints the rule but him who gave it its course to follow. In the summer, rising, it lengthens the days so as to give people more time for work. In the winter, it shortens its course, not so as to lengthen the time of cold but so that, the nights being longer, it would cooperate with human beings, promoting their rest, and with the earth to make it fruitful. Note also the harmony with which the days balance each other. In the winter they are shorter and in the summer longer, in spring and autumn they accord with one other, seeking a similar length. The night is regulated in the same way. As the psalmist says, "One day to the next hands on the message, and night to night transmits the news."[3] Day and night, with their orderly procession, cry out in unison to heretics that there is no other God than the Creator of all things, who has given them rule and order.[4] CATECHETICAL LECTURES 9.6.[5]

---

[1] Ps 19:6 (18:6 LXX). [2] Cyril alludes to the mythological theme of the sun, which is being carried by Apollo in his vehicle. [3] Ps 19:3 (18:3 LXX). [4] See Wis 11:20. [5] CTP 103:171-72.

43:6-8* THE MOON

⁶He made the moon also, to serve in its
 season^b
 to mark the times and to be an everlasting
  sign.
⁷From the moon comes the sign for feast days,
 a light that wanes when it has reached the full.
⁸The month is named for the moon,
 increasing marvelously in its phases,
an instrument of the hosts on high
 shining forth in the firmament of heaven.

---

b The Greek text of this line is uncertain * Sir 43:6-9 Vg.

OVERVIEW: *The moon is a symbol of the church, since it receives light from Christ (RA-BANUS MAURUS).*

43:8 Named for the Moon

A SYMBOL OF THE CHURCH. RABANUS MAU-RUS: After having discussed the sun, he rightly speaks also of the moon, because the church follows Christ, and as the moon is illuminated by the sun, in the same way the church is illuminated by Christ and established by his glory. Scripture recalls this in the psalm in which the prophet speaks in a mysterious way of the king and of the king's son, saying, "He will endure as the sun, like the moon through all ages."[1] The sun, in fact, is the Word of the Father, the Son of God, the Christ who remains as God and man, one from two natures and in two natures distinct and perfect. Moreover, Christ remains before the moon, that is, before the church, which gazes on him always with the light of the heart. It is right to compare the moon with the church, since it does not have a splendor of its own but receives light from the sun in certain ways that astronomers accurately explain, along with other things. In the same way, the church is apportioned light from the true Creator. In time of persecution, the light diminishes. Then, with the return of peace, it becomes full again with the joy of the clearest light. ON ECCLESIASTICUS 9.7.[2]

---

[1]Ps 72:5 (71:5 LXX). [2]PL 109:1072.

43:9-12* THE STARS AND THE RAINBOW

[9]*The glory of the stars is the beauty of heaven,*
  a gleaming array in the heights of the Lord.
[10]*At the command of the Holy One they stand as ordered,*
  they never relax in their watches.
[11]*Look upon the rainbow, and praise him who made it,*
  exceedingly beautiful in its brightness.
[12]*It encircles the heaven with its glorious arc;*
  the hands of the Most High have stretched it out.

* Sir 43:10-13 Vg.

OVERVIEW: The stars are images of the saints who adorn the church. The rainbow is an image of the Scriptures of the Old and the New Testament (RABANUS MAURUS).

43:9 The Glory of the Stars

THE SYMBOL OF THE SAINTS. RABANUS MAU-RUS: The beauty of the saints adorns the church. Those whom the most high Lord has ordained to enlighten the whole world with the preaching of the gospel and with the marks of the virtues await the judgment of God in holy words, that is, they attend with constancy to the doctrine of the true faith and are not broken by the adversities of this world. Nor do they let themselves be overcome by anger but endure all things with patience, continually caring for the flock entrusted to them, always diligently remembering in their hearts those words of the Lord, "Be ready, with your loins girded and your lamps lit. Be like those who await the master's return from the wedding."[1] "Be ready, because in an hour you do not expect, the Son of man will come."[2] "By your perseverance you will save your souls."[3] ON ECCLESIASTICUS 9.7.[4]

43:11 *Look on the Rainbow*

AN IMAGE OF SCRIPTURE. RABANUS MAURUS: God almighty set the rainbow as a sign between himself and humanity, indicating that he would never again destroy the world with a flood.[5] And this is why the rainbow has the color of both water and fire—in part light blue and in part red—so that it might testify to both judgments, to the one that is to come and to the one that has already taken place, since the world will be burned by fire and was once destroyed by the waters of the flood. For this reason we liken the rainbow to the Scripture of the New and the Old Testaments, since, in a certain way, it encircles the necks of the faithful with two curved parts. On this we read, "He has strung and aimed his bow,"[6] and thus he gives a sweet yoke to[7] to the faithful, but for rebels he proclaims himself to be a fearsome weapon. The rainbow is very beautiful in its brilliance, because the sense and intelligence of sacred Scripture are magnificent. "It encircles the heavens with a ring of glory," because it speaks abundantly of the highest things and of the lowest. ON ECCLESIASTICUS 9.7.[8]

---

[1]Lk 12:35-36. [2]Mt 24:44. [3]Lk 21:19. [4]PL 109:1072-73. [5]See Gen 9:11-13. [6]Ps 7:13. [7]See Mt 11:30. [8]PL 109:1073.

43:13-33* THE MARVELS OF NATURE

[13]*By his command he sends the driving snow*
   and speeds the lightnings of his judgment.
[14]*Therefore the storehouses are opened,*
   and the clouds fly forth like birds.
[15]*In his majesty he amasses the clouds,*
   and the hailstones are broken in pieces.
[16]*At his appearing the mountains are shaken;*
   at his will the south wind blows.
[17]*The voice of his thunder rebukes the earth;*
   so do the tempest from the north and the whirlwind.
He scatters the snow like birds flying down,
   and its descent is like locusts alighting.
[18]*The eye marvels at the beauty of its whiteness,*
   and the mind is amazed at its falling.

¹⁹He pours the hoarfrost upon the earth like salt,
   and when it freezes, it becomes pointed thorns.
²⁰The cold north wind blows,
   and ice freezes over the water;
it rests upon every pool of water,
   and the water puts it on like a breastplate.
²¹He consumes the mountains and burns up the wilderness,
   and withers the tender grass like fire.
²²A mist quickly heals all things;
   when the dew appears, it refreshes from the heat.

²³By his counsel he stilled the great deep
   and planted islands in it.
²⁴Those who sail the sea tell of its dangers,
   and we marvel at what we hear.
²⁵For in it are strange and marvelous works,
   all kinds of living things, and huge creatures of the sea.
²⁶Because of him his messenger finds the way,
   and by his word all things hold together.

²⁷Though we speak much we cannot reach the end,
   and the sum of our words is: "He is the all."
²⁸Where shall we find strength to praise him?
   For he is greater than all his works.
²⁹Terrible is the Lord and very great,
   and marvelous is his power.
³⁰When you praise the Lord, exalt him as much as you can;
   for he will surpass even that.
When you exalt him, put forth all your strength,
   and do not grow weary, for you cannot praise him enough.
³¹Who has seen him and can describe him?
   Or who can extol him as he is?
³²Many things greater than these lie hidden,
   for we have seen but few of his works.
³³For the Lord has made all things,
   and to the godly he has granted wisdom

* Sir 43:14-37 Vg.

OVERVIEW: Cold is a figure of the devil; heat is a figure of what is holy (ORIGEN). Our praise of the Holy Spirit is inferior to his glory (BASIL). Human understanding can never fully know God (AUGUSTINE).

43:20 The Cold North Wind Blows

A FIGURE OF THE HOSTILE POWERS. ORIGEN: We have been commanded to be fervent in spirit,[1] and this shows that the Word of God is a blazing fire. And Jeremiah hears from the one who gave him oracles, "Look, I have put my words in your

---

[1]See Rom 12:11.

mouth, a fire."[2] Therefore, since God is fire,[3] the angels are flames of fire,[4] and the saints should be fervent in the spirit of God. They have without a doubt cooled in their love for him and have become cold. Indeed, the Lord says that "increasing iniquity, the love of many will grow cold."[5] And all those beings that symbolize the contrary power in sacred Scripture are always cold. The devil, in fact, is called a serpent and a dragon:[6] what is colder than these? It is said that the dragon rules in the waters,[7] and this is also said of one of the evil spirits that the prophet says dwells in the sea.[8] And elsewhere the prophet says, "He will strike with the holy sword the serpent dragon that flees—the dragon, the perverse serpent—and he will kill him."[9] And in another passage, "Even if they depart from before my eyes and flee into the depths of the sea, I will command the dragon, and he will bite them."[10] And in Job this creature is called king of all the beings that are in the water.[11] The prophet announces that evils come from the north, and especially those that inhabit the earth.[12] And the north wind is indicated as cold in the Scriptures, as is written in Wisdom, "icy north wind." Without question, we must refer this to the devil. ON FIRST PRINCIPLES 2.8.3.[13]

43:30 Exalt the Lord

PRAISE THE HOLY SPIRIT WITH ALL POWER.
BASIL THE GREAT: You expect to be glorified with Christ ("If we suffer with him, we will also be glorified with him"[14]). You would not, however, glorify the Spirit of holiness along with Christ, as though he were not worthy to have the same honors that you have. You hope to reign with Christ, but you insult the Spirit of grace, relegating him to the rank of a slave and a servant. And I say these things not to show all that is due to the Spirit in glorification but to confound the bad faith of those who do not concede it to him, fleeing as impious the communion of the glory of the Spirit with the Son and with the Father. Who could allow these things to happen without weeping? Is it not obvious, to the point

where even a child could understand it, that the present state presages the abandonment of the faith that threatens us?[15] Incontestable things become doubtful. We believe in the Spirit and oppose him precisely in our professions of faith. We are baptized[16] and still fight. We invoke him as the author of life,[17] yet we despise him as a companion in slavery. We received him with the Father and the Son, and we dishonor him as if he were part of the creation. Those who do not know what to ask for in prayer,[18] if they are moved to express something sacred regarding the Spirit, limit the flow of their words to maintain measure, as though they had already given him enough honor. One should mourn their weakness; we, however, do not have words to express thanks for all the gifts of which we experience the effects. The Spirit in fact surpasses all knowledge[19] and thwarts the possibility of any speech that fails to conform to at least a minimum of his dignity, according to the words of the book called Wisdom:[20] "Exalt him as you can, because he is higher still. In exalting him, you will increase your strength. Do not grow weary; otherwise you will not reach him." ON THE HOLY SPIRIT 28.70.[21]

43:31 Who Can Describe God?

GOD IS BEYOND OUR UNDERSTANDING.
AUGUSTINE: Indeed, with what understanding can a person apprehend God when he does not even apprehend that very intellect of his own by which he wants to know God? And if he does already understand this, let him diligently consider then that there is nothing better in his nature than his intellect. Let him see, then, if he

---

[2]Jer 1:9. [3]See Deut 4:24; Heb 12:29. [4]See Ps 104:4 (103:4 LXX); Heb 1:7. [5]Mt 24:12. [6]See Rev 12:9; 20:2. [7]See Ezek 29:3. [8]See Ezek 32:2. [9]Is 27:1. [10]Amos 9:3. [11]Job 41:25. [12]See Jer 1:14. [13]Simonetti UTET 308-9. [14]Rom 8:17. [15]See Lk 18:8. [16]Basil reminds us that we invoke the Holy Spirit in the baptismal profession of faith and have been baptized also in his name. [17]Cf. Acts 3:15. [18]See Rom 8:26. [19]See Phil 4:7. [20]Basil mentions only the beginning of the Greek title: Wisdom of Sirach. [21]CTP 106:188-89.

discovers in it any features of form, brilliance of colors, spatial broadness, distance of parts, extension of mass, spatial dislocation, or anything else of this kind. Certainly we find nothing of this sort in that which is best in us, that is, in our intellect, with which we attain wisdom to the extent we are able. So then, what we do not find in what is best in us, we must not look for in him who is much better than what is best in us. We conceive, therefore—if we can and to the extent we can—of good without quality, greatness without quantity, creator without necessity,

in the first place without location, containing all things but without exteriority, entirely present everywhere without place, eternal without time, author of changeable things while remaining absolutely unchanged and foreign to all passivity. Whoever conceives of God in this way, though he still cannot discover perfectly what he is, at least avoids, with pious diligence and to the extent possible, attributing to him what he is not. ON THE TRINITY 5.1.2.[22]

[22]NBA 4:235-37.

44:1-15 GOD'S GLORY IN HISTORY: THE PRAISE OF THE ANCESTORS

[1]*Let us now praise famous men,*
and our fathers in their generations.
[2]*The Lord apportioned to them[c] great glory,*
his majesty from the beginning.
[3]*There were those who ruled in their kingdoms,*
and were men renowned for their power,
giving counsel by their understanding,
and proclaiming prophecies;
[4]*leaders of the people in their deliberations*
and in understanding of learning for the people,
wise in their words of instruction;
[5]*those who composed musical tunes,*
and set forth verses in writing;
[6]*rich men furnished with resources,*
living peaceably in their habitations—
[7]*all these were honored in their generations,*
and were the glory of their times.
[8]*There are some of them who have left a name,*
so that men declare their praise.
[9]*And there are some who have no memorial,*
who have perished as though they had not lived;
they have become as though they had not been born,

and so have their children after them.
[10]*But these were men of mercy,*
   whose righteous deeds have not been forgotten;
[11]*their prosperity will remain with their descendants,*
   and their inheritance to their children's children.[d]
[12]*Their descendants stand by the covenants;*
   their children also, for their sake.
[13]*Their posterity will continue for ever,*
   and their glory will not be blotted out.
[14]*Their bodies were buried in peace,*
   and their name lives to all generations.
[15]*Peoples will declare their wisdom,*
   and the congregation proclaims their praise.

c Heb: Gk *created*   d Heb Compare Vg Syr: The Greek of this verse is uncertain

OVERVIEW: No one will even remember the sinners of this world (RABANUS MAURUS).

44:9 Some Have No Memorial

THE MEMORY OF SINNERS WILL DISAPPEAR.
RABANUS MAURUS: The godless and sinners were not worthy of memory, because if the Scripture says something of them, it does so not to praise them but to blame. In the psalm it is written of them, "The fortresses of the enemy have been pulled down forever, the memory of the city you destroyed has disappeared. Their memory has disappeared with a roar."[1] At the end of the world, in fact, to the devil's joy, those who it has been determined belong to his city will fall, and their memory will perish with a fantastic din when they go to eternal punishment. ECCLESIASTICUS 10.1.[2]

[1]Ps 9:7, variant.   [2]PL 109:1083.

44:16-18* ENOCH AND NOAH

[6]*Enoch pleased the Lord, and was taken up;*
   he was an example of repentance to all generations.

[17]*Noah was found perfect and righteous;*
   in the time of wrath he was taken in exchange;
therefore a remnant was left to the earth
   when the flood came.
[18]*Everlasting covenants were made with him*
   that all flesh should not be blotted out by a flood.

* Sir 44:16-19 Vg.

OVERVIEW: Enoch was the first of the saints of the Old Testament (RABANUS MAURUS).

44:16 Enoch Pleased the Lord

PRAISE AND MISSION OF ENOCH. RABANUS MAURUS: It is right that he began to enumerate the holy fathers, not from Adam, who transgressed the divine commandment and was expelled from paradise, but from Enoch, who walked with God and was taken up into paradise.[1] And in this way the splendor of the saints shines, because from the pains of this world they are taken up to the peace of the heavenly kingdom. It is believed that he will return together with Elijah at the end of the world, to counsel men and women so that they would turn from their sins to repentance. In this way, together with his companion, he will pay the debt of death in the persecution of the antichrist.[2] ON ECCLESIASTICUS 10.3.[3]

---

[1]See Gen 5:24. [2]This text alludes to a very old tradition, which appears for the first time in the Apocalypse of Peter (beginning of the second century). [3]PL 109:1084.

44:19-23* ABRAHAM, ISAAC AND JACOB

¹⁹*Abraham was the great father of a multitude of nations,*
  and no one has been found like him in glory;
²⁰*he kept the law of the Most High,*
  and was taken into covenant with him;
he established the covenant in his flesh,
  and when he was tested he was found faithful.
²¹*Therefore the Lord^e assured him by an oath*
  that the nations would be blessed through his posterity;
that he would multiply him like the dust of the earth,
  and exalt his posterity like the stars,
and cause them to inherit from sea to sea
  and from the River to the ends of the earth.
²²*To Isaac also he gave the same assurance*
  for the sake of Abraham his father.

²³*The blessing of all men and the covenant*
  he made to rest upon the head of Jacob;
he acknowledged him with his blessings,
  and gave him his inheritance;^f
he determined his portions,
  and distributed them among twelve tribes.

e Gk *he*   f Heb: Gk *by inheritance*   * Sir 44:20-27 Vg.

OVERVIEW: The narratives of Abraham and his posterity prefigure the church, Christ, the saints and triune teaching (RABANUS MAURUS).

44:21 *Assurance from the Lord*

ABRAHAM AND HIS OFFSPRING. RABANUS MAURUS: The inheritance that he was promised symbolizes two things. The comparison with the sand of the sea indicates the Jews, who are sterile. And the comparison with the stars of heaven[1] designates all the people who believe in Christ, who by the light of the resurrection will shine like the stars of heaven. "Every star in fact differs from another in splendor. So also in the resurrection."[2] His descendents will inherit "from one sea to the other, from the river to the ends of the earth," since Christ, born of the descendents of Abraham, rules from one sea to the other and from the river to the ends of the earth,[3] and his church, his very body, fills all the limits of the world. One also notes that Abraham represents in himself three things. In the first place, the Savior, who, leaving his family,[4] came into this world.[5] Second, the Father, when he sacrificed his only Son.[6] Third, by the fact that he had welcomed three men and adored one of them,[7] he symbolized the saints, who joyfully received the coming of Christ in the flesh. This mystery of the incarnation is the work of the entire holy Trinity but was realized only in the Son. "And the Word was made flesh and came to dwell among us."[8] ON ECCLESIASTICUS 10.5.[9]

---

[1]Cf. Gen 22:17 [2]1 Cor 15:41-42. [3]Cf. Ps 72:8 (71:8 LXX) [4]See Gen 12:1. [5]See Jn 1:9. [6]See Gen 22:2-13. [7]See Gen 18:2-3. [8]Jn 1:14. [9]PL 109:1085.

45:1-5* MOSES

[1]From his descendants the Lord⁸ brought forth a man of mercy,
    who found favor in the sight of all flesh
and was beloved by God and man,
    Moses, whose memory is blessed.
[2]He made him equal in glory to the holy ones,
    and made him great in the fears of his enemies.
[3]By his words he caused signs to cease;
    the Lord⁸ glorified him in the presence of kings.
He gave him commands for his people,
    and showed him part of his glory.
[4]He sanctified him through faithfulness and meekness;
    he chose him out of all mankind.
[5]He made him hear his voice,
    and led him into the thick darkness,

and gave him the commandments face to face,
    the law of life and knowledge,
to teach Jacob the covenant,
    and Israel his judgments.

g Gk *he*   * Sir 45:1-6 Vg.

OVERVIEW: Moses is an image of Christ (RA-BANUS MAURUS).

45:4 Sanctified Through Faithfulness and Meekness

MOSES IS AN IMAGE OF CHRIST. RABANUS MAURUS: It is certain that his faith and his meekness made holy and acceptable to God the one who was chosen by the divine providence to govern all. While the sons of Israel listened, the Lord gave him the law on Mount Sinai and established the precepts of life, speaking with him in the cloud so that he would teach his people and instruct them in how to live justly. And though he would symbolize many things at different times, by the fact that he brought the people of God out of Egypt through the waters of the Red Sea and led them through the desert, while the cloud guided and indicated the way, he is the image of the Law. Under the guidance of Christ, the Law freed the faithful from the spiritual Egypt and from the power of the true pharaoh by the waters of baptism, so that in the desert of this world, instructed and taught by the divine precepts, they would reach the promised land, the heavenly homeland, where they will have every good thing in abundance and will enjoy eternal life. ON ECCLESIASTICUS 10.8.[1]

[1]PL 109:1087.

45:6-22* AARON

[6]*He exalted Aaron, the brother of Moses,*[b]
    a holy man like him, of the tribe of Levi.
[7]*He made an everlasting covenant with him,*
    and gave him the priesthood of the people.
He blessed him with splendid vestments,
    and put a glorious robe upon him.
[8]*He clothed him with superb perfection,*
    and strengthened him with the symbols of authority,
    the linen breeches, the long robe, and the ephod.
[9]*And he encircled him with pomegranates,*

with very many golden bells round about,
to send forth a sound as he walked,
    to make their ringing heard in the temple
    as a reminder to the sons of his people;
¹⁰*with a holy garment, of gold and blue*
    and purple, the work of an embroiderer;
with the oracle of judgment, Urim and Thummim;
    ¹¹*with twisted scarlet, the work of a craftsman;*
with precious stones engraved like signets,
    in a setting of gold, the work of a jeweler,
for a reminder, in engraved letters,
    according to the number of the tribes of Israel;
¹²*with a gold crown upon his turban,*
    inscribed like a signet with "Holiness,"
a distinction to be prized, the work of an expert,
    the delight of the eyes, richly adorned.
¹³*Before his time there never were such beautiful things.*
    No outsider ever put them on,
but only his sons
    and his descendants perpetually.
¹⁴*His sacrifices shall be wholly burned*
    twice every day continually.
¹⁵*Moses ordained him,*
    and anointed him with holy oil;
it was an everlasting covenant for him
    and for his descendants all the days of heaven,
to minister to the Lordⁱ and serve as priest
    and bless his people in his name.
¹⁶*He chose him out of all the living*
    to offer sacrifice to the Lord,
incense and a pleasing odor as a memorial portion,
    to make atonement for the people.^j
¹⁷*In his commandments he gave him*
    authority and statutes and^k judgments,
to teach Jacob the testimonies,
    and to enlighten Israel with his law.
¹⁸*Outsiders conspired against him,*
    and envied him in the wilderness,
Dathan and Abiram and their men
    and the company of Korah, in wrath and anger.
¹⁹*The Lord saw it and was not pleased,*
    and in the wrath of his anger they were destroyed;
he wrought wonders against them
    to consume them in flaming fire.
²⁰*He added glory to Aaron*

and gave him a heritage;
he allotted to him the first of the first fruits,
 he prepared bread of first fruits in abundance;
[21]*for they eat the sacrifices to the Lord,*
 which he gave to him and his descendants.
[22]*But in the land of the people he has no inheritance,*
 and he has no portion among the people;
 for the Lord[l] himself is his[m] portion and inheritance

h Gk *him* i Gk *him* j Other authorities read *thy people* k Heb: Gk *in covenants of* l Gk *he* m Other authorities read *your* * Sir 45:7-27 Vg.

OVERVIEW: The garb of the high priest is a symbol of virtues (RABANUS MAURUS).

45:8 Clothed with Perfection

SYMBOLS OF VIRTUES. RABANUS MAURUS: The vestments of the high priest are nothing other than the works of the virtues and the wise doctrine that truly adorn the priest of the Lord, since he must constantly possess these. And for this reason he said, "You have crowned him with instruments of virtue."[1] The wise in heart,[2] who have been filled by God with a spirit of prudence so as to make those very vestments, are the prophets and apostles, as well as the other doctors of the truth. They show us with the greatest clarity how priests and ministers of the altar must live and how they must teach, by example and action or with words of exhortation. The vestments made by Moses and his brother Aaron—that is, the sacred Scriptures—are what Paul indicates and recommends to leaders, saying, "Bishops, as administrators of God, must be beyond reproach: not arrogant, not quick-tempered, not given to wine, not violent, not avid for dishonest gain, but hospitable, loving the good, sensible, just, pious, self-controlled, holding fast to sure doctrine according to the teaching that has been handed down."[3] ON ECCLESIASTICUS 10.9.[4]

[1]Sir 45:8, variant of Vg. [2]See Ex 35:10. [3]Tit 1:7-9. [4]PL 109:1087-88.

45:23-26* PHINEHAS

[23]*Phinehas the son of Eleazar is the third in glory,*
 for he was zealous in the fear of the Lord,
and stood fast, when the people turned away,
 in the ready goodness of his soul,
 and made atonement for Israel.
[24]*Therefore a covenant of peace was established with him,*
 that he should be leader of the sanctuary and of his people,

that he and his descendants should have
the dignity of the priesthood for ever.
²⁵A covenant was also established with David,
the son of Jesse, of the tribe of Judah:
the heritage of the king is from son to son only;
so the heritage of Aaron is for his descendants.
²⁶May the Lordⁿ grant you wisdom in your heart
to judge his people in righteousness,
so that their prosperity may not vanish,
and that their glory may endure throughout their generations.^o

n Gk *he* o The Greek of this line is obscure * Sir 47:28-31 Vg.

OVERVIEW: Phinehas, son of a priest, is an image of Christ the priest (RABANUS MAURUS).

45:24 Leader of the Sanctuary

PHINEHAS IS AN IMAGE OF CHRIST. RABANUS MAURUS: In a mysterious sense, it is right that the dignity of the eternal priesthood is promised to Phinehas, son of Eleazar the priest, for the zeal that he had against the fornicators.[1] Indeed, whoever, moved by godly zeal, makes an effort to suppress the impulses of his flesh or reproves and restrains those under him, so as to not let them deviate from the truth out of lust and sexual desire, will have the dignity of the eternal priesthood in the church of God, which rightly belongs to that priest of whom it is written, "Like Melchizedek, you are a priest forever."[2] He will possess, with him, the eternal kingdom in heavenly light. ON ECCLESIASTICUS 10.10.[3]

[1]See Num 25:7-8. [2]Ps 110:4 (109:4 LXX). [3]PL 109:1090.

46:1-6* JOSHUA

¹Joshua the son of Nun was mighty in war,
and was the successor of Moses in prophesying.
He became, in accordance with his name,
a great savior of God's^p elect,
to take vengeance on the enemies that rose against them,
so that he might give Israel its inheritance.
²How glorious he was when he lifted his hands
and stretched out his sword against the cities!
³Who before him ever stood so firm?
For he waged the wars of the Lord.

[4]Was not the sun held back by his hand?
And did not one day become as long as two?
[5]He called upon the Most High, the Mighty One,
when enemies pressed him on every side,
[6]and the great Lord answered him
with hailstones of mighty power.
He hurled down war upon that nation,
and at the descent of Beth-horon[q] he destroyed those who resisted,
so that the nations might know his armament,
that he was fighting in the sight of the Lord;
for he wholly followed the Mighty One.

p Gk *his*   q Compare Joshua 10.11: Greek lacks *of Beth-horon*   * Sir 46:1-8 Vg (46:1-7a LXX).

OVERVIEW: Joshua is an image of Christ in his name and his deeds (RABANUS MAURUS).

46:1 *Joshua Was Mighty in War*

JOSHUA-JESUS. RABANUS MAURUS: Joshua son of Nun showed himself by his name[1] and his actions to be a figure of the Savior, to whom God the Father "has given the name that is above every other name, so that at the name of Jesus every knee would bend in the heavens, on the earth and under the earth."[2] And since this name is above every other name, for generations it was not borne by anyone. Moses wrote the book of Genesis, in which we read of Abraham and of those born to him, of whom many are righteous but none of whom merited to be called Jesus. Not even Abel was called Jesus, nor he who began to invoke the name of the Lord God[3] nor he who pleased God and was taken away and did not know death.[4] Nor Noah, who was the only just person of his generation before God.[5] And not Abraham, who received the promises of the covenant,[6] nor Isaac, born of him, nor Jacob the deceiver[7] nor any of his sons. Moses was faithful in all his house,[8] but not even he was called Jesus. Rather, I find the name of Jesus for the first time in the book of Exodus. I want to reiterate when the name of Joshua-Jesus is first mentioned, "Amalek came to fight against Israel, and Moses said to Joshua at Rephidim."[9] This is the first mention of the name Joshua-Jesus: "Choose some brave men from among the sons of Israel to fight against Amalek tomorrow."[10] He is the one who was given command after the death of Moses, who led the army and fought against Amalek and, as is symbolized by the hands stretched out on the mountain,[11] nailed the principalities and powers to his victorious cross.[12] ON ECCLESIASTICUS 10.11.[13]

---

[1]The names of Joshua and Jesus are the same in Hebrew and Greek. Their distinction is due to the Latin translations and continues in most modern languages. [2]Phil 2:9-10. [3]Seth; see Gen 4:26. [4]Enoch; see Gen 5:22-24. [5]See Gen 6:9. [6]See Gen 15:18; 17:2-21. [7]See Gen 27:36; Hos 12:4. [8]See Num 12:7. [9]Ex 17:8-9. [10]Ex 17:9 Vg. [11]See Ex 17:11-12. [12]Col 2:14-15. [13]PL 109:1090-91.

46:7-10* CALEB

⁷And in the days of Moses he did a loyal deed,
    he and Caleb the son of Jephunneh:
they withstood the congregation,ʳ
    restrained the people from sin,
    and stilled their wicked murmuring.
⁸And these two alone were preserved
    out of six hundred thousand people on foot,
to bring them into their inheritance,
    into a land flowing with milk and honey.
⁹And the Lord gave Caleb strength,
    which remained with him to old age,
so that he went up to the hill country,
    and his children obtained it for an inheritance;
¹⁰so that all the sons of Israel might see
    that it is good to follow the Lord.

r Other authorities read *the enemy*   * Sir 46:9-12 Vg (46:6b-10 LXX).

OVERVIEW: Caleb is an image of the wise person who opposes the pagan philosophers and the heretics (RABANUS MAURUS).

46:9 The Lord Gave Caleb Strength

CALEB IS AN IMAGE OF THE WISE. RABANUS MAURUS: What Caleb says, "As my vigor was then, so it is now,"[1] indicates that all the saints and the wise of heart have the same vigor in things present as in those past, in things recent as in those ancient, in the Gospels and in the Law. This is therefore what he says, the one who is vigorous now under Jesus as he was vigorous then under Moses, since a vigilant heart remains vigorous in the mysteries of both Testaments. But we also see the request made by the same Caleb, son of Jephunneh, to Joshua: "Give me this mountain, of which the Lord spoke in that day."[2] The saint asks for nothing earthly or lowly, nothing that lies in the deep valleys, but asks for a very high mountain, a mountain on which there is a great, fortified city.[3] He asks for it because he knew how to fight, as it is written, "The wise man storms a city of warriors and breaks down the stronghold in which it trusted."[4] Hearing these words of Solomon, do you think his intent was to teach us that the wise man had taken a city and destroyed fortresses made of stone? Or rather, does he indicate that the cities and walls are the dogmas of the godless and the syllogisms of the philosophers by which they compose impiety and what is opposed to the divine law, as practiced by the pagans and barbarians? But it must be assumed that the fortified cities set on the mountains are those things that heretics base on the statements of the Scriptures, as on high mountains. The wise man will therefore destroy

---

[1]Josh 14:11. [2]Josh 14:12. [3]See Num 13:28. [4]Prov 21:22.

the cities, preaching the word of truth and overthrowing the lying fortresses with the battering ram of truth, as Paul also said: "Destroying arguments and every bulwark that raises itself against the knowledge of God."[5] ON ECCLESIASTICUS 10.11.[6]

---

[5]2 Cor 10:5. [6]PL 109:1093.

46:11-12* THE JUDGES

[11]*The judges also, with their respective names,*
those whose hearts did not fall into idolatry
and who did not turn away from the Lord—
may their memory be blessed!
[12]*May their bones revive from where they lie,*
and may the name of those who have been honored
live again in their sons!

* Sir 46:13-15 Vg.

OVERVIEW: The judges of the people prefigure the apostles and ministers of the church (RABANUS MAURUS).

46:11 The Memory of the Judges

THE MEMORY OF THE JUST REMAINS FOREVER. RABANUS MAURUS: After Joshua son of Nun, the people of God were ruled by judges, who governed them and defended them from enemies. In the same way, after the passion, resurrection and ascension into heaven of our Savior, the church of God had the apostles and the apostolic leaders who instructed it with holy admonitions, fortifying it, with good merits and with holy prayers, against spiritual iniquity and against all enemies. For this reason it is right to say that "their hearts were not corrupted, and they did not turn away from the Lord,"[1] since they persevered to the end of their lives in right faith and in the true religion, to such an extent that their memory has been honored by a perennial blessing[2] and the power of their good works was rewarded with an eternal prize. Thus the memory of their name will be handed down to their posterity with glory. Indeed, all peoples will recount their wisdom, and the entire assembly of the saints sings their praises.[3] ON ECCLESIASTICUS 10.11.[4]

---

[1]Sir 46:11 Vg. [2]Sir 46:14 Vg. [3]Sir 46:15 Vg. [4]PL 109:1094.

46:13-20* SAMUEL

[13]*Samuel, beloved by his Lord,*
a prophet of the Lord, established the kingdom
and anointed rulers over his people.
[14]*By the law of the Lord he judged the congregation,*
and the Lord watched over Jacob.
[15]*By his faithfulness he was proved to be a prophet,*
and by his words he became known as a trustworthy seer.
[16]*He called upon the Lord, the Mighty One,*
when his enemies pressed him on every side,
and he offered in sacrifice a sucking lamb.
[17]*Then the Lord thundered from heaven,*
and made his voice heard with a mighty sound;
[18]*and he wiped out the leaders of the people of Tyre*
and all the rulers of the Philistines.
[19]*Before the time of his eternal sleep,*
Samuel[s] called men to witness before the Lord and his anointed:
"I have not taken any one's property,
not so much as a pair of shoes."
And no man accused him.
[20]*Even after he had fallen asleep he prophesied*
and revealed to the king his death,
and lifted up his voice out of the earth in prophecy,
to blot out the wickedness of the people.

s Gk *he*   * Sir 46:16-23 Vg.

OVERVIEW: Job is a model of virtue in every age, as was Samuel (ANONYMOUS ANOMOEAN).

46:19 No One Accused Him

IN PRAISE OF JOB AND SAMUEL. ANONYMOUS ANOMOEAN: Blessed is that man who was testified to by God, exalted by the angels and admired even by the devil, because he did not give in when faced with the most horrific sores and the deepest sorrows. He was thus a man "foreign to evil,"[1] because he was a stranger to every crime, without blemish, exempt from all criticism. He was "foreign to evil" before God and human beings,[2] before angels and spirits, before what is corruptible and what is incorruptible. He was "foreign to evil" because he manifested in himself the type of the new grace, where it is prescribed that "a bishop should be above reproach."[3] He was "foreign to evil" in his soul and in his body, in his decisions and in his thoughts, in his words and in his works, in his commit-

---

[1]Job 1:1. [2]See 2 Cor 8:21. [3]1 Tim 1:7.

ments and in his conversations. In everything, therefore, his life was "foreign to evil." The same was said of Samuel in the praises of the fathers: "And no one found fault with him."[4] That is, that man was not accused, because he was "foreign to evil," as Job had been in the past. COMMENTARY ON JOB 1.9.[5]

---

[4]Sir 46:19 (46:22 Vg). The Vulgate translates the Greek text literally. [5]CSEL 96:100-101.

47:1-11* NATHAN AND DAVID

[1]And after him Nathan rose up
   to prophesy in the days of David.
[2]As the fat is selected from the peace offering,
   so David was selected from the sons of Israel.
[3]He played with lions as with young goats,
   and with bears as with lambs of the flock.
[4]In his youth did he not kill a giant,
   and take away reproach from the people,
when he lifted his hand with a stone in the sling
   and struck down the boasting of Goliath?
[5]For he appealed to the Lord, the Most High,
   and he gave him strength in his right hand
to slay a man mighty in war,
   to exalt the power[t] of his people.
[6]So they glorified him for his ten thousands,
   and praised him for the blessings of the Lord,
   when the glorious diadem was bestowed upon him.
[7]For he wiped out his enemies on every side,
   and annihilated his adversaries the Philistines;
   he crushed their power[t] even to this day.
[8]In all that he did he gave thanks
   to the Holy One, the Most High, with ascriptions of glory;
he sang praise with all his heart,
   and he loved his Maker.
[9]He placed singers before the altar,
   to make sweet melody with their voices.
[10]He gave beauty to the feasts,
   and arranged their times throughout the year,[u]
while they praised God's[v] holy name,

and the sanctuary resounded from early morning.
¹¹The Lord took away his sins,
and exalted his power^w for ever;
he gave him the covenant of kings
and a throne of glory in Israel.

t Gk *born*   **u** Gk *to completion*   **v** Gk *his*   **w** Gk *born*   * Sir 47:1-13 Vg.

OVERVIEW: Nathan the prophet was full of the grace of the Holy Spirit (RABANUS MAURUS).

47:2 Selected from the Peace Offering

NATHAN THE PROPHET. RABANUS MAURUS: When it says that Nathan, like the fat of salvation,[1] was separated from the meat, it indicates

that he was full of the grace of the Holy Spirit and that his conduct and his life were far from and foreign to those of carnal and sinful people.[2] ON ECCLESIASTICUS 10.13.[3]

[1]Sir 47:2 Vg. [2]Rabanus applies to Nathan this verse, which traditionally is applied to David. [3]PL 109:1095.

47:12-22* SOLOMON

¹²After him rose up a wise son
who fared amply^x because of him;
¹³Solomon reigned in days of peace,
and God gave him rest on every side,
that he might build a house for his name
and prepare a sanctuary to stand for ever.
¹⁴How wise you became in your youth!
You overflowed like a river with understanding.
¹⁵Your soul covered the earth,
and you filled it with parables and riddles.
¹⁶Your name reached to far-off islands,
and you were loved for your peace.
¹⁷For your songs and proverbs and parables,
and for your interpretations, the countries marveled at you.
¹⁸In the name of the Lord God,
who is called the God of Israel,
you gathered gold like tin
and amassed silver like lead.

¹⁹*But you laid your loins beside women,*
and through your body you were brought into subjection.
²⁰*You put a stain upon your honor,*
and defiled your posterity,
so that you brought wrath upon your children
and they were grieved^y at your folly,
²¹*so that the sovereignty was divided*
and a disobedient kingdom arose out of Ephraim.
²²*But the Lord will never give up his mercy,*
nor cause any of his works to perish;
he will never blot out the descendants of his chosen one,
nor destroy the posterity of him who loved him;
so he gave a remnant to Jacob,
and to David a root of his stock.

x Gk *lived in a broad place*   y Other authorities read *I was grieved*   * Sir 47:14-25 Vg.

OVERVIEW: Solomon was led astray by his women, who are symbols of pagan idolatry and philosophy (ORIGEN).

47:19 Brought into Subjection

SOLOMON HAD MANY WOMEN. ORIGEN: If you reread what is written of Solomon, you will find that he, though being extremely wise,[1] "drew near to many women," whereas the law of God says, "Do not have many wives, that they might make you commit fornication against your God."[2] Even he, though extremely wise and of great merit before God, was nonetheless deceived, because he gave himself to many women. I think that the many women refer to the many dogmas and the various philosophies of the peoples: wanting to know and investigate them, as a man rich in knowledge and wisdom, he could not keep himself within the rule of the divine law. He was seduced by the philosophy of Moab, which persuaded him to sacrifice to the idol of Moab, and likewise to that of the Ammonites and of the other peoples. It is said that he received many women, building temples and sacrificing to their idols.[3] Therefore: it is a great thing and truly a work of God to mix with many dogmas as with women and nevertheless to not deviate from the rule of truth but to say firmly, "There are sixty queens, and eighty concubines and young maidens without number, but one alone is my dove, my perfect one, the only daughter of her mother, the only daughter of the one who bore her."[4] HOMILIES ON NUMBERS 20.3.3.[5]

[1]See Eccles 12:9. [2]Deut 17:17. [3]See 1 Kings 11:7-8. [4]Song 6:8-9. [5]CTP 76:284-85; ACTHN 127*.

47:23-25* REHOBOAM AND JEROBOAM

²³*Solomon rested with his fathers,*
and left behind him one of his sons,
ample in^z folly and lacking in understanding,
Rehoboam, whose policy caused the people to revolt.
Also Jeroboam the son of Nebat, who caused Israel to sin
and gave to Ephraim a sinful way.
²⁴*Their sins became exceedingly many,*
so as to remove them from their land.
²⁵*For they sought out every sort of wickedness,*
till vengeance came upon them.

z Heb (with a play on the name Rehoboam) Syr: Gk *the people's*   * Sir 47:26-31 Vg.

OVERVIEW: Christ frees and purifies us (RABANUS MAURUS).

47:25 They Sought Out Wickedness

CHRIST FREES AND CLEANSES. RABANUS MAURUS: This wicked innovation was perpetuated among the people of the ten tribes until the Lord enacted his revenge and they were deported to Assyria. When it says, "Until their justification came, and he freed them from all their sins,"[1] I think it refers to the justification and freedom of our Savior, who at his coming frees and protects from every enemy those who have turned to faith in him and have been purified from all their sins through baptism in him. ON ECCLESIASTICUS 10.16.[2]

---

[1]Sir 47:25 (47:31 Vg).   [2]PL 109:1099.

48:1-11* ELIJAH

¹*Then the prophet Elijah arose like a fire,*
and his word burned like a torch.
²*He brought a famine upon them,*
and by his zeal he made them few in number.
³*By the word of the Lord he shut up the heavens,*
and also three times brought down fire.

⁴*How glorious you were, O Elijah, in your wondrous deeds!*
  And who has the right to boast which you have?
⁵*You who raised a corpse from death*
  and from Hades, by the word of the Most High;
⁶*who brought kings down to destruction,*
  and famous men from their beds;
⁷*who heard rebuke at Sinai*
  and judgments of vengeance at Horeb;
⁸*who anointed kings to inflict retribution,*
  *and prophets to succeed you.*ᵃ
⁹*You who were taken up by a whirlwind of fire,*
  in a chariot with horses of fire;
¹⁰*you who are ready*ᵇ *at the appointed time, it is written,*
  to calm the wrath of God before it breaks out in fury,
to turn the heart of the father to the son,
  and to restore the tribes of Jacob.
¹¹*Blessed are those who saw you,*
  *and those who have been adorned*ᶜ *in love;*
  *for we also shall surely live.*ᵈ

a Heb: Gk *him*   b Heb: Gk *are for reproofs*   c Other authorities read *who have died*   d The text and meaning of this verse are uncertain   * Sir 48:1-12 Vg.

OVERVIEW: Sin is like thorns that must be burned by Christ's forgiveness (ORIGEN).

48:1 *His Word Burned Like a Torch*

FORGIVENESS BURNS THE THORNS OF SIN. ORIGEN: If we understand what it means to be subject to Christ, especially in light of the passage, "And when everything is subject, he also, the Son, will subject himself to him who made everything subject to him,"[1] then we will understand the lamb of God who takes on himself the sin of the world[2] in a way worthy of the goodness of the God of the universe. And yet the lamb does not take on himself the sins of all, if they do not suffer and experience torment until their sins are taken from them. There are in fact thorns that are not merely loose but firmly stuck in the hands of whoever is so drunk with vice as to even forget the state of sobriety, as it says in Proverbs, "Thorns are hidden in the hands of a drunkard."[3] Must we spend words describing what troubles such implanted evils cause to the one who accepts them in the body of his soul? One who has accepted moral evil so deeply in his soul as to become a land that produces thorns[4] needs to be deeply cut by the living Logos of God, which is "effective and sharper than any two-edged sword,"[5] hotter than any fire. Into a soul reduced to this state, that fire must be sent that is capable of finding the thorns[6] and getting at them in virtue of its divinity, without setting fire to the stems and ears of the fields. Many are the ways in which the Lamb of God takes away the sins of the world,[7] in the first place through the sacrifice of himself. Some of these ways can be shown to the many, while others are hidden to them and known only to those considered worthy of the divine wisdom. COMMENTARY ON THE GOSPEL OF JOHN 6.57-58.[8]

---

[1]1 Cor 15:28.   [2]See Jn 1:29, 36.   [3]Prov 26:9.   [4]See Gen 3:18.   [5]Heb 4:12.   [6]See Ex 22:6.   [7]See Jn 1:29, 36.   [8]Trad. Corsini 374-75.

48:12-14* ELISHA

^{12}*It was Elijah who was covered by the whirlwind,*
and Elisha was filled with his spirit;
in all his days he did not tremble before any ruler,
and no one brought him into subjection.
^{13}*Nothing was too hard for him,*
and when he was dead his body prophesied.
^{14}*As in his life he did wonders,*
so in death his deeds were marvelous.

* Sir 48:13-15 Vg.

OVERVIEW: Elijah is a symbol of Christ, and Elisha is a figure of the church (RABANUS MAURUS).

48:12 Elijah and Elisha

FIGURES OF CHRIST AND THE CHURCH.
RABANUS MAURUS: How is it possible that Elisha, when Elijah his master gave him the opportunity, asked for a double portion of the spirit of Elijah? The Lord says in the Gospel, "The disciple is not greater than the master. But everyone who is well prepared will be like his master."[1] But if we examine the mystery of this request, we will find that it is not an inopportune one but necessary. In fact, "Elijah said to Elisha, Ask what I must do for you before I am taken from you. Elisha responded, I beg you that a double portion of your spirit be in me. And he responded, You have asked a difficult thing. Nevertheless, if you see me when I am taken away from you, it will be granted to you. If not, it will not be granted you."[2] What does Elijah symbolize here but our head, that is, the Lord our Redeemer, and Elisha his body, which is the church?[3] Elijah, then, gives the occasion to ask, because in the Gospel it says, "Ask, and it will be given you."[4] And also, "Ask, and you will receive, that your joy may be full."[5] Having received this assurance from the Lord, Elisha, that is, the Christian people, asks that the spirit of Christ be doubled in him, which is to say, a double grace of the Holy Spirit, for the remission of sins and for the conferral of virtue. Our Redeemer, who had no sin, and neither did he commit sin, nor was deception found in his mouth,[6] had no need for the remission of sins, not having any sin,[7] but carried out the works of the Holy Spirit. He says this to the Jews in the Gospel: "If I cast out demons by the finger of God, it is because the kingdom of God has come on you."[8] ON ECCLESIASTICUS 10.18.[9]

---

[1]Lk 6:40. [2]2 Kings 2:9-10 (4 Kings 2:9-10 LXX). [3]See Col 1:14. [4]Mt 7:7. [5]Jn 16:24. [6]See Is 53:9; 1 Pet 2:22. [7]See Jn 8:46. [8]Lk 11:20. [9]PL 109:1103-4.

48:15-16* UNFAITHFULNESS AND PUNISHMENT

¹⁵*For all this the people did not repent,*
and they did not forsake their sins,
till they were carried away captive from their land
and were scattered over all the earth;
the people were left very few in number,
but with rulers from the house of David.
¹⁶*Some of them did what was pleasing to God,^e*
but others multiplied sins.

e Gk lacks *to God*   * Sir 48:16-18 Vg.

OVERVIEW: After David, the kings and the people of Israel fluctuated between faithfulness and unfaithfulness to God (RABANUS MAURUS).

48:15 Unrepentance and Captivity

A SUMMARY OF THE HISTORY OF ISRAEL. RABANUS MAURUS: When it says, "There remained only a people very few in number, with a prince of the house of David. Some of them did what was pleasing to God, but others multiplied sins," it indicates that the descendents of the house of David and the tribes of Judah and of Benjamin did not completely reject the worship of God and his temple, as did the ten tribes that were in Samaria. But some of them were idolaters, such as Joram,[1] Ahaziah,[2] Manasseh,[3] Jehoiachin[4] and Zedekiah.[5] Others adhered to their God, as did Jehoshaphat,[6] Hezekiah[7] and Josiah.[8] Similarly, their subjects also acted in different ways: some followed the right way, others stumbled into error. For this reason it later happened that when many had already deviated from the truth, they were punished with imprisonment, so that those who had worshiped idols in their own land would also worship them in a foreign land.[9] ON ECCLESIASTICUS 10.18.[10]

---

[1]See 2 Kings 8:18 (4 Kings 8:18 LXX). [2]See 2 Kings 8:27 (4 Kings 8:27 LXX). [3]See 2 Kings 21:1-2 (4 Kings 21:1-2 LXX). [4]See 2 Kings 24:8-9 (4 Kings 24:8-9 LXX). [5]See 2 Kings 24:18-19 (4 Kings 24:18-19 LXX). [6]See 1 Kings 22:41-43 (3 Kings 22:41-43 LXX). [7]See 2 Kings 18:1-3 (4 Kings 18:1-3 LXX). [8]See 2 Kings 22:1-2 (4 Kings 22:1-2 LXX). [9]Cf. Jer 5:19. [10]PL 109:1103.

48:17-21* HEZEKIAH

¹⁷*Hezekiah fortified his city,*
    and brought water into the midst of it;
he tunneled the sheer rock with iron
    and built pools for water.
¹⁸*In his days Sennacherib came up,*
    and sent the Rabshakeh;[f]
he lifted up his hand against Zion
    and made great boasts in his arrogance.
¹⁹*Then their hearts were shaken and their hands trembled,*
    and they were in anguish, like women in travail.
²⁰*But they called upon the Lord who is merciful,*
    spreading forth their hands toward him;
and the Holy One quickly heard them from heaven,
    and delivered them by the hand of Isaiah.
²¹*The Lord[g] smote the camp of the Assyrians,*
    and his angel wiped them out.

f Other authorities add *and departed* **g** Gk *he* * Sir 48:19-24 Vg.

OVERVIEW: Hezekiah's fortified city is an image of the church (RABANUS MAURUS).

48:17 *Tunnels and Pools*

JERUSALEM IS AN IMAGE OF THE CHURCH.
RABANUS MAURUS: What it says in this passage, "He dug a canal in the rock with iron and built cisterns for water," mysteriously indicates the holy city, of which it is written, "The Savior is our fortified city,"[1] which cannot remain hidden since it is built on a hill.[2] Elsewhere it is also written, "The rush of the river gladdens the city of God,"[3] and, "Marvelous things are said of you, city of God."[4] He founded it and fortified it. And the Father says, "He built my city"[5] and restores all the walls—which were in part knocked down by the malice of the pagans or of the heretics—with correct faith and true religion, raising the towers of the virtues and putting another wall without, a bulwark.[6] In the building of forts these are called parapets, and they teach us to hold on to the efficacy of good works. It is not enough in fact to have the wall of faith, if this faith is not reinforced by good works.[7] This wall and this bulwark are in fact made of living stones,[8] which, according to the prophet, turn on the earth.[9] The king made every kind of armor and shield, establishing the various testimonies of Scripture and commanding the evangelical doctrine in defense of his church. He established doctors who would lead the spiritual warriors and guide all the armies in a just and reasonable way, adequately defending the church's camps against every enemy.[10] ON ECCLESIASTICUS 10.19.[11]

---

[1] Is 26:1, variant. [2] See Mt 5:14. [3] Ps 46:5 (45:5 LXX). [4] Ps 87:2 (86:2 LXX). [5] Is 45:13. [6] See Is 26:1. [7] See Jas 2:14-26. [8] See 1 Pet 2:5. [9] See Zech 9:16. [10] See Heb 11:34. [11] PL 109:1105.

48:22-25* ISAIAH

²²For Hezekiah did what was pleasing to the Lord,
    and he held strongly to the ways of David his father,
which Isaiah the prophet commanded,
    who was great and faithful in his vision.
²³In his days the sun went backward,
    and he lengthened the life of the king.
²⁴By the spirit of might he saw the last things,
    and comforted those who mourned in Zion.
²⁵He revealed what was to occur to the end of time,
    and the hidden things before they came to pass.

* Sir 48:25-28 Vg.

OVERVIEW: The sun went backwards to indicate the additional life that would be granted to Hezekiah, just as the sun was eclipsed when Christ died (CYRIL OF JERUSALEM).

48:23 The Sun Went Backwards

A SIGN FOR HEZEKIAH AND FOR CHRIST.
CYRIL OF JERUSALEM: For Hezekiah, by now without hope, according to the words of the prophet who told him the judgment, his life was extended fifteen years.¹ The sun, continuing on its way, he made to retreat.² This was a sign. The sun went backwards for Hezekiah³ but was eclipsed for Christ.⁴ In both phenomena, the retreat and the eclipse, a sign was given, although with different meaning with respect to Hezekiah and to Jesus. If Hezekiah managed to have the divine judgment revoked, would Jesus not give the remission of sins? Be converted, therefore, and mourn over your sins,⁵ close the door and pray to obtain the forgiveness of sins⁶ and avoid the burning flames, since confession has the power to put out the fire itself,⁷ just as it has the strength to tame lions.⁸ CATECHETICAL LECTURES 2.15.⁹

¹Cf. Is 38:5; 2 Kings 20:6 (4 Kings 20:6 LXX). ²Cf. Is 38:8; 2 Kings 20:11 (4 Kings 20:11 LXX). ³See Sir 48:23 (48:26 Vg). ⁴See Lk 23:45. ⁵See Is 30:15. ⁶See Mt 6:6. ⁷Cf. Pr Azar 26-27 (Dan 3:49-50 LXX). ⁸Cf. Dan 6:17-23; Bel 31-42 (Dan 14:31-42 LXX). ⁹CTP 103:60-61.

49:1-3* JOSIAH

*¹The memory of Josiah is like a blending of incense
    prepared by the art of the perfumer;
it is sweet as honey to every mouth,
    and like music at a banquet of wine.
²He was led aright in converting the people,
    and took away the abominations of iniquity.
³He set his heart upon the Lord;
    in the days of wicked men he strengthened godliness.*

* Sir 49:1-4 Vg.

OVERVIEW: The purification enacted by Josiah is an image of the cleansing enabled by Christ (RABANUS MAURUS).

49:2 Converting the People

JOSIAH AND CHRIST THE PURIFIERS. RABANUS MAURUS: According to the allegory, Josiah is a figure of the saving Lord, he who is called the salvation and strength of the Lord, since Scripture says of him, "The mighty Lord, the Lord strong in battle."[1] And elsewhere, "He will save his people from their sins."[2] In fact, out of zeal for God, he who said through the prophet, "Zeal for your house consumes me,"[3] purifies the land of Judah and Jerusalem from all filth and abomination. Of him John says, "His winnowing fork is in his hand, and he will clear his threshing floor."[4] ON ECCLESIASTICUS 10.21.[5]

[1]Ps 24:8 (23:8 LXX). [2]Mt 1:21. [3]Ps 69:10 (68:10 LXX). [4]Mt 3:12. [5]PL 109:1107.

49:4-10* LAST KINGS AND PROPHETS

*⁴Except David and Hezekiah and Josiah
    they all sinned greatly,
for they forsook the law of the Most High;
    the kings of Judah came to an end;
⁵for they gave their power to others,*

and their glory to a foreign nation,
⁶who set fire to the chosen city of the sanctuary,
    and made her streets desolate,
    according to the word^h of Jeremiah.
⁷For they had afflicted him;
    yet he had been consecrated in the womb as prophet,
to pluck up and afflict and destroy,
    and likewise to build and to plant.

⁸It was Ezekiel who saw the vision of glory
    which God^i showed him above the chariot of the cherubim.
⁹For God^i remembered his enemies with storm,
    and did good to those who directed their ways aright.^j

¹⁰May the bones of the twelve prophets
    revive from where they lie,
for they comforted the people of Jacob
    and delivered them with confident hope.

---

h Gk *by the hand* **i** Gk *he* **j** The text and meaning of this verse are uncertain * Sir 49:5-12 Vg.

OVERVIEW: Ezekiel predicted the forgiveness of sins brought about by Christ (RABANUS MAURUS).

49:9 God Remembered His Enemies

EZEKIEL PREDICTED CHRIST. RABANUS MAURUS: Ezekiel, whose name is translated "confirmed by God"[1] and who, in Babylon, predicted to the sinful masses the coming imprisonment, though promising forgiveness of sins to those who would turn and do penance, points in a mysterious way to the Lord and Savior, who is the power and wisdom of God[2] and was called by the prophet the arm of the Lord.[3] He has visited us, we who were in the prison of this world, foretelling future punishments for sinners and promising eternal healing to those who were repentant. ON ECCLESIASTICUS 10.23.[4]

---

[1]This interpretation is traditional. [2]See 1 Cor 1:24. [3]Cf. Is 53:1.
[4]PL 109:1109.

49:11-13* ZERUBBABEL, JOSHUA AND NEHEMIAH

¹¹How shall we magnify Zerubbabel?
    He was like a signet on the right hand,
    ¹²and so was Jeshua the son of Jozadak;

in their days they built the house
    and raised a temple^k holy to the Lord,
    prepared for everlasting glory.

---

¹³*The memory of Nehemiah also is lasting;*
he raised for us the walls that had fallen,
and set up the gates and bars
and rebuilt our ruined houses.

k Other authorities read *people*   * Sir 49:13-15 Vg.

Overview: Zerubbabel is an image of Christ's incarnation (Rabanus Maurus).

49:11 *Like a Signet on the Right Hand*

Zerubbabel Is an Image of Christ. Rabanus Maurus: How he is a seal in the right hand of Israel is what the prophet Haggai shows at the end of his book: "In that day, says the Lord of hosts, I will take you, Zerubbabel, son of Shealtiel, my servant, says the Lord of hosts, and I will place you like a seal, because I have chosen you, says the Lord of hosts."[1] In the end, he is commanded to speak only to Zerubbabel,[2] since he preceded Christ as his image, having assumed the flesh of the line of David.[3] He is told, therefore, what will happen at the end, that this world will pass away[4] and that he will destroy every principality, power and might, pull down the thrones of kings and destroy the power of kingdoms and nations, and the chariots, the horses and the riders.[5] "In that day, says the Lord of hosts, I will take you, Zerubbabel, son of Shealtiel, my servant."[6] He calls him "servant" because of the human body, since "then he also, the Son, will be subjected to the one who subjected all things to him,"[7] and with all things subjected it will be seen that he also is subjected. But when all of this is fulfilled, God will put a seal in his hands. God the Father marks him, and he is the image of the invisible God,[8] his imprint and his substance,[9] and whoever will believe in God will be sealed as with a ring. On Ecclesiasticus 10.25.[10]

[1]Hag 2:23. [2]See Hag 2:21. [3]See Mt 1:13. [4]See 1 Cor 7:31. [5]See Hag 2:22. [6]Hag 2:23. [7]1 Cor 15:28. [8]See Col 1:15. [9]See Heb 1:3. [10]PL 109:1110.

49:14-16* SUMMARY

¹⁴*No one like Enoch has been created on earth,*
for he was taken up from the earth.
¹⁵*And no man like Joseph*ˡ *has been born,*
and his bones are cared for.
¹⁶*Shem and Seth were honored among men,*
and Adam above every living being in the creation.

l Heb Syr: Greek adds *the leader of his brothers, the support of the people*   * Sir 49:16-19 Vg.

Overview: Enoch's ascent prefigures Christ's ascension (Rabanus Maurus).

49:14 *No One Like Enoch*

Enoch Prefigures Christ's Ascension. Rabanus Maurus: What was set forth at first and again recapitulated concerning Enoch, if not that his being taken away prefigured the ascension into heaven of our Lord Jesus Christ, who became incarnate in the last days of the world[1] and was testified to by all the patriarchs and prophets?[2] It is rightly said of him that "no one was created on earth equal to Enoch," which means consecration,[3] as one who has consecrated his church, consecrating it with his blood. He came into the world without sin and was received into heaven in glory. Of him the psalmist says, "You are the most beautiful among the sons of men,"[4] and, "Ascending on high, he took prisoners with him; he gave gifts to human beings."[5] ON ECCLESIASTICUS 10.27.[6]

[1]See Heb 1:2; 1 Pet 1:20. [2]See Heb 1:1. [3]This interpretation is poorly attested. [4]Ps 45:3 (44:3 LXX). [5]Eph 4:8; Ps 68:19 (67:19 LXX). [6]PL 109:1112.

50:1-24* SIMON THE PRIEST

[1]*The leader of his brethren and the pride of his people*[m]
  was Simon the high priest, son of Onias,
who in his life repaired the house,
  and in his time fortified the temple.
[2]*He laid the foundations for the high double walls,*[n]
  the high retaining walls for the temple enclosure.
[3]*In his days a cistern for water was quarried out,*[o]
  a reservoir like the sea in circumference.
[4]*He considered how to save his people from ruin,*
  and fortified the city to withstand a siege.
[5]*How glorious he was when the people gathered round him*
  as he came out of the inner sanctuary![p]
[6]*Like the morning star among the clouds,*
  like the moon when it is full;
[7]*like the sun shining upon the temple of the Most High,*
  and like the rainbow gleaming in glorious clouds;
[8]*like roses in the days of the first fruits,*
  like lilies by a spring of water,
  like a green shoot on Lebanon[q] *on a summer day;*
[9]*like fire and incense in the censer,*
  like a vessel of hammered gold
  adorned with all kinds of precious stones;
[10]*like an olive tree putting forth its fruit,*
  and like a cypress towering in the clouds.

¹¹When he put on his glorious robe
    and clothed himself with superb perfection
and went up to the holy altar,
    he made the court of the sanctuary glorious.
¹²And when he received the portions from the hands of the priests,
    as he stood by the hearth of the altar
with a garland of brethren around him,
    he was like a young cedar on Lebanon;
and they surrounded him like the trunks of palm trees,
    ¹³all the sons of Aaron in their splendor
with the Lord's offering in their hands,
    before the whole congregation of Israel.
¹⁴Finishing the service at the altars,
    and arranging the offering to the Most High, the Almighty,
¹⁵he reached out his hand to the cup
    and poured a libation of the blood of the grape;
he poured it out at the foot of the altar,
    a pleasing odor to the Most High, the King of all.
¹⁶Then the sons of Aaron shouted,
    they sounded the trumpets of hammered work,
they made a great noise to be heard
    for remembrance before the Most High.
¹⁷Then all the people together made haste
    and fell to the ground upon their faces
to worship their Lord,
    the Almighty, God Most High.
¹⁸And the singers praised him with their voices
    in sweet and full-toned melody.^r
¹⁹And the people besought the Lord Most High
    in prayer before him who is merciful,
till the order of worship of the Lord was ended;
    so they completed his service.
²⁰Then Simon^s came down, and lifted up his hands
    over the whole congregation of the sons of Israel,
to pronounce the blessing of the Lord with his lips,
    and to glory in his name;
²¹and they bowed down in worship a second time,
    to receive the blessing from the Most High.

²²And now bless the God of all,
    who in every way does great things;
who exalts our days from birth,
    and deals with us according to his mercy.
²³May he give us^t gladness of heart,
    and grant that peace may be in our days in Israel,

as in the days of old.
[24]*May he entrust to us his mercy!*
And let him deliver us in our[u] *days!*

m Heb Syr: Greek lacks this line. Compare 49.15   n The meaning of this phrase is obscure   o Cn Compare Heb: Gk *was diminished*   p Gk *the house of the veil*   q Or *a sprig of frankincense*   r Other authorities read *in sweet melody throughout the house*   s Gk *he*   t Other authorities read *you*   u Other authorities read *his*   * Sir 50:1-26 Vg.

OVERVIEW: Job is praised as a just man who is like an emerald in the mud (ANONYMOUS ANOMOEAN). The brass trumpets are images of the apostolic preaching (ORIGEN).

50:6 Like the Morning Star

IN PRAISE OF JOB. ANONYMOUS ANOMOEAN: "There was a man in the land of Uz."[1] He was like a dove in the middle of ravenous eagles, like a lamb in the middle of predatory wolves,[2] like a star in the middle of fearsome clouds. "A man" righteous among the unrighteous, holy among the profane, innocent among the unclean, pious among the godless, good among the wicked, like an emerald in the mud, like a pearl in the sand. COMMENTARY ON JOB 1.7.[3]

50:16 Making a Great Noise

THE SOUND OF THE APOSTOLIC PREACHING. ORIGEN: When our Lord Jesus comes (his coming was prefigured by the ancient son of Nun)[4] he sends his priests, the apostles, who carry trumpets hammered out of metal,[5] that is, the magnificent, heavenly teaching of their preaching. Matthew, in his Gospel, first sounded the priestly trumpet. Mark, Luke and John also each blew their priestly trumpets. Peter also makes the trumpets resound in his two epistles, as do James and Jude. John continues to sound the trumpet in his epistles, as does Luke when he describes the deeds of the apostles. And finally the one arrives who says, "I believe that God has placed us, the apostles, in the last place,"[6] and hurling lightning bolts with the trumpets of his fourteen epistles, he makes the walls of Jericho—the contrivances of idolatry and the opinions of philosophers—collapse on their foundations.[7] HOMILIES ON JOSHUA 7.1.[8]

---

[1]Job 1:1.   [2]See Mt 10:16; Lk 10:3.   [3]CSEL 96:97-98.   [4]Joshua and Jesus are two different translations of the same Hebrew name.   [5]See Num 10:2; Ps 98:6 (97:6 LXX).   [6]1 Cor 4:9.   [7]Cf. Josh 6:20. This list of New Testament books does not match Origen's list. It might have been adapted by Rufinus.   [8]CTP 108:117.

50:25-26* A NUMERICAL PROVERB

[25]*With two nations my soul is vexed,*
   and the third is no nation:
[26]*Those who live on Mount Seir,*[v] *and the*
   Philistines,
   and the foolish people that dwell in
   Shechem.

v Heb Vg: Gk *on the mountain of Samaria*   * Sir 50:27-28 Vg.

OVERVIEW: This passage has application to the Jews, the nations and the heretics (RABANUS MAURUS).

50:25 Vexed with Two Nations

JEWS, PAGANS AND HERETICS. RABANUS MAURUS: He says that he hated two peoples. One of these is the Jewish people subject to the letter of the law, which was also known by the name of Seir, which means "shaggy" or "hairy." Seir is Esau,[1] whose name means "red,"[2] the older son of Isaac and Rebecca; the younger was called Jacob. But why was Esau all red and hairy, if not because the first people was stained by the blood of the prophets and of Christ and lived in the squalor of sin and wickedness? For this reason the younger one grabbed onto his heel,[3] since the younger people would mysteriously surpass the older. This is in fact "a perverse and adulterous generation,"[4] according to the truthful voice of the Gospel, that "kills the prophets and stones those who are sent to them."[5] In the last days they did not fear to raise their impious hands against the heir, killing the Son of God.[6] . . . The other people are the Philistines, whose name means "double ruin"[7] and symbolizes the people of the nations, contaminated by both idolatry and perverse conduct and thus making themselves hateful, since in error they have strayed far from the way of truth. The third is then the assembly of heretics, the foolish people living at Shechem,[8] in the sides of the mountain and in discomfort, because, writing and teaching perverse things every day, they foolishly waste their effort. The fact that they are not even considered a people shows that heretics do not have a single origin or a single error but have arisen in many different places and fallen into many errors. And they even contradict each other. ON ECCLESIASTICUS 10.30.[9]

---

[1]Both Seir as another name for Esau and the etymology are traditional. [2]Cf. Gen 25:25. [3]See Gen 25:26. [4]Mt 16:4. [5]Mt 23:27; Lk 13:34. [6]See Mt 21:38; Mk 12:7; Lk 20:14. [7]This etymology seems to be unknown. [8]Cf. Sir 50:26. [9]PL 109:1118-19.

50:27-29* CONCLUSION

[27]*Instruction in understanding and knowledge*
    I have written in this book,
Jesus the son of Sirach, son of Eleazar, of Jerusalem,[w]
    who out of his heart poured forth wisdom.
[28]*Blessed is he who concerns himself with these things,*
    and he who lays them to heart will become wise.
[29]*For if he does them, he will be strong for all things,*
    for the light of the Lord is his path.

w The text of this line is uncertain   * Sir 50:29-31 Vg.

OVERVIEW: The creation makes known the Trinity (AUGUSTINE).

50:29 Strong for All Things

FROM THE CREATION TO THE KNOWLEDGE OF THE TRINITY. AUGUSTINE: All of the works of the divine art show in themselves a certain unity, form and order. Each constitutes something of a unity, such as bodily natures and the characters of souls. And they are constituted according to a certain form, like the figures and qualities of bodies or the theories and techniques of the soul. And they follow or have a specific order, like the weights and positions of bodies or the loves and pleasures of the soul. It is necessary, therefore, that knowing the Creator through his works,[1] we rise to the Trinity, of whom the creation, in a sure and just proportion, bears the traces.[2] ON THE TRINITY 6.10.12.[3]

---

[1]See Rom 1:20. [2]Sir 50:29 (50:31 Vg), variant. [3]NBA 4:287.

51:1-12* HYMN OF THANKSGIVING

[1]*I will give thanks to thee, O Lord and King,*
    and will praise thee as God my Savior.
I give thanks to thy name,
    [2]*for thou hast been my protector and helper*
and hast delivered my body from destruction
    and from the snare of a slanderous tongue,
    from lips that utter lies.
Before those who stood by
    thou wast my helper, [3]*and didst deliver me,*
    in the greatness of thy mercy and of thy name,
from the gnashings of teeth about to devour me,[x]
    from the hand of those who sought my life,
    from the many afflictions that I endured,
[4]*from choking fire on every side*
    and from the midst of fire which I did not kindle,
[5]*from the depths of the belly of Hades,*
    from an unclean tongue and lying words—
    [6]*the slander of an unrighteous tongue to the king.*
My soul drew near to death,
    and my life was very near to Hades beneath.
[7]*They surrounded me on every side,*
    and there was no one to help me;

I looked for the assistance of men,
  and there was none.
⁸*Then I remembered thy mercy, O Lord,*
  and thy work from of old,
that thou dost deliver those who wait for thee
  and dost save them from the hand of their enemies.
⁹*And I sent up my supplication from the earth,*
  and prayed for deliverance from death.
¹⁰*I appealed to the Lord, the Father of my lord,*
  not to forsake me in the days of affliction,
  at the time when there is no help against the proud.
¹¹*I will praise thy name continually,*
  and will sing praise with thanksgiving.
My prayer was heard,
  ¹²*for thou didst save me from destruction*
and rescue me from an evil plight.
Therefore I will give thanks to thee and praise thee,
  and I will bless the name of the Lord.

x Cn Compare Vg: Gk *when I was about to be devoured*   * Sir 51:1-17 Vg.

OVERVIEW: Fire may kill the bodies but not the souls of the martyrs (RABANUS MAURUS).

51:4 Fire on Every Side

THE SUFFERINGS OF THE MARTYRS. RABANUS MAURUS: We read that this happened frequently in the passions of the martyrs. Like the three young men, who remained unhurt in the intense flames of the furnace,[1] they also would not have suffered harm from the consuming flames. But since this has not been granted to all the martyrs of God, since many of them were burned bodily by the fire, though their souls arrived freely in the heavenly places, it is better to understand this fire and this flame as the intense heat of persecution, which, although it can afflict the saints of God for a little while, cannot go so far as to cause them to lose their souls. ON ECCLESIASTICUS 10.31.[2]

---

[1]See Dan 3. [2]PL 109:1120.

51:13-30* POEM ON THE SEARCH OF WISDOM

¹³*While I was still young, before I went on my travels,*
  I sought wisdom openly in my prayer.
¹⁴*Before the temple I asked for her,*

and I will search for her to the last.
¹⁵From blossom to^y ripening grape
    my heart delighted in her;
my foot entered upon the straight path;
    from my youth I followed her steps.
¹⁶I inclined my ear a little and received her,
    and I found for myself much instruction.
¹⁷I made progress therein;
    to him who gives me wisdom I will give glory.
¹⁸For I resolved to live according to wisdom,^z
    and I was zealous for the good;
    and I shall never be put to shame.
¹⁹My soul grappled with wisdom,^z
    and in my conduct I was strict;^a
I spread out my hands to the heavens,
    and lamented my ignorance of her.
²⁰I directed my soul to her,
    and through purification I found her.
I gained understanding^b with her from the first,
    therefore I will not be forsaken.
²¹My heart was stirred to seek her,
    therefore I have gained a good possession.
²²The Lord gave me a tongue as my reward,
    and I will praise him with it.

²³Draw near to me, you who are untaught,
    and lodge in my school.
²⁴Why do you say you are lacking in these things,^c
    and why are your souls very thirsty?
²⁵I opened my mouth and said,
    Get these things^d for yourselves without money.
²⁶Put your neck under the yoke,
    and let your souls receive instruction;
    it is to be found close by.
²⁷See with your eyes that I have labored little
    and found for myself much rest.
²⁸Get instruction with a large sum of silver,
    and you will gain by it much gold.
²⁹May your soul rejoice in his mercy,
    and may you not be put to shame when you praise him.
³⁰Do your work before the appointed time,
    and in God's^e time he will give you your reward.

y Other authorities read *As from*   z Gk *her*   a The Greek text of this line is uncertain   b Gk *heart*   c Cn Compare Heb Syr: The Greek text of this line is uncertain   d Greek lacks *these things*   e Gk *his*   * Sir 51:18-38 Vg, with great differences. The Vulgate adds also Sir 52:1-13, which repeats 1 Kings 8:22-31 (3 Kings 8:22-31 LXX).

OVERVIEW: Ask for wisdom when you are still young (RABANUS MAURUS). The church is the place where we are taught such wisdom as we learn to live properly and forever (AUGUSTINE).

51:14 *Search for Wisdom to the Last*

ASKING FOR WISDOM. RABANUS MAURUS: After the prayer offered by the author of this book, speaking as the church, he tells how he had sought wisdom from his childhood, having asked it of the Lord. When he says that he sought wisdom before his youth, before the opportune time[1] to ask, he shows to have desired it prior to the errors of childhood and adolescence, and even before his youth, and to have asked insistently that God would give it to him, promising to seek it always. Adolescence and youth are fraught with dangers, because the actions of the exterior person[2] dominate, as Solomon says in the book of Proverbs, confessing that he does not know "the way of a youth in his adolescence,"[3] and the prophet asks the Lord, "Do not recall the sins of my youth and of my ignorance."[4] For this reason philosophers, representing human life with the letter Y, assign the lefthand stroke to infancy and adolescence and the righthand stroke to the more mature age, when the intellect is more robust and rejects the earlier foolishness of the senses. In fact, this letter was first used by Pythagoras as an example of human life, in such a way that the bottom stroke, thinner than a comma, would indicate the uncertain condition of the earliest age, not yet given to either vice or virtue. The junction above it begins with adolescence, of which the right side is difficult but tends to a blessed life, and the left is easier but leads to perdition and death. ON ECCLESIASTICUS 10.31.[5]

51:23 *Lodge in My School*

THE PLACE OF INSTRUCTION. AUGUSTINE: The Word of God was directed to us. It was proclaimed to exhort us, as the Scripture says: "Receive instruction in the house of instruction."[6] Instruction is given so as to instruct, and the house of instruction is the church of Christ. Let us ask ourselves the object and purpose of this instruction: who is instructed, and who imparts the instruction. One learns to live well, and the purpose for which he learns to live well is so as to live forever. To this end Christians are taught, and Christ is the one who teaches. SERMON 399.1.1.[7]

---

[1]The Vulgate has *tempus* ("time") instead of *templum* ("shrine"). Rabanus comments on the variant. [2]Cf. 2 Cor 4:16. [3]Prov 30:19, variant. [4]Ps 25:7 (24:7 LXX), variant. [5]PL 109:1122. [6]Sir 51:23, 28 (51:31, 36 Vg). Augustine joins the two verses, which are both very different from the Greek, in one phrase: Sir 51:23 [Sir 51:31 Vg] "Approach me, you that have not been instructed and gather in the house of instruction" and the beginning of Sir 51:28 [Sir 51:36 Vg], "Receive the instruction ..." [7]NBA 34:732-33.

BARUCH

1:1-14 BARUCH AND THE ASSEMBLY OF THE JEWS IN BABYLON

¹These are the words of the book which Baruch the son of Neraiah, son of Mahseiah, son of Zedekiah, son of Hasadiah, son of Hilkiah, wrote in Babylon, ²in the fifth year, on the seventh day of the month, at the time when the Chaldeans took Jerusalem and burned it with fire. ³And Baruch read the words of this book in the hearing of Jeconiah the son of Jehoiakim, king of Judah, and in the hearing of all the people who came to hear the book, ⁴and in the hearing of the mighty men and the princes, and in the hearing of the elders, and in the hearing of all the people, small and great, all who dwelt in Babylon by the river Sud.

⁵Then they wept, and fasted, and prayed before the Lord; ⁶and they collected money, each giving what he could; ⁷and they sent it to Jerusalem to Jehoiakim the high priest,ᵃ the son of Hilkiah, son of Shallum, and to the priests, and to all the people who were present with him in Jerusalem. ⁸At the same time, on the tenth day of Sivan, Baruchᵇ took the vessels of the house of the Lord, which had been carried away from the temple, to return them to the land of Judah—the silver vessels which Zedekiah the son of Josiah, king of Judah, had made, ⁹after Nebuchadnezzar king of Babylon had carried away from Jerusalem Jeconiah and the princes and the prisoners and the mighty men and the people of the land, and brought them to Babylon.

¹⁰And they said: "Herewith we send you money; so buy with the money burnt offerings and sin offerings and incense, and prepare a cereal offering, and offer them upon the altar of the Lord our God; ¹¹and pray for the life of Nebuchadnezzar king of Babylon, and for the life of Belshazzar his son, that their days on earth may be like the days of heaven. ¹²And the Lord will give us strength, and he will give light to our eyes, and we shall live under the protectionᶜ of Nebuchadnezzar king of Babylon, and under the protectionᶜ of Belshazzar his son, and we shall serve them many days and find favor in their sight. ¹³And pray for us to the Lord our God, for we have sinned against the Lord our God, and to this day the anger of the Lord and his wrath have not turned away from us. ¹⁴And you shall read this book which we are sending you, to make your confession in the house of the Lord on the days of the feasts and at appointed seasons."

a Gk *the priest* b Gk *he* c Gk *in the shadow*

OVERVIEW: The historical context is set during the time five years after the destruction of Jerusalem, when Baruch went to Babylon (THEODORET). Out of respect, the text records the names of Baruch's ancestors and establishes Baruch's authority. The book of Baruch mentions the fact that although the Jerusalem temple had been razed, the people continued to offer sacrifices on the spot where it had stood because it was unlawful to sacrifice anywhere else

(OLYMPIODORUS). The king of Babylon, Nebuchadnezzar, becomes a symbol of fortitude when he is afflicted (DOROTHEUS).

1:1 The Genealogy of Baruch

THE HISTORICAL CONTEXT. THEODORET OF CYR: The worthy Baruch accompanied the fleeing Jews into Egypt, as we have seen.[1] Five years after the destruction of the city, he went to Babylon. Those who distributed the food of goodness dedicated themselves in any case to helping the weak and guiding them to truth. Once he had reached Babylon, he read the prophecy of Jeremiah to the deportees, and in particular to Jeconiah, who was taken prisoner after a brief reign—and he was struck to the heart. Indeed, Baruch made them aware of the sins of the past, so they would know the reasons for their disgrace and would shed many tears and that each might offer money to send to the priests at Jerusalem to buy offerings to sacrifice to the Lord. COMMENTARY ON BARUCH 1.[2]

BARUCH'S ANCESTORS. OLYMPIODORUS OF ALEXANDRIA: Perhaps he mentions Baruch's ancestors because they were worthy of respect. FRAGMENTS ON BARUCH 1.1.[3]

1:3 In the Hearing of Jeconiah

THE NAME OF THE KING. OLYMPIODORUS OF ALEXANDRIA: He had earlier been deported to Babylon by Nebuchadnezzar: the same Jeconiah, son of Jehoiakim, was also called Eliakim, because he had two names. FRAGMENTS ON BARUCH 1.3.[4]

1:10 Sacrifices Offered to God

IN THE PLACE WHERE THE TEMPLE WAS. OLYMPIODORUS OF ALEXANDRIA: Even though the temple had been razed to the ground, they offered sacrifices on the spot where it was built. In fact, it was unlawful to offer sacrifices in a place other than Jerusalem. FRAGMENTS ON BARUCH 1.10.[5]

1:11 Praying for Nebuchadnezzar and Belshazzar

AN IMAGE OF PATIENT RESISTANCE TO TEMPTATION. DOROTHEUS OF GAZA: The Fathers call sexual desire "Egypt," meaning the body's inclination toward its own satisfaction and the mind's focus on pleasure. They understand by "Assyrians" the passionate, all-consuming thoughts that trouble and confuse the mind as they fill it with impure images and violently drag it down with sin, even when it does not want that sin around. . . . Before one gives into passion, even if his thoughts rise up against him, he is still free in his own city; indeed, he also has God helping him. If, therefore, such a person humbles himself before God and bears the yoke of his affliction of temptation with thanksgiving and puts up even a small fight, the help of God will surely deliver him. If instead he flees hard work and lowers himself to the desires of the body, then he is deported with force and violence to the land of the Assyrians, where he must serve them even if he does not want to. But then the prophet still says, "Pray for the life of Nebuchadnezzar because in his life is your salvation." "Nebuchadnezzar" stands for someone who does not become discouraged at the affliction of temptation that comes, nor does he rebel but endures it with humility, suffering it like something he deserves and considering that he is not worthy to be freed from this weight. Indeed, he understands that his trial deserves to last even longer and should be even more severe. He is someone who, whether he is aware or not that the cause of his troubles lies with himself or his circumstances at the moment, believes that nothing that comes from God is without justice. SPIRITUAL INSTRUCTIONS 13.143.[6]

---

[1]See Jer 43:6-7 (50:6-7 LXX). [2]PG 81:760-61. [3]PG 93:761. [4]PG 93:761. [5]PG 93:761. [6]CTP 21.197-98.

1:15–2:10 THE CONFESSION OF SINS

¹⁵*And you shall say: "Righteousness belongs to the Lord our God, but confusion of face, as at this day, to us, to the men of Judah, to the inhabitants of Jerusalem,* ¹⁶*and to our kings and our princes and our priests and our prophets and our fathers,* ¹⁷*because we have sinned before the Lord,* ¹⁸*and have disobeyed him, and have not heeded the voice of the Lord our God, to walk in the statutes of the Lord which he set before us.* ¹⁹*From the day when the Lord brought our fathers out of the land of Egypt until today, we have been disobedient to the Lord our God, and we have been negligent, in not heeding his voice.* ²⁰*So to this day there have clung to us the calamities and the curse which the Lord declared through Moses his servant at the time when he brought our fathers out of the land of Egypt to give to us a land flowing with milk and honey.* ²¹*We did not heed the voice of the Lord our God in all the words of the prophets whom he sent to us, but we each followed the intent of his own wicked heart by serving other gods and doing what is evil in the sight of the Lord our God.*

² *"So the Lord confirmed his word, which he spoke against us, and against our judges who judged Israel, and against our kings and against our princes and against the men of Israel and Judah.* ²*Under the whole heaven there has not been done the like of what he has done in Jerusalem, in accordance with what is written in the law of Moses,* ³*that we should eat, one the flesh of his son and another the flesh of his daughter.* ⁴*And he gave them into subjection to all the kingdoms around us, to be a reproach and a desolation among all the surrounding peoples, where the Lord has scattered them.* ⁵*They were brought low and not raised up, because we sinned against the Lord our God, in not heeding his voice.*

⁶*"Righteousness belongs to the Lord our God, but confusion of face to us and our fathers, as at this day.* ⁷*All those calamities with which the Lord threatened us have come upon us.* ⁸*Yet we have not entreated the favor of the Lord by turning away, each of us, from the thoughts of his wicked heart.* ⁹*And the Lord has kept the calamities ready, and the Lord has brought them upon us, for the Lord is righteous in all his works which he has commanded us to do.* ¹⁰*Yet we have not obeyed his voice, to walk in the statutes of the Lord which he set before us."*

OVERVIEW: God's punishment was just (OLYMPIODORUS), visited on those who are ingenious in their wickedness (THEODORET). Such wickedness was seen during the siege, which elicited atrocities including the eating of human flesh; divine punishment was swift (THEODORET).

1:15 Confused Faces

GOD'S JUSTICE. OLYMPIODORUS OF ALEXAN-DRIA: God punished us justly, and today we are ashamed to be justly made prisoners. FRAGMENTS ON BARUCH 1.15.[1]

GOD'S JUST JUDGMENT. THEODORET OF CYR: God's judgment against us is extremely just: we deserve shame, all of us having transgressed. Indeed, like the kings, even the priests have done

---

[1]PG 93:764.

what is forbidden. COMMENTARY ON BARUCH 1.15-16.[2]

1:19 Negligent in Not Heeding God

INGENIOUS IN WICKEDNESS. THEODORET OF CYR: "We are stubborn," not to mention "we have devised every kind of sin." Paul says of them that they are "ingenious in wickedness."[3] COMMENTARY ON BARUCH 1.19.[4]

2:3 Eating Human Flesh

THE TRAGEDY OF HUNGER. THEODORET OF CYR: The siege led to hunger, which forced them to eat human flesh.[5] As it says, the pagans around us rejoiced over this. COMMENTARY ON BARUCH 2.3.[6]

2:9 Calamities Ready

THE LORD IS PATIENT BUT ALSO PUNISHES. THEODORET OF CYR: He calls his punishment "the swiftness of the Lord." The Scripture often calls his patience "sleep."[7] Moreover, recalling the punishment, they affirm that the Lord is just. Indeed, it was because they had transgressed and did not want to be healed that he punished them. Then they humbly beg him, remembering the ancient freedom that their fathers enjoyed, when they were freed from the bitter servitude of Egypt.[8] COMMENTARY ON BARUCH 1.9.[9]

---

[2]PG 81:761. [3]Rom 1:30. [4]PG 81:761. [5]Likely Theodoret is alluding to the siege of Jerusalem in A.D. 70; see Flavius Josephus *The Jewish War* 6.208. [6]PG 81:764. [7]See Ps 78:65 (77:65 LXX). [8]See Bar 2:11. [9]PG 81:764.

2:11-3:8 SUPPLICATION

[11]*And now, O Lord God of Israel, who didst bring thy people out of the land of Egypt with a mighty hand and with signs and wonders and with great power and outstretched arm, and hast made thee a name, as at this day,* [12]*we have sinned, we have been ungodly, we have done wrong, O Lord our God, against all thy ordinances.* [13]*Let thy anger turn away from us, for we are left, few in number, among the nations where thou hast scattered us.* [14]*Hear, O Lord, our prayer and our supplication, and for thy own sake deliver us, and grant us favor in the sight of those who have carried us into exile;* [15]*that all the earth may know that thou art the Lord our God, for Israel and his descendants are called by thy name.* [16]*O Lord, look down from thy holy habitation, and consider us. Incline thy ear, O Lord, and hear;* [17]*open thy eyes, O Lord, and see; for the dead who are in Hades, whose spirit has been taken from their bodies, will not ascribe glory or justice to the Lord,* [18]*but the person that is greatly distressed,[d] that goes about bent over and feeble, and the eyes that are failing, and the person that hungers, will ascribe to thee glory and righteousness, O Lord.* [19]*For it is not because of any righteous deeds of our fathers or our kings that we bring before thee our prayer for mercy, O Lord our God.* [20]*For thou hast sent thy anger and thy wrath upon us, as thou didst declare by thy servants the prophets, saying:* [21]*"Thus says the Lord: Bend your shoulders and serve the king of Babylon, and you will remain in the land which I gave to your fathers.* [22]*But*

if you will not obey the voice of the Lord and will not serve the king of Babylon, ²³I will make to cease from the cities of Judah and from the region about Jerusalem the voice of mirth and the voice of gladness, the voice of the bridegroom and the voice of the bride, and the whole land will be a desolation without inhabitants."

²⁴But we did not obey thy voice, to serve the king of Babylon; and thou hast confirmed thy words, which thou didst speak by thy servants the prophets, that the bones of our kings and the bones of our fathers would be brought out of their graves;ᵉ ²⁵and behold, they have been cast out to the heat of day and the frost of night. They perished in great misery, by famine and sword and pestilence. ²⁶And the house which is called by thy name thou hast made as it is today, because of the wickedness of the house of Israel and the house of Judah.

²⁷Yet thou hast dealt with us, O Lord our God, in all thy kindness and in all thy great compassion, ²⁸as thou didst speak by thy servant Moses on the day when thou didst command him to write thy law in the presence of the people of Israel, saying, ²⁹"If you will not obey my voice, this very great multitude will surely turn into a small number among the nations, where I will scatter them. ³⁰For I know that they will not obey me, for they are a stiff-necked people. But in the land of their exile they will come to themselves, ³¹and they will know that I am the Lord their God. I will give them a heart that obeys and ears that hear; ³²and they will praise me in the land of their exile, and will remember my name, ³³and will turn from their stubbornness and their wicked deeds; for they will remember the ways of their fathers, who sinned before the Lord. ³⁴I will bring them again into the land which I swore to give to their fathers, to Abraham and to Isaac and to Jacob, and they will rule over it; and I will increase them, and they will not be diminished. ³⁵I will make an everlasting covenant with them to be their God and they shall be my people; and I will never again remove my people Israel from the land which I have given them."

3 O Lord Almighty, God of Israel, the soul in anguish and the wearied spirit cry out to thee. ²Hear, O Lord, and have mercy, for we have sinned before thee. ³For thou art enthroned for ever, and we are perishing for ever. ⁴O Lord Almighty, God of Israel, hear now the prayer of the dead of Israel and of the sons of those who sinned before thee, who did not heed the voice of the Lord their God, so that calamities have clung to us. ⁵Remember not the iniquities of our fathers, but in this crisis remember thy power and thy name. ⁶For thou art the Lord our God, and thee, O Lord, will we praise. ⁷For thou hast put the fear of thee in our hearts in order that we should call upon thy name; and we will praise thee in our exile, for we have put away from our hearts all the iniquity of our fathers who sinned before thee. ⁸Behold, we are today in our exile where thou hast scattered us, to be reproached and cursed and punished for all the iniquities of our fathers who forsook the Lord our God.

d The meaning of the Greek is uncertain   e Gk *their place*

OVERVIEW: God does not close his eyes to sin. Thus, the people of Israel were reduced to a remnant (THEODORET). Sin, blindness of the soul and future punishment await those who rebel against God (OLYMPIODORUS), and even the tombs of their ancestors will be desecrated in this life (THEODORET). Those who are faithful, however, should recall God's promises (THEO-DORET) in the midst of their wearied spirit. One might also note that in Scripture the word *spirit* has several meanings (ATHANASIUS).

Sitting at the right of the Father indicates that the Son has equal dignity with the Father (BASIL). Sitting is a symbol of God's power to judge and his immutability (CHRYSOSTOM). The Word did not undergo a change of nature with the incarnation (Theodotus). At the end, he will judge the dead, whose prayers are futile (Olympiodorus).

2:13 Few in Number

We Have Become Few. Theodoret of Cyr: We acknowledge the justice of your punishment. We ask you to bring it to an end. Indeed, we have become few, we who at one time were compared with the grains of sand.[1] Commentary on Baruch 2.13.[2]

2:17 O Lord, See

God Behaves Differently from Human Beings. Theodoret of Cyr: People who are ill-disposed usually close their eyes when they see someone who has injured them and look away when those who have offended them beg forgiveness. But these things are said in a human way, because the divinity is not composite but simple and infinite.[3] Commentary on Baruch 2.17.[4]

2:18 Greatly Distressed

The Weight of Sin. Olympiodorus of Alexandria: Those who carry a great weight bend over due to their weakness. And the soul that is tormented and greatly saddened by its sins also confesses to be bowed down and weak. Fragments on Baruch 2.18.[5]

Two Possible Kinds of Blindness. Olympiodorus of Alexandria: Their eyes are failing perhaps in a concrete sense, due to misfortune, or perhaps it refers to those whose minds are darkened and do not reason. Fragments on Baruch 2.18.[6]

2:24 Bones Brought from Graves

Future Judgment. Olympiodorus of Alexandria: After death, their bones were to suffer as a sign of the future judgment. Fragments on Baruch 2.24.[7]

Desecration of Tombs. Theodoret of Cyr: And not only have we who are alive been given over to servitude, but also the tombs of our ancestors, in particular those of the kings, were destroyed to their foundations, and their bones were scattered and exposed to the open air to be corroded by the elements. Commentary on Baruch 2.19.[8]

2:27 God's Great Compassion

God's Promises. Theodoret of Cyr: They also recall the threats written in the Law. In the canticle of Moses the different ways that evils would happen to them were described. "The teeth of wild beasts I will send among them."[9] By wild beasts he meant their enemies. Then he adds, "I will deprive them of children by the foreign sword,"[10] and, "I will scatter them."[11] They recall these threats, but they also remember the promise of good things: "You said that you would grant mercy to those who were repentant, freeing them from servitude and restoring their former freedom to them." Commentary on Baruch 2.27.[12]

3:1 Crying Out to God

Different Meanings of the Word Spirit. Athanasius: You might have known, by consulting with learned persons, that there are different meanings of the word *spirit*. The Scripture, in fact, also speaks of the "spirit of man [a person]," as David sings, "I spoke with my heart by night, and my spirit was afflicted."[13] And Baruch prays, saying, "An anguished soul and a saddened spirit raises its cry to you." And in the canticle of the three young men, "Spirits and souls of the just, bless the Lord."[14] For his

---

[1]See Gen 22:17; Heb 11:12, etc. [2]PG 81:764. [3]Theodoret explains that the human attributes used by the Scripture to describe God's actions should be interpreted as metaphors. [4]PG 81:765. [5]PG 93:764. [6]PG 93:764. [7]PG 93:764. [8]PG 81:765. [9]Deut 32:24. [10]Deut 32:25. [11]Deut 32:26. [12]PG 81:765-68. [13]Ps 77:7 (76:7 LXX). [14]Pr Azar 64 (Dan 3:86 LXX).

part, the apostle writes, "The Spirit attests to our spirit that we are children of God. And if children, we are also heirs."[15] And, "No one knows what is in a person except the spirit of the person that is within him."[16] Moreover, in the letter to the Thessalonians he prays "that your whole spirit, soul and body would be kept irreproachable at the coming of Jesus Christ our Lord."[17] Winds are also called "spirit," as for example in Genesis, "And God made a spirit sweep over the earth, and the waters subsided."[18] And in the book of Jonah, "the Lord brought a great spirit over the sea and made a great tempest in the sea, so that the ship was in danger of breaking up."[19] Also in Psalm 106 it is written, "He spoke, and a hurricane spirit was stirred up over the waves."[20] And in Psalm 148, "Praise the Lord from the earth, fish of the sea and the abyss, fire, hail, snow, ice and tempest spirit, that carry out his word."[21] And in Ezekiel, in the lamentation over Tyre, "Your oarsmen brought you to the heart of the sea, into deep waters. The spirit of the east smashed you."[22] If you were also to read the sacred Scriptures, you would find that the meaning itself of the divine words is also called "spirit," as when Paul writes, "He has made us fit to be ministers of the new covenant, not of the letter but of the spirit: the letter in fact kills, but the spirit gives life."[23] "Letter" is that by which an expression is materially composed, but the spiritual meaning contained in it is called "spirit." LETTER TO SERAPION 1.7.1–1.8.1.[24]

3:3 God Enthroned Forever

THE SON ENJOYS THE SAME DIGNITY AS THE FATHER. BASIL THE GREAT: If someone says the Father deserves a higher place and the only-begotten Son deserves to sit in a lower place, he will find himself imagining that all the resulting conditions of the body attach to this creature of his imagination. These are the deliriums of drunken delusion that stretch the limits of insanity. The Lord taught that "he who does not honor the Son does not honor the Father."[25]

Therefore, how can anyone consider himself a follower of true religion if he refuses to worship and glorify with the Father him who in nature, in glory and in dignity is joined with the Father? What can we say? What just defense will we have in the day of the awful universal judgment of all creation? The Lord has clearly announced that he will come "in the glory of his Father."[26] Stephen saw Jesus standing at the right hand of the Father.[27] Paul testified in the Spirit concerning Christ "that he is at the right hand of God."[28] The Father says, "Sit at my right hand."[29] The Holy Spirit attests that he has sat down at "the right hand of the majesty" of God.[30] Shall we attempt to degrade him from his condition of equality to a lower state when he shares the honor and the throne with the Father? The fact that he sits as opposed to standing suggests, I believe, a nature that is fixed and absolutely stable, as Baruch also said when he wanted to exhibit God's immutability and immobility: "You sit forever while we are forever perishing."[31] Moreover, the place at the right hand indicates, in my judgment, equality of honor. ON THE HOLY SPIRIT 6.15.[32]

GOD JUDGES AND IS UNCHANGED. JOHN CHRYSOSTOM: "I saw the Lord seated."[33] To be seated on a throne is always a symbol of judgment, as David says: "You are seated on a throne, you who administer justice."[34] And Daniel, "Three thrones were set up, and the tribunal sat down."[35] By contrast, the prophet says that simply being seated is a symbol of something else. Of what? Stability, durability, proceeding onward, immutability, eternity, infinite life. Thus it is said, "You who are seated forever, and we who perish forever." You, it is said, who en-

---

[15]Rom 8:16-17. [16]1 Cor 2:11. [17]1 Thess 5:23. [18]Gen 8:1. In Greek the same word (*pneuma*) can mean a "puff of air," the "wind" and the "spirit." [19]Jon 1:4. [20]Ps 107:25 (106:25 LXX). [21]Ps 148:7-8. [22]Ezek 27:25-26. [23]2 Cor 3:6. [24]CTP 55:51-53. [25]Jn 5:23. [26]Acts 7:55. [27]See Acts 7:55-56. [28]Rom 8:34. [29]Ps 110:1 (109:1 LXX). [30]See Acts 2:34. [31]For the sake of his argumentation, Basil understands the verse literally. [32]CTP 106:105-6; NPNF 2 8:9-10**. [33]Is 6:1. [34]Ps 9:5. [35]Dan 7:9-10.

dure: who are, who live and are always thus. The comparison makes it clear that he was not speaking of a seat but "you who are seated forever, and we who perish." To sit on a throne is to judge. COMMENTARY ON ISAIAH 6.2.[36]

THE WORD REMAINS UNCHANGED IN THE INCARNATION. THEODOTUS OF ANCYRA: The Word was God before all time, coeternal with the Father.[37] But he wanted to become man for human beings. It was not through a change in the divine nature but by the miracle and will of God that he accepted birth as the beginning of his humanity. Thus, as a man he was born, but as God the Word, he preserved Mary's virginity. Not even our own word corrupts the integrity of the mind in the moment it is conceived.[38] It is the same with the Word of God. Being substantial and enhypostatic, when he chose to be born he nonetheless did not corrupt her virginity. What took place is beyond the logic of nature, and it consequently does not in any way descend to nature's way of reasoning: I am talking about a miracle. This does not proceed according to reason: I am speaking of God who was born, who chose to be born and yet did not thereby start being God at that moment. Although being God, he was born. It was not the birth that made him God. He remained what he was and became what he was not. Because he wanted to become what he was not for the plan of salvation, he chose birth as the beginning of that plan. He became man without changing his nature and thereby upsetting the terms of the divine being. Sacred Scripture says, "You are always the same, and your years have no end."[39] And, "You who reign forever," thus showing the immutability of the divine being. And he says further, "I, God, am always the same, and do not change."[40] He therefore became man without there being any change in the being of God or its being changed into another nature. What happened would not have been a miracle if he had manifested another nature through a change of nature. With us, many changes of this kind occur. But in this case God worked the miracle of becoming what he was not while remaining what he was. Referring to this event the great apostle said, "He, being in the form of God."[41] He says "being," and not "he was at one time," to show the perdurance of the nature. "Being in the form of God, he did not consider it robbery to be equal to God."[42] He says "to be equal to God," not as though he had been so only at one time. And he goes on to say, "But he humbled himself, assuming the form of a servant."[43] See how he remained what he was and at the same time humbled himself in the form of a servant? Though being God, he became a servant. HOMILY 2.2.[44]

3:4 Hear the Prayer of the Dead

PUNISHMENT AFTER DEATH. OLYMPIODORUS OF ALEXANDRIA: Those who have received condemnation for sin are dead. These words clearly indicate the immortal nature of the soul. FRAGMENTS ON BARUCH 3.4.[45]

---

[36]CTP 162:170. [37]See Jn 1:1-2. [38]The Fathers often compare the eternal generation of the Word with a human word, which the mind produces without modifying itself. Theodotus applies the same concept to the incarnation. [39]Ps 102:28 (101:28 LXX). [40]Mal 3:6. [41]Phil 2:6. [42]Phil 2:6. [43]Phil 2:7. [44]CTP 97:83-84. [45]PG 93:764.

3:9–4:4 WISDOM, A PREROGATIVE OF ISRAEL

⁹*Hear the commandments of life, O Israel;*
  give ear, and learn wisdom!
¹⁰*Why is it, O Israel, why is it that you are in the land of your enemies,*
  that you are growing old in a foreign country,
that you are defiled with the dead,
  ¹¹*that you are counted among those in Hades?*
¹²*You have forsaken the fountain of wisdom.*
¹³*If you had walked in the way of God,*
  you would be dwelling in peace for ever.
¹⁴*Learn where there is wisdom,*
  where there is strength,
  where there is understanding,
that you may at the same time discern
  where there is length of days, and life,
  where there is light for the eyes, and peace.

¹⁵*Who has found her place?*
  And who has entered her storehouses?
¹⁶*Where are the princes of the nations,*
  and those who rule over the beasts on the earth;
¹⁷*those who have sport with the birds of the air,*
  and who hoard up silver and gold,
in which men trust,
  and there is no end to their getting;
¹⁸*those who scheme to get silver, and are anxious,*
  whose labors are beyond measure?
¹⁹*They have vanished and gone down to Hades,*
  and others have arisen in their place.

²⁰*Young men have seen the light of day,*
  and have dwelt upon the earth;
but they have not learned the way to knowledge,
  nor understood her paths,
  nor laid hold of her.
²¹*Their sons have strayed far from her* ʲ *way.*
²²*She has not been heard of in Canaan,*
  nor seen in Teman;

²³*the sons of Hagar, who seek for understanding on the earth,*
  the merchants of Merran and Teman,
  the story-tellers and the seekers for understanding,
have not learned the way to wisdom,
  nor given thought to her paths.

²⁴*O Israel, how great is the house of God!*
  And how vast the territory that he possesses!
²⁵*It is great and has no bounds;*
  it is high and immeasurable.
²⁶*The giants were born there, who were famous of old,*
  great in stature, expert in war.
²⁷*God did not choose them,*
  nor give them the way to knowledge;
²⁸*so they perished because they had no wisdom,*
  they perished through their folly.

²⁹*Who has gone up into heaven, and taken her,*
  and brought her down from the clouds?
³⁰*Who has gone over the sea, and found her,*
  and will buy her for pure gold?
³¹*No one knows the way to her,*
  or is concerned about the path to her.
³²*But he who knows all things knows her,*
  he found her by his understanding.
He who prepared the earth for all time
  filled it with four-footed creatures;
³³*he who sends forth the light, and it goes,*
  called it, and it obeyed him in fear;
³⁴*the stars shone in their watches, and were glad;*
  he called them, and they said, "Here we are!"
  They shone with gladness for him who made them.
³⁵*This is our God;*
  no other can be compared to him!
³⁶*He found the whole way to knowledge,*
  and gave her to Jacob his servant
  and to Israel whom he loved.
³⁷*Afterward she appeared upon earth*
  and lived among men.

4 *She is the book of the commandments of God,*
  and the law that endures for ever.
All who hold her fast will live,
  and those who forsake her will die.
²*Turn, O Jacob, and take her;*

walk toward the shining of her light.
³*Do not give your glory to another,*
   or your advantages to an alien people.
⁴*Happy are we, O Israel,*
   for we know what is pleasing to God.

---

f Other authorities read *their*

OVERVIEW: The preceding chapters were a letter to the deportees in the form of a confession. Having confessed their sin, the prophecy begins; they are then instructed in the commandments that are a source of life for those who observe them and of death for those who do not (ORIGEN, OLYMPIODORUS). Hearing these words and trying to put them into practice, one quickly recognizes how difficult it is to get rid of passions or pride (CASSIAN).

The persons of the Trinity are called water and light (ATHANASIUS). Water is a symbol of baptism (JEROME). Threats, exhortations and pardon are for the blessed (CLEMENT OF ALEXANDRIA). Christ is the way, the light and peace (OLYMPIODORUS). The future world is a garden where virtues bloom in our life with God (METHODIUS).

Human beings are similar to beasts (OLYMPIODORUS). Do not follow the false wisdoms of the fortune tellers and false observance of the Law (OLYMPIODORUS). Do not follow vain things, like the Jews do (OLYMPIODORUS). The world has been given to all, rich and poor (AMBROSE). The church grows towards perfection (OLYMPIODORUS). Christ incarnated did not abandon the heavens (FULGENTIUS). The devils are also called giants (OLYMPIODORUS).

People and angels are called to praise the magnificence of God's work (CHRYSOSTOM). Baruch tells us that God appears among human beings and is seen, but no one can see the Father except the Son, so the one who must have been seen was the Son whom Baruch referred to as God (HILARY OF POITIERS). Thus we have a prophecy of Christ's incarnation accompanied by another prophecy of the appearance of his apostles among us (IRENAEUS, OLYMPIODORUS, QUODVULTDEUS). Knowledge and prudence are sources of virtue (CLEMENT OF ALEXANDRIA). These words are addressed to the historical Israel and to the spiritual Israel (OLYMPIODORUS).

3:9 *Hear the Commandments of Life*

THE SOURCE OF LIFE AND DEATH. ORIGEN: It seems good to me to attempt to explain why the prescriptions, judgments[1] and commandments of the law have been given. The text says, "In order to put them to the test [to see] if they would listen to the voice of the Lord and keep his commandments."[2] In fact, what was there about the commandments that was so good and perfect if the former people of God were found still murmuring and rebelling? Shortly thereafter, in fact, they even returned to the idols and forgot all about the benefits and wonders that God had done, erecting the statue of a year-old calf.[3] This therefore is why the precepts were given, in order to put them to the test. This is also why, through the mouth of Ezekiel the prophet, the Lord says to them, "I gave you ordinances and prescriptions that were not good, in which you cannot live."[4] Notice how when they were put to the test in the precepts of the Lord they were not found faithful. Therefore "the commandment that was ordained for life was found to be death for them."[5] The same commandment, if it is observed, generates life, but if it is not observed, it generates death. In so far, therefore, as the commandments generate death for those who do not

---

[1]See Ex 15:25. [2]Ex 15:26. [3]See Ex 32:4. [4]Ezek 20:25. [5]Rom 7:10.

observe them, they are called "commandments that are not good, in which they cannot live."[6] But since the wood of the cross of Christ has been mixed in with them and has changed them into sweetness[7] and they are observed, being understood in the spirit, those same commandments have come to be called commandments of life, as it also says elsewhere, "Hear, O Israel, the commandments of life."

But let us see what it promises if they are observed. It says, "If you will observe my ordinances, I will not bring on you all the diseases that I brought on the Egyptians."[8] What does he mean to say? That if one observes the commandments he will not suffer disease, that is, he will not have a fever or suffer other pains of the body? I do not believe that these are the kinds of promises given to those who observe the divine commandments. In another place there is the example of Job, the most just and observant of every religious act of mercy who is struck by malignant ulcers from head to foot.[9] Therefore one cannot say that those who keep the commandments are free from diseases but that they will not have the diseases that the Egyptians have; in fact, the world is figuratively called Egypt. HOMILIES ON EXODUS 7.2.[10]

THE BEGINNING OF PROPHECY. OLYMPIODORUS OF ALEXANDRIA: This is the beginning of Baruch's prophecy. All of the preceding words are part of the letter of the deportees to Babylon and are in the form of a confession. FRAGMENTS ON BARUCH 3.9.[11]

3:10 In the Land of Your Enemies

IT IS DIFFICULT TO ESCAPE THE YOKE OF PRIDE. JOHN CASSIAN: When the children of Israel had been taken captive by Necho, king of Egypt, Nebuchadnezzar, king of Assyria, came up and brought them back from the borders of Egypt to the land of Palestine, not meaning to restore them to their former liberty and their native land but meaning to carry them off to his own land and to transport them to a still more distant country than the land of Egypt in which they had been prisoners.[12] And this illustration exactly applies to the case before us. For though there is less harm in yielding to the sin of pride than to fornication, still it is more difficult to escape from the yoke of pride. In the same way, in fact, the slave who is carried off to a greater distance will have more difficulty in returning to his native land and the freedom of his ancestors. The prophet's rebuke will be deservedly aimed at him, "Because you are grown old in a strange country," since one is rightly said to have grown old in a strange country if he has not gotten rid of the yoke of his passions. CONFERENCES 1.5.12.[13]

3:12 Forsaking Wisdom

WATER AND LIGHT REFRACT TRIUNE TEACHING. ATHANASIUS: The Father is called source and light: "They have abandoned me, the source of living water."[14] And in Baruch, "How is it, Israel, that you are in the land of your enemies? You have abandoned the source of wisdom." And according to John, "Our God is light."[15] The Son, in relation to the source, is called a river: "The river of God is full of waters."[16] In relation to light, he is called splendor, as Paul says, "He is the splendor of the glory and the imprint of his being."[17] The Father is thus light and the Son his splendor (we need not fear repeating the same things often, especially in these matters). Now, it is possible to see in the Son also the Spirit, in whom we are enlightened, "that he would give you," it is said, "the Spirit of wisdom and of revelation, in the knowledge of him, by enlightening the eyes of the heart."[18] Enlightened then by the Spirit, it is Christ who enlightens in him. It is said, in fact, that "he was the true light that enlightens every person who comes into

---

[6]Ezek 20:25. [7]Cf. Ex 15:25. [8]Ex 15:26. [9]See Job 2:7. [10]CTP 27:131-31. [11]PG 93:764. [12]See 2 Kings 23–24 (4 Kings 23–24 LXX). [13]CTP 155:221. [14]Jer 2:13. [15]1 Jn 1:5. [16]Ps 65:10 (64:10 LXX). [17]Heb 1:3. [18]Eph 1:17.

the world."[19] Analogously, then, if the Father is the source and the Son is called river, we drink of the Spirit, as it is written, "We have all been given to drink of the one Spirit."[20] But, at the same time, drinking of the Spirit we drink of Christ: "They drank from the spiritual rock that followed them, and the rock was Christ."[21] LETTER TO SERAPION 1.19.2-5.[22]

THE FATHER A DRY SPRING WITHOUT THE SON. ATHANASIUS: If God is and is called the fountain of wisdom and life[23] . . . as in the book of Baruch it is written, "You have forsaken the fountain of wisdom," this implies that life and wisdom are not foreign to the essence of the fountain but are proper to it. Nor were they at any time without existence but always existed. Now the Son is all this, who says, "I am the life,"[24] and, "I Wisdom dwell with prudence."[25] Is it then irreligious to say, "Once the Son was not,"[26] for it is the same thing as saying, "Once the fountain was dry, destitute of life and wisdom." But then it would cease to be a fountain. DISCOURSES AGAINST THE ARIANS 1.6.19.[27]

WATER IS A SYMBOL OF BAPTISM. JEROME: "As the deer longs for springs of water, so my soul longs for you, O God."[28] It is characteristic of deer that they do not fear the poison of serpents, so much so that, blowing into their lairs through their noses, they force them out so as to kill and eat them.[29] And when the poison they have thus swallowed begins to burn their insides, though it is not fatal, it nevertheless ignites a fire in them that creates a tremendous thirst. They then go in search of springs, and in the pure waters they extinguish the fire of the poison. In the same way, then, that deer desire springs of water, so also our deer—those who, fleeing the Egypt of this world, have killed Pharaoh and have drawn out all of his army[30] with the waters of baptism— after having killed the devil desire nothing but the springs of the church: the Father, the Son and the Holy Spirit. That the Father is a spring is written Jeremiah, "They have abandoned me,

the spring of living water, to dig for themselves leaky cisterns, unable to hold water."[31] About the Son, it is written somewhere, "They have abandoned the source of wisdom."[32] Finally, of the Holy Spirit it is written, "From the one who drinks the water that I will give him, a fountain will spring up, welling up to eternal life,"[33] and the Evangelist immediately provides an explanation, saying that the Savior's words here referred to the Holy Spirit.[34] This is the clearest proof that the three springs of the church are the mystery of the Trinity. And it is these springs that the soul of the believer longs for.[35] The soul of the believer is interiorly drawn to them, so much so as to say, "My soul thirsts for God, the living spring."[36] Indeed, it is not merely foolish ambition to want to see God but an intense desire, a thirst that burns all. Before receiving baptism these souls spoke to themselves asking, "When can I come into the presence of God?"[37] Now their desire is fulfilled: they have arrived, they are in God's presence, they have been presented before the altar, face to face with the sacrament of the Savior. HOMILIES ON THE PSALMS 41.[38]

3:13 If You Had Obeyed

THREATS, EXHORTATIONS AND PARDON ARE BLESSINGS. CLEMENT OF ALEXANDRIA: And still another form of instruction is benediction. "And blessed is he," he says by David, "who has

---

[19]Jn 1:9. [20]1 Cor 12:13. [21]1 Cor 10:4. [22]CTP 55:73-74. [23]Athanasius quotes Jer 2:13; 17:12-13. [24]Jn 14:6. [25]Prov 8:12. [26]As Arius said. [27]NPNF 2 4:317*. See also Athanasius *Defense of the Nicene Definition* 3.12. [28]Ps 42:2 (41:2 LXX). [29]Jerome refers to a very ancient tradition that states that deer are hunters of vipers but are immune to their poison. [30]See Ex 15:1-17. [31]Jer 2:13. [32]Jerome does not mention his source, since for him the canonicity of Baruch is questionable. [33]Jn 4:13-14. [34]See Jn 7:37-39. [35]See Ps 42:2 (41:2 LXX). We note here that English usage must distinguish between "source" (Bar 3:12), "fountain" (Jn 4:14) and "spring" (Ps 42:2), but the Greek word *pēgē* and its Latin counterpart *fons* are more comprehensive, and both embrace all these meanings. In every instance, Jerome's discourse is about running water that the patristic tradition calls "living water" as opposed to "stagnant water," which is unfit for baptism. [36]Ps 42:3 (41:3 LXX). [37]Ps 42:3 (41:3 LXX). [38]CTP 88:189-90.

not sinned; and he shall be as the tree planted near the channels of the waters, which will yield its fruit in its season, and its leaf shall not wither"—which is an allusion to the resurrection—"and whatever he will do will prosper with him."[39] This is what he wants us to be so that we may be blessed. Again, showing the opposite scale of the balance of justice, he says, "But not so the ungodly—not so; but as the dust that the wind sweeps away from the face of the earth."[40] By showing the punishment of sinners and how easily they are dissipated and carried off by the wind, the Teacher[41] dissuades us from crime by means of punishment. And, by holding up the penalty we deserve, he shows the goodness of his beneficence in the most skillful way in order that we may possess and enjoy its blessings. He invites us to knowledge also when he says by the mouth of Jeremiah, "If you had walked in the way of God, you would have lived forever in peace." Thus, when he exhibits the reward of knowledge here, he invites those who are wise to its love. And, granting pardon to him who has erred, he says, "Turn, turn, as a grape gatherer to his basket."[42] Do you see the goodness of justice, in that it counsels to repentance? CHRIST THE EDUCATOR 1.10.92.1-3.[43]

FOLLOWING THE PATH OF CHRIST. OLYMPIODORUS OF ALEXANDRIA: The Lord says, "I am the way."[44] The one who walks in imitation of him[45] follows his way. FRAGMENTS ON BARUCH 3.13.[46]

3:14-15 Light and Peace

CHRIST IS LIGHT AND PEACE. OLYMPIODORUS OF ALEXANDRIA: Obviously, in the Lord, "the one who believes in me, will never die."[47] In fact, the Lord says, "I am the light of the world."[48] And the apostle, "He indeed is our peace."[49] FRAGMENTS ON BARUCH 3.14.[50]

A GARDEN WHERE VIRTUES BLOOM. METHODIUS: As soon as souls have left this world, it is said that the angels meet them with much rejoicing and conduct them to those very pastures to which they were longing to come, imagining them from far away when, still dwelling in their bodies, they dreamed of the divine world. When, therefore, they have come there, they see wonderful and glorious and blessed things of beauty, and such as cannot be spoken to humanity. They see there righteousness, prudence, love, truth, temperance and other flowers and plants of wisdom, equally splendid. We see here only the shadows and apparitions of them, as in dreams, and think that they consist of human actions because there is no clear image of them here but only dim copies that themselves we often see when making dark copies of them. No one, in fact has been able to contemplate with his own eyes the greatness, the magnificence and the beauty of the justice, the intelligence or the peace. But there, in him whose name is I AM,[51] they are seen perfect and clear as they are. For there is a tree of temperance and of love and of understanding, just as there are plants of the fruits that grow here—as of grapes, pomegranates and apples. And so, too, the fruits of those trees are gathered and eaten and do not perish and wither. Instead, those who gather them grow toward immortality and a likeness to God. Just as he from whom all are descended, before the fall and the blinding of his eyes, being in paradise, enjoyed its fruits, God appointing man to dress and to keep the plants of wisdom.[52] For it was entrusted to the first Adam[53] to cultivate those fruits. Now Jeremiah saw that these things exist in a certain particular place, removed a great distance from our world, where, deploring the state of those who have fallen from that good state, he says, "Learn where wisdom is found, where strength is, where understanding is so that you may also know where length of days,

---

[39]Ps 1:1-3. [40]Ps 1:4. [41]Christ. [42]Jer 6:9. [43]CTP 181:117-18. [44]Jn 14:6. [45]See Mt 11:29. [46]PG 93:764. [47]Jn 11:26. [48]Jn 8:12. [49]Eph 2:14. [50]PG 93:765. [51]Cf. Ex 3:14; Rev 1:4, 8, etc. [52]See Gen 2:15. [53]See 1 Cor 15:45.

life, the light of the eyes and peace are. Who has found her place or who has come on her treasures? SYMPOSIUM OR BANQUET OF THE TEN VIRGINS 8.2-3.[54]

3:16-17 Beasts and Birds

LIKE BEASTS. OLYMPIODORUS OF ALEXANDRIA: The leaders of the nations are the wise of this age who ruled over human beings who behaved like beasts. FRAGMENTS ON BARUCH 3.16.[55]

FALSE WISDOM. OLYMPIODORUS OF ALEXANDRIA: They are those who look for omens in the birds. Or, they are called this because their wisdom is earthly, beastly, diabolical. FRAGMENTS ON BARUCH 3.17.[56]

3:22-23 Lacking Wisdom

FALSE OBSERVANCE OF THE LAW. OLYMPIODORUS OF ALEXANDRIA: Those who followed the letter of the law were judged like the pagans who had not received the law. In fact, "seeing, they see not, and hearing, they hear not."[57] FRAGMENTS ON BARUCH 3.22.[58]

DO NOT PURSUE VAIN THINGS. OLYMPIODORUS OF ALEXANDRIA: He calls them merchants because they have no experience with cultivation. Asked to make wine, they gathered wild grapes instead of domestic grapes.[59] Merran and Teman are barbarous peoples. They represent the uncouth manners of those who remain entangled in the vanity of this life. FRAGMENTS ON BARUCH 3.23.[60]

FOLLOWING RITUAL. OLYMPIODORUS OF ALEXANDRIA: They are those who esteemed ablutions of cups and bowls instead of the commandment and judgments of God.[61] And having violated justice, mercy and faith, they paid tithes of rue and mint.[62] FRAGMENTS ON BARUCH 3.23.[63]

3:24-25 The House and Territory of God

THE WORLD WAS GIVEN TO ALL. AMBROSE: The elements have been given to all for their common use. The splendid ornaments of the world are enjoyed by the rich and poor alike. Are perhaps the gilded ceilings of the palaces of the wealthy more beautiful than the glistening stars that gild the sky? Are perhaps the estates of the rich more expansive than the surface of the earth? For this is what was said to those who were adding house to house, villa to villa: "Will you alone dwell over the earth?"[64] You, though poor, have a larger house in which when you raise your voice it is heard and listened to. "O Israel," says the prophet, "how great is the house of God and how vast the place of his possession! It is large and has no end, immense and high." The house of God belongs to the rich and poor alike; it is difficult, however, for the rich to enter into the kingdom of heaven.[65] HEXAMERON 9.8.52.[66]

THE CHURCH GROWS TOWARD PERFECTION. OLYMPIODORUS OF ALEXANDRIA: This treats of the church and of the nature of the mystery, since now "our knowledge is imperfect,"[67] and the perfection of knowledge has not yet arrived.[68] He refers to compassion as territory, which increases as one grows toward the good. FRAGMENTS ON BARUCH 3.24.[69]

WHEN CHRIST BECAME INCARNATE. FULGENTIUS OF RUSPE: Not the Trinity but Christ, who is God above all things, who ascended to heaven in the flesh under the gaze of the disciples and who will come from heaven in the flesh.[70] He who did not leave heaven when he took on flesh on earth and did not leave his own on earth when he ascended into heaven in the flesh, because of his divinity. Indeed, he promised this, saying, "See, I am with you all days, until the end of the world."[71] He is that God, there-

---

[54]CTP 152:114-16. [55]PG 93:765. [56]PG 93:765. [57]Mt 13:13. [58]PG 93:765. [59]See Is 5:2. [60]PG 93:768. [61]See Mt 23:25; Lk 11:39. [62]See Lk 11:42; Mt 23:23. [63]PG 93:768. [64]Is 5:8. [65]See Mt 19:23. [66]CTP 164:286. [67]1 Cor 13:9. [68]See Cor 13:10. [69]PG 93:768. [70]Cf. Acts 1:9, 11; Lk 24:51. [71]Mt 28:20.

fore, who according to the prophecy of blessed Jeremiah "is great and without limits, sublime and immense" in the divine nature and of whom a little later the same prophet says, "He is our God, and no other can be compared with him. He has searched every way of knowledge and has given it to Jacob his servant, and to Israel his beloved." It is this God who made himself for a little while lower than the angels,[72] taking on the nature of a servant,[73] as the same prophet says, "After these things he appeared on the earth and lived among human beings." The faithless thought he was a mortal and changeable human being, but he is precisely the same one that those who truly believe in him will see—now that their hearts have been cleansed from sin—as the immortal and unchangeable God according to his own nature. LETTERS 17.10.18.[74]

3:26 The Giants, Famous of Old

A NAME FOR DEVILS. OLYMPIODORUS OF ALEXANDRIA: This refers to demons, who in the beginning were part of the ranks of angels and were cast down from the highest heaven for their lack of respect. They are famous because their condition was foretold. They were tall in stature, though proud. "Experts in war," since demons, or rather heretics, being unworthy of the peace of Christ,[75] are committed to fighting him. FRAGMENTS ON BARUCH 3.26.[76]

3:35 None Can Compare with Our God

SINGING THE MAGNIFICENCE OF GOD'S WORKS. JOHN CHRYSOSTOM: It is ordained that not only we human beings but also the angels, the archangels, the celestial nations and all we who are on earth give praise. "Bless the Lord," it says, "all you works of his."[77] His good works are no small achievement; rather, they exceed all speech, intellect and human understanding. The prophets announce these things every day, each in various ways publishing this splendid triumph. One says, "You have gone up on high, you have led captivity captive, and you have received gifts among people."[78] And, "The Lord strong and powerful in battle."[79] And another says, "He will divide the spoils of the strong."[80] For this is why he came, in order to announce freedom to the prisoners and the recovery of sight to the blind.[81] And raising aloud the cry of victory against over death, he said, "Where, O death, is your victory? Where, O grave, is your sting?"[82] And another, in its turn, announcing good news of the most profound peace, said, "They will forge their swords into plowshares and their spears into pruning hooks."[83] And while one invokes Jerusalem, saying, "Rejoice greatly, daughter of Zion, because your king comes to you, meek, riding on a beast of burden, a young colt,"[84] another proclaims his second coming, thus saying, "The Lord, whom you seek, will come, and who will abide the day of his coming? Leap as calves set free from their bonds."[85] And another again, amazed at such similar events, said, "This is our God; no other will be compared with him." HOMILIES ON THE GOSPEL OF MATTHEW 19.9.[86]

A PROPHECY ABOUT THE APOSTLES. OLYMPIODORUS OF ALEXANDRIA: They speak who obeyed the apostolic calling without delay and "have the desire to be set free from the body so as to be with Christ,"[87] preferring nothing to the fulfillment of the commandments. FRAGMENTS ON BARUCH 3.36.[88]

GOD SEEN ON EARTH. HILARY OF POITIERS: Listen now to Jeremiah: "This is our God, and there shall be no one else like him who has found out all the way of knowledge and has given it to Jacob his servant and to Israel his beloved. Afterward he showed himself on earth and dwelled among people." For previously he had said, "And he is human, and who shall know him?"[89] Thus

---

[72]See Heb 2:9. [73]See Phil 2:7. [74]CTP 149:414. [75]See Col 3:15. [76]PG 93:768. [77]Ps 103:22 (102:22 LXX). [78]Ps 68:19 (67:19 LXX). [79]Ps 24:8 (23:8 LXX). [80]Is 53:12. [81]See Lk 4:18. [82]1 Cor 15:55. [83]Is 2:4. [84]Zech 9:9. [85]Mal 3:1-2, 20. [86]CTP 170:378. [87]Phil 1:23. [88]PG 93:769.

you have God seen on earth and dwelling among people. Now I ask you what sense you would assign to "no one has seen God at any time, except the only-begotten Son who is in the bosom of the Father,"[90] when Jeremiah proclaims God seen on earth and dwelling among people? The Father most assuredly cannot be seen except by the Son. Who then is this who was seen and lived among us? He must be our God, for he is God visible in human form, whom human beings can handle. On the Trinity 4.42.[91]

3:37 Knowledge Lived Among Mortals

THE PROPHETIC ANNOUNCEMENT OF CHRIST'S ADVENT. IRENAEUS: The prophets, receiving the prophetic gift from the same Word, announced his advent according to the flesh, by which the blending and communion of God and man took place, according to the good pleasure of the Father, the Word of God foretelling from the beginning that God should be seen by human beings and interacting with them on the earth; that he would confer with them and be present with his own creation, saving it and becoming capable of being perceived by it, and freeing us from the hands of all who hate us, that is, from every spirit of wickedness; and causing us to serve him in holiness and righteousness all of our days,[92] in order that humanity, having embraced the Spirit of God, might pass into the glory of the Father. . . .

Inasmuch, then, as the Spirit of God pointed out by the prophet what would happen in the future, forming and adapting us beforehand for the purpose of our being made subject to God—but it was a future thing that humanity, through the good pleasure of the Holy Spirit should see God—it was necessarily the case those who were used as instruments for announcing the future events should themselves see God, whom they intimated was to be seen by human beings. This was so that God and the Son of God, and the Son and the Father, should not only be prophetically announced but also that he should also be

seen by all of his members who are sanctified and instructed in the things of God. AGAINST HERESIES 4.20.4, 8.[93]

PROPHECIES ABOUT CHRIST'S INCARNATION. QUODVULTDEUS: The prophet David says, "He sent his word and healed them."[94] And Jeremiah, "He is our God, and there is no other but him, who has searched all the ways of wisdom and given it to Jacob, his beloved. After that he appeared on earth and dwelled among human beings." And the prophet Habakkuk says, "The word will depart and go out into the fields."[95] And the prophet Isaiah, "Their heart is completely weighed down. He is a man, and who will know him?"[96] John the Evangelist confirms this, saying, "The Word became flesh and dwelled among us."[97] Paul also attests this: "He, being by nature equal to God, did not consider it a good to be equal to God but made himself nothing, taking the nature of a servant, becoming like human beings and being as a man."[98] And the Sibyl confesses, "Certainly to judge the flesh and the world with his presence."[99] THE BOOK OF PROMISES AND PREDICTIONS OF GOD 3.3.[100]

4:4 What Is Pleasing to God

KNOWLEDGE AND PRUDENCE. CLEMENT OF ALEXANDRIA: He clearly calls us to goodness by Solomon when he says, "Blessed is the one who has found wisdom and the mortal who has found understanding."[101] "For goodness is found by him who seeks it and is likely to be seen by him who has found it."[102] By Jeremiah, too, he sets forth prudence when he says, "Blessed are we, Israel; for what is pleasing to God is known by us"—and it is known by the Word, by whom we

---

[89]Jer 17:9 LXX. [90]Jn 1:18. [91]NPNF 2 9:84*. [92]Lk 1:74-75.
[93]ANF 1 488-90*. [94]Ps 107:20 (106:20 LXX). [95]Hab 3:5. [96]Jer 17:9. Quodvultdeus confuses Isaiah with Jeremiah. [97]Jn 1:14.
[98]Phil 2:6-7. [99]Sibylline Oracles 8:219. Until the Renaissance, the Sibylline Oracles were often used as pagan prophecies concerning Christ. However, this text and the whole of book 8 is a Christian addition. See also the Introduction. [100]CTP 82:226. [101]Prov 3:13.
[102]See Mt 7:7; Lk 9:9.

are blessed and wise. For wisdom and knowledge are mentioned by the same prophet when he says, "Hear, O Israel, the commandments of life, and listen to know understanding."[103] CHRIST THE EDUCATOR 1.10.91.3.[104]

HISTORICAL ISRAEL AND SPIRITUAL ISRAEL. OLYMPIODORUS OF ALEXANDRIA: He urges the Israelites to be the first to take hold of grace.

In fact, "it was necessary that the Word of God first be announced to them."[105] The spiritual Israel speaks in this way, to whom the Savior addresses himself, saying, "Blessed are your eyes because they see, and your ears, because they hear."[106] FRAGMENTS ON BARUCH 4.4.[107]

---

[103]Bar 4:9. [104]CTP 181:116-17. [105]Acts 13:46. [106]Mt 13:16. [107]PG 93:769.

4:5–5:9 JERUSALEM'S LAMENTATIONS AND HOPES

[5]*Take courage, my people,*
*   O memorial of Israel!*
[6]*It was not for destruction*
*   that you were sold to the nations,*
but you were handed over to your enemies
*   because you angered God.*
[7]*For you provoked him who made you,*
*   by sacrificing to demons and not to God.*
[8]*You forgot the everlasting God, who brought you up,*
*   and you grieved Jerusalem, who reared you.*
[9]*For she saw the wrath that came upon you from God,*
*   and she said:*
"Hearken, you neighbors of Zion,
*   God has brought great sorrow upon me;*
[10]*for I have seen the captivity of my sons and daughters,*
*   which the Everlasting brought upon them.*
[11]*With joy I nurtured them,*
*   but I sent them away with weeping and sorrow.*
[12]*Let no one rejoice over me, a widow*
*   and bereaved of many;*
I was left desolate because of the sins of my children,
*   because they turned away from the law of God.*
[13]*They had no regard for his statutes;*
*   they did not walk in the ways of God's commandments,*
*   nor tread the paths of discipline in his righteousness.*
[14]*Let the neighbors of Zion come;*

remember the capture of my sons and daughters,
   which the Everlasting brought upon them.
¹⁵For he brought against them a nation from afar,
   a shameless nation, of a strange language,
who had no respect for an old man,
   and had no pity for a child.
¹⁶They led away the widow's beloved sons,
   and bereaved the lonely woman of her daughters.
¹⁷"But I, how can I help you?
¹⁸For he who brought these calamities upon you
   will deliver you from the hand of your enemies.
¹⁹Go, my children, go;
   for I have been left desolate.
²⁰I have taken off the robe of peace
   and put on the sackcloth of my supplication;
   I will cry to the Everlasting all my days.

²¹"Take courage, my children, cry to God,
   and he will deliver you from the power and hand of the enemy.
²²For I have put my hope in the Everlasting to save you,
   and joy has come to me from the Holy One,
because of the mercy which soon will come to you
   from your everlasting Savior.ᵍ
²³For I sent you out with sorrow and weeping,
   but God will give you back to me with joy and gladness for ever.
²⁴For as the neighbors of Zion have now seen your capture,
   so they soon will see your salvation by God,
which will come to you with great glory
   and with the splendor of the Everlasting.
²⁵My children, endure with patience the wrath that has come upon you from God.
Your enemy has overtaken you,
   but you will soon see their destruction
   and will tread upon their necks.
²⁶My tender sons have traveled rough roads;
   they were taken away like a flock carried off by the enemy.

²⁷"Take courage, my children, and cry to God,
   for you will be remembered by him who brought this upon you.
²⁸For just as you purposed to go astray from God,
   return with tenfold zeal to seek him.
²⁹For he who brought these calamities upon you
   will bring you everlasting joy with your salvation."

³⁰Take courage, O Jerusalem,
   for he who named you will comfort you.

³¹Wretched will be those who afflicted you
   and rejoiced at your fall.
³²Wretched will be the cities which your children served as slaves;
   wretched will be the city which received your sons.
³³For just as she rejoiced at your fall
   and was glad for your ruin,
   so she will be grieved at her own desolation.
³⁴And I will take away her pride in her great population,
   and her insolence will be turned to grief.
³⁵For fire will come upon her from the Everlasting for many days,
   and for a long time she will be inhabited by demons.

³⁶Look toward the east, O Jerusalem,
   and see the joy that is coming to you from God!
³⁷Behold, your sons are coming, whom you sent away;
   they are coming, gathered from east and west,
at the word of the Holy One,
   rejoicing in the glory of God.

5 Take off the garment of your sorrow and affliction, O Jerusalem,
   and put on for ever the beauty of the glory from God.
²Put on the robe of the righteousness from God;
   put on your head the diadem of the glory of the Everlasting.
³For God will show your splendor everywhere under heaven.
⁴For your name will for ever be called by God,
   "Peace of righteousness and glory of godliness."

⁵Arise, O Jerusalem, stand upon the height
   and look toward the east,
and see your children gathered from west and east,
   at the word of the Holy One,
   rejoicing that God has remembered them.
⁶For they went forth from you on foot,
   led away by their enemies;
but God will bring them back to you,
   carried in glory, as on a royal throne.
⁷For God has ordered that every high mountain and the everlasting hills be made low
   and the valleys filled up, to make level ground,
   so that Israel may walk safely in the glory of God.
⁸The woods and every fragrant tree
   have shaded Israel at God's command.
⁹For God will lead Israel with joy,
   in the light of his glory,
   with the mercy and righteousness that come from him.

g Or from the Everlasting, your Savior

OVERVIEW: Christ rescued us (OLYMPIODORUS). The Lord accuses his people of having deserted him (CHRYSOSTOM). A prophecy about Israel likens it to a widow (OLYMPIODORUS). The symbolism of distant and wicked foreigners may apply to the Babylonians and Romans or to false teachers (OLYMPIODORUS). Sinners, Jews and Jerusalem do not see God (OLYMPIODORUS). The Scriptures proclaim the eternity and the divinity of the Son (ATHANASIUS). The Lord protects his weakest creatures (AMBROSE). Christ consoles us (OLYMPIODORUS). The new Jerusalem of which Baruch speaks (IRENAEUS) also causes us to look forward to Christ's return (OLYMPIODORUS). The new garment of baptism means we have put off our old desires and are clothed with Christ (OLYMPIODORUS). The diadem of glory is an allusion to the church or to baptism (OLYMPIODORUS). Christ's peace is a distinguishing sign of the new Jerusalem (OLYMPIODORUS).

4:6 You Were Sold

CHRIST RESCUED US. OLYMPIODORUS OF ALEXANDRIA: The devil in fact had a written note for our debt,[1] but Christ redeemed us with his own blood.[2] FRAGMENTS ON BARUCH 4.6.[3]

4:7 You Provoked God

ABANDONING GOD. JOHN CHRYSOSTOM: "And my people has not understood me."[4] They have not understood me, he says, that I am more brilliant than the sun. "Woe to a sinful people."[5] This also is typical of the prophets, to grieve over one who is sick with an incurable illness. Jeremiah does this in many places, and Christ as well, saying, "Woe to you, Chorazin, woe to you, Bethsaida,"[6] because this also is a form of instruction. In fact, one who has not been brought back by reasoning can often be corrected by someone's grief. "People full of sins."[7] Another accusation: all are so, and gravely. "Perverse race."[8] He does not accuse their birth but indicates that their wickedness began from the earliest age. Just as

John, when he said, "serpents, children of vipers,"[9] did not depreciate their nature (otherwise he would not have said, "Produce fruit, then, worthy of repentance,"[10] if they had been such by nature and by birth), so also here, in saying "Perverse race,"[11] the prophet does not accuse their birth. "Lawless children."[12] He did not say, "outside of the law," but "without law," with a disposition in no way better than those who had received no law at all, thus showing that the difference is in their previous choice. "You have abandoned the Lord, angering him."[13] He said this expressively: the name of God would have been enough to establish the accusation. It is what Jeremiah reproves, saying, "Since they have departed from him and are drawn near to demons." "The Holy One of Israel."[14] This is the culmination of the accusation, by the fact that though he was the common Lord of all, it was to them that he had made himself known. COMMENTARY ON ISAIAH 1.3.[15]

4:12 Widowed and Bereaved

A PROPHECY ABOUT ISRAEL. OLYMPIODORUS OF ALEXANDRIA: He calls her a widow because she was without the divine care, alone and desolate[16]—clearly she who is now alone. Or, furthermore, the only one to have had the divine temple. Or the only one to have been encircled by the Assyrians but not conquered, because in fact "the Lord tried me harshly but did not give me over to death."[17] But above all it is the synagogue that deserves the name widow, which, having acted arrogantly toward Christ her spouse, has been abandoned. FRAGMENTS ON BARUCH 4.12.[18]

4:15 A Nation from Afar

DISTANT AND WICKED FOREIGNERS. OLYMPIODORUS OF ALEXANDRIA: God "removed our sins

---

[1]See Col 2:14. [2]See Gal 3:13; Acts 20:28. [3]PG 93:769. [4]Is 1:3. [5]Is 1:4. [6]Mt 11:21. [7]Is 1:4. [8]Is 1:4. [9]Mt 3:7; Lk 3:7; cf. Mt 22:33. [10]Lk 3:8; cf. Mt 3:8. [11]Is 1:4. [12]Is 1:4. [13]Is 1:4. [14]Is 1:4. [15]CTP 162:56-57. [16]See Mt 24:15; Mk 13:14; Lk 21:20. [17]Ps 118:18 (117:18 LXX). [18]PG 93:7769.

from us,"[19] but we are attracted to them, and for them we are punished. It says that he sends, because nothing happens without God's consent. The "perverse nation" was first the Babylonians, then the Romans. This can also be understood as those who teach false knowledge,[20] resorting to the deceptions of the sophists. FRAGMENTS ON BARUCH 4.15.[21]

4:19 Left Desolate

SINNERS, THE JEWS AND JERUSALEM. OLYMPIODORUS OF ALEXANDRIA: I remain alone because of God's absence. This could have been said by the saints, who made the condition of sinners their own; or by the synagogue of the Jews, when because of its arrogance toward Christ it was said to it, "See, your house will be left desolate"[22]; or by the city, because of the desolation of the inhabitants. FRAGMENTS ON BARUCH 4.19.[23]

4:20 The Robe of Peace, the Sackcloth of Supplication

THE ETERNITY AND DIVINITY OF THE SON. ATHANASIUS: Paul reasonably has said, "his eternal power and godhead,"[24] thereby signifying the Son. He said this while accusing the Greeks of contemplating the harmony and order of the creation without reflecting on the framing Word within it (for the creatures witness to their own Framer) so as through the creation to apprehend the true God and abandon their worship of it. And where the sacred writers say, "who exists before the ages,"[25] and, "by whom he made the ages,"[26] they thereby as clearly preach the eternal and everlasting being of the Son, even while they are designating God. Thus, if Isaiah says, "The everlasting God, the creator of the ends of the earth,"[27] and Susanna said, "O everlasting God,"[28] and Baruch wrote, "I will cry unto the Everlasting in my days," and shortly after, "My hope is in the Everlasting, that he will save you, and joy is come to me from the Holy One,"[29] yet as the apostle, writing to the Hebrews, says, "who

being the radiance of his glory and the expression of his person,"[30] and David too in the psalm, "And the brightness of the Lord be on us,"[31] and, "In your light shall we see light,"[32] who has so little sense as to doubt of the eternity of the Son? DISCOURSES AGAINST THE ARIANS 1.4.12.2-5.[33]

4:26 Traveling Rough Roads

THE LORD PROTECTS HIS WEAKEST CREATURES. AMBROSE: How great is the providence of the Lord! Where there is a fruit of a softer quality, the thickness of the leaves offers a more protective covering for its defense, as we see in the example of the fig tree. Therefore the more delicate creatures must be protected from the other sturdier ones, as the same Lord teaches by the mouth of Jeremiah, saying, "Like these good figs, thus I will regard the deported ones of Judah that I have sent from this place into the land of the Chaldeans for their good and will fix my eyes on them for their good."[34] In fact, when they were exposed to offenses he encircled them, so to speak, with a more protective covering of his mercy so that those tender fruits would not perish prematurely. Moreover, he later on also says about them, "The creatures of my possession have walked rough ways," and he says more to them further on, "Be brave, my children, and cry to the Lord." This is the sole inviolable protection, the impregnable defense against all the storms and the injuries. Where there are delicate fruits, the protection and the defense of the leaves is thicker; on the contrary, where there are more resistant fruits, there the leaves are more delicate, as in the case of the apple. HEXAMERON 5.14.59.[35]

4:30 God Will Comfort You

CHRIST CONSOLES US. OLYMPIODORUS OF

---

[19]Ps 103:12 (102:12 LXX). [20]See 1 Tim 6:20. [21]PG 93:772. [22]Mt 23:28. [23]PG 93:772. [24]Rom 1:20. [25]Ps 55:20 (54:20 LXX). [26]Heb 1:2. [27]Is 40:28. [28]Sus 42 (Dan 13:42 LXX). [29]Bar 4:22, variant. [30]Heb 1:3. [31]Ps 90:17 (89:17 LXX, variant). [32]Ps 36:10 (35:10 LXX). [33]CTP 173:55-56. [34]Jer 24:5-6. [35]CTP 164:129.

ALEXANDRIA: That is, the Word of God, who became incarnate for us[36] and made the church worthy to be called his spouse.[37] FRAGMENTS ON BARUCH 4.30.[38]

4:36 Look Towards the East, O Jerusalem

THE FUTURE KINGDOM. IRENAEUS: Jeremiah the prophet has pointed out that as many believers as God has prepared for this purpose, to multiply those left on earth, should both be under the rule of the saints to minister to his Jerusalem and that his kingdom shall be in it, saying, "Look around Jerusalem towards the east, and behold the joy that comes to you from God. Behold, your children shall come whom you have sent forth; they shall come in a band from the east even to the west by the word of that Holy One, rejoicing in that splendor from your God."[39] Now all these things being such as they are, they cannot be understood in reference to supercelestial matters, "for God," it is said, "will show the whole earth that is under heaven your glory."[40] But in the times of the kingdom, the earth has been called again by Christ to its pristine condition, and Jerusalem will be rebuilt after the pattern of Jerusalem above,[41] of which the prophet Isaiah says, "Behold, I have depicted your walls on my hands, and you are always in my sight.[42] John, the Lord's disciple, says that the new Jerusalem above shall then descend, as a bride adorned for her husband,[43] and that this is the tabernacle of God, in which God will dwell with humanity.[44] Of this Jerusalem the former one is an image—the Jerusalem of the former earth in which the righteous are disciplined beforehand for incorruption and prepared for salvation. AGAINST HERESIES 5.35.1-2.[45]

EXPECTING CHRIST. OLYMPIODORUS OF ALEXANDRIA: Look toward the sun of justice,[46] toward our Lord Jesus Christ. FRAGMENTS ON BARUCH 4.36.[47]

5:1 The Garment of Sorrow and Affliction

THE NEW GARMENT OF BAPTISM. OLYMPIODORUS OF ALEXANDRIA: Put off the old humanity with its desires,[48] since "as many of you as have been baptized in Christ have clothed yourselves with Christ."[49] FRAGMENTS ON BARUCH 5.1.[50]

5:2 The Diadem of the Glory of the Everlasting

ALLUSION TO THE CHURCH OR BAPTISM. OLYMPIODORUS OF ALEXANDRIA: That is, the cross of Christ, which is marked on the foreheads of believers.[51] Or it is said of the Lord, since Christ is the head of the church.[52] FRAGMENTS ON BARUCH 5.2.[53]

5:4 Peace of Righteousness

JERUSALEM AND CHRIST'S PEACE. OLYMPIODORUS OF ALEXANDRIA: These are the distinguishing signs of the new Jerusalem. He added the term "justice."[54] Because, however, he is the peace of sinners,[55] as David says, for this reason the Lord adds, "My peace I leave you, my peace I give you."[56] In fact, the enemies' attacks can no longer destroy the peace of justice or defeat the glory of piety. And moreover, because Christ is our peace,[57] he is also our justice and our glory and is the model for our behavior according to justice, and by him we also have been called. FRAGMENTS ON BARUCH 5.4.[58]

---

[36]Cf. Jn 1:14. [37]See Eph 5:22-33. [38]PG 93:772. [39]Bar 4:36-37. [40]Bar 5:3. [41]Cf. Gal 4:26. [42]Is 49:16. [43]Rev 21:2. [44]Cf. Rev 21:3. [45]ANF 1:565-66*. [46]See Mal 4:2 (3:20 LXX). [47]PG 93:773. [48]See Col 3:9. [49]Gal 3:27. [50]PG 93:773. [51]Olympiodorus alludes to the baptismal rite of imposing the cross on the forehead. [52]See Eph 1:22; 5:23; Col 1:18. [53]PG 93:773. [54]This diverges from the traditional interpretation of Jerusalem as the "vision of peace." [55]See Ps 28:3 (27:3 LXX). In the psalm, the word *peace* is a euphemism that means "their wickedness." For the sake of his argumentation, Olympiodorus, however, interprets it literally, giving it a positive meaning. [56]Jn 14:27. [57]See Eph 2:14. [58]PG 93:773.

THE LETTER OF JEREMIAH

^{1b}*A copy of a letter which Jeremiah sent to those who were to be taken to Babylon as captives by the king of the Babylonians, to give them the message which God had commanded him.*

^{2}*Because of the sins which you have committed before God, you will be taken to Babylon as captives by Nebuchadnezzar, king of the Babylonians.* ^{3}*Therefore when you have come to Babylon you will remain there for many years, for a long time, up to seven generations; after that I will bring you away from there in peace.* ^{4}*Now in Babylon you will see gods made of silver and gold and wood, which are carried on men's shoulders and inspire fear in the heathen.* ^{5}*So take care not to become at all like the foreigners or to let fear for these gods^i possess you, when you see the multitude before and behind them worshiping them.* ^{6}*But say in your heart, "It is thou, O Lord, whom we must worship."* ^{7}*For my angel is with you, and he is watching your lives.*

^{8}*Their tongues are smoothed by the craftsman, and they themselves are overlaid with gold and silver; but they are false and cannot speak.* ^{9}*People^j take gold and make crowns for the heads of their gods, as they would for a girl who loves ornaments;* ^{10}*and sometimes the priests secretly take gold and silver from their gods and spend it upon themselves,* ^{11}*and even give some of it to the harlots in the brothel. They deck their gods^k out with garments like men—these gods of silver and gold and wood,* ^{12}*which cannot save themselves from rust and corrosion. When they have been dressed in purple robes,* ^{13}*their faces are wiped because of the dust from the temple, which is thick upon them.* ^{14}*Like a local ruler the god^l holds a scepter, though unable to destroy any one who offends it.* ^{15}*It has a dagger in its right hand, and has an axe; but it cannot save itself from war and robbers.* ^{16}*Therefore they evidently are not gods; so do not fear them.*

^{17}*For just as one's dish is useless when it is broken, so are the gods of the heathen,^{m} when they have been set up in the temples. Their eyes are full of the dust raised by the feet of those who enter.* ^{18}*And just as the gates are shut on every side upon a man who has offended a king, as though he were sentenced to death, so the priests make their temples secure with doors and locks and bars, in order that they may not be plundered by robbers.* ^{19}*They light lamps, even more than they light for themselves, though their gods^n can see none of them.* ^{20}*They are^o just like a beam of the temple, but men say their hearts have melted, when worms from the earth devour them and their robes. They do not notice* ^{21}*when their faces have been blackened by the smoke of the temple.* ^{22}*Bats, swallows, and birds light on their bodies and heads; and so do cats.* ^{23}*From this you will know that they are not gods; so do not fear them.*

^{24}*As for the gold which they wear for beauty—they will not shine unless some one wipes off the rust; for even when they were being cast, they had no feeling.* ^{25}*They are bought at any cost, but there is no breath in them.* ^{26}*Having no feet, they are carried on men's shoulders, revealing to mankind their worthlessness.* ^{27}*And those who serve them are ashamed because through them these* gods[n] are made to stand, lest they fall to the ground. If any one sets one of them upright, it cannot move of itself; and if it is tipped over, it cannot straighten itself; but gifts are placed before them just as before the dead. [28]The priests sell the sacrifices that are offered to these gods[p] and use the money; and likewise their wives preserve some with salt, but give none to the poor or helpless. [29]Sacrifices to them may be touched by women in menstruation or at childbirth. Since you know by these things that they are not gods, do not fear them.

[30]For why should they be called gods? Women serve meals for gods of silver and gold and wood; [31]and in their temples the priests sit with their clothes rent, their heads and beards shaved, and their heads uncovered. [32]They howl and shout before their gods as some do at a funeral feast for a man who has died. [33]The priests take some of the clothing of their gods[q] to clothe their wives and children. [34]Whether one does evil to them or good, they will not be able to repay it. They cannot set up a king or depose one. [35]Likewise they are not able to give either wealth or money; if one makes a vow to them and does not keep it, they will not require it. [36]They cannot save a man from death or rescue the weak from the strong. [37]They cannot restore sight to a blind man; they cannot rescue a man who is in distress. [38]They cannot take pity on a widow or do good to an orphan. [39]These things that are made of wood and overlaid with gold and silver are like stones from the mountain, and those who serve them will be put to shame. [40]Why then must any one think that they are gods, or call them gods?

Besides, even the Chaldeans themselves dishonor them; [41]for when they see a dumb man, who cannot speak, they bring him and pray Bel[r] that the man may speak, as though Bel[s] were able to understand. [42]Yet they themselves cannot perceive this and abandon them, for they have no sense. [43]And the women, with cords about them, sit along the passageways, burning bran for incense; and when one of them is led off by one of the passers-by and is lain with, she derides the woman next to her, because she was not as attractive as herself and her cord was not broken. [44]Whatever is done for them is false. Why then must any one think that they are gods, or call them gods?

[45]They are made by carpenters and goldsmiths; they can be nothing but what the craftsmen wish them to be. [46]The men that make them will certainly not live very long themselves; how then can the things that are made by them be gods? [47]They have left only lies and reproach for those who come after. [48]For when war or calamity comes upon them, the priests consult together as to where they can hide themselves and their gods.[t] [49]How then can one fail to see that these are not gods, for they cannot save themselves from war or calamity? [50]Since they are made of wood and overlaid with gold and silver, it will afterward be known that they are false. [51]It will be manifest to all the nations and kings that they are not gods but the work of men's hands, and that there is no work of God in them. [52]Who then can fail to know that they are not gods?[u]

[53]For they cannot set up a king over a country or give rain to men. [54]They cannot judge their own cause or deliver one who is wronged, for they have no power; they are like crows between heaven and earth. [55]When fire breaks out in a temple of wooden gods overlaid with gold or silver, their priests will flee and escape, but the gods[v] will be burnt in two like beams. [56]Besides, they can offer no resistance to a king or any enemies. Why then must any one admit or think that they are gods?

[57]Gods made of wood and overlaid with silver and gold are not able to save themselves from thieves and robbers. [58]Strong men will strip them of their gold and silver and of the robes they wear, and go off with this booty, and they will not be able to help themselves. [59]So it is better to be a king who shows his courage, or a household utensil that serves its owner's need, than to be these false gods; better even the door of a house that protects its contents, than these false gods; better also a wooden pillar in a palace, than these false gods.

⁶⁰*For sun and moon and stars, shining and sent forth for service, are obedient.* ⁶¹*So also the lightning, when it flashes, is widely seen; and the wind likewise blows in every land.* ⁶²*When God commands the clouds to go over the whole world, they carry out his command.* ⁶³*And the fire sent from above to consume mountains and woods does what it is ordered. But these idolsʷ are not to be compared with them in appearance or power.* ⁶⁴*Therefore one must not think that they are gods nor call them gods, for they are not able either to decide a case or to do good to men.* ⁶⁵*Since you know then that they are not gods, do not fear them.*

⁶⁶*For they can neither curse nor bless kings;* ⁶⁷*they cannot show signs in the heavens andˣ among the nations, or shine like the sun or give light like the moon.* ⁶⁸*The wild beasts are better than they are, for they can flee to cover and help themselves.* ⁶⁹*So we have no evidence whatever that they are gods; therefore do not fear them.*

⁷⁰*Like a scarecrow in a cucumber bed, that guards nothing, so are their gods of wood, overlaid with gold and silver.* ⁷¹*In the same way, their gods of wood, overlaid with gold and silver, are like a thorn bush in a garden, on which every bird sits; or like a dead body cast out in the darkness.* ⁷²*By the purple and linenʸ that rot upon them you will know that they are not gods; and they will finally themselves be consumed, and be a reproach in the land.* ⁷³*Better therefore is a just man who has no idols, for he will be far from reproach.*

h The King James Version prints *The Epistle of Jeremy* as Chapter 6 of the book of Baruch, and the chapter and verse numbers are here retained
i Gk *for them*   j Gk *They*   k Gk *them*   l Gk *he*   m Gk *of them*   n Gk *they*   o Gk *It is*   p Gk *to them*   q Gk *them*   r Or *they bring Bel and pray*   s Gk *he*   t Gk *them*   u The Greek text of this verse is uncertain   v Gk *they*   w Gk *these things*   x Other ancient authorities omit *and*   y Cn: Gk *marble*, Syr *silk*

OVERVIEW: The letter is to give the Hebrew captives in Babylon a response to protection against idolatry (OLYMPIODORUS). We should not fear idols and arrogant people (QUODVULT-DEUS). Idols, heretic and carnal persons are moved by the devil (OLYMPIODORUS). No light is comparable with that of the Law and the Prophets, but the soul of the idolatrous is in darkness (OLYMPIODORUS).

6:1 A Copy of the Letter[1]

HISTORICAL CONTEXT. OLYMPIODORUS OF ALEXANDRIA: Instructed by the Spirit that the Jews would be deported, the prophet is commanded by God to write the letter even before the deportation, so that when the time of their imprisonment had arrived, it would be a protection for them so that they would not let themselves be deceived or worship the idols of the Babylonians. FRAGMENTS ON THE LETTER OF JEREMIAH.[2]

6:3 Seven Generations

CHRONOLOGICAL QUESTION. OLYMPIODORUS OF ALEXANDRIA: He calculates ten years for each generation. FRAGMENTS ON THE LETTER OF JEREMIAH 2.[3]

6:4 Gods of Silver, Gold and Wood

WE SHOULD NOT FEAR IDOLS OR ARROGANT PEOPLE. QUODVULTDEUS: Joshua, son of Nun, and Caleb, son of Jephunneh, who explored the country together with the priests Moses and Aaron, fulfill their pious duty and dissuade the people from the purpose of a despairing will,[4] saying, "Do not fear the people of this region— we will swallow·them in one gulp. The favorable

[1]In the Septuagint, the Letter of Jeremiah is obviously an independent book, since it is transmitted alone, after Lamentations. That is why it has an independent title in Greek. Nevertheless, in the Vulgate and in several modern translations it is the last chapter of Baruch. [2]PG 93:773. [3]PG 93:776. [4]See Num 14:5-6.

time has passed for them. The Lord is with us. Do not fear."[5] All of these things regarding the destruction of idols pertain also to the Christian people, so that no one would be apostate from God, fearing the demons from whom they have been freed by God's grace. And it is precisely their vain procession that Jeremiah describes when he says, "Among other things, when you have entered Jerusalem, you will see there gods of gold and silver carried on their shoulders." These are made by hands and are nothing and can do neither good nor evil, by the fact that they are nothing. "Do not fear them. Sanctify the Lord in your hearts[6] and let him be the object of your fear."[7] Isaiah[8] describes the worshipers of demons as "those giants were there, who are called experts in war. But the Lord did not choose them, nor did he give them the way of knowledge. And they perished for lack of wisdom."[9] And Solomon says, "At the beginning, when the proud giants perished."[10] Against their pride, Christ's humble people rose victorious. The Book of Promises and Predictions of God 2.9.16.[11]

6:17 Eyes Full of Dust

The Devil's Dust. Olympiodorus of Alexandria: He speaks of idols but says the same of the leaders of the heretics and of those who are preoccupied with earthly things. Their eyes are full of the devil's dust, so they truly cannot see the diabolical impulses that enter them. Fragments on the Letter of Jeremiah 16.[12]

6:19 Lighting Lamps

Lights Without Comparison. Olympiodorus of Alexandria: Along with idols he considers those who have been drawn into error and are not enlightened by the law of God, of which it is written, "Your law is light for my feet,"[13] or by the word of the prophets, "lighted like a lamp that shines in a dark place."[14] Fragments on the Letter of Jeremiah 18.[15]

6:20 Faces Blackened

Darkness in the Souls of the Idolatrous. Olympiodorus of Alexandria: Idolaters are similar to idols. Indeed, it is written, "The one who makes them will be like them."[16] And for all those who are moved by demons, the face of the soul is deprived of light, darkened by the diabolical smoke that is in their hearts. Fragments on the Letter of Jeremiah 20.[17]

---

[5]Num 14:9. [6]1 Pet 3:14-15. [7]Is 8:13. [8]Likely Quodvultdeus confuses Isaiah with Jeremiah, who, in turn, is often portrayed as the real author of the words of Baruch, who was Jeremiah's secretary. [9]Bar 3:26-28. [10]Wis 14:16. [11]CTP 82:143-44. [12]PG 93:776. [13]Ps 119:104 (118:104 LXX). [14]2 Pet 1:19. [15]PG 93:776. [16]Ps 115:8 (113:16 LXX); 135:18 (134:18 LXX). [17]PG 93:776.

THE PRAYER OF AZARIAH AND
THE SONG OF THE THREE YOUNG MEN

1-27* THE PRAYER OF AZARIAH

^{1}And they walked about in the midst of the flames, singing hymns to God and blessing the Lord.
^{2}Then Azariah stood and offered this prayer; in the midst of the fire he opened his mouth and said:
^{3}"Blessed art thou, O Lord, God of our fathers, and worthy of praise;
   and thy name is glorified for ever.
^{4}For thou art just in all that thou hast done to us,
   and all thy works are true and thy ways right,
   and all thy judgments are truth.
^{5}Thou hast executed true judgments in all that thou hast brought upon us
   and upon Jerusalem, the holy city of our fathers,
   for in truth and justice thou hast brought all this upon us because of our sins.
^{6}For we have sinfully and lawlessly departed from thee,
   and have sinned in all things and have not obeyed thy commandments;
^{7}we have not observed them or done them,
   as thou hast commanded us that it might go well with us.
^{8}So all that thou hast brought upon us,
   and all that thou hast done to us,
   thou hast done in true judgment.
^{9}Thou hast given us into the hands of lawless enemies, most hateful rebels,
   and to an unjust king, the most wicked in all the world.
^{10}And now we cannot open our mouths;
   shame and disgrace have befallen thy servants and worshipers.
^{11}For thy name's sake do not give us up utterly,
   and do not break thy covenant,
   ^{12}and do not withdraw thy mercy from us,
for the sake of Abraham thy beloved
   and for the sake of Isaac thy servant
   and Israel thy holy one,
^{13}to whom thou didst promise
   to make their descendants as many as the stars of heaven
   and as the sand on the shore of the sea.
^{14}For we, O Lord, have become fewer than any nation,

and are brought low this day in all the world because of our sins.
¹⁵*And at this time there is no prince, or prophet, or leader,*
no burnt offering, or sacrifice, or oblation, or incense,
no place to make an offering before thee or to find mercy.
¹⁶*Yet with a contrite heart and a humble spirit may we be accepted,*
as though it were with burnt offerings of rams and bulls,
and with tens of thousands of fat lambs;
¹⁷*such may our sacrifice be in thy sight this day,*
and may we wholly follow thee,
for there will be no shame for those who trust in thee.
¹⁸*And now with all our heart we follow thee,*
we fear thee and seek thy face.
¹⁹*Do not put us to shame,*
but deal with us in thy forbearance
and in thy abundant mercy.
²⁰*Deliver us in accordance with thy marvelous works,*
and give glory to thy name, O Lord!
Let all who do harm to thy servants be put to shame;
²¹*let them be disgraced and deprived of all power and dominion,*
and let their strength be broken.
²²*Let them know that thou art the Lord, the only God,*
glorious over the whole world."

²³*Now the king's servants who threw them in did not cease feeding the furnace fires with naphtha, pitch, tow, and brush.* ²⁴*And the flame streamed out above the furnace forty-nine cubits,* ²⁵*and it broke through and burned those of the Chaldeans whom it caught about the furnace.* ²⁶*But the angel of the Lord came down into the furnace to be with Azariah and his companions, and drove the fiery flame out of the furnace,* ²⁷*and made the midst of the furnace like a moist whistling wind, so that the fire did not touch them at all or hurt or trouble them.*

*The Prayer of Azariah and the Song of the Three Young Men is inserted within the Greek book of Daniel, between Dan 3:23 and Dan 3:24 (RSV) and is numbered as Dan 3:24-90. It exists under two different Greek forms: the original translation of the Septuagint and its revision by Theodotion. Even if the latter predominates in the manuscript witnesses of the Greek Bible, the former was also occasionally used by ecclesiastical authors, mostly for critical purposes, as can be seen from the correspondence between Origen and Julius Africanus. Since the differences between the two recensions are comparatively small, the abbreviation LXX is used throughout except when it can be ascertained that Theodotion's revision (Th) has been quoted. The verse numbering of the RSV follows mostly Theodotion (occasionally the Septuagint has a different order or verse division).

OVERVIEW: The Song of the Three Young Men does not exist in the Hebrew text (ORIGEN). Even in tribulation the first thought of the just is to glorify God (THEODORET). Thus, the prayer these young men offer first glorifies God and recognizes that his decisions are just (ORIGEN, JEROME). God can be praised in any circumstances (THEODORET). Their confession of faith, as ours, covers over sin (CYRIL OF JERUSALEM, CHRYSOSTOM). The prayer that the three young men pray is not for themselves but for the people (JEROME). They followed the commandments of God, which ultimately proved to be for their good since the commandments were not given for God but for our own good (THEODORET). As saints, we acknowledge our unworthiness before God and ask for his intervention since we know and have seen the proof of his goodness as is evidenced in his treatment of these faithful young men (Chrysostom, Theodoret). Their faith grew because of this experience, which proved to be a blessing to them, just as the growth of God's people is always received as a blessing from God (Chrysostom).

Our sins sometimes get in the way of God's promises, just as the sins of the people in this story got in the way of God's blessings (Theodoret). Although the Jews were not able to worship and comply with the Law in the exile, their contrite and humble heart was better than any sacrifice of blood (Chrysostom, Theodoret, Pseudo-Chrysostom). When we face opposition, just as they did, we should remember that nothing is greater than God (Eucherius). God was the one who commanded the fire to spare the young men (Jerome, Severian). If we invoke God, he sends us the angel of his word (Jerome). The young men were spared from the flames surrounding them, but sometimes those flames can refine us, ultimately bringing glory to God and saving us from ourselves (Chrysostom).

The Hebrew Text Lacks the Song. Origen: In comparison with the Hebrew codices, our codices have many more verses according to the version circulating in the churches, "Thus therefore Ananiah, Azariah and Misael praised and blessed the Lord"[1] down to, "All you faithful worship the Lord, bless the God of gods, praise him and celebrate, because his grace endures forever. Then king Nebuchadnezzar heard them singing hymns, and he saw them that they were still alive."[2] Or, according to another version, it moves from, "And as they took a walk in the middle of the flames, they praised God and blessed the Lord"[3] down to, "All you faithful, worship the Lord, bless the God of gods, praise him and celebrate, because his grace endures forever."[4] But in the Hebrew codices, "these three men Sadràch, Mesàch and Abdènego fell down bound in the middle of the fire"[5] are immediately followed by the verse, "Then king Nebuchad-

nezzar was immediately astonished and rising up in a hurry, he addressed his ministers."[6] This in fact is how Aquila has written the text, following the Hebrew.[7] Letter to Julius Africanus 4.[8]

1 (3:24 LXX) *Singing Praise*

Praising God Among Tribulations. Theodoret of Cyr, "They walked about in the middle of the flames singing praises to God and praising the Lord." These words provide an indication of the essence of their faith. For, instead of asking to be freed from the evil that had befallen them, they celebrated it, singing the praises of the one who was in control of their situation and who had allowed them to make this most honorable confession. There is a similarity here that can be observed between the old and the new. When the blessed apostles Peter and John were condemned to a similar fate by the Pharisees, they left rejoicing since they had been considered worthy to be punished for the name of Jesus.[9] The blessed Paul with Silas, also being inflicted with the tortures of the magistrates of Philippi, remained in jail, bound in shackles. However, at midnight, the text says, "they prayed and sang to the Lord."[10] Thus also these blessed young people insisted on going back and forth inside the furnace offering praises to God. Commentary on Daniel 3.23.[11]

2 (3:25 LXX) *In the Middle of the Fire*

Examples of Prayer for Glorifying God. Origen: Regarding prayer,[12] we have examples in Daniel, "And Azariah, standing up, prayed in this way, and opening his mouth in the middle of the fire he said. . . ."[13] And in Tobit, "And I

---

[1]Pr Azar 1 (Dan 3:24 LXX). [2]Pr Azar 68 + Dan 3:24 (Dan 3:90-91 LXX). [3]Pr Azar 1 (Dan 3:24 Th). [4]Pr Azar 68 (Dan 3:90 Th). [5]Dan 3:23. [6]Dan 3:24 (Dan 3:91 LXX). [7]In other words, Aquila omits the Prayer of Azariah. [8]SC 302:524-26. [9]See Acts 5:41. [10]Acts 16:25. [11]CTP 188:106-7. [12]Origen distinguishes four kinds of prayer: supplication, glorification, intercession and thanksgiving. [13]Pr Azar 2 (Dan 3:25 LXX).

prayed with tears saying, 'You are just, O Lord, and all your works are just, and all your ways are mercy and truth. And your judgments that you offer are true and just forever.' "[14] Since the passage cited in Daniel has been obelized because it is not found in the Hebrew and those of the circumcision reject the book of Tobit as not canonical, I will quote the words of Anna from the first book of Kings: "And she prayed to the Lord and cried with many tears and made a vow saying, 'Lord of hosts, if you will look down on the lowliness of your servants,' etc. . . ."[15] Also, in Habakkuk, "A prayer of Habakkuk, the prophet, with song, 'Lord, I have heard your voice, and I was afraid. Lord, I considered your works, and I was astonished. In the middle of two animals you will be known; in the approaching of the years you will be known.'"[16] This example illustrates very well the definition of the term *proseuchē*[17] in that it combines prayer with the attempt to give glory. But also in the book of Jonah, "Jonah prayed to the Lord his God out of the belly of the fish, saying, 'I cried in my tribulation to the Lord my God, and he listened to me; from the heart of the grave you heard the screams of my voice; you threw me into the depths, in the heart of the sea, and the waters encircled me.' "[18] ON PRAYER 14.4.[19]

3 (3:26 LXX) Blessed Are You, O Lord

GOD'S DECISIONS ARE JUST. JEROME: Whenever we are oppressed by various difficulties, let us repeat this same prayer with our whole heart. And whatever may happen to us, let us confess that it is only right that we endure it. In this way the Scripture may be fulfilled in us: "The daughters of Judah, O Lord, have exulted and rejoiced in all your judgments.[20] COMMENTARY ON DANIEL 3:26-28A.[21]

GOD CAN BE PRAISED IN EVERY CIRCUMSTANCE. THEODORET OF CYR: Who would not admire the dignity of the tone of the wisdom of the introduction? It is not in prosperity and good fortune and not even in a favorable circumstance of life that it celebrates God the creator of the universe, but inside this furnace. The prolog calls him God of the ancestors, demonstrating his prudent judgment and announcing the virtue of the ancestors. It says, "We praise you, O Lord, that we have those ancestors whose God you intended to be called. You in fact have said to your servant Moses, 'I am the Lord of Abraham, the God of Isaac and the God of Jacob.' "[22] This your name is worthy of praise and glory, not on just one occasion and a specified time but for all ages. COMMENTARY ON DANIEL 3.26.[23]

4 (3:27 LXX) Just in All That You Have Done

LIKE WATER THAT EXTINGUISHES A FIRE. CYRIL OF JERUSALEM: Recall what happened to Ananiah and his companions. From which sources did they make water flow or how many vessels of water did they use to extinguish the fire that rose up forty-nine cubits high? Even when the flame rose a little too high, faith was poured out there to extinguish the fire like a river when all confessed their sin, saying, "You are right, O Lord, in all this that you have made; yes, we have sinned in committing evil." And their confession dissipated the flames. CATECHETICAL LECTURES 2.16.[24]

6 (3:29 LXX) We Have Sinfully Departed from You

REMEMBERING OUR SINS. JOHN CHRYSOSTOM: There is none, there is no remedy better able to destroy sins than to continually recall them and to continually accuse oneself. In this way the publican could cancel his innumerable sins by saying, "God, have mercy on me, a sinner."[25] And

---

[14]Tob 3:1-2. [15]1 Sam 1:10-11. [16]Hab 3:1. [17]*Proseuchē* is the general Greek word used for prayer. [18]Jon 2:2-4. [19]CTP 138:81-82. [20]Ps 97:8 (96:8 LXX). [21]Trad. Cola 59. [22]Ex 3:6. [23]CTP 188:107. [24]CTP 103:61. [25]Lk 18:13.

thus also the Pharisee remained unjustified because, taking no care to think of his own sins, he condemned everyone else, saying, "I am not like other people, greedy and avaricious, or even like this publican."[26] Thus also Paul exhorted, "Let each one examine his own conduct, and then he will find reason to boast only in himself and not in others."[27] Did you know that even in the Old Testament the righteous accused themselves? Listen to them speak as with one voice. David said, "My iniquities have gone over my head. They oppress me like a heavy burden."[28] And Isaiah cried out, "Woe is me, wretched man, because I am a man of unclean lips!"[29] The three young men, while they were in the furnace and offered their bodies to death for God, counted themselves among the greatest of sinners, saying, "We have sinned, we have done every kind of evil." And yet what was more brilliant, more pure than they? And even if they had committed some sins, the nature of the flames would have cancelled all of them. They did not look at their virtues, however, but thought of their sins. ON THE OBSCURITY OF PROPHECIES 2.9.[30]

THEY DO NOT SPEAK ABOUT THEMSELVES. JEROME: The three young people surely did not sin, nor were they old enough at the time they were deported to Babylon to justify being punished for their personal faults. Thus, it must mean that they were, therefore, speaking as representatives of the people in the same way as the apostle when he said, "What I do is not what I want, the actions that I do are those which I do not want to do,"[31] and so it goes throughout the rest of that passage in a similar context. COMMENTARY ON DANIEL 3:29.[32]

7 (3:30 LXX) We Have Not Observed the Commandments

GIVEN FOR OUR GOOD. THEODORET OF CYR: The observance of the laws and the prescriptions, he says, add nothing to the lawgiver, but to us they provide an abundance of resources. It is for this reason that God has established these laws, so that through their observance he might supply us with an occasion for salvation. COMMENTARY ON DANIEL 3.30.[33]

10 (3:33 LXX) We Cannot Open Our Mouths

THE SAINTS KNOW THEY ARE UNWORTHY BEFORE GOD. JOHN CHRYSOSTOM: "And I said, Woe is me, I am stunned, because though I am a man with unclean lips and live among a people of unclean lips, I have seen with my eyes the Lord of Sabaoth."[34] The vision astonished the prophet, it caused him suddenly to start, it threw him into great fear, it moved him to a confession, it disposed him to know the faintheartedness of his own being more clearly. All the saints are like this: the more they are honored, precisely then do they humble themselves the more. Thus also Abraham, when he spoke with God, called himself dirt and dust.[35] And Paul, when he was honored by receiving that vision, called himself an abnormal birth.[36] Therefore this prophet also declares his own meanness, first because of his nature, saying, "Woe is me, I am stunned, because I am a man," and then because of the state of his soul, "And I have unclean lips." I believe he called his lips impure in comparison with the fervent mouths of those pure powers[37] and with the service they rendered with the utmost exactness. He did not stop here but makes his confession for the whole people, adding the words, "I live among a people of impure lips." And why does he accuse his lips? To show his inability to speak freely. Given that the three young men said practically the same thing in the furnace—"We cannot open our mouths"—here also, which was a moment for hymns and praise (and indeed he saw the heavenly powers just doing this), it is right that he speaks of his lips, which above all else are called to that ministry. COMMENTARY ON ISAIAH 6.4.[38]

---

[26]Lk 18:11. [27]Gal 6:4. [28]Ps 38:5 (37:5 LXX). [29]Is 6:5. [30]VS 12:161-63. [31]Rom 7:19. [32]Trad. Cola 59-60. [33]CTP 188:108-9. [34]Is 6:5. [35]See Gen 18:27. [36]See 1 Cor 15:8. [37]That is, the angelic hosts in Isaiah's vision. [38]CTP 162:175-76.

11 (3:34 LXX) *Do Not Give Us Up*

THE JUST ASK FOR GOD'S INTERVENTION.
THEODORET OF CYR: We dare to speak thus,
since we have many testimonies of your goodness. In the first instance, the same name, that
one for which we call you "Lord"; then, your
immeasurable mercy that you employ in guiding all things; besides this, the agreement you
made with our ancestors: in fact, you promised
them that you would make the Hebrew people
illustrious and worthy of praise. The prophet
remembers therefore the names of his ancestors, recalling the good Lord to compassion by
mentioning those righteous ones. COMMENTARY
ON DANIEL 3.34.[39]

14 (3:37 LXX) *Fewer Than Any Nation*

THE GROWTH OF THE PEOPLE. JOHN CHRYSOS-
TOM: "May the Lord make you fruitful, you and
your children."[40] Have you seen another kind of
blessing, the increase of the people? For this same
reason it says elsewhere that the contrary is a
punishment: "We have become smaller than any
other nation; we are now humiliated throughout
the earth." And in fact they enjoyed this blessing when they were in Egypt, despite the infinite
number of things forbidden them, the forced
labor, the tribulations, the cruelty of their persecutors. But nothing caused the Word of God to
fail, and the blessing acted in such a way that in
two hundred years, they had become six hundred
thousand people.[41] ON THE PSALM 113.5.[42]

GOD'S PROMISES ARE NOT FALSIFIED. THEO-
DORET OF CYR: You have not been giving false
promises, O Lord. Rather, it was we who violated the agreements. Although we had become
many due to the promise you made, because of
our sins we were reduced to only a few. He implies this, in fact, when he asserts, "We have become fewer once more." He does not, in fact, say,
"We are few in comparison with all the other
peoples," but, "We have become fewer," that is:

We were beyond number due to your promise,
but once we violated that agreement with you,
from many we became only a few. Then he
provides God with the details of the misfortune
that had hit them. He does not, however, inform
him as if he thought that the Lord was ignorant
of what had happened but summons him to
mercy through the enumeration of the misfortunes. COMMENTARY ON DANIEL 3.37.[43]

15 (3:38 LXX) *No Place Left to Make an Offering*

**IN EXILE, THE JEWS COULD NOT WORSHIP
OR KEEP THE LAW.** JOHN CHRYSOSTOM: When
they were in Babylon and their enemies wanted
to make them sing, they neither listened nor
obeyed, because they were prisoners and the
servants of masters who maltreated them. But
having been deprived of their homeland and
their freedom (and even their lives were in
danger) and compelled by the hands of their
enemies as in a trap, when they were commanded to sing that song with their harps,
they said, "By the rivers of Babylon we sat and
wept, because those who deported us asked us
to sing. How can we sing the songs of the Lord
in a foreign land?"[44] We must not say that they
acted thusly because they had no harps. They
give the reason: "How can we sing the songs of
the Lord in a foreign land?" And they had their
harps with them: "On the poplars of that land
we hung up our harps."[45] But they were not
allowed even to fast. This is what the prophet
had said to them: " 'Have you fasted for these
seventy years?' says the Lord."[46] That the offering of sacrifices or libations was prohibited
is what the three young men say: "We have
neither prince, nor prophet, nor leader nor
place to offer you the firstfruits and to find
mercy." They do not say, "We have no priest,"

---

[39]CTP 188:109-10. [40]Ps 115:14 (113:22 LXX). [41]See Ex 12:37.
[42]PG 55:311. [43]CTP 188:110-11. [44]Ps 137:1, 3-4 (136:1, 3-4 LXX).
[45]Ps 137:2 (136:2 LXX). [46]Zech 7:5, variant.

for in fact there were priests. But so that you would know that everything depended on the place and the entire law was linked to it, it says, "There is no place." And why speak of sacrifices and libations? It was not allowed even to read the Law (which another prophet reproves, "And they read out the Law and proclaimed the confession")[47] or to celebrate the Passover, Pentecost, the Feast of Booths. AGAINST JEWS AND GENTILES 17.[48]

16 (3:39 LXX) *A Contrite Heart*

HUMILITY IS BETTER THAN ANY SACRIFICE. PSEUDO-CHRYSOSTOM: I declare that this sacrifice (I am referring to humility) has always been superior to the Jewish sacrifice, not only now but also in the past. In fact, those three young men who in the furnace of Babylon changed the flames into mud; who were mere lads but elders; small but stronger than the many; prisoners but more powerful than the king; they who lost their homeland but not their faith; naked but clothed; poor but well-off; servants but above the free; they who changed the furnace into dew, transforming the elements; who extinguished the strength of the flames; who were bound by the tyrant and loosed by the fire—they sang a hymn, saying, "We have sinned, we have done every kind of evil, departing from you, we have fallen short in every way. We have neither prince, nor leader, nor prophet, nor holocaust, nor sacrifice, nor oblation, nor incense nor place to offer you the firstfruits and to find mercy. May we be received with a contrite heart and a humble spirit." HOMILY 2 ON PSALM 50.[49]

A CONTRITE HEART REPLACES THE SACRIFICE. THEODORET OF CYR: Since, it says, your law does not allow the customary sacrifices to be offered in every place, we offer a contrite and humble heart in place of the rams, the bulls, the countless sheep, and we ask that this sacrifice be more pleasing to you than any other, since you are accustomed to freeing from all dishonor those who trust in you. This holy man does not pronounce these words about himself but was schooled by David the prophet, who in the psalm asserts, "If you had wanted sacrifice, we would have given it to you; you will not be pleased with burnt offerings: a contrite spirit is the appropriate sacrifice to the Lord. God will not refuse a contrite and humble heart."[50] And again, from the mouth of God, "Surely I do not eat the meat of bulls, nor do I drink the blood of goats. Sacrifice to God an offering with praises, and pay your vows to the most High, and call to me in the day of your trouble, and I will have mercy on you, and you will praise me."[51] And a little later, "You will honor me with a sacrifice of praise, and here is the path in which I will show him my salvation."[52] This divine man, following the instruction of such words, begged God to accept the contrite heart in place of every other offering. COMMENTARY ON DANIEL 3.39-40.[53]

22 (3:45 LXX) *Let Them Know You Are the Lord*

NOTHING IS GREATER THAN GOD. EUCHERIUS: I speak of our God. You could burn for him with a fire as great as it is holy: it is enough, however, that in place of your former passions, you would yield to desires having value. If you were impressed with a lofty person's prestige, nothing is higher than God. If you were awed by things apt and tending to glory, there is nothing more glorious than God. If you could not help but admire the splendor of shiny things, is there perhaps something more brilliant than God? If the sight of beautiful things attracted you, nothing is more beautiful than God. If you thought you perceived truth in someone, there is nothing truer than God is. If you felt yourself obliged to

---

[47]Amos 4:5. [48]PG 48:835-36. [49]PG 55:587. [50]Ps 51:16-17 (50:18-19 LXX). Theodoret, like all the patristic tradition, uses the Septuagint numbering of the Psalms. [51]Ps 50:13-15 (49:13-15 LXX). [52]Ps 50:23 (49:23 LXX). [53]CTP 188:112.

admire someone for his generosity, nothing is more generous than God. Do you admire what is pure and simple? Nothing is more limpid than that goodness. Do great riches tempt you? Nothing is more abundant than that prosperity. Are you fond of someone because he is faithful? What could be more secure than God's fidelity? Do you like something because it suits you? But nothing could be more suitable than God's love. Is there something that attracts you by its unaffected air or its pleasantness? There is nothing more terrible or more benign than that greatness,[54] than that indulgence. RENUNCIATION OF THE WORLD.[55]

23 (3:46 LXX) *Naphtha, Pitch, Tow and Brush*

COMMENTARY ON FEEDING THE FIRE. JEROME: Sallust in his history[56] says that the naphtha is a species of tinder used in Persia, most apt in feeding fires. Others believe that naphtha is the name given to olive pits that are thrown away when the dregs of the oil have dried up. They assert that in the same way, the Greek term *pyrinē* comes from its property of feeding the fire (*pyr*). COMMENTARY ON DANIEL 3:46.[57]

25 (3:48 LXX) *The Chaldeans Burned by the Furnace*

GOD COMMANDS THE FIRE. SEVERIAN OF GABALA: God commands the fire to consume the Chaldeans, so they would not believe that the fire's energy had been weakened by the miracle and deny its truth. For this reason those who were inside remained unhurt, while outside the fire attacked the Chaldeans, to firmly convince the onlookers that, in regard to the saints, the fire was not ignorant of its own nature but rather honored piety. Thus also the lions did with Daniel.[58] SERMON ON THE THREE YOUNG MEN.[59]

26 (3:49 LXX) *The Angel of the Lord Came into the Furnace*

IF WE INVOKE THE LORD. JEROME: When the spirit is suffocated from inner turmoil and taken up with various kinds of restlessness, having been deprived for the moment of any hope of human aid and turning totally to the Lord, an angel of the Lord descends near to it. In other words, the divine word descends to the aid of the servant and brushes aside the burning blazes of passion so that the heated darts of the enemy[60] do not penetrate the inner citadel of our heart and the enemy cannot hold us in his fiery furnace. COMMENTARY ON DANIEL 3.49-30.[61]

27 (3:50 LXX) *Scattering the Flames*

VIRTUOUS POVERTY IS LIKE A FURNACE. JOHN CHRYSOSTOM: Let us also imitate those young people. Indeed, even now too there is a gold statue,[62] the tyranny of mammon. But let us not pay attention to the tambourines, the flutes, the harps of ten cords[63] or the other forms of the pomp of wealth. Yes, even if we must fall into the furnace[64] of poverty, we prefer it, so as not to adore that statue, and in its midst there will be a wind of dew. Let us not then be afraid to speak about the furnace of poverty. In fact, back then, those who fell into the furnace were shown to be more glorious, while those who worshiped the statue perished. But then it happened all at once; now instead some things will take place down here, some up there, others both here now and in the day that will come. Those who prefer poverty rather than worshiping mammon will be more glorious both here now and also then in the future, while those who down here become rich unjustly then will endure the more serious punishment.

Lazarus also came out of this furnace too, no less glorious than those young people, while

---

[54]See Ps 145:5 (144:5 LXX). [55]CTP 139:128-29. [56]Histories 4, fragment 61. [57]Trad. Cola 61. [58]Cf. Dan 6:17-23; Bel 31-42 (Dan 14:31-42 LXX). [59]PG 56:597. [60]Cf. Eph 6:16. [61]Trad. Cola 61. [62]See Dan 3:1. [63]See Dan 3:5. [64]See Dan 3:6.

the rich man who was in the place of those who were worshipers of the statue was condemned to Gehenna.[65] Indeed, much of what has been said about these young people was a prefiguration of this. Just as those who fell in the furnace suffered no harm, while those who were outside of the furnace were seized with great violence,[66] thus it will be also then. The saints, walking through the river of fire,[67] will not suffer any pain—in fact, they will be resplendent—while the worshipers of the statue will see the fire attacking them more ferociously than any wild animal, and it will drag them within. HOMILIES ON THE GOSPEL OF MATTHEW 4.19.[68]

---

[65]See Lk 16:23. [66]See Dan 3:22. [67]See Dan 7:10. [68]CTP 170:103-4.

28-68 THE SONG OF THE THREE YOUNG MEN

[28]*Then the three, as with one mouth, praised and glorified and blessed God in the furnace, saying:*
[29]*"Blessed art thou, O Lord, God of our fathers,*
  and to be praised and highly exalted for ever;
[30]*And blessed is thy glorious, holy name*
  and to be highly praised and highly exalted for ever;
[31]*Blessed art thou in the temple of thy holy glory*
  and to be extolled and highly glorified for ever.
[32]*Blessed art thou, who sittest upon cherubim and lookest upon the deeps,*
  and to be praised and highly exalted for ever.
[33]*Blessed art thou upon the throne of thy kingdom*
  and to be extolled and highly exalted for ever.
[34]*Blessed art thou in the firmament of heaven*
  and to be sung and glorified for ever.

[35]*"Bless the Lord, all works of the Lord,*
  sing praise to him and highly exalt him for ever.
[36]*Bless the Lord, you heavens,*
  sing praise to him and highly exalt him for ever.
[37]*Bless the Lord, you angels of the Lord,*
  sing praise to him and highly exalt him for ever.
[38]*Bless the Lord, all waters above the heaven,*
  sing praise to him and highly exalt him for ever.
[39]*Bless the Lord, all powers,*
  sing praise to him and highly exalt him for ever.

⁴⁰Bless the Lord, sun and moon,
  sing praise to him and highly exalt him for ever.
⁴¹*Bless the Lord, stars of heaven,*
  sing praise to him and highly exalt him for ever.
⁴²*Bless the Lord, all rain and dew,*
  sing praise to him and highly exalt him for ever.
⁴³*Bless the Lord, all winds,*
  sing praise to him and highly exalt him for ever.
⁴⁴*Bless the Lord, fire and heat,*
  sing praise to him and highly exalt him for ever.
⁴⁵*Bless the Lord, winter cold and summer heat,*
  sing praise to him and highly exalt him for ever.
⁴⁶*Bless the Lord, dews and snows,*
  sing praise to him and highly exalt him for ever.
⁴⁷*Bless the Lord, nights and days,*
  sing praise to him and highly exalt him for ever.
⁴⁸*Bless the Lord, light and darkness,*
  sing praise to him and highly exalt him for ever.
⁴⁹*Bless the Lord, ice and cold,*
  sing praise to him and highly exalt him for ever.
⁵⁰*Bless the Lord, frosts and snows,*
  sing praise to him and highly exalt him for ever.
⁵¹*Bless the Lord, lightnings and clouds,*
  sing praise to him and highly exalt him for ever.
⁵²*Let the earth bless the Lord;*
  let it sing praise to him and highly exalt him for ever.
⁵³*Bless the Lord, mountains and hills,*
  sing praise to him and highly exalt him for ever.
⁵⁴*Bless the Lord, all things that grow on the earth,*
  sing praise to him and highly exalt him for ever.
⁵⁵*Bless the Lord, you springs,*
  sing praise to him and highly exalt him for ever.
⁵⁶*Bless the Lord, seas and rivers,*
  sing praise to him and highly exalt him for ever.
⁵⁷*Bless the Lord, you whales and all creatures that move in the waters,*
  sing praise to him and highly exalt him for ever.
⁵⁸*Bless the Lord, all birds of the air,*
  sing praise to him and highly exalt him for ever.
⁵⁹*Bless the Lord, all beasts and cattle,*
  sing praise to him and highly exalt him for ever.
⁶⁰*Bless the Lord, you sons of men,*
  sing praise to him and highly exalt him for ever.
⁶¹*Bless the Lord, O Israel,*
  sing praise to him and highly exalt him for ever.
⁶²*Bless the Lord, you priests of the Lord,*

sing praise to him and highly exalt him for ever.
⁶³*Bless the Lord, you servants of the Lord,*
sing praise to him and highly exalt him for ever.
⁶⁴*Bless the Lord, spirits and souls of the righteous,*
sing praise to him and highly exalt him for ever.
⁶⁵*Bless the Lord, you who are holy and humble in heart,*
sing praise to him and highly exalt him for ever.
⁶⁶*Bless the Lord, Hananiah, Azariah, and Mishael,*
sing praise to him and highly exalt him for ever;
for he has rescued us from Hades and saved us from the hand of death,
and delivered us from the midst of the burning fiery furnace;
from the midst of the fire he has delivered us.
⁶⁷*Give thanks to the Lord, for he is good,*
for his mercy endures for ever.
⁶⁸*Bless him, all who worship the Lord, the God of gods,*
sing praise to him and give thanks to him,
for his mercy endures for ever."

OVERVIEW: The hymn of praise that the three young men offer stems from their love of God (THEODORET). It is a contemplation of the divine nature, which is higher than our understanding could ever hope to achieve (CYRIL OF JERUSALEM). These men, and those who imitate them, are like the martyrs, who are close to the angels (CHRYSOSTOM) in heaven (AMBROSE). In their song, the three young men list all that has been created, including the angels, offering this song as praise to the God of heaven and against idolatry (SEVERIAN, THEODORET, JOHN OF DAMASCUS).

Scripture here distinguishes between the soul and the spirit, and it uses the plural instead of the singular and vice versa (ORIGEN, FULGENTIUS). Whether speaking of soul or spirit, when the just are dead, they praise the Lord (CASSIAN) in thanksgiving for the humbleness of spirit that the Lord provides us an example (AUGUSTINE), an example imitated by these three young men, who place themselves in the last place because of their humility (THEODORET).

29 (3:52 LXX) *Blessed Is the God of Our Ancestors*

A HYMN OF PRAISE. THEODORET OF CYR:

These words indicate a fervent and unending love: although stricken with it, they search for definitions capable of celebrating the dignity of the one who is to be praised, and, since they cannot find any, they punctuate their phrases with superlatives, speaking of God in terms of him being "highly praised and praised more than any other." And they not only say this but also add that his name is worthy of praise. And they do well to constantly assert that he is "Lord and God of our ancestors," agreeing in this way that they are not worthy of being called by this name. COMMENTARY ON DANIEL 3.53.[1]

32 (3:55 LXX; 3:54 Th) *One Seated on the Cherubim*

DIVINE NATURE IS HIGHER THAN OUR UNDERSTANDING. CYRIL OF JERUSALEM: Do you want to have proof concerning the incomprehensibility of the divine nature? Try looking at the three children who praised the Lord in the fiery furnace, saying, "Blessed are you who behold the depths and sit over the cherubim." Tell me the nature of the cherubim, and then look on him or

---

[1]CTP 188:115.

the nature of him who sits over them! And yet, Ezekiel within the limits of possibility offered a description of them, saying, "Every one has four faces, the first of a man, the second one of lion, the third of an eagle and the last one of a year-old calf; every one has six wings and has eyes on every side; under each there is a spinning wheel of four sides."[2] But in spite of these descriptions that he made, we cannot succeed in constructing for ourselves an exact idea of what he was talking about. If we cannot understand what the throne is that the prophet has described, how will we succeed in comprehending the one who sits on the throne, when he is invisible and mysterious? It is impossible then to construct an idea of the divine nature; it is possible only to offer up praises for the works that it has made and that are before our eyes. CATECHETICAL LECTURES 9.3.[3]

LIKE THE ANGELS. JOHN CHRYSOSTOM: Here you see not only the yoke of an animal but also the chariots of the infinitude of martyrs and God who is above these chariots and leads them to heaven. Regarding the souls of the saints being the chariots of God, listen to what the prophet says, "The chariots of God are thousands on thousands."[4] What he gave to the heavenly powers, he has also given to our nature. He is seated on the cherubim, as the psalm says, "He rode on a cherub and flew,"[5] and, "He who sits on the cherubim and looks into the depths." And this is what he has also given to us. He sits on them; he dwells in us. "I will dwell in you and walk among you."[6] They became a chariot; we become a temple.[7] Have you noticed the relationship of honor? Have you noticed how he has mollified both what is higher and what is lower?[8] For this reason, if we desire it, we differ from the angels in nothing. SERMON ON THE HOLY MARTYRS.[9]

34-63 (3:56-85 LXX) All the Works of the Lord

HEAVEN AND FIRMAMENT ARE NOT THE

SAME. AMBROSE: "Let a firmament be made in the middle of the water."[10] It should not astonish us . . . that above[11] he speaks about the heavens and here about the firmament, because David also says, "The heavens narrate the glory of God and the firmament announces the work of his hands."[12] In other words, the created world, when it is introduced to our sight, gives praise to its Creator: his invisible majesty is acknowledged through the things that are seen. And it seems to me that the term "heavens" is a generic term,[13] because the Scripture attests the existence of many heavens. The term "firmament," however, is more specific since here also we read, "And he called the firmament heaven."[14] He seems to have said above, in a general sense, that in the beginning the heavens were created[15] in order to comprise all the work of the creation of the sky and that here instead he has indicated the specific solidity of this external support that he calls firmament.[16] This is called the firmament of the sky, as we read in the hymn of the prophet, "Blessed are you in the firmament of the sky." HEXAMERON 2.4.15.[17]

EVERY CREATED BEING INVITED TO PRAISE GOD. THEODORET OF CYR: Since you are every-where, they are saying, you fill the universe, em-bracing every creature. Having sung such praises, they call every created nature—not only those creatures endowed with reason but also those that are irrational and inanimate—to offer this com-mon praise. COMMENTARY ON DANIEL 3.56.[18]

ALL CREATION IS CALLED TO RESIST IDOLA-TRY. SEVERIAN OF GABALA: Consider the godless

---

[2]See Ezek 1:6-15. [3]CTP 103:170. [4]Ps 68:18 (67:18 LXX). [5]Ps 18:11 (17:11 LXX). [6]Lev 26:11-12; 2 Cor 6:16. [7]See 1 Cor 3:16. [8]See Col 1:20. [9]PG 50:645-46. [10]Gen 1:6. [11]See Gen 1:1. [12]Ps 19:2 (18:2 LXX). [13]This is implicated in the frequent usage of the plural "heavens," even if, strictly speaking, the plural is a Semitism; see Mt 6:9. [14]Gen 1:8. [15]See Gen 1:1. [16]The etymology of "fir-mament" is connected with the notion of firmness. In the patristic period, this meaning of the word was derived from the Greek word *stereōma*, which has the same connection with the idea of "firm-ness." [17]CTP 164:76-77. [18]CTP 188:116.

person, how he stumbles over the same things by which the faithful are justified. He sees the moon and worships it. He sees the stars and venerates them. He sees the sea and calls it divine. Those who entered the furnace in Babylon after their salvific and laudable confession praised God through his works in a hymn, saying, "Bless the Lord, all you works of the Lord." Having said this, they could have ended the hymn. God does not pay attention to the length of the hymn but to the intention of those who sing. By saying "all you works," everything was in fact included, and there was no need to add anything else. But since they were not proclaiming this to themselves but praising God, and with the hymn they also taught the Chaldeans who were present, the hymn necessarily runs through the entire creation. Thus the Chaldeans, who were lost in error, would learn who it was that was sung to and who it was that sang. On the Prodigal Son.[19]

Angels Are Creatures. Theodoret of Cyr: The divine Scriptures teach us with clarity that, with the exception of the holy Trinity, the angels and the archangels and every other incorporeal being has a created nature. In fact, David the prophet orders them to offer praise: "Praise him, all you angels, praise him all of you his hosts,"[20] and adds explaining the reason, "Since he spoke and it was created; he commanded and it was made."[21] Moreover, in another psalm, "He who makes his angels spirits and his ministers a burning flame."[22] And the three young people rejoiced in the furnace when they composed the divine hymn, when, after having begun with that excellent and most fitting premise, "Bless the Lord, all you works of the Lord," they immediately added, "Bless the Lord, you angels of the Lord," "Bless the Lord, all you powers of the Lord." Questions on Genesis 2.[23]

Rain, Dew and Winds Are Creatures. Severian of Gabala: Frequently there are droughts and violent and unexpected winds. Those who listen to lies and entertain vain

thoughts are in the habit of ascribing everything out of the ordinary to matter and to something perverse, without knowing that nothing escapes the Lord or happens to no purpose but that God arranges all of this for the people's instruction and to drive away godlessness. The proper functioning of creatures would seem to proclaim the Creator, whereas disorder contradicts the worship of creatures. If the rain or the winds were something divine or sacred, they would not violate order, given that what is divine is not susceptible to disorder. This is why they say, "All rain and dew and all spirits, bless the Lord." In fact, even the rain and the wind were worshiped, the one as the giver of food and the other as the cultivator of the fruits of earth. They also worshiped the earth, and its fruits were assigned to various demons, saying that vines were the gift of Dionysius, the olive of Athena, and so on. Sermon on the Three Young Men.[24]

Mountains, Hills and Springs Are Creatures. Severian of Gabala: But perhaps the mountains and hills were excluded? Not at all. But since the wicked rites of demons were performed on the hills and idols were worshiped there, it says, "Mountains and hills, bless the Lord."[25] Mentioning the hills, they also recall springs and rivers, because these also were divinized. In fact, springs were called nymphs and the sea Poseidon, together with the sirens and the nereids. Of the fact that the rivers were worshiped we have proof in our own day in Egypt, where they sacrificed at the swelling of the Nile, not marveling at God through nature but worshiping the water itself as God. This is why rivers, springs and the sea are included in the hymn. Sermon on the Three Young Men.[26]

---

[19]PG 59:630. [20]Ps 148:2. [21]Ps 148:5, variant. [22]Ps 104:4 (103:4 LXX). The Hebrew, followed by modern translations, says, "You make the winds your messengers, the flames your servants." But in Greek another interpretation is possible, since *angelos* means both "messenger" and "angel," whereas *pneumata* indicates both the "winds" and the "spirits." [23]LEC (CUAP) 1:10. [24]PG 56:598. [25]Pr Azar 59 (Dan 3:75 LXX). [26]PG 56:598.

BIRDS AND ANIMALS ARE CREATURES.
SEVERIAN OF GABALA: Then they also add the
birds of the air and the animals. Not even these
escaped divinization: in fact, they adored the
eagle and the raven, and the Egyptians honored
wild beasts and domestic animals as though
they were gods. And the error had such power
that cities were named after animals: among
them one finds cities with the names of Dogs,
of Sheep, of Wolves and of Lions.[27] SERMON ON
THE THREE YOUNG MEN.[28]

ANOTHER NAME FOR THE AIR. JOHN OF DA-
MASCUS: It is customary in the divine Scripture
to speak of the air also as heavens, because we
see it above us. "Bless him," it says, "all you birds
of the heaven,"[29] meaning of the air. For it is the
air and not the heaven that is the region in which
birds fly. ORTHODOX FAITH 2.6.[30]

64 (3:86 LXX) *Spirits and Souls of the Righteous*

**THE SCRIPTURE DISTINGUISHES BETWEEN
SOUL AND SPIRIT.** ORIGEN: Someone might
ask, "If the soul of Elijah was not first in the
Tishbite and then in John, what might that be
in both which the Savior in both cases called
Elijah?"[31] I answer that Gabriel in his reply to
Zachariah had already suggested that it was the
same being that was in Elijah and John. He says,
in fact, "He will lead back many sons of Israel to
the Lord God ,and he will go before him in the
spirit and power of Elijah."[32] For, note well: he
did not say "in the soul of Elijah," in which case,
the doctrine of the transmigration of souls might
have some ground, but "in the spirit and the
power of Elijah." The Scriptures clearly know
the difference between "spirit" and "soul," since
the text, "May the God of peace sanctify you
wholly, and may your spirit and soul and body be
preserved entire, without blame at the coming of
our Lord Jesus Christ,"[33] and the other passage,
"Blessed the Lord, you spirits and souls of the
righteous," as it is recorded in the book of Daniel

(according to the version of the Seventy), which
indicates the difference between soul and spirit.
John therefore is called Elijah not because of
the soul but because of the spirit and the power,
and if these things existed before in Elijah and
then in John, this is not at all in conflict with
the teaching of the church. But "the spirits of
the prophets are subject to the prophets,"[34] not
the souls of the prophets, which are not subject
to the prophets. COMMENTARY ON MATTHEW
13.2.[35]

THE JUST PRAISE THE LORD. JOHN CASSIAN:
But there are many also who while still living
in this body are dead and incapable of praising
God while lying in the grave. However, there
are others of us who, although dead in the body,
bless and praise God in the spirit, according to
the words of the text, "Bless the Lord, spirits
and souls of the righteous," and "Let every living
spirit praise the Lord."[36] And in the Apocalypse
it is said that the spirits of those who have been
killed not only praise God but also speak directly with him.[37] CONFERENCES 1.1.14.[38]

**SCRIPTURE INTERCHANGES PLURAL AND SIN-
GULAR.** FULGENTIUS OF RUSPE: We are not ignorant of the fact that through the grace of God it
can happen that many people can be designated
with a singular term such as in the passage . . .
"the multitude of the believers had one heart and
one soul,"[39] where nevertheless it is spoken of a
single soul in order to speak of the souls generally; of the faithful, of course, and not of the
impious. The Lord spoke, in fact, to his faithful
disciples, of whom he says, "By your perseverance you will save your souls."[40] Also the blessed

---

[27]Most probably Severian alludes to Cynopolis ("City of the
Dog(s)," present-day Samallut), Thebes in Egypt (where sheep were
adored), Lykopolis ("City of the Wolf / Wolves," present-day Assiut)
and Leontopolis ("City of the Lion(s)," present-day Tell el-Yahudiy-
ye). [28]PG 56:598. [29]This is the literal meaning of the verse, which
is translated by modern versions precisely as did John of Damascus.
[30]CTP 142:100. [31]See Mt 11:14. [32]Lk 1:16-17. [33]1 Thess 5:23.
[34]1 Cor 14:32. [35]CTP 151:17-18. [36]Ps 150:5. [37]See Rev 6:9-10.
[38]CTP 155:80. [39]Acts 4:32. [40]Lk 21:19.

Peter says to the faithful, "Believing, you rejoice with ineffable joy and a pervasiveness of glory, in attaining the goal of your faith, the salvation of your souls."[41] And in the book of Wisdom it is said, "The souls of the righteous are in the hands of God."[42] We also know that the blessed apostle said to the Thessalonians that he recognized their election was from God: "May the God of peace perfectly sanctify you in all things; and may all your being: spirit, soul and body be guarded blameless for the day of our Lord Jesus Christ."[43] Also in the hymn of the three children, one also reads, "Bless the Lord, spirits and souls of the righteous." We know through the grace of God that the holy church is designated as a single virgin, since the apostle says, "I have in fact betrothed you to Christ, your only spouse, in order to present you as a pure virgin,"[44] but in that one virgin, a plural number of virgins are also designated. We read, in fact, "Virgins will be introduced to the king, after her."[45] LETTERS 14.7.[46]

65 (3:87 LXX) *Holy and Humble in Heart*

IMITATE THE HUMBLENESS OF THE LORD.
AUGUSTINE: "If therefore," he adds, "I, your Lord and master, have washed your feet, you also must wash one another's feet. I have, in fact, given you an example, so that you may do as I have done."[47] This, blessed Peter, is what you did not ascertain when you did not want the Lord to wash your feet.[48] This is what he promised to you that you would come to know afterwards, when your Lord and master terrified you into submission so that you let him wash your feet. We have learned humility from the Highest; let us do offer to one another, and with humility, what he the highest did in his humility. This is a great example of humility. And do this to one another,[49] even in the outward gesture, when they treat one another with hospitality; for this exercise of humility is generally prevalent

and finds effective expression in the very deed that makes it discernible. It is for this that the apostle, when he commends to us the ideal of the widow, emphasizes this quality: "She practices hospitality by washing the feet of the saints."[50] And wherever the custom of physically washing the feet does not exist among the faithful, what they do not do with their hands they do spiritually, if they are in the number of those people to whom the song of the three young people is addressed, "Bless the Lord, you holy and humble of heart." But it is better, and more in compliance with the truth, if the example of the Lord is followed in a material way as well. The Christian should not think it beneath him or her to do what was done by Christ. For when the body is bent at the feet of a brother or sister, the feeling of humility is ignited in the heart, or, if it was already there, such humility is fed. TRACTATES ON THE GOSPEL OF JOHN 58.4.[51]

66 (3:88 LXX) *Hananiah, Azariah and Mishael*

THE HUMBLE YOUNG MEN PLACE THEMSELVES LAST. THEODORET OF CYR: Thus they thought themselves the least of creation and the worst among all people. The blessed Paul also thought this way when he said, "To me, the most insignificant among all the saints, this grace was granted."[52] And elsewhere, "Christ descended from the heavens in order to save sinners, of which I am the foremost."[53] He names himself the first among sinners and calls himself the least among the saints. In the same way, these blessed souls exhort themselves last to sing the praises of the Lord and exalt him forever. COMMENTARY ON DANIEL 3.88.[54]

---

[41]1 Pet 1:8-9. [42]Wis 3:1. [43]1 Thess 5:23. [44]2 Cor 11:2. [45]Ps 45:15 (44:15 LXX). [46]CTP 149:275-76. [47]Jn 13:14-15. [48]Cf. Jn 13:8. [49]Cf. Jn 13:14. [50]1 Tim 5:10. [51]NBA 24:1098-99. [52]Eph 3:8. [53]1 Tim 1:15. [54]CTP 188:120.

SUSANNA

1-64* SUSANNA AND DANIEL'S JUDGMENT

¹There was a man living in Babylon whose name was Joakim. ²And he took a wife named Susanna, the daughter of Hilkiah, a very beautiful woman and one who feared the Lord. ³Her parents were righteous, and had taught their daughter according to the law of Moses. ⁴Joakim was very rich, and had a spacious garden adjoining his house; and the Jews used to come to him because he was the most honored of them all.

⁵In that year two elders from the people were appointed as judges. Concerning them the Lord had said: "Iniquity came forth from Babylon, from elders who were judges, who were supposed to govern the people." ⁶These men were frequently at Joakim's house, and all who had suits at law came to them.

⁷When the people departed at noon, Susanna would go into her husband's garden to walk. ⁸The two elders used to see her every day, going in and walking about, and they began to desire her. ⁹And they perverted their minds and turned away their eyes from looking to Heaven or remembering righteous judgments. ¹⁰Both were overwhelmed with passion for her, but they did not tell each other of their distress, ¹¹for they were ashamed to disclose their lustful desire to possess her. ¹²And they watched eagerly, day after day, to see her.

¹³They said to each other, "Let us go home, for it is mealtime." ¹⁴And when they went out, they parted from each other. But turning back, they met again; and when each pressed the other for the reason, they confessed their lust. And then together they arranged for a time when they could find her alone.

¹⁵Once, while they were watching for an opportune day, she went in as before with only two maids, and wished to bathe in the garden, for it was very hot. ¹⁶And no one was there except the two elders, who had hid themselves and were watching her. ¹⁷She said to her maids, "Bring me oil and ointments, and shut the garden doors so that I may bathe." ¹⁸They did as she said, shut the garden doors, and went out by the side doors to bring what they had been commanded; and they did not see the elders, because they were hidden.

¹⁹When the maids had gone out, the two elders rose and ran to her, and said: ²⁰"Look, the garden doors are shut, no one sees us, and we are in love with you; so give your consent, and lie with us. ²¹If you refuse, we will testify against you that a young man was with you, and this was why you sent your maids away."

²²Susanna sighed deeply, and said, "I am hemmed in on every side. For if I do this thing, it is death for me; and if I do not, I shall not escape your hands. ²³I choose not to do it and to fall into your hands, rather than to sin in the sight of the Lord."

²⁴Then Susanna cried out with a loud voice, and the two elders shouted against her. ²⁵And one of them ran and opened the garden doors. ²⁶When the household servants heard the shouting in the garden, they rushed in at the side door to see what had happened to her. ²⁷And when the elders told their tale, the servants were greatly ashamed, for nothing like this had ever been said about Susanna.

²⁸The next day, when the people gathered at the house of her husband Joakim, the two elders came, full of their wicked plot to have Susanna put to death. ²⁹They said before the people, "Send for Susanna, the daughter of Hilkiah, who is the wife of Joakim." ³⁰So they sent for her. And she came, with her parents, her children, and all her kindred.

³¹Now Susanna was a woman of great refinement, and beautiful in appearance. ³²As she was veiled, the wicked men ordered her to be unveiled, that they might feast upon her beauty. ³³But her family and friends and all who saw her wept.

³⁴Then the two elders stood up in the midst of the people, and laid their hands upon her head. ³⁵And she, weeping, looked up toward heaven, for her heart trusted in the Lord. ³⁶The elders said, "As we were walking in the garden alone, this woman came in with two maids, shut the garden doors, and dismissed the maids. ³⁷Then a young man, who had been hidden, came to her and lay with her. ³⁸We were in a corner of the garden, and when we saw this wickedness we ran to them. ³⁹We saw them embracing, but we could not hold the man, for he was too strong for us, and he opened the doors and dashed out. ⁴⁰So we seized this woman and asked her who the young man was, but she would not tell us. These things we testify."

⁴¹The assembly believed them, because they were elders of the people and judges; and they condemned her to death.

⁴²Then Susanna cried out with a loud voice, and said, "O eternal God, who dost discern what is secret, who art aware of all things before they come to be, ⁴³thou knowest that these men have borne false witness against me. And now I am to die! Yet I have done none of the things that they have wickedly invented against me!"

⁴⁴The Lord heard her cry. ⁴⁵And as she was being led away to be put to death, God aroused the holy spirit of a young lad named Daniel; ⁴⁶and he cried with a loud voice, "I am innocent of the blood of this woman."

⁴⁷All the people turned to him, and said, "What is this that you have said?" ⁴⁸Taking his stand in the midst of them, he said, "Are you such fools, you sons of Israel? Have you condemned a daughter of Israel without examination and without learning the facts? ⁴⁹Return to the place of judgment. For these men have borne false witness against her."

⁵⁰Then all the people returned in haste. And the elders said to him, "Come, sit among us and inform us, for God has given you that right." ⁵¹And Daniel said to them, "Separate them far from each other, and I will examine them."

⁵²When they were separated from each other, he summoned one of them and said to him, "You old relic of wicked days, your sins have now come home, which you have committed in the past, ⁵³pronouncing unjust judgments, condemning the innocent and letting the guilty go free, though the Lord said, 'Do not put to death an innocent and righteous person.' ⁵⁴Now then, if you really saw her, tell me this: Under what tree did you see them being intimate with each other?" He answered, "Under a mastic tree."ᵃ ⁵⁵And Daniel said, "Very well! You have lied against your own head, for the angel of God has received the sentence from God and will immediately cutᵃ you in two."

⁵⁶Then he put him aside, and commanded them to bring the other. And he said to him, "You offspring of Canaan and not of Judah, beauty has deceived you and lust has perverted your heart.

⁵⁷This is how you both have been dealing with the daughters of Israel, and they were intimate with you through fear; but a daughter of Judah would not endure your wickedness. ⁵⁸Now then, tell me: Under what tree did you catch them being intimate with each other?" He answered, "Under an evergreen oak."ᵇ ⁵⁹And Daniel said to him, "Very well! You also have lied against your own head, for the angel of God is waiting with his sword to sawᵇ you in two, that he may destroy you both."

⁶⁰Then all the assembly shouted loudly and blessed God, who saves those who hope in him. ⁶¹And they rose against the two elders, for out of their own mouths Daniel had convicted them of bearing false witness; ⁶²and they did to them as they had wickedly planned to do to their neighbor; acting in accordance with the law of Moses, they put them to death. Thus innocent blood was saved that day.

⁶³And Hilkiah and his wife praised God for their daughter Susanna, and so did Joakim her husband and all her kindred, because nothing shameful was found in her. ⁶⁴And from that day onward Daniel had a great reputation among the people.

a The Greek words for *mastic tree* and *cut* are so similar that the use of *cut* is ironic wordplay **b** The Greek words for *evergreen oak* and *saw* are so similar that the use of *saw* is ironic wordplay *The story of Susanna is located variously in the versions: in the Old Latin, Coptic and Arabic as well as Theodotion's Greek it precedes Daniel 1; in the Septuagint and Vulgate it follows the protocanonical book, serving as Daniel 13.

OVERVIEW: The story of Susanna is a Greek addition to the text of Daniel (JULIUS AFRICANUS). It does not fit chronologically with the narrative flow of the rest of the book of Daniel (HIPPOLYTUS).

Susanna was a holy daughter, born from a holy family. She was instructed in the Law and faithfully followed the Law even in the face of unfounded accusations (HIPPOLYTUS, ORIGEN-JEROME) that were brought to Nebuchadnezzar, who, at this time, demonstrated his goodness and kindness toward the Jews (HIPPOLYTUS). The two elders who brought the unjust accusations against Susanna are figures of the persecutors of the church; their names are to be found in Jeremiah (HIPPOLYTUS, ORIGEN-JEROME). Both the Jews and the pagans attack the church of God (HIPPOLYTUS).

This account of Susanna's testing is also a source of advice for the practical life (ORIGEN-JEROME). THE example of the good and the wicked reflect the Christian challenge of every age (HIPPOLYTUS). Passions attack the souls of the wicked as well as the good, but with different reactions from the subject of the attack (ORIGEN-JEROME). Sometimes these attacks can lead to death, which also is another name for sin (ORIGEN-JEROME). Those who give in to these attacks and do not repent are the wicked who then are judged (HIPPOLYTUS), but there is salvation for those who avail themselves of repentance and baptism (HIPPOLYTUS).

The elders, however, were unrepentant, reflecting the image of the devil and of the persecutors of the church (HIPPOLYTUS). GOD was not fooled by their appearance of piety, nor is he fooled by ours (AUGUSTINE). Susanna was ultimately vindicated despite their accusations against her, just as believers will one day be vindicated despite the cry of the wicked against them before the world (HIPPOLYTUS). The wicked do not share the devil's nature, but they do follow his suggestions (DIDYMUS). We must guard ourselves against the snares of the devil, which can manifest itself in those who seek to seduce through their appearance (HIPPOLYTUS). At times such as these, we should offer up a silent prayer to the Lord, which he will hear in the face of temptation and trial (AUGUSTINE). Daniel had such trust in his Lord and was inspired by the Holy Spirit when he offered his prayer to God (CYRIL OF JERUSALEM). God hears the prayer of those who are sometimes hidden (HIPPOLYTUS). Let us pray lest we become Canaanites who dwelled apart from God's people

(ORIGEN), realizing that our salvation depends on faith and not on the flesh or our own strength (HILARY OF POITIERS).

The curse spoken against the elders reminds us of the messiness and unforeseen consequences of sin, as God's curse passes on from parents to their children (CHRYSOSTOM). This story and some of the names contained in it not only demonstrate that the story itself was originally composed in Greek (JEROME) but also have significance beyond the immediate narrative, as the names of the characters are symbols of the church (AMMONIUS).

A GREEK ADDITION. JULIUS AFRICANUS: This episode is an elegantly written text, but apart from this, it can be demonstrated that it is clearly a work of literary fiction that should be rejected as more recent for many reasons. When Susanna was condemned to death,[1] she protests that the decision was unjust.[2] First of all, Daniel consistently prophesies in a different way, by means of visions and dreams or by receiving the manifestation of an angel but never by prophetic inspiration.[3] . . . When one of the elders says, "Under a mastic tree"[4] (*prinos*), he answers that "the angel will cleave him in two"[5] (*prisein*). And in a similar way he threatens the other who says, "Under an evergreen oak"[6] (*schinos*) and that he will hew you down (*schisthenai*). It happens that in Greek these words introduce assonances (*prinos* with *prisai* and *schinos* with *schisai*), while in Hebrew they are completely different sounding.[7] Instead, all the admitted parts of the Old Testament from the Hebrew have been translated from the Hebrew into Greek. . . . The more important fact is that this episode, together with the other two that are at the end,[8] are not found in the text of Daniel received from the Hebrew. LETTER TO ORIGEN 3-5, 7.[9]

1 (13:1 LXX) *In Babylon*

CHRONOLOGY IS NOT ALWAYS FOLLOWED IN THE SCRIPTURE. HIPPOLYTUS: What is nar-

rated here happened at a later time, although it is placed at the beginning of the book.[10] For it was a custom with the writers to narrate many things in an inverted order in their writings. We also find in the prophets some visions recorded in the past tense but which were fulfilled only later. Again, some are recorded as future events but have already been fulfilled. And this was done by the disposition of the Spirit so that the devil might not understand the things spoken in parables by the prophets and might not a second time lay his snares and ruin humanity. COMMENTARY ON DANIEL 1.5.2-4.[11]

2-4 (13:2-4 LXX) *The Family and Training of Susanna*

SUSANNA'S FAMILY. HIPPOLYTUS: This Joakim who lived in Babylon took Susanna as his wife. She was the daughter of Hilkiah,[12] the priest who had found the Book of the Law in the house of the Lord when King Josiah had ordered him to purify the holy of holies.[13] His brother is Jeremiah the prophet, who, like those who remained after the deportation of the people to Babylon, went to Egypt and lived in Taphne,[14] where he was stoned to death by them while he was prophesying.[15] Susanna, being of the priestly line, of the tribe of Levi, intermarried with the tribe of Judah, thus in herself joining these two righteous tribes from whom the righteous seed

---

[1]Sus 41 (Dan 13:41 LXX). [2]Sus 46-49 (Dan 13:46-49 LXX). [3]Perhaps this phrase voices some skepticism about the prophetical nature of the book of Daniel, which was controversial in Judaism. [4]Sus 58 (Dan 13:58 LXX). [5]Sus 59 (Dan 13:59 LXX). [6]Sus 54 (Dan 13:54 LXX). [7]The same objection reappears in Jerome, who is quoted below. [8]Julius Africanus is referring to the stories of Bel and the dragon (Dan 14 LXX). [9]SC 302:514-18. [10]Hippolytus follows Theodotion's revision, which places the story of Susanna before the beginning of Daniel, whereas in the Septuagint it is Dan 13. [11]SC 14:78. [12]The description of Susanna's kin appears in several ancient authors, but it has no scriptural foundation. [13]See 2 Kings 22:3-10 (4 Kings 22:3-10 LXX); 2 Chron 14:8-14. [14]The city of Taphne, called Daphne in the Hellenistic period, is the present-day Defenneh, in northern Egypt. [15]See Jer 43:7-9 (50:7-9 LXX); 44:1 (51:1 LXX). The legend of Jeremiah's stoning appears in several apocryphal texts, namely, in the Lives of the Prophets.

of Christ would appear, and thus he who was born from them in Bethlehem[16] was manifested as a priest of God.[17] Matthew, in fact, wanting to follow the pure and untainted genealogy along the line of Joseph,[18] when he reached Josiah, omitted his five sons and mentioned Jeconiah, who was born in Babylon from Susanna, passing over one righteous seed in favor of another righteous seed. It says, in fact, "Josiah begat Jeconiah and his siblings at the time of the deportation of Babylon."[19] COMMENTARY ON DANIEL 1.12.2-6.[20]

A HOLY DAUGHTER FROM HOLY PARENTS. HIPPOLYTUS: Trees are easily recognized from the fruit they have produced.[21] Being devout and full of zeal for the law[22] they bear to the world worthy sons of God, that is, the prophet and witness of Christ[23] and the one who from Babylon has been found tested and faithful,[24] who has manifested the holiness and the wisdom of the blessed Daniel. COMMENTARY ON DANIEL 1.13.2.[25]

DAUGHTERS ALSO SHOULD LEARN THE LAW. ORIGEN (VIA JEROME): It is well to make use of this testimony in order to exhort parents to educate with the divine law and testimony of God not only their sons but also their daughters. STROMATEIS 10 (VIA ON DANIEL 13.3).[26]

NEBUCHADNEZZAR'S GOODNESS. HIPPOLYTUS: It is opportune to ask how those who were captives and had been enslaved by the Babylonian could gather together in the same place as if they were free. It must be known that after he deported them, Nebuchadnezzar dealt with them in a humane way and permitted them to meet together and to do all things according to the law. COMMENTARY ON DANIEL 1.13.4-5.[27]

5 (13:5 LXX) *Two Elderly Men Elected Judges*

FIGURES OF THE PERSECUTORS OF THE CHURCH. HIPPOLYTUS: Susanna had to endure this from of old, and we still must endure under the princes of Babylon. Susanna was a figure of the church; her husband Joakim, a figure of Christ. The garden that was found near the house represented the communion of saints, planted like fruitful trees[28] in the middle of the church. Babylon is the world. The two elders are figures of the two peoples who conspire against the church, one of the circumcision and the other of the Gentiles.[29] COMMENTARY ON DANIEL 1.14.5-6.[30]

JEREMIAH INDICATES THEIR NAMES. ORIGEN (VIA JEROME): A Hebrew informed us that they were Achiah and Zedekiah, those whom "the king of Babylon roasted in the fire because their conduct in Israel was an outrage, having committed adultery with the wives of their neighbors."[31] STROMATEIS 10 (VIA ON DANIEL 13.5A).[32]

7 (13:7 LXX) *Susanna Walks in Her Husband's Garden*

ADVICE FOR PRACTICAL LIFE. ORIGEN (VIA JEROME): "In the morning"[33] Susanna went to take a walk. It is not at all out of place (in order to pacify those who find examples in the sacred writing for everything that we do) to take a walk at a time such as this, for example, since back then one did well to take a walk in order to keep his own body healthy. STROMATEIS 10 (VIA ON DANIEL 13.8B-9).[34]

8-11 (13:8-11 LXX) *Taken by a Burning Passion for Her*

SCRIPTURE RECORDS THE ACTIONS OF THE

---

[16]See Mt 2:1-6; which indicates the tribe of Judah. [17]The tribe of Levi. [18]See Mt 1:16. [19]Mt 1:11. [20]SC 14:90-92. [21]See Mt 12:33; Lk 6:43. [22]See Acts 21:20. [23]Allusion to Jeremiah. [24]Susanna. [25]SC 14:94. [26]Trad. Cola 203. [27]SC 14:94-96. [28]See Ps 1:3. [29]Hippolytus writes at the beginning of the third century, when Christians were still actively persecuted. [30]SC 14:96-98. [31]Jer 29:22-23. [32]Trad. Cola 203. [33]With a variant of unknown origin, since Susanna's walk is placed "in the afternoon" or the evening (LXX) and "after noon" by Theodotion. [34]Trad. Cola 204.

GOOD AND THE BAD. HIPPOLYTUS: The leaders of the Jews want to eliminate this episode from the Scriptures,[35] insinuating that none of this happened in Babylon, because they are ashamed of what the elders did then. The economy of the Father does not acknowledge this line of argument since the sacred Scriptures, without qualification and with all frankness, tell us everything, not only the just actions of the people who were saved by what they accomplished but also the scandalous lives of some whose conduct led to their own perdition. In such a way, fortified by the fear of God, we will hurry to imitate the righteous in order to be saved like they were, but those who have done the opposite will have under their eyes the sentence that will be sent from God. COMMENTARY ON DANIEL 1.14.2-4.[36]

THOSE WHO ALREADY ARE WICKED. ORIGEN (VIA JEROME): The Greek word *pathos* is better rendered for us with the term "disturbance"[37] rather than with the term "passion." Therefore this disturbed and covetous desire stimulated, or rather it churned violently, in the heart of the elders. But because their souls were like plowed soil and they could only think about getting what they desired, their own feelings became perverted, and, once perverted, their eyes were turned toward earth so that they did not see the celestial truths, and they forgot about sound judgment, they forgot about God, about honesty, about the nature oriented toward the good inborn in every person. STROMATEIS 10 (VIA ON DANIEL 13.8B-9).[38]

DISAGREEMENT BETWEEN THE PERSECUTORS OF THE CHURCH. HIPPOLYTUS: These words are easily understood: the two peoples, incited by Satan who is working in them, never stop trying to raise up persecutions and tribulations against the church. They try to destroy it, but they are not in agreement with each other. COMMENTARY ON DANIEL 1.15.4.[39]

13 (13:13 LXX) *Time for Lunch*

DISAGREEMENT BETWEEN JEWS AND PAGANS. HIPPOLYTUS: These words indicate that, with regard to food, the Jews are not in agreement with the Gentiles; but in their ideas and in all the other affairs of this world, they are of one mind and can agree with one another. COMMENTARY ON DANIEL 1.15.5.[40]

14 (13:14 LXX) *Each Confessed His Passion*

THE VERDICT ON THE WICKED. HIPPOLYTUS: Thus in revealing themselves to each other they look toward the time when suddenly they will be interrogated by the angels in order to render to God an account of all the sins they have done, according to the word of Solomon, "The interrogation will destroy the impious."[41] COMMENTARY ON DANIEL 1.15.6.[42]

15 (13:15 LXX) *A Favorable Opportunity*

AN IMAGE OF BAPTISM. HIPPOLYTUS: Which is the favorable day if not that of Passover? This is the day in which the laver is prepared in the garden for those who burn with lust; and the church, washed like Susanna, is presented to God as a young and pure spouse. And, like the two attendants who accompanied Susanna,[43] faith and charity prepare the oil and the ointments for those who come to be washed. What do the ointments signify? The commandments of the Word. The oil is nothing other than the gifts of the Spirit. With these the faithful come scented with the anointing that takes place after the laver of washing. These things were prefigured here in the blessed Susanna for our sake. COMMENTARY ON DANIEL 1.16.2-4.[44]

---

[35]Hippolytus knows that the stories are absent from Daniel's Semitic text. [36]SC 14:96-97. [37]In other words, to be disturbed greatly. [38]Trad. Cola 204. [39]SC 14:98. [40]SC 14:98. [41]Prov 1:32 LXX. [42]SC 14:98. [43]Cf. Sus 15 (Dan 13:15 LXX). [44]SC 14:100.

18 (13:18 LXX) *Entering by the Side Gate*

THE NARROW DOOR OF BAPTISM. HIPPOLY-TUS: Thus here it is symbolized that anyone who wants to partake of the water that flows in the garden[45] must renounce the gate that is wide and enter through the tight and narrow door.[46] COMMENTARY ON DANIEL 1.18.3.[47]

THE ELDERS ARE IMAGES OF THE DEVIL. HIPPOLYTUS: Thus just as in paradise the devil hid in the snake, also now, hidden in the elders, it has conceived desire in order to corrupt Eve anew.[48] COMMENTARY ON DANIEL 1.18.4.[49]

21 (13:21 LXX) *We Will Accuse You*

THE STRATAGEMS OF THE PERSECUTORS. HIPPOLYTUS: Listening to these words, the blessed Susanna was troubled in her heart and set a watch on her mouth since she did not want to be contaminated by the impious elders. It is possible to truly understand what happened to Susanna, you see, since you find the same thing fulfilled now also with the church. When, in fact, the two peoples come to an agreement in order to corrupt some of the saints, they wait for the appropriate moment and then penetrate into the house of God, while all are praying and singing hymns to God, and they drag outside some of those they seize, saying, "Come, consent with us and worship our gods; otherwise we will denounce you." If they do not consent, they drag them before the court and accuse them of acting contrary to the law of Caesar and condemn them to death. COMMENTARY ON DANIEL 1.20.1-3.[50]

22 (13:22 LXX) *Trapped on Every Side*

ANOTHER NAME FOR SIN. ORIGEN (VIA JEROME): He calls sin death. In the same way, therefore, that for the one who commits adultery, adultery is death, so every sin that leads to death must be called death. And we are convinced that we die every time we sin mortally, whereas we rise again and recover life every time we do works worthy of life. STROMATEIS 10 (VIA ON DANIEL 13.22).[51]

23-24 (13:23-24 LXX) *Susanna Chooses Not to Sin*

GOD SEES BEYOND APPEARANCE. AUGUSTINE: "It is better for me not to escape your hands than to sin in front of God." She refused the proposals she heard because she feared him who she could not see and to whose divine gaze, however, she was very visible. Because she did not happen, in fact, to see God does not mean that God did not see her. God saw what he was building up: he inspected his work, inhabited his temple. He was there; he was answering their insidious trap. If the giver of chastity had abandoned her, chastity also would have been extinguished. Therefore she said, "I am trapped on every side." But she waited for the one who would save her from weakness of spirit and from the fury of the false witnesses who were like stormy winds. Between these winds and that storm, however, chastity did not suffer shipwreck because the Lord guided the route. She screamed. People came. The process began, and the case came up for judgment. The servants of Susanna believed what the imposter elders said against their mistress. It seemed to them that it would be against their religion not to believe the elders, even though the innocent and stainless life Susanna had led up to this point seemed to offer valid testimony of her chastity. No such chatter had been made on her account. There they were, false witnesses, but God noticed. The household believed one thing; God saw another. But what God saw, human beings did not know, and it seemed right to believe the elders. Therefore she had to die, but if her flesh were to die, her chastity still would have triumphed. Instead, the

---

[45]Allusion to baptism, which is received in the garden, as a symbol of the church. [46]See Mt 7:13-14; Lk 13:23-24. [47]SC 14:106-7. [48]See Gen 3:1-7. [49]SC 14:106. [50]SC 14:108-10. [51]Trad. Cola 205.

Lord was present to whom she prayed, and he heard because he knew her. SERMON 343.1.[52]

THE WICKED CRY OUT AGAINST BELIEVERS. HIPPOLYTUS: And to whom did Susanna cry out? She cried out to God, as Isaiah says, "Then you will call, and the Lord will answer you; while you are still speaking, he will say, Here I am."[53] "And the two elders cried out against her." The wicked never stop crying out against us and say, Away with such people from the earth, for it is not fitting that they should live.[54] COMMENTARY ON DANIEL 1.23.2-3.[55]

28 (13:28 LXX) *Perverse Intention*

THE WICKED GIVE THE DEVIL ROOM. DIDYMUS THE BLIND: The devil does not fill someone or dwell in him by participation in his nature or being, as some think, but is thought to dwell in someone whom he has filled with confusion, deception and wickedness. With this same deception he entered the old men, who became cruel toward Susanna, and filled their souls with the passion of lust and the belated will of old age. In fact, it is written, "The two old men arrived, full of evil intentions." He also filled the entire Jewish people with these deceptions. As the prophet says, "Woe to you, sinful nation, a people full of sins, evil seed, corrupt children."[56] "Evil seed" is the devil, and his children are called "sinners" because of their surpassing wickedness. If, therefore, those who are called "his children" in the Scriptures do not possess the devil according to a participation in being—because this has been shown, more than once, to be impossible in creatures—then neither can anyone else receive him by participation in his being but only by taking on an extremely treacherous will. ON THE HOLY SPIRIT, APPENDIX.61.[57]

31 (13:31 LXX) *Delicate in Appearance*

BEAUTY IS MORE THAN SKIN DEEP. HIPPOLYTUS: Her beauty was not, in fact, the beauty of the body of a prostitute, like the beauty painted on the body of Jezebel[58] or the face that is made up with makeup of all colors. Rather, it was the beauty of faith, wisdom and holiness. COMMENTARY ON DANIEL 1.25.3.[59]

44 (13:44 LXX) *The Lord Heard Susanna*

THE LORD HEARS ALSO A SILENT PRAYER. AUGUSTINE: "With my voice I have cried to the Lord." I have not, that is, cried with the voice of the body, whose sound is made from the vibration of the air, but with the voice of the heart that is silent for human beings but sounds like an outcry to God. Susanna was heard by this voice. With this voice the Lord has taught to us to pray without sound in the secret places, that is, in the recesses of the heart.[60] Nor would one say that we pray less intensely because of the fact that no word comes out of our mouth. In fact, when we pray silently in our heart, if alien thoughts come to distract the mind of one who prays, we cannot anymore say, "With my voice I have cried to the Lord."[61] We can rightly say these words only when the soul—without being dragged down with the flesh and having no sexual purposes in mind—alone speaks to the Lord. Then this prayer can be truly called an "outcry" because of the vigor of the tension that the soul experiences. "And he has heard me from his holy mountain."[62] From the prophet the Lord called a mountain where it is written that the stone that was cut without human hands has grown into the grandeur of a mountain.[63] EXPOSITIONS OF THE PSALMS 3.4.[64]

45 (13:45 LXX) *The Lord Stirred the Spirit of Daniel*

DANIEL WAS INSPIRED BY THE HOLY SPIRIT. CYRIL OF JERUSALEM: The Spirit endued the soul

---

[52]NBA 34:37-39. [53]Is 58:9. [54]Acts 22:22. [55]SC 14:112. [56]Is 1:4 LXX. [57]CTP 89:154. [58]See 2 Kings 9:30 (4 Kings 9:30 LXX). [59]SC 14:114-15. [60]See Mt 6:6. [61]Ps 3:5. [62]Ps 3:5. [63]See Dan 2:35. [64]NBA 25:21-23.

of Daniel with wisdom so that, young as he was, he became a judge of elders. The chaste Susanna was condemned as a wanton harlot. There was no one to plead her case, for who was to deliver her from the rulers? She was led away to death; she was now in the hands of the executioners. But her Helper was close at hand, the Comforter, the Spirit who sanctifies every rational nature. Come here to me, he says to Daniel. Even though you are young, convict old men infected with the sins of youth. For it is written, God raised up the Holy Spirit on a young lad; and nevertheless (to pass on quickly) by the sentence of Daniel that chaste woman was saved. We bring this forward as testimony since this is not the time for expounding further. Nebuchadnezzar also knew that the Holy Spirit was in Daniel because he says to him, "O Belteshazzar, master of the magicians, I know about you that the Holy Spirit of God is in you."[65] One thing he said truly, and one falsely. Daniel did have the Holy Spirit, that was true; but he was not the master of the magicians because he was no magician. His wisdom came through the Holy Spirit. And before this he had also interpreted for Nebuchadnezzar the vision of the image that he who had seen it did not himself understand.[66] For he says, Tell me the vision, which I who saw it do not know.[67] See the power of the Holy Spirit: those who saw it did not know, while those who did not see it did know and interpreted. CATECHETICAL LECTURES 16.31.[68]

46 (13:46 LXX) *Innocent of Her Blood*

GOD INTERVENES FOR THOSE WHO ARE HIS. HIPPOLYTUS: Let us examine why this visitation of the Lord did not take place before her condemnation but at the moment in which they were taking her away to death. This happens so that the power of God would shine forth. When he wants to save one of his servants, he saves him when he wants to and how he wants to. When he wants the trial to end, he waits patiently, to glorify and crown his servant like

a good athlete. When Susanna finished praying and was heard, the angel of the Lord was sent to her, he who is the avenger and helper, to defeat her enemies. When Daniel saw the angel's haste, being a prophet and having the Spirit of God, he shouted, "I am innocent of her blood!" so as not to be responsible for her death with the others. Pilate acted in the same way before the Lord, washing his hands and saying, "I am not responsible for this blood."[69] COMMENTARY ON DANIEL 1.27.[70]

54 (13:54 LXX) *Under a Mastic Tree*

A WORD PLAY WITH THE GREEK NAMES OF THE TREES. JEROME: "And a little while after the elder said, 'Under the mastic tree.' And Daniel answered him, 'You have lied well—but against your own head; here in fact is the angel of God with a sword for cleaving you in two.'" Since the Hebrews do not accept the story of Susanna asserting that it is not contained in the book of Daniel, we must carefully assess if the words *schini* and *prini* (which mean mastic tree and evergreen oak) exist in the Jewish language and what their etymology is—if, that is, in their [i.e., the Hebrew] language *schino* derives from the word "to cleave" and *prino* from the word "to divide" or "to saw."[71] If we do not succeed in this attempt, we are necessarily forced to accept those whose position is that this pericope only exists in Greek because it contains etymology that is found only in the Greek and not in the Hebrew. But if someone finds that the words "to cleave" and "to divide" also have the same etymological root as those two trees in the Hebrew, then we will be able to accept this pericope as Scripture as well.

---

[65]Dan 4:6. [66]Cf. Dan 2:31-45. [67]See Dan 2:26. [68]CTP 103:372-73. [69]Mt 27:24. This quotation implies that the Jews, and not the Roman authorities, were responsible for Jesus' death. [70]SC 14:119-21. [71]Jerome explains that the story uses word plays that are possible only in Greek: in Sus 54-55 between *schinos* ("mastic tree") and *schizō* ("to divide, to tear"); in Sus 58-59 between *prinos* ("evergreen oak") and *katapriō* ("to saw"). This fact confirms his dismissal of the parts that are not extant in Hebrew.

COMMENTARY ON DANIEL 13.54-55.[72]

56 (13:56 LXX) *Seduced and Perverted*

LET US NOT BECOME AS THE CANAANITES.
ORIGEN: Let us pay attention, just as Joshua
says, so that we can prevail over the Canaanites,[73] because if they prevail over us and hold
us captive, they may turn us from Israelites to
Canaanites, just as it happened to him who was
won over by the enticements of the flesh, to
which the prophet said, "Race of Canaan and
not of Judah, beauty has seduced you." Let it not
happen to us, therefore, that we hear, "race of
Canaan," because "cursed is the son of Canaan;
he will be a servant to his brothers."[74] May the
Lord instead grant that we may be children of
Abraham, Isaac and Jacob, heirs according to
the promise[75] and brought forth from stones[76] so
that we may be children of Abraham, in Christ
Jesus our Lord. HOMILIES ON JOSHUA 22.6.[77]

SALVATION COMES FROM FAITH. HILARY OF
POITIERS: Salvation was awaited by and offered
to Israel but not to the carnal Israel. "In fact, it is
not the children of the flesh who are the children
of God, but the children of the promise who are
considered his offspring."[78] As John also attests,
the children of Abraham are not the children according to the flesh, since they are also children
of vipers,[79] and God can raise up children of
Abraham from rocks.[80] The Lord taught that
the right of succession is constituted by works
of faith and that we must not think of the birth
of children according to carnal generation, when
he says, "If you were children of Abraham, you
would do the works that Abraham did."[81] And
Daniel also, condemning the old men, does not
say, "offspring of Abraham," but, "offspring of
Canaan and not of Judah." Ezekiel also, confronting the people with their iniquities, says,
"Your father was a Canaanite, your mother a
Hittite. Your origin and your birth are of the
land of Canaan."[82] We are not dealing, therefore,
with this Israel that comes from carnal succes-

sion and to which is attributed the birth of a
generation that is wholly profane because of its
unbelief. It is not to this Israel, therefore, that
salvation is given, because they did not accept it
when it was offered, but to that other who, their
slavery ended, has become the people of God.
HOMILIES ON THE PSALMS 52.19.[83]

**GOD'S CURSES PASS FROM PARENTS TO
CHILDREN.** JOHN CHRYSOSTOM: Ham receives
the sentence so that he might come to his
senses, and he is punished through his son,[84]
so that you would learn that even if one is old,
the punishment will pass to the child. And this
makes his life bitter and painful, knowing that
even after his death his son will be punished for
what he did. And that the son will be miserable
from birth and all his descendants detestable
and inclined to evil is what the Scripture says
instead of pronouncing a curse: "Your father was
an Amorite and your mother a Hittite."[85] And
elsewhere it says scornfully, "offspring of Canaan
and not of Judah." HOMILIES ON GENESIS 29.7.[86]

63 (13:63 LXX) *Hilkiah, Susanna, Joakim*

THE NAMES ARE SYMBOLS OF THE CHURCH.
AMMONIUS OF ALEXANDRIA: This is the text of
the story, but an allegory can also be drawn from
the letter. Hilkiah in fact means "alteration of
God" or "praise of God." Susanna means "their
praise" or "apostolic lily." Joakim, "disposition
of the Lord" or "praise of the Lord." Daniel,
"judgment of God" and "God is judge."[87] When,
therefore, the joy of the souls of the church, who
are pleasing to God—that is, the apostolic lily,
the sweet-smelling flower, the spiritual aroma,
the daughter of Hilkiah who learned from her
parents to act according to the tradition of the
prophets (who are the food and the inheritance

[72]Trad. Cola 207. [73]See Josh 17:18. [74]Gen 9:25. [75]See Gal
3:9. [76]See Mt 3:9; Lk 3:8; see also Mt 16:18. [77]CTP 108:283-84.
[78]Rom 9:8. [79]See Mt 3:7; Lk 3:7. [80]See Mt 3:9; Lk 3:8. [81]Jn 8:39.
[82]Ezek 16:3. [83]CTP 185:234-35. [84]See Gen 9:25. [85]Ezek 16:3.
[86]PG 53:270-71. [87]Such etymologies are fairly common.

of Israel)—unites with Christ, the spiritual spouse, who is Joakim, the spiritual spouse of the church—the one who prepares for the faithful the goods of the world to come, announcing the kingdom of heaven and making them participants of the Holy Spirit[88] (who is worthy of praise forever, amen)—then the godless judges of the people will suddenly arise. If, however, they cannot corrupt her soul with forbidden dogma, killing it (this is in fact the death of the soul), then they give the body over to the senseless, unreasoning mob to be sacrificed. And if God permits the suffering of the spouse, he places the crown of martyrdom on her. And

if instead he frees her from the hands of her enemies,[89] then also he honors her, keeping her near himself. Those who plot against her are in any case condemned to Gehenna by God's just judgment,[90] pronounced over them by Daniel, whose name is translated "judgment of God." The old men have no name, like the rich man spoken of by Luke, who did not pity Lazarus's sores.[91] FRAGMENT.[92]

---

[88]See Heb 6:4. [89]See Ps 31:16 (30:16 LXX). [90]See 2 Macc 9:18. [91]See Lk 16:20-25. [92]PG 85:1368-69.

BEL AND THE DRAGON

1-22* DANIEL AND THE PRIESTS OF BEL

^{1}When King Astyages was laid with his fathers, Cyrus the Persian received his kingdom. ^{2}And Daniel was a companion of the king, and was the most honored of his friends.

^{3}Now the Babylonians had an idol called Bel, and every day they spent on it twelve bushels of fine flour and forty sheep and fifty gallons of wine. ^{4}The king revered it and went every day to worship it. But Daniel worshiped his own God.

^{5}And the king said to him, "Why do you not worship Bel?" He answered, "Because I do not revere man-made idols, but the living God, who created heaven and earth and has dominion over all flesh."

^{6}The king said to him, "Do you not think that Bel is a living God? Do you not see how much he eats and drinks every day?" ^{7}Then Daniel laughed, and said, "Do not be deceived, O king; for this is but clay inside and brass outside, and it never ate or drank anything."

^{8}Then the king was angry, and he called his priests and said to them, "If you do not tell me who is eating these provisions, you shall die. ^{9}But if you prove that Bel is eating them, Daniel shall die, because he blasphemed against Bel." And Daniel said to the king, "Let it be done as you have said."

^{10}Now there were seventy priests of Bel, besides their wives and children. And the king went with Daniel into the temple of Bel. ^{11}And the priests of Bel said, "Behold, we are going outside; you yourself, O king, shall set forth the food and mix and place the wine, and shut the door and seal it with your signet. ^{12}And when you return in the morning, if you do not find that Bel has eaten it all, we will die; or else Daniel will, who is telling lies about us." ^{13}They were unconcerned, for beneath the table they had made a hidden entrance, through which they used to go in regularly and consume the provisions. ^{14}When they had gone out, the king set forth the food for Bel. Then Daniel ordered his servants to bring ashes and they sifted them throughout the whole temple in the presence of the king alone. Then they went out, shut the door and sealed it with the king's signet, and departed. ^{15}In the night the priests came with their wives and children, as they were accustomed to do, and ate and drank everything.

^{16}Early in the morning the king rose and came, and Daniel with him. ^{17}And the king said, "Are the seals unbroken, Daniel?" He answered, "They are unbroken, O king." ^{18}As soon as the doors were opened, the king looked at the table, and shouted in a loud voice, "You are great, O Bel; and with you there is no deceit, none at all."

^{19}Then Daniel laughed, and restrained the king from going in, and said, "Look at the floor, and notice whose footsteps these are." ^{20}The king said, "I see the footsteps of men and women and children."

²¹*Then the king was enraged, and he seized the priests and their wives and children; and they showed him the secret doors through which they were accustomed to enter and devour what was on the table.* ²²*Therefore the king put them to death, and gave Bel over to Daniel, who destroyed it and its temple.*

*In the manuscripts, the story of Bel is placed at the end of the book of Daniel. Modern editions make various choices, either publishing it as an independent account or as Daniel 14, or even as Daniel 13, if Susanna is considered a separate story.

OVERVIEW: The Scripture uses the word *flesh* to designate the human being (ATHANASIUS). God, however, has no need of the things of the flesh as though he would get hungry or tired (PSEUDO-CHRYSOSTOM). The temptations of the flesh, such as eating and drinking in excess, are the cause of most of the ills of humanity (PALLADIUS).

5 (14:5 LXX) *God Has Dominion Over All Flesh*

THE WORD FLESH INDICATES THE HUMAN BEING. ATHANASIUS: "The Logos," as John said, "was made flesh."[1] Scripture, in fact, has the habit of indicating people with the term "flesh," as when it says by the mouth of the prophet Joel, "I will pour out my Spirit on all flesh,"[2] and as Daniel said to Astyages, "I do not adore idols made by the hands of people, but the living God, who has created the sky and the earth and has power over all flesh,"[3] for he and Joel identify the flesh with the human race. DISCOURSES AGAINST THE ARIANS 3.30.5.[4]

6 (14:6 LXX) *Bel Not a Living God?*

GOD NEEDS NO MATERIAL OBJECTS. PSEUDO-CHRYSOSTOM: Ah! What a great sign of acknowledgment—that a god eats and drinks a lot! Daniel did not say, "Master, this could never be God" (the king in fact was a weak person) but instead explained, "I speak to you about the God who created the earth and the sky,[5] and you speak to me about such utter nonsense? Surely this would not be something that matters to God. God in fact does not have hunger, nor does he get tired."[6] ON DANIEL 13.[7]

15 (14:15 LXX) *The Priests Ate and Drank Everything*

EATING AND DRINKING IN EXCESS. PALLADIUS: Which damage does not derive from the excess of eating and drinking? Diseases, strife and all kinds of problems derive from the satiety of the belly, with all their consequences. When did it happen that Eve went out looking for something outside of paradise? Was it not perhaps when she listened to the snake and ate of the fruit of the tree in order to please herself with the fruit that had been forbidden to her?[8] When did it happen that Cain decided to commit the abomination of killing his brother? Was it not perhaps when he tasted the fruit of the firstfruits, reserving the best for his own appetite?[9] When did it happen that the sons of Job suddenly found their tombs in the same place as they were eating? Was it not perhaps while they were attempting to eat and to drink [to excess]?[10] When did it happen that Esau fell from divine blessing? Was it not perhaps when, for the attraction of the gullet, he became a slave to his belly?[11] When did it happen that Saul fell from his royal status? Was it not perhaps when he ate the meat of the precious sheep against the prohibition of the law?[12] When did it happen that the people of Israel provoked the temper of

---

[1]Jn 1:14. [2]Joel 2:28. [3]Bel 5 (Dan 14:5 LXX). Athanasius makes reference to the Greek text, where the word *sarx* (literally "flesh") is used. In the Septuagint, *sarx* carries over the additional meanings of the Hebrew as "living being" or even "human being." In modern translations it is more common to find one of these expanded meanings. [4]CTP 173:287. [5]See Gen 1:1. [6]Is 40:28. [7]PG 56: 244. [8]See Gen 3:1-13, 22-24. [9]See Gen 4:3-8. [10]See Job 1:11-19. [11]See Gen 25:29-34. [12]See 1 Sam 15:1-23.

God? Was it not perhaps when they mourned for the dishes of the Egyptians, expecting from their leader meats and pots of stew?[13] Hofni and Phineas, Eli's sons, how is it that they did not survive even a single hour but were killed in battle? Was it not perhaps because they secretly stole the offerings of meat destined for the sacrifice?[14] And as for Jacob, one who was naturally blameworthy, is it not that he began revolting "when he ate and was not filled up, he grew fat and became thick and broad"?[15] And when did it happen that the Sodomites took to stimulating themselves against the laws of nature? Was it not perhaps when they corrupted their minds in their continuous banquets?[16] This in fact is what Ezekiel recalls to their shame when he says, "In the abundance of the wine and the satiety of the bread they abandoned helping others,"[17] and he says this regarding the city of Sodom. But then he adds, "And also her daughters," namely, the suburbs that always imitate the customs of the city. And what happened when the purpose of temperance was abandoned by that ancient people? Was it not perhaps when, in a similar way, they got older they began to lie around on the couch, which is how they are described with some disdain by the prophet: "They eat lambs from the flock, and the year-old calves are removed from the stable still nursing. And they drink filtered wine, after which they are massaged with precious ointments; they abandon themselves to the comfort of their couches, while they suffer nothing over the ruin of Joseph"?[18] And Isaiah, against whom has he turned his complaints? Is it not perhaps against those who rise up early in the morning in order to feast? And thus he exclaims, "Woe to those who rise up early in the morning and go in search of inebriating drinks, who hang around late in the evening until they are inflamed in their faces with wine; they drink the wine, accompanied by the lyre and harp, but they do not attend to the deeds of the Lord."[19] And when the priests of Bel were confounded by Daniel? Was it not perhaps when they left a trail through the ashes that their treachery was uncovered because they had gone to take the food and drinks meant for Daniel? DIALOGUE ON THE LIFE OF SAINT JOHN CHRYSOSTOM 12.[20]

---

[13]See Ex 16:2-3. [14]1 Sam 2:12-17; 4:11. [15]See Deut 32:15 LXX. [16]See Gen 13:13; Lk 17:28-29. [17]Ezek 16:49. [18]Amos 6:4-6. [19]Is 5:11-12. [20]CTP 125:186-88.

23-30 DANIEL KILLS THE DRAGON

[23]*There was also a great dragon, which the Babylonians revered.* [24]*And the king said to Daniel, "You cannot deny that this is a living god; so worship him."* [25]*Daniel said, "I will worship the Lord my God, for he is the living God.* [26]*But if you, O king, will give me permission, I will slay the dragon without sword or club." The king said, "I give you permission."*

[27]*Then Daniel took pitch, fat, and hair, and boiled them together and made cakes, which he fed to the dragon. The dragon ate them, and burst open. And Daniel said, "See what you have been worshiping!"*

²⁸*When the Babylonians heard it, they were very indignant and conspired against the king, saying, "The king has become a Jew; he has destroyed Bel, and slain the dragon, and slaughtered the priests." ²⁹Going to the king, they said, "Hand Daniel over to us, or else we will kill you and your household." ³⁰The king saw that they were pressing him hard, and under compulsion he handed Daniel over to them.*

OVERVIEW: The martyrs led the fight against the idols (PSEUDO-EPHREM).

THE MARTYRS' FIGHT AGAINST THE IDOLS.
PSEUDO-EPHREM: Christ has given to the martyred saints the power to defeat the inhuman plans of the tyrants. He has given to his soldiers all the necessary armor for this war, surrounding them from every side with "the shield of faith,"[1] with the armor of love[2] and a strong mind. He has provided their ramparts with "the sword of the Spirit,"[3] with which they cut off the head of the adversary. He has devastated the foundations of the temples of the idols, crushing the carved images as if they were light powder. He overturns the temples and the altars of the impure sacrifices and the illicit libation offerings, condemning to the fire the hideous dress of their caretakers and driving away the demons of the effigy who have been deceiving them and leading them to Gehenna. Seeing these things, the glorious martyrs, energized from the power of Christ, have conceived a desire more burning than to suffer for the power of his name. With their own hands they have overturned the images, casting down to earth all these monstrosities. And anywhere they found an effigy, they shattered it, throwing it down into the mud for the ultimate shame and derision of those who venerated and adored it. And they said to the governors and the tyrants, "Here is what you adored," things impotent, blind[4] and immovable—these weak things that you honored. You, equipped of reason, venerate dumb things, you, whom God has honored with his own image,[5] so that you would recognize his power and adore him with fear and trembling when you come to stand before him and come to understand who he is. He is in fact the God who is without beginning, strong, frightening and powerful, most glorious and invisible. Leaving the adoration of him who has made you, you adored the creation instead of the Creator.[6] He made the sun in order to illumine the day, so that enjoying its light and the heat, you would always glorify your Creator. And so he has allowed you to enjoy it. Instead, like blind people, you abandoned the Creator, preferring to adore the creature. Similarly, the Creator created the moon for you in order to dissipate the shadow of the night; you, like fools, imagining that the moon has replaced God, adore it instead of him. PRAISE OF THE MARTYRS.[7]

---

[1]Eph 6:16. [2]See 1 Thess 5:8. [3]Eph 6:17. [4]See Hab 2:18. [5]See Gen 1:26-27. [6]See Rom 1:25. [7]*ESOO* 2:310.

31-42 DANIEL IN THE LIONS' DEN

³¹*They threw Daniel into the lions' den, and he was there for six days.* ³²*There were seven lions in the den, and every day they had been given two human bodies and two sheep; but these were not given to them now, so that they might devour Daniel.*

³³*Now the prophet Habakkuk was in Judea. He had boiled pottage and had broken bread into a bowl, and was going into the field to take it to the reapers.* ³⁴*But the angel of the Lord said to Habakkuk, "Take the dinner which you have to Babylon, to Daniel, in the lions' den."* ³⁵*Habakkuk said, "Sir, I have never seen Babylon, and I know nothing about the den."* ³⁶*Then the angel of the Lord took him by the crown of his head, and lifted him by his hair and set him down in Babylon, right over the den, with the rushing sound of the wind itself.*

³⁷*Then Habakkuk shouted, "Daniel! Daniel! Take the dinner which God has sent you."* ³⁸*And Daniel said, "Thou hast remembered me, O God, and hast not forsaken those who love thee."* ³⁹*So Daniel arose and ate. And the angel of God immediately returned Habakkuk to his own place.*

⁴⁰*On the seventh day the king came to mourn for Daniel. When he came to the den he looked in, and there sat Daniel.* ⁴¹*And the king shouted with a loud voice, "Thou art great, O Lord God of Daniel, and there is no other besides thee."* ⁴²*And he pulled Daniel[a] out, and threw into the den the men who had attempted his destruction, and they were devoured immediately before his eyes.*

a Gk *him*

OVERVIEW: The story of Habakkuk shows that Jesus' ascension to heaven is possible (CYRIL OF JERUSALEM). It also reminds us that we should not forget our unworthiness before God (BARSANUPHIUS AND JOHN).

36 (14:36 LXX) *The Angel of the Lord Took Him*

HABAKKUK'S STORY SHOWS THAT JESUS REALLY ASCENDED TO HEAVEN. CYRIL OF JERUSALEM: When they object by saying that the ascension of the Savior is impossible, it will be well for you to recall to your memory what I have said to you about the carrying away of Habakkuk: if it were possible for an angel to take Habakkuk away by the hair of his head and to transport him from one place to another, there is even all the more reason for it to be possible for the Lord of the prophets and the angels to go up on a cloud and to ascend by virtue of his own power and with more power from on high from the Mount of Olives to the sky.[1] CATECHETICAL LECTURES 14.25.[2]

38 (14:38 LXX) *You Have Remembered Me, O God*

BEFORE GOD, WE ARE UNWORTHY. BARSANUPHIUS AND JOHN: How then, when you go to converse with others, is it that you move from charity and joy to exasperation and rancor, and

---

[1]See Lk 24:50-51; Acts 1:9. [2]CTP 103:311-12.

reproach your neighbor instead of yourself and do not say, "I am the dishonorable one," but even quite approve of yourself? Because, if the occasion arises, you say, "Speak, for I have spoken and will listen gladly." Who believes that they listen to your words gladly? Are you Elijah the prophet? Accuse yourself, and know that all of this that happens to you does not happen without the will of God, whether it is in the matter of rest that you yield thanks or an affliction that requires patience. Where is the word in Scripture, "You endure it when someone hits you in the face,"[3] and so on? For this is why we are far from God.

Therefore, if you want to learn the way, it is this: to consider the one who persecutes you like the one who cares for you; the one who despises you like the one who praises you; the one who insults you like the one who honors you; and the one who plagues you like the one who provides you with rest. And whether if, by forgetfulness or deliberately, they do not treat you in the way to which you are accustomed, do not get upset but say instead: If God intended this, they would have come. And when they do come, you receive them with a joyful face, rejoicing and thinking: the Lord has had mercy on me although I was unworthy; like Daniel, when the Lord went to visit him, he said only this: "You have remembered, Lord," judging himself unworthy. Book of Letters 68.[4]

---

[3]See 2 Cor 11:20. [4]CTP 93:142-43; cf. FC 113:91.

Early Christian Writers and the Documents Cited

The following table lists all the early Christian documents cited in this volume by author, if known, or by the title of the work. The English title used in this commentary is followed in parentheses with the Latin designation and, where available, the Thesaurus Linguae Graecae (=TLG) digital references or Cetedoc Clavis numbers. Printed sources of original language versions may be found in the bibliography of works in original languages.

Ambrose

Cain and Abel (*De Cain et Abel*)	Cetedoc 0125
Duties of the Clergy (*De officiis ministrorum*)	Cetedoc 0144
Expositions on the Psalms (*Enarrationes in XII Psalmos Davidicos*)	Cetedoc 0140
Hexameron (*Exameron*)	Cetedoc 0123
On Abraham (*De Abraham*)	Cetedoc 0127
On the Christian Faith (*De fide*)	Cetedoc 0150
On the Holy Spirit (*De Spiritu Sancto*)	Cetedoc 0151

Ambrosiaster

Commentary on the First Letter to the Corinthians (*Commentarius in Pauli epistulam ad i Corinthios*)	
Commentary on the Letter to the Romans (*Commentarius in Pauli epistulam ad Romanos*)	Cetedoc 0184c

Ammonius of Alexandria
Fragment (*Fragmenta*)

Andrew of Crete
Marian Homilies (*Homiliae XXI*)

Anonymous Anomoean
Commentary on Job (*In Job commentarius*)

Anonymous Italian
Sermons (*Sermones*)

Athanasius

Discourses Against the Arians (*Orationes tres contra Arianos*)	TLG 2035.042
Festal Letters (*Epistulae festales*)	TLG 2035.x01
Letter to Serapion (*Epistulae quattuor ad Serapionem*)	TLG 2035.043
On the Incarnation (*De incarnatione verbi*)	TLG 2035.002

Augustine

Christian Combat (*De agone christiano*)	Cetedoc 0296
Christian Instruction (*De doctrina Christiana*)	Cetedoc 0263
City of God (*De civitate Dei*)	Cetedoc 0313
Confessions (*Confessionum libri tredecim*)	Cetedoc 0251
Expositions of the Psalms (*Enarrationes in Psalmos*)	Cetedoc 0283
Newly Discovered Sermons (*Sermones*)	Cetedoc 0284
Of True Religion (*De vera religione*)	Cetedoc 0264
On Eighty-three Varied Questions (*De diversis quaestionibus octoginta tribus*)	Cetedoc 0289
On Genesis, Against the Manicheans (*De Genesi contra Manichaeos*)	Cetedoc 0265
On Lying (*De mendacio*)	Cetedoc 0303
On the Literal Interpretation of Genesis (*De Genesi ad litteram libri duodecimo*)	Cetedoc 0266
On the Trinity (*De Trinitate*)	Cetedoc 0329
On Various Questions to Simplicianus (*De diversis quaestionibus ad Simplicianum*)	Cetedoc 0290
Questions on the Heptateuch (*Quaestionum in heptateuchum libri septem*)	Cetedoc 0270
Retractations (*Retractationum libri duo*)	Cetedoc 0250
Sermons (*Sermones*)	Cetedoc 0284
Tractates on the Gospel of John (*In Johannis evangelium tractatus*)	Cetedoc 0278
Unfinished Literal Commentary on Genesis (*De Genesi ad litteram imperfectus liber*)	Cetedoc 0268
Unfinished Tractate Against Julian (*Contra Julianum opus imperfectum*)	Cetedoc 0356

Barsanuphius and John

Book of Letters

(*Quaestiones et responsiones*)	TLG 2851.001
(*Quaestiones et responsiones ad coenobitas [Epistulae 224-616]*)	TLG 2851.002
(*Quaestiones et responsiones ad laicos et episcopos [Epistulae 617-848]*)	TLG 2851.003

Basil the Great

On the Holy Spirit (*De Spiritu Sancto*)	TLG 2040.003
On the Martyr Julitta (*Homilia in martyrem Julittam*)	TLG 2040.023

Bede the Venerable

Homilies on the Gospels (*Homiliarum evangelii libri ii*)	Cetedoc 1367
On Tobit (*In librum beati patris Tobiae*)	Cetedoc 1350

Callinicus

Life of Hypatius (*Vita sancti Hypatii*)	TLG 2770.001

Cassian, John
Conferences (*Collationes*)   Cetedoc 0512

Cassiodorus
Explanation of the Psalms (*Expositio psalmorum*)   Cetedoc 0900
The Institutes (*Institutiones*)   Cetedoc 0906

Chromatius of Aquileia
Sermons (*Sermones*)   Cetedoc 0217 and 0217+
Tractate on Matthew (*Tractatus in Matthaeum*)   Cetedoc 0218

Clement of Alexandria
Christ the Educator (*Paedagogus*)   TLG 0555.002

Clement of Rome
1 Clement (*Epistula i ad Corinthios*)   TLG 1271.001

Cyprian of Carthage
The Dress of Virgins (*De habitu virginum*)   Cetedoc 0040
On Envy and Jealousy (*De zelo et livore*)   Cetedoc 0049
On Mortality (*De mortalitate*)   Cetedoc 0044
Works and Almsgiving (*De opere et eleemosynis*)   Cetedoc 0047

Cyril of Alexandria
Commentary on Malachi (*Commentarius in xii prophetas minores*)   TLG 4090.001
Commentary on Romans (*Fragmenta in sancti Pauli epistulam ad Romanos*)   TLG 4090.003
Commentary on the Gospel of John (*Commentarii in Joannem*)   TLG 4090.002
Commentary on Zachariah (*Commentarius in xii prophetas minores*)   TLG 4090.001
Fragment on 2 Corinthians (*Fragmenta in sancti Pauli epistulam ii ad Corinthios*)   TLG 4090.005

Cyril of Jerusalem
Catechetical Lectures (*Catecheses ad illuminandos*)   TLG 2110.003

Cyril/John of Jerusalem
Mystagogical Lectures (*Mystagogiae [Sp.]*)   TLG 2110.002

Dhuoda
Manual (*Manuale*)

Didymus the Blind
On Ecclesiastes (*In Ecclesiasten [11-12]*)   TLG 2102.007
On the Holy Spirit (*Liber de Spiritu Sancto*)   Cetedoc 0615
On the Psalms
    (*Commentarii in Psalmos*)   TLG 2102.018
    (*Commentarii in Psalmos*)   TLG 2102.019

Dionysius of Alexandria
To Dionysius of Rome (*Epistulae*)   TLG 2952.001

Dorotheus of Gaza
Spiritual Instructions (*Expositiones et doctrinae diversae animabus perutiles*)

Epiphanius of Salamis
Ancoratus (*Ancoratus*)   TLG 2021.001

Eucherius of Lyons
Book of Formulas (*Formulae spirituales*)
In Praise of Solitude (*De laude eremi*)
Renunciation of the World (*De contemptu mundi*)

Eusebius of Caesarea
Commentary on the Psalms (*Commentaria in Psalmos*)   TLG 2018.034

Evagrius of Pontus
Chapters on Prayer (*De oratione*)   TLG 4110.024

Fastidiosus
Sermons (*Sermo*)   Cetedoc 0708

Faustus of Riez
On Grace (*De gratia libri duo*)   Cetedoc 0961

Fulgentius of Ruspe
Against Fabianus (*Contra Fabianum fragmenta*)   Cetedoc 0824
Book to Victor Against the Sermon of Fastidiosus the Arian
   (*Liber ad Victorem contra sermonem Fastidiosi Ariani*)   Cetedoc 0820
Letter to Monimus (*Ad Monimum libri III*)   Cetedoc 0814
Letter to Peter on the Faith (*De fide ad Petrum seu De regula fidei*)   Cetedoc 0826
Letters (*Epistulae*)   Cetedoc 0817
On the Forgiveness of Sins (*Ad Euthymium de remissione peccatorum libri II*)   Cetedoc 0821
On the Incarnation (*Sermo dubius 2: Incarnationis divinae mysterium*)   Cetedoc 0841
On the Trinity, To Felix (*Liber de Trinitate ad Felicem*)   Cetedoc 0819
On the Truth of Predestination
   (*De veritate praedestinationis et gratiae libri III ad Johannem et Venerium*)   Cetedoc 0823
Sermons (*Sermones*)
Three Books to Trasamundus (*Ad Trasamundum libri III*)   Cetedoc 0816

Gaudentius of Brescia
Sermons (*Tractatus vel Sermones*)
To Benivolus (*Ad Benevolum*)

Gregory of Elvira
On the Faith (*De fide orthodoxa*)   Cetedoc 0551

Gregory of Nazianzus
On the Holy Lights, Oration 39 (*In sancta lumina*)   TLG 2022.047

Gregory of Nyssa
On Virginity (*De virginitate*)   TLG 2017.043

Gregory the Great
Dialogues (*Dialogorum libri iv*)   Cetedoc 1713
Homilies on Ezekiel (*Homiliae in Hiezechihelem prophetam*)   Cetedoc 1710
On the Seven Penitential Psalms (*Expositio in septem Psalmos*)
Pastoral Rule (*Regula pastoralis*)   Cetedoc 1712
Six Books on 1 Kings (*In librum primum Regum expositionum libri vi*) Cetedoc 1719

Hesychius of Jerusalem
Homilies on Job (*Homélies sur Job version Arménienne I: Homélies I-XI*)

Hilary of Poitiers
Homilies on the Psalms (*Tractatus super psalmos I-XCI*)   Cetedoc 0428
Letter or Booklet (*Epistola seu Libellus*)
On the Trinity (*De Trinitate*)   Cetedoc 0433

Hippolytus
Commentary on Daniel (*Commentarium in Danielem*)   TLG 2115.030

Ildefonsus of Toledo
On Mary's Perpetual Virginity (*De virginitate perpetua sanctae Mariae*)

Irenaeus of Lyons
Against Heresies (*Adversus haereses*)   Cetedoc 1154 f

Isaac of Nineveh
Ascetical Homilies (*De perfectione religiosa*)

Jerome
Commentary on Daniel (*Commentarii in Danielem*)   Cetedoc 0588
Commentary on Hosea (*Commentarii in prophetas minores*)   Cetedoc 0589
Commentary on Malachi (*Commentarii in prophetas minores*)   Cetedoc 0589
Homilies on Mark (*Tractatus in Marci evangelium*)   Cetedoc 0594
Homilies on the Psalms (*Tractatus lix in psalmos*)   Cetedoc 0592

John Chrysostom
Against Jews and Gentiles (*Contra Judaeos et gentiles, quod Christus sit Deus*)   TLG 2062.372

Against the Opponents of the Monastic Life
  (*Adversus oppugnatores vitae monasticae*)   TLG 2062.003
Baptismal Instructions
  (*Ad illuminandos catecheses 1-2 [series prima et secunda]*)   TLG 2062.025
  (*Catecheses ad illuminandos 1-8 [series tertia]*)   TLG 2062.382
Commentary on Galatians (*In epistulam ad Galatas commentarius*)   TLG 2062.158
Commentary on Isaiah (*In Isaiam*)   TLG 2062.497
Homilies on Genesis (*In Genesim [homiliae 1-67]*)   TLG 2062.112
Homilies on Hosea (*Homiliae in Oseam*)
Homilies on the Gospel of Matthew (*In Matthaeum [homiliae 1-90]*)   TLG 2062.152
Letter to the Fallen Theodore (*Ad Theodorum lapsum [lib. 1]*)   TLG 2062.002
On the Obscurity of Prophecies (*De prophetiarum obscuritate [homiliae 1-2]*)   TLG 2062.150
On the Priesthood (*De sacerdotio*)   TLG 2062.085
On the Psalms (*Expositiones in Psalmos*)   TLG 2062.143
On Vainglory and the Right Way for Parents to Bring up Their Children
  (*De inani gloria et de educandis liberis*)   TLG 2062.378
On Virginity (*De virginitate*)   TLG 2062.009
Sermon on the Holy Martyrs (*De sanctis martyribus*)   TLG 2062.050
To Stagirius Who Was Tormented by a Devil
  (*Ad Stagirium a daemone vexatum [lib. 1-3]*)   TLG 2062.006

John of Damascus
Homily for Holy Saturday (*Homilia in sabbatum sanctum*)   TLG 2934.056
Homily on the Dormition (*Homilia i in dormitionem Mariae*)   TLG 2934.023
Orthodox Faith (*Expositio fidei*)   TLG 2934.004
Three Treatises on Divine Images (*Orationes de imaginibus tres*)   TLG 2934.005

Julian of Eclanum
Tractate (via Augustine "Unfinished Tractate Against Julian"
  in *Retractationum libri duo*)   Cetedoc 0250

Julian Pomerius
On the Contemplative Life (*De vita contemplativa*)

Julius Africanus
Letter to Origen (*Epistula ad Origenem*)   TLG 2956.003

Leander of Seville
Letter to His Sister Florentine (*Liber de institutione virginum et contemptu mundi*)

Leo the Great
Sermons (*Tractatus septem et nonaginta*)   Cetedoc 1657

Maximus of Turin
Sermons (*Collectio sermonum antiqua*)   Cetedoc 0219 a

Methodius of Olympus
Symposium or Banquet of the Ten Virgins
    (Symposium sive Convivium decem virginum)   TLG 2959.001

Nicetas of Remesiana
Instruction on the Faith of the Trinity *(Libelli instructionis [de ratione fidei])*
Prayer, Vigil and Hymns of Praise *(De vigiliis, de utilitate hymnorum)*

Olympiodorus of Alexandria
Fragments on Baruch *(Commentarii in Baruch [in catenis])*   TLG 2865.005
Fragments on the Letter of Jeremiah *(Commentarii in Jeremiae epistulam)*   TLG 2865.006

Optatus
Against the Donatists *(De schismate Donatistarum adversus Parmenianum)*

Origen
Commentary on Matthew
    (Commentarii in evangelium Matthaei [lib. 10-11])   TLG 2042.029
    (Commentarium in evangelium Matthaei [lib.12-17])   TLG 2042.030
Commentary on the Gospel of John
    (Commentarii in evangelium Joannis [lib. 1, 2, 4, 5, 6, 10, 13])   TLG 2042.005
    (Commentarii in evangelium Joannis [lib. 19, 20, 28, 32])   TLG 2042.079
Commentary on the Song of Songs *(Commentarium in Canticum Canticorum)*   Cetedoc 0198 2
Fragments on the Gospel of John *(Fragmenta in evangelium Joannis [in catenis])*   TLG 2042.006
Homilies on Exodus *(Homiliae in Exodum)*   TLG 2042.023
Homilies on Ezekiel *(Homiliae in Ezechielem)*   TLG 2042.027
Homilies on Genesis *(Homiliae in Genesim)*   TLG 2042.022
Homilies on Isaiah *(Homiliae in Isaiam)*
Homilies on Jeremiah
    (In Jeremiam [homiliae 1-11])   TLG 2042.009
    (In Jeremiam [homilae 12-20])   TLG 2042.021
Homilies on Joshua *(In Jesu nave homiliae xxvi)*   TLG 2042.025
Homilies on Leviticus *(Homiliae in Leviticum)*   TLG 2042.024
Homilies on Numbers *(In Numeros homiliae)*   Cetedoc 0198 0
Homilies on the Book of Judges *(Homiliae in librum Iudicum)*   Cetedoc 0198 7
Homilies on the Gospel of Luke *(Homiliae in Lucam)*   TLG 2042.016
Homilies on the Psalms *(Selecta in Psalmos [Dub.; fragmenta e catenis])*   TLG 2042.058
Letter to Julius Africanus *(Epistula ad Africanum)*   TLG 2042.045
On First Principles *(De principiis)*   TLG 2042.002
On Prayer *(De oratione)*   TLG 2042.008

Origen (via Jerome)
Stromateis *(Stromateis)* [via On Daniel *(Commentarii in Danielem)*]

Palladius of Helenopolis
Dialogue on the Life of St. John Chrysostom
  (*Dialogus de vita Joannis Chrysostomi*)   TLG 2111.004

Paterius
Exposition of the Old and New Testament
  (*Liber de expositione veteris ac novi testamenti*)

Paulinus of Nola
Letters (*Epistulae*)   Cetedoc 0202

Pelagius (?) (via Pseudo-Augustine)
On the Christian Life (*De vita Christiana*)   Cetedoc 0730

Peter Chrysologus
Sermons (*Collectio sermonum*)   Cetedoc 0227+

Prosper of Aquitaine
The Call of All Nations (*De vocatione omnium gentium*)

Pseudo-Ambrose
The Contest Between Vices and Virtue (*Liber de vitiorum virtutumque
  conflictu [Incertus]*)
On the Book of Revelation (*Expositio super septem visiones libri Apocalypsis*)
On the Trinity (*De Trinitate, alias In symbolum apostolorum tractatus*)
Prayer (*Precationes duae [hactenius Ambrosio attributae]*)
Sermons (*Sermones sancto Ambrosio hactenus ascripti*)

Pseudo-Augustine
Book on the Spirit and the Soul (*De spiritu et anima*)
Hypomnesticon (*Hypomnesticon vulgo libri hypognosticon*)
Manual (*Manuale [incertus]*)
Mirror (*Speculum [incertus]*)
Questions from Both Testaments (*Quaestiones veteris et novi testamenti
  [incertus]*)
Questions from the Old Testament (*Quaesiones aliae veteris et novi testamenti
  [incertus]*)
Sermon on the Creed (*Sermones. De symbolo sermo ad catechumenos*)
Sermons (*Sermones supposititii. Classis II. De Tempore*)

Pseudo-Chrysostom
Homily 2 on the Psalm 50 (*In Psalmum 50 [homilia 2; Sp.]*)   TLG 2062.200
On Daniel (*Interpretatio in Danielem prophetam [Sp.]*)   TLG 2062.209
On Lazarus Dead Since Four Days
  (*In quatriduanum Lazarum = Contra Anomoeos, homilia 9 [Sp.]*)   TLG 2062.017

Pseudo-Cyprian of Carthage
Book on the Vanity of Idols (*De idolorum vanitate [dubium]*)   Cetedoc 0057

Pseudo-Ephrem
Praise of the Martyrs (*De laude martyrii*)

Quodvultdeus
The Book of Promises and Predictions of God
   (*Liber promissionum et praedictorum Dei*)   Cetedoc 0413

Rabanus Maurus
On Ecclesiasticus (*Commentariorum in Ecclesiasticum libri decem*)

Rufinus of Aquileia
The Blessings of the Patriarchs (*De benedictionibus patriarcharum*)   Cetedoc 0195

Salvian the Presbyter of Marseilles
Against Avarice (*Ad ecclesiam [sive Adversus avaritiam]*)
The Governance of God (*De gubernatione Dei*)   Cetedoc 0485

Severian of Gabala
On the Prodigal Son (*In parabolam de filio prodigo*)
   [included in TLG under the authorship of John Chrysostom]   TLG 2062.231
On the Verse "Put Your Hand"
   (*In illud Abrahae dictum, Pone manum tuam sub femur meum*)
Sermon on the Three Young Men (*De tribus pueris*)   TLG 4139.067

Severus of Antioch
Cathedral Homilies (*Homiliae cathedrales*)

Sophronius of Jerusalem
Homilies (*Homiliae*)

Stephen of Hnes
Life of Apollo the Archimandrite (*Vita di Apollo archimandrita*)

Theodore bar Koni
Book of Scholia (Seert) (*Liber scholiorum*)

Theodoret of Cyr
Commentary on Baruch (*Interpretatio in Jeremiam*
   [*including Baruch and Lamentations*])   TLG 4089.026
Commentary on Daniel (*Interpretatio in Danielem*)   TLG 4089.028
Ecclesiastical History (*Historia ecclesiastica*)   TLG 4089.003
Questions on Genesis (*Quaestiones in Octateuchum*)   TLG 4089.022

Theodotus of Ancyra
Homilies *(Homiliae)*

Valerian of Cimiez
Homilies *(Homiliae)*

Victor of Cartenna
On Penance *(De paenitentia)*

Victor of Vita
Book of the Catholic Faith *(Liber fidei catholicae)*

Vigilius of Thapsus
Against the Arians *(Contra Arianos)*
Against Varimadus *(Opus contra Varimadum Arianum)*   Cetedoc 0364
On the Trinity *(De Trinitate)*

Biographical Sketches & Short Descriptions of Select Anonymous Works

This listing is cumulative, including all the authors and works cited in this series to date.

Abba John (date unknown). Noted monk in John Cassian's *Conferences* who presided over a coenobitic community in the desert of Scetis and was sought out for his wisdom.

Abba Moses (c. 332-407). Moses the Ethiopian or Moses the Black. He began as a house slave of a government official, later dismissed for robbery, a life he continued after his dismissal. After his conversion, he became a monk of Scetis and then a priest trained by Isidore the Priest. He retired to Petra where he was martyred with seven others by barbarian invaders.

Abba Pior (d. 373). An Egyptian desert father. He left his family while still a boy. His sister sought him out fifty years later, trying to persuade him to return from his life of solitude, but she was unsuccessful. He was known as a generous monk who was willing to put up with much discomfort, living in a horrible cell that no one who followed after him could stand to live in.

Abraham of Nathpar (fl. sixth-seventh century). Monk of the Eastern Church who flourished during the monastic revival of the sixth to seventh century. Among his works is a treatise on prayer and silence that speaks of the importance of prayer becoming embodied through action in the one who prays. His work has also been associated with John of Apamea or Philoxenus of Mabbug.

Acacius of Beroea (c. 340-c. 436). Syrian monk known for his ascetic life. He became bishop of Beroea in 378, participated in the council of Constantinople in 381, and played an important role in mediating between Cyril of Alexandria and John of Antioch; however, he did not take part in the clash between Cyril and Nestorius.

Acacius of Caesarea (d. c. 365). Pro-Arian bishop of Caesarea in Palestine, disciple and biographer of Eusebius of Caesarea, the historian. He was a man of great learning and authored a treatise on Ecclesiastes.

Acts of Paul and Thecla (second century). A story about a disciple of Paul known for her continence and miraculous deliverances from martyrdom. Originally a part of *The Acts of Paul*, the work was judged a forgery by Tertullian who opposed its use in the advocacy of female preaching and baptizing. Nonetheless, the work was widely popular and translated into several languages.

Acts of Peter (c. 190). An apocryphal account of the apostle's life and ministry, including his conflicts with Simon Magus and his death via inverted crucifixion.

Acts of Thomas (c. 225). A widely circulated apocryphal account of the missionary and wonderworking activities of Thomas, which includes the earliest report of the apostle's martyrdom in India.

Adamantius (early fourth century). Surname of Origen of Alexandria and the main character in the dialogue contained in *Concerning Right Faith in God*. Rufinus attributes this work to Origen. However, trinitarian terminology, coupled with references to Methodius and allusions to the fourth-century Constantinian era bring this attribution into question.

Adamnan (c. 624-704). Abbot of Iona, Ireland, and author of the life of St. Columba. He was influential in the process of assimilating the Celtic church into Roman liturgy and church order. He also wrote *On the Holy Sites*, which influenced Bede.

Alexander of Alexandria (fl. 312-328). Bishop of Alexandria and predecessor of Athanasius, on whom he exerted considerable theological influence during the rise of Arianism. Alexander excommunicated Arius, whom he had appointed to the parish of Baucalis, in 319. His teaching regarding the eternal generation and divine substantial union of the Son with the Father was eventually confirmed at the Council of Nicaea (325).

Ambrose of Milan (c. 333-397; fl. 374-397). Bishop of Milan and teacher of Augustine who defended the divinity of the Holy Spirit and the perpetual virginity of Mary.

Ambrosiaster (fl. c. 366-384). Name given to the author of an anonymous Pauline commentary once thought to have been composed by Ambrose.

Ammonas (fourth century). Student of An-tony the Great and member of a colony of anchorite monks at Pispir in Egypt. He took over leadership of the colony upon Antony's death in 356. He was consecrated by Athanasius as bishop of a small unknown see. He died by 396. Fourteen letters and eleven sayings in the Apophthegmata Patrum are attributed to him, although it is unlikely that all of the identified sayings are his.

Ammonius of Alexandria (late fifth-early sixth century). Alexandrian presbyter who was one of the more moderate anti-Chalcedonian theologians of Alexandria and served as a prominent representative of Alexandrian theology and Christology in his day. His exegetical method, however, exhibits more affinity with Antioch than Alexandria. Fragments from his commentary on John number over 600, and he is often identified as the author of catena fragments from commentaries on both the Old and New Testament (see PG 85:1362-1814), though, due to the prevalence of this name in Egypt and the existence of other possible authors, attribution remains uncertain.

Amphilochius of Iconium (b. c. 340-345; d. c. 398-404). An orator at Constantinople before becoming bishop of Iconium in 373. He was a cousin of Gregory of Nazianzus and active in debates against the Macedonians and Messalians.

Anastasius I of Antioch (d. 598/599). Patriarch of Antioch (559-570 and 593-598), exiled by Justinian II and restored by Gregory the Great. His writing significantly influenced later theologians, though only his five-part treatise on orthodox belief survives in its entirety.

Anastasius of Sinai (d. c. 700). Abbot of the monastery of St. Catherine. He argued against various heresies in his dogmatic and polemical works. His main treatise, the *Hodegos* or "Guide," is primarily an attack on monophysism.

Andreas (c. seventh century). Monk who

collected commentary from earlier writers to form a catena on various biblical books.

Andrew of Caesarea (early sixth century). Bishop of Caesarea in Cappadocia. He produced one of the earliest Greek commentaries on Revelation and defended the divine inspiration of its author.

Andrew of Crete (c. 660-740). Bishop of Crete, known for his hymns, especially for his "canons," a genre which supplanted the *kontakia* and is believed to have originated with him. A significant number of his canons and sermons have survived and some are still in use in the Eastern Church. In the early Iconoclastic controversy he is also known for his defense of the veneration of icons.

Antony (or Anthony) the Great (c. 251-c. 356). An anchorite of the Egyptian desert and founder of Egyptian monasticism. Athanasius regarded him as the ideal of monastic life, and he has become a model for Christian hagiography.

Aphrahat (c. 270-350; fl. 337-345). "The Persian Sage" and first major Syriac writer whose work survives. He is also known by his Greek name Aphraates.

Apollinaris of Laodicea (310-c. 392). Bishop of Laodicea who was attacked by Gregory of Nazianzus, Gregory of Nyssa and Theodore for denying that Christ had a human mind.

Aponius/Apponius (fourth-fifth century). Author of a remarkable commentary on Song of Solomon (c. 405-415), an important work in the history of exegesis. The work, which was influenced by the commentaries of Origen and Pseudo-Hippolytus, is of theological significance, especially in the area of Christology.

Apostolic Constitutions (c. 381-394). Also known as *Constitutions of the Holy Apostles* and thought to be redacted by Julian of Neapolis. The work is divided into eight books, and is primarily a collection of and expansion on previous works such as the *Didache* (c. 140) and the *Apostolic Traditions*. Book 8 ends with eighty-five canons from various sources and is elsewhere known as the *Apostolic Canons*.

Apringius of Beja (mid sixth century). Iberian bishop and exegete. Heavily influenced by Tyconius, he wrote a commentary on Revelation in Latin, of which two large fragments survive.

Arator (c. 490-550). Roman subdeacon appointed by Pope Vigilius. From Liguria, Italy, he served as an imperial ambassador for the Gothic court prior to his appointment as subdeacon. A poet at heart, his *De actibus apostolorum*, a poetic paraphrase and allegorical expansion of the book of Acts, was popular in the Middle Ages.

Arethas of Caesarea (c. 860-940). Byzantine scholar and disciple of Photius. He was a deacon in Constantinople, then archbishop of Caesarea from 901.

Aristides (second century). Christian philosopher and early apologist. Reputed to be from Athens, he wrote his *Apologia*, addressed either to Hadrian or Antoninus Pius, to defend the Christian understanding of God against that of the barbarian, Greek and Jewish traditions.

Arius (fl. c. 320). Heretic condemned at the Council of Nicaea (325) for refusing to accept that the Son was not a creature but was God by nature like the Father.

Armenian Liturgy (c. fourth or fifth century). Ancient Christian liturgy based in part on Syrian rites used by early missionaries to Armenia and similar in structure to the old rite of Antioch. The Armenian liturgy also incorporates unique elements and influences from a variety of traditions. The invention of a national script in the fifth century allowed for the translation of the liturgy into Armenian.

Arnobius of Sicca (d. c. 327). Teacher of rhetoric at Sicca Veneria in Numidia in North Africa and opponent of Christianity, he converted late in life and became an apologist for the faith he formerly opposed. According to Jerome, Arnobius's one extant work, *Against the Nations*, was written at the request of his bishop, who wanted proof that his conversion was genuine. It was probably composed during the persecution under Diocletian.

Arnobius the Younger (fifth century). A participant in christological controversies of the fifth century. He composed *Conflictus cum Serapione*, an account of a debate with a monophysite monk in which he attempts to demonstrate harmony between Roman and Alexandrian theology. Some scholars attribute to him a few more works, such as *Commentaries on Psalms*.

Asterius the Homilist (late fourth-early fifth century). Author of thirty-one homilies on Psalms 1–15 and 18, abbreviated versions of which are preserved under the name of John Chrysostom. This otherwise unknown preacher, sometimes identified with Asterius of Amasea and Asterius the Sophist, lived in or near Antioch.

Athanasian Creed (c. fourth or fifth century). One of the three ecumenical creeds in Western Christianity. Also known as the *Quicumque vult*, it expounds in great detail the doctrines of the Trinity and Incarnation. Traditionally attributed to Athanasius, the creed's origin and date are now disputed; it likely arose in Southern Gaul.

Athanasius of Alexandria (c. 295-373; fl. 325-373). Bishop of Alexandria from 328, though often in exile. He wrote his classic polemics against the Arians while most of the eastern bishops were against him.

Athenagoras (fl. 176-180). Early Christian philosopher and apologist from Athens, whose only authenticated writing, *A Plea Regarding Christians*, is addressed to the emperors Marcus Aurelius and Commodus, and defends Christians from the common accusations of atheism, incest and cannibalism.

Augustine of Hippo (354-430). Bishop of Hippo and a voluminous writer on philosophical, exegetical, theological and ecclesiological topics. He formulated the Western doctrines of predestination and original sin in his writings against the Pelagians.

Babai (c. early sixth century). Author of the *Letter to Cyriacus*. He should not be confused with either Babai of Nisibis (d. 484) or Babai the Great (d. 628).

Babai the Great (d. 628). Syriac monk who founded a monastery and school in his region of Beth Zabday and later served as third superior at the Great Convent of Mount Izla during a period of crisis in the Nestorian church.

Bardesanes (154-222). Philosopher who sought to reconcile Christian thought with contemporary astrological theories, while rejecting Zoroastrian determinism. His ideas, including arguments against the Marcionites, were recorded by a disciple in the *Book of the Laws of the Lands*. He also wrote 150 doctrinal hymns.

Barsanuphius and John (fifth to sixth century). Two anchorite friends who served as spiritual directors to coenobites at a monastery near Gaza. The two communicated with others, including one another, almost exclusively through letters. Little is known of them apart from their correspondence, included among 850 letters of Barsanuphius. Dorotheus of Gaza was one of Barsanuphius's most important disciples.

Basil of Seleucia (fl. 444-468). Bishop of Seleucia in Isauria and ecclesiastical writer. He took part in the Synod of Constantinople in 448 for the condemnation of the Eutychian errors and the deposition of their great champion, Dioscurus of Alexandria.

Basil the Great (b. c. 330; fl. 357-379). One of the Cappadocian fathers, bishop of Caesarea and champion of the teaching on the Trinity propounded at Nicaea in 325. He was a great administrator and founded a monastic rule.

Basilides (fl. second century). Alexandrian heretic of the early second century who is said to have believed that souls migrate from body to body and that we do not sin if we lie to protect the body from martyrdom.

Bede the Venerable (c. 672/673-735). Born in Northumbria, at the age of seven he was put under the care of the Benedictine monks of Saints Peter and Paul at Jarrow and given a broad classical education in the monastic tradition. Considered one of the most learned men of his age, he is the author of *An Ecclesiastical History of the English People*.

Benedict of Nursia (c. 480-547). Considered the most important figure in the history of Western monasticism. Benedict founded many monasteries, the most notable found at Montecassino, but his lasting influence lay in his famous Rule. The Rule outlines the theological and inspirational foundation of the monastic ideal while also legislating the shape and organization of the cenobitic life.

Besa the Copt (fifth century). Coptic monk, disciple of Shenoute, whom he succeeded as head of the monastery. He wrote numerous letters, monastic catecheses and a biography of Shenoute.

Book of Steps (c. 400). Written by an anonymous Syriac author, this work consists of thirty homilies or discourses which specifically deal with the more advanced stages of growth in the spiritual life.

Braulio of Saragossa (c. 585-651). Bishop of Saragossa (631-651) and noted writer of the Visigothic renaissance. His *Life* of St. Aemilianus is his crowning literary achievement.

Byzantine Order. Eastern rite incorporating diverse local traditions from throughout the empire. Byzantine liturgy, which fused into a more standard order in the late Middle Ages, is marked by a variety of rich cultural influences, especially lyrical and mystical elements.

Caesarius of Arles (c. 470-543). Bishop of Arles renowned for his attention to his pastoral duties. Among his surviving works the most important is a collection of 238 sermons that display an ability to preach Christian doctrine to a variety of audiences.

Callinicus (mid fifth century). Disciple and biographer of Hypatius, third abbot of the monastery at Rufiniane near Chalcedon and Constantinople. Callinicus's *Life of Hypatius* shows clear borrowings from Athanasius's *Life of Antony*, but nevertheless gives insight into the development of monastic life near Constantinople.

Callistus of Rome (d. 222). Pope (217-222) who excommunicated Sabellius for heresy. It is very probable that he suffered martyrdom.

Cassia (b. c. 805; d. between 848 and 867). Nun, poet and hymnographer who founded a convent in Constantinople.

Cassian, John (360-432). Author of the *Institutes* and the *Conferences*, works purporting to relay the teachings of the Egyptian monastic fathers on the nature of the spiritual life which were highly influential in the development of Western monasticism.

Cassiodorus (c. 485-c. 580). Founder of the monastery of Vivarium, Calabria, where monks transcribed classic sacred and profane texts, in Greek and Latin, preserving them for the Western tradition.

Chromatius (fl. 400). Bishop of Aquileia, friend of Rufinus and Jerome and author of tracts and sermons.

Clement of Alexandria (c. 150-215). A highly educated Christian convert from paganism, head of the catechetical school in Alexandria and pioneer of Christian scholarship. His major works, Protrepticus, Paedagogus and the Stromata, bring Christian doctrine face to face with the ideas and achievements of his time.

Clement of Rome (fl. c. 92-101). Pope whose *Epistle to the Corinthians* is one of the most important documents of subapostolic times.

Commodian (probably third or possibly fifth century). Latin poet of unknown origin (possibly Africa, Syria, Rome or Gaul) whose two surviving works suggest chiliast and patripassionist tendencies.

Constantine (d. 337). Roman emperor from 306, with his fellow-emperor Licinius. The two proclaimed religious tolerance in the *Edict of Milan* in 313, allowing Christianity to be practiced freely. He became sole emperor in 324 and sought to preserve the unity and structure of the church for the good of the state. Constantine issued decrees against schisms and summoned the Council of Nicaea (325) to settle the Arian controversy.

Constitutions of the Holy Apostles. *See* Apostolic Constitutions.

Cosmas of Maiuma (c. 675-c. 751). Adopted son of John of Damascus and educated by the monk Cosmas in the early eighth century. He entered the monastery of St. Sabas near Jerusalem and in 735 became bishop of Maiuma near Gaza. Cosmas in his capacity as Melodus ("Songwriter") is known for his canons composed in honor of Christian feasts. An alternate rendering of his name is Kosmas Melodos.

Council of Chalcedon (451). The fourth of seven ecumenical councils. The council was summoned by Emperor Marcian in response to a controversy over the person and nature of Christ. The Definition of Chalcedon, informed by Leo's *Tome*, affirmed the statements of Nicaea (325) and Constantinople (381) while further defining the relationship between the two natures in the one person of Christ as unmixed, unchangeable, indivisible and inseparable. The Oriental Orthodox Church refused to accept Chalcedon's definition of the faith, preferring to stay with the *miaphysite* Christology of Cyril of Alexandria.

Council of Constantinople (381). The second ecumenical council, convened by Theodosius I to unify the Eastern Church. The council endorsed the Nicene Creed of 325, expanding it at certain controverted points in order to answer to challenges from, among others, the Eunomians and Pneumatomachians who denied the divinity of the Holy Spirit, while also condemning the Apollinarian denial of Christ's full humanity.

Council of Rome (382). Called by Damasus in response to the Council of Constantinople, this gathering affirmed the Council of Constantinople while also seeking to establish the primacy of the Roman see. The first three chapters of the *Decretum Gelasianum*, which

list a hierarchy of authoritative sources and a biblical canon, may have been produced by this council.

Council of Toledo (447). Affirmed the earlier Council of Toledo I (400) and the liturgical practice already established in the West of including the procession of the Spirit from the Father *and the Son (filioque)*, which had been added to the recitation of the creed by some in the West in order to combat the heresy of Arianism which subordinated the Son to the Father.

Cyprian of Carthage (fl. 248-258). Martyred bishop of Carthage who maintained that those baptized by schismatics and heretics had no share in the blessings of the church.

Cyril of Alexandria (375-444; fl. 412-444). Patriarch of Alexandria whose extensive exegesis, characterized especially by a strong espousal of the unity of Christ, led to the condemnation of Nestorius in 431.

Cyril of Jerusalem (c. 315-386; fl. c. 348). Bishop of Jerusalem after 350 and author of Catechetical Homilies.

Cyril of Scythopolis (b. c. 525; d. after 557). Palestinian monk and author of biographies of famous Palestinian monks. Because of him we have precise knowledge of monastic life in the fifth and sixth centuries and a description of the Origenist crisis and its suppression in the mid-sixth century.

Damasus of Rome (c. 304-384). Appointed pope in 366, following a conflict with Ursinus settled by Valentinian I. Damasus solidified the authority of Rome, attacked heresy using councils and strategic partnerships, promoted the cult of the martyrs, and commissioned Jerome's production of the Vulgate.

Dhuoda (ninth century). Wife of Bernard, Duke of Septimania, and author of a work on Christian virtue, *Manual*, which she wrote for her eldest son, William.

Diadochus of Photice (c. 400-474). Antimonophysite bishop of Epirus Vetus whose work *Discourse on the Ascension of Our Lord Jesus*

Christ exerted influence in both the East and West through its Chalcedonian Christology. He is also the subject of the mystical *Vision of St. Diadochus Bishop of Photice in Epirus.*

Didache (c. 140). Of unknown authorship, this text intertwines Jewish ethics with Christian liturgical practice to form a whole discourse on the "way of life." It exerted an enormous amount of influence in the patristic period and was especially used in the training of catechumen.

Didascalia Apostolorum (Teaching of the Twelve Apostles and Holy Disciples of Our Savior) (early third century). A Church Order composed for a community of Christian converts from paganism in the northern part of Syria. This work forms the main source of the first six books of the *Apostolic Constitutions* and provides an important window to view what early liturgical practice may have looked like.

Didymus the Blind (c. 313-398). Alexandrian exegete who was much influenced by Origen and admired by Jerome.

Diodore of Tarsus (d. c. 394). Bishop of Tarsus and Antiochene theologian. He authored a great scope of exegetical, doctrinal and apologetic works, which come to us mostly in fragments because of his condemnation as the predecessor of Nestorianism. Diodore was a teacher of John Chrysostom and Theodore of Mopsuestia.

Dionysius of Alexandria (d. c. 264). Bishop of Alexandria and student of Origen. Dionysius actively engaged in the theological disputes of his day, opposed Sabellianism, defended himself against accusations of tritheism and wrote the earliest extant Christian refutation of Epicureanism. His writings have survived mainly in extracts preserved by other early Christian authors.

Dorotheus of Gaza (fl. c. 525-540). Member of Abbot Seridos's monastery and later leader of a monastery where he wrote *Spiritual Instructions.* He also wrote a work on traditions of Palestinian monasticism.

Dracontius (fifth century). Latin poet and legal scholar. During imprisonment (484-c. 496) for angering the ruler of Carthage, Dracontius produced his *Satisfactio* and *Laudes Dei,* which explore, in particular, biblical themes of mercy.

Egeria (or Etheria, Aetheria) (fourth century). Possible name for the author of an *Itinerary* or pilgrimage diary that records valuable details on early liturgy, traditions, and church and monastic structure. Through letters to her religious community, likely in Gaul, Egeria describes a journey (c. 381-384) to Egypt, Palestine and Asia Minor.

Ennodius (474-521). Bishop of Pavia, a prolific writer of various genre, including letters, poems and biographies. He sought reconciliation in the schism between Rome and Acacius of Constantinople, and also upheld papal autonomy in the face of challenges from secular authorities.

Ephrem the Syrian (b. c. 306; fl. 363-373). Syrian writer of commentaries and devotional hymns which are sometimes regarded as the greatest specimens of Christian poetry prior to Dante.

Epiphanius of Salamis (c. 315-403). Bishop of Salamis in Cyprus, author of a refutation of eighty heresies (the *Panarion*) and instrumental in the condemnation of Origen.

Epiphanius the Latin. Author of the late fifth-century or early sixth-century Latin text *Interpretation of the Gospels,* with constant references to early patristic commentators. He was possibly a bishop of Benevento or Seville.

Epistle of Barnabas. See *Letter of Barnabas.*

Epistula Apostolorum (mid second century). A self-purported letter of doubtful authenticity from the apostles to the churches of the world that emphasizes the divinity and sonship of Jesus along with his childhood miracles.

Ethiopian Liturgy. Liturgical rite similar to the rite of Alexandria. Ethiopian liturgy has evolved since the introduction of Coptic liturgy to Ethiopia, traditionally by St. Frumentius in the fourth century. Significant Eastern and Jewish influences were added over time.

Eucherius of Lyons (fl. 420-449). Bishop of Lyons c. 435-449. Born into an aristocratic family, he, along with his wife and sons, joined the monastery at Lérins soon after its founding. He explained difficult Scripture passages by means of a threefold reading of the text: literal, moral and spiritual.

Eugippius (b. 460). Disciple of Severinus and third abbot of the monastic community at Castrum Lucullanum, which was made up of those fleeing from Noricum during the barbarian invasions.

Eunomius (d. 393). Bishop of Cyzicyus who was attacked by Basil and Gregory of Nyssa for maintaining that the Father and the Son were of different natures, one ingenerate, one generate.

Eusebius of Caesarea (c. 260/263-340). Bishop of Caesarea, partisan of the Emperor Constantine and first historian of the Christian church. He argued that the truth of the gospel had been foreshadowed in pagan writings but had to defend his own doctrine against suspicion of Arian sympathies.

Eusebius of Emesa (c. 300-c. 359). Bishop of Emesa from c. 339. A biblical exegete and writer on doctrinal subjects, he displays some semi-Arian tendencies of his mentor Eusebius of Caesarea. ·

Eusebius of Gaul, or Eusebius Gallicanus (c. fifth century). A conventional name for a collection of seventy-six sermons produced in Gaul and revised in the seventh century. It contains material from different patristic authors and focuses on ethical teaching in the context of the liturgical cycle (days of saints and other feasts).

Eusebius of Vercelli (fl. c. 360). Bishop of Vercelli who supported the trinitarian teaching of Nicaea (325) when it was being undermined by compromise in the West.

Eustathius of Antioch (fl. 325). First bishop of Beroea, then of Antioch, one of the leaders of the anti-Arians at the council of Nicaea. Later, he was banished from his seat and exiled to Thrace for his support of Nicene theology.

Euthymius (377-473). A native of Melitene and influential monk. He was educated by Bishop Otreius of Melitene, who ordained him priest and placed him in charge of all the monasteries in his diocese. When the Council of Chalcedon (451) condemned the errors of Eutyches, it was greatly due to the authority of Euthymius that most of the Eastern recluses accepted its decrees. The empress Eudoxia returned to Chalcedonian orthodoxy through his efforts.

Evagrius of Pontus (c. 345-399). Disciple and teacher of ascetic life who astutely absorbed and creatively transmitted the spirituality of Egyptian and Palestinian monasticism of the late fourth century. Although Origenist elements of his writings were formally condemned by the Fifth Ecumenical Council (Constantinople II, A.D. 553), his literary corpus continued to influence the tradition of the church.

Eznik of Kolb (early fifth century). A disciple of Mesrob who translated Greek Scriptures into Armenian, so as to become the model of the classical Armenian language. As bishop, he participated in the synod of Astisat (449).

Facundus of Hermiane (fl. 546-568). African bishop who opposed Emperor Justinian's postmortem condemnation of Theodore of Mopsuestia, Theodoret of Cyr and Ibas of Ebessa at the fifth ecumenical council. His written defense, known as "To Justinian" or "In Defense of the Three Chapters," avers that ancient theologians should not be blamed for errors that became obvious only upon later theological reflection. He continued in the tradition of Chalcedon, although his Christology was supplemented, according to Justinian's decisions, by the theopaschite formula *Unus ex Trinitate passus est* ("Only one of the three suffered").

Fastidiosus (late fifth-early sixth century).

African Catholic priest who converted to Arianism. The text of one of his sermons survives in a refutation by Fulgentius.

Fastidius (c. fourth-fifth centuries). British author of *On the Christian Life*. He is believed to have written some works attributed to Pelagius.

Faustinus (fl. 380). A priest in Rome and supporter of Lucifer and author of a treatise on the Trinity.

Faustus of Riez (c. 400-490). A prestigious British monk at Lérins; abbot, then bishop of Riez from 457 to his death. His works include *On the Holy Spirit*, in which he argued against the Macedonians for the divinity of the Holy Spirit, and *On Grace*, in which he argued for a position on salvation that lay between more categorical views of free will and predestination. Various letters and (pseudonymous) sermons are extant.

The Festal Menaion. Orthodox liturgical text containing the variable parts of the service, including hymns, for fixed days of celebration of the life of Jesus and Mary.

Filastrius (fl. 380). Bishop of Brescia and author of a compilation against all heresies.

Firmicus Maternus (fourth century). An anti-Pagan apologist. Before his conversion to Christianity he wrote a work on astrology (334-337). After his conversion, however, he criticized paganism in *On the Errors of the Profane Religion.*

Firmilian of Caesarea (fl. c. 230-c. 268). Influential bishop of Caesarea in Cappadocia. He studied under Origen and became involved in the controversies over the return of the lapsed into the church and rebaptism, having written to Cyprian concerning the latter issue.

First Creed of the Council of Antioch (341). Eastern bishops' response to charges of Arianism from Western leaders. At a gathering that marked the dedication of the Golden Church at Antioch, the bishops put forth four creeds as alternatives to the Nicene formula.

Flavian of Chalon-sur-Saône (d. end of sixth century). Bishop of Chalon-sur-Saône in Burgundy, France. His hymn *Verses on the Mandate in the Lord's Supper* was recited in a number of the French monasteries after the washing of the feet on Maundy Thursday.

Fructuosus of Braga (d. c. 665). Son of a Gothic general and member of a noble military family. He became a monk at an early age, then abbot-bishop of Dumium before 650 and metropolitan of Braga in 656. He was influential in setting up monastic communities in Lusitania, Asturia, Galicia and the island of Gades.

Fulgentius of Ruspe (c. 467-532). Bishop of Ruspe and author of many orthodox sermons and tracts under the influence of Augustine.

Gaudentius of Brescia (fl. 395). Successor of Filastrius as bishop of Brescia and author of twenty-one Eucharistic sermons.

Gennadius of Constantinople (d. 471). Patriarch of Constantinople, author of numerous commentaries and an opponent of the Christology of Cyril of Alexandria.

Germanus of Constantinople (c. 640-c. 733). Patriarch of Constantinople (715-730). He wrote the *Historia Ecclesiastica*, which served for centuries as the explanation of the divine liturgy of the Byzantine Church, written during the outbreak of the great iconoclastic controversies in Eastern Christianity. One of the leading theologians of the Sixth Ecumenical Council (680-681), which condemned monothelitism.

Gerontius (c. 395-c. 480). Palestinian monk, later archimandrite of the cenobites of Palestine. He led the resistance to the council of Chalcedon.

Gildas (sixth century). British monk and historian. His major work is *De excidio Britanniae*, a history focused on the pagan invasion of Britain and the vices of contemporary Britons. Fragments of letters and a Penitential are also attributed to Gildas.

Gnostics. Name now given generally to followers of Basilides, Marcion, Valentinus, Mani and others. The characteristic belief is that matter is a prison made for the spirit by an evil or ignorant creator, and that redemption depends on fate, not on free will.

Gospel of Peter (late second century). An early apocryphal writing with Docetic aspects that likely originated in Syria. It was referred to by Serapion (c. 190) and Origen, though only one section survives in an eighth-century manuscript.

Gospel of Philip (second or third century). A Gnostic collection of sayings, including several attributed to Jesus, on the process of salvation. This Coptic document, discovered at Nag Hammadi, is probably unconnected with the *Gospel of Philip* cited by Epiphanius.

Gospel of Truth (second century). One of the Coptic texts found at Nag Hammadi. This Gnostic treatise discusses the nature, ministry and death of Jesus, and includes several unique speculations. Some scholars have connected it with the second-century Gnostic Valentinus. Irenaeus referred to it disparagingly as the so-called *Gospel of Truth*, which he found to be in conflict with the four canonical Gospels.

Gregory of Elvira (fl. 359-385). Bishop of Elvira who wrote allegorical treatises in the style of Origen and defended the Nicene faith against the Arians.

Gregory of Narek (950-1003). Armenian monk, philosopher, mystic and poet who lived in the monasteries of Narek (greater Armenia, now Turkey). He wrote a mystical interpretation of the Song of Songs and the Armenian Prayer book and liturgy. The latter, which he authored in his mature years, he referred to as his "last testament."

Gregory of Nazianzus (b. 329/330; fl. 372-389). Cappadocian father, bishop of Constantinople, friend of Basil the Great and Gregory of Nyssa, and author of theological orations, sermons and poetry.

Gregory of Nyssa (c. 335-394). Bishop of Nyssa and brother of Basil the Great. A Cappadocian father and author of catechetical

orations, he was a philosophical theologian of great originality.

Gregory of Tours (c. 538-594). Bishop of Tours elected in 573. Gregory produced hagiographical and historical works. His *Historia Francorum*, a fragmentary yet valuable source, begins with creation and highlights sixth-century Gaul.

Gregory Thaumaturgus (fl. c. 248-264). Bishop of Neocaesarea and a disciple of Origen. There are at least five legendary *Lives* that recount the events and miracles which led to his being called "the wonder worker." His most important work was the *Address of Thanks to Origen*, which is a rhetorically structured panegyric to Origen and an outline of his teaching.

Gregory the Great (c. 540-604). Pope from 590, the fourth and last of the Latin "Doctors of the Church." He was a prolific author and a powerful unifying force within the Latin Church, initiating the liturgical reform that brought about the Gregorian Sacramentary and Gregorian chant.

Hegemonius (fl. early fourth century). Author of *Acta disputationis*, traditionally believed to have been written in fourth-century Syria. This work is a fictitious debate between a Mesopotamian bishop and a Manichaean.

Hegesippus (second century). An author, possibly of Jewish descent, who served as a source for Eusebius and is best known for five books of anti-Gnostic polemic.

Heracleon (fl. c. 145-180). Gnostic teacher and disciple of Valentinus. His commentary on John, which was perhaps the first commentary to exist on this or any Gospel, was so popular that Ambrose commissioned Origen to write his own commentary in response, providing a more orthodox approach to the Fourth Gospel.

Hesychius of Jerusalem (fl. 412-450). Presbyter and exegete, thought to have commented on the whole of Scripture.

Hilary of Arles (c. 401-449). Archbishop of Arles and leader of the Semi-Pelagian party.

Hilary incurred the wrath of Pope Leo I when he removed a bishop from his see and appointed a new bishop. Leo demoted Arles from a metropolitan see to a bishopric to assert papal power over the church in Gaul.

Hilary of Poitiers (c. 315-367). Bishop of Poitiers and called the "Athanasius of the West" because of his defense (against the Arians) of the common nature of Father and Son.

Hippolytus (fl. 222-245). Recent scholarship places Hippolytus in a Palestinian context, personally familiar with Origen. Though he is known chiefly for *The Refutation of All Heresies*, he was primarily a commentator on Scripture (especially the Old Testament) employing typological exegesis.

Horsiesi (c. 305-c. 390). Pachomius's second successor, after Petronius, as a leader of cenobitic monasticism in Southern Egypt.

Hyperechius (c. fifth century). A monk known only from his *Exhortation to the Monks*, 160 statements in Greek on monastic virtues, and the collection *Sayings of the Fathers*, which quotes eight of these exhortations.

Ignatius of Antioch (c. 35-107/112). Bishop of Antioch who wrote several letters to local churches while being taken from Antioch to Rome to be martyred. In the letters, which warn against heresy, he stresses orthodox Christology, the centrality of the Eucharist and unique role of the bishop in preserving the unity of the church.

Ildefonsus of Toledo (mid seventh century). Archbishop of Toledo (657-667). Previously a monk, he served as abbot of Agalí, and later as archbishop. Only a portion of his works is extant, including some theological works and letters. He is best known for his *De viris illustribus* (Lives of Illustrious Men) continuing the catalog begun by Isidore of Seville. His extant writing reflects his Marian piety.

Irenaeus of Lyons (c. 135-c. 202). Bishop of Lyons who published the most famous and influential refutation of Gnostic thought.

Isaac of Nineveh (d. c. 700). Also known as Isaac the Syrian or Isaac Syrus, this monastic writer served for a short while as bishop of Nineveh before retiring to live a secluded monastic life. His writings on ascetic subjects survive in the form of numerous homilies.

Isaiah of Scete (late fourth century). Author of ascetical texts, collected after his death under the title of the *Ascetic Discourses*. This work was influential in the development of Eastern Christian asceticism and spirituality.

Isho'dad of Merv (fl. c. 850). Nestorian bishop of Hedatta. He wrote commentaries on parts of the Old Testament and all of the New Testament, frequently quoting Syriac fathers.

Isidore of Pelusium (d. c. 440). Egyptian ascetic. Born to a prominent Egyptian family in Alexandria, he left behind his wealth to live on a mountain near Pelusium, and was often consulted by church and civic leaders alike, such as Cyril of Alexandria and Theodosius II, for his wisdom and his counsel of moderation. Many of his letters also have come down to us, some of which provide keen insight into the interpretation of Scripture.

Isidore of Seville (c. 560-636). Youngest of a family of monks and clerics, including sister Florentina and brothers Leander and Fulgentius. He was an erudite author of comprehensive scale in matters both religious and sacred, including his encyclopedic *Etymologies*.

Jacob of Nisibis (d. 338). Bishop of Nisibis. He was present at the council of Nicaea in 325 and took an active part in the opposition to Arius.

Jacob of Sarug (c. 450-c. 520). Syriac ecclesiastical writer. Jacob received his education at Edessa. At the end of his life he was ordained bishop of Sarug. His principal writing was a long series of metrical homilies, earning him the title "The Flute of the Holy Spirit."

Jerome (c. 347-420). Gifted exegete and exponent of a classical Latin style, now best known as the translator of the Latin Vulgate. He defended the perpetual virginity of Mary, attacked Origen and Pelagius and supported extreme ascetic practices.

John Chrysostom (344/354-407; fl. 386-407). Bishop of Constantinople who was noted for his orthodoxy, his eloquence and his attacks on Christian laxity in high places.

John of Antioch (d. 441/42). Bishop of Antioch, commencing in 428. He received his education together with Nestorius and Theodore of Mopsuestia in a monastery near Antioch. A supporter of Nestorius, he condemned Cyril of Alexandria, but later reached a compromise with him.

John of Apamea (fifth century). Syriac author of the early church who wrote on various aspects of the spiritual life, also known as John the Solitary. Some of his writings are in the form of dialogues. Other writings include letters, a treatise on baptism, and shorter works on prayer and silence.

John of Carpathus (c. seventh/eighth century). Perhaps John the bishop from the island of Carpathus, situated between Crete and Rhodes, who attended the Synod of 680/81. He wrote two "centuries" (a literary genre in Eastern spirituality consisting of 100 short sections, or chapters). These were entitled *Chapters of Encouragement to the Monks of India* and *Chapters on Theology and Knowledge* which are included in the *Philokalia*.

John of Damascus (c. 650-750). Arab monastic and theologian whose writings enjoyed great influence in both the Eastern and Western Churches. His most influential writing was the *Orthodox Faith*.

John of Jerusalem (John II of Jerusalem) (late fourth-early fifth century). Successor of Cyril as bishop of Jerusalem (386-417). Engaged with Epiphanius in the first Origenist controversy and became involved in the Pelagian controversy. He is probably the author of the five Mystagogical Lectures attributed to Cyril.

John the Elder (c. eighth century). A Syriac author also known as John of Dalyatha or John Saba ("the elder") who belonged to monastic circles of the Church of the East and lived in the region of Mount Qardu (northern Iraq). His most important writings are twenty-two homilies and a collection of fifty-one short letters in which he describes the mystical life as an anticipatory experience of the resurrection life, the fruit of the sacraments of baptism and the Eucharist.

John the Monk. Traditional name found in *The Festal Menaion*, believed to refer to John of Damascus. *See* John of Damascus.

Joseph of Thebes (fourth century). One of the desert fathers of Scetis, also known as Abba Joseph, who taught the most important virtue of a monk was to remain in complete submission to a spiritual father in total renunciation of one's own will.

Joseph's Bible Notes (Hypomnestikon) (fourth or fifth century). A pastiche of biblical and historical questions drawn from various writers, including the Jewish historian, Josephus. It was believed to have been written by Josephus Christianus, derived from the brief poem appended at the end of the book, but the author ultimately is unknown. It evidences an Alexandrian Christology.

Josephus, Flavius (c. 37-c. 101). Jewish historian from a distinguished priestly family. Acquainted with the Essenes and Sadducees, he himself became a Pharisee. He joined the great Jewish revolt that broke out in 66 and was chosen by the Sanhedrin at Jerusalem to be commander-in-chief in Galilee. Showing great shrewdness to ingratiate himself with Vespasian by foretelling his elevation and that of his son Titus to the imperial dignity, Josephus was restored his liberty after 69 when Vespasian became emperor.

Julian of Eclanum (c. 385-450). Bishop of Eclanum in 416/417 who was removed from office and exiled in 419 for not officially opposing Pelagianism. In exile, he was accepted by Theodore of Mopsuestia, whose Antiochene exegetical style he followed. Although he was never able to regain his ecclesiastical position, Julian taught in Sicily until his death. His works include commentaries on Job and parts of the Minor Prophets, a translation of Theodore of Mopsuestia's commentary on the Psalms, and various letters. Sympathetic to Pelagius, Julian applied his intellectual acumen and rhetorical training to argue against Augustine on matters such as free will, desire and the locus of evil.

Julian Pomerius (late fifth-early sixth century). Author of *On the Contemplative Life* and a teacher of Caesarius of Arles. Originally from Mauretania, Julian moved to southern Gaul where he was ordained as a priest. He eventually settled in Arles as a teacher of rhetoric.

Julian the Arian (c. fourth century). Antiochene, Arian author of *Commentary on Job*, and probably a follower of Aetius and Eunomius. The 85 *Apostolic Canons*, once part of the *Apostolic Constitutions*, and the Pseudo-Ignatian writings are also attributed to him.

Julius Africanus (c. 160-c. 240). First Christian chronographer who influenced later historians such as Eusebius. Born in Jerusalem, he was charged with organizing a library in the Pantheon at Rome. He was acquainted with Origen during the time he studied in Alexandria and corresponded with him. He died in Palestine.

Justin Martyr (c. 100/110-165; fl. c. 148-161). Palestinian philosopher who was converted to Christianity, "the only sure and worthy philosophy." He traveled to Rome where he wrote several apologies against both pagans and Jews, combining Greek philosophy and Christian theology; he was eventually martyred.

Justinian the Emperor (482-565). Emperor of Byzantium, 527-565. As the second member of the Justinian Dynasty, he instituted an ambitious, though failed, restoration of the Byzantine Empire. He sought theological unity through a politicized Christianity that persecuted perceived heretics and apostates along with Jews and pagans. Many of his writings are extant, including twenty-one letters and four dogmatic works.

Lactantius (c. 260-c. 330). Christian apologist removed from his post as teacher of rhetoric at Nicomedia upon his conversion to Christianity. He was tutor to the son of Constantine and author of *The Divine Institutes.*

Leander (c. 545-c. 600). Latin ecclesiastical writer, of whose works only two survive. He was instrumental in spreading Christianity among the Visigoths, gaining significant historical influence in Spain in his time.

Leo the Great (regn. 440-461). Bishop of Rome whose *Tome to Flavian* helped to strike a balance between Nestorian and Cyrilline positions at the Council of Chalcedon in 451.

Letter of Barnabas (c. 130). An allegorical and typological interpretation of the Old Testament with a decidedly anti-Jewish tone. It was included with other New Testament works as a "Catholic epistle" at least until Eusebius of Caesarea (c. 260/263-340) questioned its authenticity.

Letter to Diognetus (c. third century). A refutation of paganism and an exposition of the Christian life and faith. The author of this letter is unknown, and the exact identity of its recipient, Diognetus, continues to elude patristic scholars.

Liturgy of St. Basil (fourth century and onward). The liturgical collections of the Byzantine liturgy containing an anaphora attributed to Basil the Great. The liturgy has evolved considerably over the centuries.

Liturgy of St. James. A liturgy adopted throughout the East, including by the Syrian Orthodox Church. Traditionally attributed to St. James the bishop of Jerusalem, it survives in both Greek and Syriac versions.

Liturgy of St. Mark (fourth century). Traditional Eucharistic liturgy of the Alexandrian Church. First adopted by the Egyptian Melchites, its extant manuscripts are based on an early Egyptian text, and forms of the rite are still used by the Coptic and Ethiopian Churches.

Liturgy of the Blessed Apostles (first or second

century). One of the earliest Christian liturgies. Attributed to Addai (Addaeus) and Mari (Maris), Christian missionaries to Edessa and surrounding areas of Syria, the liturgy was also celebrated in Mesopotamia and Persia. It was likely used in the Syrian church and was also taken up later by the Nestorians.

Liturgy of the Coptic Jacobites (sixth century). Liturgy of the West Syrian Church named after the monophysite Jacob Baradaeus (d. 578) who used this rite, in the Coptic language, to solidify the hierarchy of monophysitism. Many of the anaphorae can be traced back in their basic structure to the church of Jerusalem in apostolic times.

Liturgy of the Hours (third century). Early liturgy for prayers throughout the day. The church community, especially monastics, offered prayer at set times of the day: morning prayer, prayers of terce (third hour), sext (sixth hour) and none (ninth hour) that correspond to the hours of Christ's crucifixion and death. Evening prayer was associated with the nighttime rest of the world itself. More elaborate and extended divisions of the hours followed that included Lauds, Prime, Terce, Sext, None, Vespers and Compline, reflective of a theology of time that celebrates the rhythm of life as God's people communicate with him.

Lucifer (d. 370/371). Bishop of Cagliari and vigorous supporter of Athanasius and the Nicene Creed. In conflict with the emperor Constantius, he was banished to Palestine and later to Thebaid (Egypt).

Luculentius (fifth century). Unknown author of a group of short commentaries on the New Testament, especially Pauline passages. His exegesis is mainly literal and relies mostly on earlier authors such as Jerome and Augustine. The content of his writing may place it in the fifth century.

Macarius of Egypt (c. 300-c. 390). One of the Desert Fathers. Accused of supporting Athanasius, Macarius was exiled c. 374 to an island in the Nile by Lucius, the Arian successor of Athanasius. Macarius continued his teaching of monastic theology at Wadi Natrun.

Macrina the Younger (c. 327-379). The elder sister of Basil the Great and Gregory of Nyssa, she is known as "the Younger" to distinguish her from her paternal grandmother. She had a powerful influence on her younger brothers, especially on Gregory, who called her his teacher and relates her teaching in *On the Soul and the Resurrection*.

Manichaeans. A religious movement that originated circa 241 in Persia under the leadership of Mani but was apparently of complex Christian origin. It is said to have denied free will and the universal sovereignty of God, teaching that kingdoms of light and darkness are coeternal and that the redeemed are particles of a spiritual man of light held captive in the darkness of matter (*see* Gnostics).

Marcellus of Ancyra (d. c. 375). Wrote a refutation of Arianism. Later, he was accused of Sabellianism, especially by Eusebius of Caesarea. While the Western church declared him orthodox, the Eastern church excommunicated him. Some scholars have attributed to him certain works of Athanasius.

Marcion (fl. 144). Heretic of the mid second century who rejected the Old Testament and much of the New Testament, claiming that the Father of Jesus Christ was other than the Old Testament God (*see* Gnostics).

Marius Victorinus (b. c. 280/285; fl. c. 355-363). Grammarian of African origin who taught rhetoric at Rome and translated works of Platonists. After his conversion (c. 355), he wrote works against the Arians and commentaries on Paul's letters.

Mark the Hermit (c. sixth century). Monk who lived near Tarsus and produced works on ascetic practices as well as christological issues.

Martin of Braga (fl. c. 568-579). Anti-Arian metropolitan of Braga on the Iberian peninsula. He was highly educated and presided over the provincial council of Braga in 572.

Martyrdom of Polycarp (c. 160). A letter

written shortly after the death of the eighty-six-year-old bishop of Smyrna which provides, in sometimes gruesome detail, the earliest account of Christian martyrdom outside of the New Testament.

Martyrius. *See* Sahdona.

Maximinus (the Arian) (b. c. 360-65). Bishop of an Arian community, perhaps in Illyricum. Of Roman descent, he debated publicly with Augustine at Hippo (427 or 428), ardently defending Arian doctrine. Besides the polemical works he wrote against the orthodox, such as his *Against the Heretics, Jews and Pagans*, he also wrote fifteen sermons that are considered much less polemical, having been previously attributed to Maximus of Turin. He is also known for his twenty-four *Explanations of Chapters of the Gospels*.

Maximus of Turin (d. 408/423). Bishop of Turin. Over one hundred of his sermons survive on Christian festivals, saints and martyrs.

Maximus the Confessor (c. 580-662). Palestinian-born theologian and ascetic writer. Fleeing the Arab invasion of Jerusalem in 614, he took refuge in Constantinople and later Africa. He died near the Black Sea after imprisonment and severe suffering, having his tongue cut off and his right hand mutilated. He taught total preference for God and detachment from all things.

Melito of Sardis (d. c. 190). Bishop of Sardis. According to Polycrates, he may have been Jewish by birth. Among his numerous works is a liturgical document known as *On Pascha* (ca. 160-177). As a Quartodeciman, and one intimately involved in that controversy, Melito celebrated Pascha on the fourteenth of Nisan in line with the custom handed down from Judaism.

Methodius of Olympus (d. 311). Bishop of Olympus who celebrated virginity in a *Symposium* partly modeled on Plato's dialogue of that name.

Minucius Felix (second or third century). Christian apologist who was an advocate in Rome. His *Octavius* agrees at numerous points with the *Apologeticum of Tertullian*. His birthplace is believed to be in Africa.

Montanist Oracles. Montanism was an apocalyptic and strictly ascetic movement begun in the latter half of the second century by a certain Montanus in Phrygia, who, along with certain of his followers, uttered oracles they claimed were inspired by the Holy Spirit. Little of the authentic oracles remains and most of what is known of Montanism comes from the authors who wrote against the movement. Montanism was formally condemned as a heresy before by Asiatic synods.

Muratorian Fragment (second century). Earliest known list of New Testament books, preserved in an eighth-century manuscript. The document is missing its first lines yet includes all but five books of the final canon. It also discusses various contested writings, several of which are clearly rejected.

Nemesius of Emesa (fl. late fourth century). Bishop of Emesa in Syria whose most important work, *Of the Nature of Man*, draws on several theological and philosophical sources and is the first exposition of a Christian anthropology.

Nestorius (c. 381-c. 451). Patriarch of Constantinople (428-431) who founded the heresy which says that there are two persons, divine and human, rather than one person truly united in the incarnate Christ. He resisted the teaching of theotokos, causing Nestorian churches to separate from Constantinople.

Nicetas of Remesiana (fl. second half of fourth century). Bishop of Remesiana in Serbia, whose works affirm the consubstantiality of the Son and the deity of the Holy Spirit.

Nilus of Ancyra (d. c. 430). Prolific ascetic writer and disciple of John Chrysostom. Sometimes erroneously known as Nilus of Sinai, he was a native of Ancyra and studied at Constantinople.

Novatian of Rome (fl. 235-258). Roman theologian, otherwise orthodox, who formed a schismatic church after failing to become pope.

His treatise on the Trinity states the classic Western doctrine.

Odes of Solomon (early second century). A collection of forty-two pseudo-Solomonic poems containing commentary on the liturgy of a Judeo-Christian community in Syria. The poems are permeated with soteriological concerns, though they never mention the name Jesus.

Oecumenius (sixth century). Called the Rhetor or the Philosopher, Oecumenius wrote the earliest extant Greek commentary on Revelation. Scholia by Oecumenius on some of John Chrysostom's commentaries on the Pauline Epistles are still extant.

Olympiodorus (early sixth century). Exegete and deacon of Alexandria, known for his commentaries that come to us mostly in catenae.

Optatus (fourth century). Bishop of Milevis in North Africa. He wrote a treatise against Donatism. These six books emphasize the uniqueness of the Catholic Church and include a list of documents on the Donatist controversy.

Origen of Alexandria (b. 185; fl. c. 200-254). Influential exegete and systematic theologian. He was condemned (perhaps unfairly) for maintaining the preexistence of souls while purportedly denying the resurrection of the body. His extensive works of exegesis focus on the spiritual meaning of the text.

Pachomius (c. 292-347). Founder of cenobitic monasticism. A gifted group leader and author of a set of rules, he was defended after his death by Athanasius of Alexandria.

Pacian of Barcelona (c. fourth century). Bishop of Barcelona whose writings polemicize against popular pagan festivals as well as Novatian schismatics.

Palladius of Helenopolis (c. 363/364-c. 431). Bishop of Helenopolis in Bithynia (400-417) and then Aspuna in Galatia. A disciple of Evagrius of Pontus and admirer of Origen, Palladius became a zealous adherent of John Chrysostom and shared his troubles in 403. His *Lausaic History* is the leading source for

the history of early monasticism, stressing the spiritual value of the life of the desert.

Papias of Hierapolis (c. early second century). Bishop of Hierapolis in Phrygia who may have known the apostle John. Through his writings, which are extant only in fragments preserved in Eusebius's *Ecclesiastical History*, Papias influenced later theologians including Irenaeus, Hippolytus and Victorinus, and provided an important witness to traditions about the origins of the Gospels.

Paschasius of Dumium (c. 515-c. 580). Translator of sentences of the Desert Fathers from Greek into Latin while a monk in Dumium.

Paterius (c. sixth-seventh century). Disciple of Gregory the Great who is primarily responsible for the transmission of Gregory's works to many later medieval authors.

Patrick (d. c. 492). Saint known as the apostle to Ireland. Born in Britain and later kidnapped at the age of sixteen by pirates, Patrick was taken to Ireland where he worked as a shepherd. He later returned to Britain and undertook training in Gaul and possibly also Lerins for the apostolate. According to tradition, he was consecrated a bishop and returned to northern Ireland in 432 where he preached the gospel and established his see at Armagh, which was extended to the continent via Irish missionaries. His two works that survive are *Epistle to the Soldier Coroticus* and *Confession*, written toward the end of his life. His feast day is March 17.

Paulinus of Milan (late 4th-early 5th century). Personal secretary and biographer of Ambrose of Milan. He took part in the Pelagian controversy.

Paulinus of Nola (355-431). Roman senator and distinguished Latin poet whose frequent encounters with Ambrose of Milan (c. 333-397) led to his eventual conversion and baptism in 389. He eventually renounced his wealth and influential position and took up his pen to write poetry in service of Christ. He also wrote many letters to, among others,

Augustine, Jerome and Rufinus.

Paulus Orosius (b. c. 380). An outspoken critic of Pelagius, mentored by Augustine. His *Seven Books of History Against the Pagans* was perhaps the first history of Christianity.

Pelagius (c. 354-c. 420). Contemporary of Augustine whose followers were condemned in 418 and 431 for maintaining that even before Christ there were people who lived wholly without sin and that salvation depended on free will.

Peter Chrysologus (c. 380-450). Latin archbishop of Ravenna whose teachings included arguments for adherence in matters of faith to the Roman see, and the relationship between grace and Christian living.

Peter of Alexandria (d. c. 311). Bishop of Alexandria. He marked (and very probably initiated) the reaction at Alexandria against extreme doctrines of Origen. During the persecution of Christians in Alexandria, Peter was arrested and beheaded by Roman officials. Eusebius of Caesarea described him as "a model bishop, remarkable for his virtuous life and his ardent study of the Scriptures."

Philip the Priest (d. 455/56) Acknowledged by Gennadius as a disciple of Jerome. In his *Commentary on the Book of Job*, Philip utilizes Jerome's Vulgate, providing an important witness to the transmission of that translation. A few of his letters are extant.

Philo of Alexandria (c. 20 B.C.-c. A.D. 50). Jewish-born exegete who greatly influenced Christian patristic interpretation of the Old Testament. Born to a rich family in Alexandria, Philo was a contemporary of Jesus and lived an ascetic and contemplative life that makes some believe he was a rabbi. His interpretation of Scripture based the spiritual sense on the literal. Although influenced by Hellenism, Philo's theology remains thoroughly Jewish.

Philoxenus of Mabbug (c. 440-523). Bishop of Mabbug (Hierapolis) and a leading thinker in the early Syrian Orthodox Church. His extensive writings in Syriac include a set of thirteen *Discourses on the Christian Life*, several works on the incarnation and a number of exegetical works.

Phoebadius of Agen (d. c. 395). Bishop of Agen whose *Contra arianos* attacked the 357 pro-Arian formula of Sirmium. Phoebadius was the last leader induced to sign the formula of Ariminum in 359, a compromise widely viewed as an Arian triumph.

Photius (c. 820-891). An important Byzantine churchman and university professor of philosophy, mathematics and theology. He was twice the patriarch of Constantinople. First he succeeded Ignatius in 858, but was deposed in 863 when Ignatius was reinstated. Again he followed Ignatius in 878 and remained the patriarch until 886, at which time he was removed by Leo VI. His most important theological work is *Address on the Mystagogy of the Holy Spirit*, in which he articulates his opposition to the Western filioque, i.e., the procession of the Holy Spirit from the Father and the Son. He is also known for his *Amphilochia* and *Library* (*Bibliotheca*).

Poemen (c. fifth century). One-seventh of the sayings in the *Sayings of the Desert Fathers* are attributed to Poemen, which is Greek for shepherd. Poemen was a common title among early Egyptian desert ascetics, and it is unknown whether all of the sayings come from one person.

Polycarp of Smyrna (c. 69-155). Bishop of Smyrna who vigorously fought heretics such as the Marcionites and Valentinians. He was the leading Christian figure in Roman Asia in the middle of the second century.

Possidius (late fourth-fifth century). A member of Augustine's monastic community at Hippo from 391, then bishop of Calama in Numidia sometime soon after 397. He fled back to Hippo when Vandals invaded Calama in 428 and cared for Augustine during his final illness. Returning to Calama after the death of Augustine (430), he was expelled by

Genseric, Arian king of the Vandals, in 437. Nothing more is known of him after this date. Sometime between 432 and 437 he wrote *Vita Augustini*, to which he added *Indiculus*, a list of Augustine's books, sermons and letters.

Potamius of Lisbon (fl. c. 350-360). Bishop of Lisbon who joined the Arian party in 357, but later returned to the Catholic faith (c. 359?). His works from both periods are concerned with the larger Trinitarian debates of his time.

Primasius (fl. 550-560). Bishop of Hadrumetum in North Africa (modern Tunisia) and one of the few Africans to support the condemnation of the Three Chapters. Drawing on Augustine and Tyconius, he wrote a commentary on the Apocalypse, which in allegorizing fashion views the work as referring to the history of the church.

Proclus of Constantinople (c. 390-446). Patriarch of Constantinople (434-446). His patriarchate dealt with the Nestorian controversy, rebutting, in his *Tome to the Armenian Bishops*, Theodore of Mopsuestia's Christology where Theodore was thought to have overly separated the two natures of Christ. Proclus stressed the unity of Christ in his formula "One of the Trinity suffered," which was later taken up and spread by the Scythian monks of the sixth century, resulting in the theopaschite controversy. Proclus was known as a gifted preacher and church politician, extending and expanding Constantinople's influence while avoiding conflict with Antioch, Rome and Alexandria.

Procopius of Gaza (c. 465-c. 530). A Christian exegete educated in Alexandria. He wrote numerous theological works and commentaries on Scripture (particularly the Hebrew Bible), the latter marked by the allegorical exegesis for which the Alexandrian school was known.

Prosper of Aquitaine (c. 390-c. 463). Probably a lay monk and supporter of the theology of Augustine on grace and predestination. He collaborated closely with Pope Leo I in his doctrinal statements.

Prudentius (c. 348-c. 410). Latin poet and hymn writer who devoted his later life to Christian writing. He wrote didactic poems on the theology of the incarnation, against the heretic Marcion and against the resurgence of paganism.

Pseudo-Clementines (third-fourth century). A series of apocryphal writings pertaining to a conjured life of Clement of Rome. Written in a form of popular legend, the stories from Clement's life, including his opposition to Simon Magus, illustrate and promote articles of Christian teaching. It is likely that the corpus is a derivative of a number of Gnostic and Judeo-Christian writings. Dating the corpus is a complicated issue.

Pseudo-Dionysius the Areopagite (fl. c. 500). Author who assumed the name of Dionysius the Areopagite mentioned in Acts 17:34, and who composed the works known as the *Corpus Areopagiticum* (or *Dionysiacum*). These writings were the foundation of the apophatic school of mysticism in their denial that anything can be truly predicated of God.

Pseudo-Macarius (fl. c. 390). An anonymous writer and ascetic (from Mesopotamia?) active in Antioch whose badly edited works were attributed to Macarius of Egypt. He had keen insight into human nature, prayer and the inner life. His work includes some one hundred discourses and homilies.

Quodvultdeus (fl. 430). Carthaginian bishop and friend of Augustine who endeavored to show at length how the New Testament fulfilled the Old Testament.

Rabanus (Hrabanus) Maurus (c. 780-856). Frankish monk, theologian and teacher, student of Alcuin of York, then Abbot of Fulda from 822 to 842 and Archbishop of Mainz from 848 until his death in 856. The author of poetry, homilies, treatises on education, grammar, and doctrine, and an encyclopedia titled *On the Nature of Things*, he also wrote commentaries on Scripture, including the books of Kings and Esther. Though he is technically an early medieval writer, his works are included as they reflect earlier thought.

Riddles in the Apocalypse (eighth century). Commentary on Revelation of unknown authorship. *De Enigmatibus ex Apocalypsi* in Latin, the commentary explores the enigmatic symbolism of the book. It is contained in the one volume commentary known as the *Irish Reference Bible*, or *Das Bibelwerk* which dates from the late eighth century (see also CCL 7:231-95).

Romanus Melodus (fl. c. 536-556). Born as a Jew in Emesa not far from Beirut where after his baptism he later became deacon of the Church of the Resurrection. He later moved to Constantinople and may have seen the destruction of the Hagia Sophia and its rebuilding during the time he flourished there. As many as eighty metrical sermons (*kontakia*, sg. *kontakion*) that utilize dialogical poetry have come down to us under his name. These sermons were sung rather than preached during the liturgy, and frequently provide theological insights and Scriptural connections often unique to Romanus. His Christology, closely associated with Justinian, reflects the struggles against the Monophysites of his day.

Rufinus of Aquileia (c. 345-411). Orthodox Christian thinker and historian who nonetheless translated and preserved the works of Origen, and defended him against the strictures of Jerome and Epiphanius. He lived the ascetic life in Rome, Egypt and Jerusalem (the Mount of Olives).

Sabellius (fl. 200). Allegedly the author of the heresy which maintains that the Father and Son are a single person. The patripassian variant of this heresy states that the Father suffered on the cross.

Sahdona (fl. 635-640). Known in Greek as Martyrius, this Syriac author was bishop of Beth Garmai. He studied in Nisibis and was exiled for his christological ideas. His most important work is the deeply scriptural *Book of Perfection* which ranks as one of the masterpieces of Syriac monastic literature.

Salvian the Presbyter of Marseilles (c. 400-c. 480). An important author for the history of his own time. He saw the fall of Roman civilization to the barbarians as a consequence of the reprehensible conduct of Roman Christians. In *The Governance of God* he developed the theme of divine providence.

Second Letter of Clement (c. 150). The so called *Second Letter of Clement* is an early Christian sermon probably written by a Corinthian author, though some scholars have assigned it to a Roman or Alexandrian author.

Sedulius, Coelius (fl. 425-450). Author of the *Paschale carmen*, a poem in five books, which focuses on the miraculous character of Christ's suffering. Sedulius learned philosophy in Italy and was later converted to Christianity by the presbyter Macedonius. He has at times been confused with the poet Sedulius Scotus (ninth century). He is also known for the similarly themed *Paschale opus*, among other works.

Seventh Council of Carthage Under Cyprian (256). One of many Carthaginian councils convened in response to the controversy surrounding rebaptisms. All bishops present, including Cyprian, deemed that baptism administered by heretics was invalid and necessitated rebaptism, a position later revised by Augustine.

Severian of Gabala (fl. c. 400). A contemporary of John Chrysostom, he was a highly regarded preacher in Constantinople, particularly at the imperial court, and ultimately sided with Chrysostom's accusers. He wrote homilies on Genesis.

Severus of Antioch (fl. 488-538). A monophysite theologian, consecrated bishop of Antioch in 522. Born in Pisidia, he studied in Alexandria and Beirut, taught in Constantinople and was exiled to Egypt.

Shenoute (c. 350-466). Abbot of Athribis in Egypt. His large monastic community was known for very strict rules. He accompanied Cyril of Alexandria to the Council of Ephesus in 431, where he played an important role in deposing Nestorius. He knew Greek but wrote in Coptic, and his literary activity includes homilies, catecheses on monastic subjects, letters, and a couple of theological treatises.

Shepherd of Hermas (second century). Divided into five *Visions*, twelve *Mandates* and ten *Similitudes*, this Christian apocalypse was written by a former slave and named for the form of the second angel said to have granted him his visions. This work was highly esteemed for its moral value and was used as a textbook for catechumens in the early church.

Sibylline Oracles (second century B.C.-second century A.D.) An apocryphal collection of Greek prophecies. Spanning the second century B.C. to the second century A.D., the collection is the product of Christian redaction of Jewish adaptations and expansions of pagan Greek oracles.

Socrates (Scholasticus) (c. 380-450). Greek historian and lawyer from Constantinople. His *Ecclesiastical History*, meant to continue the work of Eusebius, comprises seven books, each covering the reign of one emperor between 306 and 439.

Sophronius of Jerusalem (Sophronius Sophistes) (c. 550-638). Patriarch of Jerusalem (634-638) and opponent of monothelitism. Born in Damascus of Arabic descent, Sophronius became a monk and friend to John Moschus at a monastery near Jerusalem, though he also ministered in Sinai, Egypt and Italy.

Stephen of Hnes (Stephen of Heracleopolis Magna) (seventh century?). Bishop of Hnes who built two small chapels, or monasteries, in the district of Cusae in upper Egypt. He wrote a panegyric to Apollo the archimandrite of the monastery of Isaac. Apollo, who had met the Patriarch Severus of Antioch just before his death in 538, was Stephen's spiritual father. He wrote another encomium to St. Helias who was later venerated by her followers in the cult of St. Helias.

Sulpicius Severus (c. 360-c. 420). An ecclesiastical writer from Bordeaux born of noble parents. Devoting himself to monastic retirement, he became a personal friend and enthusiastic disciple of St. Martin of Tours.

Symeon the New Theologian (c. 949-1022). Compassionate spiritual leader known for his strict rule. He believed that the divine light could be perceived and received through the practice of mental prayer.

Syncletica (fifth century). Egyptian nun known from collected sayings and a fifth-century *Life*. Syncletica began ascetic practices in her parents' Alexandria home and after their death retired to desert life. Until succumbing to illness in her eighties, she was a spiritual leader to women who gathered to learn from her piety.

Synesios of Cyrene (c. 370-c. 413). Bishop of Ptolemais elected in 410. Born of a noble pagan family, Synesios studied in Alexandria under the neoplatonist philosopher Hypatia. His work includes nine hymns that present a complex Trinitarian theology with neoplatonic influences.

Synod of Alexandria (362). A gathering of Egyptian bishops and Nicene delegates, called by Athanasius after the death of Constantius. The synod published a letter that expressed anti-Arian agreement on Trinitarian language.

Tarasius of Constantinople (d. 806). Patriarch of Constantinople from 784. Tarasius promoted reconciliation between Eastern and Western churches. At his urging Empress Irene II called the Second Council of Nicaea (787) to address debates over iconoclasm.

Tatian (second century). Christian apologist from the East who studied under Justin in Rome, returning to his old country after his mentor's martyrdom. Famous for his Gospel harmony, the *Diatessaron*, Tatian also wrote *Address to the Greeks*, which was a defense of Christianity addressed to the pagan world.

Tertullian of Carthage (c. 155/160-225/250; fl. c. 197-222). Brilliant Carthaginian apologist and polemicist who laid the foundations of Christology and trinitarian orthodoxy in the West, though he himself was later estranged from the catholic tradition due to its laxity.

Theodore bar Koni (d. 845). Important Nestorian author and apologist who taught at the school of Kashkar [Iraq] in Beth Aramaye and later became metropolitan of Beth Garmai. Numerous works are attributed to him, though only a collection of scholia on the Old and New Testaments which offers a defense of East Syrian Christianity and refutations of Islam and various heresies is extant. He also wrote an ecclesiastical history that provided a glimpse into the lives of Nestorian patriarchs, a book on logic, and treatises against monophysitism and Arianism.

Theodore of Heraclea (d. c. 355). An anti-Nicene bishop of Thrace. He was part of a team seeking reconciliation between Eastern and Western Christianity. In 343 he was excommunicated at the council of Sardica. His writings focus on a literal interpretation of Scripture.

Theodore of Mopsuestia (c. 350-428). Bishop of Mopsuestia, founder of the Antiochene, or literalistic, school of exegesis. A great man in his day, he was later condemned as a precursor of Nestorius.

Theodore of Tabennesi (d. 368) Vice general of the Pachomian monasteries (c. 350-368) under Horsiesi. Several of his letters are known.

Theodoret of Cyr (c. 393-466). Bishop of Cyr (Cyrrhus), he was an opponent of Cyril who commented extensively on Old Testament texts as a lucid exponent of Antiochene exegesis.

Theodotus of Ancyra (d. before 446). Bishop of Ancyra in Galatia and friend-turned-enemy of Nestorius. He fought against John of Antioch who consequently excommunicated him. Several of his works are extant.

Theodotus the Valentinian (second century). Likely a Montanist who may have been related to the Alexandrian school. Extracts of his work are known through writings of Clement of Alexandria.

Theophanes (775-845). Hymnographer and bishop of Nicaea (842-845). He was persecuted during the second iconoclastic period for his support of the Seventh Council (Second Council of Nicaea, 787). He wrote many hymns in the tradition of the monastery of Mar Sabbas that were used in the *Paraklitiki*.

Theophilus of Alexandria (d. 412). Patriarch of Alexandria (385-412) and the uncle of his successor, Cyril. His patriarchate was known for his opposition to paganism, having destroyed the Serapeion and its library in 391, but he also built many churches. He also was known for his political machinations against his theological enemies, especially John Chrysostom, whom he himself had previously consecrated as patriarch, ultimately getting John removed from his see and earning the intense dislike of Antioch Christians. He is, however, venerated among the Copts and Syrians, among whom many of his sermons have survived, although only a few are deemed authentically his. His *Homily on the Mystical Supper*, commenting on the Last Supper, is perhaps one of his most well known.

Theophilus of Antioch (late second century). Bishop of Antioch. His only surviving work is *Ad Autholycum*, where we find the first Christian commentary on Genesis and the first use of the term Trinity. Theophilus's apologetic literary heritage had influence on Irenaeus and possibly Tertullian.

Theophylact of Ohrid (c. 1050-c. 1108). Byzantine archbishop of Ohrid (or Achrida) in what is now Bulgaria. Drawing on earlier works, he wrote commentaries on several Old Testament books and all of the New Testament except for Revelation.

Third Council of Constantinople (681). The Sixth Ecumenical Council, convoked by Constantine IV to resolve the Monothelite controversy. The council's decree affirmed the doctrine that Christ's two natures correspond to two distinct wills and two energies.

Treatise on Rebaptism (third century). An anonymous treatise arguing, possibly against Cyprian, that those receiving baptism by heretics in the name of Jesus ought not be rebaptized.

Tyconius (c. 330-390). A lay theologian and exegete of the Donatist church in North Africa who influenced Augustine. His *Book of Rules* is the first manual of scriptural interpretation in the Latin West. In 380 he was excommunicated by the Donatist council at Carthage.

Valentinian Exposition (second century). A type of secret catechism for those who were to be initiated into the Valentinian version of gnosis. It provided an exposition of the origin of creation and was also concerned with the process of how our salvation is achieved in light of the myth of Sophia. There are references to the sacramental rituals of baptism and the Eucharist and also early evidences of the disagreements and theological controversies that existed among Valentinian theologians.

Valentinus (fl. c. 140). Alexandrian heretic of the mid second century who taught that the material world was created by the transgression of God's Wisdom, or Sophia (*see* Gnostics).

Valerian of Cimiez (fl. c. 422-439). Bishop of Cimiez. He participated in the councils of Riez (439) and Vaison (422) with a view to strengthening church discipline. He supported Hilary of Arles in quarrels with Pope Leo I.

Venantius Fortunatus (c. 530-c. 610). Latin poet. In 597 Venantius was appointed bishop of Poitiers, where he had served the community of former queen Radegunde since 567. His works include lives of saints and two hymns that were soon incorporated into Western liturgy.

Verecundus (d. 552). An African Christian writer, who took an active part in the christological controversies of the sixth century, especially in the debate on Three Chapters.

He also wrote allegorical commentaries on the nine liturgical church canticles.

Victor of Cartenna (fifth century). Bishop of Cartenna in Mauretania Caesariensis to whom Gennadius attributed *Adversus Arianos*. Other works have been attributed to him, including select works associated with Pseudo-Ambrose and Pseudo-Basil.

Victor of Vita (fl. 480/481-484). Bishop of Vita in the Byzacena province and author of a history of the Vandal persecution in Africa. There is disagreement over the details of his life.

Victorinus of Petovium (d. c. 304). Latin biblical exegete. With multiple works attributed to him, his sole surviving work is the *Commentary on the Apocalypse* and perhaps some fragments from *Commentary on Matthew*. Victorinus expressed strong millenarianism in his writing, though his was less materialistic than the millenarianism of Papias or Irenaeus. In his allegorical approach he could be called a spiritual disciple of Origen. Victorinus died during the first year of Diocletian's persecution, probably in 304.

Vigilius of Thapsus (fl. c. 484). Bishop of Thapsus, who took part in talks between Catholics and Arians at Carthage in 484. Vigilius was the author of *Contra Eutychetem* and the *Dialogus contra arianos, sabellianos et photinianos*, and probably *Contra Felicianum*.

Vincent of Lérins (d. before 450). Monk who has exerted considerable influence through his writings on orthodox dogmatic theological method, as contrasted with the theological methodologies of the heresies.

Walafridius (Walahfrid) Strabo (808-849). Frankish monk, writer and student of Rabanus Maurus. Walafridius was made abbot of the monastery of Reichenau in 838 but was exiled in 840, when one of the sons of Emperor Louis the Pious—to whom Walafridius was loyal— invaded Reichenau. He was restored in 842 and died in 849. His writings include poetry, commentaries on scripture, lives of saints and a historical explanation of the liturgy. Though he is technically an early medieval writer, his works are included

Zephyrinus (d. 217). Bishop of Rome from 199 to 217. Renewed his predecessor Victor's condemnation of the adoptionism being taught in Rome by Theodotus of Byzantium and re-admitted the excommunicated modalist bishop Natalius upon the latter's repentance, but as a layperson. Much of what we know about him is from the work of Hippolytus, whose negative opinion of Zephyrinus may have been colored by his antagonism toward Zephyrinus's successor, Callistus. The epistles attributed to Zephyrinus are now considered spurious (part of the so-called False Decretals of the ninth century) but are included as possibly reflecting earlier thought.

Timeline of Writers of the Patristic Period

Location	British Isles	Gaul	Spain, Portugal	Rome* and Italy	Carthage and Northern Africa
Period					
2nd century				Clement of Rome, fl. c. 92-101 (Greek)	
				Shepherd of Hermas, c. 140 (Greek)	
				Justin Martyr (Ephesus, Rome), c. 100/110-165 (Greek)	
				Tatian (Rome/Syria), 2nd cent. (Greek)	
				Muratorian Fragment, 2nd cent. (Latin [orig. Greek])	
				Valentinus the Gnostic (Rome), fl. c. 140 (Greek)	
				Hegesippus, 2nd cent. (Greek)	
		Irenaeus of Lyons, c. 135-c. 202 (Greek)		Marcion (Rome), fl. 144 (Greek)	
				Heracleon, 145-180 (Greek)	
3rd century				Zephyrinus (Rome), regn. 199-217	Tertullian of Carthage, c. 155/160-c. 225 (Latin)
				Callistus of Rome, regn. 217-222 (Latin)	
				Minucius Felix of Rome, fl. 218-235 (Latin)	
				Hippolytus (Rome, Palestine?), fl. 222-235/245 (Greek)	
				Novatian of Rome, fl. 235-258 (Latin)	Cyprian of Carthage, fl. 248-258 (Latin)
					Seventh Council of Carthage Under Cyprian, 256 (Latin)
					Treatise on Rebaptism, 3rd cent. (Latin)
				Victorinus of Petovium, 230-304 (Latin)	

*One of the five ancient patriarchates

Alexandria* and Egypt	Constantinople* and Asia Minor, Greece	Antioch* and Syria	Mesopotamia, Persia	Jerusalem* and Palestine	Location Unknown
Philo of Alexandria, c. 20 B.C. - c. A.D. 50 (Greek)				Flavius Josephus (Rome), c. 37-c. 101 (Greek)	
Basilides (Alexandria), 2nd cent. (Greek)	Polycarp of Smyrna, c. 69-155 (Greek)	Ignatius of Antioch, c. 35-107/ 112 (Greek)			
	Martyrdom of Polycarp, c. 160 (Greek)	*Didache* (Egypt?), c. 100 (Greek)			
Letter of Barnabas (Syria?), c. 130 (Greek)	Aristides, 2nd cent. (Greek)	*Odes of Solomon* (perhaps also Palestine or Egypt), early 2nd cent. (Syriac/Aramaic)			
Gospel of Truth (Egypt?), 2nd cent. (Coptic/Greek)	Papias of Hierapolis, c. early 2nd cent. (Greek)				*Second Letter of Clement* (spurious; Corinth, Rome, Alexandria?) c. 150, (Greek)
Valentinian Exposition, 2nd cent. (Greek)					
Theodotus the Valentinian, 2nd cent. (Greek)	Athenagoras (Greece), fl. 176-180 (Greek)				
Epistula Apostolorum, mid 2nd cent. (Greek [Coptic/ Ethiopic])					
	Melito of Sardis, d. c. 190 (Greek)			Julius Africanus, c. 160-c. 240 (Greek)	
	Acts of Paul and Thecla, 2nd cent. (Greek)	*Gospel of Peter*, late 2nd cent. (Greek)			
Clement of Alexandria, c. 150-215 (Greek)	*Acts of Peter*, c. 190 (Greek)	Theophilus of Antioch, c. late 2nd cent. (Greek)			
	Montanist Oracles, late 2nd cent. (Greek)				
Sabellius (Egypt), 2nd-3rd cent. (Greek)		*Gospel of Philip* (Syria, Egypt?) 2nd or 3rd cent. (Coptic/ Greek)			
Letter to Diognetus, 3rd cent. (Greek)		Bardesanes, 154-222 (Syriac)			
		Acts of Thomas, c. 225 (Syriac)	Mani (Manichaeans), c. 216-276 (Persian/ Syriac)		Pseudo-Clementines 3rd cent. (Greek)
Origen (Alexandria, Caesarea of Palestine), 185-254 (Greek)	Firmilian of Caesarea, fl. c. 230-c. 268 (Greek)	*Didascalia Apostolorum*, early 3rd cent. (Syriac)			
	Gregory Thaumaturgus (Neocaesarea), fl. c. 248-264 (Greek)				
Dionysius of Alexandria, d. 264/5 (Greek)					
	Methodius of Olympus (Lycia), d. c. 311 (Greek)				

Timeline of Writers of the Patristic Period

Location	British Isles	Gaul	Spain, Portugal	Rome* and Italy	Carthage and Northern Africa
Period					
4th century		Lactantius, c. 260-330 (Latin)			
				Firmicus Maternus (Sicily), fl. c. 335 (Latin)	Arnobius of Sicca, d. c. 327 (Latin)
			Hosius of Cordova, d. 357 (Latin)	Marius Victorinus (Rome), fl. 355-363 (Latin)	
		Hilary of Poitiers, c. 315-367 (Latin)	Potamius of Lisbon, fl. c. 350-360 (Latin)	Eusebius of Vercelli, fl. c. 360 (Latin)	
			Gregory of Elvira, fl. 359-385 (Latin)	Lucifer of Cagliari (Sardinia), d. 370/371 (Latin)	
				Damasus of Rome, c. 304-384 (Latin)	Optatus of Milevis, 4th cent. (Latin)
				Ambrosiaster (Italy?), fl. c. 366-384 (Latin)	
				Filastrius of Brescia, fl. 380 (Latin)	
			Pacian of Barcelona, 4th cent. (Latin)	Faustinus (Rome), fl. 380 (Latin)	
			Prudentius, c. 348-c. 410 (Latin)	Faustus of Riez, fl. c. 380 (Latin)	
					Isaiah of Scete, late 4th cent. (Greek)
		Egeria, 4th cent. (Latin)		Gaudentius of Brescia, fl. 395 (Latin)	Paulus Orosius, b. c. 380 (Latin)
		Phoebadius of Agen, d. c. 395 (Latin)			
		Athanasian Creed, c. 4th or 5th cent. (Latin)		Ambrose of Milan, c. 333-397; fl. 374-397 (Latin)	Augustine of Hippo, 354-430 (Latin)
5th century	Fastidius (Britain), c. 4th-5th cent. (Latin)	*Joseph's Bible Notes*, 4th or 5th cent. (Latin)		Paulinus of Milan, late 4th-early 5th cent. (Latin)	Synesios of Cyrene (Alexandria, Cyrene), c. 370-c. 413 (Greek)
					Possidius, late 4th-5th cent. (Latin)
		Sulpicius Severus (Bordeaux), c. 360-c. 420/425 (Latin)		Rufinus (Aquileia, Rome), c. 345-411 (Latin)	
		John Cassian (Palestine, Egypt, Constantinople, Rome, Marseilles), 360-432 (Latin)		Chromatius (Aquileia), fl. 400 (Latin)	
				Aponius, fl. 405-415 (Latin)	
					Luculentius, 5th cent. (Latin)
	Sedulius, Coelius, fl. 425-450 (Latin)	Vincent of Lérins, d. 435 (Latin)		Pelagius (Britain, Rome), c. 354-c. 420 (Greek)	
		Valerian of Cimiez, fl. c. 422-449 (Latin)		Maximus of Turin, d. 408/423 (Latin)	Quodvultdeus (Carthage), fl. 430 (Latin)
		Eucherius of Lyons, fl. 420-449 (Latin)		Paulinus of Nola, 355-431 (Latin)	
		Hilary of Arles, c. 401-449 (Latin)		Peter Chrysologus (Ravenna), c. 380-450 (Latin)	Dracontius, 5th cent. (Latin)
				Julian of Eclanum, 386-454 (Latin)	

*One of the five ancient patriarchates

Alexandria* and Egypt	Constantinople* and Asia Minor, Greece	Antioch* and Syria	Mesopotamia, Persia	Jerusalem* and Palestine	Location Unknown
	Constantine, d. 337 (Greek)		Hegemonius, fl. early 4th cent. (Greek)		
Antony, c. 251-355 (Coptic /Greek)	Theodore of Heraclea (Thrace), fl. c. 330-355 (Greek)	Eustathius of Antioch, fl. 325 (Greek)	Aphrahat (Persia) c. 270-350; fl. 337-345 (Syriac)	Eusebius of Caesarea (Palestine), c. 260/ 263-340 (Greek)	Commodian, c. 3rd or 5th cent. (Latin)
Peter of Alexandria, d. c. 311 (Greek)	Marcellus of Ancyra, d. c. 375 (Greek)	Eusebius of Emesa, c. 300-c. 359 (Greek)			
Arius (Alexandria), fl. c. 320 (Greek)	Epiphanius of Salamis (Cyprus), c. 315-403 (Greek)	Ephrem the Syrian, c. 306-373 (Syriac)	Jacob of Nisibis, fl. 308-325 (Syriac)		
Alexander of Alexandria, fl. 312-328 (Greek)	Basil (the Great) of Caesarea, b. c. 330; fl. 357-379 (Greek)	Julian the Arian, c. 4th cent. (Greek)			
Pachomius, c. 292-347 (Coptic/Greek?)	Macrina the Younger, c. 327-379 (Greek)	First Creed of the Council of Antioch, 341 (Greek)			
Theodore of Tabennesi, d. 368 (Coptic/Greek)	Apollinaris of Laodicea, 310-c. 392 (Greek)				
Athanasius of Alexandria, c. 295-373; fl. 325-373 (Greek)	Gregory of Nazianzus, b. 329/330; fl. 372-389 (Greek)	Nemesius of Emesa (Syria), fl. late 4th cent. (Greek)			Maximinus, b. c. 360-365 (Latin)
Abba Pior, d. 373 (Coptic/Greek)	Gregory of Nyssa, c. 335-394 (Greek)	Diodore of Tarsus, d. c. 394 (Greek)		Acacius of Caesarea (Palestine), d. c. 365 (Greek)	
Horsiesi, c. 305-390 (Coptic/Greek)	Amphilochius of Iconium, c. 340/ 345- c. 398/404 (Greek)	John Chrysostom (Constantinople), 344/354-407 (Greek)		Cyril of Jerusalem, c. 315-386 (Greek)	
Macarius of Egypt, c. 300-c. 390 (Greek)	Evagrius of Pontus, 345-399 (Greek)	Apostolic Constitutions, c. 375-400 (Greek)		John (II) of Jerusalem, late 4th-early 5th cent. (Greek)	
Abba John, date unknown (Coptic/Greek)		Didascalia, 4th cent. (Syriac)			
Didymus (the Blind) of Alexandria, 313-398 (Greek)	Eunomius of Cyzicus, fl. 360-394 (Greek)	Theodore of Mopsuestia, c. 350-428 (Greek)			
Tyconius, c. 330-390 (Latin)	Pseudo-Macarius (Mesopotamia?), late 4th cent. (Greek)	Acacius of Beroea, c. 340-c. 436 (Greek)			
Joseph of Thebes, 4th cent. (Coptic/Greek)	Nicetas of Remesiana, d. c. 414 (Latin)	Asterius the Homilist (Antioch), late 4th- early 5th (Greek)		Diodore of Tarsus, d. c. 394 (Greek)	
Ammonas, 4th cent. (Syriac)		Book of Steps, c. 400 (Syriac)		Jerome (Rome, Antioch, Bethlehem), c. 347-420 (Latin)	
Abba Moses, c. 332-407 (Coptic/Greek)	Socrates (Scholasticus), c. 380-450 (Greek)	Severian of Gabala, fl. c. 400 (Greek)			
Theophilus of Alexandria, d. 412 (Greek)	Theodotus of Ancyra, d. before 446 (Greek)				
Palladius of Helenopolis (Egypt), c. 365-425 (Greek)	Proclus of Constantinople, c. 390-446 (Greek)		Eznik of Kolb, fl. 430-450 (Armenian)	Philip the Priest (d. 455/56)	
	Nestorius (Constantinople), c. 381-c. 451 (Greek)			Hesychius of Jerusalem, fl. 412-450 (Greek)	
Cyril of Alexandria, 375-444 (Greek)	Basil of Seleucia, fl. 440-468 (Greek)				
Isidore of Pelusium, d. c. 440 (Greek)		Nilus of Ancyra, d. c. 430 (Greek)		Euthymius (Palestine), 377-473 (Greek)	
Hyperechius, c. 5th cent. (Coptic/Greek)	Diadochus of Photice (Macedonia), 400-474 (Greek)	John of Antioch, d. 441/2 (Greek)			

Timeline of Writers of the Patristic Period

Location / Period	British Isles	Gaul	Spain, Portugal	Rome* and Italy	Carthage and Northern Africa
5th century (cont.)		Eusebius of Gaul, 5th cent. (Latin)			Victor of Cartenna, 5th cent. (Latin)
		Prosper of Aquitaine, c. 390-c. 463 (Latin)		Leo the Great (Rome), regn. 440-461 (Latin)	
		Salvian the Presbyter of Marseilles, c. 400-c. 480 (Latin)		Arnobius the Younger (Rome), fl. c. 450 (Latin)	
		Gennadius of Marseilles, d. after 496 (Latin)		Ennodius (Arles, Milan, Pavia) c. 473-521 (Latin)	Victor of Vita, fl. 480/481-484 (Latin)
6th century		Julian Pomerius, late 5th-early 6th cent. (Latin)		Epiphanius the Latin, late 5th-early 6th cent. (Latin)	Vigilius of Thapsus, fl. c. 484 (Latin)
		Caesarius of Arles, c. 470-543 (Latin)	Paschasius of Dumium (Portugal), c. 515-c. 580 (Latin)	Eugippius, c. 460- c. 533 (Latin)	Fulgentius of Ruspe, c. 467-532 (Latin)
	Gildas, 6th cent. (Latin)		Apringius of Beja, mid-6th cent. (Latin)	Benedict of Nursia, c. 480-547 (Latin)	Fastidiosus, late 5th-early 6th cent. (Latin)
			Leander of Seville, c. 545-c. 600 (Latin)	Cassiodorus (Calabria), c. 485-c. 540 (Latin)	Verecundus, d. 552 (Latin)
		Gregory of Tours, c. 538-594 (Latin)	Martin of Braga, fl. 568-579 (Latin)	Arator, c. 490-550 (Latin)	Primasius, fl. 550-560 (Latin)
7th century		Flavian of Chalon-sur-Saône, fl. 580-600 (Latin)	Isidore of Seville, c. 560-636 (Latin)	Gregory of Agrigentium, d. 592 (Greek)	Facundus of Hermiane, fl. 546-568 (Latin)
			Braulio of Saragossa, c. 585-651 (Latin)	Gregory the Great (Rome), c. 540-604 (Latin)	
			Ildefonsus of Toledo, mid 7th cent. (Latin)	Paterius, 6th/7th cent. (Latin)	
		Venantius Fortunatus (Gaul, Italy), c. 530-c. 610 (Latin)	Fructuosus of Braga, d. c. 665 (Latin)		
8th-12th century	Adamnan, c. 624-704 (Latin)				
	Bede the Venerable, c. 672/673-735 (Latin)	Rabanus Maurus (Frankish), c. 780-856 (Latin)			
	Riddles in the Apocalypse, 8th cent. (Latin)	Walafridius Strabo (Frankish), 808-849 (Latin)			
		Dhuoda, 9th cent. (Latin)			

*One of the five ancient patriarchates

Alexandria* and Egypt	Constantinople* and Asia Minor, Greece	Antioch* and Syria	Mesopotamia, Persia	Jerusalem* and Palestine	Location Unknown
Syncletica, 5th cent. (Coptic/Greek)	Callinicus, mid 5th cent. (Greek)				
Poemen, 5th cent. (Greek)	Gennadius of Constantinople, d. 471 (Greek)	Theodoret of Cyr, c. 393-466 (Greek)		Gerontius of Petra c. 395-c. 480 (Syriac)	
Besa the Copt, 5th cent. (Sahidic)		Pseudo-Victor of Antioch, 5th cent. (Greek)			
Shenoute, c. 350-466 (Coptic)		John of Apamea, 5th cent. (Syriac)			
Ammonius of Alexandria, late 5th-early 6th cent. (Greek)				Barsanuphius and John, 5th/6th cent. (Greek)	
Olympiodorus, early 6th cent. (Greek)	Andrew of Caesarea (Cappadocia), early 6th cent. (Greek)	Philoxenus of Mabbug (Syria), c. 440-523 (Syriac)	Jacob of Sarug, c. 450-520 (Syriac)	Procopius of Gaza (Palestine), c. 465-530 (Greek)	Pseudo-Dionysius the Areopagite, fl. c. 500 (Greek)
	Oecumenius (Isauria), 6th cent. (Greek)	Severus of Antioch, c. 465-538 (Greek)	Babai, early 6th cent. (Syriac)	Dorotheus of Gaza, fl. 525-540 (Greek)	
	Romanus Melodus, fl. c. 536-556 (Greek)	Mark the Hermit (Tarsus), c. 6th cent. (4th cent.?) (Greek)		Cyril of Scythopolis, b. c. 525; d. after 557 (Greek)	
	Justinian the Emperor, 482-565 (Greek)	Anastasius I of Antioch, d. 598/599 (Latin)	Abraham of Nathpar, fl. 6th-7th cent. (Syriac)		(Pseudo-) Constantius, before 7th cent.? (Greek)
	Maximus the Confessor (Constantinople), c. 580-662 (Greek)		Babai the Great, c. 550-628 (Syriac)		
Anastasius of Sinai (Egypt, Syria), d. c. 700 (Greek)	Germanus of Constantinople, c. 640-c. 733 (Greek)	Sahdona/Martyrius, fl. 635-640 (Syriac)	Isaac of Nineveh, d. c. 700 (Syriac)	Sophronius of Jerusalem, c. 550-638 (Greek)	Andreas, c. 7th cent. (Greek)
	Andrew of Crete, c. 660-740 (Greek)	John of Damascus (John the Monk), c. 650-750 (Greek)		Cosmas Melodus, c. 675-751 (Greek)	
Stephen of Thes, 7th cent. (Coptic)	John of Carpathus, 7th-8th cent. (Greek)		John the Elder of Qardu (north Iraq), 8th cent. (Syriac)		
	Tarasius of Constantinople, d. 806 (Greek)				
	Theophanes (Nicaea), 775-845 (Greek)	Theodore bar Koni, d. 845 (Syriac)			
	Cassia (Constantinople), c. 805-c. 848/867 (Greek)				
	Photius (Constantinople), c. 820-891 (Greek)		Isho'dad of Merv, d. after 852 (Syriac)		
	Arethas of Caesarea (Constantinople/Caesarea), c. 860-940 (Greek)				
	Gregory of Narek, 950-1003 (Armenian)				
	Symeon the New Theologian (Constantinople), 949-1022 (Greek)				
	Theophylact of Ohrid (Bulgaria), 1050-1126 (Greek)				

BIBLIOGRAPHY OF WORKS
IN ORIGINAL LANGUAGES

This bibliography refers readers to original language sources and supplies Thesaurus Linguae Graecae (=TLG) or Cetedoc Clavis (=Cl.) numbers where available. The edition listed in this bibliography may in some cases differ from the edition found in TLG or Cetedoc databases.

Ambrose. "De Abraham." In *Sancti Ambrosii opera omnia*. Edited by J.-P. Migne. PL 14, cols. 419-500. Paris: Migne, 1844-1865. Cl. 0127.

———. "De Cain et Abel." In *Sancti Ambrosii opera omnia*. Edited by J.-P. Migne. PL 14, cols. 315-60. Paris: Migne, 1844-1865. Cl. 0125.

———. "De fide ad Gratianum Augustum libri quinque." In *Sancti Ambrosii opera omnia*. Edited by J.-P. Migne. PL 16, cols. 527-698. Paris: Migne, 1844-1865. Cl. 0150.

———. "De officiis." In *Sancti Ambrosii opera omnia*. Edited by J.-P. Migne. PL 16, cols. 23-184. Paris: Migne, 1844-1865. Cl. 0144.

———. "De Spiritu Sancto." In *Sancti Ambrosii opera omnia*. Edited by J.-P. Migne. PL 16, cols. 703-816. Paris: Migne, 1844-1865. Cl. 0151.

———. "Exameron." In *Sancti Ambrosii opera*. Edited by Karl Schenkl. CSEL 32, pt. 1, pp. 1-261. Vienna, Austria: F. Tempsky; Leipzig, Germany: G. Freytag, 1897. Cl. 0123.

———. "Enarrationes in XII Psalmos Davidicos." In *Sancti Ambrosii opera*. Edited by J.-P. Migne. PL 14, cols. 921-1180. Paris: Migne, 1844-1865. Cl. 0140.

Ambrosiaster. *Commentarius in epistulas Paulinas*: Vol. 2: *In epistulas ad Corinthios*. Edited by H. J. Vogels. CSEL 81.2. Vienna: Hoelder-Pichler-Tempsky, 1968.

———. *Commentarius in epistulas Paulinas*: Vol. 1: *In epistulam ad Romanos*. Edited by H. J. Vogels. CSEL 81.1 Vienna: Hoelder-Pichler-Tempsky, 1966. Cl. 0184c.

Ammonius of Alexandria. "Fragmenta." In *Opera omnia*. Edited by J.-P. Migne. PG 85, Cols. 1362-1608. Paris: Migne, 1857-1866.

Andrew of Crete. "Homiliae XXI." In *Opera omnia*. Edited by J.-P. Migne. PG 97, cols. 806-1301. Paris: Migne, 1857-1866.

Anonymous Anomoean. *Anonymi in Job commentarius*. Edited by Kenneth B. Steinhauser, Hildegund Müller and Dorothea Weber. CSEL 96. Vienna, Austria: Verlag der Österreichischen Akademie der Wissenschaften, 2006.

Anonymous Italian. *Sermones*. In *Homélies (quatorze) du IXe siècle d'un auteur inconnu de l'Italie du Nord*. Edited by Philippe Mercier. SC 161. Paris: Éditions du Cerf, 1970.

Athanasius. "De incarnatione verbi." In *Sur l'incarnation du verbe*. Edited by C. Kannengiesser. SC 199, pp. 258-468. Paris: Éditions du Cerf, 1973. TLG 2035.002.

———. "Epistulae festales." In *Sancti Athanasii: Syriace et Latine*. Edited by Leonis Allatii. NPB 6. Rome: Typis Sacri Consilii Propagando Christiano Nomini, 1853. TLG 2035.x01

————. "Epistulae quattuor ad Serapionem." In *Opera omnia*. Edited by J.-P. Migne. PG 26, cols. 525-676. Paris: Migne, 1887. TLG 2035.043.

————. "Orationes tres contra Arianos." In *Opera omnia*. Edited by J.-P. Migne. PG 26, cols. 813-920. Paris: Migne, 1887. TLG 2035.042.

Augustine. *Confessionum libri tredecim*. Edited by L. Verheijen. CCL 27. Turnhout, Belgium: Brepols, 1981. Cl. 0251.

————. *Contra Iulianum opus imperfectum*. Edited by Michaela Zelzer. CSEL 85.1. Vienna, Austria: Hoelder-Pichler-Tempsky, 1974. See also PL 45, cols. 1337-1608. Cl. 0356.

————. "De Agone Christiano." In *Sancti Aurelii Augustini opera omnia*. Edited by J.-P. Migne. PL 40, cols. 289-310. Paris: Migne, 1844-1865. Cl. 0296.

————. "De civitate Dei." In *Sancti Aurelii Augustini opera omnia*. Edited by J.-P. Migne. PL 41, cols. 13-804. Paris: Migne, 1844-1865. Cl. 0313.

————. *De diversis quaestionibus ad Simplicianum*. In *Sancti Aurelii Augustini opera omnia*. Edited by Almut Mutzenbecher. CCL 44. Turnhout, Belgium: Brepols, 1970. Cl. 0290.

————. "De diversis quaestionibus octoginta tribus." In *Sancti Aurelii Augustini opera omnia*. Edited by Almut Mutzenbecher. CCL 44A, pp. 11-249. Turnhout, Belgium: Brepols, 1975. Cl. 0289.

————. "De doctrina christiana." In *Sancti Aurelii Augustini opera omnia*. Edited by J.-P. Migne. PL 34, cols. 15-122. Paris: Migne, 1844-1865. Cl. 0263.

————. "De Genesi ad litteram imperfectus liber." In *Sancti Aureli Augustini De Genesi ad litteram libri duodecim*. Edited by Joseph Zycha. CSEL 28.1, pp. 459-503. Vienna, Austria: F. Tempsky; Leipzig, Germany: G. Freytag, 1894. Cl. 0268.

————. "De Genesi contra Manichaeos." In *Sancti Aurelii Augustini opera omnia*. Edited by J.-P. Migne. PL 34, cols. 173-220. Paris: Migne, 1844-1865. Cl. 0265.

————. "De mendacio." In *Sancti Aureli Augustini opera*. Edited by Joseph Zycha. CSEL 41, pp. 413-66. Vienna, Austria: F. Tempsky, 1900. Cl. 0303

————. *De Trinitate*. In *Aurelii Augustini opera*. Edited by William John Mountain. CCL 50-50A. Turnhout, Belgium: Brepols, 1968. Cl. 0329.

————. "De vera religione." In *Sancti Aurelii Augustini opera omnia*. Edited by J.-P. Migne. PL 34, cols. 121-72. Paris: Migne, 1844-1865. Cl. 0264.

————. *Enarrationes in Psalmos*. In *Aurelii Augustini opera*. Edited by Eligius Dekkers and John Fraipont. CCL 38, 39, 40. Turnhout, Belgium: Brepols, 1956. Cl. 0283.

————. "In Johannis evangelium tractatus." In *Aurelii Augustini opera*. Edited by R. Willems. CCL 36. Turnhout, Belgium: Brepols, 1954. Cl. 0278.

————. "Quaestionum in heptateuchum libri septem." In *Sancti Aurelii Augustini opera omnia*. Edited by J.-P. Migne. PL 34, cols. 547-824. Paris: Migne, 1844-1865. Cl. 0270.

————. *Sancti Aurelii Augustini Retractationum libri II*. Edited by Almut Mutzenbecher. CCL 57. Turnhout, Belgium: Brepols, 1984. Cl. 0250.

————. *Sermones*. In *Sancti Aurelii Augustini opera omnia*. Edited by J.-P. Migne. PL 38 and 39. Paris: Migne, 1844-1865. Cl. 0284.

Barsanuphius and John. "Quaestiones et responsiones." In *Barsanuphe et Jean de Gaza, Correspondance, tome I-II*. Edited and translated by F. Neyt and P. de Angelis-Noah. SC 426 and 427. Paris: Éditions du Cerf, 1997-98. TLG 2851.001.

————. "Quaestiones et responsiones ad coenobitas (Epistulae 224-616)." In *Correspondance* (Volume 2, Aux cénobites: Tome I, Lettres 224-398; Tome II, Lettres 399-616). Edited and translated by F. Neyt and P. de Angelis-Noah. SC 450 and 451. Paris: Éditions du Cerf, 2000. TLG 2851.002.

———. "Quaestiones et responsiones ad laicos et episcopos (Epistulae 617-848)." In *Correspondance* (Volume 3, Aux laïcs et aux évêques, Lettres 617-848). Edited and translated by F. Neyt and P. de Angelis-Noah. SC 468. Paris: Éditions du Cerf, 2002. TLG 2851.003.

Basil the Great. *De Spiritu Sancto*. In *Basile de Césarée: Sur le Saint-Esprit*. 2nd ed. Edited and translated by B. Pruche. SC 17 bis. Paris: Éditions du Cerf, 1968. TLG 2040.003.

———. *Homilia in martyrem Julittam*. In *Opera omnia*. Edited by J.-P. Migne. PG 31, cols. 372-85. Paris: Migne, 1857-1866. TLG 2040.023.

Bede. "Homiliarum evangelii." In *Bedae opera*. Edited by D. Hurst. CCL 122, pp. 1-378. Turnhout, Belgium: Brepols, 1955. Cl. 1367.

———. *In librum beati patris Tobiae*. In *Bedae opera*. Edited by D. Hurst. CCL 119B, pp. 3-190. Turnhout, Belgium: Brepols, 1983. Cl. 1350.

Callinicus. *Vita sancti Hypatii*. In *Callinicos. Vie d'Hypatios*. Edited by G. J. M. Bartelink. SC 177, pp. 62-298. Paris: Éditions du Cerf, 1971. TLG 2770.001.

Cassian, John. *Collationes xxiv*. Edited by Michael Petschenig. CSEL 13. Vienna, Austria: F. Tempsky; Leipzig, Germany: G. Freytag, 1886. Cl. 0512.

Cassiodorus. *Expositio psalmorum*. Edited by Mark Adriaen. CCL 97 and 98. Turnhout, Belgium: Brepols, 1958. Cl. 0900.

———. "In psalterium expositio." In *Magni Aurellii Cassiodori opera omnia*. Edited by J.-P. Migne. PL 70, cols. 25-1056. Paris: Migne, 1844-1865. Cl. 0900.

———. *Institutiones*. Edited by R. A. B. Mynors. Oxford: Clarendon Press, 1961. Cl. 0906.

Chromatius of Aquileia. "Sermones." In *Opera*. Edited by R. Étaix and J. Lemarié. CCL 9A, pp. 3-182. Turnhout, Belgium: Brepols, 1974. Cl. 0217 and 0217+.

———. *Tractatus in Matthaeum*. In *Opera*. Edited by R. Étaix and J. Lemarié. CCL 9A, p. 185-489; SL9A supplementum, p. 624-36. Turnhout, Belgium: Brepols, 1974. Cl. 0218.

Clement of Alexandria. "Paedagogus." In *Le pédagogue (par) Clement d'Alexandrie*. Translated by Mauguerite Harl, Chantel Matray and Claude Mondésert. Introduction and notes by Henri-Irénée Marrou. SC 70, 108 and 158. Paris: Éditions du Cerf, 1960-1970. TLG 0555.002.

Clement of Rome. "Epistula i ad Corinthios." In *Clément de Rome: Épître aux Corinthiens*. Edited by Annie Jaubert. SC 167. Paris: Éditions du Cerf, 1971. TLG 1271.001.

Cyprian. "De habitu virginum." In *Sancti Thascii Caecilii opera omnia*. Edited by J.-P. Migne. PL 4, cols. 439-64. Paris: Migne, 1844-1865. Cl. 0040.

———. "De mortalitate." In *Sancti Thascii Caecilii opera omnia*. Edited by J.-P. Migne. PL 4, cols. 581-602. Paris: Migne, 1844-1865. Cl. 0044.

———. "De opere et eleemosynis." In *Sancti Cypriani episcopi opera*. Edited by Manlio Simonetti. CCL 3A, pp. 55-72. Turnhout, Belgium: Brepols, 1976. Cl. 0047.

———. "De zelo et livore." In *Sancti Thascii Caecilii opera omnia*. Edited by J.-P. Migne. PL 4, cols. 637-52. Paris: Migne, 1844-1865. Cl. 0049.

Cyril of Alexandria. "Commentarii in Joannem." In *Sancti patris nostri Cyrilli archiepiscopi Alexandrini in D. Joannis evangelium*. Edited by P. E. Pusey. Culture et Civilisation. Oxford: Clarendon Press, 1872; repr. Brussels, 1965. TLG 4090.002.

———. "Commentarius in xii prophetas minores." In *Sancti patris nostri Cyrilli archiepiscopi Alexandrini in xii prophetas*. 2 vols. Edited by P. E. Pusey. Oxford: Clarendon Press, 1868 (repr. 1965). TLG 4090.001.

————. "Fragmenta in sancti Pauli epistulam ii ad Corinthios." In *Sancti patris nostri Cyrilli archiepiscopi Alexandrini in D. Joannis evangelium*, vol. 3, pp. 320-60. Edited by P. E. Pusey. Oxford: Clarendon Press, 1872 (repr. 1965). TLG 4090.005.

Cyril of Jeruslaem. "Catecheses ad illuminandos 1-18." In *Cyrilli Hierosolymorum archiepiscopi opera quae supersunt omnia."* Vol. 1, pp. 28-320; vol. 2, pp. 2-342. Edited by Wilhelm Karl Reischl and Joseph Rupp. Munich: Lentner, 1860 (repr. Hildesheim: Olms, 1967). TLG 2110.003.

Cyril/John of Jerusalem. "Mystagogiae 1-5 (Sp.)." In *Cyrille de Jérusalem: Catéchèses, mystagogigues*. 2nd. ed. Edited by Auguste Piédagnel. SC 126, pp. 82-174. Paris: Éditions du Cerf, 1988. TLG 2110.002.

Dhuoda. "Liber Manualis." In *Manuel pour mon fils*. Edited by Pierre Riché. Translated by Bernard de Vregille and Claude Mondésert. SC 225. Paris: Éditions du Cerf, 1975.

Didymus the Blind. "Commentarii in Ecclesiasten (11-12)." In *Didymos der Blinde. Kommentar zum Ecclesiastes*, pt. 6. Edited by G. Binder and L. Liesenborghs. PTA 9, pp. 2-244. Bonn: Habelt, 1969. TLG 2102.025.

————. "Commentarii in Psalmos 29-34." In *Didymus der Blinde: Psalmenkommentar*, pt. 3. Edited by M. Gronewald. PTA 8, pp. 2-414. Bonn: Rudolf Habelt Verlage, 1969. TLG 2102.018.

————. "Commentarii in Psalmos 35-39." In *Didymus der Blinde: Psalmenkommentar*, pt. 4. Edited by M. Gronewald. PTA 6, pp. 2-314. Bonn: Rudolf Habelt Verlage, 1969. TLG 2102.019.

————. "Liber de Spiritu Sancto." In *Opera*. PL 23, cols. 109-62. Edited by J.-P. Migne. Paris: Migne, 1844-1865. Cl. 0615.

Dionysius of Alexandria. "Epistulae ad Dionysium Romanum." In *Opera*. PL 5, cols. 117-28. Edited by J.-P. Migne. Paris: Migne, 1844-1865.

Dorotheus of Gaza. "Expositiones et doctrinae diversae animabus perutiles." In *Opera omnia*. Edited by J.-P. Migne. PG 88, cols. 1611-1838. Paris: Migne, 1857-1866.

Epiphanius of Salamis. *Ancoratus*. In *Epiphanius, Band 1: Ancoratus und Panarion*. GCS 25, pp. 1-149. Edited by K. Holl. Leipzig, Germany: Hinrichs, 1915. TLG 2021.001.

Eucherius. "De contemptu mundi (Epistola paraenetica ad Valerianum cognatum)." In *Opera*. PL 50, cols. 711-26. Edited by J.-P. Migne. Paris: Migne, 1844-1865.

————. "De laude eremi." In *Opera*. PL 50, cols. 701-12. Edited by J.-P. Migne. Paris: Migne, 1844-1865.

————. "Formulae Spirituales." In *Opera*. PL 50, cols. 727-72. Edited by J.-P. Migne. Paris: Migne, 1844-1865.

Eusebius of Caesarea. *Commentaria in Psalmos*. In *Opera omnia*. PG 23, cols. 66-1396; PG 24, cols. 9-76. Edited by J.-P. Migne. Paris: Migne, 1857. TLG 2018.034.

Evagrius of Pontus. "De oratione." (Under the name of Nilus of Ancyra.) In *Opera omnia*. PG 79, cols. 1165-2000. Edited by J.-P. Migne. Paris: Migne, 1865. TLG 4110.024.

Fastidiosus. "Sermo." In *Opera*. Edited by J. Fraipont. CCL 91, p. 280-83. Turnhout, Belgium: Brepols, 1968. Cl. 0708.

Faustus of Riez. "De gratia libri duo." In *Opera*. Edited by A. Engelbrecht. CSEL 21, pp. 3-96. Vienna, Austria: F. Tempsky; Leipzig, Germany: G. Freytag, 1891. Cl. 0961.

Fulgentius of Ruspe. "Ad Euthymium de remissione peccatorum libri II." In *Opera*. Edited by J. Fraipont. CCL 91A, pp. 458-548. Turnhout, Belgium: Brepols, 1968. Cl. 0821.

————. "Ad Felicem Notarium De Trinitate Liber Unus." In *Sancti Fulgentii opera omnia*. Edited by J.-P. Migne. PL 65, cols. 497-508. Paris: Migne, 1844-1865. Cl. 0819.

————. "Ad Monimum libri III." In *Opera*. Edited by J. Fraipont. CCL 91, pp. 1-64. Turnhout, Belgium: Brepols, 1968. Cl. 0814.

————. "Ad Monimum libri III." In *Sancti Fulgentii opera omnia*. Edited by J.-P. Migne. PL 65, cols. 151-206. Paris: Migne, 1844-1865. Cl. 0814.

————. "Ad Trasimundum libri III." In *Sancti Fulgentii opera omnia*. Edited by J.-P. Migne. PL 65, cols. 223-304. Paris: Migne, 1844-1865. Cl. 0816.

————. "Contra Fabianum fragmenta." See "Fidei Catholicae Instrumenta [Excerpta]." In *Sancti Fulgentii opera omnia*. Edited by J.-P. Migne. PL 65, cols. 749-834. Paris: Migne, 1844-1865. Cl. 0824.

————. "Contra Sermonem Fastidiosi Ariani Ad Victorem Liber Unus." In *Opera*. Edited by J.-P. Migne. PL 65, cols. 507-28. Paris: Migne, 1844-1865. Cl. 0820.

————. "De fide ad Petrum seu de regula fidei." In *Opera*. Edited by J. Fraipont. CCL 91A, pp. 711-60. Turnhout, Belgium: Brepols, 1968. Cl. 0826.

————. "De veritate praedestinationis et gratiae Dei" In *Sancti Fulgentii opera omnia*. Edited by J.-P. Migne. PL 65, cols. 603-72. Paris: Migne, 1844-1865. Cl. 0823.

————. "Epistulae." In *Opera*. Edited by J. Fraipont. CCL 91, pp. 189-273, 362-381, 387-444; CCL 91A, pp. 447-457, 563-624. Turnhout, Belgium: Brepols, 1968. Cl. 0817.

————. "Liber ad Victorem contra sermonem Fastidiosi Ariani." In *Opera*. Edited by J. Fraipont. CCL 91, p. 283-308. Turnhout, Belgium: Brepols, 1968. Cl. 0820.

————. "Sermo dubius 2: Incarnationis divinae mysterium." In *Opera*. Edited by J. Fraipont. CCL 91A, pp. 953-59. Turnhout, Belgium: Brepols, 1968. Cl. 0841.

————. "Sermones." In *Sancti Fulgentii opera omnia*. Edited by J.-P. Migne. PL 65, cols. 719-50; 855-954. Paris: Migne, 1844-1865.

Gaudentius of Brescia. "Ad Benivolum." In *Opera omnia*. Edited by Anton Polascheck. CSEL 68. Vienna, Austria: Hoelder-Pichler-Tempsky, 1936.

————. "Tractatus vel Sermones." In *Opera omnia*. PL 20, cols. 843-1002. Edited by J.-P. Migne. Paris: Migne, 1845.

Gregory of Elvira [attributed to Ambrose by Migne]. "De fide orthodoxa." In *Sancti Ambrosii opera omnia*. Edited by J.-P. Migne. PL 17, cols. 549-68. Paris: Migne, 1844-1865. Cl. 0551.

Gregory of Nazianzus. "In sancta lumina (orat. 39)." In *Opera omnia*. Edited by J.-P. Migne. PG 36, cols. 336-60. Paris: Migne, 1886. TLG 2022.047.

Gregory of Nyssa. "De virginitate." In *Grégoire de Nysse: Traité de la virginité*. Edited by M. Aubineau. SC 119, pp. 246-560. Paris: Éditions du Cerf, 1966. TLG 2017.043.

Gregory the Great. *Dialogorum libri iv*. In *Dialogues: Grégoire le Grand*. Edited by A. de Vogüé. SC 260; 265. Paris: Éditions du Cerf, 1979-1980. Cl. 1713.

————. "Expositio in septem Psalmos." In *Sancti Gregorii Papae i opera omnia*. PL 79, cols. 549-659. Edited by J.-P. Migne. Paris: Migne, 1844-1865.

————. "Homiliae in Hiezechihelem prophetam." In *Opera*. Edited by Mark Adriaen. CCL 142, 3-398. Turnhout, Belgium: Brepols, 1971. Cl. 1710.

————. "In librum primum Regum variarum expositionum libri vi." In *Sancti Gregorii Papae i opera omnia*. Edited by J.-P. Migne. PL 79, cols. 17-468. Paris: Migne, 1844-1865. Cl. 1719 [dubium].

————. *Regula pastoralis*. Edited by F. Rommel and R. W. Clement. CCL 141. Turnhout, Belgium: Brepols, 1982. Cl. 1712.

Hesychius of Jerusalem. *Homélies sur Job version Arménienne I: Homélies I-XI*. Edited by Charles

Renoux and Charles Mercier. PO 42 (191). Turnhout, Belgium: Brepols, 1983.

Hilary of Poitiers. *De trinitate*. Edited by P. Smulders. CCL 62, 62A. Turnhout, Belgium: Brepols, 1979-1980. Cl. 0433.

———. "Epistola seu Libellus." In *Sancti Hilarii opera omnia*. PL 10, cols. 733-50. Edited by J.-P. Migne. Paris: Migne, 1844-1865.

———. "Tractatus super psalmos I-XCI." In *Sancti Hilarii opera omnia*. Edited by J.-P. Migne. PL 9, cols. 231-890. Paris: Migne, 1844-1865. Cl. 0428.

Hippolytus. *Commentarium in Danielem*. In *Hippolyte: Commentaire sur Daniel*. Edited by M. Lefèvre SC 14, pp. 70-386. Paris: Éditions du Cerf, 1947. TLG 2115.030.

Ildefonsus of Toledo. "De virginitate perpetua sanctae Mariae." In *Opera*. PL 96, cols. 53-110. Edited by J.-P. Migne. Paris: Migne, 1844-1865.

Irenaeus. "Adversus haereses, livre 3, 5." In *Contre les hérésies*. Edited by A. Rousseau and L. Doutreleau (Book 3, 5) and C. Mercier (Book 3). SC 100, 152-53, 210-11, 263-64, 293-94. Paris: Éditions du Cerf, 1965-82. Cl. 1154 f.

Isaac of Nineveh. "De perfectione religiosa." In *Mar Isaacus Ninivita de perfectione religiosa*, pp. 1-99. Edited by Paul Bedjan. Leipzig, Germany: Harrassowitz, 1909.

Jerome. *Commentarii in Danielem*. Edited by F. Glorie. CCL 75A. Turnhout, Belgium: Brepols, 1964. Cl. 0588.

———. "In Malachiam." In *Hieronymi opera omnia*. Edited by J.-P. Migne. PL 25, cols. 1541-78. Paris: Migne, 1844-1865. Cl. 0589.

———. "In Osee." In *Commentarii in prophetas minores*. Edited by M. Adriaen. CCL 76, pp. 1-158. Turnhout, Belgium: Brepols, 1969. Cl. 0589.

———. "Tractatus in Marci evangelium." In *Opera*. Edited by G. Morin. CCL 78, pp. 451-500. Turnhout, Belgium: Brepols, 1958. Cl. 0594.

———. "Tractatus lix in psalmos." In *Opera*. Edited by G. Morin. CCL 78, pp. 3-352. Turnhout, Belgium: Brepols, 1958. Cl. 0592.

John Chrysostom. "Ad illuminandos catecheses 1-2 (series prima et secunda)." In *Opera omnia*. Edited by J.-P. Migne. PG 49, cols. 223-40. Paris: Migne, 1857-1866. TLG 2062.025.

———. "Ad Stagirium a daemone vexatum (lib. 1-3." In *Opera omnia*. Edited by J.-P. Migne. PG 47, cols, 423-94. Paris: Migne, 1857-1866. TLG 2062.006.

———. "Ad Theodorum lapsum (lib. 1)." In *Jean Chrysostome: A Théodore*. Edited by J. Dumortier. SC 117, pp. 46-78. Paris: Éditions du Cerf, 1966. TLG 2062.002.

———. "Adversus oppugnatores vitae monasticae." In *Opera omnia*. Edited by J.-P. Migne. PG 47, cols. 319-86. Paris: Migne, 1857-1866. TLG 2062.003.

———. Catecheses ad illuminandos 1-8 (series tertia). In *Jean Chrysostome: Huit catéchèses baptismales*. 2nd ed. Edited by A. Wenger. SC 50, pp. 108-260. Paris: Éditions du Cerf, 1970. TLG 2062.382.

———. "Contra Judaeos et gentiles, quod Christus sit Deus." In *Opera omnia*. Edited by J.-P. Migne. PG 48, cols. 811-38. Paris: Migne, 1857-1866. TLG 2062.372.

———. "De inani gloria et de educandis liberis." In *Jean Chrysostome: Sur la vaine gloire et l'éducation des enfants*. Edited by A.-M. Malingrey. SC 188, pp. 64-196. Paris: Éditions du Cerf, 1972. TLG 2062.378.

———. "De prophetiarum obscuritate (homiliae 1-2)." In *Opera omnia*. Edited by J.-P. Migne. PG 56, cols. 163-192. Paris: Migne, 1857-1866. TLG 2062.150.

———. "De sacerdotio." In *Jean Chrysostome: Sur le sacerdoce*. Edited by A.-M. Malingrey. SC 272, pp. 60-362. Paris: Éditions du Cerf, 1980. TLG 2062.085.

———. "De sanctis martyribus." In *Opera omnia*. Edited by J.-P. Migne. PG 50, cols. 645-54. Paris: Migne, 1857-1866. TLG 2062.050.

———. "De virginitate." In *Jean Chrysostome: La virginité*. Edited by B. Grillet and H. Musurillo. SC 125, pp. 92-394. Paris: Éditions du Cerf, 1966. TLG 2062.009.

———. "Expositiones in Psalmos." In *Opera omnia*. Edited by J.-P. Migne. PG 55, cols. 39-498. Paris: Migne, 1857-1866. TLG 2062.143.

———. "Homiliae VI in Oziam." In *Opera omnia*. Edited by J.-P. Migne. PG 56, cols. 93-142. Paris: Migne, 1857-1866.

———. "In epistulam ad Galatas commentaries." In *Opera omnia*. Edited by J.-P. Migne. PG 61, cols. 611-82. Paris: Migne, 1857-1866. TLG 2062.158.

———. "In Genesim (homiliae 1-67)." In *Opera omnia*. Edited by J.-P. Migne. PG 53, cols. 21-385; PG 54, cols. 385-580. Paris: Migne, 1857-1866. TLG 2062.112.

———. "In Isaiam." In *Jean Chrysostome: Commentaire sur Isaïe*. Edited by J. Dumortier. SC 304, pp. 36-356. Paris: Éditions du Cerf, 1983. TLG 2062.497.

———. "In Matthaeum (homiliae 1-90)." In *Opera omnia*. Edited by J.-P. Migne. PG 57, cols.13-472; PG 58, cols. 471-794. Paris: Migne, 1857-1866. TLG 2062.152.

John of Damascus. "Expositio fidei." In *Die Schriften des Johannes von Damaskos*, vol. 2. Edited by P. B. Kotter. *Patristische Texte und Studien* 12, pp. 3-239. Berlin: De Gruyter, 1973. TLG 2934.004.

———. "Homilia in Sabbatum sanctum." In *Opera omnia*. Edited by J.-P. Migne. PG 96, cols. 601-44. Paris: Migne, 1857-1866. TLG 2934.056.

———. "Homilia i in dormitionem Mariae." In *Die Schriften des Johannes von Damaskos*, vol. 5. Edited by P. B. Kotter. *Patristische Texte und Studien* 29, pp. 483-500. Berlin and New York: De Gruyter, 1988. TLG 2934.023.

———. "Orationes de imaginibus tres." In *Die Schriften des Johannes von Damaskos*, vol. 3. Edited by P. B. Kotter. *Patristische Texte und Studien* 17, pp. 65-200. Berlin: De Gruyter, 1975. TLG 2934.005.

Julian of Eclanum. "Tractatus." In "Opus imperfectum contra Julianum." See *Sancti Aurelii Augustini Retractationum libri II*. In *Aurelii Augustini opera*. Edited by Almut Mutzenbecher. CCL 57. Turnhout, Belgium: Brepols, 1984. Cl. 0250.

Julian Pomerius. "De vita contemplative." In *Opera omnia*. Edited by J.-P. Migne. PL 59, cols. 415-520. Paris: Migne, 1857-1866.

Julius Africanus. "Epistula ad Origenem." In Origen, *Philocalie, 1-20, Sur les Écritures et La Lettre à Africanus sur l'histoire de Suzanne*. Translation and Text by Nicholas de Lange. SC 302. Paris: Éditions du Cerf, 1983. TLG 2956.003.

Leander of Seville. "Liber de institutione virginum et contemptu mundi." In *Opera omnia*. Edited by J.-P. Migne. PL 72, cols. 873-94. Paris: Migne, 1857-1866.

Leo the Great. "Tractatus septem et nonaginta." In *Opera*. Edited by A. Chavasse. CCL 138-138A. Turnhout, Belgium: Brepols, 1973. Cl. 1657.

Maximus of Turin. "Collectio sermonum antique." In *Opera*. Edited by A. Mutzenbecher. CCL 23. Turnhout, Belgium: Brepols, 1962. Cl. 0219a.

Methodius. "Symposium sive Convivium decem virginum." In *Méthode d'Olympe: Le banquet*. Edited by V.-H. Debidour and H. Musurillo. SC 95, pp. 42-332. Paris: Éditions du Cerf, 1963. TLG 2959.001

Nicetas of Remesiana. "De vigiliis, de utilitate hymnorum." Edited by C. Turner. *Journal of Theological Studies* 24 (1923): 225-52.

———. "De Ratione fidei." In *Opera omnia.* Edited by J.-P. Migne. PL 52, cols. 847-52. Paris: Migne, 1857-1866.

Olympiodorus of Alexandria. "Commentarii in Baruch in catenis." In *Opera omnia.* Edited by J.-P. Migne. PG 93, cols. 761-73. Paris: Migne, 1857-1866. TLG 2865.005.

———. "Commentarii in Jeremiae epistulam." In *Opera omnia.* Edited by J.-P. Migne. PG 93, cols. 773-80. Paris: Migne, 1857-1866. TLG 2865.006.

Optatus. "De Schismate Donatistarum Adversus Parmenianum." In *Opera omnia.* Edited by J.-P. Migne. PL 11, cols. 883-1104. Paris: Migne, 1857-1866.

Origen. "Commentarii in evangelium Joannis (lib. 1, 2, 4, 5, 6, 10, 13)." In *Origène. Commentaire sur saint Jean.* 3 vols. Edited by C. Blanc. SC 120, 157 and 222. Paris: Éditions du Cerf, 1966-1975. TLG 2042.005.

———. "Commentarii in evangelium Joannis (lib. 19, 20, 28, 32)." In *Origenes Werke,* vol. 4. Edited by E. Preuschen. GCS 10, pp. 298-480. Leipzig, Germany: Hinrichs, 1903. TLG 2042.079.

———. "Commentarii in evangelium Matthaei (lib. 10-11)." In *Origène. Commentaire sur l'évangile selon Matthieu,* vol. 1. Edited by R. Girod. SC 162, pp. 140-386. Paris: Éditions du Cerf, 1970. TLG 2042.029.

———. "Commentarium in Canticum Canticorum" In *Origenes Werke,* vol. 8. Edited by W. A. Baehrens. GCS 33, pp. 61-241. Leipzig, Germany: Teubner, 1925. Cl. 0198.2.

———. "Commentarium in evangelium Matthaei (lib.12-17)." In *Origenes Werke,* vol. 10.1-10.2. Edited by E. Klostermann. GCS 40.1-40.2. Leipzig, Germany: Teubner, 1935-1937. TLG 2042.030.

———. "De oratione." In *Origenes Werke,* vol. 2. Edited by P. Koetschau. GCS 3, pp. 297-403. Leipzig, Germany: Hinrichs, 1899. TLG 2042.008.

———. "De principiis." In *Origenes vier Bücher von den Prinzipien,* pp. 462-560, 668-764. Edited by H. Görgemanns and H. Karpp. Darmstadt, Germany: Wissenschaftliche Buchgesellschaft, 1976. TLG 2042.002.

———. "De principiis (Periarchon). In *Origenes Werke.* Edited by P. Koetschau. GCS 22, pp. 7-364. Leipzig, Germany: Teubner, 1913. Cl. 0198 E.

———. "Epistula ad Africanum." In *Philocalie, 1-20, Sur les Écritures La Lettre à Africanus sur l'histoire de Suzanne: Origene.* Translation and Text by Nicholas de Lange. SC 302. Paris: Éditions du Cerf, 1983. TLG 2042.045.

———. "Fragmenta in evangelium Joannis (in catenis)." In *Origenes Werke,* vol. 4. Edited by E. Preuschen. GCS 10, pp. 483-574. Leipzig, Germany: Hinrichs, 1903. TLG 2042.006.

———. "Homiliae in Exodum." In *Origenes Werke,* vol. 6. Edited by W. A. Baehrens. GCS 29, pp. 217-30. Leipzig, Germany: Teubner, 1920. TLG 2042.023.

———. "Homiliae in Ezechielem." In *Origenes Werke,* vol. 8. Edited by W. A. Baehrens. GCS 33, pp. 319-452. Leipzig, Germany: Teubner, 1925. TLG 2042.027.

———. "Homiliae in Genesim." In *Origenes Werke,* vol. 6. Edited by W. A. Baehrens. GCS 29, pp. 23-30. Leipzig, Germany: Teubner, 1920. TLG 2042.022.

———. "Homiliae in visiones Isaiae." In *Origenes Werke,* vol. 8. Edited by W. A. Baehrens. GCS 33, pp 242-89. Leipzig, Germany: Teubner, 1925.

———. "Homiliae in Leviticum." In *Origenes Werke,* vol. 6. Edited by W. A. Baehrens. GCS 29, pp. 332-334, 395, 402-416. Leipzig, Germany: Teubner, 1920. TLG 2042.024.

————. "Homiliae in librum Judicum." In *Origenes Werke*, vol. 7. Edited by W. A. Baehrens. GCS 30, pp. 464-522. Leipzig, Germany: Teubner, 1921. Cl. 0198.7.

————. "Homiliae in Lucam." In *Origenes Werke*, vol. 9. 2nd ed. Edited by M. Rauer. GCS 49 (35), pp. 3-222. Berlin: Akademie Verlag, 1959. TLG 2042.016.

————. "In Jeremiam (homiliae 1-11)." In *Origène. Homélies sur Jérémie*, vol. 1. Edited by P. Nautin. SC 232, pp. 196-430. Paris: Éditions du Cerf, 1976. TLG 2042.009.

————. "In Jeremiam (homilae 12-20)." In *Origenes Werke*, vol. 3. Edited by E. Klostermann. GCS 6, pp. 85-194. Leipzig, Germany: Hinrichs, 1901. TLG 2042.021.

————. "In Jesu nave homiliae xxvi." In *Origenes Werke*, vol. 7. Edited by W. A. Baehrens. GCS 30, pp. 290-463. Leipzig, Germany: Teubner, 1921. TLG 2042.025.

————. "In Numeros homiliae." In *Origenes Werke*, vol. 7. GCS 30, pp. 3-285. Edited by W. A. Baehrens. Leipzig, Germany: Teubner, 1921. Cl. 0198 O.

————. "Selecta in Psalmos." In *Opera omnia*. Edited J.-P. Migne. PG 12, cols. 1053-1320, 1368-1369, 1388-1389, 1409-1685. Paris: Migne, 1857-1866. TLG 2042.058.

————. "Stromateis." In *Opera omnia*. Edited by J.-P. Migne. PG 11, cols. 99-108. Paris: Migne, 1857-1866.

Palladius. "Dialogus de vita Joannis Chrysostomi." In *Palladii dialogus de vita S. Joannis Chrysostomi*, p. 3-147. Edited by P. R. Coleman-Norton. Cambridge: Cambridge University Press, 1928. TLG 2111.004.

Paterius. "Liber de expositione veteris ac novi testamenti." In *Opera omnia*. Edited by J.-P. Migne. PL 79, cols. 683-1136. Paris: Migne, 1857-1866.

Paulinus of Nola. "Epistulae." In *Opera*. Edited by G. Hartel and A. Goldbacher. CSEL 29, 34.1 and 34.2. Vienna, Austria: F. Tempsky; Leipzig, Germany: G. Freytag, 1894-1898. Cl. 0202.

Pelagius (?). "De vita Christiana" (attributed to Pseudo-Augustine). In *Augustini opera omnia*. Edited by J.-P. Migne. PL 40, cols. 1031-1046. Paris: Migne, 1844-1865. Cl. 0730.

Peter Chrysologus. "Collectio sermonum." Edited by A. Olivar. CCL 24, 24A, 24B. Turnhout, Belgium: Brepols, 1975. Cl. 0227+.

Prosper of Aquitaine. "De vocatione omnium gentium." In *Opera*. Edited by J.-P. Migne. PL 51, cols. 647-722. Paris: Migne, 1844-1865.

Pseudo-Ambrose. "De Trinitate, alias In symbolum apostolorum tractatus." In *Sancti Ambrosii opera omnia*. Edited by J.-P. Migne. PL 17, cols. 509-46. Paris: Migne, 1844-1865.

————. "Expositio Super Septem Visiones Libri Apocalypsis." In *Sancti Ambrosii opera omnia*. Edited by J.-P. Migne. PL 17, cols. 765-970. Paris: Migne, 1844-1865.

————. "Liber De Vitiorum Virtutumque Conflictu [Incertus]." In *Sancti Ambrosii opera omnia*. Edited by J.-P. Migne. PL 17, cols. 1057-74. Paris: Migne, 1844-1865.

————. "Precationes Duae Hactenius Ambrosio Attributae." In *Sancti Ambrosii opera omnia*. Edited by J.-P. Migne. PL 17, cols. 751-62. Paris: Migne, 1844-1865.

————. "Sermones sancto Ambrosio hactenus ascripti." In *Opera omnia*. Edited by J.-P. Migne. PL 17, cols. 603-704. Paris: Migne, 1844-1865.

Pseudo-Augustine. "De spiritu et anima (incertus)." In *Sancti Aurelii Augustini opera omnia*. Edited by J.-P. Migne. PL 40, cols. 779-832. Paris: Migne, 1844-1865.

————. "Hypomnesticon." In *Sancti Aurelii Augustini opera omnia*. Edited by J.-P. Migne. PL 45, cols. 1611-64. Paris: Migne, 1844-1865.

————. "Manuale (incertus)." In *Sancti Aurelii Augustini opera omnia*. Edited by J.-P. Migne. PL 40, cols. 951-68. Paris: Migne, 1844-1865.

———. "Speculum (incertus)." In *Sancti Aurelii Augustini opera omnia*. Edited by J.-P. Migne. PL 40, cols. 967-84. Paris: Migne, 1844-1865.

———. "Quaestiones veteris et novi testamenti (incertus)." In *Sancti Aurelii Augustini opera omnia*. Edited by J.-P. Migne. PL 35, cols. 2207-2386. Paris: Migne, 1844-1865.

———. "Quaestiones aliae veteris et novi testamenti (incertus)." *Sancti Aurelii Augustini opera omnia*. Edited by J.-P. Migne. PL 35, cols. 2385-2416. Paris: Migne, 1844-1865.

———. "Sermones. De symbolo sermo ad catechumenos." In *Sancti Aurelii Augustini opera omnia*. Edited by J.-P. Migne. PL 40, cols. 637-52. Paris: Migne, 1844-1865.

———. "Sermones supposititii. Classis II. De Tempore." In *Sancti Aurelii Augustini opera omnia*. Edited by J.-P. Migne. PL 39, cols.1973-2096. Paris: Migne, 1844-1865.

Pseudo-Chrysostom. "In Psalmum 50 (homilia 2) [Sp.]." In *Joannis Chrysostomi opera omnia quae exstant*. Edited by J.-P. Migne. PG 55, cols. 575-88. Paris: Migne, 1857-1866. TLG 2062.200.

———. "In quatriduanum Lazarum = Contra Anomoeos, homilia 9 [Sp.]." In *Sur l'égalité du père et du fils: contre les anomeens homelies VII-XII*. SC 396. Paris: Éditions du Cerf, 1994. TLG 2062.017.

———. "Interpretatio in Danielem prophetam." In *Joannis Chrysostomi opera omnia quae exstant*. Edited by J.-P. Migne. PG 56, cols. 193-246. Paris: Migne, 1857-1866. TLG 2062.209.

Pseudo-Cyprian of Carthage. "De Idolorum Vanitate." In *Sancti Thascii Caecilii opera omnia*. Edited by J.-P. Migne. PL 4, cols. 563-82. Paris: Migne, 1844-1865.

Pseudo-Ephrem. "De laude martyrii." In *Sancti Patris nostri Ephraem Syri opera omnia quae exstant Graece, Syriace, Latine, in sex tomos distributa*, Vol. 2. Rome: Ex Typographia Vaticana, 1732-1746.

Quodvultdeus. "Liber promissionum et praedictorum Dei." In *Opera*. Edited by R. Braun. CCL 60, pp. 1, 11-223. Turnhout, Belgium: Brepols, 1976. Cl. 0413

Rabanus Maurus. "Commentariorum in Ecclesiasticum libri decem." In *Opera*. Edited by J.-P. Migne. PL 109, cols. 763-1126. Paris: Migne, 1844-1865.

Rufinus of Aquileia. "De benedictionibus patriarcharum." In *Opera*. Edited by M. Simonetti. CCL 20, pp. 189-228. Turnhout, Belgium: Brepols, 1961. Cl. 0195.

Salvian the Presbyter. "Ad ecclesiam (sive Adversus avaritiam)." In *Opera*. Edited by J.-P. Migne. PL 53, cols. 173-228. Paris: Migne, 1844-1865.

———. *De gubernatione Dei*. Edited by G. Lagarrigue. SC 220. Paris: Éditions du Cerf, 1975. Cl. 0485.

Severian of Gabala. "De tribus pueris." (Under the authorship of John Chrysostom.) In *Joannis Chrysostomi Opera omnia quae exstant*. Edited by J.-P. Migne. PG 56, cols. 593-600. Paris: Migne, 1857-1866. TLG 4139.067.

———. "In illud Abrahae dictum, Pone manum tuam sub femur meum." In *Joannis Chrysostomi opera omnia quae exstant*. Edited by J.-P. Migne. PG 56, cols. 553-64. Paris: Migne, 1857-1866.

———. "In parabolam de filio prodigo." (Under the authorship of John Chrysostom.) In *Joannis Chrysostomi opera omnia quae exstant*. Edited by J.-P. Migne. PG 59, cols. 515-522. Paris: Migne, 1857-1866. TLG 2062.231.

Severus of Antioch. *Les Homiliae cathedrals de Sévère d' Antioche: Homélies XL à XLV*. Edited by Jacques d'Édesse. PO 36, fasc. 1, no. 167. Turnhout, Belgium: Brepols, 1971.

Sophronius of Jerusalem. "Homiliae." *Le omelie: Sophronius Saint, Patriarch of Jerusalem*. Translated and edited by Antonino Gallico. CTP 92. Rome: Città Nuova, 1991.

Stephen of Hnes (Stephen Bishop of Heracleopolis Magna). "Vita di Apollo archimandrite." *A Panegyric on Apollo Archimandrite of the Monastery of Isaac.* Edited by K. Heinz Kuhn. Scriptores Coptici 39, 40; CSCO 394, 395. Louvain, Belgium: Secrétariat du CorpusSCO, 1978.

Theodore bar Koni. *Liber scholiorum.* Edited by A. Scher. CSCO 69. Louvain, Belgium: Secrétariat du Corpus, 1912.

Theodoret of Cyr. "Historia ecclesiastica." In *Theodore: Kirchengeschichte.* 2nd ed. Edited by L. Parmentier and F. Scheidweiler. GCS 44, pp. 1-349. Berlin: Akademie Verlag, 1954. TLG 4089.003.

————. *Interpretatio in Danielem.* In *Opera omnia.* Edited by J.-P. Migne. PG 81, cols. 1256-1546. Paris: Migne, 1857-1866. TLG 4089.028.

————. "Interpretatio in Jeremiam" (including Baruch and Lamentations). In *Opera omnia.* Edited by J.-P. Migne. PG 81, cols. 496-805. Paris: Migne, 1857-1866. TLG 4089.026.

————. "Quaestiones in Octateuchum." In *Theodoreti Cyrensis quaestiones in Octateuchum.* Edited by N. Fernández Marcos and A. Sáenz-Badillos. Textos y Estudios "Cardenal Cisneros" 17, pp. 3-318. Madrid: Poliglota Matritense, 1979. TLG 4089.022.

Theodotus of Ancyra. *Homiliae.* In *Opera omnia.* Edited by J.-P. Migne. PG 77, cols. 1349-1431. Paris: Migne, 1857-1866.

Valerian of Cimiez. "Homiliae." In *Opera omnia.* Edited by J.-P. Migne. PL 52, cols. 691-758. Paris: Migne, 1845.

Victor of Cartenna. "De paenitentia." In *Opera.* Edited by J.-P. Migne. PL 17, cols. 971-1004. Paris: Migne, 1844-1865.

Victor of Vita. *Liber tertius: professio fidei catholicorum.* In *Opera omnia.* Edited by J.-P. Migne. PL 58, cols. 219-234. Paris: Migne, 1844-1865.

Vigilius of Thapsus. "Contra Arianos." In *Opera.* Edited by J.-P. Migne. PL 62, cols. 155-180. Paris: Migne, 1844-1865.

————. "De Trinitate." In *Opera.* Edited by J.-P. Migne. PL 62, cols. 237-334. Paris: Migne, 1844-1865.

————. "Opus contra Varimadum Arianum." In *Eugyppii opera omnia.* Edited by J.-P. Migne. PL 62, cols. 351-434. Paris: Migne, 1844-1865. Cl. 0364.

Bibliography of Works in English Translation

Ambrose. "Hexameron." In *Hexameron, Paradise, and Cain and Abel*, pp. 3-283. Translated by John J. Savage. FC 42. Washington, D.C.: The Catholic University of America Press, 1961.

Ambrosiaster. "1 Corinthians." In *Commentaries on Romans and 1-2 Corinthians*, pp. 119-206. Translated and edited by Gerald L. Bray. Ancient Christian Texts. Downers Grove, Ill.: IVP Academic, 2009.

———. "Romans." In *Commentaries on Romans and 1-2 Corinthians*, pp. 1-118. Translated and edited by Gerald L. Bray. Ancient Christian Texts. Downers Grove, Ill.: IVP Academic, 2009.

Andrew of Crete. "Marian Homily." See "On the Dormition of Our Most Holy Lady, the Mother of God," in *On the Dormition of Mary: Early Patristic Homilies*, pp. 83-152. Translated by Brian Daley. Popular Patristics Series. Crestwood, N.Y.: St. Vladimir's Seminary Press, 1998

Athanasius. "Discourses Against the Arians." In *Selected Works and Letters*, pp. 306-447. Translated by Archibald Robertson. NPNF 4. Series 2. Edited by Philip Schaff and Henry Wace. 14 vols. 1890-1900. Reprint, Peabody, Mass.: Hendrickson, 1994.

———. "Festal Letters." In *Selected Works and Letters*, pp. 506-53. Translated by Archibald Robertson. NPNF 4. Series 2. Edited by Philip Schaff and Henry Wace. 14 vols. 1890-1900. Reprint, Peabody, Mass.: Hendrickson, 1994.

———. "Letter to Serapion." See C. R. B. Shapland, *The Letters of Saint Athanasius Concerning the Holy Spirit*. New York: Philosophical Library, 1951.

———. "On the Incarnation." In *Christology of the Later Fathers*, pp. 55-110. Translated by Archibald Robertson. Edited by Edward Rochie Hardy. LCC 3. Philadelphia: Westminster Press, 1954.

Augustine. *Confessions*. Translated by Vernon J. Bourke. FC 21. Washington, D.C.: The Catholic University of America Press, 1953.

———. "Confessions." In *The Confessions and Letters of Augustin, with a Sketch of His Life and Work*, pp. 27-207. Translated by J. G. Pilkington. NPNF 1. Series 1. Edited by Philip Schaff. 14 vols. 1886-1890. Reprint, Peabody, Mass.: Hendrickson, 1994.

———. *Expositions of the Psalms*. Translated by Maria Boulding. WSA 3 15-20. Edited by John E. Rotelle. New York: New City Press, 2000-2004.

———. *Expositions on the Book of Psalms*. Edited from the Oxford translation by A. Cleveland Coxe. NPNF 8. Series 1. Edited by Philip Schaff. 14 vols. 1886-1890. Reprint, Peabody, Mass.: Hendrickson, 1994.

———. "On the Literal Meaning of Genesis." In *On Genesis*, pp. 168-506. Translated by Edmund Hill. *WSA* 1 13. Edited by John E. Rotelle. New York: New City Press, 2002.

———. "On the Trinity." In *St. Augustine: On the Holy Trinity, Doctrinal Treatises, Moral Treatises*, pp. 14-238. Translated by A. W. Haddan. NPNF 3. Series 1. Edited by Philip Schaff. 14 vols. 1886-1890. Reprint, Peabody, Mass.: Hendrickson, 1994.

———. *Sermons.* Translated by Edmund Hill. *WSA* 3 1-11. Edited by John E. Rotelle. New York: New City Press, 1990-1997.

———. "Tractates on the Gospel of John." In *Homilies on the Gospel of John, Homilies on the First Epistle of John, Soliloquies*, pp. 7-452. Translated by John Gibb and James Innes. NPNF 7. Series 1. Edited by Philip Schaff. 14 vols. 1886-1890. Reprint, Peabody, Mass.: Hendrickson, 1994.

Barsanuphius and John. *Letters.* 2 vols. Translated by John Chryssavgis. FC 113, 114. Washington, D.C.: The Catholic University of America Press, 2006-2007.

Basil the Great. "On the Holy Spirit." In *Letters and Select Works*, pp. 1-50. Translated by Blomfield Jackson. NPNF 8. Series 2. Edited by Philip Schaff. 14 vols. 1890-1900. Reprint, Peabody, Mass.: Hendrickson, 1994.

Bede. *Bede: On Tobit and on the Canticle of Habakkuk.* Translated by Seán Connolly. Dublin: Four Courts Press, 1997.

———. *Homilies on the Gospels.* 2 vols. Translated by Lawrence T. Martin and David Hurst. CS 110, 111. Kalamazoo, Mich.: Cistercian Publications, 1991.

Cassian, John. "Conferences." In *Sulpicius Severus, Vincent of Lerins, John Cassian*, pp. 293-546. Translated by Edgar C. S. Gibson. NPNF 11. Series 2. Edited by Philip Schaff and Henry Wace. 14 vols. 1890-1900. Reprint, Peabody, Mass.: Hendrickson, 1994.

Cassiodorus. "The Institutes." See *An Introduction to Divine and Human Readings by Cassiodorus Senator.* Translated by L. W. Jones. New York: Columbia University Press, 1969.

Clement of Alexandria. *Christ the Educator.* Translated by Simon P. Wood. FC 23. Washington, D.C.: The Catholic University of America Press, 1953.

Clement of Rome. *1 Clement.* See "The Letter to the Corinthians," in *The Apostolic Fathers*, pp. 1-64. Translated by Francis X. Grimm. FC 1. Washington, D.C.: The Catholic University of America Press, 1947.

Cyprian. "Works and Almsgiving." In *Treatises*, pp. 225-53. Translated by Roy J. Defarrari. FC 36. Washington, D.C.: The Catholic University of America Press, 1958.

Cyril of Alexandria. *Commentary on the Gospel According to Saint John.* 2 vols. Translated by Philip Edward Pusey and Thomas Randell. Edited by Henry Parry Liddon. Library of Fathers of the Holy Catholic Church 43, 48. Oxford: James Parker, 1874-1885.

Cyril of Jerusalem. "Catechetical Lectures." In *S. Cyril of Jerusalem, S. Gregory Nazianzen*, pp. 1-143. Translated by Edward Hamilton Gifford et al. NPNF 7. Series 2. Edited by Philip Schaff and Henry Wace. 14 vols. 1886-1900. Reprint, Peabody, Mass.: Hendrickson, 1994.

———. "Mystagogical Lectures." In *S. Cyril of Jerusalem, S. Gregory Nazianzen*, pp. 144-202. Translated by Edward Hamilton Gifford et al. NPNF 7. Series 2. Edited by Philip Schaff and Henry Wace. 14 vols. 1886-1900. Reprint, Peabody, Mass.: Hendrickson, 1994.

Dorotheus of Gaza. "Spiritual Instructions." In *Discourses and Sayings.* Translated by Eric P. Wheeler. CS 33. Kalamazoo, Mich.: Cistercian Publications, 1977.

Fulgentius of Ruspe. "Letters." In *Fulgentius: Selected Works*, pp. 277-568. Translated by Robert B. Eno. FC 95. Washington, D.C.: The Catholic University of America Press, 1997.

———. "On the Forgiveness of Sins." In *Fulgentius: Selected Works*, pp. 109-84. Translated by Robert B. Eno. FC 95. Washington, D.C.: The Catholic University of America Press, 1997.

Gregory the Great. *The Homilies of St. Gregory the Great on the Book of the Prophet Ezekiel*. Translated by Theodosia Gray. Edited by Juliana Cownie. Etna, Calif.: Center for Traditionalist Orthodox Studies, 1990.

———. "Pastoral Rule." In *Leo the Great, Gregory the Great*, part 2, pp. 1-72. Translated by Charles Feltoe et al. NPNF 12. Series 2. Edited by Philip Schaff and Henry Wace. 14 vols. 1890-1900. Reprint, Peabody, Mass.: Hendrickson, 1994.

Irenaeus. "Against Heresies." In *The Apostolic Fathers with Justin Martyr and Irenaeus*, pp. 309-567. Translated by A. Cleveland Coxe. ANF 1. Edited by Alexander Roberts and James Donaldson. 10 vols. 1885-1887. Reprint, Peabody, Mass.: Hendrickson, 1994.

Isaac of Nineveh. *The Ascetical Homilies of Saint Isaac the Syrian*. Translated by the Holy Transfiguration Monastery. Brookline, Mass.: Holy Transfiguration Monastery, 1984.

Jerome. *Jerome's Commentary on Daniel*. Translated by G. L. Archer Jr. Grand Rapids: Baker, 1977.

———. "Homilies on Mark." In *The Homilies of Saint Jerome*, vol. 2, pp. 121-192. Translated by Marie Liguori Ewald. FC 57. Washington, D.C.: The Catholic University of America Press, 1966.

———. "Homilies on the Psalms." In *The Homilies of Saint Jerome*, vol. 1. Translated by Marie Liguori Ewald. FC 48. Washington, D.C.: The Catholic University of America Press, 1964.

John Chrysostom. "Baptismal Instructions." See "Two Instructions to Candidates for Baptism," in *Saint Chrysostom: On the Priesthood, Ascetic Treatises, Select Homilies and Letters, Homilies on the Statutes*, pp. 159-71. Translated by T. P. Brandram. NPNF 9. Series 1. Edited by Philip Schaff. 14 vols. 1886-1890. Reprint, Peabody, Mass.: Hendrickson, 1994.

———. *Homilies on the Gospel of Matthew*. Translated by George Prevost, revised by M. B. Riddle. NPNF 10. Series 1. Edited by Philip Schaff. 14 vols. 1886-1890. Reprint, Peabody, Mass.: Hendrickson, 1994.

———. "Letter to Theodore." In *Saint Chrysostom: On the Priesthood, Ascetic Treatises, Select Homilies and Letters, Homilies on the Statutes*, pp. 83-116. NPNF 9. Series 1. Edited by Philip Schaff. 14 vols. 1886-1890. Reprint, Peabody, Mass.: Hendrickson, 1994.

———. "On the Priesthood." In *Saint Chrysostom: On the Priesthood, Ascetic Treatises, Select Homilies and Letters, Homilies on the Statutes*, pp. 33-83. NPNF 9. Series. 1. Edited by Philip Schaff. 14 vols. 1886-1890. Reprint, Peabody, Mass.: Hendrickson, 1994.

John of Damascus. "Homily on the Dormition." See *On the Dormition of Mary: Early Patristic Homilies*, pp. 183-202. Translated by Brian Daley. Popular Patristics Series. Crestwood, N.Y.: St. Vladimir's Seminary Press, 1998.

———. "On the Orthodox Faith." In *Writings*, pp. 165-406. Translated by Frederic H. Chase. FC 37. Washington, D.C.: The Catholic University of America Press, 1958.

———. *Three Treatises on the Divine Images*. Translated by Andrew Louth. Popular Patristics Series. Crestwood, N.Y.: St. Vladimir's Seminary Press, 2003.

Maximus of Turin. *The Sermons of St. Maximus of Turin*. Translated by Boniface Ramsey. ACW 50. New York: Newman Press, 1989.

Methodius of Olympus. "Banquet of the Ten Virgins." In *Gregory Thaumaturgus, Dionysius the Great, Julius Africanus, Anatolius and Minor Writers, Methodius, Arnobius*, pp. 309-55. Translated by William R. Clark. ANF 6. Edited by Alexander Roberts and James Donaldson. 10 vols. 1885-1887. Reprint, Peabody, Mass.: Hendrickson, 1994.

Nicetas. "On the Trinity." In *Niceta of Remesiana, Sulpicious Severus, Vincent of Lerins, Prosper of Aquitaine*, pp. 9-76. Translated by Gerald G. Walsh. FC 7. New York: Fathers of the Church, 1949.

Optatus. *Against the Donatists*. Translated by Mark Edwards. Translated Texts for Historians. Liverpool: Liverpool University Press, 1997.

Origen. "Commentary on Matthew." In *The Gospel of Peter, The Diatessaron of Tatian, The Apocalypse of Peter, The Vision of Paul, . . .* , pp. 413-512. Translated by John Patrick. ANF 9. Edited by Allan Menzies. 10 vols. 1885-1887. Reprint, Peabody, Mass.: Hendrickson, 1994.

———. *Commentary on the Gospel According to John, Books 1-10 and 13-32*. Translated by Ronald E. Heine. FC 80, 89. Washington, D.C.: The Catholic University of America Press, 1989-1993.

———. *Homilies on Genesis and Exodus*. Translated by Ronald E. Heine. FC 71. Washington, D.C.: The Catholic University of America Press, 1982.

———. *Homilies on Jeremiah, Homily on 1 Kings 28*. Translated by John Clark Smith. FC 97. Washington, D.C.: The Catholic University of America Press, 1998.

———. *Homilies on Joshua*. Translated and Edited by Barbara J. Bruce and Cynthia White. FC 105. Washington, D.C.: The Catholic University of America Press, 2002.

———. *Homilies on Leviticus: 1-16*. Translated by Gary Wayne Barkley. FC 83. Washington, D.C.: The Catholic University of America Press, 1990.

———. *Homilies on Numbers*. Translated by Thomas P. Scheck. Edited by Christopher Hall. Ancient Christian Texts. Downers Grove, Ill.: IVP Academic, 2009.

———. "On First Principles." In *Tertullian (IV); Minucius Felix; Commodian; Origen (I and III)*, pp. 239-384. Translated by Frederick Combie. ANF 4. Edited by Alexander Roberts and James Donaldson. 10 vols. 1885-1887. Reprint, Peabody, Mass.: Hendrickson, 1994.

———. "On Prayer." In *Prayer; Exhortation to Martyrdom*, pp. 15-140. Translated by John J. O'Meara. ACW 19. Westminster, Md.: Newman Press, 1954.

———. *The Song of Songs: Commentary and Homilies*. Translated and annotated by R. P. Lawson. ACW 26. New York: Newman Press, 1956.

Paulinus of Nola. "Letter 13 to Pamachius." In *Letters of St. Paulinus of Nola*, vol. 1, pp. 117-43. Translated by P. G. Walsh. ACW 35. New York: Paulist Press, 1966.

Peter Chrysologus. "Sermons." In *Saint Peter Chrysologus Selected Sermons and Saint Valerian Homilies*, vol. 1, pp. 25-282. Translated by George E. Ganss. FC 17. New York: Fathers of the Church, 1953.

———. *St. Peter Chrysologus: Selected Sermons*, vols. 2 and 3. Translated by William B. Palardy. FC 109, 110. Washington, D.C.: Catholic University of America Press, 2004, 2005.

Prosper of Aquitaine. *The Call of All Nations*. Translated by P. de Letter. ACW 14. Westminster, Md.: Newman Press, 1952.

Salvian the Presbyter. "Against Avarice." See "The Four Books of Timothy to the Church," in *The Writings of Salvian, the Presbyter*, pp. 267-371. Translated by Jeremiah F. O'Sullivan. FC 3. Washington, D.C.: The Catholic University of America Press, 1962.

———. "The Governance of God." In *The Writings of Salvian, the Presbyter*, pp. 21-232. Translated by Jeremiah F. O'Sullivan. FC 3. Washington, D.C.: The Catholic University of America Press, 1962.

Theodoret of Cyr. *Commentary on Daniel*. Translated by Robert C. Hill. Writings from the Greco-

Roman World 7. Atlanta: Society of Biblical Literature, 2006.

———. *The Questions on the Octateuch: On Genesis and Exodus.* Greek text revised by John F. Petruccione. Translated by Robert C. Hill. LEC (CUAP) 1. Washington, D.C.: The Catholic University of America Press, 2007.

Victor of Vita. "Book of the Catholic Faith." In *Victor of Vita: History of the Vandal Persecution.* Translated with introduction by John Moorhead. Liverpool: Liverpool University Press, 1992.

Author/Writings Index

Subject Index

Scripture Index